The Expansion of Latin Europe, 1000–1500

Internal Colonization in Medieval Europe

THE EXPANSION OF LATIN EUROPE, 1000-1500

General Editors: James Muldoon and Felipe Fernández-Armesto

Part I

1 The Medieval Frontiers of Latin Christendom: Expansion, Contraction, Continuity
Edited by James Muldoon and Felipe Fernández-Armesto

2 Internal Colonization in Medieval Europe
Edited by Felipe Fernández-Armesto and James Muldoon

3 The North Atlantic Frontier of Medieval Europe: Vikings and Celts
Edited by James Muldoon

4 The North-Eastern Frontiers of Medieval Europe: Scandinavia and the Baltic
(Provisional title)

5 The Medieval Latin Frontiers in Central Europe
(Provisional title)

6 The Islamic Frontier of Medieval Europe: The Eastern Mediterranean
(Provisional title)

7 The Islamic Frontier of Medieval Europe: The Western Mediterranean
(Provisional title)

8 Spain and the Atlantic Frontier of Medieval Europe
(Provisional title)

Part II

9 Medieval Ethnographies: European Perceptions of the World Beyond
Edited by Joan Pau Rubiés

10 Travelers, Intellectuals, and the World Beyond Medieval Europe
Edited by James Muldoon

11 Religion and Expansion: The Medieval Missionary Impulse
Edited by James F. Ryan

Part III

12 The Expansion of Orthodox Europe: Byzantium, the Balkans and Russia
Edited by Jonathan Shepard

13 The Mongol Empire and its Impact
(Provisional title)

14 Islamic Expansion in the Later Middle Ages
(Provisional title)

The Expansion of Latin Europe, 1000–1500

Volume 2

Internal Colonization in Medieval Europe

edited by
Felipe Fernández-Armesto and James Muldoon

ASHGATE
VARIORUM

Published in **The Expansion of Latin Europe, 1000-1500 Series** by

Ashgate Publishing Limited
Wey Court East
Union Road
Farnham,
Surrey GU9 7PT
England

Ashgate Publishing Company
Suite 420
101 Cherry Street
Burlington, VT 05401-4405
USA

ISBN 978-0-7546-5972-3

Ashgate website: http://www.ashgate.com

British Library Cataloguing in Publication Data
Internal colonization in medieval Europe. - (The expansion of Latin Europe, 1000-1500)
1. Economic development - Europe - History - To 1500
2. Civilization, Medieval 3. Europe - History - 476-1492
4. Europe - Economic conditions - To 1492 5. Europe - Social conditions - To 1492
I. Fernández-Armesto, Felipe II. Muldoon, James
940.1'7

US Library of Congress Control Number 2008924411

This book is printed on acid free paper.

Mixed Sources
Product group from well-managed forests and other controlled sources
www.fsc.org Cert no. SGS-COC-2482
© 1996 Forest Stewardship Council
FSC

Printed and bound in Great Britain by
TJ International Ltd, Padstow, Cornwall

THE EXPANSION OF LATIN EUROPE, 1000-1500 – VOL 2

Contents

Acknowledgements

The chapters in this volume are taken from the sources listed below, for which the editor and publishers wish to thank their authors, original publishers or copyright holders for the permission to use their materials as follows:

Chapter 1: Karl Leyser, 'The Ascent of Latin Europe', An Inaugural Lecture delivered before the University of Oxford on 7 November 1984 (Oxford, 1986), pp. 1–28.

Chapter 2: Léopold Génicot, 'On the Evidence of Growth of Population from the Eleventh to the Thirteenth Century', Sylvia Thrupp (ed.), *Change in Medieval Society*, (New York, 1964), pp. 14–29.

Chapter 3: Jacques Heers, 'The "Feudal" Economy and Capitalism: Words, Ideas and Reality', *Journal of European Economic History* (1974), pp. 609–53.

Chapter 4: Lynn White, Jr 'Cultural Climates and Technological Advance in the Middle Ages', *Viator*, 2 (1971), pp. 171–201.

Chapter 5: Richard C. Hoffmann, 'Economic Development and Aquatic Ecosystems in Medieval Europe', *American Historical Review*, 101 (1996), pp. 631–69.

Chapter 6: Margaret Ley Bazeley, 'The Extent of the English Royal Forest in the Thirteenth Century,' *Transactions of the Royal Historical Society*, 4th s., 4 (1921), pp. 140–72. Copyright © 1921 The Royal Historical Society, published by Cambridge Univeristy Press, reproduced with permission.

Chapter 7: R.S. Lopez, 'The Evolution of Land Transport in the Middle Ages', *Past and Present*, 9 (1956), pp. 17–29.

Chapter 8: Marjorie Nice Boyer, 'A Day's Journey in Medieval France', *Speculum*, 26 (1951), pp. 597–608.

Chapter 9: R.A. Donkin, 'The Cistercian Order and the Settlement of Northern England', *Geographical Review*, 59 (1969), pp. 403–16.

Chapter 10: M. Postan, 'Chronology of Labour Services', *Transactions of the Royal Historical Society*, 4th s., 20 (1937), pp. 169–93. Copyright © 1937 The Royal Historical Society, published by Cambridge Univeristy Press, reproduced with permission.

Chapter 11: P.J. Jones, 'An Italian Estate, 900-1200', *The Economic History Review*, 2nd s., 7 (1954), pp.18–32. Published by Blackwell Publishing, reproduced with permission.

Chapter 12: M. Toch, 'Lords and Peasants: A Reappraisal of Medieval Economic Relationships', *The Journal of European Economic History*, 15, (1986), pp. 163–82.

Chapter 13: E.M. Carus-Wilson, 'An Industrial Revolution of the Thirteenth Century,' *The Economic History Review*, 11 (1941), pp. 39–60. Published by Blackwell Publishing, reproduced with permission.

Chapter 14: M. Lombard, 'L'évolution urbaine pendant le haut Moyen Âge', *Annales: Économies, Sociétés, Civilisations*, 12 (1957), pp. 7–28. Translated by Philip Simpson. Copyright © 2008 Ashgate Publishing.

Chapter 15: D. Nicholas, 'Settlement Patterns, Urban Functions and Capital Formation in Medieval Flanders', *Annales: Économies, Sociétés, Civilisations,* 33 (1978), pp. 501–27.

Illustrations

Subsistence fishing? St Peter is depicted as a successful angler in a fragment from an anonymous English Gospel lectionary done in the style of the Canterbury school about 1000 AD. Collection of the J. Paul Getty Muesum, Malibu, California, MS. 9 (85. MS. 79), fol. 2v. Used with permission of The J. Paul Getty Museum, Los Angeles, California.

A fishmonger's stall. Marginal illumination in a 1290 French antiphonary from the monastery of Beaupré near Gramont, now in Walters Art Gallery, Baltimore, Maryland, MS 759, fol. 108r. The Beaupré Antiphonary, Catholic Church, Flemish, after 1904, parchment, 18 15/16 x 13 5/8 in.

General Editors' Preface

This series began with a suggestion that a volume dealing with medieval European expansion would make an interesting prologue to the *Expanding World: The European Impact on World History 1450–1800* series that was already appearing. Several of the volumes in that series did include articles dealing with aspects of the medieval background, but the medieval 'expansion of Europe' – within and along the frontiers of Latin Christendom – lay outside the terms of reference. So did an important part of the medieval prelude to the story of the 'expanding world': the growth of neighboring cultures with which Latin Christendom collided.

Motives, practices, and tools characteristic of modern European expansion were creations or developments of the Middle Ages. 'The internal colonization of Europe' was the basis of subsequent overseas colonization. Along the edges of Latin Christendom, expanding societies encountered Celts, Scandinavians, Slavs, and others who were organizing societies of their own that could block or redirect European expansion, initiate cultural exchange, and exercise varying degrees of influence on the way Europeans thought about themselves and the world. As medieval Christian society expanded further, Europeans encountered other societies with which they competed or cooperated.

The introductory volume for the entire series will deal with the expansion of European society during the Middle Ages in terms of the frontier experience, setting the stage for the entire series. Gradually or fitfully, with occasional reversals, between the late ninth and mid-fourteenth centuries, the culture of Latin Christendom spread outwards in all directions from the heartlands of western Europe. In spite of the contraction of Latin Christendom after the Black Death, the check to the outward growth of the frontier, and the continuing expansion of Islam, the basic motives for expansion remained, as did knowledge of institutional structures employed in developing overseas trade and colonization.

Other volumes will deal with the expansion of Europe in geographical terms. The first will examine the internal colonization of Europe that began around 1000 as the population began to increase, previously unfarmed areas were transformed into arable land, and new towns created. This period of growth provided impetus for acquiring new lands to settle and for developing the techniques of colonization, techniques that were to have a long history. Remaining volumes will deal with European expansion along specific frontiers. While European expansion possessed some general qualities, each frontier had its own particular characteristics.

The first external frontier to be considered is with the Muslim world. One volume devoted to the Muslim frontier deals with the crusades and related efforts to block or reverse Muslim expansion in the Mediterranean. The crusades were also early examples of colonization as the crusaders established permanent settlements and a kind of European feudal government in the reconquered territories occupied by an urban population of Christians, heretical and schismatic, Jews, and Muslims.

The second volume dealing with Christian expansion along the frontier with the Muslim world will examine the *reconquista* in the westward-facing parts of Spain and Portugal, a process that not only led to the creation of the Spanish and Portuguese kingdoms, but also to Christian occupation of parts of the African coast, exploration of the Atlantic, and the discovery of several island chains. These efforts in turn led to Columbus's voyages and to Portuguese explorations that eventually linked the Atlantic to the trade routes of the Indian Ocean.

Along other frontiers, European Christians expanded into lands occupied by a variety of societies, often employing religious motives to justify their actions as they had done in the crusades to regain the Holy Land. For example, expansion along the Celtic frontier brought Anglo-Norman conquerors of England into contact with Scots, Welsh, and Irish, all Christians yet, by continental standards, 'uncivilized'. Expansion here meant not only conquest but also, as in the case of Ireland, a responsibility for reforming the Church as well. There was also the task of transforming the pastoral societies of the Celtic fringe into agricultural societies that the intruders assumed to be the basis for fully civilized society. On the northern, southern, and eastern shores of the Baltic where unevangelized Slavs and Baltic peoples dwelled, and – further south – along the Danube and inland from the Dalmatian coast, Christian Scandinavians, Germans, Slavs and Magyars faced a variety of intractable infidels who deployed modest levels of material culture in terrain classifiable, according to the values of the time, as savage.

English and Spanish medieval experience of dealing with the peoples encountered along the frontier shaped initial responses to peoples encountered in the Americas. When they came to the New World they came with perceptions about people who lived on the frontier and with institutions for dealing with them. Europeans saw, or thought they saw, in the Americas societies like those that they had encountered in the course of their medieval expansion so they attempted apply lessons learned from that expansion to the Americas. Within two generations, however, colonizers began to recognize that the Americas were different and that the lessons learned in the course of medieval expansion were not necessarily directly applicable to the New World.

The second set of volumes deals with two inter-related issues; first, the role of religion in shaping the medieval response to the world beyond Europe and the perceptions of non-Europeans that circulated throughout Europe. The Christian responsibility for preaching to all mankind encouraged missionaries to move beyond the geographical frontiers of Christendom to preach to infidels who lived along those frontiers. Early modern overseas expansion, Catholic and Protestant, renewed this notion of mission on a large scale. A further volume in this category deals with European knowledge of the world beyond Europe. Much of this knowledge came from missionaries, especially Franciscan friars, and from merchants such as Marco Polo who had visited China, India, and the Islamic world. Missionaries and merchants subsequently wrote down their observations about these worlds, providing their fellow Europeans with the earliest first-hand information about the eastern world, information that shaped the fifteenth-century search for a new route to Asia.

The third group of volumes focuses on the other expanding societies that Latin Christians encountered in the course of expansion. These volumes demonstrate how expansion led to interaction with other societies, some expanding, others contracting. The Byzantine Empire ruled a Christian society that became increasingly estranged from the Latin West over theological and cultural issues between the eleventh and the thirteenth centuries. To some extent, the Byzantines found themselves caught between two expanding societies, the Latin

Christians of Europe and the Muslims who had emerged from Arabia in the seventh century, eventually conquering a great deal of territory that the Byzantines once ruled. The crusades that Europeans launched at the end of the eleventh century aimed at assisting in the defense of the Byzantine Empire and at freeing the Holy Land from Muslim hands. As things turned out, however, the crusaders were not interested in restoring the lands to Byzantine control. They sought instead to carve out kingdoms for themselves at the expense of both the Muslims and the Byzantines.

Muslim expansion was not only at the expense of the Byzantines, however. From the mid-seventh century to the late seventeenth, Muslim expansion also had a serious impact on Western European development. Christian armies encountered Muslim societies in Iberia where a several-centuries long series of wars led to the creation of numerous small states. At the other end of Europe, Muslim expansion through the Balkans from the fourteenth century to the seventeenth century blocked European expansion eastward and pushed the boundaries of Latin Christendom back as traditionally Christian kingdoms such as Hungary fell to Turkish armies. European expansion into the African Atlantic began in the fifteenth century partly in order to find a route to Asia that would outflank the Muslim-dominated eastern Mediterranean.

Another society whose expansion impinged on Europe was the Mongol Empire that Genghis Khan (1162–1227) created. On the one hand, the Mongols wrought a great deal of havoc on the eastern frontiers of Christian Europe as well as on the Muslims in the Near East. On the other hand, Mongol control of the routes between Europe and Asia made it possible for European merchants and missionaries to travel back and forth, thus providing Europeans with more accurate knowledge about the East than they had ever possessed before.

The collapse of the Mongol Empire in the fourteenth century made possible the creation of new states out of the Mongol domain. From the perspective of Western Europe the most important of these successor states was Moscow whose rulers embarked upon a policy of expansion that eventually led to the creation of a Russian Empire. This empire not only succeeded to the Mongol hegemony in Central Asia, it also took over the Byzantine Emperor's role as leader and defender of Orthodox Christianity, identifying Moscow as the Third Rome and heir to the Byzantine tradition. Subsequent expansion brought the Russians into conflict with peoples of the Latin West, Islam, and China. Russian expansion eventually extended through Siberia, across the Bering Strait to the North American mainland.

The expansion of Europe between 1000 and 1492 provided the foundation upon which modern expansion built. This first stage of European expansion was a part of a larger process, global age of expansion. This series traces the origins of a vital aspect of modernity back into the Middle Ages and sets an early chapter of the rise of Europe in the context of the history of the world.

James Muldoon and Felipe Fernández-Armesto

General Editors

Introduction

Expansion does not only happen outwards: there are often inward crevices and gaps to fill, slack to take up. From the 11th to the early 14th centuries, while the frontiers of Latin Christendom dilated, a process of internal expansion was also under way. Population grew. New resources were exploited, while new technologies enhanced the productivity of old ones. New lands were cultivated, sometimes with new crops, or turned from wilderness to pasture. Forests fell. Bogs were drained. Settlement encroached on marginal soils and headed uphill. New kinds of economic activity became possible in growing towns. Church and state grasped communities formerly isolated by forest, marsh or mountain – Europe's inner barbarians, whose evangelization, before this period, was sometimes sketchy and whose habitats were often blanks on the map. Traffic grew and people moved peacefully in increasing numbers – as migrants, merchants, pilgrims and 'wandering scholars' – along new arteries of what would now be called the infrastructure of Europe: roads and bridges and newly reconnoitred routes. Latin Christendom emerged as a genuinely expanding world, as it stretched between increasingly remote horizons.[1]

New settlement and new forms of exploitation converted previously uninhabited or sparsely inhabited environments. In mountain settings, western civilization spread up slopes formerly unoccupied or abandoned to the domain of hostile highlanders, whom their lowland neighbours despised as barbarians. The new accessibility of highlands to settlement from below is intelligible against a long background of climate change: a 'warm spell', which lasted from the late 10th to the mid-13th centuries, with effects which only began to fade when a 'little ice age' drove settlers from late-colonized uplands in the 14th century.[2] Meanwhile, other environments were transformed and ecologies disturbed, as the riverbankers of western

---

1 Valuable overviews are provided by Robert Fossier, *Enfance de l'Europe: XIe au XIIe siècles, aspectséconomiques et sociaux,* 2 vols (Paris, 1982); Robert Bartlett, *The Making of Europe: Conquest, Colonisation and Cultural Change, 950–1350* (Princeton, 1993); M. Balard and A. Ducellier (eds), *Coloniser au Moyen Âge* (Paris, 1995) concentrates on expansion outwards from Europe.

2 On climate see J.M. Grove and R. Suitsur, 'Glacial Evidence for the Medieval Warm Period', *Climatic Change,* xxxvi (1994), pp. 143–69. For particular studies of mountain regions, see C. Wickham, *The Mountains and the City: the Tuscan Appenines in the Early Middle Ages;* C. Bartels, *'Montani* und *Silvani* im Harz: mittelalterlicher und frühneuzeitlicher Bergbau und seine Einflüsse auf die Umwelt', in *Bergbau, Verhütting und Waldnuttung in Mittelalter* (1996), pp. 112–27; Michael Toch, 'Peasants of the Mountains, Peasants of the Valleys and Medieval State Building: the Case of the Alps', in J.-F. Bergier (ed.), *Montagnes, fleuves, forêts dans l'histoire* (St-Katharinen, 1989), pp. 65–70; M. Durany Castrillo, 'El paisaje medieval a través del ejemplo berciano', *Paisajes rurales y paisajes urbamos* (1999), pp. 29–64; E. Jurand, 'Couvert forestièr et élevage pastoral dans les Abruzzes (Italie): à l'origine de la "montagne chauve"', *Mélanges de la Casa de Velázquez,* xxx, part 1 (1994), pp. 275–89.

Europe conquered the wild wood. This was more than an economic enterprise: it was a sacred undertaking – a kind of reconquista, reclaiming for God part of the terrain of paganism. The forest was stained with pagan sensuality and alive with sprites, demons, and 'wild men of the woods'. Trees hallowed by unenlightened generations fell to pious axe-strokes.[3]

The most famous example is the best. Unable to sleep 'on a certain night' in 1122, Abbot Suger of Saint-Denis rose to search the forest for twelve trees mighty enough to frame the new sanctuary he was planning for his abbey church, built – he hoped – to be full of light and 'to elevate dull minds to the truth'. The foresters smiled at him and wondered if the abbot was 'quite ignorant of the fact that nothing of the kind could be found in the entire region'; but he found what he needed 'with the courage of faith'.[4] It was a representative incident in a vast project for the domestication of little-exploited and under-exploited environments.[5] Gothic architecture, erected by means which economized on wood, was a style adapted to shrinking forests.[6]

Christianity was, in a sense, an ideology of environmental adaptation, sanctifying human stewardship of nature. Religious orders were agents of Europe's inward colonialism, just as they were often patrons and facilitators of outward conquest.[7] The Cistercians, one of the most dynamic new monastic orders of the period, directed their efforts into 'deserts' where habitation was sparse and nature hostile. They disputed Suger's views on aesthetics – advocating simplicity and austerity in worship – but favoured building and tree-felling on at least a comparable scale. They razed woodlands and made rough places plain, driving flocks and ox-teams into wildernesses where now, all too often, the vast abbeys lie ruined in their turn. Sometimes, in their craving to escape the glutinous secular society that imperilled souls, Cistercians actually drove existing settlers away from their lands, extending the frontiers of colonization even further as peasants imitated their practices on even more marginal lands.[8]

3 Felipe Fernández-Armesto, *Civilisations: Culture, Ambition and the Transformation of Nature* (New York, 2001), pp. 119–30.

4 The text is superbly edited and amplified in Erwin Panovsky, *Abbot Suger on the Abbey of St-Denis and its Art Treasures* (Princeton, 1946).

5 R. Bechmann, *Des arbres et des hommes: la forêt au Moyen Âge* (Paris, 1984); H. Darby, 'The Clearing of the Woodland in Europe', in W.L. Thomas (ed.), *Man's Role in Changing the Face of the Earth* (Chicago, 1956); C. Wickham, 'European Forests in the Early Middle Ages', in *Land and Power: Studies in Italian and European Social History, 400–1200* (London, 1994), pp. 155–99.

6 R. Bechmann, *Les racines des cathédrales: l'architecture gothique, expression des conditions du milieu* (Paris, 1981).

7 M. Amouroux, 'L'Église régulière, outil de la colonisation de la Syries par lkes croisés aux XIIe et XIIIe siècles', in Lombard and Ducellier, (eds), pp. 281–95.

8 On depopulation see R.A. Donkin, 'Settlement and Depopulation on Cistercian Estates during the Twelfth and Thirteenth Centuries', *Bulletin of the Institute of Historical Research,* xxxiii (1960), pp. 141–65. On the Cistercian project in general, the most important works are C. Higounet, 'Les types d'exploitation cisterciennes et prémontrées du XIIIe siècle', *Annales de l'Est* (1959); Georges Duby, 'Le Monachisme et l'économie rurale', in *Hommes et structures du Moyen Âge* (Paris, The Hague, 1973), pp. 381–94; T. Kinder, *L'Europe cistercienne* (Paris, 1997); L. Pressouyre, *L'Espace cistercienne* (Paris, 1994).

Engineering came to the aid of environmental adaptation.[9] According to Lynn White, Jr (*infra*, p. 91ff.), the word 'engineer' first appears in a document of 1170 'and is very common in the 13th century': not surprisingly, as the applications of engineering multiplied. Drainage helped extend humans' habitable domain.[10] In Holland, rapid population growth seems closely linked with the success of Floris V's project to reclaim waterlogged land after soil subsidence.[11] Even where waterlogged soils did not demand attention, the aquatic environment underwent modifications at human hands. The navigability of rivers was improved by embanking and canalization.[12] The impact on eco-systems was sometimes dramatic, as explained in Hoffman's paper in this volume (*infra*, p. 123ff.). Building roads and bridges was an urgent task of public utility, for which monarchs accepted some responsibility and for which – for example – Domingo de la Calzada, who built causeways and bridges for pilgrims to Compostela, was made a saint.[13] Human mobility accelerated and developed in range.

Behind the expanding frontiers, modest technical revolutions were boosting production. Among inventions originating in Europe at this time were windmills, ground lenses and clocks; others, brought there thanks to improved communications across Eurasia, were paper, the compass, the blast-furnace and cannon. Large, heavy ploughs with curved blades bit deeply into the land; more efficient mills, more exact metallurgy and new products, especially in arms and glassware, extended the range of business and the flow of wealth.[14] An 'agricultural revolution' spread hesitantly, faintly from the world of Islam, promoting improved farming

9 Jean Gimpel, *The Medieval Machine: the Industrial Revolution of the Middle Ages* (London, 1988); Frances and Joseph Gies, *Cathedral, Forge and Waterwheel: Technology and Invention in the Middle Ages* (New York, 1994).

10 See William Te Brake, *Medieval Frontier: Culture and Economy in Rijnland* (College Station, 1985); D.E.H. De Boer et al. (eds), *Holland en het water in de middeleeuwen: strijd tegen het water en beheersing en gebruik van het water* (Hilversum, 1997), which deals with fisheries as well as drainage. For recent particular case-studies see C. Dekker, 'De ontginning', in *Geschiedenis van de provincie Utrecht tot* 1528 (Utrecht, 1999), pp. 131–42, 156–68, 352–60; D. Hodgma, ''s-Hertogenbosch hoog en droog: de binnendieze en de historisches bouwlocaties', in *De Oudste steen boven* (2000), pp. 190–6, 228–9.

11 J.M. Bos, 'Landschap en politiek: het gemaakte landschap van de dertiende eeuw', in D.E.H. De Boer et al. (eds), *Wi Florens: de Hollandse graf Floris V in de samenleving van de XIIIe Eeuw* (Utrecht, 1996), pp. 80–8.

12 J.-P. Braunaud, 'La flottage du bois et le changement du paysage fluviale des montagnes françaises,' *Médiévales*, xxxvi (1999), pp. 53–61.

13 J. Houbert, 'Les routes du Moyen Âge', in *Les Routes de France: colloque des Cahiers de Civilisation* (Paris, 1959), pp. 22–56; R.H. Bautier, 'Recherches sur les routes de l'Europe médiévale', *Bulletin philologique et historique,* (1960), pp. 99–143; N. Ohler, *Reisen in Maittelalter* (Düsseldorf, 1986); on pilgrimage and road-building and maintenance see *El camino de Santiago y la articulación del espacio hispánico: XX Semana de Estudios Medievales en Estella, 1994* (Pamplona, 1996); N. Yates and J.M. Gibson, *Traffic and Politics: the Construction and Maintenance of Rochester Bridge, AD 43–1900* (Woodbridge, 1994).

14 For a superb recent summary of the state of debate on whether and how farming techniques might have stimulated social change, see C. Dyer, 'Medieval Farming and Technology: Conclusion', in G. Astill and J. Langdon, (eds), *Medieval Farming and Technology: the Impact of Agricultural Change in Northwest Europe* (Brill, 1997), pp. 293–312. On metallurgy see Gimpel, op. cit.

with new strains of wheat and – where it would grow – of rice.[15] Although the respective roles of 'feudalism' and 'free peasants' in extending tillage and coaxing new wealth from the soil are much debated, it seems clear that the colonization of new lands created opportunities of enrichment at all social levels. More food meant more people – or was it the other way round?[16] The population of Europe may well have doubled while these changes took place.[17]

New trade-routes enmeshed Atlantic and Mediterranean seaboards in a single economy. Naturally, western Europe has two economies – Mediterranean and northern – separated by a strait with widely different sailing conditions along the two seaboards and a chain of breakwaters which determines the flow of rivers and, therefore the directions of exchange. For much of Europe's history, communication between these two zones was not easy. Limited access through the Toulouse gap, the Rhone corridor and the Alpine passes kept restricted forms of commerce alive, even in periods when commercial navigation from sea to sea was abandoned. In the thirteenth century, Mediterranean craft, mainly from Genoa, Majorca and Catalonia, resumed large-scale ventures along Atlantic coasts. German merchants unified the northern seas in a similar way, linking London and Bruges with Lübeck and Riga. Lübeck, founded in 1143, was the pioneer-city of what became the Hanseatic League.[18]

Exchange across vast distances made geographical specialization and genuine industrialization possible. All the industries served, for instance, by the trade of Genoa depended on geographical specialization. Textiles depended on concentrating wools and dyestuffs from widely separated places of origin; food processing relied on the matching of fresh foodstuffs with salt. Shipbuilding demanded a similar marriage of raw materials – wood, iron, sailcloth and pitch. 'Industrial revolution' and *Wirschaftswunder* have become part of the historical lexicon for the period.

Expansion was more than colonization and commerce: it was a process of the export of culture. The self-conscious town remained, as it had been in antiquity, a defining feature of western civilization.[19] Even the oldest-established cities might experience a renewal of civic spirit. The commune of Verona is displayed in the tympanum of the cathedral in its moment of creation, when the patron saint, Zeno 'with a serene heart, grants to the people a

15 A.M. Watson, 'Arab and European Agriculture in the Middle Ages: a Case of Restricted Diffusion', in Del Sweeney, (ed.), *Agriculture in the Middle Ages: Technology, Practice and Representation* (Philadelphia, 1995), pp. 62–75; 'The Arab Agricultural Revolution and its Diffusion, 700–1100', *Journal of Economic History,* xxxiv (1974), pp. 8–35.

16 See Gimpel, op. cit. and G. De Boe and F. Verhaeghe (eds), *Environment and Subsistence in Medieval Europe: Papers of the Medieval Europe Brugge 1997, Conference 9* (Zellick, 1997).

17 Josiah Cox Russell, 'Population in Europe, 500–1500', in Carlo M. Cipolla (ed.), *The Fontana Economic History of Europe,* i (1972), pp. 25–70; A. Higounet-Nadal, 'La Démographie des villes françaises au Moyen Âge,' *Annales de démographie historique* (1980), pp. 187–211; N. Bulst, 'L'Essor (Xe–XIVe siècles),' *Histoire des populations de l'Europe,* i (2000), pp. 160–84, 583–623.

18 P. Dollinger, *La Hanse* (1964) remains the best general study of this subject. There is an English translation, *The German Hansa,* trans. and ed. D.S. Ault and S.H. Steinberg (Stanford, 1970).

19 Jacques Le Goff, 'The Town as an Agent of Civilisation', in Carlo M. Cipolla, (ed.), op. cit., pp. 71–106; C. Higounet, 'Congregare Populationem', *Annales de démographie historique* (1979), pp. 135–44, on southern Europe.

standard worthy of defence'. The façade of Sant'Ambrogio in Milan has a similar scene of Saint Ambrose conjuring the commune into being. At times of assembly, in sight of designs such as these, civic identity was symbolized and reinforced. Though independent city-states remained rare outside Italy, urban awareness grew, as the number and dimensions of town grew, all over Europe.[20] Urban growth can be measured in the multiplication of parishes and the colonization of cities by mendicant communities, anxious to meet the spiritual needs of deracinated masses.[21]

Neglected peoples were brought into the candle-glow of scholarship. For the pilgrim-guide writer known as 'Aiméry Picaud', the forests and mountains that had to be crossed by pilgrims to Compostela housed misplaced exotics of egregious degrees of vice. A mule was as good as a woman for the Basques' perverted purposes, he thought, and the Navarrese poisoned rivers to increase the sale of their wines.[22] Yet alongside the self-indulgence of prejudice, some realistic images of marginal peoples and their societies emerged from genuine ethnographic 'fieldwork'.[23]

Matrix: Mentality and Demography

The first group of essays offers a broad picture of the foundations of European expansion. The opening chapter sets the scene with Karl Leyser's inaugural lecture as Chichele Professor of Medieval History at Oxford (1984). In *The Ascent of Latin Christendom*, Leyser used texts left by 11th-century historians to reconstruct their perceptions of their own times. The result is a vivid set of insights into a civilization enlivened by the conviction that it was experiencing expansion and was on the verge of great achievements. What is especially interesting is that Europeans themselves were aware that significant developments were occurring and that their world was becoming transformed.

The second chapter deals with population growth, a prerequisite for expansion of the kind Europe experienced in this period. The fact of such growth is obvious, but the problems of quantifying it seemed insuperable before Léopold Génicot's pioneering essay of 1953. The data is quite limited in quantity and from widely scattered times and places so that it is difficult to make judgements about the size of the population, but it is possible to draw some rough conclusions about growth. One of the most important but perhaps easily overlooked

20 On France, for example, see A. Chédeville, J. Le Goff, J. Rossiaud, *La Ville en France au Moyen Âge des carolingiens à la Renaissance* (Paris, 1998).

21 Jacques Le Goff, 'Apostolat mendiant et fait urbain dans la France médiévale', *Annales: Économies, sociétés, civilisations,* xxiii (1968), pp. 335–52.

22 J. Viellard, *Le guide du pélerin* (Mâcon, 1950), p. 32.

23 See J.-P. Massaut and M.-E. Henneau, (eds), *La christianisation des campagnes: Actes du colloque du CIHEC, 25-27 août, 1994* (Brussels, 1996); Robert Bartlett, *Gerald of Wales* (Oxford,1982); Felipe Fernández-Armesto, 'Medieval Ethnography', *Journal of the Anthropological Society of Oxford,* xiii (1982), pp. 275–86.

facts about such growth is that it was not evenly distributed throughout Europe. Some places grew faster than others while other places, some planned towns for example, never grew to fulfill the hopes of their founders.

One of the theoretical issues that the expansion of Europe generated concerns the relation of the medieval feudal, agricultural economy to the modern commercial, capitalistic economy. At the highest level of analysis, scholars have long been obsessed with the problem of how far medieval expansion foreshadowed or even pre-determined the modern 'rise of the west'; as far as internal changes within Latin Christendom are concerned, this problem may be expressed as that of the relationship between the extension and diversification of the medieval economy and the growth experienced in modern times. Did 'feudalism' yield to 'capitalism' and, if so, when and how? The third chapter contains the reflections of Jacques Heers in 1974, that captured, and to some extent, fixed the terms of debate.[24] This also raised the question of the degree to which feudalism contributed to or hindered the rise of Europe.

Any serious discussion of European expansion, medieval or modern, inevitably raises the question of the role of technology in expansion. Modern European overseas expansion is often linked to the development of military technology, above all the large cannon-bearing warship. Lynn White, a veritable apostle of the study of medieval technology, saw medieval expansion linked to several developments of a more mundane sort, the horse collar, the stirrup, and the mill. In his most famous work, *Medieval Technology and Social Change* he demonstrated the impact of these developments on medieval society.[25] In chapter 4, White argues that technological development was not a matter of serendipity, a matter of unexpected good fortune, but a consequence of a cultural context that encouraged and rewarded innovation, what he called the 'cultural climate' of the past. This essay brilliantly represents his thinking as well as capturing the key issues in the debate. He also set the problem in global context, raising but not resolving, the issue of why and how Europe became a *mise-en-scène* of technical progress.

Infrastructure and Ecology

The internal colonization – or re-colonization – of Europe had an enormous impact on the physical environment of medieval Europe, a topic that has attracted great interest in recent years. With the collapse of the Roman Empire in the West, the general decline in the indigenous population, and the influx of various new peoples, the amount of land under cultivation declined, giving way to forests and wastelands. The expansion that began *c.*1000 was rooted in a growing population leading to the need to reclaim forests and waste. Chapter 5 presents Richard Hoffman's illuminating essay that points out that the process of environmental

24 It can usefully be compared with the approach taken later by Thomas N. Bisson, 'The Feudal Revolution', *Past and Present,* no. 142 (1994), pp. 6–42.

25 Lynn White, Jr., *Medieval Technology and Social Change* (Oxford, 1962).

transformation was not restricted to the land. In addition to the obvious uses of water for farming and personal use, some of the areas that were cleared were wetlands that had to be drained in order to make the soil productive. The mills that Lynn White discussed were often water mills that required the damming of streams and the creation of millponds in order to provide a steady supply of water to move the wheel. Other waterways had to be cleared to allow small boats, a significant form of transport, to operate. Finally, to supplement the diet, fish were often raised in manorial ponds.

In Chapter 6 Margaret Ley Bazeley, in a paper read before the Royal Historical Society in London in 1921, demonstrates that the pressure to clear the forests encountered man-made opposition as kings and great lords sought to retain forests for as hunting preserves. Much forest land in England was reserved from peasant colonization, leading for demands to remove lands from protected status as royal forest subject to the harsh terms of the Forest Law and leave them open to exploitation. Bazeley was interested in the juridical status of forests and the political and legal conflicts involving those seeking access to forests and those who sought to restrict access. As a result legal issues such as efforts to secure 'disafforestment', that is removal of forests from the jurisdiction of the Forest Law, were her primary focus. In today's environmentally aware world, however, what is interesting in this essay is not the issue of 'disafforestment' but that of 'deforestation', the cutting down of forests for settlement and the legal debates that reflected differing visions of the most appropriate use of natural resources.[26]

The essays by professors Lopez and Boyer, Chapters 7 and 8, describe the difficulties of land travel in a world that is in the process of being cleared. Lopez made the striking point that medieval roads did not always follow the famous roads that the Romans established, because the medieval roads were created to serve the needs of commerce not the needs of imperial administration, the purpose of the Roman road system. Furthermore, medieval land routes faced competition from water-borne trade commerce, so those who laid them out tended to seek the routes that would compete with water routes most efficiently. In effect a new road network was gradually developed not from the perspective of a central authority seeking a tool of administrative control but from the economic interests of local and regional populations. Professor Boyer's essay carefully works out the distance that a traveller could be expected to cover in day, an illustration of the problems affecting those who wished to travel. The competition that land routes faced from water routes is also another reminder of the importance of water that Hoffman discussed.

Chapter 9 deals with what has become one of the most controversial topics in the study of medieval economic development, the role of the monks of the Cistercian Order in the development of the medieval rural economy. It is often argued that in order to remain faithful to their austere beginnings, the Cistercians established new monasteries in marginal lands that would require constant effort to maintain if the community was to survive. R.A. Donkin revises our understanding of how the Cistercians operated by examining one of the most

26 For a more recent account, see Charles R. Young, *The Royal Forests of Medieval England* (Philadelphia, 1979).

famous areas of Cistercian expansion, northern England. He concluded that rather than clearing and taming wastelands, the Cistercians took over existing small properties, often evicting the peasant inhabitants in the process, and then engaged in activities designed to improve agricultural production. In effect, rather than being the pioneers of colonization of marginal lands, the monks came after the initial stages of colonization and acted as managers of large-scale agricultural operations rather than path-breaking colonizers.[27]

The Rural Economy

Somewhat more particularly, the debate over the origins of modernity raised the question of how changing methods of environmental exploitation affected the role of labour: did the role of lords relax, and that of peasants grow in the expanding countryside? This is a still unresolved debate, but the part Michael M. Postan played was long dominant in it. Chapter 10 contains his 1937 piece on what he called 'the chronology of labour services' which anticipated views he maintained more or less intact throughout his long life.[28] The crux of the issue was how the manorial system based on the management of an estate worked by peasants was gradually transformed into a capitalist system operated by rent-paying peasants. Postan argued that the general perception of a gradual smooth passage from the medieval economy to the modern based on the commutation of medieval labour services to modern cash payment is misleading. In fact, while there was commutation in some places, in others labour services were reintroduced, particularly in the later Middle Ages as many landlords became more directly involved in farming their desmans. Postan's essay emphasized the importance of detailed studies of economic conditions in specific times and places before making broad generalizations.

As is often the case, a forceful position on an important topic, as Postan's essay was, led both to further work along the lines that he suggested and to revisionism, not a rejection of his position but modification and adjustment based on later research. An example of the first consequence of Postan's work are the studies of P.J. Jones in Italian contexts. Chapter 11 contains his enormously helpful retracing of events on the rural scene in Tuscany from the 12th to the 13th centuries, first published in 1954.[29] This was a response to Postan's call for more detailed studies of the medieval economy.

27 For a more recent work that that developed this theme: see Constance H. Berman, co-editor, *Medieval Agriculture, the Southern-French Countryside, and the Early Cistercians* (Philadelphia, 1986).

28 For a later summary, see Michael M. Postan, 'The Economic Foundations of Medieval Society', in *Essays on Medieval Agriculture and General Problems of the Medieval Economy* (Cambridge, 1973), pp. 3–27.

29 See also 'From Manor to Mezzadria: A Tuscan Case-Study in the Medieval Origins of Modern Agrarian Society', in Nicolai Rubinstein (ed.), *Florentine Studies* (1968), pp. 193–241.

Chapter 12, M. Toch's revisionist essay of 1986, is an example of another response to Postan's work. He argued that lordship remained important, and seigniorial initiative was vital in encouraging settlement and developing new economic initiatives; but that the liberation of labour at low social levels was clearly also a stimulus to production as well.[30]

In 1941, the classic essay of E.M. Carus-Wilson on 'An Industrial Revolution of the Thirteenth Century', Chapter 13 of this volume, ended one area of debate about the transformation of the economy from a rural base to an urban one in the later Middle Ages. It convinced the scholarly world that cloth output actually grew in a period when it seemed to be diminishing or vanishing in some urban centres: the explanation was that it was being re-located to rural settings.[31] He pointed out that fulling mills, usually associated with urban development, one of the fundamental pieces of machinery in the cloth-making process, were often established in rural areas by the lords of manors, demonstrating, as Postan had argued, that the path from medieval to modern was not a straightforward one moving inevitably from the countryside to the city.

Urban and Commercial Expansion

The process of internally colonizing Europe had one other important consequence, the revival of urban life. The revival of urban life was associated with the revival of trade and commerce, but the nature of that relationship is unclear and had engendered a good deal of scholarly controversy, much of it associated with the work of the Belgian scholar Henri Pirenne.[32] Pirenne had argued that Muslim domination of the Mediterranean had ended the Roman cultural and economic world that was centered on the Mediterranean and moved the center of gravity of the emerging medieval world to northern Europe.[33] Basing his assertions on his own extensive research on the development of the Netherlands, Pirenne drew a number of conclusions about the origins and development of cities that he believed applicable to Europe in general. Although the stated focus of his research was the point at which the Roman cultural and economic world ceased to dominate European society, it had important consequences for the long-term study of urban development throughout Europe. The issues involved included the origins and functions of medieval cities and the sources of population for them.

30 See Fossier, op. cit., pp. 964–79; Timothy Reuter, (ed.), *The Medieval Nobility* (Amsterdam, 1978).

31 Cf. E. Coornaert, 'Draperies rurales, draperies urbaines', *Revue belge de philologie et d'histoire,* 28 (1950), pp. 60–96.

32 An old but still useful introduction to Pirenne's work is *The Pirenne Thesis: Analysis, Criticism, and Revision*, Alfred F. Havighurst (ed.) (Boston, 1958). This volume contains critiques of Pirenne's work by two authors represented in the present volume, Robert S. Lopez and Lynn White, Jr.

33 Pirenne presented his views in two important books: *Mohammed and Charlemagne*, trans. Bernard Miall (London, 1929); and *Medieval Cities: Their Origins and the Revival of Trade*, trans. Frank D. Halsey (Princeton, 1925; reprinted 1969).

Pirenne's work attracted a great deal of attention and generated a large body of research, much of it critical. Maurice Lombard, the author of Chapter 14, emphasized that the medieval city was a walled centre of production and trade, not the administrative centre of a region characterized by public spaces such as temples and a forum. Furthermore, Lombard suggests that Pirenne was wrong in stressing the break between the medieval Christian and Muslim economies. Instead, he pointed to the strong economic links between Europe and the Muslim world beginning in the eighth century that contributed to the urban revival in the West. Finally, in Chapter 15, David Nicholas, another critic of Pirenne, argues that Pirenne overemphasized the role of the travelling merchant in the formation of towns and underestimated the importance of a pre-existing settled population whose needs the merchant would serve.

The medieval extension of the frontiers of Christendom becomes intelligible against this background of expansion at home. In recent years, scholarly attention has focused with increasing interest and concentration on these inward 'frontiers' and the colonization and exploitation of the environment western Christians occupied.[34] Yet the broad outlines of the story have long been understood: indeed, they are obvious. The evidence of the dynamism and wealth of western Europe in the period preceding the disasters of the fourteenth century is abundant and inescapable in the surviving art and building of the era; it infuses the landscapes and streetscapes which are still apparent today and were laid down in the era. The essays in this volume therefore cover a long period of scholarly foundation-laying for our present understanding, from the 1920s to the 1990s. As usual in this series and its companion-series, *An Expanding World*, edited by A.J. Russell-Wood, the emphasis is on uniting, for readers' convenience, important essays in English (and, exceptionally, where of indispensable importance, in other languages) from journals, rarely-available conference proceedings, or recondite publications.

Bibliography

Abulafia, David and Nora Berend, *Medieval Frontiers: Concepts and Practices* (Aldershot, 2002).

Aston, Michael, D. Austin and C. Dyer (eds), *The Rural Settlements of Medieval England* (Oxford, 1989).

Bateson Mary, 'The Laws of Breteuil', *English Historical Review* 15 (1900), pp. 73–8, 302–18, 496–523, 754–7; 16 (1901), pp. 92–110, 332–45.

Beresford, Maurice, *New Towns of the Middle Ages: Town Plantation in England, Wales and Gascony* (London, 1967; reprinted. Gloucester, 1988).

34 W. Rössner, *Peasants in the Middle Ages* (Cambridge, 1992), pp. 33–44; see the recent conference proceedings: G. De Boe and F. Verhaeghe, (eds), *Rural Settlements in Medieval Europe: Papers of the Medieval Europe Brugge 1997, Conference 6* (Zellick, 1997), and M. Colardelle et al., (eds), *L'Homme et la nature au Moyen Âge: paléoenvironnement des sociétés occidentales: Actes du Ve Congrès Internationale d'archéologie médiévale* (Paris, 1996).

Berlow, R.K., 'The Development of Business Techniques Used at the Fairs of Champagne from the End of the XIIth Century to the middle of the XIIIth Century', *Studies in Medieval and Renaissance History* 8 (1971), pp. 8–32.

Birrell, Jean, 'Peasant Craftsmen in the Medieval Forest', *Agricultural History Review* 17 (1969), pp. 91–107.

Bloch, Marc, *French Rural History: An Essay on Its Basic Characteristics*, trans. Janet Sondheimer (Berkeley, CA, 1966).

Burns, Robert I., *The Crusader Kingdom of Valencia: Reconstruction on a Thirteenth-Century Frontier*, 2 vols. (Cambridge, MA, 1967).

Bradley, John, 'Planned Anglo-Norman Towns in Ireland', in H.B. Clarke and Anngret Simms (eds), *The Comparative History of Urban Origins in Non-Roman Europe*, British Archaeological Reports, International Series, 255, 2 vols. (Oxford, 1985), Vol. 2, pp. 411–67.

Citarella, Armando, 'The Relations of Amalfi with the Arab World before the Crusades', *Speculum* 42 (1967), pp. 299–312.

Darby, H.C., 'The Clearing of Woodland in Europe', in W.L. Thomas (ed.) *Man's Role in Changing the Face of the Earth* (Chicago, 1956), pp. 183–216.

Darby, H.C., 'The Fenland Frontier in Anglo-Saxon England', *Antiquity* 8 (1934), pp. 185–201.

Davies, Rees, *Domination and Conquest: The Experience of Ireland, Scotland and Wales 1100–1300* (Cambridge, 1991).

Down, Kevin, 'The Agricultural Economy of Colonial Ireland', in Art Cosgrove (ed.) *New History of Ireland*, Vol. 2, *Medieval Ireland, 1169–1534* (Oxford, 1987), pp. 450–81.

Duby, Georges, *Rural Economy and Country Life in the Medieval West*, trans. Cynthia Poston (London, 1968).

Duby, Georges, *The Early Growth of the European Economy: Warriors and Peasants from the Seventh to the Twelfth Century*, trans. H.B. Clarke, (New York, 1974).

Duffy, P. J., 'The Nature of the Medieval Frontier in Ireland', *Studia Hibernica* 22–23 (1982–1983), pp. 21–38.

Dvornik, Francis, *The Making of Central and Eastern Europe* (London, 1949).

Empey, C.A., 'Conquest and Settlement: Patters of Anglo-Norman Settlement in North Minster and South Leinster', *Irish Economic and Social History* 13 (1986), pp. 5–31.

Focillon, Henri, *The Year 1000* (New York, 1971).

Hallem, H.E., (ed.) *The Agrarian History of England and Wales*, Vol. 2, *1042–1350* (Cambridge, 1988).

Hensel, Witold, 'The Origins of Western and Eastern European Slav Towns', in M.W. Barlkey (ed.), *European Towns: Their Archaeology and Early History* (London and New York, 1977), pp. 373–90.

Hoffmann, Richard, *Land, Liberties and Lordship in a Late Medieval Countryside: Agrarian Structures and Change in the Duchy of Wroclaw* (Philadelphia, 1989).

Howe, John M., 'The Conversion of the Physical World: The Creation of a Christian Landscape', in James Muldoon (ed.), *Varieties of Religious Conversion in the Middle Ages* (Gainesville, FL, 1997), pp. 63–78.

Hurst, J.G., 'The Changing Medieval Village in England', in J.A. Raftis (ed.), *Pathways to Medieval Peasants* (Toronto, 1981), pp. 27–62.

Kahl, Hans-Dietrich, *Slawen und Deutsche in der brandenburgischen Geschiichte des zwölften Jahrhunderts*, 2 vols (Cologne, 1964).

Kahl, Hans-Dietrich, 'Compellere intrare: Die Wendenpolitik Bruns von Querfurt im Lichte hochmittelalterlichen Missions- und Vökerrechts', in Helmut Beumann (ed.), *Heidenmission und Kreuzzugsgedanke in der deutschen Ostpolitik des Mittelalters* (Darmstadt, 1963), pp. 177–274.

Knoll, Paul, 'Economic and Political Institutions on the Polish-German Frontier in the Middle Ages: Action, Reaction, Interaction', in Robert Bartlett and Angus MacKay (eds), *Medieval Frontier Societies* (Oxford, 1989), pp. 151–74.

Knoll, Paul, *The Rise of the Polish Monarchy: Piast Poland in East Central Europe 1320–1370* (Chicago, 1972).

Koebner, Richard, 'The Settlement and Colonization of Europe', in J.H. Clapham and Eileen Power (eds), *The Agrarian Life of the Middle Ages*, 2nd ed., Vol. 1, *The Cambridge Economic History of Europe* (Cambridge, 1966), pp. 1–91.

Kuhn, Walter, 'German Town Foundations of the Thirteenth Century in Western Pomerania', in H.B. Clarke and Anngret Simms (eds), *The Comparative History of Urban Origins in Non-Roman Europe*, British Archaeological Reports, International Series 255, 2 vols (Oxford, 1985), Vol. 2, pp. 547–80.

Kuhn, Walter, *Vergleichende Untersuchen zur mittelalterlichen Ostsiedlung* (Cologne and Vienna, 1973).

Latouche, Robert, *The Birth of Western Economy: Economic Aspects of the Dark Ages*, trans. E.M. Wilkinson (London, 1967).

Leyser, Karl, *Medieval Germany and its Neighbours* (London, 1982).

Lourie, Elena, 'Free Muslims in the Balearics Under Christian Rule in the Thirteenth Century', *Speculum* 45 (1970), pp. 624–49.

MacKay, Angus, *Spain in the Middle Ages: From Frontier to Empire, 1000–1500* (New York, 1977).

McNeill, J.R., *The Mountains of the Mediterranean World: an Environmental History* (Cambridge, 1990).

McCrank, Lawrence J., *Medieval Frontier History in New Catalonia* (Aldershot, 1996).

Nef, John U., 'Mining and Metallurgy in Medieval Civilisation', *The Cambridge Economic History of Europe,* 2 (Cambridge, 1952), pp. 693–761.

Nitz, Hans-Jürgen, 'The Church as Colonist: The Benedictine Abbey of Lorsch and Planned *Waldhufen* Colonization in the Odenwald', *Journal of Historical Geography* 9 (1983), pp. 105–26.

Pryor, J.H., 'The Origins of the Commenda Contract', *Speculum* 52 (1977), pp. 5–37.

Russell, Josiah Cox, *British Medieval Population* (Albuquerque, NM, 1948).

Schlesinger, Walter (ed.), *Die deutsche Ostsiedlung als Problem der europäischen Geschichte* (Sigmaringen, 1975).

Slichter van Bath, B.H., *Agrarian History of Western Europe, A.D. 500–1850*, trans. Olive Ordish (London, 1963).

Thompson, James Westfall, 'The German Church and the Conversion of the Baltic Slavs', *American Journal of Theology* 20 (1916), pp. 205–30.

Titow, J.Z., 'Some Evidence of the Thirteenth-Century Population Increase', *Economic History Review*, 2nd ser. 14 (1961), pp. 218–24.

Vlasto, A.P., *The Entry of the Slavs into Christendom* (Cambridge, 1970).

1
The Ascent of Latin Europe

Karl Leyser

My task tonight has not been made easier by the resplendent examples I must follow. Yet am I wholly fortunate and privileged to have Sir Richard Southern and Michael Wallace-Hadrill as my predecessors and judges. My indebtedness to them both is huge and continuous and it goes back many years, to the days when Richard Southern was in charge of Sir Maurice Powicke's seminar in 1947 and then, when Michael Wallace-Hadrill from Merton and in his writings, taught me my first faltering steps in early medieval historiography. I acknowledge it gladly and I should also recall here the impulse I owe to Geoffrey Barraclough's *Mediaeval Germany*. Strictly speaking—and I say this without effrontery—I have no predecessors at all. A Chichele Chair of Medieval History did not exist until very recently indeed and I am its first occupant. I take this designation to mean no more than that I have spoken prose all my working life. It was the Regius Professor who recently, in a review, well defined the business of an Inaugural Lecture: it should crystallize thought.[1] It can, however, do a number of other things as well. It can survey and take stock of the situation of its subject. Where has the study of Medieval Europe and England got to and in which direction is it moving? Are these the right marching goals? Furthermore it can pause and dwell on the favourite authors and foremost sources the speaker is most deeply engaged with and what they tell us about the world he most wishes to evoke and illuminate. These are the two beacon-lights Sir Richard and Michael have lit and I shall try to steer by both of them and hope to present a crystal or two of my thinking at the same time.

My title may sound strange but it was not chosen casually. Rises can be soaring and meteoric, an ascent always suggests effort, labour, and trouble, and occasional halts to fetch breath. It is one of these or, as I hope to show, but the semblance of a pause, I would like to dwell on today, the first half of the eleventh century before the turmoil and shrillness of what we sometimes call the age of Gregorian Reform. Now anyone wishing to reflect on Latin Europe must of course at once resort to the works of two outstanding scholars who, well over thirty years ago, re-charted our way into this topic, Ernst Curtius and Erich Auerbach. Yet Curtius, in his *European Literature and the Latin Middle Ages*, rather ignored what lay between the Carolingian and the Twelfth-Century Renaissance as an intermediate period and in his *Mimesis* at least, Auerbach gave this moment of Latin writing and thought a miss too.[2] Later he dwelt on some tenth-century authors but their styles and expressive devices appealed to him more than the substance of what they had to say.[3] Curtius went further and in a lecture appended to the English version of his great book he considered that medieval thought and expression became creative only around the year 1050.[4] This is a very challengeable verdict and it shall be challenged here. However, the historian of Europe on the eve of the turmoil, taking stock, the historian who wishes to know how, when, and why Latin Europe began its climb to military, economic, and cultural dominance, how, when, and why it took the shape and shell it lived in until 1939, must above all face and come to terms with the commanding heights of recent and current French scholarship.

Its inspiration and aims lay in a new relationship between the pursuit of history and the social sciences which was proclaimed in a celebrated paper by Ferdinand Braudel published in the *Annales* in 1958.[5] It gave short shrift to Curtius whose magisterial theme is characterized thus: the study of a cultural system which prolonged and, by its own preferences, disfigured the civilisation of the later Roman Empire which was itself weighed down by an oppressive heritage. More damning still was his view of the human sciences in crisis: They remained 'in the grip of a retrograde and insidious humanism which can no longer serve as their framework.'[6] The construction of a new framework, almost a new language—Braudel used the word—thus became the urgent and foremost task realised by, amongst others, a band of French medievalists. It was led by Georges Duby whose study of the Mâconnais, largely based on the charters of Cluny appeared some five years before Braudel's article and the statement of his aims can be taken as programmatic: 'To approach human beings directly without isolating them from their milieu, to follow the history of families and fortunes closely, to carry on simultaneously the study of activities and diverse institutions and to seize upon the bonds which united them.'[7] This alone can prepare the great syntheses and the search for them became, one can say, a consuming purpose. An undercurrent of scientific certainty, of geographical, ethnological, and economic model-making, of thinking in terms of structures, carried all before it. Georges Duby's Maconnais was followed by Fossier's Picardy, Chédeville's Chartrain, Magnou-Nortier's South-West, Toubert's Latium and Bonassie's justly acclaimed Catalonia.[8] The most characteristic product of this band of scholars is thus the microcosmic and all-embracing regional study. The headlines for this were written some twenty years ago by Jacques Le Goff in the preface to his collection of papers, *Pour un autre moyen age: Temps, travail et culture en Occident* translated under the title *Time, Work and Culture in the Middle Ages.* The aim here was a historical anthropology of the pre-industrial West and it should be mentioned that Le Goff's Middle Ages stretch from the Later Roman Empire until the Industrial Revolution of the eighteenth and ninteenth centuries. They were to him the primordial past in which our collective identity acquired certain of its essential characteristics. Le Goff has, of course, endorsed 'l' histoire à longue durée', as Braudel prescribed it. 'Vulgar' Marxism is rejected but 'material civilisation and culture must interpenetrate one another within a socio-economic analysis'.[9] It might be said that in this post-marxist analysis we have a kind of historical materialism without the eschatology, without the immediate, unacceptable consequences for the present, just like a puritanism that has outlived the religious beliefs that had once given birth to it.

And the result? Here we have a grandiose recent synthesis, the work of Robert Fossier, two volumes in the *Nouvelle Clio* series entitled *Enfance de l'europe*. It is a magisterial survey of the struggles of early medieval societies to break through their poverty trap, to enlarge and enrich themselves without doing so only at the expense of one another. Here again we encounter the restless and ceaseless search for *syntheses* and *structures* and, in particular, Fossier wishes to unfold three closely joined developments: first, the population increase—the insistently swelling wave of people, the greatest, he thinks, in the whole history of the continent. With it arose the settlements and villages as they are still today, on the whole, together with the more immediate phenomenology of new enterprise and expansion: religious, military and mercantile. Next comes, as a consequence, a loosening of familial bonds and their enrichment by other horizontal and vertical forms of association. Lastly Fossier presents, and here he is most emphatic not to say dogmatic, a process he calls 'encellulement', 'cellularization' in the seignorial mould which left all initiatives in the hands of a few clerks and warriors.[10] The lives of most men, he points out, were dominated by the exploitive routines applied by these masters, the harsh institutions of local justice and labour services, and the *châteaux* on which they depended. There seems to be a remarkable unanimity about the all-importance of the ban, the rights and powers of coercion as a dominant theme of the eleventh century. A man was either under it and subject to its humiliating burdens and sanctions, and most men were, or he escaped it, that is to say he belonged to the handful of *potentes* who enforced it or was one of the *milites* and clerks who helped them.

Yet however important these institutions became as modes of life, as the cast-iron order of economic and social concentration, *encellulement* did not, it seems to me, destroy all larger identities across the boundaries of castellany and lordship and must not become a sole dominant theme. It is here that the historiography of the tenth and early eleventh centuries comes to our help. Its horizons were scaled by latinity and Latin *christianitas*. History in the tenth and early eleventh century was the temporal framework of divine purpose manifesting itself. Through it, fallible human beings might fitfully apprehend what that purpose was. For men who had lived for generations through anxious seasons of war, heathen invasions, plunder and *depopulatio* and also the self-lacerations of *christianitas*, it is not surprising that history became one of their first preoccupations when the clouds began to lift and conditions became a little easier to comprehend and reflect upon. Historiography was the most creative and also the most enduring achievement of later Ottonian and early eleventh-century Europe, much more so than Curtius and Auerbach allowed. It was also the way of bringing about a new and larger cohesion both among lay and clerical elites. Above all it had the critical task of integrating newcomers like the Polish, Magyar and Scandinavian aristocracies into Latin Christianity and it succeeded in performing it.

The Roman Empire eventually collapsed because it was no longer able to absorb wave after wave of barbarians into its fabric. The Latin West and Centre in the early eleventh century were able to do just that, to resist militarily and to impose culturally, not least of all through the agency of historical writing. Where military resistance failed, as in

Aethelred II's England, the cultural ascendancy nonetheless triumphed. It was only as a *rex christianus*, seen in the company of the Emperor Conrad II at his coronation in Rome that Canute could hope to stabilize, rule, and transmit his conquests.[11] The Empire too was now ringed by Christian eastern and south-eastern neighbours. These converts, whether they liked it or not, had to merge their own oral memories into a larger christological and eschatological context. For their symbiosis with Christian Latin neighbours they had to find a place for themselves in a much larger past than they had known hitherto. For this process they often depended on teachers borrowed from their patrons and godfathers. Dudo of St Quentin, the first historian of the Normans, was a clerk from Vermandois. The first historian of Poland, the Gallus Anonymus, seems to have come from Flanders.[12]

The historians of the late tenth and early eleventh century not only masked and documented a process of expansion which thus gives them their special place in the ascent of Latin Europe, they also unfold new forms of self-awareness, new ways of portraying both themselves and social relations. There was a new breadth as well as intimacy such as we do not quite find in the historical writings of the Carolingian world. Let us begin with Adémar of Chabannes.[13] Adémar was a monk at St Cybard in Angoulême but through his uncles he had close links with, and often stayed in, St Martial, at Limoges. Born in 988 he enjoyed an excellent education at St Martial and wrote first of all a history of its abbots, albeit as a monk of another house. His *Chronique*, in three books, is much the most essential historical work bearing on Aquitaine in the tenth and early eleventh centuries. There is scarely another. To begin with a history of the Franks under the Merowingians and Carolingians based on sources like the *Liber Historiae Francorum*, the *Continuation of Fredegarius* and the *Annales regni Francorum*, from chapter xvi of the third book, the *Chronique* becomes Adémar's own. But this is not all. The all-consuming business and interest of Adémar's life was his passionate attempt to prove that St Martial of Limoges had been one of Christ's disciples and one of the apostles. To this end he wrote a celebrated *Letter* which he sought to propagate widely, and on this topic he addressed councils, in particular one in 1028, when he preached and disputed on his hobby-horse of a subject. Though of noble birth, Adémar was not a man particularly close to any court. He described the ambiance of Duke William the Great of Aquitaine (993/4–1030) but there is almost nothing atypical in his account: the pilgrimages, the presents exchanged with other princes and the Emperor Henry II, the constant attendance of bishops near his person, the pious patronage of monasteries, the advice of monks in the *administratio regni*, and the efforts to have the good-will of Abbot Odilo of Cluny: they are all part of a quasi-regal repertoire.[14] We hear much also about the counts of Angoulême in the *Chronique*, but if Adémar was an occasional visitor of their court he did not belong to it. Nor does he ever seem to have held an abbey and yet he was an important and prominent man. His numerous sermons at gatherings to propagate the peace movement, and its oaths, have survived. He accumulated and possessed a splendid library and was an industrious copier of manuscripts whose autographs have survived and been identified. He bequeathed his books to St Martial before setting out on a pilgrimage to Jerusalem from which he did not return and perhaps had not wanted to. He died in 1034. Altogether it is striking how influential and eminent a literate and erudite monk could be in early eleventh-century France and we shall meet other examples. In his obit notice it is set down that he commanded a Life of St Martial to be written in golden letters and many other books.[15] He had a large noble kin and was evidently a man of means.

Adémar's Letter about the Apostolate of St Martial was addressed not only to a number of local clerical notables, like the Bishop of Limoges, canons, monks, an architect, all at Limoges, learned men in the vicinity and various abbots, but it was also meant for the Bishop of Rodez, for Bishop Dietrich II of Metz, the Empress Cunigunde, Henry II's widow, the Emperor Conrad II, and Duke William, 'grammatico, orthodoxo et potentissimo Aquitanorum duci'.[16] Adémar seems to have liked to use *grammaticus* for 'literate'. It was finally meant also for Pope John XIX. For the assessment of the emperor's place at the peak of the worldly hierarchy the inscription is worth remembering. His notice and approval were regarded as important and it was deemed right to try and gain them and not only the goodwill of Adémar's own prince, the duke of Aquitaine. Here, as elsewhere, it is apparent that the world before the Investiture Conflict had an inner cohesion which did not survive that upheaval into the twelfth century. Adémar's horizons were large and he knew, if in a somewhat blurred way, about men and events in the later Ottonian *Reich*. He knew, for instance, that Duke Henry of Bavaria, struggling for the kingship in 1002 had gained possession of the *insignia* by some determined arm-twisting, forcing Archbishop Heribert of Cologne to surrender them. He wrote about the foundation of Bamberg and the Pope's consecration of it and that Henry II too cultivated Odilo of Cluny, listing his presents to the abbey. His report of Conrad II's election and succession is elaborate if confused. Here the bishops and *proceres* who elevated him were not called 'Saxons' as West-Frankish writers sometimes described all their Eastern neighbours. Once, at least, Adémar spoke of the *terra Theodisca*.[17]

Most of what he wrote about Duke William V, we have said, belonged to a well-rehearsed genre of panegyric. Yet in one respect he enlarged on this and hit upon a theme that is central in his vision. William, he wrote, had been taught letters from boyhood and possessed a good knowledge of scriptures. He kept a fine library in his palace and when he took a break from the hubbub of ruling he applied himself to reading for nights on end until sleep overtook him. Not content with this, Adémar linked his hero with a tradition of princely literacy. This is what Louis (the Pious) and his father Charlemagne used to do. More still, Theodosius 'victor Augustus' in the hall of his *palatium* not only read but even wrote with great zeal. Adémar concluded this reflection with a mention of Caesar: 'Octavianus Caesar Augustus' he called him who after his *lectio* wrote of his battles, Roman history, and other things with his own hand. Lupus of Ferrières had occasionally exhorted Charles the Bald to study and imitate the deeds of Trajan and Theodosius. Here a duke is praised for following and aligning himself with the examples from both Christian and pagan Antiquity. Evidently Adémar deeply approved of the continuity he thought he saw.[18]

In his very next chapter he described the Irish and Ireland. The island, he wrote, had twelve *civitates* with ample bishoprics and one king. It had its own language but Latin letters, 'propriam linguam, sed latinas litteras'. St Patrick, a Roman, had converted it. The importance Adémar attached to the latinity of the Irish is heightened by the context in which he mentioned it, a massive Norse attack. The Norseman, according to him, suffered a crushing defeat, none of them escaped.[19] It is not clear whether our Aquitanian author knew much about Ireland's religious past. For him it was a rather remote outpost of Latin Europe and *Christianitas* but its successful defence mattered to the whole of which it formed part. In an earlier chapter Adémar had described how William Longue-Epée succeeded Rollo in Normandy. He had been baptised as a boy and the whole body of Normans who lived close to *Francia* accepted the faith. They forsook their heathen speech and got used to Latin, *sermo latinus*.[20] This must not be taken literally. Nothing could show more clearly how much an observant Latin writer of the early eleventh century was aware of the shifting and uncertain frontiers of christianity and latinity and there is his note of evident satisfaction about the internal reconquest, as he saw it. Conversely Dudo of St Quentin, in verses addressed to his patron (1014–1015), Count Rudolf, made him the heir of Roman heroic *virtus*. Scipio, Pompey and Cato, when they were consuls, Rome was aglow, now the Normans are on top and the *culmen honoris* belongs to Duke Richard I. Whether Dudo succeeded in flattering his Norman hosts by naturalizing them in a Roman past we don't know. His work was after all dedicated to so deep-dyed an old fox as Bishop Adalbero of Laon, but at least he tried.[21]

Adémar's sensitivity to speech has left other marks in his *Chronique*. Not long after the year 1000 the Moors of Cordoba attacked Narbonne suddenly and hoped to take it by sorcery. The Christians inside took the sacraments— Adémar's counterpoint—prepared for death and assaulted the enemy. They won and took many prisoners whom they enslaved and sold. Twenty huge Moors, however, they gave to St Martial at Limoges. The abbot Gosfred kept two and Adémar remarked that their language was not that of the Saracens but they seemed to bark like dogs. Perhaps this meant they did not speak Arabic but some North-African Berber dialect.[22]

It would be quite wrong to ignore Adémar as the splendid source that he is for some of the processes so well analysed by Georges Duby and Robert Fossier. He tells us much about the peace movement with the relics of saints brought to huge assemblies where peace was preached but also intensive prayer against rampant disease offered. There are throngs of knights holding *beneficia* from a powerful abbot.[23] In a mid-winter campaign between Jordan of Chabanais and Bishop Alduin of Limoges, the former was suddenly attacked and struck down by an unknown *miles* when he was already victoriously on his way back with many prisoners. Characteristically the construction of a castle lay behind the war. Castles again were the key to lordship and the objects of savage warfare elsewhere in the area under Adémar's purview.

There was much blinding, even of a choir-bishop, and revenge. Duke William when he could not hurt the real culprit maimed his brother instead.[24] Yet there was also an example of Christian forgiveness. When Count William of Angoulême fell ill less than a year after his joyful return from a Jerusalem pilgrimage a woman was accused of having procured his disease by *maleficia*. The case was tried by a judicial duel in which the champion of the accusation defeated the defence. Nonetheless the count refused to let the woman, who had not confessed, be tortured again. He died of his illness on 6 April 1028. His son and successor proved to be less forbearing and according to another version of the *Chronique* had the woman and the accomplices burnt.[25] Adémar ends his *Chronique* with the story of a successful military operation against Saracens in Spain whence the Gascon participants return with much booty. The northwards flow of wealth from the Taifa kingdoms had begun.[26] The process of *encellulement* did not bar a larger framework of action and vision.

Adémar of Chabannes had a contemporary whose historical writings even more than his own proclaim awareness of a new order, the birth of a new *ensemble* of peoples in a Christian *orbis Romanus*. That historian was Rodulf Glaber, (the bald).[27] What is more he seems to welcome this new order, to stress its discontinuity rather than bonds with the ancient Roman world and to approve of its political pluralism. Instead of one empire there were now two kingdoms and rulers, those of the Franks (W. Francia) and the Saxons. Under their new kings the world began to flourish once more and thanks to their mutual peace the kingdom of Christ began to subject tyrants everywhere by the baptismal font. Glaber here celebrated above all the conversion of the Magyars, as elsewhere he was jubilant about the reopening of the land-route to Constantinople and Jerusalem which led necessarily through their settlements. He welcomed also the massive upsurge of the pilgrimage movement even though he did not conceal from himself or his readers the conceit and boasting of many who had made the journey chiefly to be admired by their neighbours. To those who thought that the mass prilgrimage heralded the coming of Anti-Christ he replied calmly that, all the same, the devoted labour of the faithful who went would receive its reward from a just judge.[28]

Rodulf Glaber was born about 985, almost certainly of noble parents though he may have been illegitimate. In his great historical work, the *Historiarum Libri Quinque* which he wrote between 1026 and 1045, he is much more autobiographical than was Adémar. At the age of twelve, he related in Book V, a maternal uncle (and one cannot stress the importance of that relationship for the early middle ages enough) placed him in a monastery, St Leger-de-Champeaux, which was, however, subject to St Germain d'Auxerre. As a monk his life is more notable for constant movement, travel and migration than *stabilitas*. He is found at Moutiers, Bèze, at, above all, St Bénigne, Dijon, Cluny, and at Rome. He knew and stood close to St William of Dijon, whose *Life* he wrote shortly after 1031, and also Odilo of Cluny to whom he dedicated his *Histories*. He also knew Bishop Odalrich of Orléans who told him events and incidents, things he had experienced on his pilgrimage to Jerusalem. Once again, then, here is a monk who never rose to any prelacy but, nevertheless, was a man of importance whose company was sought after by his superiors who entrusted him with weighty tasks. He tells us how and why. In his early years Rodulf had been anything but a willing recruit to the regular life and while at St Germain or St Leger, he wrote, he exasperated his betters, his equals, and his juniors. Eventually they expelled him but they had no qualms about his future because he was a man of letters, he possessed what he called *litteratoriam notionem*, and those who drove him out felt that he would never want a roof over his head and a place to stay, on that account. Rodulf, moreover, nodded assent: it was the general experience.[29]

Men of letters in the West would not always be so confident.

Rodulf's *Histories* had of course many themes in common with Adémar's *Chronique* and this in itself is valuable evidence for what mattered to the *cognoscenti* of the early eleventh century. There again was the peace movement with its assemblies from near and far to which the relics and bodies of the saints were carried by their guardians, monks and clerks, to overawe the lay warriors and instil into them a sense of fear and sacrilege and so make them swear the oaths. Both writers shared the shock and concern about the discovery of heresy among a clerical élite in Orléans. Its very existence and luxuriant self-assurance can be read as a sign of well-being rather than crisis. Rodulf, like Adémar, mentioned the flow of booty from Spain, this time to the altars of Cluny, and he too told the tale of a count killed by a humble *miles* in action. Again there is much fighting round castles.[30]

Rodulf's *Histories*, all the same, differ profoundly from Adémar's *Chronique* in that they explore inwards as well as outwards. The demons that frightened him as he lay in his little bed were a part of himself with which he struggled.[31] Their power was, like that of the heretics, all too real and fearsome. Adémar had revealed a society in which the saints sometimes had to do duty for the want of effective government. His *Chronique* is also a great monument to Aquitaine and its links with *Latinitas* at large. Rodulf addressed himself chiefly to another, and perhaps more profound, function of medieval historiography of which mention has already been made: it was to give a secure temporal framework to the succession of events, to place them in a christological and eschatological context. Through it men could identify themselves with a larger scheme, and escaped from the chaos of accidents, from a succession of violent happenings, into a divine plan bounded at one end by the Old and the New Testament, and the struggles of the early Church and martyrs, and at the other by the second coming. Rodulf achieved this in his very preface when he announced that there had not been anyone for two hundred years who would tell future generations of the things that had come to pass in the churches of God and in the people, not since Bede and Paul the Deacon.[32] The imposing Frankish historiography in between he ignored, and his *Histories* were dominated and orientated by the year 1000, and the thousandth anniversary of the Passion. These dates did not portend for him any imminent disasters; rather they pointed to a hopeful future. Rodulf was sparing with dates but he was deeply aware of differing reckonings of time. Some of his critics have blamed him for chronological vagueness but he did indeed see and write 'histoire à longue durée'.

Rodulf also wrote reflective history. He wanted to ponder over the many things and the men who had been renowned in the *orbis Romanus* from the year 900, but particularly round the year 1000. He also wanted to think about events and contingencies beyond and outside the *orbis Romanus*, overseas and in barbarous regions. Rodulf, too, is well aware of Latin Europe's frontiers and also, as we shall see, of frontiers within it. As a Burgundian he wanted to record what he had heard and lived to see 'in sacris ecclesiis et utroque populo', i.e. what befell the churches and both peoples, the Saxons and the Western Franks (these were his words for Germans and French).[33] Their rulers, the Emperor Henry II and Robert the Pious, he regarded as equals and the foremost in this part of the world. The Anglo-Saxons entered his horizons later, and like Adémar he knew of Canute's conquest, but little more. Rodulf, as I have already said, welcomed the end of Carolingian rule because he thought the Carolingians' disappearance had brought peace between the royal families of East and West and so made possible Christianity's advance. His optimism lives through a famous passage when he described how, around the year 1002, in Italy and Gaul churches were being built and rebuilt like new white clothes for the whole world, not only cathedrals and monasteries but also village chapels. This served only to introduce two munificent builders and donors, Hervey, the treasurer of Tours who rebuilt St Martins and William of Dijon.[34] But Rodulf's optimism and confidence went further still. In Book V of his *Histories* he explained: Christ when walking on the waters had allowed St Peter, whom he had set over his Church, to walk with him, and by this he signified to the faithful that when all peoples had been subdued, but not altogether destroyed and extirpated, his kingdom would be established and endure for all times. The sea stood for the secular world. Here a programme of limitless aggression, of conquest and (forcible?) conversion emerges from the scriptural exposition, and already in Book IV Rodulf has reported a major Christian victory over the Saracens and Conrad II's successful campaign against the Slav and heathen Liutizi (1036). In Rodulf then the ascent of the *orbis Romanus* has already begun, and so he told his readers.[35]

This does not mean that he was silent about the calamities and disasters of his time, men's backslidings and the Church's situation in the midst of them. A terrible and prolonged famine preceeded the thousandth anniversary of the Passion when the harvests recovered and there was plenty. The outbreak seems to have been confined to Burgundy but for Rodulf there was nothing accidental about it. He describes the manifestations and horrors of the catastrophe, no less vividly than do our television cameras today. The liquidation of church treasures did not always help the starving crowds because the food, bought at enormous cost, often reached them too late so that it killed rather than saved. Rodulf ended his account of the famine with a stark observation. He noted that this arcane misfortune of divine wrath did not lead men to contrition or pious supplication. Too much suffering dulled rather than roused religious sensibilities.[36] The Church was thus not always master of the situation and men in despair did not always turn first to its ministrations for comfort. Rodulf had peace and plenty follow these years of climatic disaster and mortality, to teach his readers the lesson of their creator's *magnanimitas*. We take belief in the populace and in the higher echelons of eleventh-century society for granted. In reality it was a struggle and insecure, something that had to be fought for constantly.

In Book V of his *Histories* Rodulf turned to man's links with the supernatural and in these spheres monks were the expert interpreters, almost the scientists. Here also he looked at the monastic condition and experience and we can learn from him better than from any other source I know of what it was like to be a monk in the early eleventh century. Here also the demon of self-doubt came to the fore with his insinuations: Why do you monks bother so with vigils, fasts, psalmodies and humiliations 'beyond the common usages of other men'? Are not countless laymen, steeped in disgraceful deeds up to the end of their days to receive the same rest as you? One day, one hour (of repentance) could suffice to earn the rewards, the eternal bliss of your justice. So why do you trouble to rise at the sound of the bell when you might go on sleeping? The demon addressing his victim—it is usually another monk, not Rodulf himself—continues: 'I'll tell you a secret though it is damaging to our, the devil's side. Each year on the day of his Resurrection Christ spoils all hell and leads his own back to the better world [ad supera]. So you have nothing to fear and can indulge what you fancy by way of carnal pleasure and desires.'[37] Rodulf here reveals a remarkable body of beliefs: that the harrowing of hell was a continuous process. The author is thus voicing gnawing doubts, whether monastic asceticism and intercession were essential in the scheme of salvation either for the living or the dead. He hastened to refute these doubts by the Gospels: not all were so brought back but Rodulf did not slam the door altogether on such insinuations. The falsest demons sometimes uttered things that were not wholly wrong. These apparitions could even lead to self-improvement, but in general those to whom prodigies are shown, either by good or by evil spirits, don't live very long.

It is noticeable how many of these spasms of anguish, the encounters with the demon, occur in Rodulf's text when the bells rang for Matins, the time for rising at dawn or before. It seems to have been the critical moment in the monk's day when devotion most often threatened to break down. Rodulf also tells his readers how his communities dealt with coarse human habits, like spitting and how monks occasionally ran away to spend a few weeks in the world.[38] In his *Vita domni Willelmi* Rodulf was a fervent advocate of reform and its demand for strict and rigorous uniformity. All the more remarkable is his frank avowal of the strains and, for some, the almost unbearable tensions which communal disciplines, old and new, could impose.

The apex of Rodulf Glaber's *orbis Romanus* was the papacy rather than any secular ruler and its casing the Church. In another celebrated passage the Roman coronation of the emperor was not a matter of course or of ritual only, but of papal choice and even examination, and this two centuries before Innocent III. The candidate had to be worthy of it. The criterion of *idoneitas* is more than implied. The pope would not crown any tyrant who thrust himself forward, as had happened formerly. The orb with the cross, which Pope Benedict VIII gave Henry II in 1014, taught a lesson of service and obligation. Henry II, according to Rodulf, learned it respectfully and sent the *sphaira*, like so many other good things, to Cluny.[39] Rodulf almost certainly saw it there and was gratified. Equally firm was he in the rejection of Byzantine attempts to vindicate a certain ecclesiastical autonomy. Without his *Histories* nothing would be known about the Greeks' approach to Pope John XIX in 1024 asking him to allow their Church to be called universal within its own sphere. If Rome was compliant, corruptible or politic, the zealots from the camp of monastic renewal were not and insisted on the *magisterium Petri*, the supreme power to bind and loose. Here attitudes were hardening and Byzantium's exclusion and separateness lay already firmly embedded in Rodulf's world picture.[40]

Lastly, he was not merely aware of but, if anything, helped to propagate cultural frontiers within the *orbis Romanus*. It was precisely the plurality of rulers and *regna* that appealed to him and where again he pointed to the future. When Robert the Pious married his Queen Constance, between 1001 and 1003 she brought with her a large following from Aquitaine and the Auvergne. Their levity of manners, clothes, weapons, horse-harness, hair-styles and shoes were greeted with deep dismay and bitterly denounced by William of Dijon and his mouth-piece, Rodulf. Burgundians, hitherto decent folk, were infected and tarnished by these satanic fashions. Abbot William stood fast and declared that if anyone who had adopted them died, he could only with difficulty be saved.[41] Rodulf ended Book III with a poem where vestiary and moral turpitude went hand in hand. He was, moreover, not alone in his censures for a letter of exactly the same tenor has survived which Abbot Siegfried of Gorze addressed to Poppo of Stavelot damning Henry III's forthcoming match with Agnes of Poitou in 1043. The *honestas regni* in arms and horsemanship was at stake with the advent of French fashions, even before the marriage—besides the tonsure of beards, indecent clothes, and other things unheard of in the days of the Ottos and Henry II.[42] Here too dress and styles stood for a change of *mores* for the worse. Rigorists like William, Siegfried, and Poppo not only ruled their monks with a rod of iron they also sought to control and to police the bearing of the lay aristocracy. But even here the preachers' horizons were regional rather than local.

So far we have seen the early eleventh century through the eyes of an Aquitanian and a Burgundian monk. It is significant that Reims and the Isle de France were for the moment silent. There was so far no Abbot Suger, no Guibert of Nogent, though we must not overlook Fulbert of Chartres. Even the *Life of Robert the Pious*, however, was written by a monk from the Loire Valley, Helgaud of Fleury. The centres of gravity were all somewhere different from where they were going to be in the High Middle Ages. Further East they lay not yet in the Rhine Valley but in the Marches of Saxony, along the Elbe and the Saale. Here in the homeland of the Ottonians there had been a massive build-up of wealth, material culture and display resting on military strength and success which now, however, were no longer unequivocal and unchallenged. Eastern Saxony too was a land covered with recently built and dedicated, magnificent churches: cathedrals and monasteries, with markets, mints, and the beginnings of towns. There were rich silver mines, and the capacity to work in iron and make things, even to export some of them. There was now a Latin literature in which history once again stood to the fore. It flourished in monastic foyers, but there were also schools of wider learning in Magdeburg, Hildesheim and Halberstadt. Here in East Saxony we meet a morose *esprit* who has confided in us, consciously addressing a posthumous audience with passion, deeply-grounded beliefs, and also a style of his own: I mean of course Thietmar of Merseburg.

Writers like Widukind of Corvey and Liudprand of Cremona achieve a rare literary stature. Relatively little known and rarely read as they are they belong, all the same, to a timeless category that transcends its own contingencies, so vivid a picture they convey of their worlds, their societies, and values. The same is true of that great and sombre memorial, the *Chronicon* of Thietmar of Merseburg.[43] Thietmar defies all the generalizations which have been advanced about the evolution of medieval historiography. He is individual and idiosyncratic and reveals himself in all his quirks, his remorses and, at the same time, his deep concern for the salvation of others, friends, and acquaintances. Yet, according to current rules and generalizations, he should echo models and be typecast. He is also intimate about himself, his family, his rulers, and archbishops where he should, under the canons of criticism in vogue, wear a mask of iron. Thietmar's sense of society is very infectious and his was already a complex society. Take, for instance, his own career. It had been intended by his father, Siegfried of Walbeck, that he should be a monk at Berge, the Magdeburg monastery, but in the end the count could not place him there and he joined the cathedral community instead. The canons were given a feast, lasting two days, when he entered.[44] One wonders what stood in the way at Berge where a younger brother, Siegfried, to whom he dedicated the *Chronicon*, later served. It is easy to see why Thietmar was to have become a monk. He was physically a little handicapped and rather a sight. The Ottonians liked good-looking bishops in the secular church—men of stature, literally, who stood out over the shoulders of the crowd as rulers should. Thietmar was small, he had a facial swelling and a broken nose that had never healed properly. The last was caused by an accident in his boyhood but he has not told us how it happened.[45] He had, however, an indefatigable memory, and an irresistible urge to record and write about himself, his kin, his contemporaries, and the Ottonian *Reich* at large. His prompting stemmed from a restless conscience, a vivid capacity for self-reproach which, in his case, could not be assuaged by acts of penance but only by writing about it, and so we are the gainers.

Thietmar's panorama is *christianitas*. He had, however, inherited from Widukind an ethos which marked barbarians off from Christians, and even newly-converted ones could not always at once and automatically bridge the gap in his esteem. A distinction between us and them underlay his judgment, not only between his aristocratic milieu and the *plebs* but also his Saxon stem-pride towards Poles, Czechs, not to mention Elb-Slavs and others. For their heathen sanctuaries and religion, however, he is by far the most acute observer who mastered a slavonic dialect and commanded much personal knowledge of the Sorabian and Liutizi tribes. Seen in this light Thietmar can be regarded as one of the first of the ethnological experts who later became so characteristic of the expanding Latin West. Adam of Bremen in the eleventh century is another. Organized geographical and historical knowledge and a growing body of historical and ethnological literature became thus essential tools and pre-suppositions for practical measures and the employment of men, arms, and resources in the eastwards enlargement of the *Reich*. And Thietmar's work was not forgotten but entered and soon belonged to a swirling current of Saxon historiography, a current which became a broad stream in the twelfth century. Nor must his knowledge of Anglo-Saxon England under Danish assault, of the troubles and feuds of the Lower Rhenish region, his occasional news of France, his excellent news of the Burgundian kingdom, his interest in Byzantine shipping, and Italian astuteness, be ignored when we seek to put together his horizons.[46]

He was, all the same, not unique for he shared with Rodulf Glaber the autobiographical vein, and the penchant for self-reproach, and Adémar of Chabannes, the historian of Aquitaine, captured the same episodical and personally-linked form of treating recent and contemporary events. Unlike Thietmar, only Adémar, as we saw, had a bee under his bonnet, the apostolate of St Martial to which he devoted so much time and attention. To prove his point he would stop at very little in his writings and sermons. Thietmar, more modestly, only misdealt some of the cards, i.e. he tampered with charters on behalf of his beloved and only recently-revived see, the bishopric of Merseburg. All three men had more profound things in common: their historiography rested on the belief that the historical process was divinely directed and that men, if they acted rightly, would experience God's mercy and gifts. Conversely, if they sinned, they must endure setbacks and catastrophes. These were divine punishments. This meant, however, that just as men could strive for their personal salvation so they could by collective good conduct avert misfortunes, starvation, heathen raids, or whatever. In this roundabout way then, as well as by the employment of their *virtus*, men made their own history and were by no means subject to blind chance or incomprehensible forces. The idea that man made his own history, as Vico taught it, may have been secularized but that does not make it any less a legacy from the Latin Middle Ages.[47]

The characteristics of this early eleventh-century historiography must be looked for in both its treatment of social relations, and individuality. Medievalists are, perhaps understandably, inclined to illuminate their themes through climaxes. The growth of self was a slower and perhaps more varied process, with more markers, than the great presences of, say, a Lupus of Ferrières or an Abelard might suggest. Here the early eleventh century with Adémar, Rodulf Glaber, and Thietmar once again heaves into sight. The political world of Thietmar was imposing, well-ordered, and magnificent, that of the two other men at any rate improving. Their decades were a moment of balance, relative calm, and cultural cohesion, before the great crisis of Gregorian Reform in the Secular Church and the Investiture Conflict. For the South of France that was damaging and the prelude to heresy. In the *Reich* it proved a tragedy, dividing Germany, forming lasting fronts, associations and aversions within it, such as had not existed before. It also isolated Germany from its Western neighbours, an isolation that became almost permanent. The voluminous writings about the right relations between *ecclesia* and *regnum* were in the *Reich* for local audiences only. They did not ring the changes in France or in England. Here lay perhaps another tragedy. The Anglo-Norman coalescence heightened the acuteness of the Franco-German frontier even if Anglo-Norman kings sometimes allied with Salian emperors.

In a fundamental way then the early eleventh century mattered for the configuration of Latin Europe. Its new pluralistic self-awareness, growing confidence, and capacity to reshape the horizons of newcomers, however violent, now began to form a groundwork of attitudes that proved to be remarkably resilient and enduring. Ascent was not just a matter of increasing resources, well deployed, of new military skills, well marshalled. It was, as I hope to have shown, also the work of a society exceptionally well served and well instructed by its historians who were really (forgive the military metaphor) the 'intelligence-officers' of its aims and directions. Here lay one of the Latins' special strengths. Byzantine historiography had above all the task of preserving and safeguarding a past, and to defend it against all comers.

To conclude, I'd like to remind you of an Oxford tradition in medieval historical studies. It goes back to Sir Maurice Powicke and is very much alive in the work of Sir Richard Southern and Michael Wallace-Hadrill. It is the intuitive practice of allowing imagination and literary sensibilities to open up direct lines of communication between the historian and his subjects, not least of all his medieval forebears. While they must be understood and interpreted with the help of all the arsenal of critical and philological scholarship, they can and should be also encountered directly, and enjoyed, like any great literature, immediately. Cultural history is therefore not only a reflection of material conditions and predicaments. It is also a timeless dialogue in which, without mystification, we can and must join. The words, images and conceptual moulds of these three, and many other, early- and high-medieval historians are still related to our inner selves, our modes of speech, imagination and feeling. They, like the survivors of the visual arts, are part of our roots and should be cultivated. The humanism still needed to do so, if I may contradict

Ferdinand Braudel, is neither retrograde nor insidious. This is no polemic against the search for new and more bridges between history and the social sciences but a passionate reminder not to neglect or forsake, but to look after and share, this awesome and wonderful legacy.

NOTES

1. M. Howard, *TLS* No. 4253 (5 Oct. 1984), p. 114.
2. E. R. Curtius, *European Literature and the Latin Middle Ages*, tr. W. R. Trask (Princeton, 1953) and E. Auerbach, *Mimesis: The Representation of Reality in Western Literature*, tr. W. R. Trask (Princeton, 1953).
3. E. Auerbach, *Literary Language and its Public in Late Latin Antiquity and in the Middle Ages*, tr. R. Manheim (London, 1965), ch. 2. See, for example, his comments on Rather of Verona and Liudprand of Cremona, pp. 133–56.
4. Curtius, 'The Medieval Bases of Western Thought', op. cit., Appendix, p. 589.
5. F. Braudel, 'Histoire et sciences sociales à longue durée', *Annales économies sociétés, civilisations*, 13 (1958), 725–53.
6. Braudel, ibid., pp. 732, 725.
7. G. Duby, *La Société aux XI*[e] *et XII*[e] *siècles dans la région mâconnaise* (Bibliothèque générale de l'école pratique des hautes études, VIe section, Paris, 1953), p. ix.
8. R. Fossier, *La Terre et les hommes en Picardie jusqu'à la fin du XIII*[e] *siècle*, (2 vols., Paris and Louvain, 1968); A. Chédeville, *Chartres et ses campagnes XI*[e]*–XIII*[e] *siècles* (Paris, 1973); E. Magnou-Nortier, *La Société laique et l'Église dans la province ecclésiastique de Narbonne de la fin du VIII*[e] *à la fin du XI*[e] *siècle* (Toulouse, 1974); P. Toubert, *Les Structures du Latium médiéval* (Bibliothèque des écoles françaises d'Athènes et de Rome, 2 vols., Rome, 1973); P. Bonnassie, *La Catalogne du milieu du X*[e] *à la fin du XI*[e] *siècle: Croissance et mutations d'une société* (2 vols., Toulouse, 1975–6).
9. J. Le Goff, Time, Work and Culture in the Middle Ages, tr. A. Goldhammer (Chicago and London, 1980), pp. ix–xiii. The quotation, from Maurice Lombard, is on p. xiii.
10. R. Fossier, *Enfance de l'Europe X*[e]*–XII*[e] *siècles: Aspects économiques et sociaux*, I: *L'Homme et son espace, Nouvelle Clio*, 17 (Paris, 1982), pp. 71–2; 288; 290; 301; 364–422.
11. Wipo, *Gesta Chuonradi II. Imperatoris*, ch. 16, in H. Bresslau (ed.), *Die Werke Wipos, Monumenta Germaniae Historica* [henceforth *MGH*], *Scriptores*

Rerum Germanicarum in usum scholarum [henceforth *SRG*] (3rd edn., Hanover and Leipzig, 1915), p. 36; *Florentii Wigorniensis Monachi Chronicon ex Chronicis*, ed. B. Thorpe, *English Historical Society* (London, 1848), I. 185–9.

12. On Dudo, see now E. Searle, 'Fact and Pattern in Heroic History: Dudo of St Quentin', *Viator*, 15 (1984), 119–37, and his editor, J. Lair, (below, n. 21). The origins of the Gallus Anonymus remain disputed. See W. Wattenbach and R. Holtzmann, *Deutschlands Geschichtsquellen im Mittelalter: Deutsche Kaiserzeit* (Tübingen, 1948), I. iv. 812–3 and, in particular, pt. 3, ed. F.-J. Schmale (Darmstadt, 1971), pp. 228–30.*
13. Adémar de Chabannes, *Chronique*, ed. J. Chavanon, *Collection de textes pour servir à l'étude et à l'enseignement de l'histoire* (Paris, 1897). On Adémar see the two articles by L. Halphen in his *A travers l'histoire du moyen âge* (Paris, 1950) and also, K. F. Werner, 'Ademar von Chabannes und die Historia pontificum et comitum Engolismensium', *Deutsches Archiv für Erforschung des Mittelalters*, 19 (1963), 297–325; Wattenbach–Holtzmann, pp. 310–11; Wattenbach–Schmale, pp. 99–100*; M. Manitius, *Geschichte der lateinischen Literatur des Mittelalters*, ii (Munich, 1923), 284–94. For an incisive critique of Adémar as a source for Charles the Bald's reign, see J. Gillingham, 'Adémar of Chabannes and the history of Aquitaine in the reign of Charles the Bald', in *Charles the Bald: Court and Kingdom*, ed. M. Gibson and J. Nelson, with the assistance of D. Ganz, *BAR International Series*, 101 (1981), 3–14.
14. Adémar, *Chronique*, iii, 41, pp. 163–5.
15. Adémar, *Chronique*, preface, p. x n. 3.
16. Adémar, *Epistola de Apostolatu Martialis, Migne Patrologiae: Series Latina Prior*, cxli, col. 89.
17. Adémar, *Chronique*, iii. 33, pp. 155–6; iii. 37, p. 160; iii. 62, pp. 187–8.
18. Adémar, *Chronique*, iii. 54, pp. 176–7.
19. Adémar, *Chronique*, iii. 55, p. 177.
20. Adémar, *Chronique*, iii. 27, p. 148: 'omnisque eorum Normannorum, qui juxta Frantiam inhabitaverunt, multitudo fidem Christi suscepit, et gentilem linguam obmittens, latino sermone assuefacta est.'
21. *De moribus et actis primorum Normanniae ducum auctore Dudone Sancti Quintini decano*, ed. J. Lair (Caen, 1865), p. 125: 'Versus ad comitem Rodulfum, hujus operis relatorem', ii. 1–10.
22. Adémar, *Chronique*, iii. 52, p. 175: 'more catulorum loquentes, glatire videbantur.'

NOTES 27

23. Adémar, *Chronique*, iii. 45, p. 168.

24. Adémar, *Chronique*, iii. 42, p. 166: 'Casu ab ignoto milite impetitus . . . interit.' On the blinding, see iii. 25, p. 147; iii. 28, p. 150.

25. Adémar, *Chronique*, iii. 66, pp. 190–2. For the other version see G. Waitz's edition of Adémar in *MGH, Scriptorum Tomus IV* (Hanover, 1841), pp. 146 n. 2; 147 n. 2, and in J. Boussard (ed.), *Historia Pontificum et Comitum Engolismensium* (Bibliothèque elzévirienne, nouvelle série: Études et Documents; Paris, 1957), pp. 19–20. On the incident, a very early witchcraft trial, see M. Blöcker, 'Ein Zauberprozess im Jahre 1028', *Schweizerische Zeitschrift für Geschichte*, 29 (1979), 533–55. The sources stress that the count had hitherto enjoyed rude good health: 'solebat enim robusto et sano corpore vigere' (*Chronique*, p. 191). It was precisely this that roused the need to account for his languishing illness and so prompted the charges of witchcraft. The parallel with the situations described by E. E. Evans-Pritchard, *Witchcraft, Oracles and Magic among the Azande* (Oxford, 1937), pt. I. iv; pt. IV. v, is very striking.

26. Adémar, *Chronique*, iii. 70, pp. 194–5.

27. Raoul Glaber: Les cinq livres de ses histoires (900–1044), ed. M. Prou (Collection de textes; Paris, 1886). On Rodulf, see Manitius, ii. 347–53, Wattenbach–Holtzmann, i. 2, pp. 302–4; Wattenbach–Schmale, pp. 92–3*; and N. Bulst, 'Rodulfus Glabers Vita domni Willelmi abbatis', *Deutsches Archiv*, 30 (1974), p. 451 n. 3 for further literature. On Rodulf's theodicy, proclaimed through the created world, see J. France, 'The Divine Quaternity of Rodulfus Glaber', *Studia Monastica*, 17 (1975), 283–94. I have not discussed this here.

28. Rodulf Glaber, *Historiarum Libri Quinque*, I.v. 22, p. 21; III. i. 2, p. 52; IV. vi. 18, pp. 106–7; IV. vi, 21. p. 109.

29. Rodulf Glaber, *Historiarum Lib.*, v i. 3, p. 116.

30. Compare Adémar, *Chronique*, iii. 35, p. 158; III. 69, p. 194, and Rodulf Glaber, *Historiarum Lib.*, IV. v. 14–16, pp. 103–5. Both authors, and, in particular, Adémar's numerous sermons bearing on the peace movement, are discussed by H. Hoffman, *Gottersfriede und Treuga Dei* (Schriften der *MGH*, 20; Stuttgart, 1964), pp. 27–31; 33–40; 54–6; 81–7 (Treuga Dei); 257–9. On the Orléans heretics, compare Adémar, *Chronique*, iii. 59, p. 184–5, and Rodulf Glaber *Historiarum Lib.*, III. viii. 26–31, pp. 74–81. On booty from Spain, see Rodulf Glaber*Historiarum Lib.*, IV. vii. 22, pp. 109–10. On Count Rainald of Autun being killed by a *miles* 'generis infimi', see Rodulf Glaber, *Historiarum Lib.*, IV. ix. 26, p. 113.

NOTES

31. Rodulf Glaber, *Historiarum Lib.*, v. i. 2, pp. 115–16.
32. Rodulf to Abbot Odilo of Cluny, *Historiarum Lib.*, pp. 1–2.
33. Rodulf Glaber, *Historiarum Lib.*, I, i. 4, p. 5.
34. Rodulf Glaber, *Historiarum Lib.*, III. iv–v. 13–16, pp. 62–6.
35. Rodulf Glaber, *Historiarum Lib.*, v. i. 10, p. 122; and see IV. vii. 22–viii, 23, pp. 109–11 (victories over the Saracens and the Liutizi).
36. For the famine of 1031–2 Rodulf is the principal source: *Historiarum Lib.*, IV. iv. 10–13, pp. 99–103.
37. Rodulf Glaber, *Historiarum Lib.*, v. i. 1, pp. 114–15.
38. Rodulf Glaber, *Historiarum Lib.*, v. i. 7, p. 119.
39. Rodulf Glaber, *Historiarum Lib.*, I. v. 23, pp. 21–2.
40. Rodulf Glaber, *Historiarum Lib.*, IV. i. 2–4, pp. 92–4; and compare, I. iv. 16, p. 17.
41. Rodulf Glaber, *Historiarum Lib.*, III. ix. 40, pp. 89–90.
42. For the text of Abbot Siegfried's letter see W. von Giesebrecht, *Geschichte der deutschen Kaiserzeit*, ii, 5th edn. (Leipzig, 1885), pp. 714–18, in particular p. 718.
43. *Thietmari Merseburgensis Episcopi Chronicon*, ed. R. Holtzmann, *MGH, SRG, nova series* ix, 2nd edn. (Berlin, 1955). On Thietmar see H. Lippelt, *Thietmar von Merseburg Reichsbischof und Chronist*, *Mitteldeutsche Forschungen*, 72 (Cologne and Vienna, 1973), and K. Leyser, *Rule and Conflict in an Early Medieval Society Ottonian Saxony* (London, 1979), *passim*, but in particular, pp. 33–4; 39–42; and K. Leyser, *Medieval Germany and its Neighbours* (London, 1982), p. 246.
44. Thietmar, *Chronicon*, IV. 16, p. 150.
45. Thietmar, *Chronicon*, IV. 75, p. 218.
46. Thietmar, *Chronicon*, VII. 36–7, 39–43, viii, 7, pp. 442–3, 446–50, 502 on England; VII. 47–9, pp. 456–8 on the Lower Rhine; vii. 27–30, pp. 430–4 on the Kingdom of Burgundy; iii. 23, p. 126 on Byzantine ships; and vii. 2, p. 400 on Italian guile.
47. I. Berlin, 'Vico's Concept of Knowledge', in H. Hardy (ed.), *Against the Current* (Oxford, 1981), pp. 111–19, and compare p. 95.

2

On the Evidence of Growth of Population in the West from the Eleventh to the Thirteenth Century

Léopold Génicot

ECONOMIC EXPANSION, religious ferment, renaissance of letters and development of science, creation of an original art, territorial gains at the expense of the infidel world, all these phenomena of which the life of Christian Europe was woven between the 11th century and the 13th are in some way related to a net growth of the population. Consequently, almost all historians hold that, during what Marc Bloch called the second feudal age, the West went through a strong demographic surge.

This virtual unanimity is, however, a little deceptive: no one ordinarily doubts the fact or its importance yet we really know little about it. Actually, no one has had the courage to study it very closely. The documentation is so poor as at first sight to seem unable to sustain more than vague general conclusions. It has not been interrogated methodically, for fear that the effort would be futile.[1] Perhaps this pessimism is justified, but how can we tell? We cannot be certain until at least one scholar has carried out systematic and exhaustive research in some definite region, and has then tried to draw together all the forms of evidence that reveal the shape of demographic trends from the post-Carolingian period up to the end of the Middle Ages.

This article tries to show what types of research would be feasible. It offers, not a finished history of the population of the different regions of the West between the years 1000 and 1300—indeed, the present state of knowledge would barely permit of an outline—but a list of the various indices of population growth that the monographs we need ought to collect and analyze. We shall illustrate the uses and the significance of each of these indices. Perhaps this will stimulate more careful research into "demographic prehistory". In any case I hope it will show that, although some historians may have exaggerated in speaking of the "demographic revolution of the 11th, 12th, and 13th centuries" and although our knowledge is still far from precise, the impression that population was growing is well founded.

To speak of demography means that we must seek quantitative measures, even though the figures may only partially reflect the reality and be no more than a basis for interpretation. Accordingly, we shall classify the numerous and varied indices of population growth in order of decreasing precision, that is to say, according as they may be expressed in more or less rigorous mathematical form, or better still—for history is concerned with evolution—, in statistical series. They might be ranged as follows: the evidence given in military or fiscal documents; information gained from inventories of seigneurial property and rights; birth rates to be deduced from genealogical study and from the descriptions of families to be found in many charters; long-term price trends, in particular of agricultural prices; the multiplication and expansion of towns; land clearance, technological advances, and the fragmentation of traditional land holdings; changes in ecclesiastical geography and construction or alteration of public buildings, especially of churches and chapels; and colonization of the vast regions seized from the Infidel.

Medievalists do not hope to find a complete census of any population. They are happy enough to find incomplete or indirect data, such as lists of men liable to military service, or accounts of hearth taxes or poll taxes. The former are rather rare and late; only in Italy do we have any that antedate the 14th century.[2] Again, they concern only the towns and we cannot be certain that urban population fluctuated in the same way as rural population. And their use depends on the calculation of a multiplier, usually on uncertain grounds, that will represent the ratio between the number of men capable of bearing arms and the total population.[3] The second type of data, as presented by the celebrated "Etat des paroisses et des feux" of 1328 and the Poll tax returns of 1377, is more valuable because it ordinarily covers a wide region, not just a single town. But it raises even more difficult problems. What was a hearth and what is the average number of individuals it indicates?[4] Or what was the ratio between the number of adults who paid a poll tax and the number of children? What percentage of the population did exempt groups form—clergy, often nobles and their households, and vagrants? Were the enumerators and collectors conscientious? Was it hard to evade payment? How are we to fill the frequent gaps in the records? To what extent and under what conditions is it legitimate to argue from the part to the whole? All these questions are extremely delicate.[5] On the other hand, again with exceptions in Italy (the *generales subventiones* of Frederick II and Charles of Anjou [6]), the fiscal records, like the military lists, are all later than 1300. Yet for our purpose they are still relevant and useful, even for the earlier period. They furnish figures which, when compared with earlier data from other sources, show very convincingly that the population of the West had grown before the 14th century, and they help us to form a rough idea of the amplitude and the rhythm of this growth. Without the poll tax referred to above, J. C. Russell would not have been able to establish so firmly the fact that the population of England more than tripled in some 250 years, between 1086 and 1346.[7]

Among the oldest of the other auxiliary sources are the surveys known as the polyptyques. Sometimes these give a fully detailed inventory of all the lands and dues belonging to a lay or ecclesiastical lord. In the 13th century many great and middling lords whose classical manorial regime had weathered a crisis drew up surveys of this kind in order, so to speak, to take their bearings.[8] Sometimes the survey is merely a concise description of a single manor, compiled on the occasion of a pious donation or of a dispute or of what was later called a *dénombrement* of a fief. But whatever their form or scope, the polyptyques all contain similar statistical data: the number of settlements on the estate, for at least from the 11th century this often comprised more than one; the number of holdings of each type; the total area, in the ancient and the current measures, of fields and meadows [9]; the number of tenants and the average extent of their holdings [10]; and finally, in so far as one can tell from figures based on dues levied on individuals or on hearths, the total population and its density.[11] If one has, then, for all or part of an estate, several polyptyques or related documents, such as accounts, it is possible to establish these facts at a series of dates and hence to deduce, more or less exactly, the demographic trend of the period and region in question. New settlements may appear,[12] or the older ones may come to be more densely populated. For example, the 81 people living on the lands of Weedon Beck in 1248 had by 1300 grown to 110.[13] Such a record is a valid measure of population growth if all other things remain equal at the two dates, namely, the area of land in question and the hearth or household unit. We must also be certain that an increase in one item is not offset by a decrease in another, for example, that an increase in the number of tenants does not simply reflect a decrease in the number of sub-tenants or of landless people.

Another way of measuring population change is through calculations of the average number of children per household. With luck, if our documentation is good enough, there will be two ways of doing this. One is through compiling genealogies. If genealogies compiled in the middle ages are used they of course have to be checked, and may sometimes be amplified, by new research.[14] In this way it was discovered that the eldest branches of two of the greatest families of the region of Namur in each generation between the dates 1000 and 1250, had respectively a minimum of 5.75 and 4.30 children who came of age.[15] The method is however applicable only in the case of great families.[16] And the average number of children surviving may have varied considerably between one social level and another. There is however another procedure, one that to my knowledge has never been tried,[17] namely, the gathering of the descriptions of complete families to be found in charters.[18] These quite often, when referring to pious donations of land, or in the case of *liberi* who donated themselves or of serfs who were donated to a religious foundation, name parents and their children.[19] This information should be classified by date, by social class, by regions, etc. It would then show how the average number of children altered between one period and another. It might also resolve other problems, especially the question whether, as many historians have maintained, the serfs died out through having a particularly low birth rate. Having obtained the average by one or the other of these methods, one then has to estimate the number of children per couple, in the period and region in question, that would have been requisite simply to maintain the population level. Ideally one would deduce this from local documents of the period. In practice the best plan is to take a coefficient calculated by modern specialists, say 2.7, modifying it in the light of differences in the relevant variables. We are unable to take account of infant mortality, because the documents mention only children who have lived for some years, indeed usually only those who have grown up. But we have to take account of the nuptuality rate. This was undoubtedly lower in the Middle Ages than today because of a more pronounced disequilibrium between the sexes and because of more frequent entry into religious orders.[20] Again, we have to bear in mind that the average duration of life was also lower in that age of all too frequent famine and epidemic.[21]

Price trends, especially in agricultural prices, also demand attention. They are or may be, to an extent which has to be determined for every case, a function of demographic change.[22] A fall in the rent of fields and meadows, accompanied by a rise in wages, especially of farm hands, such as we see in 14th-century England [23], is an unequivocal sign of a fall in population. Inversely, a rise in the value of arable land, above all if it is accompanied by a fall in wages, is a clue to population increase. Although we may never be able to trace the course of wages with any exactness before 1300, it is possible to form a general idea of their movement in the regions that are better documented. As to land values, at least in the 13th century, it is quite easy to show that they were rising: one may do so either by comparing average figures in successive years [24] or, more surely, by charting the course of the rents on specific pieces of land.[25]

Other indices lend themselves less easily to measurement, chief among these being the growth of towns. In some regions, such as the Low Countries, these probably originated in the 9th century; in others, such as Lombardy, they were revivified in the 10th century; everywhere they were in full expansion between the 11th century and the 13th.[26] Proof of this lies in the continual enlargement of their bounds that is revealed by the successive construction of new outworks and by the reordering of their ancient parish divisions.[27] The extension of their areas was not, however, exactly proportionate to increase in the number of inhabitants, for the density of urban population was not a constant. It varied from one town to another and within the same town, not only from one period to another but from one quarter to another, as, for example, between the market quarter and what modern architects would call the residential quarters, or from the ancient *civitas* to newly built suburbs. Besides, the walled area was seldom if ever completely built up; especially towards the close of the Middle Ages, it might include fields and meadows and other vacant sites. Yet in default of any more exact measure, the extension of the area enclosed is of some significance. To cite only two instances, the area enclosed by the fortifications of Ghent, one of the greatest towns of the age, had by the 14th century grown from 80 hectares to 644; the fortified area of Aix, a lesser town, grew from 50 hectares to 175.[28]

Parallel with this urban movement ran another which some historians overlook: the transformation of villages into little towns.[29] Places that had hitherto been simply agricultural acquire market rights and a market place, and sometimes a fair. They become petty commercial centers.

One should beware of exaggerating the demographic significance of these urban phenomena. Urban growth is not a precise index of total population growth. Even if the area of Ghent grew almost tenfold in 250 years or the population of some town in central Italy grew in the same period from 5,000 to 30,000 [30], it does not follow that the population of Flanders or of Tuscany or of Umbria had grown tenfold or sixfold. Towns have always [31] tended to absorb the people of their immediate environs; in some regions, as in Italy, they have attracted the artisans of whole regions [32], and even the peasants.[33] They have continually drained the open country. All the same, and this is the point to be emphasized here, they did not empty the countryside.[34] They drained off only its surplus human output.

They did not even take the whole of that surplus. Between the 11th and the 13th century, the rural population grew appreciably. The considerable extension of arable land during this period is sufficient evidence of this.[35] For this was the age of the great work of dyking and drainage in fenlands. In Flanders, nature and man combined in the 11th century to push back the sea.[36] In Lombardy, bishops, monasteries, and finally communes, endeavoured to tame the Po and make its valley fertile.[37] By 1250 the work was finished: Milan by then, for instance, had its great irrigation canal, the Muzza, while downstream, between the tributaries of the Oglio and the Molinella, the river was well under control.[38]

This is also, notably in such regions of France as the Parisian basin, the great age of the "villes neuves". The "villes neuves" were new settlements founded on open waste and in forest clearings by enlightened lords and their colonists (*hôtes*).[39] We have the foundation charters of some of these places. For others the place name attests their origin [40] by referring to new foundation (the French *Villeneuve*) or to the proprietor (Créon, Libourne), or by indicating their privileged status (the Italian *Villafranca*), or by copying the name of some great city far off (Bruges or Ghent in Béarn), or above all, by preserving the memory of the ancient forests and of the clearing process which eroded it, as in the German place names ending in *rade, raut, rode, roth, reut, riet, holz, wald, forst, hausen, hain, hagen, bruch, brand, scheid, schlag,* etc. Often the ground plan [41] is our evidence, a grid pattern or the angling of intersections proving that the whole place was laid out in one operation.

Even where there was no dyking, no drainage, and no planting of new settlements, there was still new activity, although it may be more difficult for us to trace it. Yet careful examination of the old landscapes and attentive reading of the documents relating to them will often reveal that arable and pasture areas were being enlarged. Sometimes the structure of villages is significant, as in the intercalary type of settlement. Here there is a nucleus around which lie hamlets, scattered houses, or, less frequently, isolated manors. Records and source data prove these to be relatively new. They may, for example, be mentioned as inhabited places only rather late; they may be served by a little chapel dependent on the church in the central settlement, or they may be located in the middle of a huge tract of land owned by a single tenant, while the surrounding lands lie in open fields cultivated in strips, etc.[42] Sometimes holdings are classified in such a way as to indicate that new clearing has taken place. A 13th century polyptyque, for instance, distinguishes the older tenements—manses, *més,* quarters, and *masale* land—from the assarts (newly broken land). Or study of the names of fields and holdings reveals the presence of *courts, vents, artigues, arsis,* and *mesnils,* dating from Roman or early Frankish times. Again, the documents may speak of the tithes known as *novales,* those levied on newly cultivated land, which may go back to a 9th century origin but more often only to the 11th century.[43] Finally, a charter or a saint's life may mention the new development of forest or wasteland: for example, a property may be deeded to an individual or to a religious foundation to be cleared (*ad extirpandum*), or someone struck by paralysis has to lease out land that he had brought under cultivation.[44]

All of these indices of the advance of cultivation have been known to us for a long time. The need now is to examine them in a more methodical and rigorous way. Research should focus on clearly defined areas and should exploit every existing source of information.[45] Local study should deal simultaneously with water problems, with the appearance [46], the number and the importance of *villes neuves* [47], and with clearing operations within older lands in order to identify and date each assart.[48] By doing so, it would be possible to measure the advance of cultivation in the region in question as accurately as possible.

The increase of the cultivated area would be a main clue to the degree of population growth. Yet although the two phenomena certainly move together, there is nothing to show that they must vary equally. Conceivably the breaking in of more land might be due less to an increase in population than to a fall in the number of the landless, or to a general rise in standards of living. The problem in each case would be to decide how far the movement was the result of population pressure. To know the motivation of the people or the communities concerned would be helpful. The founding of a *ville neuve* by a king or a territorial prince whose aims were political, strategic, or fiscal rather than truly economic [49] and whose call for immigrants drew a response mainly from more or less remote countries [50], or the creation of a grange (outlying farm) by some Cistercian abbey would be less significant for the region we were studying [51] than clearing planned by the cadets of seigneurial families or by peasants. Work of this kind was often more important than has been generally recognized.[52]

To attack forest and wasteland is one means of dealing with population pressure. Another way is to improve technique. Agricultural methods progressed through fallowing every third year instead of every second and, on some plots, by sowing legumes in the fallow, through plowing more frequently and more deeply and fertilizing the soil more, and by specialization, for example, in vine culture or market gardening. All this was going on in the valley of the Rhine in the 12th and 13th centuries.[53] What was achieved there may have been achieved elsewhere. In studying the demographic history of a region, it is important to look into all this.

But not everyone with too many children made an effort to get more land or to farm better. When population began to grow families at first continued to live on their patrimony. After a time, if juridical and other customs permitted [54], they would simply divide it. Fragmentation of manorial units, both of a whole vill and of the peasant *mansus*, was thus to some extent [55] a consequence [56] of population growth. It is one of our indices. It is true that the movement began well before 1100; in some places, for example in Lorraine [57], it was by then general. Of greater interest for us is the further fragmentation of the units, especially the quarter, into which the ancient manse had been split, but its occurrence is not easy to date.

Population growth bore not only on the secular "cell" of the social organism, the vill, but also on its religious "cell", the parish. Sometimes the parish disintegrated, though less often than has been supposed.[58] The proprietors and the incumbents of the old churches, both rural and urban, defended their privileges fiercely and often victoriously.[59] Thus the spiritual problems consequent on the growth of the flock had to be met by other means than subdivision of parishes. The old churches, and the bodies of clergy serving them, had to be enlarged [60] or else new *loci religiosi* had to be set up, that is, chapels served more or less regularly by a priest, so that the faithful could at least hear Sunday Mass.[61] Construction or alteration of churches and chapels is thus evidence of population growth [62]; here the historian should consult the archeologist.

Finally, along with chance references to the development of this or that rural industry, we have clear proof of a rise in the population curve–in the expansion of the West. *Reconquista,* the feudal operations of the Hautevilles and their rivals in Southern Italy and Sicily, Crusades, and the *Drang nach Osten*–these movements are too familiar and too far-reaching to be discussed here. Between the 11th century and the 13th, and even into the 14th century, they were drawing colonists from all parts of the Christian West.[63] In research in the population history of a region one must never forget to find out whether any of its people emigrated–either in large groups, like the Flemish peasants who went off to the Baltic fenlands, or singly, like the barons of Perche or of Béarn who straggled off to Spain.[64] One should also try to find out why they went. Land hunger need not have been the only motive.

These then are the kinds of evidence which tend to show that from 1000 or 1050 to 1300 or 1350 the Christian West was becoming more thickly settled. Taken by itself, each piece of evidence is debatable. For example, the clearing of new land is not in itself "decisive evidence of an unusual growth of population, of a demographic revolution [65]". It is the consistency of the evidence that brings conviction. Increase in the number of households or of individuals within a given area, birth rates higher than would have been necessary to mere maintenance of the population, a rise in land values coinciding with a probable fall in wages, growth in the size and number of towns, the promotion of more and more villages to the status of a little town and the rise of God knows how many new villages and hamlets, the pushing back of seas, marshes, wasteland, and forest by the advance of fields and pastures, improvements in the yield of land, fragmentation of old manorial units, subdivision of parishes or enlargement of churches and building of chapels, the expansion of the West to the South and to the East—how are we to explain all this going on at the same time, except by a net increase of population?

But though the nature of the process is clear enough, its working is in many respects still hazy. The evidence has not been systematically interrogated. We are still much in the dark about the starting points, the duration, the intensity and the phasing of the movement. When did it begin? We say, in the mid-11th century. But is this true of Italy? [66] Or of Germany? [67] Or of the Low Countries, Flanders or Normandy? [68] When did it die down? Most historians would say, in the 14th century; many towns were then stagnating or declining, while marginal lands and even whole villages [69] were being deserted. But there is still controversy as to whether these developments came in the early or middle years of the century. Those who believe that they came around 1300 point to the impossibility of bringing any more land under wheat, and to evidence of soil exhaustion on many of the assarts.[70] They argue that in these circumstances population must already have ceased to grow and may already have begun to fall. But the majority still holds to the contrary thesis that the Black Death was responsible for reversing the trend.[71] Again, some researchers take an entirely different view of the phasing of the movement. One writer claims that the Bavarian plain was already fully exploited by the end of the 12th century and the mountain zones not yet fully exploited at the end of the 13th.[72] Another claims, after comparing two fiscal records, that between 1312 and 1427 the population of the Tirol grew by 50%.[73]

The extent to which population grew is also a matter of debate. To speak of a revolution is perhaps to exaggerate. Even by the rather generous estimates of Levasseur or of Lamprecht, the average annual increase comes out far below that of England or Germany between 1800 and 1850—a percentage of 3.8 or 4.8 instead of 14 or 11.[74] As to the possible phases of the movement, we are still unable to distinguish and describe them.

Almost everything that we know or postulate on this subject therefore requires to be verified and restated in quantitative terms. This can be done only through meticulously careful regional study. We cannot even be certain of reaching precise quantative results. But the attempt has to be made, for although it has been long neglected [75], the problem is nonetheless important. Indeed, in all medieval history there are few questions so fundamental as this one.

P.S. On reading the manuscript of this article my esteemed colleague and friend Professor Philippe Wolff of the University of Toulouse suggested to me that the improvement in the status of peasants, especially the relaxation of the bonds attaching them to the soil, may equally be a consequence of population growth. This is certainly true, yet the interpretation of this index is a particularly delicate matter, one that does not lend itself well to statistical study.

NOTES

1 This seems to be the conviction of C. Cipolla, J. Dhondt, M. Postan, and P. Wolff, authors of the remarkable "Rapport sur la démographie au moyen âge" presented at the Ninth International Congress of the Historical Sciences and published in Vol. I of the *Rapports* of that Congress (Paris, 1950), pp. 55ff.

2 K. J. Beloch, *Bevölkerungsgeschichte Italiens* (Berlin and Leipzig, 1937), vol. I, pp. 1ff.

3 Good examples of the use of these lists are offered for the Flemish towns, which in the 14th century rivalled the Italian cities, by Jos. De Smet, "L'effectif des milices brugeoises et la population de la ville en 1340", *Revue belge de philologie et d'histoire*, t. XII (1933), pp. 636ff. and H. van Werveke, "Het bevolkingscijfer van de stad Gent in de veertiende eeuw", *Miscellanea historica in honorem L. van der Essen*, t. I (Brussels and Paris, 1947), pp. 345ff.

K. Bücher, *Die Bevölkerung von Frankfurt-am-Main* (Leipzig, 1886) is still useful for anyone interested in the history of the medieval urban population.

4 There is no doubt that this average varied from one region to another with the strength or weakness of a communal spirit, with conceptions of the family, and with inheritance customs; it varied also from one period to another according as the population was tending to grow, to become stabilized, or to fall. The search for a multiplier valid for all countries and all periods, on which some authors are bent, is therefore futile and seriously mistaken.

5 On the handling of these questions see especially J. Cuvelier, "Les dénombrements de foyers en Brabant (XIVe–XVIe siècle)", *Publications de la Commission royale d'histoire de Belgique* (Brussels, 1912) and F. Lot, "L'état des paroisses et des feux de 1328", *Bibliothèque de l'Ecole des Chartes*, t. XC (1929), p. 51.

6 K. J. Beloch, *op. cit.*, pp. 91ff.

7 J. C. Russell, *British Medieval Population* (Albuquerque, 1948). If the auxiliary calculations of this author, such as the average expectation of life, are debatable, the total figures that he suggests for the years 1086, 1346, and 1377 are more certain. On the basis of the Polyptyque of Saint-Germain-des-Prés, compiled at the end of the reign of Charlemagne or early in that of Louis the Pious, and on *L'Etat des paroisses et des feux* of 1328, E. Levasseur, in *La population française* (Paris, 1889), t. I, pp. 139 and 160, proposed the figures of 8 to 9 million inhabitants for France in the Carolingian period and of 20 to 22 million for the first third of the 14th century. But he almost immediately modified these figures by reason of the analysis of A. Longnon, *Polyptyques de l'abbaye de Saint-Germain-des-Prés* (Paris, 1895), t. I, p. 250. His inquiries were resumed with more rigor by F. Lot, "Conjectures démographiques sur la France au IXe siècle", in *Le Moyen Age*, t. XXXII (1921), pp. 1ff. For this scholar the density of rural population in France about 810–820 was between 34 and 39 per square kilometer. These new conclusions were confirmed with the help of the polyptyque of Saint-Bertin relating to French Flanders, by H. van Werveke, "De bevolkingsdichtheid in de IXe eeuw. Poging tot schatting", *XXXe Congrès de la Fédération archéologique et historique de Belgique* (Brussels, 1935), *Annales* (Brussels, 1936), pp. 107ff. On the other hand, in his edition of the Etat of 1328, F. Lot estimated the density of population at this date as between 35 and 38 per square kilometer, a figure sharply rejected by so learned a scholar as E. Perroy, "A l'origine d'une économie contractée. Les crises du XIVe siècle", *Annales. Economies. Sociétés. Civilisations* (4e Année, 1949), p. 168, n. 1. This would imply that between the age of Charlemagne and that of Philip VI, the population of the

French countryside did not grow or that if it increased after 1050 this merely compensated for probable losses between 850 and 1050, as M. Bloch believed, "Les invasions: occupation du sol et peuplement", *Annales d'histoire sociale,* II (1945), p. 26. These deductions are much more speculative than those of English researchers, especially because the basis of Lot's estimates for the Carolingian period is so much narrower than that of Domesday Book. To generalize about France as a whole from about twenty estates is indeed reckless. Surely the polyptyques of Saint-Germain and of Saint-Bertin refer to estates better furnished with manpower than neighboring estates, simply because they were monastic and also because they refer to regions that were drawing immigrants? Even supposing that their populations were as large in 800 as in 1300, would it follow that this was true throughout France? Besides, is it certain that the French population had not grown between these dates? The only way to be certain of this would be to study identical estates at different dates from the point of view of the extent of cultivated land, the number of tenants and of hearths, etc.

8 See, for England, J. C. Russell, *op. cit.,* pp. 76ff. and, for the continent, L. Verriest, *Institutions médiévales* (Mons et Frameries, 1946), p. 117.

9 Conversion into modern measures is always hazardous. It is usually done with the help of tables drawn up at the end of the Ancien Régime or at the beginning of the 19th century, on the assumption that no modification had occurred since the Middle Ages. It is best, therefore, not to use these unless it is necessary, that is to say, unless one needs to compare data from different estates.

10 From the post-Carolingian age, indeed in some cases earlier, there ceases to be any correlation between the number of tenures and the number of tenants. Calculation of the latter runs up against the difficulty of vague references to partners (*conparticipes*) or by the recurrence in the lists of the same names, which may or may not refer to the same people.

11 As A. E. Levett has noted, *Studies in Manorial History* (Oxford, 1938), p. 249, it is rash to deduce the number of inhabitants from the number of tenants. The former included, besides the tenants, the following categories whose importance varied from estate to estate: subtenants, farmhands lodging with their masters, artisans without a scrap of land—perhaps not even their own house and garden—, rear-vassals of whom polyptyques usually give no hints, and small independent freeholders.

12 It was by counting inhabited centers as they appeared in the documents that K. Lamprecht, *Deutsches Wirtschaftsleben im Mittelalter* (Leipzig, 1885), I, pp. 163ff. and II, pp. 17ff., thought he had discovered the phases of demographic history in the Moselle valley between the 10th century and the 15th. The method is defensible, since new settlements usually indicate new population. However, in striving to be statistical the German historian laid himself open to serious criticism. He proceeded as though he had full information on all the inhabited places in the years 1000, 1050, 1100, etc., or as though the percentage that he did not know was a constant; this is to suppose that one's documentation is either complete or bears a constant relation to the facts throughout the whole period. He gave the same weight to all inhabited centers, although in an age of intensive clearing the new settlements are usually mere hamlets or isolated farms, with many fewer inhabitants than the old settlements. He overlooked the abandonment of some villages between the 11th century and the 13th. From the fact that there appeared to have been no new settlements in this region after 1240, he arbitrarily concluded that population ceased to grow at that date.

13 M. Morgan, *The English Lands of the Abbey of Bec* (Oxford, 1946), p. 111.

14 For examples of the ancient genealogies, useful but to be checked with extreme care, see "Chronicon Hanoniense quod dicitur Balduini Avennensis", ed. J. Heller, in *Monumenta Germaniae Historica. Scriptores,* XXV, pp. 421ff.

15 L. Génicot, *L'économie rurale namuroise au bas moyen âge,* T. I, *La seigneurie foncière* (Louvain and Namur, 1943), p. 66. The same method has been applied by P. Feuchère, "Histoire sociale et généalogie. La noblesse du Nord de la France", *Annales. Economies. Sociétés. Civilisations,* VI (1951), pp. 315ff.

16 At least for the 11th, 12th, and 13th century. From the late Middle Ages and espe-

cially from 1400, it is possible to draw up most interesting genealogies of bourgeois families, like that of the Rohrbachs of Frankfurt-am-Main, analyzed by H. Boos, *Geschichte der rheinischen Städtekultur* (2nd ed., Berlin, 1899), III, p. 44, and set out in detail in H. Grotefend, ed., *Quellen zur Frankfürter Geschichte* (Frankfurt, 1884), table 19, pp. 434ff.

17 The example in *Beilage V: Beispiele der Kinderfrequenz der abhängigen Bevölkerung* for the Carolingian age, established from the *libri traditionum* of Fulda and other German abbeys in K. Th. von Inama-Sternegg, *Deutsche Wirtschaftsgeschichte* (2nd ed., Leipzig, 1909), is only a rough sketch of what could be done.

18 Obviously other types of documents may be used for this purpose, such as the polyptyques, like that of Irminon, and for the later Middle Ages tax rolls, like the Tyrolese rolls of 1427 used by K. Schadelbauer, "Die Kopfzahl der bäuerlichen Familien in Tirol im 15 Jahrhundert", in *Quellen zur Steuer-, Bevölkerungs- und Sippengeschichte des Landes Tirol im 13, 14, und 15 Jahrhundert. Festgabe zum 80 Lebensjahre O. Redlichs. Schlern-Schriften,* Heft 44 (Innsbrück, 1939).

19 One must of course always make sure that the data are clearly representative. For example, one cannot exclude the possibility that figures drawn from pious donations are above the average, such transactions being sometimes the alternative to excessive fragmentation. In that case, however, a statistician would term the error a more or less strictly systematic one, which would not invalidate the evolutionary study of which we are speaking. On account of this bias one should not, however, mix data drawn from pious donations with those drawn from other sources.

20 On this point see K. Kulischer, *Allgemeine Wirtschaftsgeschichte des Mittelalters und der Neuzeit* (Munich and Berlin, 1927), I, p. 173 or the well-known book of K. Buecher, *Die Frauenfrage im Mittelalter* (2nd ed., Leipzig, 1910), summarized in *Abhandlung XI* of the first volume of *Die Entstehung der Volkswirtschaft* (17th ed., Tübingen, 1926).

21 With the exception of some historians of medicine who have dealt with this briefly and indirectly and whose chief works are listed in E. Keyser, *Bevölkerungsgeschichte Deutschlands* (2nd ed., Leipzig, 1941) (the only edition I was able to procure), the epidemics and plagues of our period have received little attention from 20th century researchers. We still have little to go on beyond F. Curschmann, *Hungersnöte im Mittelalter* (Leipzig, 1900) or even older works, such as A. Corradi, *Annali delle Epidemie occorse in Italia* (Bologna, 1865), or L. Torfs, *Fastes des calamités publiques survenues dans les Pays-Bas,* 2 vols. (Paris and Tournay, 1859), or chapter 21 in L. Delisle, *Etudes sur la condition de la classe agricole et l'état de l'agriculture en Normandie au moyen âge* (Evreux, 1851) and appendix 1 to vol. I of K. Lamprecht, *op. cit.*, pp. 1537ff.

22 Agricultural prices seem to me to be more closely related to the demographic situation and more likely to show changes in this if they are expressed in wheat and not in money or when they move in a different direction from other prices or have a different amplitude in their fluctuations.

23 M. Postan, "Some Economic Evidence of Declining Population in the later Middle Ages", *Economic History Review,* 2nd series, vol. II, no. 3 (1950), pp. 225ff. See also W. Abel, "Bevölkerungsgang und Landwirtschaft im ausgehenden Mittelalter im Lichte der Preis und Lohnbewegung", *Schmoller's Jahrbücher,* 58th year (1934), pp. 33ff.

24 This is the method used in France by d'Avenel and in Germany by Lamprecht and used again by W. Abel, *Agrarkrisen und Agrarkonjunktur in Mitteleuropa vom 13 bis zum 19 Jahrhundert* (Berlin, 1935), pp. 24ff. It is also the one which J. R. Strayer, in *The Royal Domain in the Bailliage of Rouen* (Princeton, 1936) suggested applying to Normandy when he wrote (p. 24) that it is sometimes possible to make a comparison between the prices given in the document which he was publishing and those of 1180–1200, that is, 70 or 80 years before, given by L. Delisle in ch. XX of the work cited in n. 21.

25 We have indicated this method in a table on p. 289 of the work cited above in n. 15.

26 The best general exposition is still that of H. Pirenne, "Le mouvement économique

et social au moyen âge, du XIe au milieu du XVe siècle" in G. Glotz, ed., *Histoire générale,* 2nd part, *Histoire du moyen âge* (Paris, 1933), VIII (reprinted in *Histoire économique de l'Occident médiéval,* pp. 155ff.). However, it needs revision in the way indicated in R. Latouche, *Les origines de l'économie occidentale, IVe–XIe siècle* (Paris, 1956), pp. 271ff. and in my *Lignes de faîte du moyen âge* (2nd ed., Tournai and Paris, 1962), p. 334, n. 27.

27 The criteria of urban growth have been very carefully analyzed by F. L. Ganshof, *Over stadsontwikkeling tusschen Loire en Rijn gedurende de Middeleeuwen* (2nd ed., Brussels, 1944) and in remarks reported in the *Acts* of the Ninth International Congress of the Historical Sciences (Paris), II, pp. 34–35.

28 Figures drawn from the work of Ganshof just cited. For other important examples see F. Lot, *Recherches sur la population et la superficie des cités remontant à la période gallo-romaine* (*Bibliothèque de l'Ecole des Hautes Etudes. Sciences historiques et philologiques*) (Paris, 1945 and 1950), vols. 287 and 296; L. Blondel, "Le développement urbain de Genève à travers les siècles", *Cahiers de préhistoire et d'archéologie* (Geneva and Nyon, 1946), III, and also I. von Strampf, *Die Entstehung und mittelalterliche Entwicklung der Stadt Nürnberg* (Erlangen, 1929).

29 A. E. Levett, *op. cit.,* p. 181, remarked on this.

30 G. Luzzatto, *Storia economica d'Italia* (Rome, 1949), vol. I, p. 241, writes that many Italian towns between 1100 and 1250 grew from 5 to 6,000 souls to 30 or 40,000; the bounds sometimes finally enclosed an area tenfold the size of the original area yet building still went on beyond them.

31 On this point see very precise data in E. Keyser, *op. cit.,* pp. 268ff.

32 Italian historians have paid particular attention to the process of urbanization. See the survey by G. Luzzatto, "L'inurbamento delle popolazioni rurali in Italia nei secoli XII e XIII", *Studi di storia e diritto in onore di E. Besta* (Milan, 1939), II, pp. 185ff.

33 E. Lipson, *The Economic History of England* (10th ed., London, 1949), I, p. 185, says that at the end of the 13th century half the inhabitants of Colchester lived by agriculture.

34 Except for a narrow radius of four or five kilometers around little towns; see M. C. Daviso, "I piu antichi catasti del commune di Chieri (1253)", *Bollettino storico-bibliografico subalpino,* vol. XXXIX (1937), p. 75.

35 See R. Koebner's excellent survey on this matter in *The Cambridge Economic History of Europe* (Cambridge, 1941), I, pp. 61ff., and G. Duby, *L'économie rurale et la vie des campagnes dans l'Occident médiéval* (Paris, 1962), pp. 133–169.

36 F. L. Ganshof, *La Flandre sous les premiers comtes,* 2nd ed., p. 54, in the collection *Notre Passé* (Brussels, 1944) and S. J. Fockerma-Andreae, "Embanking and Drainage Authorities in the Netherlands in the Middle Ages", *Speculum,* XXVII (1952), pp. 158ff.

37 G. Mickwitz in the *Cambridge Economic History,* I, pp. 323ff. and G. Luzzatto, *Storia economica d'Italia,* p. 212.

38 On work on the Po, see especially P. Torelli, *Un comune cittadino in territorio ad economia agricola,* in *Pubblicazioni della R. Accademia Virgiliana di Mantova. Serie miscellanee,* III (1930), vol. I, pp. 105ff.

39 M. Bloch, *Les caractères originaux de l'histoire rurale française* (Oslo, 1931 and Paris), pp. 5ff.

40 See A. Longnon, *Les noms de lieu de la France* (Paris, 1920–1929), pp. 515ff.

41 Typical plans will be found in P. Lavendan, *Histoire de l'urbanisme* (Paris, 1926), I, pp. 296ff.; M. Bloch, *op. cit.,* pl. I in the appendix; *Cambridge Economic History,* I, p. 45.

42 See a study of my own, "Le destin d'une famille noble. Les Noville aux XIIIe et XIVe siècles", *Annales de la Société archéologique de Namur,* t. XLVI (1952), p. 216.

43 A. Poeschl, "Der Neubruchzehent", *Archiv für katholisches Kirchenrecht,* t. XCVIII (1918), pp. 33ff.

44 "Miracles de la Sainte Croix de Brogne", l. 3, c. 8, ed. by F. Baix in the *Annales de la Société archéologique de Namur,* vol. XLV (1950), p. 260. Needless to say, the indices listed here are only the most obvious ones. Others can be found, such as a

fall in the number of pigs that a village can fatten: see H. E. Darby, *An Historical Geography of England before 1800* (Cambridge, 1936), p. 181.

45 It is better to take a compact district than to pick villages here and there, if only to rule out the effect of local migration.

46 There has been a good deal of systematic study of the *villes neuves* of Southwest France, called *bastides*. One of the most recent contributions is by L. Higounet, "Cisterciens et Bastides", in *Le Moyen Age*, vol. LVI (1950), pp. 69ff.

47 As names by themselves are deceptive—there was clearing before the 11th and even before the 10th century!—, it may be useful, in the interests of exactness, to follow the methods of A. Helbok, *Grundlagen der Volksgeschichte Deutschlands und Frankreichs* (Leipzig and Berlin, 1937), maps 53ff.: draw two series of maps, one showing the various types of place names, the other showing the first mention of each place in a document, and then construct colonization maps after comparing these two. In default of maps the data of place names and of documents may simply be tabulated as in A. Bach, "Die Siedlungsnamen des Taunusgebiets in ihrer Bedeutung für die Besiedlungsgeschichte", in *Veröffentlichungen des Instituts für geschichtliche Landeskunde der Rheinlande an der Universität Bonn. Herausgegeben von F. Steinbach* (Bonn, 1927), vol. I, pp. 207ff.

48 On this see C. Higounet, "Les artigues dans les vallées luchonnaises", *Mélanges géographiques offerts en hommage à Monsieur le doyen D. Faucher* (Toulouse, 1948–1949), vol. II, pp. 555ff. and "Contribution à l'étude de la toponymie du défrichement: les artigues du Bordelais et du Bazadais", in *IIIe Congrès international de toponymie et anthroponymie. Vol. III: Actes et Mémoires* (Louvain, 1951), pp. 595ff.

49 On all of the towns of central Flanders and some of the Norman towns, see J. Dhondt, "Développement urbain et initiative comtale au XIe siècle", *Revue du Nord*, vol. XXX (1948), pp. 133ff. and J. F. Lemarignier, *Revue du moyen âge latin*, vol. IV (1948), p. 191. The first-mentioned author seems to me to exaggerate the role of material factors in the birth of these towns.

50 There were undoubtedly migrations even in the heart of the Christian West: see R. Boutruche, "Les courants de peuplement dans l'Entre-Deux-Mers", *Annales d'histoire économique et sociale*, vol. VII (1935), pp. 13ff. and 124ff.

51 Their significance is chiefly for the regions from which settlers are drawn or for places victualled by the grange.

52 Most authors follow F. L. Ganshof (*Cambridge Economic History*, I, pp. 279ff.) and Marc Bloch (*Les caractères originaux, loc. cit.*), in so emphasizing magnates and abbeys as founders of *villes neuves* as to give the reader the impression that assarting within old lands by petty lords or peasants was of only secondary importance. This is probably an error; in regard to peasant clearing see T. A. M. Bishop, "Assarting and the Growth of the Open Fields", *Economic History Review*, VI, no. 1 (1935), pp. 17ff. and R. Latouche, "Agrarzustände im westlichen Frankreich während des Hochmittelalters", *Vierteljahrschrift für Sozial- und Wirtschaftsgeschichte*, XXIX (1930), p. 111, and on the work of petty lords see my article cited in n. 42.

53 W. Abel, *Agrarkrisen*, p. 22. An increasing yield is the best proof we can get of more rational exploitation. The data on this point have, however, to be handled with great care, even for England, where the statistical data are best. See M. K. Bennet, "British Wheat Yield per Acre for Seven Centuries", *Economic History. A supplement of The Economic Journal*, III, no. 10 (February, 1935), pp. 12–20, and B. A. Slicher van Bath, "De oogstophengsten van verschillende gewassen, voornamelijk granen, in verhouding tot het Zaaizaad *ca.* 810–1820", in *A. A. G. Bijdragen*, vol. 9 (1963), pp. 29–126.

54 Several factors may have contributed to keep manorial units stable. For example, it was in the interests of royal power and lords to keep the manse intact as a fiscal unit, and local inheritance customs could have the same effect. The reciprocal of our proposition therefore does not hold, that is to say, the survival of the old units does not prove demographic stagnation. At Bobbio the manse was preserved throughout the Middle Ages solely for fiscal reasons; see C. M. Cipolla, "Per la storia della crisi del sistema curtense in Italia. Lo sfaldamento del manso nell'Appennino bob-

biese", *Bollettino dell'Istituto Storico Italiano per il Medio Evo ed Archivie Muratoriano,* n. 62 (1950), pp. 283ff.

55 The splitting up of estates could occur through pious donations or subinfeudation; see my *Economie rurale namuroise,* I, pp. 37ff.

56 It would usually follow after a lag; as a consequence of the practice of indivision, the splitting up of holdings frequently happened one or two generations after the growth of population.

57 C. E. Perrin, *Recherches sur la seigneurie rurale en Lorraine d'après les plus anciens censiers (IXe–XIIe siècles)* (Paris, 1935), pp. 634ff.

58 A. Hauck, *Kirchengeschichte Deutschlands,* vol. IV (3rd ed., Leipzig, 1913), pp. 24ff.

59 This also introduced a lag.

60 See R. Rey, *L'art roman et ses origines. Archéologie pré-romane et romane* (Toulouse and Paris, 1945), p. 147 and K. Lamprecht, *op. cit.,* I, p. 164.

61 The monasteries that multiplied from the 11th century on helped to meet this need.

62 Although they can constitute proof, they need not; a chapel might have been founded through piety and a church altered simply because architectural taste was changing.

63 M. Postan, *Cambridge Economic History* (Cambridge, 1952), II, p. 160.

64 For North Germany see R. Koebner and H. Aubin, *Cambridge Economic History,* I, pp. 80ff. and 364ff. and E. Keyser, *op. cit.,* pp. 212ff., and for Belgium, R. Doehaerd, *L'expansion économique belge au moyen âge,* in the collection *Notre Passé* (Brussels, 1946), pp. 38ff. For Spain see M. Defourneaux, *Les Français en Espagne aux XIe et XIIe siècles* (Paris, 1949), pp. 214ff. and the remarks of J. M. Lacarra in the *IXe Congrès international des Sciences historiques,* II, p. 43.

65 The phrase is taken from R. Koebner, *loc. cit.,* p. 69. He may not have intended to exaggerate. It may be admitted as true, if the emphasis is on the word revolution.

66 G. Luzzatto, *Storia economica,* p. 212, thinks that the Italian growth began in the 10th century. P. Torelli, *Un comune cittadino, op. cit.,* pp. 151ff., takes the same view.

67 R. Koetzschke, *Allgemeine Wirtschaftsgeschichte des Mittelalters,* in the *Handbuch der Wirtschaftsgeschichte,* ed. G. Brodnitz (Iena, 1924), II, pp. 361–362, in view of new settlements in Lower Saxony, in the Harz region, at the edges of the forest in Thuringia, and in Austria, described German population growth between the Carolingian and the Hohenstaufen period as "not negligible". H. Aubin, *op. cit.,* p. 365, also sees German colonization of Austria as occurring between 800 and 1100. P. Dollinger, *L'évolution des classes rurales en Bavière* (Paris, 1949), p. 79, holds that though new settlement in Bavaria was interrupted by the Hungarian invasion, it was vigorously resumed from the mid-10th century.

68 H. van der Linden, *De Cope* (Assen, 1955); C. E. Perrin, *Les classes rurales et le régime seigneurial au moyen âge* (mimeographed, Paris, 1949), p. 134; F. L. Ganshof, *op. cit.,* p. 278.

69 See in general W. Abel, "Wachstumsschwankungen mitteleuropäischer Völker seit dem Mittelalter", *Jahrbücher für Nationalökonomie und Statistik,* CXLII (1935), pp. 675ff.; and on Germany his "Die Wüstungen des ausgehenden Mittelalters. Ein Beitrag zur Siedlungs- und Agrargeschichte Deutschlands", *Quellen und Forschungen zur Agrargeschichte* (2nd ed., Iena, 1955), vol. I. Signs of the desertion of land multiply in the 15th century.

70 See M. Postan, *loc. cit.* above, n. 23. Similarly in France, according to G. d'Avenel, *Histoire économique de la propriété, des salaires, des denrées et de tous les prix en général depuis l'an 1200 jusqu'en l'an 1800* (2nd ed., Paris, 1914), II, p. 508. The price of land ceased to rise from the beginning of the 14th century.

71 See especially J. C. Russell, *op. cit.* and F. Luetge, "Das 14–15 Jahrhundert in der Sozial- und Wirtschaftsgeschichte", *Jahrbücher für Nationalökonomie und Statistik,* CLXII (1950), pp. 165ff.

72 P. Dollinger, *loc cit.*

73 O. Stolz, "Zur Statistik der Haushalte nach den Listen von 1312 und 1427", pp. 5 and 6 (in the Redlich Festschrift, cited above in n. 18). R. Koetzschke, "Grundzüge

On the Evidence of Growth of Population in the West 29

der deutschen Wirtschaftsgeschichte bis zum 17 Jahrhundert" (2nd ed.), *Grundriss der Geschichtswissenschaft* (Leipzig and Berlin, 1923), 2nd series, fasc. I, p. 116, although he believes that the Black Death reduced German population, estimates that for the 13th and 14th century it had a density of 20 to 30 per square kilometer and that in "favorable situations" the density around 1450 may have been from 30 to 40.

74 K. F. Helleiner, "Population Movement and Agrarian Depression in the Later Middle Ages", *Canadian Journal of Economics and Political Science,* XV (1949), p. 371.

75 None of the classical textbooks of medieval and modern economic history devotes even a section of a chapter to this problem.

3
The 'Feudal' Economy and Capitalism: Words, Ideas and Reality

Jacques Heers

It is now a very considerable time since economic historians first began trying to contrast the material and mental skills and structures of that period in the history of Western Europe which we call « medieval », with those of so-called 'modern' times. Through habit, reluctance to embark on any real research, or else through narrow loyalty to some sort of ideology, there are still those who continue to draw such contrasts. But it is this type of *a priorism* which has to a large extent dulled the researchers' curiosity, which has paralysed serious research of any scope or depth, which is responsible for major gaps in our knowledge and which still, even today, leads historians to seek refuge in comfortable and convenient conformities. Words such as « medieval », « feudal » (this one in particular), « archaic », « primary » have become all-purpose slogans to be used both wrongly and inaccurately at the first opportunity. They conceal, however, a much more complex reality.

Assertions such as these seem to be based on two sets of ideas, both equally contestable. First there is the unshaken belief in a sudden break, a threshold, a moment of departure between the « Middle Ages » and « modernity ». This break is described in technical, and even quantitative and structural terms, and is traced in attitudes as well. Secondly there is the conviction that the nascent and then conquering capitalism, such as could be found in 15th century Italy, developed only amongst the great merchants, and in fact affected only a very narrow fringe of the urban population leaving the countryside quite untouched. « Capitalist » techniques and attitudes did not then affect society as a whole and did not reach humbler and less well-to-do social groups.

A New Departure; Can we speak of « feudal » attitudes and structures?

The concept of a threshold between the « medieval » and « modern » period now seems to be fairly solidly established. But there is nothing which can justify it. It is based on a series of postulates which do not withstand much critical reflection. The first of these is the concept that the « Middle Ages » existed in its own right, that there was a well defined « medieval » time, as well as a « medieval » society. Such expression are, of course, no more than linguistic conveniences. The « Middle Ages » only exist as a result of the desire and the wishes of historians and pedagogues who are keen to set limits to well defined periods but while this is of long standing, it is no less artificial for that.[1] A second is the myth of a « Renaissance » which was victorious both in artistic and intellectual terms, and which in a superficial and almost inevitable way these same authors cheerfully amalgamate more or less explicitly with a renewal of economic activities, techniques and structures. There is a final credo which is even more pronounced — the belief that economic techniques and structures evolved, not in a way that was unseen, riddled with complexities, similarities, hesitations and which as a result becomes extremely difficult either to define or to place chronologically, but that on the contrary they were pushed forward by sudden starts and by revolutions.

---

1 Cf. the view expressed some time ago by A. Sapori, *Moyen Age et Renaissance en Italie*, in « Annales. Economies. Société. Civilisation. » 1956, who disputed the very existence of a Renaissance. Unfortunately this view has received little support and attention from historians who continue to maintain the traditional distinction.

Of course the historians who have stuck to these theories have been aware of the difficulty of defining this new departure with any precision. Some have seen it as a transition rather than a single step. Others have claimed that the traditional dates, drawn almost exclusively from political or military events, or from the change of dynasties or even of reigns, are not sufficient from any social or economic point of view for defining the « Middle Ages ». So economic historians have had to look for other signs which although less spectacular are certainly more representative. They have focused their attention on skill and on scale — the study of trade volumes and the circulation of money for example. Some have attempted to revise the traditional divisions, and claim that the advent of « capitalism » or « precapitalism » considerably preceded the end of the « Middle Ages » as they are traditionally considered and that there is no inevitable and absolute identity between « feudal » society and economy and the « medieval » era. So after situating the point of departure in the years between 1480 and 1500 these scholars, or their disciples, then put forward much earlier dates and draw support from a large number of historians of the modern period — the « modernists ». Recently this tendency has become established, largely due to one of the reforms of higher education in France (which was applied for only one year, in 1967) which made the « modern » period start at around the year 1400 and two important publishing houses then adopted a similar starting point for their historical publications — one took the 1350's, even 1300.

But these are false problems — a sort of game which, if not puerile, is at least free. It is quite clear that the evolution was neither general nor uniform. In fact, even if one accepts this framework the chronological break must of necessity vary according to individual countries, even according to individual towns and social groups. It is obvious that the indications of evolution, and even more so of revolution, are neither easy to define or even to find. It is obviously extremely difficult to apply any rigorous quantitative or statistical history to this period, in which continuous series of documents of a similar type are lacking, where their interpretation is often extremely difficult, and where the historian, no matter what his enthusiasm, almost always has the impression of dealing « pretty much with the uncertain ».

This is one of the reasons for the emphasis on technical history, which is also extremely difficult and complex in this period. The vast, spectacular but rather hasty theories of « revolutions » in material techniques are in fact based only on written documentation and iconography which is quite inadequate, debatable, and often mis-interpreted. Such theses enjoyed, and still enjoy, a considerable success with a certain academic public and also with those scholars who are bound to some form of historical materialism. They crop up every day with great confidence in our popular histories and our textbooks, yet they cannot withstand the critical examination of specialist historians.[2] At the same time the study of so-called intellectual techniques or skills, such as accountancy and book-keeping, the bill of exchange, on the issue and circulation of credit notes, has been conducted more carefully and is based on a wider range of documents, the interpretation of which would at first sight seem to be more straightforward but is still far from being completely satisfactory. In most cases the historian looks first of all for the first indication of a development which he considers to be decisive, that is to say he looks for the earliest document which announces the modern or contemporary way of organizing business affairs — the first bill of exchange, the first insurance contract which is free of the older, restrictive forms, the first endorsement or the first double-entry account books. This type of research obviously relies to a large extent on the chance preservation of such documents. It is rather like our childhood treasure hunts, and the way in which archaeologists in the past in their search for decisive works of art sacrificed all the most fundamental structures

2 An example is the eternal question of the horse's harness to which important improvements were made in the XIIIth century, thus permitting the more effective use of draught animals and being decisive in bringing about the end of slavery. This theory was first expounded in 1931, with some panache and great boldness, by G. Lefebvre des Noëtte, *L'attelage et cheval de selle à travers les âges*, 2 vols., Paris 1931. It is still very often quoted and even accepted without examination, although it has no solid factual basis. It is now refuted in all serious studies. Cf. H. Polge, *L'Amélioration de l'attelage a-t-elle réellement fait reculer le servage?*, in « Journal des Savants », 1967, pp. 5-42.

of their excavation sites and took no notice of objects considered to be of « minor » interest.

There are very few serious studies which have analysed the business practices of the « Middle Ages » in their own right without constant reference to contemporary forms.[3] Very few authors have understood or wished to accept that in banking and finance similar results might have been perfectly obtained with the procedures which we are tempted to call archaic simply because they are different from our own. For example, the absence of an authentic paper money, and even the uncertain and rare use of endorsement, does not necessarily imply that the circulation of money was slow and scarce. In the world of commerce, right down to the level of the humblest artisans, it would appear that ordinary account books performed that function, in Italy, at least, through simple transfer operations, the *giri di partite*.[4] These were performed in their dozens every day with the greatest of ease and without any formal obligation being made, simply on written or verbal instructions. Even at this time, then, monetary transactions involving the exchange of specie represented only a very small percentage of total transactions, perhaps less than one tenth of the total.

Was capitalism foreign to the « medieval » mentality?

It is now twenty or thirty years since the studies by A. Sayous, Y. Renouard and A. Sapori, followed by those of R. De Roover and F. Melis, began to launch a sustained offensive against the thesis of W. Sombart, Max Weber and R.H. Tawney. The latter provided us with an extremely systematic picture of a « medieval »

3 Among the very first successful studies in this field were those by F. Melis, *Storia della Ragioneria*, Bologna 1950; *Note di Storia della Banca nel Trecento*, Pisa 1935; *I primi secoli delle assicurazioni (secoli XIII-XVI)*, Rome 1965. A very recent, masterly analysis of specific documents and various accounting, mercantile and financial methods is provided by *Documenti per la Storia economica dei Secoli XIII-XVI*, Florence 1972, completed by the *Guida della Mostra internazionale della Banca. Secoli XIII-XVI*, Siena 1973.

4 R. De Roover, *The Development of Accounting prior to Luca Pacioli according to the Account books of Medieval merchants*, in « Studies in the History of Accounting », London 1956, and a more concrete study on Florence by F. Melis, *Aspetti della vita economica medievale (Studi nell'Archivio Datini di Prato)*, vol. 1, Siena 1962.

world which was dominated and ruled in every aspect, including the sphere of purely economic activity, by religious prohibitions. It was these theses that created the picture of the « medieval » merchant haunted constantly by the idea of sin, which led him to reject the single-minded pursuit of profit. He was seen as a mere « artisan » of commerce, working empirically with limited resources and paying respect to moral laws and rules imposed by the Church. But this simplistic picture in fact was based on no serious study of mercantile practices. Its validity was first contested for the towns of Italy, and it now seems that it is no more than an ideological construct which cannot be applied in practice to any Western country, including even those of Germany.[5]

But although such theories find practically no following today, they have certainly left a trace, like some distant memory. The belief in an absolute incompatibility between the « medieval » mentality, essentially a reflection of Christianity, and the concept of credit, whatever its form, at every material or occupational level, still lingers. There is a fixed picture which always intrudes and which seems to be unshakeable: the Church forbade usury, that is to say any form of money lending;[6] this prohibition weighed heavily on men's consciences and behaviour and so restrained significantly, if not decisively, the development of « modern » techniques and practices (for example, insurance, exchange operations, interest-bearing loans) and also the advent of true capitalism. This incompatibility accepted *a priori* also explains the existence of a series of outrageous theses and alternatives established without even consulting the facts. For instance there is the theory that in the « Middle Ages » lenders were always or preferably non-Christians, in particular Jews, who as a result escaped ecclesiastical condemnation. In this view the money lender becomes a man living on the

---

5 Cf. in particular the studies published in the collection: *L'opera di Werner Sombart nel centenario della nascita*, Milan 1965; see also R. De Roover, *The Concept of Just Price. Theory and Economic Policy*, in « Journal of Economic History », 1958.

6 Among the many studies on this topic are those by G. Le Bras, *La doctrine ecclésiastique de l'usure à l'époque classique*, in « Dictionnaire de théologie catholique », edited by A. Vacant and E. Mangenot, Paris 1950, article *Usure*; B.N. Nelson, *The Idea of Usury*, Princeton 1950; R. De Roover, *La pensée économique des Scholastiques: Doctrines et méthodes*, Montreal 1971.

edge of society, a pariah marked out by infamy and shut away in some sort of ghetto. Or again there is the theory that the Church's opposition to business loans and to the development of capitalism and banking provides an explanation of the origins of protestantism; the financiers preferred to break with the Church rather than be subject to its bans and restraints.[7] Finally, the idea still persists that everywhere and at all times usury was abusive and disguised, that credit was rare, and so dear that interest rates on money loans were very high, infinitely higher than anything to be found in the so-called « modern » period.

It is time to state emphatically that all these fine theories must now be relegated to that arsenal of ideas that have been tried and found wanting. None of them can be accepted without detailed scrutiny — which none of them will survive for long.

Materialist explanations which give pride of place — if not exclusive importance — to economic factors in bringing about the Reformation were among the first to drive in the wedge.[8] All the most recent studies on the activities of Jews in the countryside and the towns, and L. Poliakov's extremely perceptive work in particular, show that there was a wide range of occupations within the Jewish communities, which themselves were often well integrated with the town as a whole, occupied a wide range of districts and were tied by bonds of business and friendship to the Christians. When these Jews did undertake usury, which was certainly very common, they were often acting as intermediaries, and loaned to Christians money belonging to other Christians.[9]

But what one must emphasize above all is the astonishing development of credit operations of extreme, and sometimes incompre-

---

7 This interpretation of the Reformation as the « daughter of capitalism », which was inspired, like many other hastily elaborated and completely erroneous theories, by Marx or Engels, still received vigorous support in the 1930's, especially from A. MARTI, *Economic Causes of the Reformation in England*, London 1929, and C. BARBAGALLO, *Età Moderna*, vol. VI, part. 2. *Introduzione* 1st ed. 1936; new ed. Turin 1958.

8 Cf. for criticism of these theories the works quoted by J. DELUMEAU, *Naissance et Affirmation de la Réforme*, Paris 1965, p. 262 et seq.

9 L. POLIAKOV, *Les Banchieri Juifs et le Saint Siège*, Paris 1965. See also P. NORSA, *I Norsa; contributo alla storia di una famiglia di banchieri. Parte prima. Secoli XIV-XV*, Milan 1959.

hensible, complexity among the Christians themselves in different settings and at different times during the so-called « Middle Ages ».[10] The contradiction between moral or religious ruling and daily practice would seem to have been particularly flagrant. But even the Church often hesitated; learned doctors often had the greatest of difficulty in reaching agreement in defining, in relation to actual practices, the sin of usury. In fact the doctrines themselves seem to have changed considerably during the XVth century,[11] doubtless because of pressure from business men themselves and with the assent or with the involvement of mendicants, in particular the Dominicans.[12] But it remains true, however, that the condemnation remained very much in force. It would appear to have been both a dogmatic stance and a form of loyalty to traditional precepts, but also the reflection of a collective belief. But having said that, it remains clear that in practice these rules were ignored more or less openly and it is clear that those scholars who try to argue from the prohibitions themselves in order to deny the existence of credit or « capitalism » show an extraordinary degree of naïvety. The multiplication of these bans, their repeal and their modification proved, on the contrary, their ineffectiveness, for they were always being transgressed and avoided in some new way in ordinary day-to-day life. The historian however should study reality, rather than the rules — in other words, the numerous concessions, and also the circumstances in which the condemnations were in fact effectively carried out. And this, of course, can only be done by studying lawsuits and verdicts.

There are few things more complex and more exciting than the exploration of this contradiction between doctrine and prac-

10 As early as 1928 M. M. Postan (*Credit in Medieval Time*, in « Economic History Review » 1928) drew the attention of historians to credit practices and money lending in the Middle Ages. See also the study by E. B. Fryde and M. M. Fryde, *Public Credit with Special Reference to North-Western Europe*, in « Cambridge Economic History of Europe », vol. III, Cambridge 1963, pp. 430-542.

11 R. De Roover, *Il trattato di Fra Santi Rucellai sul cambio; il Monte comune e il Monte dei Doti*, in « Archivio Storicó Italiano » 1953.

12 S. Ruggiero Mazzone, *La legittimazione dei prestiti pubblici in Nicola di Anglia (scolastico domenicano del Secolo XV)*, in « Studi in onore di Amintore Fanfani », vol. III, Milan 1962, pp. 441-462.

tice because it brings us directly into the hitherto unexplored field of attitudes and reactions, to the subtle and poorly understood importance of collective mentalities. This field is still almost completely open. In any case, what we can tell in detail and with any precise way forbids us to lay down any general rule or present an overall picture with any certainty.

It seems certain, on one hand, that the prohibitions were well known and often had considerable influence. They were often reiterated by civil or ecclesiastical authorities, and they do seem to form part of a general mental equipment and express a collective disapproval that was not simply imposed from above but was generally felt in a more spontaneous way. While the prohibitions were religious, of course, they also derived from a social taboo which was tacitly accepted in varying degrees. In practical terms the pressure of this collective attitude would explain why those who most openly practised usury were often, although not necessarily, non-Christians or strangers to a particular community. The Italians (or Lombards) or Cahorsins were examples of this. The Genoese businessman, for example, who in his own native town carefully camouflaged the profits on loans recorded in his account books was prepared to indicate them and the annual rates of interest quite clearly once he had installed himself in London.

Such bans and social requirements also explain, without doubt, the attempts and devices to disguise « usurious » operations behind innocent appearances in order to make them seem similar to ordinary buying, selling and hiring operations which were quite acceptable. This was true of the first insurance contracts (fictitious sales with annulment clauses),[13] for loans pledged on land (sale by lease or sale with power of redemption), and in particular for re-exchange, the *ricorsa*, which led to an extraordinary development of exchange operations and of the localities and fairs where they were effected.[14]

13 For example: G. Stefani, *L'assicurazione a Venezia dalle origini alla fine della Serenissima,* 2 vols, Trieste 1956; F. Melis, *I primi secoli delle assicurazioni (secoli XIII-XVI),* Rome 1965.

14 R. De Roover, *Cambium ad Venetias: contribution to the History of Foreign Exchange,* in « Studi in Onore di Armando Sapori », Milan 1957; G. Mandich, *La pacte de Ricorsa et le marché italien des changes au XVIème siècle,* Paris 1963.

These sanctions favoured, then, the establishment of certain techniques and in this way influenced certain forms of capitalism.

It seems that sanctions never reduced the volume of loans, however. As far as credit and usury operations are concerned there seems to be a vast amount to put in the dossier — certainly enough to bring our whole way of looking at the « medieval » economy into question.

Money lending was practised on a very wide scale, by everybody, and at all social levels. The lender was not an outcast nor even isolated in society, nor were the Church or the authorities always hostile to him. The *Lombards* — Italians from Piacenza, then Tuscany, Piedmont, Asti and Chieri — were very well established wherever they settled. They did not conduct their business from some obscure, isolated and generally despised office but through huge companies composed of relatives, friends and associates. They had many subsidiaries, conducted their business on the basis of strict accounting procedures, corresponded with each other constantly (sending letters providing both general information and financial statements) and benefited from the mutual support of all their members.[15] Often they could count on support from the princes who had appointed them and who granted them privileges and monopolies, and even on support from prelates, bishops and cardinals or religious communities. The *Lombards* often became persons of importance and assumed public offices. They married in France, adopted a French form of their name, bought lands and manors — even *seigneuries.* In order to ensure the re-payment of their loans they obtained the support and guarantee of the authorities through *lettres obligatoires de sûreté*, which were delivered to them, in Paris, by the officers of the king, those of the *Châtelet* and even by the ecclesiastical tribunals, the courts of the dean and also those of the Official.[16]

15 A.-M. PATRONE, *Le Casane astigiane in Savoia,* in « Miscellanea storica italiana », Turin 1959; *Le Casane astigiane nella Valle d'Aosta,* in « Atti del XXXI Congresso storico subalpino », Turin 1962.

16 G. BIGWOOD, *Régime juridique et économique du commerce de l'argent en Belgique au Moyen Age,* 2 vols, Brussels 1921; A. GRUNZWEIG, *La garantie du crédit non commercial*

It is essential to point out in particular that Christians of all walks of life were generally deeply involved in money lending transactions in their own country. In the last two centuries of the « Middle Ages » bankers and money changers were above all money lenders.[17] But in fact all townsmen lent money when they could; wills, accounts of the execution of wills, and inventories made after death all reveal a considerable range of credits, whatever the profession of the deceased had been. Butchers in Paris and in the provinces were active money lenders, taking landed property as security; on their deaths their assets sometimes comprised more than a hundred different credits of various kinds amounting to very considerable sums.[18] This was also true of all merchants, in all countries: London merchants recorded loans, and eventually the repayments and profits, from these transactions, directly into their account books.[19] German merchants who had settled in Valencia, in the Spanish Levant, lent money to the nobles, the burghers and the peasants of the region[20] while Milanese businessmen did not attempt to conceal their interest from loans in their accounts.[21]

In exchange for loans, abbeys took goods as securities from seigneurs in need of money who had been practically ruined by war and the devastation of their lands. Some abbeys, it seems, turned this into a real industry after the ravages wrought by the English

dans la région de Paris au temps de Philippe-le-Bel, in « Studi in Onore di Amintore Fanfani », vol. II, Milan 1962, pp. 527-546.

17 On the role of the money changers and their activities see H. FAVREAU, *Les changeurs du royaume de France sous le règne de Louis XI*, in « Bibliothèque de l'Ecole des Chartes » 1964.

18 Mathieu, a butcher from the small town of Montbrison in Forez, left on his death in 1314, 132 different assets amounting to an astonishing 1,500 *livres*. His debtors were almost all either small artisans from the city or else peasants from the surrounding countryside. Some of these loans were accompanied by certain pledges, and often resulted in the confiscation of innovables, fields, vineyards and land. This would explain the deceased's fortune in land. Cf. E. FOURNIAL, *Les villes et l'économie d'échanges en Forez aux XIIIe et XIVe siècles*, Paris 1967, pp. 212-218.

19 Gilbert Maghfield, for example, a London merchant and lender, part of whose accounts have been edited by E. RICKERT, *Documents and Records: Extracts from a XIVth century account book*, in « Modern Philology », vol. 24, 1926-1927.

20 A. SCHULTE, *Geschichte der grossen Ravensburger Handelsgesellschaft. 1390-1530*, vol. III, Stuttgart, Berlin 1923. Merchants' letters are published in the appendix.

21 T. ZERBI, *Studi e problemi di storia economica: credito ed interesse in Lombardia nei secoli XIV e XV*, Milan 1955.

armies, and became transformed into busy money lending houses.[22] In the towns of Northern France canons at Troyes, Langres, and Paris were all in possession of numerous pledged goods, especially clothes, on their deaths. In these cases the documents do not permit us to assess the size of their profits and it seems impossible to establish even the nature of the usury... but could an absolutely « free » loan, which would have been so completely contrary to the practices of the time, have ever existed? Anyway, a more detailed study clearly shows three very active English clergymen making loans on interest to all kinds of people.[23]

In the same way, even in France the nobles and rural lords who lived in the country and took no part in the commercial traffic of the city increased their income by purchasing ground rents on peasant landholdings and even by lending money to citizens through an agent or relative who acted as a straightforward commission agent.[24]

All such practices do, in fact, appear to have been ancient. Detailed research into economic and social conditions at an earlier period would certainly reveal a huge number of different kinds of monetary loans, some more obvious than others. In Toulouse, for instance, the records of the public notaries clearly record debts and openly mention the rate of interest and the security left in guarantee. A businessman in the town, Raimundus Durandus, who enjoyed general esteem and was the consul of the city in 1198-9, acquired a considerable fortune in land in this way in Toulouse and the immediate vicinity through usury and the confiscation of securities.[25]

---

22 SÉCHÉ, *Une maison de prêts au XVe siècle*, in « Revue d'Anjou » 1905. (The abbey of Saint-Florent de Saumur); R. GENESTAL, *Rôle des monastères comme établissements de crédit étudié en Normandie du XIe à la fin du XIIIe siècle*, Paris 1901.

23 R. B. PUGH, *Some Medieval Moneylenders*, in « Speculum » 1968, pp. 274-289. Walter Longton, the Bishop of Coventry and Lichfield (who died in 1321) and William Meton, the Archbishop of York (who died in 1340) made loans against pledges and charged interest. Three clerks of the Royal Chancellery who were monks, registered, between 1335 and 1385, 220 recognizances of debts and as a result laid claim to lands given in pledge.

24 M.-TH. CARON, *Les Chalon-Tonnerre, famille noble de Bourgogne au XVe siècle.* Thèse de doctorat (3ème Cycle), Université de Paris X, 1971, p. 297.

25 J. H. MUNDY, *Un usurier malheureux*, in « Hommage à M. François Galabert »; special edition of the « Annales du Midi » 1956, pp. 117-127.

In peasant society the astonishing and apparently very early development of the sale of land leases, in other words rents guaranteed by land, is demonstrated by the large number of loans made to peasants by lords, abbeys, or other, richer, peasants. These date from as early as the year 900.[26] The idea of credit and interest rates was even involved in the direct relationship between lord and peasant, in the payment of annual tributes. The penalty that was sometimes inflicted for delay in the payment of quit-rents in kind not only indicates the desire to impose a sanction but also, perhaps, the idea that any delay, any lost time, justified financial compensation or additional profit. In the early 12th century the abbey of Beaulieu, in Limousin, pointed out in the *Notices des Coutumes de Favars* that peasants who did not pay their quit-rent in maslin (a mixture of wheat and other cereals) all at once and on a fixed date, would have to give « the prescribed quantity and in addition one full measure that is in excess of the tax ».[27]

To summarize, these very different ways of making interest bearing loans, many of which were first associated with rural life, soon spread throughout the « medieval » West. Of course towards the end of our period, the end of the « Middle Ages », these methods assumed new forms (although the older ones did not disappear) which seemed more adaptable and more directly linked to the conduct of business, to currencies and transferable securities. However any impression that credit became much more widespread at the beginning of the XVIth century is undoubtedly due mainly to the existence of a greater wealth of documents, of account books, commercial correspondence and contracts, which were better preserved than before. This does not necessarily reflect the real situation, so that the theory that there was a change in attitudes and in methods in this period, that a « pre-capitalist » attitude was

26 H. Van Werwecke, *Le mortgage et son rôle économique en France et en Lotharingie*, in « Revue belge de Philologie et d'Histoire », 1929, pp. 53-91; C. Violante, *Les prêts sur gage foncier dans la vie économique et sociale de Milan au XIe siècle*, in « Cahiers de civilisation médiévale », 1962, pp. 147-168 and 437-459; *Per lo studio dei prestiti dissimulati in territorio milanese (secoli X-XI)*, in « Studi in onore di Amintore Fanfani », Milan 1962, vol. I, pp. 643-735.

27 M. Deloche, *Cartulaire de l'Abbaye de Beaulieu en Limousin*, in « Collection de Documents inédits pour servir à l'Histoire de France », 1859, pp. 153-155.

born, results quite simply from the fortuitous nature of the documentation. This is an obstacle which the historian of « medieval » economies constantly finds in his path.

* * *

This widespread use of credit, of loans in kind or business loans does, however, explain why the borrowing of money took place on a relatively modest scale. Modern man likes to imagine that in the « Middle Ages » money matters were dominated by grasping and demanding userers, thereby forgetting the realities of our own times. Certainly the interest rate could vary considerably depending on the conditions of the moment, the situation of the market, the nature of the loans themselves and especially the social status of the borrower. In a given situation and all other things being equal, the way in which internal or external circumstances or good or bad news conditioned the borrowing of money is sometimes bewildering and surprising. But this was only the case in commercial centres where demand was bound up with the movement of ships or caravans, merchandise and capital. In the countryside, the borrowing of money on security of land seems to have been surprisingly stable.

On the whole the interest rate was not, then, very high. It could be as low as 3% *per annum* for business loans, and rise to 30% at the most difficult times. Generally it was fixed at an average of 8-10%, often less. Loans in kind naturally cost more, up to 40% in extreme cases, but most of those who lent money against articles in pledge asked only 20-24%. Between 1184 and 1208 one usurer from Toulouse lent at a rate of 16% *per annum*. Between 1450 and 1480 in Genoa and the towns of the Ligurian Riviera, the interest on money for debts raised on land was only between 10-12%.[28] The butcher from Montbrison, Mathieu Chambon, regularly lent at 7%, and in the Chartres area the rents pledged on peasants' goods cost only 4-7% interest *per*

[28] F. Robin, *Sestri Levante; bourg de la Riviera ligure au XVe siècle*. Thèse de doctorat (3e Cycle), in the press. Genova.

annum, in about 1250, and from 5-10% between 1290 and 1310.[29] These figures in themselves reveal how widespread credit operations were; money lending was not, then, a risky venture. The interest rates in this « medieval » or « feudal » society were definitely lower than those charged in Ancient Greece or Rome and much lower than those in the Muslim world during the « medieval » period and indeed much later. These figures reveal then both an economic system and attitudes that were neither archaic nor primitive nor far removed from capitalist ideas. On the contrary, they show an awareness of the enormous potential of loans and credit transactions. What is more, the interest rates were often lower than those imposed, even now, in « modern », « capitalist », countries.

This awareness was widespread at that time. « Medieval » man who possessed goods or money knew the value of time and conducted his affairs on this basis. So did the ordinary merchant or noble landowner who knew how to speculate, to store and even stockpile grain, or how to impose the *banvin* in order to sell his wine under the best possible conditions. The surprisingly complicated manipulations of money and methods of payment again provide innumerable instances of this awareness. The warrants and bills issued by the merchants of the Calais staple provide one example — these *Staplers* based authentic paper money on future customs income on English wool.[30] Another example, which is equally complex, is provided by the bewildering Genoese *lira di paghe* which was issued from about the 1450s by the famous *Casa di San Giorgio* and acted as guarantee for interest which was in fact paid three or four years later. Although its value certainly increased as the date of maturity approached, it was susceptible to all kinds of accidental and fortuitous influences so that its value always remained theoretical, or at least uncertain.[31]

---

29 A. Chédeville, *Chartres et ses campagnes. XIe-XIIIe siècles*, Paris 1973, p. 271 and 473.

30 W. I. Haward, *Financial Transactions between the Lancastrian Government and the Merchants of the Staple from 1449 to 1461*, in « Studies in English Trade in the XVth Century », London 1933; E. E. Power, *Medieval English Wool Trade*, London 1941; E. B. Fryde, *Edward III's War Finances 1337-1340. Transaction in Wool and Credit Operations*, Oxford 1947.

31 J. Heers, *Gênes au XVe siècle. Activités économiques et Problèmes sociaux*, Paris 1961, pp. 162-173.

Jacques Heers

The merchants' treatises also bear witness to this awareness of time and its value. Pegolotti's treatise, for example, analyses, at times very precisely, the seasonal conditions of the market in silver, and states the times when prices were at their highest in all the most important markets of the West — (this dates from about 1310-1340).[32] Purchases of agricultural products on credit, of grain from the south, wool from England seem to have developed even earlier and reveal the same attitude, in this case, in the relations between townsmen and peasants. Conclusive proof of this is provided by the bill of exchange, used in its simplest form from as early as the 14th century. The reason for its existence seems to have escaped banking historians, even such a specialist as R. De Roover. Legal and economic historians have been surprised that these bills of exchange, which were issued in one place and paid in another, were not discounted. As De Roover noted, however, the profit made by the drawer, the banker who issued the bill, was ensured by an artificial and favourable rate of exchange.[33] This is certainly correct, but we would point out that as the bill was payable only several weeks or two or three months later the banker derived his profit simply by investing the money during this period.

So time was money and the « medieval » period was not ignorant of the fact. In a word, what we often call the capitalist spirit — the unbridled search for profit, the search for greater gain, the speculative spirit, the desire to make money productive without performing manual labour — does not appear to have been foreign to the « medieval » mentality.

* * *

WAS THE « FEUDAL » ECONOMY INCOMPATIBLE WITH CAPITALISM?

There is nothing more irritating to the informed reader anxious to come closer to the truth than the constant, inaccurate and irresponsible use of the word « feudal » by journalists and nove-

32 FRANCESCO DI BALDUCCIO PEGOLOTTI, *La Pratica della Mercatura*, ed. A. Evans, Cambridge (Mass.) 1936.

33 R. DE ROOVER, *L'évolution de la lettre de change, XIVe-XVIIIe siècles*, Paris 1952.

lists, by the authors of textbooks and popular literature and even by badly informed and non-specialist historians. They all give the « Middle Ages » a vague, careless glance and then, through laziness or more often through their involvement with some half-digested ideology, are content to pour out ready-made, imprecise clichés which are nearly always meaningless. Their words carry some weight, however, and although they have no solid basis are often enough to create a climate of misunderstanding and even to paralyse serious study to some extent.

« Feudalism » — a real custard pie of a term which, like the term « Middle Ages » itself, is almost always weighed down with every conceivable implication of evil.[34] Need one be reminded, however, that « feudalism » purports to describe a political system which is in fact very difficult to define and which in any case varied greatly from one period and one country to another? The term is a bad choice — « vassalage » would undoubtedly be preferable, because the fief was unknown in a great many regions of the West, and in others meant quite different things. In short this system never existed in that perfect and ideal form which our textbooks describe except in a few principalities, among which, certainly, was that of the King of France around Paris. But these subjects have not yet been thoroughly studied — far from it.

In these circumstances is it not strange that such a specific term should be applied to all forms of economic and social life? We speak of « feudal » property and dues (some scholars even number tithes among them!), of « feudal » economy, or structures, and even of attitudes which are supposed to have characterized an entire age before the advent of « capitalism ».[35] Strictly speaking

---

34 The expression « the Middle Age of » is commonly, and increasingly, used to designate an archaic period, a step back in civilization. The adjective « medieval » is journalese, used to describe societies and civilizations that are more primitive than others, that arouse our compassion, cf. the title of a very recent work: R. VACCA, *Demain, le Moyen Age*, Paris 1973.

35 The confusion between the words « feudalism » and « seigneurie » is often deliberate. Some authors point out the difference between the two ideas somewhere in their work but then throughout their discussion regularly use « feudal » where obviously « seigneurial » is meant, and continually talk of « feudal regime » in discussing economic matters; cf. for example, in France, A. SOBOUL, *La civilisation et la révolution française*, vol. I: *La crise de l'Ancien Régime*, Paris 1970, and F. FURET's pertinent remarks on this point

Jacques Heers

all such expressions are meaningless and completely empty — a sheer misuse of words.

* * *

In economic terms a great many historians happily confuse the terms « feudal » and « seigniorial » which are far from identical. It is correct that throughout the « Middle Ages » (and much later, too) a considerable range of rural activities were conducted within the context of landed estates of varying sizes — the *seigneuries*. But these estates existed long before the « feudal » political system was established, their ideal form being the *villae* of Merovingian and Carolingian times, which were in the possession of kings or great abbeys. In the West it is quite impossible to establish any kind of connection between the spread of « feudalism » and that of the great landed estates. Nor can any connection be made between their ultimate fates, for the two systems — the one political and the other economic — are quite independent. It is sheer laziness, whether deliberate or not, to talk of a « feudal » economy, for the term is simply transferred from one concept to another.

The limitations of the seigneurie.

The importance, and even the characteristics, of the rural *seigneurie* tend to be little known and largely misunderstood. The *seigneurie* certainly did not impose any rigid, uniform, framework on the economy and society of the countryside. Its very structure, its extent, its powers over lands and men, the way in which it

in *Le cathéchisme révolutionnaire*, in « Annales. Economies. Sociétés. Civilisations. » 1971 (pp. 255-289) in particular p. 264. Other authors make no effort to conceal their intentions: « la démarche de l'historien » (!) in their view, can only be political, in the service of Marxist ideology. Cf. for example, C. Mazauric, *Sur la Révolution française*, Paris 1970, p. 134. « Au fond refuser l'emploi de régime féodal pour désigner, en historian, l'ensemble du système économique, social et jurisdictionnel de l'Ancien Régime est un témoignage non équivoque de conservatisme... Mais seul l'emploi de féodalité pour qualifier le régime d'exploitation féodal (féodalisme) est progressiste (*sic*) en associant à la définition du référent la conotation péjorative (*sic*), sans laquelle le travail historique sur l'Ancien Régime ne serait qu'un constat et non un combat ». This kind of work belongs to politics, not history.

affected peasant life — whether it dominated, or simply controlled it — varied considerably from one period and from one place to another, sometimes even within the same period and the same region, or from one village to another. Here there might be a single estate with one fortified manor house and thus one lord who ruled over the whole village and its lands. Nearby there might be two or three manor houses, even more, which shared the land between them. In other regions, lands and jurisdictions were extraordinarily confused, which resulted in countless and ceaseless arguments and brought about a decline, or at least a division, of authority and responsibilities which even worried contemporaries. The variable number of manors per village was itself a characteristic of the different forms of *seigneuries* and their powers. The study of these differences would undoubtedly reveal pronounced differences and dissimilarities in the structure of rural communities, as was the case in England, for example.[36] In many communities the seigniorial residence, the castle or manor or mansion, was situated in the middle of the estate, in the village itself, next to the church, and at the point where the roads and paths met. In others, the manors, mansions or fortified houses stood apart, at the approach to the village or on the edge of the inhabited areas; sometimes they were completely even isolated.[37] These different locations suggest both varying degrees of power and also varying degrees of participation in the political life and the labours of the community.

Our insufficient knowledge of the economic and social structures of the « medieval » rural world makes it impossible to determine the exact importance of the *seigneurie* in rural life. Here the historian often unwittingly commits that frequent and almost commonplace error of perspective which leads him to neglect, or pass

---

36 On the number of manors per village in the English lowlands see E. A. KOMINSKY, *Studies in the agrarian history of England in the XIIIth century*, Oxford 1956.

37 J.-M. PESEZ and F. PIPONNIER, *Les maisons fortes bourguignonnes*, in « Chateau Gaillard ». Etudes de castellogie médiévale ». V. Colloque de Hindsgavl (1970), Caen 1972; I. MARLAND, *Les maisons fortes de l'Auxois. XIIIe-XVe siècles*. Mémoire de Maîtrise. Université de Paris X, 1973; J.-M. PESEZ, *Recherches archéologiques sur un site de maison forte*, to be published in « Chateau Gaillard », vol. VI.

over, or in some cases even to deny, the existence of factors on which the documents give little or no information. Almost all the texts relating to the countryside, and all those which are in any case easily obtainable, the cartularies, terriers, rent-rolls, legal archives and account books, deal with the great landed estates and emphasize the lords' power over men. In this way the picture of the relationship between the lord and peasants that emerges is almost totally an over-simplified caricature: the lord lives off the peasants' labours, and they in turn cultivate only land which does not belong to them. This is an entirely artificial, intellectual, picture which conceals the real conditions of both sides.

In writing the history of the countryside much more attention must be given to the forms of direct farming. The definition put forward by Marc Bloch who saw the seigneur eventually becoming a mere *rentier* has gained very wide currency. It still lingers as a truth, or half truth, even after all the more recent studies have formally disproved it by showing that the seigniorial lands survived for a very long time, often showing no signs of weakening, while in some countries they were even strengthened. The abandonment of the *corvées* did not mean the abandonment of the demesne lands. The great landowner and, *a fortiori*, the less rich did not live only by collecting fixed or variable rents, for they also cultivated their land. Study of seigniorial accounts shows that often the proportion of the income of both lay and ecclesiastical lords made up of peasant rents was low — often very low. What were important were the seigneur's crops on his own lands, and in his own vineyards, and also the profits drawn from his lakes and forests.[38]

[38] See the very detailed study by G. Fourquin, *Les campagnes de la région parisienne à la fin du Moyen Age*, Paris 1964, pp. 149-159, for the accounts of income and expenditure on the lands belonging to the Abbey of Saint-Denis. Quit rents and all income from land brought in an average of 30 *livres parisis* out of a total income of 30,000 *livres parisis* between 1284 and 1304, that is, little more than 1% of the total. Feudal dues and rights of jurisdiction yielded very little. The administrators looked upon them as very minor items in their accounts. Woods alone brought in four times more than the payments made by peasants for their land. But what counted before all else were the incomes from game parks: Saint-Denis drew from them: « la quasi totalité des recettes en nature et la majeur partie des recettes en numéraire » — more than 85% of the entire « seigneurial » revenue. See also: G. Sivery, *Structures agraires et vie rurale dans le Hainaut à la fin du Moyen Age*. Thèse de doctorat d'Etat. Lille 1973, pp. 480-500 and in

It is astonishing that scholars have not, for example, stressed more often the role played by the Cistercians in the life of the countryside. These monks cleared the land and for a long time refused to have any rent payers. They had no peasant tenures on their possessions. Instead they cultivated their lands or their vines themselves, and reared their sheep with the help of their lay brothers or of wage-earning labourers. The Cistercian *granges* represented, then, a perfect model of direct farming on the great demesne lands.[39]

Very many seigneurs, and especially those who lived in the country, were then either in person or through their appointed stewards, directors of farming operations and careful entrepreneurs. The relationships which existed were those between employers and wage earners, and this wage earning structure characterised the entire social and economic life of the time. The notion of the seigneur who was content to harvest crops produced by others on fields cultivated by others, should be revised, for it does not correspond with the facts.

Seigniorial documents tend to give the impression that all the land belonged to the masters, and this has led many scholars — some through ignorance or the desire to schematize, others through sheer lack of attention — completely to neglect the peasant landholdings. But they did exist, although in very differing forms and with varying extent according to both area and period.

Here, too, the fact that attention was first drawn to certain Western regions of France which were studied earlier and more thoroughly than the others by well-known scholars with wide opportunities for communicating their ideas gave credence to the very superficial notion of a uniform rural society where the powerful *seigneuries* ruled almost without interruption. The « outlying areas » even though they were more extensive, escaped investigation

particular his analysis of the accounts of the Provost of Dourlers in 1343-44. Peasant rents on land gave an income of 26 Lb. (rather more than 10% of the total), the profits from jurisdictions gave 11% of the total, but about 78% of the total income was drawn from sales of wood, farm rents, mills and cultivated parkland.

[39] J.-B. Mahn, *L'ordre cistercien et son gouvernement des origines au milieu du XIIIe siècle*, Paris 1945.

and were not known about until much later. The same can be said of mountain areas, such as the regions of the South and the West of France, and the northern lands beyond Flanders.

We do, however, know that countries without feudal lords, like Friesland for example,[40] existed throughout the « Middle Ages » or at least until a very late date. We also know that in other areas the *seigneurie* appeared very late and in a very individual manner (in the Scandinavian countries for example)[41] or else exercised only very limited powers over free men who were able to organize themselves into powerful communities (e.g. the *sokemen* of the eastern counties of England).[42] In the South of France — Provence, Languedoc and even more so in Italy — other social influences and peculiarities were to be found.

Although few and far between, there are certain studies that have stated or indicated the importance of authentic peasant landholdings. What we call the allod (*alleu*), that is land exempted from all economic rents or servile duties was certainly of much greater importance in most countries than has been allowed.[43] The peasant tenants, who were referred to as such in the seigniorial documents might also have cultivated lands in their own possession which did not figure in these same texts. But we must also consider the concept of property itself. The free man who was not subject to any personal duties and was the tenant of some land for which

---

40 Cf. G. Duby, *L'économie rurale et la vie des campagnes dans l'Occident médieval*, 2 vol., Paris 1962, p. 379: « La Frise où la seigneurie ne s'était jamais beaucoup développée ».

41 L. Musset, *Les peuples scandinaves au Moyen Age*, Paris 1951.

42 B. Dodwell, *The sokemen of the Southern Danelaw in the XIIIth Century*, in « Bulletin of the Institute of Historical Research » 1937-1938, pp. 110-112. Cf. also W. G. Hoskins, *Midland Peasant. The Economic and Social History of a Leicestershire Village*, London 1965, who thinks that in these Danelaw countries the peasant community and not the manor was the essential form of social and political organization.

43 B. Boutruche, *Une société provinciale en lutte contre le régime féodal. L'alleu en Bordelais et en Bezadais du XIe au XVIIIe siècle*, Paris 1947; P. Feuchère, *Un obstacle aux réseaux de subordinations: alleux et alleutiers en Artois, Bourbonnais et Flandre wallonne*, in « Etudes publiées par la section belge de la Commission internationale pour l'Histoire des Assemblées d'Etat » 1955, pp. 1-32. Cf. also G. Duby, *L'économie rurale...* (op. cit., cf. above note 40); p. 379: « Partout, en réalité, les possessions seigneuriales étaient fort loin de recouvrir l'ensemble des terroirs. Elles laissaient de larges espaces où s'étendaient les alleux modestes ».

first, he paid often only an extremely low quit-rent, which was further lessened by the depreciation in the value of currency and so became reduced to a mere token, owed little to the seigneur. If this peasant could freely inherit this land, if he could alienate it, sell or hire it out for a much higher rent than the quit-rent he himself owed to the seigneur, could he not then consider himself to be — and was he not in fact — the real owner of this property? In economic terms, the difference between the allodial land and the ancient fee farms and even some new forms such as the *livelli* or emphyteuts appears to be very slight. In the rent contracts the seigniorial owner gawe way to the tenant. The complexity of rights caused confusion and the concept of ownership was illdefined. However the richest peasants everywhere were also rich landowners.

The traditional concept of rural life organized exclusively within the *seigneurie* not only exaggerates the latter's role and power, it also makes peasant society appear uniform, completely subject to the lord, all identical in condition. This is the origin of another of the caricaturist's clichés, of yet another slogan — that of the peasant « masses ». Nothing could be further from the truth. On the contrary, any reasonably precise and detailed study reveals an astonishing variation of legal or economic conditions, of levels of wealth and ways of life within the peasant world. Among freemen there was a real aristocracy of wealthy farmers,[44] labourers, yeomen,[45] and farmers who were great accumulators and engrossers of land, who owned numerous pieces of land, meadows, woods and vines. It was they alone who owned carts and draught animals.

44 For examples of the social diversity within the peasantry and the establishment of a peasant aristocracy see: H. S. Bennett, *Life on English Manors. A Study of Peasant conditions. 1150-1400*, Cambridge 1937; G. C. Homans, *The rural sociology of Medieval England*, in « Past and Present » 1953; J. A. Raftis, *Social Structures in Five East Midlands Villages*, in « Economic History Review » 1963, pp. 83-100; G. Sivery, *Structures...* (op. cit., cf. above note 38), pp. 386-392; Fr. Rapp, *L'aristocratie paysanne du Kochesberg à la fin du Moyen Age et au début des temps modernes*, in « Bulletin Philologique et Historique (jusqu'à 1610) du Comité des Travaux historiques et scientifiques » 1967, pp. 439-450; A. Rochette, *Fortunes paysannes du XIVe siècle en Forez*, in « Etudes foréziennes. Mélanges » 1972, pp. 143-172.

45 F. R. H. du Boulay, *Who were farming the English Domesnes at the End of the Middle Ages?*, in « Economic History Review » 1965.

Moreover these people were undoubtedly relatively well educated. In the XVth century the peasants of Normandy had their own seals to authenticate their documents and their children attended the village school. This peasant aristocracy established itself by various means — by obtaining seigniorial or administrative posts, or else through small businesses such as milling, by making money in small trades or in war, or else through the sheer good fortune of inheritance or an advantageous marriage. Land often changed hands, and the concept of stability or even rigidity in peasant economic organization, property ownership and tenures is also imaginary. The sources reveal, on the contrary, that there was a very active land market which was in continual movement.[46]

At the other extreme, but in the same rural communities, were the poor, that is men without land, villeins, cottagers who were reduced to tending by hand a mere garden, to living on customary rights of usage, gathering dead wood and fruits of the forest, or the ears of corn gleaned after the harvest, and above all to hiring out their services. This wage-earning proletariat was a great burden on the villages.[47] The poor strove to prevent the disappearance of their customary rights and opposed the seigneurs and the wealthy peasants whenever they attempted to enclose their lands or woods.

Many peasants owned more land than particular seigneurs — especially the needy country squires, the *hobereaux*, who were modest landowners — while their standard of living was equal, if not superior. So the division in living conditions in the villages did not simply follow the distinction between « feudal » seigneur and commoners, but operated within the peasant world which itself contained a great range of differences and inequalities. Nor did this peasant hierarchy appear only at the very end of the « Middle Ages »

46 A. R. H. Baker, *Open Fields and Partable Inheritance on a Kent Manor,* in « Economic History Review » 1964; B. Dodwell, *Holdings and Inheritance in Medieval East Anglia,* in « Economic History Review » 1967; Chr. Dyer, *A Redistribution of Incomes in XVth Century England,* in « Past and Present » 1968, pp. 11-33; J. A. Raftis, *The Structures of Commutation in a XIVth century Village,* in « Essays in Medieval History presented to Bertie Wilkinson », Toronto 1968, pp. 282-300.

47 J. B. Harley, *Population trends and agriculture developments from the Warwickshire hundred Rolls of 1279,* in « Economic History Review » 1958.

for it undoubtedly dates from a much earlier period, although the documents become much scarcer (or less noticed) the further back one goes. But as early as the XIIth century the *Coutumes de Favars* mentioned cultivators (*rustici*) who paid harvesters in sheaves of corn as a salary (*propter lucrum*).[48] Ties of economic dependence between employers and wage earners were, then, already established within non-noble rural society.

Finally, in order to stress this diversity, we should note that some lands were bought at an early date by simple artisans and craftsmen in the areas near to the towns, as for example in the wine-growing area around Lyons.[49]

Thus from the economic point of view the seigneur, the master of an estate of a size that might vary, did not dominate all rural activities, while the peasants owned some of the lands which they cultivated. There was, then, no economic predominance that was not shared.

* * *

Turning to the social aspects of the situation, much the same can be said of seigniorial authority and, to take a more concrete example, of the seigniorial duty of providing protection in return for which, in dangerous times such as these, the peasants are believed to have given up their own rights over their possessions and even over their own bodies. But it would seem to be the case that the fortified seigniorial houses, the *fertés*, the small fortified manor houses, were never used by anyone but the seigneur and his family. They served as residences, as farming centres providing room for storing crops and for stabling. Such houses were very numerous, more numerous even than the villages, but they were not places of refuge for the peasants.[50] In case of danger the latter had to go to the great castle of the main town of the district or province, often

---

48 Cf. above note 27.

49 M.-Th. Lorcin, *Le vignoble et les vignerons du Lyonnais aux XIVe et XVe siècles*, in « Le vin; production et consommation. Actes du second Colloque de la Société des Historians médiévistes de l'Enseignement supérieur, Grenoble 1971, in the press.

50 Cf. above note 37.

some considerable distance away, or to one of the great fortified abbeys or else to the nearest town. Neither the squire nor the abbot nor the citizens of the towns were necessarily their seigneurs or the owners of their land. These flights to the security of the great castles or abbeys were not part of normal routine life, and they meant that the peasants had to abandon their farms temporarily. The nature of the flimsy sheds which they built within these fortified areas symbolized the precariousness of this life.[51] In the case of less serious attack, however, men took up and organized their own defence on the spot, in their villages, against vagabonds, looters and bandits or against attacks by highwaymen or small armed bands. They built or raised the walls surrounding the village with or without their seigneur's aid and arranged strict rotas for the watch or guard duty, especially in the mountains of the South of France. Very often they fortified their churches whose windowless towers were pierced only by loopholes, embrasures or machicolations. In them they stored their livestock and valuables and used them when in need of a sudden place of refuge. The report following the inspection of the bailiwick of Caen in 1371 carried out by the bailiff on the orders of Charles V shows that, taken as a whole, there was in fact only a very small number of fortified castles (a mere dozen) while, on the other hand, there was an extraordinary number of fortified churches, one in each vilage in fact (82 in all).[52]. In the French countryside during these troubled times the fortified church represented a collective means of defence.[53] So in the village the peasants' refuge was not the seigneur's manor but the fortified enclosure with its walls and gates and even more so the parish church itself, which was both the symbol and the property of the village community as a whole. The church was built, maintained and repaired by the churchwardens,

---

51 Cf., for example, G. FOURNIER, *La défense des populations rurales pendant la Guerre de Cent Ans en Basse Auvergne*, in « Actes du XC^{ème} Congrès des Sociétés Savantes (section Archéologie) », Nice 1965, pp. 157-189.

52 A. DE CAUMONT, *Relation de la visite des forteresses du baillage de Caen en 1371*, in « Mémoires de la Société des Antiquaires de Normandie » 1840.

53 R. REY, *Les vieilles églises fortifiées du Midi de la France*, Paris 1925; G. FOURNIER, *Chartes de franchises et fortifications villageoises en Basse Auvergne au XIIIe siècle*, in « Les Libertés urbaines et rurales du XIe au XIVe siècle », Collection « Histoire », no. 19, Brussels 1968, pp. 223-244.

who were laymen and peasants whose task it was to collect funds and apportion costs and obligations.[54]

So it can be seen that neither economic nor military power were the exclusive prerogatives of the seigneur alone. This explains why the seigneurs, the masters of the land, no longer maintained exclusive control over the rights of the *ban*, that is the right to give orders. In most cases anyway this amounted to no more than the right to organize and regulate different activities on the land, fix the work calendar and stipulate rights of usage. But the right of the *ban* which imposed structures, patterns and cycles on rural life was often successfully claimed by the village itself. It was sometimes even the case that the principal seigneur himself had to obey *bans* which he had not established.[55] This decisively shatters the notion of a rural world in which both ends and means were organized, directed and authorized exclusively by the masters.

The seigniorial economy: management and investments.

In virtually every aspect, then, very little is either known or resolved about these landowning seigneurs. « Feudal seigneur » is an all-purpose expression which is intended to be specific but which in fact means nothing. The seigneurs had in common neither background nor even their political, social or cultural positions. Neither did they share a common heritage, training or at times even the same interests. The 'model' seigneur, the classic stereotype which can be found in any popular study or textbook, belonged to the « nobility »: he was a warrior (illiterate etc.), a knight and huntsman who enjoyed trampling the crops underfoot — a man who lived in the country in his fortified « feudal » castle far from the town and who was quite ignorant of market conditions. But this is not more than a crude caricature — or at any rate this schematized « social type » would in fact be applicable to only a very small number of seigneurs.

---

54 C. Boyd, *Tithes and Parish in Medieval Italy*, Ithaca, New York 1962; Ch. Drew, *Early Parochial organisation in England*, St. Anthony's Press, 1954; H.M., Jewells, *English local administration in the Middle Ages*, New York 1972.

55 G. Sivery, *Structures...* (op. cit., cf. above note 38), p. 349 *et seq.*

The position of the seigneur was in fact much more complex. The separation of town and country, which has long been taken to be an unshakable fact, disintegrates in the face of detailed studies. The knight, the noble ' feudal ' warrior was often himself a resident in the city — this was the case throughout the South of France at least. The rural seigneur was a warrior certainly, but he was also a citizen with important possessions in the town where he often lived surrounded by a circle of friends, relatives and protégés in a town mansion surmounted by a defensive tower rather like a keep. He understood well the demands and the potential of the market and also the possibilities of this or that form of speculation.

Many of the great estates, certainly the majority, were not owned by warrior seigneurs. The lands and manors had first belonged to the princes — to the emperor, the king, the appanaged prince, the count, the bishop or archbishop, all of whom had considerable landed property at their disposal. These princes, with the assistance of advisory bodies and agents and bailiffs, managed their possessions like the directors of great commercial enterprises. Often little distinction was made between the public and the private domain and both were managed in the same way. The advances made in political administration went hand in hand with those in the economic management of their lands.

It seems pointless to dwell, on the other hand, on the seigneuries which were held throughout the Western world by numerous religious communities which were of very different kinds and which took widely differing forms. They ranged from the Benedictine to the Cluniac abbeys, from cathedral chapters and collegiate churches to the headquarters of the Knights Templars and Hospitalers, to new orders created by the heremitical and pauper movements. The clerics and their leaders pursued aims that were often quite different — they shared no common ethic, interests or experiences nor even similar means. They came from a varying social background and their intellectual formation also differed. Many vast estates were held by abbeys situated in towns or in their immediate surroundings — as, for example, Saint-Denis, Saint-German-des-Prés, Saint-Martin-des-Champs in Paris. The canons who administered their prebends were important citizens who led the life of townsmen and readily assumed municipal offices as well.

Finally there are a number of works, many of which have now become traditional, which illustrate the great attraction exercised by the countryside over authentic townsmen, merchants and lawyers especially, who purchased lands and estates. These purchases were considerable in some regions and did not only involve land, farms and share-cropping tenures but very often authentic seigneuries, that contained a park with keeper's house, a manor and farm buildings and sometimes even tenures (and thus rents to be gathered from the peasants) together with rights pertaining to the *banalité*, that is over forges, mills etc... in some cases those over the forest, and in others even those of jurisdiction. We can easily imagine how shortly after the new owner of these lands would go to live in the country where he would lead a quite different kind of life. These purchases must have preceded what, without really defining the nature and inner workings of the process, we too loosely refer to as a process of *enoblissement*. But this was not always the case and some of these new seigneurs continued to lead a 'bourgeois' life in the town.[56] In any case the origins of these new masters, whether they became 'ennobled' or not, the new proprietors of such lands and seigneuries, differed from those of their predecessors. Their social position was new and so they brought with them new attitudes and new ways of managing their possessions.

So the world of the seigneurs also appears infinitely complex and varied. To look first at the question of wealth we find that while some owned several vast estates others held only a few pieces of land,[57] much less than their rich peasant neighbours. In terms of

[56] *Ibid.* p. 772 (« de l'épicerie à la noblesse »). In addition, in about 1450 one of the four manors of the village of Sherington in Buckinghamshire was purchased by one Richard Maryot, a London lawyer, who had a large clientele and represented several other citizens who were rich merchants, including John Maryot, a manufacturer and salt merchant. This Richard Maryot even acquired the master's house, the moated manor, but kept a house in the capital, in Fleet Street, and the manor remained a *co-feofee* owned by himself and his associates. Cf. A. C. CHIBNALL, *Sherington, Fiefs and Fields of a Buckinghamshire Village*, Cambridge 1965.

[57] Y. U. R. ULYANOV, *Watlington Manor, Oxfordshire. 1086-1300,* in «Sredine Veka», 1967; *The Stonor Family Estates in the XIth to the XIIIth centuries: on the problem of Genesis of small Estates in Medieval England*, ibid., 1967; G. SIVERY, *Structures...* (op. cit., cf. above no. 38), p. 775 *et seq.*

structures we find, too, that on one hand there were seigneuries owned by individuals or families while on the other hand there were those that were owned collectively or by institutions. When one considers the variety in the social and cultural background of the seigneurs, in their ways of life, in their powers and in their interests, the differences prove to be even greater. In these circumstances it is an inaccurate generalization to talk of « feudal seigneurs » and to speak, then, of a « class » of « feudal seigneurs » of common formation and culture is then a real absurdity which flies in the face of all probability.

* * *

Even today, however, and now perhaps more than ever before, there are scholars who do not hesitate to go even further. In the most simple terms they describe the « feudal economy » as being subject to these « feudal seigneurs », subject to their way of life, their preoccupations, their culture, to the ways in which they managed their estates, which were, they hold, so different from modern « capitalism ». They draw a uniform and gloomy picture. They treat the « feudal economy » in total contrast to the « capitalist » economy. They see the « feudatories » as masters of men rather than lands, who lived basically on rents both in kind and in money; they « exploited » the peasants, not the land. Their way of life and cultural background made them impervious to all ideas of progress, to any improvement in farming or even in techniques and hence also to any increase in their incomes. They were content with traditional revenues. But what typifies « feudalism » above all for such writers is the belief that these landlords wasted all their money and invested nothing. In other words they had no concept of saving, or of progress — they were first and foremost consumers and parasites. In the same way their exactions were almost intolerably high and so they reduced all the peasants to a state of misery, to a level of bare and precarious subsistence. The men who were, then, exploited to the last possible degree were obviously in turn unable to invest and improve their lands.

This is another purely subjective interpretation, another series of clichés forced on to historical reality by « historians » who generally have little, if any, knowledge of the most simple research findings, never mind the extraordinary quantity and variety of documents which are available. They would like to think, or at least seem to accept, that our knowledge of the « medieval » world can only be based on a few extracts from chronicles or lists of rents and on the « romantic » image invented a good hundred years ago by historical novelists. Their sources go back more then a hundred years and reveal the legacy of Victor Hugo and Walter Scott. Their views and ideas remain closely linked with those of the French middle classes between 1860 and 1880, all of whose clichés they have adopted once again. This is a fossilized type of « history » that has progressed very little and is incapable of progressing. These writers, be they politicians, ideologists, technocrats or « economists », sociologists or even those historians of periods which become more and more contemporary, work only in abstractions, using mere concepts, explanatory scheme or intellectual constructs. They desire only to impose explanatory systems and in short take little interest in research.

At the same time there does exist a range of sound studies based on detailed research on sources originating from within the seigneurie itself which allow us to identify both the techniques and form of management in action. These have revealed the great care shown by the seigneurs, and often their great efficiency as well. We must also dismiss from our thoughts the notion of a simple crop or even a primitive economy which was embedded in tradition or in which everything was left to chance, and also that of a « feudal » economy subject to the fortunes of inheritances and external factors. The owners of the land were very often intelligent men who farmed their lands in much the same way as the « capitalist » merchants in the towns conducted their trade or their financial operations. This idea of a separation between the management of estates and the management of business affairs has taken root so firmly that until recently we all accepted that purchases of land by merchants in the XVth century and especially in Italy were merely secondary operations in which they sought security for their capital without hope of much profit. Recent studies such as those by P. Jones, for example, show that the contrary was true and that these were deliberate investments which were very productive and that well managed land brought in a larger income than business.[58]

* * *

There are numerous sources of various kinds which support the view that the estates were managed with care and profit. They all help to rectify the long held, traditionally very gloomy view of « medieval » rural life. Among other sources there are the treatises on agriculture which abounded in England in the XIIIth century.[59] These manuals were written in the vernacular and so were intended for the lay landowners and not only for clerics. These are no vague dissertations of an ethical, moral or pseudo-philosophical nature on the nobility of labour in the fields; they are, on the contrary, detailed analyses of yields and returns which gave practical advice on how to farm and fertilize the land, how to supervise the stewards and workers, how to check accounts.[60] These textbooks reflect a real awareness of the needs and fluctuations of the market. As early as this they stated cost prices and yields, discussed foodstuffs for cattle and horses, their rations and the expenses involved in maintaining them. They also indicated the probable minimum yield of different cereals on a well managed estate, and these yields seem higher than those generally mentioned in other texts. The concepts of price, yield, and productivity which historians of the « feudal economy » rarely mention, stand out clearly in every page. One of these agronomists even invited estate keepers to calculate the separate yields for their different pieces of land, making special lists of each crop and taking account of the soil conditions and the time of year.

The great number of treatises and copies in existence at a time when not all levels of society had yet learned to write clearly indicates that they were circulated among the landowners who farmed

---

58 P. J. Jones, *Per la storia agraria nel Medioevo*, in « Rivista Storica Italiana », 1964.

59 *Traîte d'économie rurale composé en Angleterre au XIIIe siècle*, ed. E. Lacour, in « Bibliothèque de l'Ecole des Chartes » 1856; *Walter of Henley's husbandry, Seneschancie and Robert Grosseteste's rules*, ed. Lamond, 1890; *Recueil anglais dit de « La Fleta »*.

60 G. Duby, *L'économie rurale...*, op. cit., vol. I, p. 311 *et seq.* and also D. Oschinsky, *Medieval Treatises on Estate Accounting*, in « Economic History Review », 1947; *Medieval Treatises on Estate Management*, ibid., 1956.

their estates themselves. Certainly these manuals appeared relatively late and tended to be repetitive, offering identical advice based on a few models. But we should note all the same that these agricultural treatises were in circulation about a hundred years before the textbooks and new practical guides of the « capitalist » merchants of Italy which were themselves also very repetitious. Nor did these represent an isolated case. The tradition of the manuals on agriculture was continued in the highly scientific treatises which devoted much space to tree cultivation, like that by Pierre de Crescens, for example, which was written in Bologna in 1303 and was first printed in Augsburg in 1471,[61] then in Venice in 1495.[62] In France the aristocracy showed a keen interest in these agrarian treatises. Charles V had Pierre de Crescens translated[63] and also the treatise on the Art of Sheepbreeding by Jean de Brie.[64]

Other more complex sources confirm these findings and permit us to speak both for an earlier period and for the West as a whole. These are the books of instructions, inquiries and inventories. How can one talk of an archaic or casual « medieval » economy after examining such precise documents? The extremely detailed prescriptions in the famous Capitulary of Villis, written in the reign of Charlemagne or his son Louis the Pious, overwhelmed the stewards of the imperial estates with the most precise recommendations on how they should manage the estates, and they reveal, among other things, that the economy was dependent on the market for the sale of agricultural surpluses.[65] The imperial inventories describe the estates, lands, buildings and resources in detail.[66] The major religious communities had identical registers, which were just as precise, and the famous Polyptic of Irminon, the abbot

61 *Summa Agriculturae* or *Opus ruralium commodorum*, Augusta 1471.

62 *Ruralium Commodorum liber duodecim*, Venice 1495.

63 This version later appeared in several copies, one of which, a very luxurious copy illustrated by a great many miniatures, is in the Bibliothèque de l'Arsenal in Paris; another very simple copy with no illustrations and obviously intended for more practical use is in the Bibliothèque Municipale de Rouen [J, 1 (977)].

64 M.-T. Kaiser, *Le berger en France à la fin du Moyen Age*, Paris 1974.

65 *Capitulare de villis et curtis*, ed. A. Boretius, in « Monumenta Germaniae historica. Leges », vol. I, 1835, *Capitularia regum Francorum.*

66 *Breves exempla ad describendes res ecclesiastices et fiscales*, ibid.

of Saint-Germain-des-Prés,[67] is only one example of these very complete and detailed inventories which listed fields, men, cattle, sowings, equipment and stock. They were written between 800 and 850, during or just after the Norman or Hungarian invasions, in the middle of the period of anarchy and « feudality ».

* * *

The history of seigneurial account-keeping throughout the so-called « medieval » period has yet to be written. We still have little knowledge of the accounts kept by the landowners. They seem to be very rare, if not exceptional, and only English historians have been able to study management of the manors and their methods of farming.[68] But everything points to the fact that the account rolls of the great estates, because of their great age, the techniques they employ and their degree of completeness, are equal in importance to the books kept by city merchants. The English treatises on agriculture which we have already mentioned reveal beyond any doubt that as early as the XIIIth century very precise, detailed accounts were kept — at a time, that is, when mercantile accountancy was certainly no more exact or diversified, certainly not in England. From then onwards English rolls, which are much more numerous than those compiled by merchants in any other country save Italy, clearly reveal the desire not only to check the work carried out by stewards but also to calculate profits in advance.[69] Later, in the XVth century, many rolls and registers prove that these practices were very widespread in France and in the countries of the Empire. In the French countryside these agrarian account-books were much more numerous than those drawn up by the burghers, townsmen and business men of all kinds. In his study of rural Hainaut in this period, G. Sivery has been able to make an inventory for the years from 1295 to 1505 of 260 demanial

67 *Polyptique de l'Abbaye de Saint-Germain-des-Prés*, ed. A. LONGNON, Paris 1886.

68 Cf., for example, E. SEARK and B. ROSS, *Accounts of the cellaress of Battle Abbey. 1275-1513*, Sydney 1967; E. STONE, *Profit-and-Loss Accountancy at Norwich Cathedral Priory*, in « Transactions of the Royal Historical Society » 1962, pp. 25-48.

69 F. R. H. DU BOULAY, *The Lordship of Canterbury*, London 1966; R. R. DAVIES, *Baronial Accounts, Incomes and Arrears in the Later Middle Ages*, in « Economic History Review » 1968, pp. 211-229.

account books belonging to the count himself, together with several other series, among which were 119 registers for the Castellany of Blaton and Feignies (1381-1505) alone and 208 registers for the Castellany of Bouchain (1320-1502) — more than a thousand documents in all.[70] His thorough and very detailed analysis of the techniques used by the money collectors and agents of these rural farms reveals that these techniques closely resembled those employed by the Lombard merchants who were established in the area.[71] The stewards knew how to keep precise, clear books, how to draw up balances and measures their profit exactly. Everything indicates that the lords kept, or rather had specialist clerks who kept for them, financial accounts and registers which not only recorded the incomes and outgoings for the estates as a whole, but which also detailed individual accounts for such and such a part of the estate and for particular crops or products — for example, there were separate accounts for forests[72] lakes[73] and the accounts of King René's shepherd for the flocks moving to the other pastures in Haute Provence.[74]

This underlines the striving for mathematically calculated predictions, the desire to gather information and to enumerate, sometimes even a speculative spirit too. These preoccupations were especially prevalent in the countries where farming was carried out on a large scale and was carefully managed, as, for example, in the Ile-de-France and above all in England. A much greater number

70 G. Sivery, *Structures...* (op. cit., cf. above note 38), p. 17 *et seq.* Other recent studies are also based on seigneurial accounts that are more or less complete but very detailed: A. Plaisse, *La baronnie du Neubourg*, Paris 1961; L. Génicot, *La crise agricole du Bas Moyen Age dans le Namurois*, Louvain 1969; M.-T. Caron, *Les Chalon-Tonnerre* (cf. above note 24).

71 G. Sivery, *Structures...* (op. cit., cf. above note 38), pp. 468-478; extracts from documents pp. 509-513.

72 See, for example, the accounts kept by the *Office du Vin* of the Cathedral Chapter of Cambrai concerning the management of a wood in its possession (sales of wood, bundles and fagots; expenditure on felling and maintenance), Archives Départementales du Nord, 4 G 7401 *et seq.* from 1398, 25 registers.

73 Cf. the accounts for the lakes of the Chateau de Sully-sur-Loire, Paris, Bibliothèque Nationale. Nouvelles Acquisitions françaises no. 25203. 1367-1368. Also: *Comptes particuliers pour les étangs du Comte de Forez*, Archives départementales de la Loire, B. 1950.

74 M.-T. Kaiser, cf. above note 64.

of documents has survived by chance in England than elsewhere on the practice of what the English historians call « high farming », which was based on a rural economy very much conditioned by the needs of the market and organized entirely with a view to sales and profits. The great English landowners could turn for advice to the competent specialists and enlightened technicians who surrounded them and once or twice a year called a kind of council for the management of their lands. All their stewards, bailiffs or reeves attended as well as knights, neighbouring landowners, lawyers and clerics. The lord himself, or his council, drew up a programme for work and development — a sort of plan which outlined in advance, year by year, the objectives that were to be attained and the profits to be made by those who were responsible for various sectors.[75]

The idea of the seigneur « exploiting » his peasants and investing no money in his own land is also a gratuitous invention of writers who are obviously ignorant even of the existence of these accounts. The accounts reveal, on the contrary, that large annual or occasional sums were spent on the payment of salaries (for example to stewards, craftsmen, agricultural labourers) for the purchase of seed or tools, while capital was also invested in improving the condition of the land or farming techniques, or quite simply the type of farming itself.[76] This careful farming often had remarkable results, not in making for immediate gross profit but in the better quality of crops and, in the long term, better sales in markets whether near or far away. The seigneurs, the owners of large farms and vast stretches of pastureland, forests and fallow land often set about improving livestock strains in search of better quality wools and meat by introducing foreign breeds and by carrying out count-

[75] On the rôle of the *council* and its *auditors*: J. A. Raftis, *The Economy of the Estates of Ramsey Abbey. 1240-1440*, Toronto 1957; B. Somerville, *The Duchy of Lancaster Council and Court of Ducher Chamber*, in « Transactions of the Royal Historical Society » 1941, pp. 59-177; E. Halcrow, *The administration of the Estates and Household of the Priors of Durham Priory. Unpublished thesis.* Oxford; L. Fox, *The Administration of the Honor of Leicester in the XVth Century*, Leicester 1940; J. M. W. Bean, *The Estates of the Percy Family (1411-1537)*, London, Oxford 1957; G. A. Holmes, *The Estates of the Higher Nobility in the XIVth century*, England, Cambridge 1967.

[76] M. M. Postan, *Investment in Medieval Agriculture*, in « Journal of Economic History » 1967.

less patient and skilful experiments in cross breeding that could be profitable only in the long term. This led to the development in Spain and then in England of a new breed of sheep, the merino, whose wool was later to penetrate even the most exacting markets.[77] Pegolotti's merchants' handbook, written between 1310 and 1340, includes a very detailed inventory of the different qualities of wool to be bought at the abbeys and fairs of Eastern and Northern England.[78] Such a highly detailed register reveals the many close links between the demand of the Tuscan market and the efforts made far away by the producers, the sheep breeders.

The same was true for the different qualities of wine: the costly wine which was exported to quality markets in the town or to courts was what made the reputations of the great vineyards and it was produced on seigniorial, especially princely and ecclesiastical, estates.[79] In 1395 the Duke of Burgundy, Philip the Hardy, had to punish certain small landowners, mostly townsmen of poor means, who were hastily planting bad vines which rapidly produced large quantities of grapes but which made bad wine.[80]

There was nothing, however, that was more contrary to a desire for immediate profit, or to the waste of the resources of the land, than the care taken in cultivating the seigniorial forests on a rational, regular and far-sighted basis. They were marked for cutting at regular intervals that varied according to the species of timber, new plantations were laid down on land that had been cleared and new trees were protected.

How can it be said that the landowners refused to invest when the large-scale clearing of the forests and the reclamation of marshes that were carried out throughout the West for centuries took place mainly on their initiative, under their direction and using their capital? The establishment of new hamlets or villages did not only

77 R. S. Lopez, *El Origen de la Oveja Merina*, in « Estudios de Historia Moderna », Barcelona 1954, pp. 3-11.

78 R. A. Donkin, *The Disposal of Cistercian Wool in England and Wales during the XIIth and XIIIth Century*, in « Citeaux » 1957, pp. 109-131 and 181-202; *Cattle on the Estates of Medieval Cistercian Monasteries in England and Wales*, in « Economic History Review » 1962; F. G. Cowley, *The Cistercian Economy in Glamorgan 1130-1349*, in « Morgannwg » XI, 1967.

79 R. Dion, *Histoire de la vigne et du vin en France*, Doullens 1959, pp. 171-198.

80 *Ibid.*, p. 283.

mean the surrender of uncultivated, unproductive land — seed and plants, ploughshares and millstones had to be bought and on occasions even money had to be lent to the new inhabitants. In the Po valley the great abbeys either built at their own expense, using paid labourers, or else purchased outright from their funds, the drainage canals and aquaducts that successfully drained the marshes. Reclamation and building within the seigneurie meant that the landowner had to give up any income or profit for some time — perhaps for 5 or 10 years. This policy of anticipation and long term investment reveals a speculative or at least afarsighted mentality.

To sum up, the gulf between the mentality of the seigneur and that of the merchant « capitalist » is artificial. We know, to take only one essential aspect of the close links that united agrarian activities and commerce, that throughout the West the merchants of the early XIth century (when the famous « economic awakening » in these countries took place) were not necessarily adventurers or new, independent men. Quite the reverse, they were men who were protected by the seigneurs, on whose behalf they acted and in whose *familia* they lived. Such were the merchants of the great abbeys who transported products from the different farms (*curtes*) either to the central *curtis* or the town market. The abbeys and Lombard bishops in Pavia had storerooms and warehouses, a port on the river Ticino and even a *xenodochium*, a kind of inn or caravanserail for travellers. The merchants from abbeys were equally active in the North, and therefore were more influential in business than those who were specifically townsmen.[81]

* * *

The improper and completely unjustified use of such words as « feudal » and especially « feudal economy » obviously gives an inexact picture of the structures and behaviours of the « medieval »

---

81 H. Laurent, *Aspects de la vie économique dans la Gaule franque. Marchands du Palais et marchands d'Abbayes*, in « Revue Historique » 1938, pp. 281-297; F. Vercauteren, *Marchands et bourgeois dans le Pays Mosan au XIe et XIIe siècles*, in « Mélanges à F. Rousseau », pp. 655-672.

world. The landowners by no means imposed their economic policies on the peasantry as a whole, or dominated it. They were themselves, in any case, from widely differing social and cultural origins and backgrounds. Finally, neither their attitudes nor their behaviour showed any great contrast to or backwardness, when compared with the « capitalist » merchants from the city, and they can by no means simply be equated with the straightforward desire to exploit without foresight or calculation.

* * *

CAPITALISM OF THE GREAT OR OF THE PEOPLE?

How can this world of the « capitalist » merchants be portrayed in concrete terms? Here too we find that certain clichés have taken root in a spectacular and irresistible fashion. From the moment when historians accepted that certain accounting and financial techniques and associations of various kinds developed in the commercial world as early as the « Middle Ages », they have also emphasized the existence of a « capitalism of the great ». In their view the powerful merchant, the owner of vast commercial networks, the banks and companies with their branches or subsidiaries, alone dominated the life of the city. Below him the hierarchy of activity and wealth included only workers subject to his economic and political control. The social structure was reduced to a simplistic picture which was still based on a kind of Manicheism — the opposition, that is, between the very great, very rich and all-powerful, the leaders of industry on one hand, and on the other the humble workers; the oppressors, who formed only a thin layer of the active population, against the oppressed. But neither does this pretty invention, which some historians have found irresistible and which others have found very useful in assuming various ideological or political stances, stand up to any careful examination. Yves Renouard was the first to doubt that such was the social basis of capitalism in Florence and to ask what proportion of the city population the business men did in fact represent. He suggested that they were both numerous and of widely differing material positions.[82] Since then all serious studies attempting to establish the real nature and conditions of these men have confirmed Renouard's intuition. In the merchant towns of Italy and indeed in all the towns of the West, the historian meets in the « medieval » periods and even at the end of the « Middle Ages » — the time, that is, when capitalism was being frustrated (we are told), which is often taken as the root of all kinds of tension — an extreme variety in both conditions and wealth at all levels of the social hierarchy In the Tuscan wool industry very large cloth weaving concerns were very rare compared with the numerous, almost innumerable *botteghe* or workshops which were organized identically but which had very modest capital at their disposal and employed only a few workers. In about 1380, 200 wool *botteghe* in Florence were involved in cloth production and produced from 3 to 220 pieces per year.[83] G. A. Brückner has provided us with the results of detailed research on the *Ciompi* and Florentine society based on notarial records in place of the more partisan chronicles. These effectively illuminate the structure of human relationships and his dissection of social relations in Florence around 1378 clearly reveals that there were often foremen in small concerns who were themselves employers and capitalists — comb makers, carders, dyers, wool and cloth washers. In that year the roll of taxes on income referred to 150 master craftsmen *sottoposti a l'arte della lana.*[84]

So even in the towns where industrial capitalism was developing, business men could be numbered in tens not to say hundreds. This social diversity was increased by the great number of activities in which each was involved. Being registered in one craft, in one business or guild never meant that this was a man's only profession — far from it! What is more, the astonishing changeability

82 Y. Renouard, *Les hommes d'affaires italiens au Moyen Age*, 2nd ed., Paris 1968, p. 191. In 1369, 108 Florentine companies obtained the right to bring their merchandise into the port of Pisa.

83 F. Mèlis, *La formazione dei costi nell'industria laniera alla fine del Trecento*, in « Economia e Storia » 1954; R. De Roover, *Labour conditions in Florence about 1400: Theory, Policy and Reality*, in « Florentine Studies », ed. N. Rubinstein, London 1968, pp. 277-313.

84 G. A. Bruckner, *The Ciompi Revolution*, ibid.

of activities, of circumstances and fortunes meant that the use of strictly capitalist mercantile practices was not by any means restricted to a few families and passed on from one generation to another. The mercantile profession was generally part of a much wider framework and existed within a process of upward social mobility that was very complex. In very few cities were true « merchants » to be found, and in even fewer did they remain so from one generation to another.

Finally there is a subject that can be studied relatively easily but which is often overlooked. The accounting and financial techniques adopted in mercantile « capitalism » generally penetrated deep into the various strata of society through widely differing levels of wealth, sometimes even down to the humblest. We have already seen that this was true for credit and the different forms of money lending, and the same applies to insurance, sales on account, internal and external dealings, account keeping and all kind of monetary manipulations. We are often bewildered by the use of a range of currencies of different, and often distant, origins by people of very modest means. For example in Italy in the 1450's all businessmen knew how to use all the monetary system of their city, which were always very complex, and even those of neighbouring towns as well. In Genoa the notorious *lira di paghe*, a fictitious nominal currency which sometimes changed value daily, was constantly used for payments of all kinds by very modest people, and these reached a sum of more than 1,200,000 pounds in all and more than 10,000 transactions a year, because of the use of account transfers.[85]

The same familiarity with capitalist business techniques was to be found among individuals from a great variety of backgrounds, judging from study of investments in private enterprises or public banks. The studies by E. Byrne, E. Bach and R. L. Reynolds have shown clearly that the Genoese merchants trading in the Holy Land brought away with them, as early as the XIIth century, both money and merchandise entrusted to them by men from all social backgrounds, usually for small, or even very small, sums as a result of

85. Cf. above note 39.

the numerous *commande* contracts placed with them.[86] The associations between travelling merchants and sedentary « capitalists », and the firm division between capital involved in maritime and that in mercantile ventures certainly meant that the capitalists did not risk all their assets at once and so spread their risks over different operations, but it also permitted people with meagre resources to invest in distant trade to which they would not otherwise have had access. The most varied social groups, even those most removed from overseas trade, could invest and participate in the vast trade carried on by the city. And this was true not only for small merchants, master craftsmen, notaries and scribes, but also for women and ecclesiastical communities as well.[87] On the other hand relations between capital and labour were also distinguished by the fact that the active, working merchants who received money and goods from others invested their own money, in turn, in other expeditions and voyages; the active, working merchant, was in his turn also a capitalist who invested.

The practice of splitting up capital, sometimes to an extreme, was used in all kinds of operations, in the building of ships for example where people of small means, women or widows, bought *loca navis* and parts of them[88] and also in maritime insurance. They continued for a long time, until the end of the « medieval » period and beyond, in spite of the development of powerful concerns in which capital was concentrated both vertically and horizontally. Throughout this entire period the traditional methods retained great favour in Genoa, Venice and in all the mercantile towns. The records made by Domenico, a priest and notary, in

86 E. H. Byrne, *Commercial Contracts of the Genoese in the Syrian Trade of the Twelfth Century*, in « Quarterly Journal of Economics » 1916, pp. 128-170; *Genoese Shipping in the Twelfth and Thirteenth Centuries*, Cambridge (Mass.) 1930; *Genoese Trade with Syria in the Twelfth Century*, in « American Historical Review » 1920, pp. 191-219; R. L. Reynolds, *A Business Class in the Thirteenth-Century Genoa*, in « Journal of Economic History » 1945, pp. 1-19; E. Bach, *La cité de Gênes au XIIe siècle*, Copenhagen 1955, 175 p. and app.; p. 66.

87 L. Blancard, *Documents inédits sur le Commerce de Marseille au Moyen Age, Compagnies marseillaises du XIIIe siècle* (pp. 371-383). 2 vols., 1884-1885. Part III: *Les commandites commerciales des Béguines de Roubaud.*

88 M. Chiaudano, *I « loca navis » nei documenti genovesi dei secoli XII e XIII*, Milan 1939.

Venice between 1309 and 1316 reveal, among 543 agreements of various kinds, 42 contracts called *colleganza* contracts (in fact *commande* in the Genoese style) where the capital.involved varied from 10 *soldi* to 1,000 pounds; investments of less than 10 pounds were the most numerous and were made by people of modest means.[89]

In a more general way we should note that the development of the great mercantile companies did not necessarily exclude small capital. The *Grosse Ravensburger Handelsgesellschaft* had, between 1380 and 1530, more than 300 associates belonging to 120 different families. In 1490, 430,000 of its 590,000 florins belonged to the four main participants while the other members, who numbered more than 100, had invested only minimal sums.[90] In Genoa the so-called *a carati* companies, a sort of shareholding joint stock organization, saw their 24 original shares divided, and often subdivided, into very small sums which were, put on the market, sold or mortgaged. This gave rise to heavy dealings in transferable securities and the involvement of a great deal of small capital. The ease with which investments could be withdrawn at any moment from the business circuit simply through the sale of shares favoured middling and small investments.[91] Finally, if the investments made in the Medici Company by individuals who formed its *sopracorpo* were made predominantly by great persons, noblemen or ecclesiastics,[92] a study has yet to be made of investments of a more limited size in the Tuscan companies which could draw on considerable capital of widely varying size and social origin.

* * *

Lastly, as early as 1200-1250 the purchase of shares in the public debt offered many opportunities to people with small funds to invest. This explains the extraordinary development of the

89 *Domenico, prete di S. Maurizio, notaio in Venezia (1309-1315)*, ed. M. F. Tiepolo, Venice 1970.

90 Cf. above note 20.

91 J. Heers, *Gênes...* (op. cit., cf. above note 31), pp. 200-206.

92 R. De Roover, *The Rise and Decline of the Medici Bank. 1397-1494*, Harvard U. P. 1963; especially the tables p. 67 and 68.

associations of State creditors — the *Compere* or *Maone* which originated in Italy. These grouped together a large number of people who influenced the destinies of cities or states, and were subject to the strangest fortunes in all spheres of economic, political and social life.[93] In Genoa there were countless *Compere* united around the *Casa di San Giorgio* and also the famous *Maona de Chio*.[94] In Milan there was the *Banco di Sant'Ambrogio*, in Florence the *Monte*, or rather the *Monti*, while there were also the public bank of Venice[95] and the *Taulas* of Barcelona[96] and Valencia[97] Later there were the French *Partis* in Lyon.[98] Of course these State organizations paid only relatively low interest, generally with some delay. In Genoa, the interest on the shares of the *Casa di San Giorgio* varied between 1445 and 1465 from 5-8%. But they inspired confidence and seemed to offer reassuring security, so their customers were of all kinds — lay and religious communities, pious associations, charitable associations, women and widows, or else parents investing dowries for their daughters and especially people of modest means and of very varying professions. The great capitalists would seem to have been little involved here, on the whole. In Florence, especially after 1470 there were many investors in the *Monte des 7%*, generally of very modest sums.[99] In 1460, 11,315 « persons » owned shares in the *San Giorgio* of Genoa. The city then had just over 100,000 inhabitants. There were 3,072 shares, or 27% of the total subscribers and just over 9% of the capital

93 P. Usher, *The early history of Deposit Banking in Mediterranean Europe*, Cambridge 1943.

94 R. Cessi, *Studi sulle Maone medievali*, Roma 1935.

95 G. Luzzatto, *Il debito pubblico nel sistema finanziario veneziano dei secoli XII-XV*, in « Studi di Storia economica veneziana », Venice 1935; *Il debito pubblico della Repubblica di Venezia dagli ultimi decenni del XII secolo alla fine del XV*, Milan 1963 (with an appendix by F. C. Lane, *Sull'ammontare del « Monte Vecchio » di Venezia*, pp. 273-290).

96 Y. Roustit, *La dette publique à Barcelone au XVe siècle*, in « Estudios de Historia Moderna », Barcelona 1954.

97 S. Carreres Zacares, *La primitiva Taula de Cambis de Valencia*, Valencia 1957,

98 R. Doucet, *Le grand parti de Lyon au XVIe siècle*, in « Revue Historique » 1933, vol. CLXXI, pp. 473-513 et vol. CLXXII, pp. 1-41.

99 There is no general study of this question. But see: B. Barbadoro, *Le finanze della Repubblica fiorentina*, Florence 1929. Cf. also R. A. Goldthwaite, *Private Wealth in Renaissance Florence. A Study of four Families*, Princeton 1968, pp. 244-246.

invested, for sums of less than 100 *lire di luoghi* (about 50 pounds in current money), a very modest sum. The registers of the *Casa* indicate the nature of the investors and this study confirms the existence of small « capitalists » from very modest social positions. The shares were listed according to the quarter of the town and the popular areas are represented as much as the others.[100] The *San Giorgio* kept all the main taxes collected by the Commune. It had an extraordinary, financial, political, economic and social power, and after 1453 it administered the overseas colonies and on the whole appears to have been a model of good administration, constituting a veritable state within a state, which demonstrates the importance of these popular investments and also the way in which capitalist attitudes had penetrated deeply all levels of society.

Popular capitalism was indeed one of the great social novelties in this world, even though it was « medieval ». The fact must obviously contradict many *a priori* views as to the absolute, natural and irreducible opposition between capital and labour.

* * *

The ideas and the practice of « modern capitalism » were, then, established very early in the « Middle Ages » — they certainly ran throughout the period. They penetrated down into different social levels, many of which were both very humble and alien to the world of business. Such ideas and practices were far from absent from rural life and the seigneurs conducted their businesses and cultivated their lands much as the merchants and financiers organized their affairs. Far from simply « exploiting » and wasting, they knew how to keep books, invest and look ahead. « The Capitalism of the great » and, even more, « the feudal economy » are then no more than clichés that bear no relation to reality.

100 J. Heers, *Gênes*... (op. cit., cf. above note 31), pp. 174-190.

4
Cultural Climates and Technological Advance in the Middle Ages

Lynn White, Jr

To establish facts, and the more obvious relations among facts, has never satisfied the consciences of historians. We are driven to ask not only what happened but also why it happened. Historical explanation, of course, is seldom a matter of one billiard ball striking another, of "causes" in the narrow sense. It is much more often a process of gradual illumination of the fact to be explained by gathering around it other facts that, like lamps, seem to throw light on it. At last the historian arrives at a sense that the central fact on which he is focusing has become intelligible.

In 1959 when I finished the manuscript of a book on medieval technology,[1] I was painfully aware of its greatest defect: it identifies and describes a few major aspects of the unprecedented technological activity that occurred in the medieval West, but it fails to explain the phenomenon observed. To tell the truth, I was much more sure of the *what* than the *why*. Four years later I had become bold enough to publish a preliminary inventory of possible reasons, not all of equal weight but none mutually exclusive, for medieval technological advance.[2] This is not, however, the sort of problem that stands still. The present state of scholarship demands a new effort to understand it.

I

There is much to be understood. The technological creativity of medieval Europe is one of the resonant facts of history.[3] Beginning obscurely as early

[1] *Medieval Technology and Social Change* (Oxford 1962), hereafter *Med. Techn.*

[2] "What Accelerated Technological Progress in the Western Middle Ages?" in *Scientific Change*, ed. Alistair C. Crombie (London 1963) 272-291.

[3] The most comprehensive survey of medieval European technology is that by Bertrand Gille in *Histoire générale des techniques*, ed. Maurice Daumas, 1 (Paris 1962) 429-598, and 2 (1965) 2-139. See also Friedrich Klemm, *Der Beitrag des Mittelalters zur Entwicklung der abendländischen Technik* (*Beiträge zur Geschichte der Wissenschaft und der Technik* 2, Wiesbaden 1961), and my "The Expansion of Technology, 500-1500 A. D." in *The Fontana Economic History of Europe* ed. Carlo M. Cipolla, 1, chapter 4 (London 1969 issued as pamphlet).

as the sixth century, within three hundred years the northern peasantry created a novel agricultural system that, in proportion to expenditure of human labor, was probably the most productive in the world.[4] In the eighth century the Franks revolutionized their methods of warfare, and thereafter their descendants consistently maintained the initiative in improving military technology, as distinct from military organization. From about the year 1000 onward—although the movement was foreshadowed in the ninth century—the West produced new labor-saving mechanical devices and explored new applications of power to production, thus providing the industrial basis for burgher capitalism. Starting in the sixth century, but particularly after 1200, Europe led in the development of ship design and the nautical arts.

While the medieval West's cousinly cultures, Byzantium and Islam, long remained more sophisticated in most other respects, in technology they were laggards as compared with Europe. Only contemporary China—from which the West borrowed much[5]—could compare with Europe in inventiveness and eagerness for useful novelties. The emergence of the mechanical clock in the second quarter of the fourteenth century, however, by enlarging the number of craftsmen skilled in making and correlating moving metal parts in machines, led in Europe to heightened activity that soon gave to the Occident a clear technical superiority even over China.

Romans had been no less predatory than were Europeans of the late Middle Ages, but the Caesars were so ill equipped that they could not extend their rapacity greatly beyond the basin of the Mediterranean. By 1492, however, Europe had developed an agricultural base, an industrial capacity, a superiority in arms, and a skill in voyaging the ocean which enabled it to explore, conquer, loot, and colonize the rest of the globe during the next four centuries and more. This unification of world history was a unique event. Its implementation, and that of the Imperialist Age, 1500-1950, was provided largely by the Middle Ages.

Moreover, modern technology is the extrapolation of that of the Western Middle Ages not merely in detail but also in the spirit that infuses it. The later thirteenth century in Europe marks the moment of crisis in the history of mankind's relation to the natural evironment: it produced "the invention of invention" of which the practical effects were soon felt. The earlier record of technology around the globe is scattered and often lacking in continuity; it recounts a generally slow accumulation of isolated specific inventions,

[4] The salutary effect of this upon the standards of living among German peasants in the eleventh century is shown in my "The Life of the Silent Majority," in *Life and Thought in the Early Middle Ages* ed. Robert S. Hoyt (Minneapolis 1967) 85-100.

[5] No student of European technology can neglect Joseph Needham, *Science and Civilization in China*, 4 vols. in 6 to date (Cambridge, Eng. 1954-1970).

their spread and elaboration. But in the Middle Ages, in Europe alone, invention became a total and coherent project.[6] From the later Middle Ages onward, world technology was increasingly European technology.

Technicians at that time in large numbers[7] began to consider systematically all the imaginable ways of solving a problem. About 1260, the Franciscan Roger Bacon, pondering transportation, confidently prophesied an age of automobiles, submarines, and airplanes.[8] Since arrow wounds were then a medical problem, about 1267 Theodoric, successively bishop of Bitonto and Cervia, in his treatise on surgery noted that for the extraction of arrows "quotidie enim instrumentum novum, et modus novus, solertia et ingenio medici invenitur."[9] Clocks were a great problem, and proposals for their improvement were frequent before the solution was found. On the basis of the recently introduced Chinese mariner's compass, and inspired by the novel Hindu concept of perpetual motion, in 1269 Roger Bacon's friend, the military engineer Peter of Maricourt, proposed a magnetic clock to replace all others.[10] In 1271 Robert the Englishman, talking about plans for a weight-driven clock, admitted that the problem of the escapement had not been entirely conquered, but he was confident that it would be.[11] Almost at the same moment, at the court of Alfonso el Sabio of Castile, Rabbi Isaac ben Sid of Toledo described not only new kinds of waterclocks, which he claimed to be much better than any earlier models; he also depicted as an absolute novelty a weight-driven clock with a mercury brake.[12] Indeed, this was a fairly practical solution for the escapement, as a subsequent tradition of such clocks shows.[13] Before 1313 someone invented the sandglass.[14] But

[6] For a complex example of this coherence, see an inventory of the ways, between ca. 1010 and ca. 1480, in which Western technicians utilized the velocity, resistence and pressure of air, in my "The Invention of the Parachute," *Technology and Culture* 9 (1968) 462-467, and "Medieval Uses of Air," *Scientific American* 222 (Aug. 1970) 92-100.

[7] About 1235 Villard of Honnecourt, and in 1269 Peter of Maricourt, independently inform us that many men are arguing and laboring to the point of exhaustion to produce *perpetua mobilia*; *Villard de Honnecourt: Kritische Gesamtausgabe*, ed. H. R. Hahnloser (Vienna 1935) pl. 9; Peter of Maricourt, *Epistola de magnete* in *Rara magnetica 1269-1559*, ed. Gustave Hellmann (Berlin 1896) 11.

[8] *De secretis operibus*, chap. 4, in *Opera queadam hactenus inedita*, ed. J. S. Brewer (London 1859) 533.

[9] *Chirurgia* 1.22, appended to Guy de Chauliac, *Ars chirurgica* (Venice 1546) fol. 143.

[10] See my "Tibet, India and Malaya as Sources of Western Medieval Technology," *American Historical Review* 65 (1960) 522-526.

[11] Lynn Thorndike, "Invention of the Mechanical Clock about 1271 A.D.,"*Speculum* 16 (1941) 242-243.

[12] *Libros del saber de astronomia del rey D. Alfonso de Castilla*, ed. M. Rico y Sinobas (Madrid 1866) 4.67-76.

[13] Silvio A. Bedini, "The Compartmented Cylindrical Clepsydra," *Technology and Culture* 3 (1962) 115-141.

[14] *Med. Techn.* 165-166.

technicians labored from the 1260s until the 1330s before the true mechanical clock was invented.[15]

In a sermon on repentance preached at Santa Maria Novella in Florence on 23 February 1306, the Dominican Fra Giordano of Pisa, while providing our best evidence of the invention of eyeglasses in the 1280s, incidentally sang the praises of the recent invention of invention. "Not all the arts," he said, "have been found; we shall never see an end of finding them. Every day one could discover a new art . . . indeed they are being found all the time. It is not twenty years since there was discovered the art of making spectacles which help you to see well, and which is one of the best and most necessary in the world. And that is such a short time ago that a new art, which never before existed, was invented . . . I myself saw the man who discovered and practiced it, and I talked with him."[16]

By the early fourteenth century, then, Europe showed not only an unmatched dynamism in technology: it also arrived at a technological attitude toward problem solving which was to become of inestimable importance for the human condition. The profound contrast between this aspect of the

[15] The intensity and diversity of the search is indicated by the fact that, almost simultaneously, inventors reached two related solutions: the verge and the wheel escapement; Ernst Zinner, *Die ältesten Räderuhren* (Bamberg 1939) 26. The use of geared weight-operated striking trains in clepsydras by the thirteenth century, and the assimilation of the vocabulary of the water clock to the mechanical clock, make difficult exact dating of the invention of the latter; cf. *Med. Techn.* 124. The earliest firm date is 1341 when Galvano Fiamma, *De gestis Azonis vicecomitis*, ed. L. A. Muratori, *Rerum italicarum scriptores* 12 (Milan 1728) 1038, tells of the invention in Milan of mills run neither by water nor by wind "sed per pondera contra pondera sicut fieri solet in horologiis. Et sunt ibi rotae multae, et non est opus, nisi unius pueri. . . . Nec umquam in Italia tali opus fuit adinventum, *licet per multos exquisitum*" (italics added). The middle 1330s however, seem indicated by the fact that in 1338 a party of six Venetian merchants left for India taking a clock and an automatic fountain as their most valuable merchandise. In Delhi the Muslim Sultan paid to them the fantastic sum of 200,000 bezants "tam pro rellogio quam pro fontanella et aliis rebus dicte societatis"; Robert A. Lopez, "L'extrême frontière du commerce de l'Europe médiévale," *Moyen âge* 69 (1963) 488 n. 16. To command such a price, this clock must have been a great novelty, almost certainly weight-driven and escapement-controlled, since Islam was entirely familiar with elaborate water clocks, as is shown by Eilhard Wiedemann and F. Hauser, "Über die Uhren im Bereich der islamische Kultur," *Nova acta* (Halle) 100.5 (1915) 1-272.

[16] "Non sono però trovate tutte. Di trovare arti non si verrebbe a fine mai. Ognedì se ne potrebbe trovare una dell'arti . . . e sempre se ne trovano delle nuove. Non è ancora xx anni che si trovò l'arte di fare gli occhiali, che fanno vedere bene, ch' è una delle migliori arti e delle piu necessarie che'l mondo abbia: ed è cosi poco che si trovò arte novella che mai non fu. . . . Io vidi colui che prima la trovò e fece, e favellagli"; Enrico Narducci, *Tre prediche inedite del b. Giordano da Rivalto* (Rome 1857) 59-60, an offprint from *Giornale arcadico di scienze, lettere ed arti* 146 (1857) 125-126. Edward Rosen, "The Invention of Eyeglasses," *Journal of the History of Medicine and Allied Sciences* 11 (1956) 13-46, 183-218, clarifies the context.

Occident and the relative passivity toward technology in the Near East is the more significant because Byzantium, Islam, and the Western world were related societies, all in great measure, but in varying proportions, built of elements found in the Greek and Semitic legacies from Antiquity. The fact that thirteenth-century theologians in Cairo, Constantinople, and Paris were all commenting on Aristotle helps us to grasp the unity of the triune Middle Ages. The fact that in the time of Saint Thomas Aquinas labor-saving machinery was little developed in the Near East and concern for invention was minimal, whereas in the West a new sort of engineering[17] was being pursued with an enthusiasm amounting to passion, helps us to understand why the Occidental third of the Middle Ages generated what we call the modern world.

II

This technological thrust of the medieval West does not yield easily to explanation. Necessity is not the mother of invention,[18] since all necessities are common to mankind living in similar natural environments. A necessity becomes historically operative only when it is felt to be a necessity, and after prior technological development makes possible a new solution. Even then, what seems needed and feasible to one culture may be a matter of indifference to another.

For example, the lands of medieval Islam were generally so arid that, even where there was enough water for agriculture, the flow of streams was too scanty or sporadic to operate many mills to grind grain. Windmills were an "obvious" solution, since dry country is notoriously windy because sparsity of vegetation helps to generate air currents. And in fact in the tenth century of our era[19] the first functional windmills appeared in eastern Iran and Afghanistan, rotating on vertical axles. Here, surely, the Muslim world had discovered an answer to its "need" for mechanical power. But did Islam feel that need with any intensity? There is no evidence that the windmill of Sejistan ever spread to the rest of Islam: claims for windmills in Muslim Spain have not been substantiated.[20] In 1185, on the other hand, the hori-

[17] The word "engineer" first appears in 1170 and is very common in the thirteenth century; see *Med. Techn.* 160.

[18] I have not been able to trace this misconception earlier than the late 1120s when Hugh of Saint Victor, *Didascalicon* 1.9, ed. Charles H. Buttimer (Washington 1939) 17, cites a proverb of which scholars have not found the source: "Ingeniosa fames omnes excuderit artes." In 6.14 (p. 130) Hugh comes closer to the modern phrasing: "propter necessitatem inventa est mechanica."

[19] For the controversy over the date see *Med. Techn.* 86 n. 7.

[20] *Ibid.* 161; *Isis* 58 (1967) 249. To judge by the distinction achieved in Yuan China by immigrant Muslim engineers (see Herbert Franke, "Westöstliche Beziehungen im Zeit-

zontal-axle windmill appeared independently in Yorkshire,[21] seemingly invented by analogy with the Vitruvian watermill, and it spread over Europe almost explosively.[22] Within seven years it had been taken to Syria by German crusaders. Yet fourteen years after that, writing at Edessa in 1206, the leading Arabic author on engineering, al-Jazarī, remarks that the notion of mills driven by the wind is nonsense: the wind is too fickle to power such a machine.[23]

Late medieval Byzantium, although ruling a dwindling area, was economically still fairly prosperous and continued to be amazingly vigorous in the arts and in religious speculation. Its resilience fills one with admiration. But, like the Muslims, the Greeks of that age were not particularly concerned to improve their technology.[24] About 1444 Cardinal Bessarion, a learned Byzantine cleric who had emigrated to Italy, wrote to the Despot of the Morea[25] urging him to strengthen himself against the Turks by sending young men to the West to learn the mechanic arts. He was impressed by improved Western glass,[26] textiles, weapons, and ships. What most amazed him, however, was the spectacle of water wheels operating both sawmills and the bellows of blast furnaces. Yet in the Occident at that time there was no novelty in these: the first lumber mill appears at Evreux in 1204, and the first water-

alter der Mongolenherrschaft," *Saeculum* 19 [1968] 99-100), Islamic technology must have been more dynamic than the present deplorable state of scholarship would indicate. The best, but inadequate, survey is that by Gaston Wiet, Vadime Elisséeff, and Philippe Wolff "L'évolution des techniques dans le monde musulman au moyen âge," *Cahiers d'histoire mondial* 6 (1960-61) 15-44.

21 *Med. Techn.* 87.

22 By about 1322 a monk at Saint Mary's of Pipewell in Northamptonshire complains that one of the chief reasons for deforestation is the search for long timbers for the vanes of windmills: "et quot virgae molendinorum venticorum dabantur in temporibus diversorum abbatum nemo novit nisi Deus"; W. Dugdale, *Monasticon anglicanum*, ed. 2 (London 1682) 1.816.

23 E. Wiedemann, "Die Konstruktion von Springbrunnen durch muslimische Gelehrte, in *Festschrift zur Feier des hundertjährigen Bestehens des Wetterauischen Gesellschaft für die gesamte Naturkunde zu Hanau*, ed. C. Lucanus (Hanau 1908) 36.

24 K. Vogel's admirable chapter on Byzantine technology in the *Cambridge Medieval History*, ed. 2, 4.2 (1967) 299-305, and bibliography 465-470, indicates little motion after the seventh century.

25 Alex G. Keller, "A Byzantine Admirer of 'Western' Progress: Cardinal Bessarion," *Cambridge Historical Journal* 11 (1955) 343-348.

26 A symptom of European initiative is not only the fact that in this period Western glass was being widely exported to the Near East, but also that the Venetians, and probably the glass-masters of Barcelona likewise, were manufacturing mosque lamps for that market decorated both with Western floral designs and with pious Koranic inscriptions, sometimes garbled; R. J. Charleston, "The Import of Venetian Glass into the Near East, 15th-16th Century," in *Annales du 3e Congrès International d'étude historique du verre, Damas 1964* (Liège 1968) 158-168.

powered blast furnace in 1384 at Liège.[27] In much of Greece there were ever-running streams operating flour mills. Nor were medieval Greeks and Latins ignorant of each other. The essential fact is that they acted differently because they had differing notions on how it was important to act. In the medieval East, whether Byzantine or Islamic, technological innovation was not considered important. It involved no sense of necessity. Bessarion's letter shows that by 1444 he personally had become Latinized in more than his religion.

There have been efforts to refine the idea of necessity by relating the vitality of medieval Western technology either to the disappearance of slavery or to an alleged labor shortage that placed a premium on increasing the productivity of labor, whether agricultural or industrial.

Unfortunately the present state of scholarship in the comparative sociology of the various medieval subcultures does not permit assured generalization. For example, as regards slavery in Byzantium, one would assume that the military victories of Romanus I, Nicephorus II Phocas, and John I must have increased the supply of slaves from the ninth into the eleventh centuries. However, we do not yet know the extent to which slave labor was used in Byzantine industry[28] and consequently how it may have affected inventiveness in that area. About Antiquity we are somewhat better informed, and what we know does not confirm all modern presuppositions. In certain contexts slavery does not appear to be an obstacle to technological advance. The Hellenistic and early Imperial periods witnessed both the apogee of the ancient slave economy and the most rapid advances not only in engineering but also in basic inventions such as glass blowing.[29] In contrast, the urban artisan class both in Byzantium and in medieval Islam seems, as in the West, to have consisted largely of free men; yet the Near East, unlike Europe, did not make the transition from craftsmanship to widespread industrial production.

There is scanty but interesting evidence that in late Roman times scarcity of manpower was, in fact, an occasional stimulus to invention;[30] but it would appear that the antitechnological attitudes of the ruling class—a bent of

[27] Bradford B. Blaine, *The Application of Water-Power to Industry during the Middle Ages*, Ph. D. dissertation, University of California, Los Angeles (1966) 155, 134-135.

[28] Anne Hadjinicolaou-Marava, *Recherches sur la vie des esclaves dans le mond byzantin* (Athens 1950) 114.

[29] See the thoughtful discussion by Ludwig Edelstein, "New Interpretations of Ancient Science," *Journal of the History of Ideas* 13 (1952) 579-585: he concludes that the obstacles to the wide application even of those inventions lay less in social conditions than in "the basic values underlying ancient life." In particular, Edelstein notes, p. 584, that in Antiquity there was no sense that technological advance was approved by the gods.

[30] H. W. Pleket, "Technology and Society in the Graeco-Roman World," *Acta historica neerlandica* 2 (1967) 15-16.

mind propagated from generation to generation by an almost exclusively rhetorical education—made such proposals abortive.[31] In Europe until the late thirteenth century[32] the movement of assarting indicates that there was probably more land available than there were hands to cultivate it, and this may have been one of the stimuli to the improvement of agricultural methods which was so notable in the West. Yet over the world and throughout history many peoples faced with untapped resources have been slow in developing methods of exploiting them.

At the level of concrete facts it is difficult to interpret technological history from its social context. The emergence of the water mill, the first mechanical application of inanimate power, is an event of prime significance. It appears almost simultaneously, in the first century before Christ, in three widely separated regions: Jutland, northern Anatolia, and China.[33] Are we to assume that in early Germanic Scandinavia, in the Pontus of Mithradates, and in the Yellow River Valley of the Han dynasty, social relationships were so similar as to evoke, in a single inspired generation, the notion of replacing human muscle with the force of water? Similarly the cannon, a complex invention harnessing the expanding forces of gasses by means of a metal tube to propel a missile, is found first at Florence in 1326, in England in 1327,[34] and in China in 1332.[35] Are we to believe that in the early fourteenth century conditions in Italy and England on the one hand, and in Yuan China on the other, were so alike that a major innovation in the art of war was socially necessary, or at least appropriate? It is far simpler, and more consonant with the present state of the evidence, to hold that technology, like art, religion, or social forms themselves, enjoys a certain autonomy in its development, and that diffusion is sometimes swift among very different societies.

The history of papermaking likewise illustrates the difficulty of explaining technological growth as a function of social relations. Paper was invented in China, and, after A.D. 751, when the Caliph's armies captured some papermakers in Samarkand, it spread throughout Islam because it was cheaper than either papyrus or parchment. By about 1050 the Byzantines were using imported Muslim paper both for documents and for books. It is curious that there is no present evidence that medieval Greece ever manufactured its own paper: in the thirteenth and fourteenth centuries its source of supply

31 Ibid. 17-24.

32 *Med. Techn.* 67 n. 4.

33 Ibid. 80-81.

34 Carlo M. Cipolla, *Guns and Sails in the Early Phase of European Expansion, 1400-1700* (London 1965) 21, 32.

35 L. C. Goodrich, "Early Cannon in China," *Isis* 55 (1964) 193-195.

shifted increasingly from Islam to Italy.[36] The first indication of paper in the Occident is a Greek charter granted in 1101-1102 by Countess Adelasia of Norman Sicily;[37] this paper was probably imported. Despite assertions to the contrary regarding Játiva in Valencia in the middle of the twelfth century,[38] there is no proof that the production of pulp for paper was ever mechanized in Islam. In startling contrast, the first paper factory known to us in the West—it was already in operation by 1276 near Fabriano—[39] was a *mill*, using water power for pulping. So likewise was the second, in 1280 at Játiva,[40] now under Aragonese rule. There is no independent evidence that labor was scarcer in Italy or in Christian Spain at that time than it was in Islam. In the present state of historical research, the ardor for advancing technology which is observed in the medieval West cannot be explained, save marginally, by social conditions, although it is clear that technological changes were occasionally a factor in social change.[41]

In the twentieth century, new technology is composed so largely of engineering applications of scientific discoveries that we tend to assume a similar relation in the past. In fact, however, until a little more than a century ago there was small connection between science, which was a theoretical effort to understand nature, and technology, which was an empirical attempt to use nature.[42] For nearly five hundred years the world's greatest scientists wrote in Arabic, yet a flourishing science contributed nothing to the slow advance of technology in Islam. By the late thirteenth century the scientific movement in the West, which had begun in the eleventh century with a wave of translations from Greek and Arabic, had seized the global primacy that it still holds. Yet while some individuals at that time, like Roger Bacon, were concerned with both science and technology, their science does not seem to have enriched technology.[43] The slight connection was the

[36] J. Irigoin, "Les premiers manuscrits grecs écrits sur papier et le problème du bombycin," *Scriptorum* 4 (1950) 194-204, and "Les débuts de l'emploi du papier à Byzance," *Byzantinische Zeitschrift* 46 (1953) 314-319.

[37] E. Caspar, *Roger II* (Innsbruck 1904) 482, 561.

[38] E. g. in *A History of Technology* ed. Charles Singer *et al.*, 3 (Oxford 1957) 412.

[39] Aurelio Zonghi, "Le antiche carte fabrianesi," in *Monumenta chartae papyraceae historiam illustrantia*, ed. E. J. Labarre, 3 (Hilversum 1960) 114. Irigoin, in *Scriptorium* 4 (1950) 197 concludes that Italian paper was already being exported to Byzantium by 1255. Whereas Islamic paper never shows watermarks, the lively entrepreneurship of Westerners is indicated by the appearance of such trademarks in Italian paper by the 1280s; Irigoin, 194.

[40] Augustin Blanchet, *Essai sur l'histoire du papier et de sa fabrication* (Paris 1900) 52-53.

[41] Cf. *Med. Techn.*, passim.

[42] See my "Pumps and Pendula: Galileo and Technology," in *Galileo Reappraised*, ed. Carlo L. Golino (Berkeley 1966) 96-110.

[43] The idea that systematic scientific research can help to advance broad areas of technology is first clearly formulated in 1450 by Nicholas of Cusa in *De staticis experimentis* which

reverse: technology was advanced by supplying instrumentation for scientists, most notably the mechanical clock as an aid to medical astrologers.[44]

Still other hypotheses may be offered to account for the permeative technological interest of the medieval West. It has been shown in detail[45] that change leads to further change. In the early Middle Ages the West was much more deeply shaken by invasions and turmoil than were the lands of the Near East. Can this trauma have made the Occident more open to change than the Orient? Perhaps; but this does not explain why the West's penchant for change should have expressed itself so early and so notably in technology rather than in other kinds of activity.

Again: I myself once toyed with the notion[46] that since under Roman rule the Celts showed themselves to be fairly inventive, the vigor of medieval technology may have been simply an amplification of a cultural condition preexistent in Gaul. Perhaps; but this merely transfers the medieval enigma to the Roman age without illuminating it.

III

Clearly, along such paths we have little chance of reaching a satisfactory historical understanding of our problem. To find an explanation for this distinctive quality in the Western Middle Ages we must try to relate it to the general cultural climate of those centuries and places.

Unfortunately the scholarly discovery of the significance of technological advance in medieval life is so recent that it has not yet been assimilated to our normal image of the period. Moreover historians, like most humanists except archaeologists and art historians, are word-bound and therefore find it hard to appraise an activity like technology which has not usually left its traces in writing. In literate societies like those of the Middle Ages which place a high value on ancient texts, contemporary actualities are often obscured by words that are a prized ornamental veneer drawn from obsolete

is Bk. 4 of *Idiota*, ed. Ludwig Baur (Leipzig 1937); a complete French translation is available in Maurice de Gandillac, *Œuvres choisies de Nicolaus de Cues* (Paris 1942) 328-354, who notes (328 n. 166) that in the Vitruvius Strasbourg editions of 1543 and 1550, to which this dialogue is appended, the two participants, named Orator and Profanus in the original, are renamed Philosophus and Mechanicus. Throughout the conversation Mechanicus generally holds the initiative in proposing scientific experiments that might have useful applications in medicine, pharmacy, metallurgy, gem polishing, materials analysis, forecasting the weather, making bells and organ pipes, and perfecting ships and military engines.

44 *Technology and Culture* 10 (1969) 439-441.

45 Margaret Hodgen, *Change and History: A Study of Dated Distributions of Technological Innovations in England, A.D. 1000-1899* (New York 1952).

46 "What Accelerated Technological Progress." (n. 2 above) 280-282.

but revered tradition. Historians trying to understand the cultural climate of an epoch recognize that the degree and style of an era's respect for written tradition is a major element in its climate. The extent, however, to which the verbal repertory of each age may have been self-deceptive, or else inadequate for expressing reality, is not always pondered.

As compared with words, nonsymbolic actions are usually functional rather than decorative. Since many such actions are related to the state and trend of a society's technology, technologies and changes in them offer a useful means of judging how far written records reveal or distort the true state of a cultural climate. There is thus a feedback between our understanding of technology and our interpretation of the general context to which technology is integral.

Items borrowed by a culture offer simpler case studies than those originated within it since they involve no internal genetic problems.

The quality of life in central Java contemporary with Charlemagne may be judged by one of the world's most evocative monuments, Barabuḍur. The enormous Buddhist stupa presents a panorama of bas-reliefs[47] illustrating a world of much elegance, but one remarkably restricted in its technical methods. Only the ships that gave contact with India, whence most of old Indonesian civilization was derived, were in any way advanced, and these vessels were presumably built on Indian models. It may be significant of cultural values that the sole technical novelty that seems traceable to Java at that time is in the arts: the fiddle bow.[48]

Despite this innovation, instrumental music in the East Indies has continued to be primarily percussive. Carried westward on the currents of the spice trade, however, the musical bow, still with a very curved stick, reached Europe about 980[49] where it spread and developed speedily. In order to equalized tensions along the entire length of the bowstring and thus produce a uniform and smooth tone, the stick in Europe was progressively flattened. In early twelfth-century France the first form of the "frog" appeared as a link between the lower part of the stick and the bowstring, thus greatly im-

[47] Nicolaas J. Krom, *Barabudur: Archaeological Description*, 2 vols. of text, 3 of plates (The Hague 1927-1931).

[48] Mantle Hood, "The Effect of Medieval Technology on Musical Style in the Orient," *Selected Reports* of the Institute of Ethnomusicology, University of California, Los Angeles, 1 (1970) 147-170. The evidence is not conclusive but is strong: the *surendro*, a type of five-tone gamelan orchestra which distinctively includes a bowed lute, was known in eighth-century Java. Francis W. Galpin, "The Violin Bow," in *The Legacy of India*, ed. G. T. Garratt (Oxford 1937), 331-334, provides no early dating from India. Bowed instruments were introduced to China perhaps as late as the Yuan dynasty; cf. H. G. Farmer, "Reciprocal Influences in Music 'twixt the Far and Middle East," *Journal of the Royal Asiatic Society* (1934) 327-342.

[49] Curt Sachs, *History of Musical Istruments* (New York 1940) 275.

proving the musical possibilities of bowed instruments.[50] By the later Middle Ages the bow, probably Javanese and certainly Asian in origin, had acquired the dominance of Western instrumental music which it retains today.

No medieval text documents with explicit words the amazing openness of the medieval European mind to borrowings from alien cultures,[51] or shows contemporary awareness of Europe's capacity to exploit and elaborate such borrowings far beyond the level achieved in the lands that generated them. The Indic concept of perpetual motion which in India was doubtless a symbol of karma, and which in Islam was a curiosity, fostered in the Occident a generalized concept of a cosmos full of forces waiting to be used mechanically by man.[52] What Europe did to Chinese paper manufacturing has already been mentioned. India originated the stirrup and China developed it, but Charles Martel's army was the first to realize its full implication for warfare[53]. Gunpowder was Chinese, but the Near East, India, and ultimately Japan received artillery and firearms not from China but from the West.[54] Let us consider one example of such a borrowing, and its consequences, in more detail.

There has long been discussion, among architectural historians, of possible Asian contributions to the genesis of Gothic architecture. The idea generally has been rejected, particularly among the French.[55] The still dominant view that gothic architecture was spontaneously born of the efforts of medieval engineers to cope with the structural necessities of romanesque vaulting shows, however, misunderstanding of the nature of diffusion and of the not infrequent ability of a fairly simple item borrowed from an alien culture to "trigger" much more elaborate creations in the borrowing culture, especially if the intrusive idea answers a felt need.

In the late tenth and eleventh centuries, for reasons that are far from clear, the height of Europe's new churches was steadily increased. The lateral

[50] Hans Heinz Dräger, *Die Entwicklung des Streichbogens und seine Anwendung in Europa* (Berlin 1935) 25-26.

[51] I attempt a brief inventory of such items, only a minority of which were technological, in "Medieval Borrowings from Further Asia," *Medieval and Renaissance Studies* 5: *Proceedings of the Southeastern Institute for Medieval and Renaissance Studies, Summer 1969*, ed. O. B. Hardison, Jr. (Chapel Hill 1971) 3-26.

[52] See n. 10 above. The earliest repudiation of the feasibility of perpetual motion appears on the first page of Leonardo's unfinished treatise on machine design: see Ladislao Reti, "The Two Unpublished Manuscripts of Leonardo da Vinci in the Biblioteca Nacional of Madrid", *Burlington Magazine* 110 (1968) 17.

[53] *Med. Techn.* 1-28.

[54] *Ibid.* 163-164; also Delmer M. Brown, "The Impact of Firearms on Japanese Warfare," *Far Eastern Quarterly* 7 (1948) 238-253.

[55] E.g., André Godard's discussion of "l'origine de l'architecture française du moyen-âge" in "Voûtes iraniennes," *Āthār-é Īrān*: *Annales du service archéologique de l'Iran* 4 (1949) 239-256, and *Art de l'Iran* (Paris 1962) 266ff.

thrust of semicircular vaults demanded massive walls and buttresses; the loftier the vaults, the thicker the lower masonry that was required. In those days all quarrying and stone cutting was manual, and land transport was fearfully expensive, although less so than in Roman times.[56] What could be done to reduce the quantity of masonry needed for a church of the desired height? Moreover, the ground plans of great churches were becoming more elaborate with ambulatories, radial chapels, and the like. Semicircular vaulting could not easily be tailored to cover such irregular areas. Fortunately, to solve such problems a new idea came out of the East at the moment when Europe's architects most needed it.

The ogival arch, sometimes combined with pointed vaulting, is first found in Buddhist India about the second century after Christ.[57] It was used by the Sasanians, whose influence apparently brought it to Syria by A.D. 561.[58] The pointed arch, with vaults, appears at Ramla in Palestine in 789[59] and by the later ninth century was common in Muslim Egypt.[60] Thence it moved by about 1000 to Amalfi, a city intimately connected with Fatimite Egypt,[61]

[56] *Med. Techn.* 66.

[57] Although the present state of Indic studies does not permit definite statements about the priority of pointed arches among various sites, a growing opinion is expressed by Dietrich Brandenburg, *Islamische Baukunst in Ägypten* (Berlin 1966) 49, that the ogive began "in der frühesten buddhistischen Kunst Indiens, kam von dort nach dem zentralen Hochasien und von da nach dem Irak und Ägypten." This type of arch probably originated as a purely decorative form for gable ends in wooden structures; cf. a Kushan relief of the second century after Christ at Mathurā in John Rosenfield, *The Dynastic Arts of the Kushans* (Berkeley 1967) fig. 29. Small masonry pointed arches appear about the same time at Kauśambi; G. R. Sharma, "Kuṣāṅa Architecture with Special Reference to Kauśāmbi (India)," in *Kuṣāṇa Studies*, ed. G. R. Sharma (Allahabad 1968) 18-19, fig. 4 (3). Also of the second century is a pointed vaulted niche at the Buddhist monastery of Takht-i-Bāhi; Benjamin Rowland, *The Art and Architecture of India*, ed. 3, (Baltimore 1967) pl 42a. Alexander Cunningham, *Mahābodhi* (London 1892) 85, believed that the spectacular pointed arches and vaulting at this greatest of Buddhist shrines are later than the original Kushan (second century) construction; the evidence, as indicated by Rowland 98, 291, pl. 52b, is ambiguous. In any case the Gupta Hindu temple of the fifth century at Bhītārgāoṅ (Rowland fig. 20) with pointed vaulting antedates any known Iranian evidence of such construction; Rowland fig. 20 and J. P. Vogel, "The Temple of Bhītārgāoṅ, "*Archaeological Survey of India, Annual Report* (1908-1909) 5-16, pl. 3, 4.

[58] Arthur U. Pope, "Possible Iranian Contributions to the Beginning of Gothic Architecture," in *Beiträge zur Kunstgeschichte Asiens in Memoriam Ernst Diez* (Istanbul 1960) 20.

[59] Brandenburg (n. 57 above) 49.

[60] One of the earliest appearances in Egypt is in the shaft of the Nilometer (A.D. 866 or 861) built by an architect from Fergana; Pope (n. 58 above) 20.

[61] Cf. A. O. Citarella, "The Relations of Amalfi with the Arab World before the Crusades," *Speculum* 42 (1967) 299-312. Evidence of the pointed arch in Amalfi about 1000 has been available for more than three decades in the very dilatory restoration of the Old Cathedral, but has not been published. I myself saw some of the earliest discoveries in 1933.

and by 1071 a porch with pointed arches and pointed vaults graced Abbot Desiderius's new church at Monte Cassino.[62] Considering that the most remarkable monk there under Desiderius's abbacy was Constantine the African (died 1087), a native of North Africa who was the first great translator of Arabic science into Latin[63] and who dedicated his version of the *Pantegni* of 'Alī ibn 'Abbās (died 994) to Desiderius,[64] there is nothing surprising in the appearance of an architectural borrowing from Islam at that time and place.

Structurally the Monte Cassino porch was no more adventurous than its Near Eastern prototypes: it was, in Kenneth Conant's happy phrase, "a bit of chic."[65] The great technological advance involving the pointed arch occurred not in Italy but in Burgundy. In 1080 Abbot Hugh of Cluny visited Monte Cassino, and there either he or his engineers,[66] then working on the design of an enormous new church being planned for Cluny, realized that pointed arches and pointed vaults offered the key to solving the chief problems with which romanesque architects had been contending. As a result of their insight, the church at Cluny, begun in 1088 and effectively finished in 1120, contained 196 pointed arches with more in the high vault.[67] The new Cluny was the most conspicuous church of northern Europe. In 1130 Abbot Suger of the French royal abbey of Saint-Denis visited it. Between 1135 and 1144 he and his engineers produced at Saint-Denis what is usually regarded as the first true gothic church. In doing so they realized the full possibilities inherent in the novel Cluniac development of oriental architectural ideas.

Nothing is more characteristically and superbly medieval than Saint-Denis, and no monument of the twelfth century has been more often cited by historical meteorologists studying the cultural climate of that age. Yet an

62 Kenneth J. Conant, *Carolingian and Romanesque Architecture, 800 to 1200* (Baltimore 1959) 223 and pl. 8 A, corrects and amplifies an earlier drawing published in conjunction with Henry M. Willard in *Speculum* 10 (1935) 144-146, pl. 1; see their article, below 203-209.

63 See Paul O. Kristeller, "The School of Salerno," *Bulletin of the History of Medicine* 17 (1954) 151-153.

64 The text of the dedication is best found in Constantine the African, *L'arte universale della medicina* (*Pantegni*) 1.1, ed. Marco T. Malatto and Umberto de Martini (Rome 1961) 37.

65 Kenneth J. Conant, *A Brief Commentary on Early Medieval Church Architecture* (Baltimore 1942) 8.

66 Jacques Stennon, "Hézelon de Liège, architecte de Cluny III," in *Mélanges offerts à René Crozet*, ed. P. Gallois and Y. J. Riou (Poitiers 1966) 1.345-358 fails to prove his thesis: the extant evidence indicates that Hezelo may have been the major fund-raiser, not the architect, of the great church at Cluny.

67 Kenneth J. Conant, "The Pointed Arch: Orient to Occident," *Palaeologia* (Osaka) 7 (1959) 36.

essential quality of its achievement has been overlooked: that in creating this glorious synthesis of engineering and esthetics, the black-robed Benedictines of Saint-Denis were the vigorous heirs of russet-garbed Buddhist monks in India a millennium earlier.[68]

Apart from students of folklore—which of all the humanistic disciplines has the broadest geographic and sociological horizons—medievalists have been reluctant to recognize cultural connections over such distances. On its slow journey from India, however, the ogive travelled in much company. Since the middle of the eleventh century, shortly before Desiderius built his porch, a Christianized life of Buddha, transmitted from Sanskrit to Arabic, perhaps through a Manichean Turkic version, and thence through Georgian and Greek into Latin, had been circulating widely in the West, with the result that Buddha, slightly masked[69] as the ascetic Indian prince Josaphat (that is, Boddhisatva), was increasingly revered as a saint whose festival is on 27 November.[70] About 1110, as Cluny was approaching completion, the Arabic-speaking Jewish convert Petrus Alfonsi included in his very popular *Disciplina clericalis* many of the animal fables of the *Pañcatantra* which had made their way from Sanskrit through Pahlavi and Syriac into Arabic.[71] In 1138, while Saint-Denis was rising, Indic numerals appeared for the first time in the West on a coin of Roger II of Sicily.[72] In 1149, five years after Saint-Denis was finished, Robert of Chester, revising some Arabic astronomical tables to the coordinates of London, introduced into Latin

[68] So far as I can discover, no one in the Middle Ages spoke of gothic engineering as providing economies in construction. The proof that many were in fact aware of this virtue of the new style—which was quickly lost in the immense new elaboration of gothic carving, clustered pillars and the like—is that the austere order of Cistercians who hotly denounced the extravagances of Cluniac churches and permitted no towers or ornaments of any sort on their own (see François Bucher, "Cistercian Architectural Purism," *Comparative Studies in Society and History*, 3 [1960] 89-105) after an intial hesitation seized upon the gothic way of building and spread it over Europe. Hanno Hahn, *Die frühe Kirchenbaukunst der Zisterzienser* (Berlin 1957) 254-258, who holds that the usual image of the Cistercians as "missionaries of the gothic" is overdrawn, fails to distinguish gothic structure from gothic embellishment. The early Cistercian gothic churches achieved the stark beauty of pure functionalism in a period when the dominant trend of gothic towards lavish ornament was developing, as Hahn correctly indicates, in the cathedrals of northern France.

[69] The first Western suspicion that Josaphat was Buddha appears in a gloss inserted into a text of Marco Polo about 1446; cf. A. C. Moule and P. Pelliot, *Marco Polo: Description of the World* (London 1938) 1.410.

[70] See David M. Lang's introduction to [St. John Damascene] *Barlaam and Joasaph* (Cambridge, Mass. 1967).

[71] *Disciplina clericalis*, ed. Alfons Hilka and Werner Söderhjelm (*Acta Societatis scientiarum fennicae* 38.4, Helsingfors 1911); Haim Schwarzbaum, "International Folklore Motifs in Petrus Alfonsi's *Disciplina clericalis*," *Sefarad* 21 (1961) 267-299; 22 (1962) 17-59, 321-344; 23 (1963) 54-73.

[72] Lynn Thorndike, "The Relation between Byzantine and Western Science and Pseudo-Science before 1350," *Janus* 51 (1964) 18.

the Indian trigonometric concept of the sine function (in Latin *sinus*),[73] which word, by a series of mistranslations and transliterations, is derived from the Sanskrit term for sine.[74] In 1154, a decade after the completion of Saint-Denis, a Cistercian monk of Clairvaux named Lawrence who was returning from Rome, with the aid of two boys and many saints drove a herd of ten Indic buffaloes—creatures never before seen in northern parts—across the Alps to Clairvaux where they promptly propagated and spread "ex eo loco per multas jam provincias."[75] The inspired engineering of the new gothic architecture was part of a larger pattern of Eurasian relationships which was far more than technological and which we have scarcely begun to understand.

Medieval Europe's capacity for gathering and expanding insights and elements drawn from the most distant and unexpected sources is a major characteristic of its culture which, on the one hand, is underscored by the study of technology and which, on the other hand, helps to explain the vigor of that technology. Despite difficulties of travel and communication, medieval European technicians had autennae delicately adjusted to catch the vibrations of every promising novelty, however distant. If since 1500 global technology has become increasingly that of the Occident, the reason is not only the inventiveness of medieval Europe but also the fact that by 1498, when Vasco da Gama reached Calicut, Europe had already absorbed and adapted to its use a great part of the other technologies of Eurasia. The culture of the medieval West was unique in the receptivity of its climate to transplants, although the verbal statements of medieval men would not lead us to such an estimate of their mentality.

What a society does about technology is influenced by casual borrowings from other cultures, although the extent and uses of these borrowings are reciprocally affected by attitudes towards technological change. Fundamentally, however, such attitudes depend upon what people in a society think about their personal relation to nature, their destiny, and how it is good to act. These are religious questions.

IV

The most thoughtful analysis of the presuppositions of Western technology has been provided by a medieval historian, Ernst Benz[76] of the University of Marburg. Study of Buddhism and personal experience of it in Japan

[73] Charles H. Haskins, *Studies in the History of Mediaeval Science*, ed. 2 (Cambridge, Mass. 1927) 123.

[74] H. Hankel, *Zur Geschichte der Mathematik in Altertum und Mittelalter*, ed. 2 (Hildesheim 1965) 280-281.

[75] Herbertus, *De miraculis* 2.30, PL 185.1341.

[76] "Fondamenti cristiani della tecnica occidentale," in *Technica e casistica*, ed. Enrico Castelli (Rome 1964) 241-263. A more popular presentation of his thesis is contained in the chapter, "The Christian Expectation of the End of Time and the Idea of Technical

—especially of the anti-technological impulses in Zen[77]—led him to find the genesis of Europe's technological advance in Christian beliefs and attitudes. The Christian Creator God, the architect of the cosmos and the potter who shaped man from clay in his own image, commands man to rule the world and to help to fulfill the divine will in it as a creative cooperator with him. History, far from being cyclical as it is in most religions, in Christianity is unique and unilinear; it is accelarating toward a spiritual goal; there is no time to lose; therefore, work, including manual work, is an essential and pressing form of worship. Moreover, matter was created for a spiritual purpose and it is neither to be transcended nor despised: the dogmas of the incarnation and of the resurrection of the flesh vouch for this. The sense that intelligent craftsmanship is shown in the world's design, and that we participate in the divine by being ourselves good artisans; the conviction that we follow God's example when we use substance for righteous ends, that time must be saved because every moment is a unique psychic opportunity: these are characteristics of the Judeo-Christian view of reality and of destiny. They are alien to all the other major religions except Islam, which belongs to the same spiritual phylum, and possibly Zoroastranism, a related species. Since in Hellenistic times and in China there were notable and sometimes rapid advances in engineering, Christianity obviously is not essential to technological dynamism. What Benz suggests, nevertheless, is that Christianity provided, historically in Europe, a set of assumptions, a cultural climate, unusually favorable to technological advance.

One may expand Benz's thesis somewhat. In 1956 Robert Forbes[78] of Leyden and Samuel Sambursky[79] of Jerusalem simultaneously pointed out

---

Progress," in his *Evolution and Christain Hope: Man's Concept of the Future from the Early Fathers to Teilhard de Chardin* (Garden City 1966) 121-142.

[77] More research is needed on the relations of Buddhism to technology: the former is divided into many sects, which may have different influences. In the sixteenth century the Japanese were eager and metallurgically equipped to adopt European types of firearms from the Dutch and Portugese; see Brown's article, n. 54 above. In sharp contrast to the Chinese, in the nineteenth century they rapidly absorbed Western technology. Both in the sixteenth and the nineteenth centuries Buddhism would seem to have played a greater psychic role in Japan than in China. The considerable literature on the differential reactions of China and Japan towards Western technology (see particularly the thoughtful essay of Marion J. Levy, Jr., "Contrasting Factors in the Modernization of China and Japan," *Economic Development and Cultural Change* 2 [1953] 236-253) generally concludes that the essence of the divergence lies in the mentality of the aggressive feudal aristocracy of Japan as compared to that of the Confucian bureaucracy of China. Confucianism, however, cannot be considered inherently anti-technological: the Sung dunasty, the great age of Neo-Confucianism, produced achievements in engineering in which Confucian scholars participated; cf. Joseph Needham, Wang Ling, and Derek J. Price, *Heavenly Clockwork: The Great Astronomical Clocks of Medieval China* (Cambridge, Eng. 1960) esp. 129-130.

[78] "Power," in *History of Technology*, ed. Charles Singer et al. (Oxford 1956) 2.606.

[79] *The Physical World of the Greeks* (New York 1956) 241. As is emphasized by W. J.

that Christianity, by destroying classical animism, brought about a basic change in the attitude toward natural objects and opened the way for their rational and unabashed use for human ends. Saints, angels and demons were very real to the Christian, but the *genius loci*, the spirit inherent in a place or object, was no longer present to be placated if disturbed.

Undoubtedly also, there has been an element of Christian compassion motivating the development of power machinery and labor-saving devices: as early as the sixth century an abbot in Gaul, troubled by the sight of his monks grinding grain in querns, built a water mill, "hoc opere laborem monachorum relevans."[80] Pity, however, is not exclusively a Christian virtue: Antipater's pagan poem, which is our second document for the existence of water mills in the ancient Mediterranean, celebrates the new machine as harnessing the water nymphs to save the aching backs of slave women.[81]

Benz has pointed a direction by which historians can make intelligible the technological dynamism of the Middle Ages. His hypothesis, however, is defective because he fails to recognized that the Greek church held the fundamentals of the Christian faith as ardently as did the Latin, yet after Kallinikos's invention of Greek fire just before 673[82] the highly civilized regions dominated by Eastern Orthodoxy were unadventurous in technology. If, as Benz believes, the vigor of Western medieval technology is an expression of religion, the sources of that dynamism must be found less in the broader aspects of Christianity than in the distinctive qualities and moods that differentiate Occidental from Byzantine Christian piety.

It may seem ludicrous to claim that the distillation of alcohol,[83] the trebuchet,[84] the functional button,[85] the suction pump,[86] the wire-drawing

---

Verdenius, "Science grecque et science moderne," *Revue philosophique* 152 (1962) 329-331, lower-class animism was sophisticated into a deification of the cosmos among the educated which made intellectuals as reluctant as artisans to use mechanics to compel nature to submit to human wishes.

80 Gregory of Tours, *Vitae patrum* 18.2, ed. B. Krusch, MGH *Script. rer. merov.* 1 (Hanover 1885) 735.

81 *Anthologia palatina graeca*, 9.418, ed. H. Stadtmueller (Leipzig 1906) 3.402-403.

82 M. Mercier, *Le feu grégois* (Paris 1952) 14.

83 Ca. 1150, in Italy; cf. Robert J. Forbes, *A Short History of the Art of Distillation* (Leyden 1948) 87-89.

84 Ca. 1199; *Med. Techn.* 102 n. 5.

85 Some buttons were used in Central Asia, Iran, and Greece in Antiquity for ornament, but apparently not for warmth. The functional button, fastening overlapping edges of cloth, is first found ca. 1235 on the "Adamspforte" of Bamberg cathedral, and in 1239 on a closely related relief at Bassenheim; cf. Erwin Panofsky, *Deutsche Plastik des 11. bis 13 Jahrhundert* (Munich 1924) pl. 74; H. Schnitzler, "Ein unbekanntes Reiterrelief aus dem Kreise des Naumburger Meisters," *Zeitschrift des Deutschen Vereins für Kunstwissenschaft* 1 (1935) 413 fig. 13.

86 Ca. 1440, in Italy; Sheldon Shapiro, "The Origin of the Suction Pump," *Technology and Culture* 5 (1964) 566-574.

mill,[87] and the myriad other medieval inventions are ultimately *gesta Christi* where Christ was worshiped with a Latin accent. Nevertheless, the processes of the human mind are so curious that our judgment of the forces that produced Western technology must be based upon what appear to be the relevant facts even when the result contains elements of irony. Since people are often comic, so also history may be.

Historians of spirituality have long been aware of a basic contrast of tonality between the two great segments of Christendom which surely affected the development of their respective technologies. The Greeks have generally held that sin is ignorance and that salvation comes by illumination. The Latins have asserted that sin is vice, and that rebirth comes by disciplining the will to do good works. The Greek saint is normally a contemplative; the Western saint, an activist.

This difference, largely subliminal, emerges clearly in the iconography of the Creator God. During the first Christian millennium, in both East and West, God at the moment of creation is represented in passive majesty, actualizing the cosmos by pure power of thought, Platonically. Then, shortly after the year 1000, a Gospel book was produced at Winchester which made a great innovation: inspired by Wisdom 11.20, "Omnia in mensura et numero et pondere disposuisti," the monastic illuminator showed the hand of God—now the master craftsman—holding scales, a carpenter's square, and a pair of compasses.[88] This new representation spread and, probably under the influence of Proverbs 8.27, "certe lege et gyro vallabat abyssus," the scales and square were eliminated leaving only the compasses—the normal medieval and renaissance symbol of the engineer—held in God's hand. This tradition, which culminated in William Blake's "Ancient of Days,"[89] was never adopted in the Eastern Church. It was the perfect expression of Western voluntarism, but it violated Greek intellectualist sensibilities about God's nature.

As medieval machine design became more intricate, God the builder developed into God the mechanic. The term "machina mundi" is at least as old as Lucretius, but was rejected on religious grounds by Arnobius Afer. By the thirteenth century, however, it was commonly used by Latin clerical scientists and had strongly affirmative overtones.[90] The first to foreshadow the Deist concept of the clockmaker God was Nicole Oresme who died as

[87] The first secure evidence is a drawing, 1489-1494, by Dürer; Friedrich Lippmann, *Zeichnungen von Albrecht Dürer* 1 (Berlin 1873) pl. 4.

[88] Erwin Panofsky and Fritz Saxl, *Dürer's "Melencolia I"* (Leipzig 1923) 67 n. 3.

[89] A. Blunt, "Blake's 'Ancient Days': The Symbolism of the Compass," *Journal of the Warburg Institute* 2 (1938-39) 53-63.

[90] *Med. Techn.* 174.

bishop of Lisieux in 1382. He proposed that, to prevent the celestial spheres from accelerating as they turned, the Creator had provided the equivalent of a clock's escapement mechanism to keep them rotating at a constant speed.[91] The subsequent success of the simile indicates the direction of Europe's thought about God, nature and man.

Students of the history of scriptural exegesis are as helpful as art historians in laying bare structures of values that lie so deep that they are not often verbalized explicitly. For our purposes the varying treatments of Luke 10.38-42, the Mary-Martha episode, are full of meaning. Since the time of Origen at least, the Greek East has invariably assumed that Martha represents the active and Mary the contemplative life, and that Christ's rebuke to Martha validates the superiority of the contemplative over the active.[92] In the West, however, a quite different style of exegesis emerges early. Saint Ambrose, once himself a Roman official and now a bishop, feels that the sisters of Bethany are symbols of *actio* and *intentio*: both are essential, and one cannot rightly be considered better than the other.[93] Then Saint Augustine, a revolutionary in so many ways, entirely subverts the Greek exegesis, the structure of values inherent in it, and, one must add, the literal meaning of Christ's words. To him, Mary and Martha represent two stages in the perfect life: Martha, the life of the soul in time and space; Mary, in eternity. "In Martha erat imago praesentium, in Maria futurorum. Quod agebat Martha, ibi sumus; quod agebat Maria, hoc speramus."[94] Yet, since we mortals dwell in time and not eternity, we must be Marthas, troubled about many things, rather than Marys.

The Middle Ages grew increasingly restless over this pericope. In the middle of the twelfth century Richard of Saint Victor, while acquiescing in Christ's praise of Mary's choice on the Augustinian ground that contemplation anticipates our heavenly condition, nevertheless shows by his phrasing where

[91] "Excepté la violence, c'est aucunement semblable quant un homme a fait un horloge et il le lesse aler et estre meu par soi. Ainsi lessa Dieu les cielz estr meuz continuellment"; Nicole Oresme, *Le livre du ciel et du monde* 2.2, ed. Albert D. Menut and Alexander L. Denomy (Madison 1968) 288.

[92] T. Camelot, "Action et contemplation dans la tradition chrétienne," *La vie spirituelle* 78 (1948) 275. That the cultural climate of Semitic Christianity was in this particular closer to that of the West than of the Greek world is indicated by the fact that Saint Ephraem Syrus, writing in Syriac and almost uninfluenced by Platonic prejudices, adopts elaborate stratagems to avoid valuing Martha's activism below Mary's contemplation: see I. Hausherr, "Utrum sanctus Ephraem Mariam plus aequo anteposuerit," *Orientalia christiana* 30 (1933) 153-163.

[93] D. A. Csànyi, "Otima pars," *Studia monastica* 2 (1960) 56-57.

[94] Saint Augustine, *Sermo* 104.4, cited by A. M. de la Bonnardière," Marthe et Marie, figures de l'église d'après saint Augustin, " *La vie spirituelle* 86 (1952) 425.

his own sympathies lie: "Intenta erat Maria quomodo pasceretur a Domino; intenta erat Martha quomodo pasceret Dominum. Haec convivium parat Domino; in convivio Domini illa jam delectatur."[95] Two hundred years later the European affirmation of the primacy of action reaches almost absurd heights in one of Meister Eckhart's vernacular sermons on this text.[96] Martha, the older and wiser sister, fears lest the adolescent Mary may become so ecstatic in contemplation that she will not mature spiritually by realizing that action is essential to holiness. Christ's apparent rebuke to Martha and praise for Mary are, in Eckhart's opinion, the exact reverse: they are his way of telling the perceptive Martha not to be troubled by Mary's sentimental condition; she will grow out of it. The Greek Church could not have produced, much less tolerated, such a sermon. The mood of activism which Eckhart reflects surely fostered technological growth in the West.

Some degree of respect for manual labor is, along with activism, integral to massive technological development. It was generally lacking, at least among the literate classes, in the Greco-Roman world.[97] The Jews, however, considered God's command to labor six days of the week to be as binding as that to rest on the seventh.[98] In the late third century, massive conversions of pagans to Christianity around the eastern Mediterranean threatened to corrupt the Church, and quite naturally a few zealots tried to purify it by returning to its primitive, that is Jewish, tradition. One result was monasticism, which from the beginning asserted the originally Jewish thesis that work is worhip, indeed, that it is an essential kind of worship. With considerable constancy the monks of both East and West continued through the Middle Ages to work with their hands.[99] Many of them likewise were

[95] Richard of Saint Victor, *Liber exceptionum* 2.14.5, ed. Jean Chatillon (Paris 1958) 504.

[96] *Deutsche Predigten und Traktate*, ed. and trans. Josef Quint (Munich 1955) 280-289.

[97] Cf. Moses I. Finley, "Technical Innovation and Economic Progress in the Ancient World," *Economic History Review* 18 (1965) 44. Before the impact of the monastic ethic was fully felt, moral aversion to hard work was still found in the Christian West; see my "The Iconography of *Temperantia* and the Virtuousness of Technology" in *Action and Conviction in Early Modern Europe: Essays in Memory of E. H. Harbison*, ed. T. K. Rabb and J. E. Seigel (Princeton 1969) 198-199.

[98] S. Kalischer, "Die Wertschätzung der Arbeit in Bibel und Talmud," in *Judaica: Festschrift zu Hermann Cohens siebzigstem Geburtstage* (Berlin 1912) 583.

[99] The Greek ascetics may, in fact, have been even more steadily devoted to manual labor than the Latin: see P. McNulty and B. Hamilton, "Orientale lumen et magistra latinitas: Greek Influences on Western Monasticism (900-1100)," in *Le millénaire du Mont Athos, 963-1963* (Chevetogne 1963) esp. 187, 192, 212. One reason for this was that monastic reform movements in the West, combating what was regarded as corruption arising from worldly entanglements, elaborated Benedictine liturgies from the ninth century onward to the point where there was little time left for labor; cf. P. Schmitz, "L'influence de saint Benoît d'Aniane dans l'histoire de l'Ordre de saint Benoît," *Settimane di studio*

well read; indeed, for centuries monks were the most learned men of the West. This combination of education with pratical work would seem theoretically, by joining head and hand, to provide communities in the monasteries where technological innovation would thrive. Yet the contrast in this respect between the sons of Saint Basil and those of Saint Benedict is notable.

One voice of dissent in the West may illuminate the basic situation. The sole instance in Christian monasticism of an antipathy toward the mechanic arts appears in *Scholica graecarum glossarum* by Martin of Laon (died 875) who derives *mechanicus* not from *μηχανικός* but from *μοικός* "adulterer": "Moechus est adulter alterius thorum furtim polluens. Inde a maecho dicitur mechanica ars, ingeniosa atque subtilissima et paene quomodo facta vel administrata sit invisibilis in tantum, ut etiam visum conspicientium quodam modo furetur, dum non facile penetratur eius ingeniositas."[100] Martin was an immigrant Irish monk. The rule of Saint Columba is the only monastic code of East or West in which manual labor is regarded as pure penance for sin, unconnected with prayer and praise.[101] Moreover this etymology offered by Martin is the only Western occurence of the Heronic concept of technology as primarily producing machines to deceive and awe the populace: one among several indications of connections between early Christian Ireland and the Greek culture of Alexandria.[102] Yet this Irish mediation

---

del Centro Italiano di Studi sull'Alto Medioevo 5: *Il monachesimo* (Spoleto 1957) 401-415. The result was the development of *conversi*, lay brothers designated primarily for manual labor and distinguished from the choir monks whose prime duty was *opus Dei*. K. Hallinger, "Woher kammen die Laienbruder?", *Analecta sacri ordinis cisterciensis* 12 (1956) 38, shows that such *conversi* were found in many Western abbeys in the eleventh century, but not at Cluny before 1100. Greek monasticism never developed such specialized worker monks; cf. P. de Meester, *De monachico statu iuxta disciplinam byzantinam* (Vatican 1942) 93-95.

100 Max L. W. Laistner, "Notes on Greek from the Lectures of a Ninth-Century Monastery Teacher," *Bulletin of the John Rylands Library* 7 (1922-1923) 439. Martin's etymology was remembered by Hugh of Saint Victor, *Epitome Dindimi in philosophiam*, ed. Roger Baron, *Traditio* 11 (1955) 112, who speaks of *mechanica* as "adulterina" but notes (p. 111) that "de interpretationibus vero nominum pauca deducimus."

101 E. Delaruelle, "Le travail dans les règles monastiques occidentales du IVe au IXe siècle," *Journal de psychologie normale et pathologique* 41 (1948) 61.

102 Early in the seventh century an Alexandrian merchant took a ship loaded with grain to Christian Celtic Cornwall and returned to Egypt with a cargo of tin: Leontius, *Vita sancti Joannis Eleemosynarii* (d. 616), PG 93.1624-1625. About 800 the *Martyrology of Oengus the Culdee*, ed. Whitley Stokes (London 1905) 86, 80, remembers an Egyptian monk, who from the context seems to have died in Ireland. A litany of the tenth-eleventh century remembers seven Egyptian monks buried at Disert Uilaig; Charles Plummer, *Irish Litanies* (London 1925) 64. These were presumably part of the massive emigration of the Greek Orthodox elite from Egypt resulting from the Persian and Muslim conquests in the early seventh century, on which see my *Latin Monasticism in Norman Sicily* (Cambridge, Mass.

of Greek secular alienation from labor and technology was to have small influence in the West.

Part of the reason for this differential development between Latin and Greek monasticism lies in the fact that in the Byzantine world a literate laity continued to preserve the worldly aspects of high culture, with the result that Greek monks felt able to devote themselves more exclusively to sacred studies. In the West, the level of civilization for a time sank so disastrously that the monks assumed almost sole responsibility for preserving and encouraging all aspects of culture, profane as well as churchly.[103] Thus in the Occident monks tended to be more deeply involved in secular matters than in the East. The Slavic and Germanic regions into which the missionary monks of each Church penetrated were equally primitive. The Greek evangelists were very theological in their emphasis, and their labors were almost entirely religious. The Benedictines, however, concerned themselves less with doctrine than with ethics, and carried with them not merely a new religion but also new practical arts.[104]

1938, repr. 1968) 16-26. Most commentators on Egyptian influence in Ireland have supposed that it was transmitted at second hand through abbeys in southern Gaul. However, Margaret Schlauch, "On Conall Corc and the Relations of Old Ireland with the Orient," *Journal of Celtic Studies* 1 (1950) 152-166, has collected literary materials known from Coptic, Ethiopic, and Christian Arabic sources, but resting on vanished Greek writings, which appear in Ireland long before they are found elsewhere in Europe. Miss Schlauch misunderstands the nature of the seventh-century migration from Egypt: it consisted not of Monophysite Copts, who would have found the West inhospitable, but of Melchite Greeks fleeing Coptic hatred.

[103] Benedictine libraries often contained a considerable group of secular works; cf. C L. W. Laistner, *Thought and Letters in Western Europe, A.D. 500 to 900* (Ithaca 1957) 228-235. The only regional survey of Greek monastic libraries known to me—that made in 1457 of the seventy-eight foundations in Calabria before there is any indication that their holdings were being looted by neo-Hellenic enthusiasts from the North—lists some sixteen hundred MSS of which only five are secular: two Homers (one a fragment), the *Hecuba* of Euripides, a part of Aristophanes, and Galen's treaise on medications; moreover, of these the four literary MSS are found in two abbeys, Seminara and Mesiano, which were no more than twenty miles apart; see *Le "Liber visitationis" d'Athanase Chalkeopoulos (1457-1458)*, ed. M. H. Laurent and A. Guillou, Studi e testi 206 (Vatican 1960) 47, 107, 111.

[104] See the provocative essay of Richard E. Sullivan, "Early Medieval Missionary Activity: A Comparative Study of Eastern and Western Methods," *Church History* 22 (1954) 17-35. Byzantine lack of interest in technological advance infected the waters with which their Slavic converts were baptized. Novgorod, for example, was a great and free republic of merchants in constant commerce with the west; one might expect, on sociological grounds, technological movement there. Yet, on the basis of recent excavations in the city, Michael W. Thompson, *Novgorod the Great* (London 1967) xvii, remarks that "In the tenth century there was perhaps little to choose between the two, but already in the twelfth century Russian and western societies were widely separated, because the former avoided innovation and the latter welcomed it. We do not appreciate how innovating western medi-

This monastic technical tradition finds its greatest written expression in *De diversis artibus* produced by a theologically sophisticated and technologically learned German Benedictine, Theophilus, in 1122-1123.[105] It is a religiously motivated codification of all the skills available for the embellishment of a church, from the enameling of chalices and the painting of shrines to the making of organ pipes and the casting of great bells for the tower. In Theophilus's mechanisms the first flywheels appear; he is the first to record a new and cheaper way of making glass, which largely accounts for the expansion of glazed windows in his time; he is the first to mention a wire-drawing plate and likewise the first to describe the tinning of iron by immersion,[106] a technique that continued in use until the Japanese capture of Malaya in 1941 caused such a scarcity of tin elsewhere that the electrolytic process was developed.

Theophilus was not exceptional in his interests. In his contemporary life of Saint Bernard, Abbot Arnold of Bonneval pictures the rebuilding of Clairvaux in 1136 without mentioning the church but with a delighted account of all the abbey's waterpowered machines for milling, fulling, tanning, blacksmithing, and other industries.[107] Another quite independent monastic

---

eval society was until we can put it beside a part of Europe which was virtually static." The judgement is just in relation to technology, but Novgorod proved itself very original in painting and the forms, as distinct from the structural methods, of architecture.

[105] *De diuersis artibus*, ed. C. R. Dodwell (London 1961). Cyril Stanley Smith and John G. Hawthorne, *On Divers Arts*: *The Treatise of Theophilus* (Chicago 1963) have provided an excellent English translation and learned notes on the basis of Dodwell's revised text. For the date, see my "Theophilus redivivus," *Technology and Culture* 5 (1964) 226-230. Benoît Lacroix, "Travailleurs manuels du moyen âge roman: leur spiritualité," in *Mélanges Crozet*, (n. 66 above) 1.523-529, believes that in the twelfth century the Benedictine sense of religious dedication in labor—at least in the building of churches—spread to the laity. There is danger of exaggeration: there is exhilaration simply from participating in great works. A quatrain of 1110-1120 inscribed on the sarcophagus of Buschetto, architect of the new cathedral at Pisa (which was as much a product of civic pride as of faith) indicates that Buschetto was admired more for his engineering skill than for his pious construction or its beauty:

Quod vix mille boum possent iuga iuncta movere,
Et quod vix potuit per mare ferre ratis,
Busketi nisu quod erat mirabile visu,
Dena puellarum turba levabit onus.

Cited by Craig B. Fisher, "The Pisan Clergy and the Awakening of Historical Interest in a Medieval Commune," *Studies in Medieval and Renaissance History* 3 (1966) 177 n. 92.

[106] Ernest S. Hedges, *Tin in Social and Economic History* (New York 1964) 107, 161.

[107] *S. Bernardi vita prima* 2.5.31, PL 185:285. "Abundantibus sumptibus, conductis festinanter operariis, ipse fratres per omnia incumbebant operibus. Alii cadebant ligna, alii lapides conquadrabant, alii muros struebant, alii diffusis limitibus partiebantur fluvium, et extollebant saltus aquarum ad molas. Sed et fullones, et pistores, et coriarii, et fabri, aliique artifices, congruas aptabant suis operibus machinas, ut scaturiret et prodiret, ubicumque opportunum esset, in omni domo subterraneis canalibus deductus rivus ultro ebulliens."

description of Clairvaux in the same period shows the same enthusiasms: the author is particularly taken by an automatic flour sifter attached to the flourmill; he makes a little monkish joke, saying that the stamps of the fulling mill have remitted the penalty for the sins of the fullers; then he thanks God that such machines can alleviate the oppressive labors of both man and beast; and at last he offers a picture of the abstract power of water flowing through the abbey seeking every task: "coquendis, cribrandis, vertendis, terendis, rigandis, lavandis, molendis, molliendis, suum sine contradictione praestans obsequium."[108]

Nor was the commitment of Western ascetics to holy labor confined to crafts and mechanized industry: it extended to major engineering. In 1248, for example, while giving the decayed abbey of Lorsch to a community of Premonstratensian canons, the archbishop of Mainz says of them: "Invenimus viros iuxta cor nostrum. . . . Hii etenim non tantum religionis immaculate et vite habent testimonium sancte sed eciam in viis parandis, aqueductibus extruendis, paludibus exsiccandis, quibus monasterium in illa vicina nimium pergravatur, et generaliter in arte mechanica exercitati sunt non modicum et periti."[109] Thus far no similar documents have been produced from the entire Orthodox Church.

The 1120s, in which Theophilius produced his *De diversis artibus*, witnessed a moment of change in Europe's attitude towards manual labor and technology. Theophilus himself was concerned solely with the dignity of the technical arts in the life of a monk. Some of his ascetic contemporaries made labor the prime act of religion: Abbot Rupert of Deutz (died 1130) rebukes fanatics who spurn liturgical worship and "qui in opere manuum fere totam spem suam ponunt."[110] But at that time the concept of "religion" was broadening and spreading from the monastic to the lay life, particularly through channels provided by the newly vitalized groups of regular canons.[111] It was spiritually essential to transfer dignity explicitly from monastic labor to labor in the world outside the cloister.

[108] *Descriptio positionis seu situationis monasterii Claravallensis*, PL 185.570-571. The fulling mill "pedes ligneos (nam hoc nomen saltuoso fullonum negotio magis videtur congruere) alternatim elevans atque deponens, gravi labore fullones absolvit: et si joculare quidpiam licet interserere seriis, peccati eorum poenas absolvit. Deus bone, quanta pauperibus tuis procuras solatia, ne abundantiore tristitia absorbeantur! Quanta poenitentibus poenae alleviamenta dispensas, ne laboris violentia nonnumquam fortassis opprimantur! Nam quot equorum dorsa frangeret, quot hominum fatigaret brachia labor, a quo nos sine labore amnis ille gratiosus absolvit?"

[109] *Acta imperii inedita*, ed. E. Winkelmann, 2 (Innsbruck 1885) 724 no. 1041.

[110] *In s. Benedicti regulam* 3.10, PL 170:517.

[111] See M. D. Chenu, "Moines, clercs, laïcs au carrefour de la vie évangélique (XIIe siècle)," *Revue d'histoire ecclésiastique* 49 (1954) 59-89.

This task was undertaken by the Victorines in Paris.[112] At the end of *De civitate Dei*, Saint Augustine discusses technology in a mood of complete ambivalence: he exclaims over the ingenuity and variety of the arts, but considers many of them "superfluas, immo et periculosas perniciosasque"; medicaments and skills of healing are cancelled by "tot genera venenorum, tot armorum, tot machinamentorum."[113] In the face of Augustine's vast authority, Hugh of Saint Victor, one of the most original minds of the Middle Ages and, like Theophilus, a German, very deliberately developed a new and affirmative attitude toward technology.

His first effort was made in the early 1120s in the form of a curious dialogue on the nature and scope of philosophy in which Hugh's alter ego is none other than Dindimus, the leader of the Indian Brahmins who had long been regarded in the West as "instinctive" Christians, living saintly lives without the grace of revelation.[114] His intent is clear: to provide a secular schematization of all human knowledge which, for the first time, includes the mechanic arts. On Hugh's behalf Dindimus argues vehemently against the purists who would narrow the concept of philosophy to exclude not only mechanics but also grammar and logic: "conati sunt scindere et lacerare corpus universum [philosophie] ne membra sibi coherent, quia pulchritudinem totius non viderunt."[115] The unity of philosophy arises from its function of remedying man's three basic defects: ignorance, vice, and physical weakness. Speculation provides truth; ethics aids virtue; technology supports our bodily needs; recently logic or semantics (including grammar) has been added to philosophy to give it clarity and elegance of expression.[116] Of these, *mechanica* is the least in dignity; yet it is integral to philosophy not as regards its practice but because of the wisdom inherent in it.[117]

In the later 1120s Hugh expanded and elaborated his concept of the nature and elements of philosophy in his influential *Didascalicon*: at least 88 manuscripts of it are extant, of which not fewer than 50 are of the twelfth and

[112] Peter Sternagel, *Die artes mechanicae im Mittelalter*: *Begriffs- und Bedeutungsgeschichte bis zum Ende des 13. Jahrhunderts* (Regensburg 1966). In disagreement with Benz, Maurice de Gandillac, "Place et signification de la technique dans le monde médiéval," in *Tecnica e casistica*, ed. Enrico Castelli (Rome 1964) 273 n. 7, correctly asserts the contrast between Saint Augustine's and the Victorines' positions toward technology.

[113] Augustini, *De civ. Dei* 22.24, *Corpus christianorum, series latina* 48 (Turnholt 1955) 848-849.

[114] Cf. George Boas, *Essays in Primitivism and Related Ideas in the Middle Ages* (Baltimore 1947) 140-151.

[115] Hugh of Saint Victor, ed. Baron (n. 100 above) 113, 115-116. It is significant that Dindimus is likewise Hugh's spokesman in his *De grammatica* (*ibid.* 92).

[116] *Ibid.* 110.

[117] *Ibid.* 111.

thirteenth centuries.[118] Between 1153 and 1162 Richard of Saint Victor, probably a Scot, in his widely read *Liber exceptionum*, repeated and reinforced Hugh's fourfold division of the intellectual life.[119] Naturally both Hugh and Richard recongnized that, in the hierarchical society of their day, inclusion of the mechanic arts in a total scheme of knowledge might not be cordially received, so they disclaimed any revolutionary intent. Things like architecture and agriculture are proper topics for theorizing by a philosopher, but the doing of them is different: "agriculturae ratio philosophi est, administratio rustici."[120] Nevertheless, by giving an unprecendented psychic dignity and speculative interest to the mechanic arts, the Victorines provided one of the theses for an egalitarian movement which, centuries later, spread eastward to destroy a great part of the less flexible Orthodox Church.

A development akin to the Benedictine and Victorine sense of the significance of technology was the increasing Western acceptance of mechanisms as aids to the spiritual life. The Church Fathers, both Greek and Latin, had passionately opposed the use of all musical instruments, including the organ.[121] While in Byzantium organs habitually graced secular ceremonies, the Greek Church forbade them in its liturgies, insisting that only the unaccompanied human voice can worthily praise God.[122] Yet in the later tenth century, in the cathedral at Winchester where, about the same time, the iconography of the Creator God holding scales, square, and compasses appeared, Benedictines installed the first giant organ: 70 men pumped 26 bellows supplying 400 pipes.[123] Before the invention of the mechanical clock the organ was the most complex machine. In sharp contrast to the East, great organs became integral in the West first to processions, interludes, and the like, but, by the middle of the twelfth century, they were admitted to the central act of divine service, the Mass.[124] A hundred years later, in the mystery plays

118 Ed. Buttimer (n. 18 above) viii. For the study of this text the annotations by Jerome Taylor in his translation (New York 1961) are fundamental.

119 Richard of Saint Victor (n. 95 above) 105-106.

120 Hugh of Saint Victor, *Didascalicon* 1.4 (n. 18 above) 11; cf. Richard of Saint Victor, *Liber exceptionum* 4.23 (n. 95 above) 111.

121 James McKinnon, "The Meaning of the Patristic Polemic against Musical Instruments," *Current Musicology* (1965) 69-82.

122 Egon Wellesz, *History of Byzantine Music and Hymnography*, ed. 2 (Oxford 1961) 105-108; 366; cf. Jean Perrot, *L'orgue de ses origines hellénistiques à la fin du XIIIe siècle* (Paris 1965) 211 n. 5, 215.

123 *Frithegodi monachi Breviloquium vitae beati Wilfredi, et Wulfstani cantoris Narratio metrica de sancto Swithuno* ed. Alistair Campbell (Zurich 1950) 69-70, lines 141-170.

124 Edmund A. Bowles, "The Organ in the Medieval Liturgical Service" *Revue belge de musicologie* 16 (1962) 13-29. Even in the West no instrument save the organ was admitted to the Mass until the fifteenth century when trumpets began to announce the elevation of the Host; *idem*, "Were Musical Instruments Used in the Liturgical Service during the Middle Ages?", *Galpin Society Journal* 10 (1957) 40-56. This would indicate that, to the West, a higher degree of mechanization involved higher spirituality.

that by that time were presented outside the churches, an organ was the indispensable accompaniment of any representation of Paradise;[125] indeed, it became almost a symbol of Heaven.

In a separate building outside Hagia Sophia, Justinian placed a clepsydra and sundials, [126] but clocks were never permitted within or on Eastern churches: to place them there would have contaminated eternity with time. As soon, however, as the mechanical clock was invented in the West, it quickly spread not only to the towers of Latin churches but also to their interiors, often as astronomical planetaria designed to demonstrate visually the godly order of the cosmos.[127] Clearly, by the later Middle Ages, Western men felt psychically compatible with machines.

And not simply in religious contexts: the *Mittelalterliche Hausbuch*, a German manuscript of *circa* 1480, shows a garden enclosed in which garlanded youths and maidens are sporting about a fountain, while at the right, quite unobscured, appears the waterpowered force-pump that operates the fountain.[128] To the Middle Ages all the arts, including the mechanic arts, were a part of the good life—*teste* Leonardo. Modern suspicion of technology is a reversion to the ambivalence of Saint Augustine.

The earliest indication that men thought advancing technology to be an aspect of Christian virtue appears in the Utrecht *Psalter*, illuminated near Rheims *circa* 830, almost certainly by a Benedictine monk. The illustration of Psalm 63 (64) shows an armed confrontation between a small body of the Righteous, led by King David himself, and a distressingly larger host of the Ungodly. In each camp a sword is being sharpened conspicuously. The Evildoers are content to use an old-fashioned whetstone. The Godly, however, are employing the first crank recorded outside China to rotate the first grindstone known anywhere.[129] Obviously the artist is telling us that technological advance is God's will.

[125] Henri Lavoix, "La musique au siècle de Saint Louis," in Gaston Raynaud, *Recueil de motets français des XII*e *et XIII*e *siècles* (Paris 1883) 2.351.

[126] E. H. Swift, *Hagia Sophia* (New York 1940) 180.

[127] *Med. Techn.* 124-125.

[128] *Das Mittelalterliche Hausbuch*, ed. H. T. Bossert and W. F. Storck (Leipzig 1912) pl. 31-32. Edgar Wind, *Pagan Mysteries in the Renaissance* (London 1958) 96, notes that renaissance emblem books place "next to the classical columns and sirens, diamonds and laurels, salamanders, porcupines and unicorns . . . the new waterwheels, bellows, catapults, rockets, bombards and barbacanes. . . . Nature is man writ large; hence if forces in nature produce miraculous effects when they are harnessed, collected and propitiously released, they can set an example for the forces in man."

[129] *The Utrecht Psalter*, ed. Ernest DeWald (Princeton, 1932) pl. 58. I am grateful to Bruce Spiegelberg of Colby College for introducing me in 1966 to the total implication of this miniature, although as early as *Speculum* 15 (1940) 153 I had noted its purely mechanical novelties.

About 1450 European intellectuals began to become aware of technological progress not as a project (as indicated above, this came in the late thirteenth century) but as an historic and happy fact, when Giovanni Tortelli, a humanist at the papal court, composed an essay listing, and rejoicing over, new inventions unknown to the ancients.[130] At almost that moment the artists of Burgundy reaffirmed the thesis of the illuminator of the Utrecht *Psalter* that an advancing technology is morally salutary: they clothed Temperance, who had displaced Charity as the chief Virtue, with major symbols of late medieval inventiveness. On her head she wore a mechanical clock, produced some 120 years earlier; in her right hand she held eyeglasses, invented, as we have noted (above, 174) in the 1280s as the greatest boon to the mature and presbyopic intellectual; she stood on a tower windmill, which first appeared in the 1390s and which was the most spectacular power machine of that era.[131] To the artists who painted those pictures, and to their patrons —clerical, aristocratic and burgher—it was axiomatic that man was serving God by serving himself in the technological mastery of nature. Because medieval men believed this, they devoted themselves in great numbers and with enthusiasm to the process of invention.

Probably there were forces other than the religious which stimulated technological progress during the Middle Ages. The tradition of illustrated calendars has been secular. Their usual pattern from Roman times until the ninth century showed the months as static personifications holding symbolic attributes. This convention continued unbroken in Byzantium. Among the Franks, however, by 830 a new form appeared which set the style for the rest of the Middle Ages in the West. The pictures now show active scenes: plowing, haying, the harvesting of grain, wood chopping, men knocking acorns from oaks so that pigs can eat them, pig slaughtering.[132] The new illustrations breathe a coerciveness towards nature which is, indeed, consonant with Christianity but which may have arisen independently. Man and nature are two things, and man is master. Technological aggression, rather than reverent coexistence, is now man's posture toward nature.

Such aggression is the normal Western Christian attitude toward nature.[133] It may be that the emergence of this stance in the Carolingian age can be

[130] Alex G. Keller, "A Renaissance Humanist Looks at 'New' Inventions: the Article 'Horologium' in Giovanni Tortelli's *De orthographia*," *Technology and Culture* 11 (1970) 345-365.

[131] See my "Iconography of *Temperantia*" (n. 97 above).

[132] Henri Stern, *Le calendrier de 354* (Paris 1953) 356-357, and his "Poésies et représentations carolingiens et byzantins des mois," *Revue archéologique* 46 (1955) 164-166.

[133] The brief effort of Saint Francis to institute a democracy of all creatures was quickly terminated; cf. my "The Historical Roots of Our Ecologic Crisis," *Science* 155 (1967) 1203-1207, reprinted in my *Machina ex Deo: Essays in the Dynamism of Western Culture* (Cambridge, Mass. 1968).

explained apart from religion. Slightly before that time a basic change in agricultural methods had occurred in Northern Europe,[134] especially between the Loire and the Rhine, the heartland of the Frankish Empire. As early as the sixth century a new heavy plow began to spread from the Slavic East. It was far more efficient than the earlier light plow, but in place of a pair of oxen it normally required as many as eight, at least in newly cleared or sticky soil. No peasant owned eight oxen. The only way to power such a plow was to organize several peasants to pool their oxen, and to distribute plowed strips to them in proportion to their contribution. Previously land had been parceled to peasants in allotments sufficient to support a family equipped with two oxen and a light plow. The assumption was subsistence farming, plus enough surplus to pay rent. Now, however, with the heavy plow and the pooling of oxen the standard of land division was not human need but rather the capacity of a new power machine to till the soil. No more profound reversal of the peasant's relation to the land can be imagined. Formerly he had been part of nature; now he became an exploiter of nature. This alteration of attitudes might be guessed from the heavy plow itself. The iconography of the new calendars confirms the change. Neither the heavy plow nor the new style of calendar was known in Byzantium. In historical analysis, even of a very religious era, we cannot credit to religion, any more than to social relations or to any other single element in culture, absolute sovereignty over every aspect of life.

Nevertheless, it can scarcely be coincidence that the miniature in the Utrecht *Psalter* (816-834) which announces the morality of technological advance appeared simultaneously with, and in the same region as, the new style of calendar illustration (shortly before 830). It can scarcely be coincidence that in 826 Louis the Pious, who, as a contemporary remarks, was always eager to introduce to his realm "illa quae ante se inusitata erant,"[135] commissioned a Venetian priest named George, who had learned his skills presumably in Byzantium, to construct the first organ built in the medieval West for secular use in his palace,[136] and that from Aachen organs spread so quickly among the churches of South Germany that in 873 Pope John VIII wrote to Freising to secure both an organ and an organist.[137] Many forces shaped the Middle Ages, but of these the most powerful was religion.

The Semitization of the Greco-Roman *oikoumene*, which was accomplished in the fourth century by the victory of Christianity, marks the most drastic change of world view, both among intellectuals and among the common people, that, before our own time, has ever been experienced by a major

[134] *Med. Techn.* 39-78.

[135] *Vita Hludovici imperatoris* 40, ed. G. H. Pertz in MGH Script. 2.629.

[136] Perrot (n. 122 above) 276 seq.

[137] *Epp. Johannis VIII*, ed. E. Caspar in MGH Epistolae Karolini aevi 5.287.

culture. In China the indigenous Confucian-Taoist symbiosis was supplemented, not displaced, by Indic Buddhism. In India itself, Vedic Brahmanism slowly broadened and diversified to engulf all rivals except the Islamic intrusion that was totally unassimilable and which produced two societies in tragic confrontation. The Muslim annexation of the southern shores of the Mediterranean had no such result because, as Dante rightly saw (*Inferno* 28.22-31), Muhammad was a Judeo-Christian schismatic, not the founder of a new religion. In the regions thus overrun, the faith of the *Koran* confirmed basic Jewish views of the nature of time, the cosmos, and destiny which had already been spread at all levels of society by Christianity, Judaism's daughter.

The historians' habit of terminating what we call ancient history with the chaos of the third and early fourth centuries in which Christianity rose to dominance is not arbitrary: it recognizes a major alteration in the cultural climate of classical civilization. During the Middle Ages, both Eastern and Western, this new religion was the essential novelty and stimulus to innovation as well as to the decay of some forms of creativity which had thrived in the Greco-Roman world. It is, therefore, not surprising that so many religious and parareligious phenomena illuminate both the high rate of technological advance in the West, and, by contrast, its slow pace in the Byzantine world.

No great religion is an entirely uniform species. As Christianity spread it accommodated to local circumstances but it likewise developed spontaneous genetic mutations which as yet cannot be explained by Lamarckian adaptation to preexisting cultural climates: to an extraordinary degree, medieval religion created the climate of its environment. Part of the fascination of the Middle Ages lies in the observation, within an essential unity extending from Greenland to the Jaxartes, of the variety of cultural subclimates that can often be interpreted according to regional variants in the temper of religion. The slight but significant differences between Greek and Latin piety in this period help not only to make historically intelligible the accomplishment of the medieval West in technology but likewise to expose the psychic foundations of our modern technology which rests on that achievement.

Department of History
University of California
Los Angeles, California 90024, U.S.A.

5

Economic Development and Aquatic Ecosystems in Medieval Europe

Richard C. Hoffmann

WHAT COULD LATE MEDIEVAL PARISIANS eating carp instead of salmon have to do with serious history? Who but local antiquarians now cares that the Po flooded Mantua and Cremona in November 1280? After all, as Robin Fleming plainly showed in a centennial issue of the *American Historical Review*, scientific historians a century ago scorned picturesque details about foodstuffs, weather, and the like beyond the bounds of scholarly study of the European Middle Ages. The Historical Discipline would treat serious issues of politics and the higher literary and artistic activities of the human mind.[1] Yet the centennial issues have their ironic touches. Not a hundred pages after Fleming's study appears, Alfred W. Crosby indicted traditional (formerly, scientific) history for neglect of the concrete and the natural in the human past. He disdained the first professionals of the American Historical Association as being "with very few exceptions, marooned on one side of the chasm between the sciences and the liberal arts" and "immured in the past few hundred years."[2] Crosby then traced the slow birth of a self-conscious environmental history back (after some lonely precursors) to the mid-twentieth-century French discovery of the *longue durée* and a subsequent generation's environmental movement.

Few now deny that whatever humans do affects their non-human surroundings, and the non-human environment, living or not, also affects all human activity. Environmental historians explore and reconstruct these mutual interactions, bridging Crosby's chasm to identify precise and changing relationships among certain people and particular ecosystems. These historical phenomena are constitutive elements in the past and present of human societies, the human species, and the

Earlier versions of this essay were presented in whole or part at the 18th International Congress of Historical Sciences in Montreal; the 8th meeting of the Fish Remains Working Group, International Congress of Archaeozoology, in Cantoblanco; the International Congress of Medieval Studies at Western Michigan University; the Institute of Ichthyology at the University of Guelph; and the Historical Research Group at York University. Research reported here has been supported over the years by the Faculty of Arts, York University, by grants for travel from the International Research and Exchanges Board and the American Philosophical Society, and by a research grant from the Social Sciences and Humanities Research Council of Canada. I am also grateful for the help and advice of Eugene Balon, Norbert Benecke, Thomas Cohen, Anton Ervynck, Dirk Heinrich, Jacob Imhof, Terryl Kinder, Elinor Melville, Hans-Hermann Müller, Jean Richard, Paolo Squatriti, Peter Stanisic, and colleagues in the Historical Research Group who, of course, are innocent of my remaining errors of fact and reasoning.

[1] Robin Fleming, "Picturesque History and the Medieval in Nineteenth-Century America," *AHR*, 100 (October 1995): 1087–89.

[2] Alfred W. Crosby, "The Past and Present of Environmental History," *AHR*, 100 (October 1995): 1181.

planet. Certainly what matters in the selection of historical data is the question being asked, and the questions of environmental history were wholly outside the ken of medievalists and others a hundred years ago. No longer.

Scholars have examined medieval woodlands, wetlands, pastures, and fields, and in recent years have even done this from environmental as well as economic perspectives. Not so for waters, and especially not for waters as habitats for living organisms.[3] This article argues that growing human population, production, and exchange in medieval Europe interacted with the communities of plants and animals in Europe's streams and lakes. After identifying natural features of Europe's aquatic ecosystems, I describe ways in which well-known medieval economic developments altered them. In those distant times, too, growth had distinct environmental impact. As, in turn, medieval Europeans perceived changes to their environment, they both adjusted their own social relations and undertook deliberate modifications to their aquatic surroundings. To find people "managing" natural resources in the Middle Ages challenges those scholars who think the very notion an invention of Renaissance engineers and intellectuals. Agents for conscious human superiority and control over nature and came, it is here proposed, from an earlier, more pragmatic, and more popular setting. Readers with better knowledge of other pasts and presents far from medieval Europe or the water's edge will recognize historical parallels in their own experience.

This essay does not promise any comprehensive environmental history of medieval inland waters, with the necessary full unraveling of mutually interlocking relations among natural ecosystems, economic production, and cultural understandings. It concentrates instead on tracing the most direct patterns of impact and response between a growing and more complex medieval economy and life in fresh waters. Of course, even now, environmental consequences hover at the edge of human awareness, so none should be surprised to find here occasionally hypothetical reconstruction from an exiguous and often quite unintentional medieval record. Scraps of historical information are patterned by known ecological relationships and processes.[4]

READERS UNFAMILIAR WITH AQUATIC BIOLOGY or European landscapes deserve some preliminary orientation to these subjects. Natural aquatic ecosystems in Europe result from the physical geography and Pleistocene glaciation of the subcontinent.[5]

[3] Contrast the abiotic hydrology of André Guillerme, *The Age of Water: The Urban Environment in the North of France, A.D. 300–1800* (College Station, Tex., 1988) [French original, 1983], with such lively examples as Oliver Rackham, *Trees and Woodland in the British Landscape*, rev. edn. (London, 1990); Robert Delort, *Le commerce des fourrures en Occident à la fin du moyen âge (vers 1300–vers 1450)*, 2 vols. (Rome, 1978); and William TeBrake, *Medieval Frontier: Culture and Economy in Rijnland* (College Station, 1985).

[4] For the Middle Ages, Crosby, "Past and Present," 1181, is naïve to think "the data environmental historians needed were to be found in government reports and scientific journals filled with . . . numbers and charts." Besides particular items noted below to make sense of the historical data, see essential background in H. B. N. Hynes, *The Ecology of Running Waters* (Toronto, 1970).

[5] In accord with social and natural differences, this article focuses on the lands of medieval Western Christendom from the Mediterranean coasts to Scandinavia. It does not range into the Balkans or eastern Slavic territories, which belonged to the distinctive sibling culture of orthodox Christendom,

Europe projects as a peninsula from the larger land mass of Eurasia; ecologists find that a peninsular situation commonly reduces the variety of all resident life-forms (species). Speaking very generally, beyond the mountainous zones along the Mediterranean and Black Sea, the subcontinent slopes to the north and west through uneven (but not abrupt) relief and becomes more humid. From Central and Western Europe north of the Alps, only the Danube flows eastward. Terrain and climate make for many flowing waters, which provide what ecologists call "lotic" habitats, but rather few and localized permanent standing waters with still-water, or "lentic," habitats.

During the half millennium or so after the collapse of Roman populations and political authority, thick communities of native plants blanketed most of the irregular and damp landscape north of the Alps. Vegetative cover on the drier and more abrupt Italian and Iberian peninsulas continued to show aftereffects from intensive human use during ancient times.[6] Some good-sized areas throughout Europe were still under dense, wild woodland, where human activity was little noticed. More terrain held open woods and brushlands subject to intermittent and extensive use by scattered human communities and their livestock. Tight growths of woody and large herbaceous plants covered the well-irrigated margins of water-courses.[7] So protected, the land absorbed precipitation and retained both its soils and the plant nutrients in them. Fed by well-filtered and slowly released surface runoff and ground water, Europe's streams ran clear, cool, and stable. Seasonal high waters inundated only natural flood plains. Even in wetlands, rooted aquatic vegetation absorbed soluble nutrients and kept the water clear. In the late fourth century, the Gallo-Roman writer Ausonius saw the Moselle "bright as water in crystal goblets," and his "vision, when it pierces this deep stream, finds the open secrets of the bottom."[8] Limpid flows tumble through other poetic Gallic land-

---

sometimes called the "Byzantine Commonwealth," and contain vastly more complex and varied fish fauna in unglaciated (Balkans) or truly continental (Russia) habitats.

[6] Vito Fumagalli, *Landscapes of Fear: Perceptions of Nature and the City in the Middle Ages*, Shayne Mitchell, trans. (Cambridge, 1994), 99–103; C. Vita-Finzi, *The Mediterranean Valleys: Geological Change in Historical Times* (Cambridge, 1969), 65–82, 91–120; J. R. McNeill, *The Mountains of the Mediterranean World: An Environmental History* (Cambridge, 1992), 16–18, 72–74, 84–86; J. Donald Hughes, *Pan's Travail: Environmental Problems of the Ancient Greeks and Romans* (Baltimore, Md., 1994), 16–18, 77–84, 190. See also note 33 below.

[7] H. Darby, "The Clearing of the Woodland in Europe," in W. L. Thomas, ed., *Man's Role in Changing the Face of the Earth* (Chicago, 1956), 183–216, is a classic survey, but for the importance of early medieval woodland, see the pioneering essay of Charles Higounet, "Les forêts de l'Europe occidentale du Ve au XIe siècle," in *Agricoltura e mondo rurale in Occidente nell'alto medioevo* (Spoleto, 1966), 343–98; and the recent examination of its physical and economic attributes by Chris Wickham, "European Forests in the Early Middle Ages: Landscape and Land Clearance," in *L'ambiente vegetale nell'alto medioevo* (Spoleto, 1990), 2: 479–545. Stable and well-vegetated riparian zones are described in G. Petts, "Forested River Corridors, a Lost Resource," in Denis Cosgrove, ed., *Water, Engineering, and Landscape: Water Control and Landscape Transformation in the Modern Period* (London, 1990), 12–34; and other medieval examples appear in Fumagalli, *Landscapes*, 99–103; Alain Derville, "Rivières et canaux du Nord/Pas-de-Calais aux époques médiévales et moderne," *Revue du Nord*, 72 (1990): 19; Richard C. Hoffmann, *Land, Liberties, and Lordship in a Late Medieval Countryside: Agrarian Structures and Change in the Duchy of Wrocław* (Philadelphia, 1989), 13–14, 100–04, and 255–56. George Lambrick, "Alluvial Archaeology of the Holocene in the Upper Thames Basin 1971–1991: A Review," in Stuart Needham and Mark G. Macklin, eds., *Alluvial Archaeology in Britain* (Oxford, 1992), 222, notes a decline in the rate of alluviation at the start of the Saxon period.

[8] D. Magnus Ausonius, *Mosella*, Charles-Marie Ternes, ed. (Paris, 1972), ll. 22–74, notably 27–28, 61–62. A century later, Sidonius Apollinaris described another transparent river and lake in *Epistolae*,

scapes all the way to 1200.[9] In Thuringian Wolfram von Eschenbach's *Titurel* (*ca.* 1210–20), Schionatulander angled for trout and grayling while wading "through the cool and clear-running brook."[10]

Life-forms in early medieval waters had survived or repopulated the very antithesis of a freshwater habitat, the continental ice sheet. Millennia earlier, more glacial ice had flowed across Western Europe from the north than down from the ice caps of its inland mountains. As the waters chilled below the tolerance levels of aquatic organisms, those unable to move into salt water died or withdrew to the southeast, the one direction where warm fresh water was accessible.[11] Cold and salt-intolerant fishes survived the Ice Age only in the refuge of the lower Danube and other rivers running from the Balkans into the Black Sea. From there, it was a slow and partial process to recolonize the greater part of peninsular Western Europe. Hence the numbers of fish species in European watersheds fall sharply along an east-west gradient.

The clear, cool waters of post-glacial Western Europe thus held relatively simple fish communities with a low diversity of native species.[12] Most were well adapted to

---

II, 2 and 9 (W. B. Anderson, ed. and trans., *Sidonius Poems and Letters*, 2 vols. [Cambridge, Mass., 1936, 1965]).

[9] Guillerme, *Age of Water*, 76–77, provides several examples. Another is the description of convalescent monks watching fish play where the upper Aube entered the gardens of early thirteenth-century Clairvaux, which is found in "Descriptio positionis seu situationis monasterii Claraevallensis," *Patrologia Latina*, J. P. Migne, ed., 221 vols. (Paris, 1844–44, 1862–64), vol. 185, cols. 569–72. Though translated as "Description of the Position and Site of the Abbey of Clairvaux" in Samuel J. Eales, ed. and trans., *Life and Works of St. Bernard, Abbot of Clairvaux*, 2 vols., 2d edn. (London, 1912), 2: 460–65, the text postdates Bernard's death. Robert Fossier, "L'essor économique de Clairvaux," in *Bernard de Clairvaux*, Commission d'Histoire de l'Ordre de Cîteaux, ed. (Paris, 1953), 3: 110–12, treats pond building at Clairvaux.

[10] *Titurel*, strophe 159, 3, Walter J. Schröder and Gisela Hollandt, eds. (Darmstadt, 1971), 617.

[11] For a fish to survive moving between fresh and salt water, its kidneys must reverse their function to maintain its vital osmotic balance. This can only be done by certain inshore marine species (called euryhaline) such as flounder and mullet, and by so-called diadromous fishes, which split their life cycles between fresh and salt water. Freshwater fishes can naturally move from one habitat to another only through a (possibly temporary) freshwater link in which both temperature and dissolved oxygen levels fall within the tolerance of the species. For basic features of fish distribution in Europe, see Johannes Lepiksaar, "Die spät- und postglaziale Faunengeschichte der Süsswasserfische im Schweden: Übersicht der subfossilen Funde und der Versuch einer faunengeschichtlichen Analyse der rezente Artareale" (typescript, Göteborg, 1983); Margaret Varley, *British Freshwater Fishes: Factors Affecting Their Distribution* (London, 1967); A. Thienemann, *Verbreitungsgeschichte der Süsswassertierwelt Europas* (Stuttgart, 1950). A recent case study of retreat and recolonization by two warm-water species, the catfish (*Silurus glanis*) and the pike perch (*Stizostedion lucioperca*), is Dirk Heinrich, "Bemerkungen zur nordwestlichen Verbreitung des Welses, *Silurus glanis* L., unter Berücksichtigung subfossiler Knochenfunde," *Zoologische Jahrbücher: Abteilung für Systematik, Ökologie, und Geographie der Tiere*, 121 (1994): 303–20.

[12] "Western Europe is exceptional in that it has a very limited freshwater fish fauna, probably because of the Pleistocene glaciations. There the Alps prevented both retreat and recolonization, and many species must have been eliminated . . . It will be appreciated, therefore, that the ecology of fishes in European rivers is possibly somewhat simpler than it is in most other continents." Hynes, *Ecology*, 337–38.

Spain and Italy have species inventories still more abbreviated than elsewhere in Europe and few distinctive autochthonous taxa. This argues against these southern regions being major glacial refuges for freshwater fishes. Instead, Alps and Pyrenees alike barred the spread of species from the rest of Europe and accentuated the peninsular effect remarked above. Historically significant native inland fisheries in Italy are based primarily on migratory fishes, which also use the Mediterranean. See William A. Dill, *Inland Fisheries of Europe* (Rome, 1990), 255; and general remarks in N. F. Prat, *et al.*, "Llobregat," in B. A. Whitton, ed., *Ecology of European Rivers* (Oxford, 1984), 542.

cold, well-oxygenated, alkaline, running-water habitats with low levels of dissolved nutrients (called "oligotrophic"). Many fishes in drainages running to the Atlantic, North Sea, and Baltic show adaptations to marine access and to conditions in the ice-front lakes that had joined these basins while the glacier withdrew slowly down-slope to the north.[13] Varieties notably important as fish biomass and for human use in watersheds from the Garonne to the Vistula were the sturgeon (*Acipenser sturio*), the shads (*Alosa alosa* and *Alosa fallax*), and the closely related families of salmon, trout (*Salmonidae*), and whitefish (*Coregonidae*).[14] Most of these fishes are anadromous, meaning they spend their adult lives more or less at sea and return to fresh water to reproduce. Two of Western Europe's three species of lampreys (*Petromyzonidae*), eel-shaped but primitive and parasitic fishes, are also anadromous. Eel (*Anguilla anguilla*), however, a species of large and growing economic importance, have the reverse habit of "catadromy," for they enter fresh water as larvae to grow and mature, and return to the sea to spawn and die. Eel, lampreys, sturgeon, and shads were also important natives of western Mediterranean watersheds, but marine migratory salmonids do not occur there. Other ubiquitous (apart from peninsular Italy and Spain), numerous, and oft-eaten native fishes were the European representatives of two circumpolar genera, the perch (*Perca fluviatilis*), and the pike (*Esox lucius*). About 1080, the monk Ulrich compiled a dictionary of the sign language used at Cluny, then Western Christendom's most respected monastery, during times of compulsory silence. His section on foods named only six fishes, but five of them were from fresh water: salmon, trout, pike, eel, and lamprey.[15]

Other parts of the Old World have many representatives of the huge family of carp-like fishes, the *Cyprinidae*, which commonly favor warm and lentic habitats. By comparison, however, western European waters naturally held rather few members of this family; and those present, such as the barbel (*Barbus barbus*), bream (*Abramis brama*), roach (*Rutilus rutilus*), minnow (*Phoxinus phoxinus*), or gudgeon (*Gobio gobio*), were unusually adapted to cool and/or lotic conditions. Only barbel and gudgeon, two cyprinids especially suited to swiftly flowing middle reaches of

[13] Generally, for what follows, see Alwyne Wheeler, *The Fishes of the British Isles and North-West Europe* (East Lansing, Mich., 1969); and M. Blanc, *et al.*, *European Inland Water Fish: A Multilingual Catalogue* (London, 1971), and works cited in note 11 above.

[14] Shared characteristics of physiology (streamlined form, light color), habitat preferences (well-oxygenated water in main river channels, lakes, or the sea), and behavior (long-distance migration to spawn in open water over clean and unvegetated substrate) place all these taxa into an ecological assemblage called "white fish" in the analytical scheme introduced by Robin L. Welcomme and further articulated in Henry J. Regier, *et al.*, "Rehabilitation of Degraded River Ecosystems," in Douglas P. Dodge, ed., *Proceedings of the International Large River Symposium* (Ottawa, 1989), 93–96. In contrast, species they call "grey fish" are more laterally compressed, darker colored fishes of backwaters or main channel fringes, which can tolerate lower oxygen levels and move laterally into vegetated edges along the flood plain to reproduce. In temperate Europe, pike, several members of the perch family, and some members of the carp family—chub, dace, nose, etc.—may be considered "grey fish." "Black fish" have compressed or soft and elongated bodies of very dark color; they live in quiet, heavily vegetated flood-plain bodies of water, where they can survive very low oxygen levels and often guard complex nests. Western Europe has few prototypical "black fish," but the maturing eel in fresh water, tench, crucian carp, and carp have many "black" characteristics. Each association responds differently to particular alterations to the aquatic ecosystem. These correspondences will be noted below.

[15] Ulrich of Cluny, "Consuetudines Cluniacensis," II.4 (*Patrologia Latina*, vol. 149, col. 703). Note the absence of species preferring warm, still waters. Cluny, on a tributary of the Saône in southern Burgundy, is some 300 kilometers from salt water.

streams, joined perch, pike, salmon, and eel in the catches that twelfth-century sporting cleric Gui of Bazoches made in northern French waters.[16]

An ecological principle emphasizes the importance of "edge" between two adjoining habitats as affording access to resources in both. Rich populations of fishes in Europe's streams attracted many air-breathing predators, birds, mammals, and humans, to the stable boundaries between water and land.[17] Seventh-century Irish monk Gall and his Swabian deacon Hiltibod lived and fished on the shore of the Bodensee. Gall sought the wilderness up the Steinach and settled where they saw and caught many fish. In seeking one meal for visitors, Gall had help from a pair of otters that also fished that pool.[18] Contemporary proto-Polish fishers clustered along their streams in settlements called "Fish Eaters" (*Rybejady*). What they ate was what they caught. Archaeologists still find in food refuse from the unfortified habitation sites of early medieval peasants all across the north European plain the remains of those fishes that local waters supplied in abundance.[19] To this direct subsistence fishery, even the earliest Middle Ages had added indirect subsistence consumption by elite non-fishers.[20] Servants built a fish trap in the

[16] Epistola 21, ll. 70–88 (Herbert Adolfsson, ed., *Liber epistularum Guidonis de Basochis* [Stockholm, 1969], 97–98). Gui's fishing is discussed in Richard C. Hoffmann, "Fishing for Sport in Medieval Europe: New Evidence," *Speculum*, 60 (1985): 886–87.

[17] Compare Randall F. Schalk, "The Structure of an Anadromous Fish Resource," in L. R. Binford, ed., *For Theory Building in Archaeology* (New York, 1977), 207–49.

[18] Walafrid Strabo, *Vita Galli*, lib. 1, 6–7, 9–12, 28; *Vita Galli confessoris triplex*, Bruno Krusch, ed. in *Monumenta Germaniae Historica* (hereafter, *MGH*), *Scriptores rerum Merovingicarum*, Vol. 4, 229–337 (Hanover, 1902); and *The Life of St. Gall*, Maud Joynt, ed. and trans. (London, 1927). Monks at Stavelot on the Meuse then operated their own fish weir, too ("Miracula S. Remacli," *Acta Sanctorum*, Sept., I, 701).

[19] Jan Żak, "Der Fischfang in der Wirtschaft der protopolnischen Stämme des 6. bis 8. Jahrhunderts," *Offa: Berichte und Mitteilungen*, 37 (1980): 197–200. For examples of fish eaten at early medieval non-elite riparian sites, see, among others, Zygmunt Chełkowski, "Szczątki ryb w materiale wykopaliskowym z osady wszesnośredniowiecznej Szczecin-Mścięcino," *Materiały Zachodniopomorskie*, 5 (1959): 165–86, and tables; and "Wczesnośredniowieczne pozostałości ryb z Kamienia Pomorskiego," *Materiały Zachodniopomorskie*, 6 (1960): 245–64; Michał Iwaszkiewicz, "Szczątki rybie z miejscowości Szeligi, pow. Płock," in W. Szymański, ed., *Szeligi pod Płockiem na początku wczesnego średniowiecza* (Wrocław, 1967), 360; Norbert Benecke, "Die Fischreste aus den slawischen Inselsiedelungen in der Lieps und im Tollensesee," in V. Schmidt, ed., *Lieps: Eine slawische Siedlungskammer am Südende des Tollensesees* (Berlin, 1984), 118–21; and Benecke, "Die Fischreste aus einer frühmittelalterlichen Siedlung bei Menzlin, Kreis Anklam," *Bodendenkmalpflege in Mecklenburg*, Jahrbuch 1986, 225–39; Wietske Prummel, *Early Medieval Dorestad, an Archaeozoological Study* (Amersfoort, 1983), 11–13, 233–36; Jenny Coy, "Fish Bones," in G. G. Astill and S. J. Lobb, "Roman and Saxon Deposits at Wraysbury," *The Archaeological Journal*, 146 (1989): 118–20, and microfiche M1/68–74. Several of these sites also had early medieval fishing gear.

[20] Following the combined precedents of B. H. Slicher van Bath, *The Agrarian History of Western Europe A.D. 500–1850*, Olive Ordish, trans. (New York, 1963), 24; Andres von Brandt, *Fish Catching Methods of the World*, 3d edn. rev. (Farnham, Surrey, 1984), 3–4; and Alan B. McCullough, *The Commercial Fishery of the Canadian Great Lakes* (Ottawa, 1989), 7, I distinguish between subsistence, commercial, and recreational fisheries. A subsistence fishery is one in which fish are caught for consumption by the fisher and his or her household (direct subsistence) or by the fisher's master, lord, or employer (indirect subsistence) without intervention of a market. A commercial fishery is one in which fish are caught for sale, whether to the immediate consumer or through intermediaries. As will be noted, in some historical circumstances the same catch could result in transfers of fish for both indirect subsistence and sale. A commercial fishery with production units of a household or small crew may further be termed an artisanal as opposed to an industrial fishery. A recreational (sport) fishery is one in which fish are caught for pleasure (though they may then be consumed). Recreational fishing as such, though surely practiced in medieval Europe (see Hoffmann, "Fishing for Sport"), is not especially germane here. Note that the classification of fisheries is by economic purpose and bears no necessary or *a priori* relation to techniques of capture or target species.

Subsistence fishing? St. Peter is depicted as a successful angler in a fragment from an anonymous English Gospel lectionary done in the style of the Canterbury school about 1000 A.D. Collection of the J. Paul Getty Musuem, Malibu, California, MS. 9 (85. MS. 79), fol. 2v. Used with permission.

Meuse for eighth-century Bishop Hubert of Tongres-Maastricht, and fishers on the Mincio near Mantua in 813 were obliged to turn half of their catch over to Nonantola Abbey.[21] By that time, Western Christians agreed that when religious custom forbade eating meat, only fish was an acceptable substitute.[22]

OF COURSE, MEDIEVAL EUROPE did not remain, if it had ever been, a simple society sustained by the gathered bounty of local nature. Modern generations of historians have learned to recognize characteristic patterns of medieval economic growth. Put simply, some time in the tenth century, human numbers began to increase, and so with them did land under the plow for production of cereal grains. The medieval agricultural sector improved its equipment and farming methods. Higher productivity and more available surpluses permitted exponential expansion of a hitherto tiny and luxury-dependent exchange sector, and this transformed Europe's minuscule groupings of non-agricultural administrators and consumers into new and dynamic urban centers, the nodes of a market economy. Even when the demographic and agrarian upsurge petered out into stagnation and decline in the fourteenth century, commercial specialization and trading networks continued to thicken and to infiltrate formerly subsistence activities.

What had this increase in economic activity to do with aquatic life? Replacement of woodlands with intensified arable agriculture changed basic hydrological conditions, both directly and by proliferation of water-powered grain mills. Rising human populations and their concentration into towns added nutrients and contaminants to water courses, while the demand for fish as food soared. As these effects accumulated in each region, freshwater fisheries visibly came under stress.[23]

One familiar and basic change in the medieval economy needs mere re-articulation in ecological terms: growing reliance on cereal food meant permanent plowed fields replaced woodland from central Spain to Sweden and from Wales to Poland.[24] Forests slow runoff and maintain steady stream flow, and the clearance of woodlands makes the pattern of stream discharge more irregular. Rain and

21 "Vita Hugberti episcopi Traiectensis," in *MGH, Scriptores rerum Merovingicarum*, Vol. 6 (Hanover, 1913), 487–88; Giuseppe Mira, *La pesca nel medioevo nelle acque interne italiane* (Milano, 1937), 5. The interest in Alpine lake fisheries of monasteries at Tegernsee and Mondsee and of the archbishopric of Salzburg is well documented before 850 ("Passio Quirini Tegernseensis," Bruno Krusch, ed. in *MGH, Scriptores rerum Merovingicarum*, Vol. 3 [Hanover, 1896], 12; Willibald Hauthaler, ed., *Salzburger Urkundenbuch*, Vol. 1 [Salzburg, 1910], 907 and 915).

22 "Carême," *Dictionnaire de theologie catholique*, Vol. 1 (Paris, 1908), 1742–43; Hannelore Zug Tucci, "Il mondo medievale dei pesci tra realta' e immaginazione," in *L'uomo di fronte al mondo animale nell'alto Medio Evo* (Spoleto, 1985), 294–301.

23 In Regier, "Rehabilitation," 87–88 (and see works there cited), fishery ecologists argue that "conventional exploitative development" damages aquatic ecosystems through a sequence and synergy of excessive harvests, damming, destructive cultural practices, organic and toxic pollution, and urbanization without regard for environmental effects. Their ecosystem model comes primarily from comparative study of more or less modified river systems in the late twentieth century. The deeper historical record will confirm it in general but suggests greater nuance and different specific processes.

24 Darby, "Clearing"; Walther Maas, *Les moines-défricheurs: Etudes sur les transformations du paysage au Moyen Age aux confins de la Champagne et de la Lorraine* (Moulins, 1944), 22–23; Jean-Marie Jenn, "Défrichments cisterciens dans la région de Colmar au douzième siècle," *Annuaire de la Société historique et littéraire de Colmar*, 19 (1969–70), 42–48; Werner Rösener, *Bauern im Mittelalter* (Munich, 1985), 40–54, 118–33; Rackham, *Trees and Woodland*, 39–90; Helmut Jäger, *Einführung in die Umweltsgeschichte* (Darmstadt, 1994), 81–84.

meltwaters run more quickly off farmland. Larger and faster runoff exerts greater erosive force on stream beds and channels, and then falling water levels leave a contracted stream and deposits of eroded materials. One astute observer in late thirteenth-century Alsace noted how clearance of the Vosges in his own lifetime had caused much more rapid and dangerous runoff.[25] Modern scholars detect the same sequence of medieval deforestation and flooding in the Po basin and in central Poland.[26] Biologists now also know that unstable flow regimes create difficult habitats for fishes. Those living in running water must expend more energy during floods. They lose eggs and young to winter floods and suffer high mortalities when small streams dry up in summer. Species that spawn in flooded margins are adapted to consistent seasonal patterns of rising and falling water, so instability disrupts their reproductive behavior.[27]

Soil erosion and the resulting alluvial deposition is becoming a well-documented consequence of medieval agricultural expansion. First, the natural vegetative cover was removed. Then, characteristic medieval farming practices disrupted the soil surface and its structure. Plowmen drove long straight furrows or pulverized the soil to prepare it for the autumn sowing of winter grains. Bare fallow stripped all plants from a third or half of arable almost all year. Large open fields stopped neither wind nor water nor the downward creep of the soil itself. Topsoil thus flowed to the watercourses, especially during heavy winter rains and snowmelt.[28] In the Leine valley of Saxony, large sediments from eroded topsoil overlain with former subsoil yield C_{14} dates between the 790s and 850s; the Frankish conqueror Charlemagne had promoted new rural settlements and clearances there during the 780s and 790s.[29] In the upper Thames basin, valley erosion and deposition on flood plains reached an all-time high in late Saxon and early Norman times. Siltation in

[25] Writing around 1300, a Colmar Dominican compared his own times with the less developed Alsace his fellow friars had entered a century before: "Streams and rivers were then not so large as now, because the roots of trees held back in the mountains for a time the flow of [melting] snow and cloudbursts." P. Jaffé, ed., "De rebus Alsaticis ineuntis saeculi XIII," in *MGH, Scriptorum*, Vol. 17 (Hanover, 1861), 236.

[26] Fumagalli, *Landscapes*, 110–21. T. Dunin-Wąsowicz, "Natural Environment and Human Settlement over the Central European Lowland in the 13th Century," in Peter Brimblecombe and Christian Pfister, eds., *The Silent Countdown: Essays in European Environmental History* (Berlin, 1990), 94–95, 102, refers to "great changes in the hydrographic balance, which reached proportions of a natural disaster during the course of the 13th century." In the lower Harz, wet-season floods and dry-season dewatering of streams and springs followed the cutting of forests to fuel a mining and iron-working industry that grew from the late 1200s to 1400s. M. Linke, "Medieval Deserted Fields and Deserted Villages in the Lower Harz Mountains—An Interim Report," in B. K. Roberts and R. E. Glasscock, eds., *Villages, Fields and Frontiers: Studies in European Rural Settlement in the Medieval and Early Modern Periods* (Oxford, 1983), 296, 301.

[27] Compare Hynes, *Ecology*, 327–32, and the habits ascribed to "white fish" and "grey fish" by Regier, "Rehabilitation," 93–96.

[28] A point emphasized in both J. Vogt, "Aspects of Historical Soil Erosion in Western Europe," in Brimblecombe and Pfister, *Silent Countdown*, 86–88, and Martin Bell, "Archaeology under Alluvium: Human Agency and Environmental Process; Some Concluding Thoughts," in Needham and Macklin, *Alluvial Archaeology*, 272.

[29] H.-J. Nitz, "Feudal Woodland Colonization as a Strategy of the Carolingian Empire in the Conquest of Saxony: Reconstruction of the Spatial Patterns of Expansion and Colonist Settlement Morphology in the Leine-Weser Region," in Roberts and Glasscock, *Villages, Fields and Frontiers*, 178. Linke, "Medieval Deserted Fields," 296, finds similar evidence in soil profiles from the bottom of slopes on abandoned medieval fields in the Lower Harz and especially blames the bare winter fallow of a three-course rotation. A more general view of the process is taken in Wickham, "European Forests," 534, and works there cited.

backwaters along the Lys and Scarpe in Artois and Hainault is mentioned during the late 1200s.[30] Grain-growing monastic granges established about 1300 on the once-wooded shores and valley of the Lac d'Annecy in Savoy were followed by an increased rate of lake-bottom sedimentation. Today, we find that these deposits contain pollens from cultivars and field weeds and analytic features indicative of topsoil rather than channel erosion.[31] Further downstream, the Oude Rijn mouth of the Rhine in Holland silted shut by the eleventh century, and the one-time bay between Gdańsk and Elbląg was filled between the thirteenth and sixteenth centuries by the expanding delta of the Vistula.[32] Long, unavailing struggles of Ravenna against the filling of the Po delta and of Bruges against the plugging of the Zwin are historical commonplaces.[33] Such heavy silt loads make water more often turbid, reduce the penetration of light, and can smother organisms living in weed or gravel beds. Like the more dramatic alternation of floods and low water, the effects favor certain species over others.

To process the new grain supplies, a little-used late antique invention, the watermill, spread rapidly across the medieval landscape. From perhaps two hundred in King Alfred's England, they multiplied to 5,624 in the Domesday Book of 1085. In Poitou, Berry, Burgundy, and Lorraine, mills proliferated from the tenth century through the twelfth. On the Aube, where fourteen mills were recorded in the eleventh century, sixty-two could be counted in the twelfth century and almost two hundred in the early thirteenth. Then and later, their construction became a normal part of rural development in the Egerland and in central Silesia.[34] As one modern student summed it up,

[30] Lambrick, "Alluvial Archaeology," 222; Derville, "Rivières et canaux," 11, 15, 19.

[31] Reported in F. Oldfield and R. L. Clark, "Environmental History—The Environmental Evidence," in Brimblecombe and Pfister, *Silent Countdown*, 152–55, and works there cited.

[32] TeBrake, *Medieval Frontier*, 70, 147–48; J. Filuk, "Biologiczno-rybacka charakterystyka ichtiofauny zalewu wiślanego na tle badań paleoichtiologicznych, historycznych i wspólczesnych," *Pomorania antiqua*, 2 (1968): 146–48.

[33] Large areas in peninsular Italy and other parts of the classical Mediterranean had, however, already suffered permanent damage from deforestation, overgrazing, and erosion followed by coastal deposition in Roman times (Hughes, *Pan's Travail*, 90, 190), so further changes during the Middle Ages (as, for instance, at the mouth of the Tiber) were less dramatic there.

[34] For a major overview, see Terry S. Reynolds, *Stronger Than a Hundred Men: A History of the Vertical Water Wheel* (Baltimore, Md., 1983), 47–69. Regional discussions include Jean Richard, "Les étangs et le commerce du poisson en Bourgogne," in *L'eau en Bourgogne* (Dijon, 1986), 98–99; Guy Devailly, *Le Berry du Xe siècle au milieu du XIIIe: Etude politique, religieuse, sociale et économique* (Paris, 1973), 226–27; Jacques Brien, "Le développement de l'ordre cistercien en Poitou aux XIIème siècle et dans la prèmiere moitie du XIIIème siècle: Essai sur l'emplacement des monastères cisterciens" (Poitiers, 1954), 6; Maas, *Moines-défricheurs*, 71–74; Hans Muggenthaler, *Kolonisatorische und wirtschaftliche Tätigkeit eines deutschen Zisterzienserklosters im XII. und XIII. Jahrhundert* (Munich, 1924), 129–31; Willy Cnopf, *Die Entwicklung und wirtschaftliche Bedeutung der Teichwirtschaft in Mittelfranken* (Dissertation Erlangen, 1926), 9–23; Hoffmann, *Land, Liberties, and Lordship*, 261–62; Maria Dembińska, *Przetwórstwo zbożowe w Polsce średniowiecznej (X–XIV wiek)* (Warsaw, 1973), 63–175; Zofia Podwińska, "Rozmieszczenie wodnych młyno zbożowych w Małopolsce w XV wieku," *Kwartalnik Historii Kultury Materialnej*, 18 (1970): 373–402; Richard Holt, *The Mills of Medieval England* (Oxford, 1988), 107–44; John Langdon, "Lordship and Peasant Consumerism in the Milling Industry of Early Fourteenth-Century England," *Past and Present*, 145 (November 1994): 3–46; John Muendel, "The Grain Mills of Pistoia in 1350," *Bollettino Storico Pistoiese*, 74 (1972): 39–64; and "The Distribution of Mills in the Florentine Countryside during the Late Middle Ages," in J. Ambrose Raftis, ed., *Pathways to Medieval Peasants* (Toronto, 1981), 83–115.

Watermill and fish traps on the Lincolnshire estate of Sir Geoffrey Luttrell, *circa* 1330. A marginal illustration in the Luttrell Psalter, British Library, London, Additional Mss. 42130, fol. 181r. Used with permission.

> By the close of the Middle Ages watermills were in use on streams of every type. They dammed up the rivers of medieval man; they were on the banks of his brooks and creeks, in the middle of his rivers, under his bridges, and along his coastlines. They impeded navigation and created streams (in the form of mill races and power canals) and lakes (in the form of storage reservoirs behind waterpower dams) where none had existed before.[35]

In fact, the streams had existed but not the ponds. Medieval watermills commonly powered their overshot wheels by using a dam or weir to concentrate the falling water and pond a reserve supply of it. Medieval millwrights learned to do this on ever larger rivers. Dams blocked running water and created still water. As moving water slows, it drops the solids it has carried in suspension. On the Derwent in the English Midlands, two meters of gravel and silt alluvium eventually covered a one-meter timber mill dam, gate, and raceway, which have been dated by dendrochronology to the mid-twelfth century.[36] The broad surfaces of standing waters absorb more solar energy. This both warms the water and further improves conditions for the growth of rooted plants. Twelfth-century Picard charters and conveyances show slower, deeper, and weedier waters backing up behind mill dams and weirs all along the Scarpe, the Oise, and the Somme.[37] Ubiquitous watermills

[35] Reynolds, *Stronger Than a Hundred Men*, 69.

[36] Patrick Clay, "A Norman Mill Dam at Hemington Fields, Castle Donington, Leicestershire," in Needham and Macklin, *Alluvial Archaeology*, 163–68, and works there cited. Compare Zbigniew Bagniewski and Piotr Kubów, "Średniowieczny młyn wody z Ptakowic na Dolnynm Śląsku," *Kwartalnik Historii Kultury Materialnej*, 25 (1977): 3–30; and other medieval Polish mills described in Dembińska, *Przetwórstwo zbożowe*, 90–135. Luisa Chiappa Mauri, *I mulini a acqua nel Milanese (secoli X–XV)* (Rome, 1984), 152–75, emphasizes an early medieval replacement of horizontal with vertical wheels; and Germain Sicard, *Les moulins de Toulouse au Moyen Age* (Paris, 1953), 38–43, documents a shift from mills on anchored rafts to land-based mills with dams or weirs.

[37] Robert Fossier, *La terre et les hommes en Picardie jusqu'à la fin du XIIIe siècle* (Paris, 1968), 366–68, 380–89, 395–97.

formed and multiplied a new kind of aquatic habitat to be probed more deeply below.

Mills had immediate effects on existing watercourses and their native fish populations, for they blocked the movement of migratory fish. Like the concentrations at natural barriers, those at dams and weirs offered fishers profitable access to migratory species. Even deep in central Saxony, operation of a salmon trap at the mill dam at Lauenheim on the River Zschopau fueled a century of dispute (1293–1393) between Altzelle Abbey and the von Steinbach family.[38] Possession of mills was associated with the right to take eel on the Duero in Castile, the Garonne near Toulouse, the Meuse around Liege, and on the Lincolnshire estate that Sir Geoffrey Luttrell had depicted in his early fourteenth-century psalter.[39] When Henry III celebrated Christmas at Clarendon Palace in 1240, his purveyors laid in stores of shad, salmon, lamprey, and herring.[40] Only the coastal herring departs from the anadromous pattern of supply.

But impassable barrier dams kept migratory species from vital spawning habitats. Blocked runs of fish—were they trout or shad?—ascending the Sarca from Lake Garda in 1210 caused the bishop of Trento, who held sovereign fishing rights in that county, to require the removal of mill dams at Arco.[41] For the sake of the salmon, a Scottish statute of 1214 required all dams to be fitted with an opening and all barrier nets to be lifted every Saturday.[42] About 1470, a Rhineland abbot was complaining that since construction of a new dam three years earlier on the Dhünn (a Rhine tributary) "neither salmon nor [other] fish can go up."[43] Dikes built in the Rhine delta during the eleventh and twelfth centuries to drain marshes for agricultural settlement may have caused major declines in the sturgeon population.[44] These losses were especially important because, ecologists agree, the

[38] Eduard Beyer, *Das Cistercienser-Stift und Kloster Alt-Zelle in dem Bisthum Meissen* (Dresden, 1855), charters no. 216, 510, 518. Salmon fishing at mills in Denmark is mentioned in Brian P. McGuire, *The Cistercians in Denmark: Their Attitudes, Roles, and Functions in Medieval Society* (Kalamazoo, Mich., 1982), 140; and at mills in lower Normandy in Xavier Halard, "La pêche du saumon en Normandie du XIe au XVe siècle," *Journal of Medieval History*, 9 (1983): 175, 177.

[39] Javier Perez-Embid Wamba, *El cister en Castilla y Leon: Monacato y dominios rurales (siglos XII–XV)* ([Salamanca?], 1986), 137–38, 178–79; Mireille Mousnier, *L'Abbaye de Grandselve et sa place dans la société et l'économie méridionales XIIe–début XIVe siècles*, Thèse présentée pour l'obtention du Doctorat de IIIe cycle, Université de Toulouse le Mirail (Toulouse, 1982), 189–90; Sicard, *Les moulins de Toulouse*, 118–28; Denise Van Derveeghe, *Le domaine du Val Saint-Lambert de 1202 à 1387* (Paris, 1955), 63–66; *The Luttrell Psalter* [facsimile] (London, 1932), fol. 181r. Further examples include Isabel Alfonso Anton, *La colonización cisterciense en la meseta del Duero: El dominio de Moreruela (siglos XII–XIV)* (Zamora, 1986), 176–77; Brien, "Le développement," 43–44, Appendix 4; and the discussion of mills, eel, and salmon in H. C. Darby, *Domesday England* (Cambridge, 1977), 279–85.

[40] T. B. James, A. M. Robinson, *et al.*, *Clarendon Palace: The History and Archaeology of a Medieval Palace and Hunting Lodge near Salisbury, Wiltshire* (London, 1988), 30–31.

[41] Otto Stolz, *Geschichtskunde der Gewässer Tirols* (Innsbruck, 1936), 346.

[42] John Skene, *Regiam majestatem: The Auld Lawes and Constitutions of Scotland* [also known as *Veteres Leges Scotiae*] (Edinburgh, 1774), 335, translated the statute of Alexander II: "the streame of the water shall be in all parts swa free, that ane swine of the age of three zears, well feed, may turn himself within the streame, round about, swa that his snowt nor taill sall not touch the bank of the water" and noted its reenactment under James III (1460–88). Thomas Thomson and C. Innes, eds., *The Acts of the Parliaments of Scotland*, Vol. 1: *A.D. M.C.XXIV.–A.D. M.CCCC.XXII.* (Edinburgh, 1844), 374 red, attributed a Latin text of the same statute to William I (1165–1214).

[43] "dar enkan noch laeis noch vijsch up gegayn": Hans Mosler, ed., *Urkundenbuch der Abtei Altenberg*, Vol. 2: *1400–1893* (Düsseldorf, 1955), no. 206.

[44] R. Boddeke, *Vissen en vissen: Ervaringen van een visserijbioloog en sportvisser* (Amsterdam, 1971), 169–76.

spawning environment in fresh water determines the productivity and survival of anadromous fish.[45]

TURNING FROM RURAL DEVELOPMENT to other aspects of the medieval economy, human population growth and urbanization in the typically organic-based pre-industrial resource system affected both water chemistry and hydrological conditions for aquatic life.

Waste from more and larger concentrations of people, from rural monasteries to towns of twenty, or even fifty, thousand, necessarily increased the nutrient load—soluble nitrates—in watercourses.[46] The several hundred monks and lay brethren at early thirteenth-century Clairvaux were served by a diversion of the Aube, which ran through gardens, mills, brewery, fulling mill, tannery, laundry, and latrines before rejoining the main stream.[47] Long rows of latrines over channels running back into the local stream were the norm, since, at latest, the eleventh century among all monastic orders and, where location permitted, in secular palaces. During one famous incident in 1184, the hall floor in the palace of the archbishop of Mainz at Erfurt collapsed and pitched members of the imperial court into underlying cesspits (*cloaca*) through which the River Gera flowed.[48] Local streams likewise received the human (and animal) waste of towns, whether by runoff from street disposal (even with intentional diversions to flush gutters as at Goslar and Strasbourg), by purposely emptying the contents of cesspits into flowing water below the town (Cologne), or by direct siting of latrines over watercourses (Rouen, Nuremberg).[49] Robert Guillerme has argued that organic acid-based and alkaline-based processes used by early medieval textile and leather crafts caused

[45] Schalk, "Structure," 222–24. Anadromous populations not only need access to suitable spawning habitat, they characteristically adapt to specific flow regimes in both the main river and the spawning tributary, and form discrete and separate spawning stocks, even within individual river systems. When environments are changed—as by deforestation or barriers—survival of the stock will depend on natural variation in the gene pool providing some individuals more suited to the new regime. Their spawning success will, over time, modify the genetic composition and the behavior pattern of the whole surviving population. John E. Thorpe and L. Stradmeyer, "Management Examples: The Atlantic Salmon," in Thorpe, *et al.*, *Conservation of Fish and Shellfish Resources: Managing Diversity* (London, 1995), 83–85, 94. To the extent that medieval dams and weirs (always low by modern hydroelectric or flood-control standards) failed fully to block the larger streams and tributaries, salmon in particular would shift their spawning downstream in the watershed. A later observer (for example, Jäger, *Einführung*, 200–04) might miss the empty highest tributaries, see some still-extensive early modern runs, remain unaware of a half-millennium of adaptation to pre-industrial levels of human development, and think the situation still "natural."

[46] Klaus Grewe, "Wasserversorgung und -entsorgung im Mittelalter—Ein technikgeschichtlicher Überblick," in *Die Wasserversorgung im Mittelalter*, Klaus Grewe, ed., for the Frontinusgesellschaft (Mainz, 1991), 75, cites nineteenth-century calculations of an annual pre-industrial per-capita output of 34 kilograms of feces and 428 kilograms of urine, totaling 462 kilograms of nitrogen-rich excrement.

[47] "Descriptio . . . Claraevallensis." The fate of eventual effluent is not treated in Meredith Lillich's classic study, "Cleanliness with Godliness: A Discussion of Medieval Monastic Plumbing," in Benoît Chauvin, ed., *Mélanges à la mémoire du Père Anselme Dimier*, Vol. 3 (part 5) (Arbois, 1982), 123–49.

[48] Grewe, "Wasserversorgung," 74–75. The same collection [see note 46] has more information in contributions by Clemens Kosch, "Wasserbaueinrichtungen in hochmittelalterlichen Konventenanlagen Mitteleuropas," notably 96, 110–12, and 134–35, and by Paul Benoit and Monique Wabont, "Mittelalterliche Wasserversorgung in Frankreich: Eine Fallstudie; Die Zisterzienser," esp. 195, 204, and 207–16, which include orders besides the Cistercians.

[49] Grewe, "Wasserversorgung," 75–80; Guillerme, *Age of Water*, 105–07.

The sixty-seat latrine (two back-to-back rows of thirty), at Royaumont Abbey (Seine-et-Oise, France), viewed from below. For five hundred years, human wastes drained through this thirteenth-century structure into the River Oise. Photograph by Terryl Kinder. Used with permission.

"the precipitation of solid organic materials in water which river currents carried beyond city limits."[50]

And what was downstream? From the thirteenth through the sixteenth centuries, a lagoon-like shoreline on the Bodensee at Konstanz was filled with town wastes. Archaeological study of plant remains there shows disappearance of species native to clean waters and massive appearance of a filamentous algae associated with an excess of dissolved nutrients.[51] By the early 1400s, Parisian effluent was making the Seine below town "infectée et corrumpue" every summer.[52] These are symptoms of aquatic ecosystems under stress. More immediate and visible toxic effects came from slaughtering livestock at the waterside or extracting fibers from flax and hemp by wet decomposition ("retting").[53]

Activities in the urban and commercial sector further impeded the free flow of water. Since the eleventh century, castles and towns had diverted rivers to fill defensive moats; this stratagem gained popularity in the later Middle Ages.[54] An accessible market for fuel drove extensive peat-digging, which created the Norfolk Broads and smaller but more numerous pools called *plassen* in the Netherlands.[55] And between the eleventh and fourteenth centuries, still more weirs, dams, and ponds were built to power new industrial operations such as malting, fulling cloth, metal-working (hammers and bellows), sawmills, and paper making.[56]

The type and scale of physical and chemical changes that medieval economic development brought to European inland waters most directly and heavily affected small and medium-sized watercourses. Brooks, streams, and small rivers are more closely tied than are large rivers to their immediate terrestrial environments. Smaller size, high ratio of surface area to volume, and abundance in the landscape mean that human actions such as removal of bankside vegetation, local ditching, diversion, or embankment, small mill ponds and dams, and effluents from concentrations of livestock or people have profound local impact, removing the whole waterway from its natural form and sources of energy. Large rivers, in contrast, are linked to their surroundings through their multiple channels and extensive floodplains, so simple and local changes in shoreline conditions have less effect on

[50] Guillerme, *Age of Water*, 97–100.

[51] Hansjörg Küster, "Mittelalterliche Eingriffe in Naturräume des Voralpenlandes," in Bernd Herrmann, ed., *Umwelt in der Geschichte: Beiträge zur Umweltgeschichte* (Göttingen, 1989), 72. Regier, "Rehabilitation," 88, specifies this very botanical phenomenon as characteristic of an aquatic ecosystem under stress. Note further that where current speed and substrate prevent establishment of rooted aquatic vegetation, increased nitrate loads encourage suspended algae to grow and add more turbidity.

[52] As described in an ordinance against waste disposal from 1415 cited from François A. Isambert, *et al.*, eds., *Recueil général des anciennes lois françaises depuis l'an 420 jusqu'à la Révolution de 1789*, Vol. 8 (Paris, 1822), 565f, cap. 683, by Ilja Mieck, "Die Anfänge der Umweltschutzgesetzgebung in Frankreich," *Francia*, 9 (1981): 332. Later legislation (335–36) dealt in particular with tanners' and potters' wastes.

[53] Guillerme, *Age of Water*, 152; Jean Gimpel, *The Medieval Machine: The Industrial Revolution of the Middle Ages* (New York, 1976), 85–87; Günter Heine, "Umweltbezogenes Recht im Mittelalter," in Herrmann, *Umwelt in der Geschichte*, 123.

[54] Guillerme, *Age of Water*, 47–50, 118–31.

[55] J. M. Lambert, *et al.*, *The Making of the Broads: A Reconsideration of Their Origin in the Light of New Evidence* (London, 1961); G. J. Borger, "Draining—Digging—Dredging: The Creation of a New Landscape in the Peat Areas of the Low Countries," in J. T. A. Verhoeven, ed., *Fens and Bogs in the Netherlands: Vegetation, History, Nutrient Dynamics and Conservation* (Dordrecht, 1992), 153–57.

[56] Reynolds, *Stronger Than a Hundred Men*, 69–97.

them.[57] Hence the impact of pre-industrial economic development differed in degree and kind from that of industrial development. Yet the finding should not be oversimplified. The much-studied Rhine and its major tributaries, for instance, are said to have suffered little from human activity before channelizing and embanking in the early nineteenth century began a total degradation.[58] But most studies of major European rivers start from a present and retrospective standpoint with little deeper historical knowledge or awareness. The evidence of medieval landscape change is overwhelming. Watersheds are systemic continua: what enters at the top flows all the way down. Besides dams cutting off what had once been the highest spawning sites, we must recognize medieval deforestation and erosion as principal causes of more erratic flow regimes and contributors of material to the many mainstream sandbars and islands known from early modern records.

THE MOST DIRECT HUMAN IMPACT on freshwater ecosystems was the demand for fish as food. Medieval European awareness of fish as a nutritionally desirable substitute or supplement for meat is manifest in monastic customaries, in recipe collections and dietary treatises, and in literary allegories of combat between Lord Carnival's animal armies and the scaled hosts of Lord Lent.[59] Early Christians had avoided meat on ascetic and penitential grounds, which, refracted through the monastic practices of the early medieval church, became a general obligation of believers to abstain from eating the flesh of terrestrial quadrupeds about 150 days of the year. These times notably included every Friday, the forty days of Lent before the springtime festival of Easter, and shorter periods of penitence before other important feasts. Eating fish was not enjoined, and many medieval people could regularly afford little beyond the cereals that provided most of their calories. Nevertheless, traces of fish meals survive from both poor and rich settings.[60] For those who could afford it, fish on the table laid public claim to respect for wealth and ritual observance.[61] Thus, in the meticulously documented diets of monks at late medieval Westminster Abbey, the share of calories provided by fish rose in

[57] A general comparative point made in Regier, "Rehabilitation," 88–89.

[58] Antonin Lelek, "The Rhine River and Some of Its Tributaries under Human Impact in the Last Two Centuries," in Dodge, *Proceedings*, 469–87.

[59] As recently summarized in Terence Scully, *The Art of Cookery in the Middle Ages* (Woodbridge, Suffolk, 1995), 62–64, 72–79, from sources there indicated, but see also Zug Tucci, "Mondo medievale dei pesci," 294–301; and Laurence Bérard, "La consommation du poisson en France: Des prescriptions alimentaires à la prépondérance de la carpe," in Liliane Bodson, ed., *L'animal dans l'alimentation humaine: Les criteres de choix* (Paris, 1988), 171–73.

[60] Written and archaeological examples of laborers and peasants who commonly, if not frequently, ate fish occur in Sandor Bökönyi, "Die Wirbeltierfauna" [of Zalavàr], *Archaeologica Hungarica*, 41 (1963): 370; Helmut Hundsbichler, "Nahrung," in Harry Kühnel, *et al.*, *Alltag im Spätmittelalter* (Graz, 1984), 201–02; Coy, "Fish Bones" [Wraysbury].

[61] Marianne Mulon, ed., "Deux traités inédits d'art culinaire médiéval," *Bulletin philologique et historique (jusqu'à 1610) du comité des travaux historiques et scientifiques*, année 1968 (Paris, 1971), 369–70; Gerhard Jaritz, "The Standard of Living in German and Austrian Cistercian Monasteries of the Late Middle Ages," in E. Rozanne Elder, ed., *Goad and Nail: Studies in Medieval Cistercian History* (Kalamazoo, Mich., 1985), 58–59; Christopher C. Dyer, "The Consumption of Fresh-water Fish in Medieval England," in Michael Aston, ed., *Medieval Fish, Fisheries and Fishponds in England* (Oxford, 1988), 27–38.

direct proportion to staged restrictions on meat, dairy products, and eggs.[62] To a lesser degree, this would have been equally true in less prestigious and less well-recorded settings.

It is likely that early medieval Europeans ate much more freshwater than marine fish, and exigencies of transport, if no others, kept fresh inland fish competitive even after establishment of major marine fisheries.[63] A Greek-trained physician, Anthimus, assessing foods for the sixth-century Frankish king Theodoric, son of Clovis, named eleven fishes "which occur in these parts": four were entirely freshwater organisms, five had life stages in both salt and fresh water; from the sea came only sole, which he said went by two names.[64] When the learned Ekkehard IV imagined a monastic banquet at eleventh-century St. Gallen, fourteen of his twenty fish taxa[65] came from fresh water, five were migratory, and one from salt water only.[66] More than a century later, Hildegard of Bingen compiled a medico-dietary analysis of fishes that members of her religious community ate: of thirty-seven taxa, twenty-four came from fresh water, nine migrated into it, and four were of marine origin.[67] Such verbal impressions are corroborated by the surviving remains of fish Europeans actually ate. In large deposits of food waste from eleventh and twelfth-century Schleswig, bones from locally caught perch, pike, and cyprinids were as well represented as imported cod, and in the thirteenth and fourteenth centuries they outstripped all other fishes. Before about 1500, well-to-do Parisians on Rue Fromenteau ate mostly fish from fresh water, and their religious contemporaries at La Charité-sur-Loire exclusively those varieties.[68] By the thirteenth century,

[62] Barbara Harvey, *Living and Dying in England 1100–1540: The Monastic Experience* (Oxford, 1993), 57.

[63] Useful general overviews include Raymond Delatouche, "Le poisson d'eau douce dans l'alimentation médievale," *Comptes-rendus de l'Academie d'agriculture de France*, 52 (1966): 793–98; and "Le poisson d'eau douce dans l'alimentation médiévale: L'exemple du Maine," *Bulletin philologique et historique (jusqu'à 1610) du comité des travaux historiques et scientifiques*, année 1967, Vol. 1 (Paris, 1969), 171–82; Herbert Hitzbleck, *Die Bedeutung des Fisches für die Ernährungswirtschaft Mitteleuropas in vorindustrieller Zeit unter besonderer Berücksichtigung Niedersachsens* (Göttingen, 1971), 98–139; Jean Verdon, "Recherches sur la pêche et la pisciculture en occident durant le haut moyen âge," in *Actes du 102ᵉ Congrès national des Sociétés savantes (Limoges, 1977): Section d'archéologie et d'histoire de l'art; Le Limousin; Etudes Archéologiques* (Paris, 1979), 337–49; Alison Littler, "The Fisheries Industry in Medieval England down to the Reformation" (Dissertation Swansea, 1979), 8–10; Dyer, "Consumption of Fresh-water Fish."

[64] Anthimus, *De observatione ciborum ad Theodoricum regem Francorum epistula*, Eduard Liechtenhan, ed. and trans., rev. edn. (Berlin, 1963), 18–20, 41–42.

[65] Ethnobiologists and zooarchaeologists use the technical term *taxon* (plural *taxa*) to refer to "identified varieties or forms." The word subsumes species, subspecies, and, where they are ambiguous in some archaeology, pictures, and popular vocabularies, genera or families. Pike, for instance, are clearly distinguished by shape in medieval pictures of fishes; cyprinid species are not. Only certain bones allow discrimination between remains of salmon, migratory sea-trout, and resident stream trout, though local vernaculars plainly distinguish between live specimens on the basis of coloration and behavior.

[66] Ekkehard IV of St. Gallen, *Benedictiones ad mensas*, Johannes Egli, ed., as *Der Liber Benedictionum Ekkeharts IV. nebst den kleinern Dichtungen aus dem Codex Sangallensis 393* (St. Gallen, 1909). Compare current views in Johannes Duft, *Der Bodensee in Sankt-Galler Handschriften: Texte und Miniaturen aus St. Gallen*, 3d edn. rev. (St. Gallen, 1979), 21–23, 90–91.

[67] *Physica*, lib. 5, in *Patrologia Latina*, vol. 197, cols. 1265–86. Ulrich of Cluny's vocabulary (see above) had the same freshwater emphasis.

[68] Dirk Heinrich, "Temporal Changes in Fishery and Fish Consumption between Early Medieval Haithabu and Its Successor, Schleswig," in C. Grigson and J. Clutton-Brock, eds., *Animals and Archaeology*, Vol. 2: *Shell Middens, Fishes and Birds* (Oxford, 1983), 151–56; and "Untersuchungen an mittelalterlichen Fischresten aus Schleswig: Ausgrabung Schild 1971–1975," *Ausgrabungen in Schleswig:*

Belgian scholar Jan Materné has argued, this mainly urban market demand and the specialized labor that supplied it were responsible for rising exploitation of fisheries in northern Flanders.[69]

Populations of the fishes Europeans liked to eat came under evident stress. One sign is the contemporary human perception of resource destruction, commonly conceived as overfishing. A remarkably early explicit statement of the problem prefaces the first full-scale fisheries ordinance issued by French King Philip IV in 1289:

> today each and every river and waterside of our realm, large and small, yields nothing due to the evil of the fishers and the devices of [their] contriving, and because the fish are prevented by them from growing to their proper condition, nor have the fish any value when caught by them, nor are they any good for human consumption, but rather bad, and further it happens that they are much more costly than they used to be, which results in no moderate loss to the rich and poor of our realm.[70]

Philip's remedy is examined below. A more particular case of fishing pressure is reported from the Pinzgauer Zellersee, high in the Salzburg Alps. Its rich fisheries drew a mid-fourteenth-century settlement of professionals, who paid the archbishop 27,000 whitefish and 18 lake trout a year for the right to take, smoke, and sell still more. After one human generation, the whitefish catch collapsed, and a replacement planting of pike ate nearly all the trout, so the fishing community decided to rest the lake for three years and then to fish only with far fewer nets in a limited season and a restricted area.[71]

Berichte und Studien, Vol. 6 (Neumünster, 1987), 186–89; Jean Desse and Nathalie Desse-Berset, "Pêches locales, côtières ou lointaines: Le poisson au menu des parisiens du Grand Louvre, du 14ème au 18ème siècle," *Anthropozoologica*, 16 (1992): 119–26; Frèdèrique Audoin-Rouzeau, *Ossements animaux du Moyen-Age au monastère de la Charite-sur-Loire* (Paris, 1986), 146–47.

Further confirmation of significant medieval freshwater fish eating occurs in Prummel, *Early Medieval Dorestad*, 11–13, 235–36; A. Paul, "Knochenfunde aus dem mittelalterlich-neuzeitlichen Lübeck (Grabung Königstrasse 59–63)," *Lübecker Schriften zur Archäologie und Kulturgeschichte*, 2 (1980): 59–60; Floridus Röhrig, "Die materielle Kultur des Chorherrenstiftes Klosterneuburg unter besonderer Berücksichtigung der Aussage von Rechnungsbücher," in *Klösterliche Sachkultur des Spätmittelalters* (Vienna, 1980), 221; Jean Richard, "Transports par eau et péages de Chalon a Avignon: A propos des fournitures de poisson a la cour des papes," *112e Congrès national des Sociétés savantes, Lyon, 1987, Histoire médiévale* (Lyon, 1987), 40–44; *Le Ménagier de Paris*, Georgine E. Brereton and Janet M. Ferrier, eds. (Oxford, 1981), 231–36; Annie Grant, "Animal Resources," in Grenville Astill and Annie Grant, eds., *The Countryside of Medieval England* (Oxford, 1988), 170–72; Anton Ervynck, Wim Van Neer, and P. Van der Plaetsen, "De organische resten," in M. DeWilde and Anton Ervynck, eds., *"De Burcht" te Londerzeel: Bewoningsgeschiedenis van een motte en een bakstenen kasteel* (Brussels, 1992).

[69] Jan Materné, "Beroeps- en vrijetijdsvisserij op de Vlaamse binnenwateren tussen Antwerpen en Gent vóór de industriële revolutie," *Bijdragen tot de geschiedenis*, 71 (1988): 142–44.

[70] H. Duplés-Agier, "Ordonnances inédites de Philippe-le-Bel et de Philippe-le-Long sur la police de la pêche fluviale," *Bibliothèque de l'Ecole des Chartes*, 14 (1852): 49. More recent context is provided in Paul Jeulin, "L'elaboration par la monarchie de l'ancienne reglementation de la pêche fluviale," *Revue historique de droit français et étranger*, ser. 4, 40 (1962): 127–28, and 42 (1964): 728–30, who notes how these themes became a commonplace of French legislation. Comparable perceptions of fisheries damaged by too intensive use are voiced in mid-fifteenth-century enactments by communal governments at Florence: Richard Trexler, "Measures against Water Pollution in Fifteenth Century Florence," *Viator*, 5 (1974): 463–67; and Strasbourg: Hans Stromeyer, *Zur Geschichte der Badischen Fischerzünfte* (Karlsruhe, 1910), 2.

[71] Hans Freudlsperger, "Kurze Fischereigeschichte des Erzstiftes Salzburg," *Mitteilungen der Gesellschaft für Salzburger Landeskunde*, 76 (1936): 100. Likewise, Wim Van Neer and Anton Ervynck, "New Data on Fish Remains from Belgian Archaeological Sites," in Wim Van Neer, ed., *Fish Exploitation in*

Less subjective indicators allow closer description and diagnosis of fish populations under stress. Thousands of bone remains from tenth through thirteenth-century Gdańsk reveal a steady reduction in the size of sturgeon caught nearby. Like trends are more vaguely visible in some other large Central European collections predating 1200.[72] Shrinking average size indicates a population where more fish are being caught before reaching their full growth.

Shifts in species composition of medieval catches are still more telling. Investigators have diagnosed a decline of anadromous and cold-water varieties during the high and later Middle Ages in several regions of Western Europe. Using archaeological remains of sturgeon from seventeen southern Baltic sites, Norbert Benecke generalized both a reduction in average size and a fall of this species from 70 percent of fish consumed during the seventh, eighth, and ninth centuries to only 10 percent during the twelfth and thirteenth. Benecke blamed long-term overexploitation, especially of the reproductively dominant large females of this long-lived and slow-growing fish.[73] Written records supported R. Boddeke's finding of a comparable downward trend in the sturgeon catch of the Low Countries that lasted from the eleventh through the fourteenth century. He held responsible the widespread damming and diking of critical spawning waters in the upper estuary and noted that after great storm floods smashed the barrier dikes around 1400, sturgeon catches came back until new reclamation works affected them adversely in the 1800s.[74] In thirteenth-century France and England, all sturgeon were reserved for the king. By the fourteenth century, chefs in those countries were circulating a recipe to "make sturgeon" from veal, a distinct mark of the prestige and favor still attached to an almost extinct food fish.[75]

As for salmon, catches from fisheries on the small rivers of lower Normandy,

---

the Past: Proceedings of the 7th Meeting of the I.C.A.Z. Fish Remains Working Group (Tervuren, 1994), 225, argue that relatively greater reliance on marine fish in the diets of late medieval Belgian towns as compared to rural castles and monasteries demonstrates the reduction of fish populations near those urban concentrations. Jäger's (*Einführung*, 192) claim of no evidence for decline in numbers of aquatic organisms before the 1500s results from an unrealistic assumption that only governmental records of catches constitute "scientific" data.

[72] W. Susłowska and K. Urbanowicz, "Szczętlu kostne ryb z wczesnośredniowiecznego Gdańska (X–XIII w.)," *Gdańsk wczesnośredniowieczny*, 6 (1967): 53–65. Early medieval remains of fish distinctly larger than later norms for the same species are also remarked by Z. Kozikowska, "Ryby w pokarmie średniowiecznych (X–XIV w.) mieszkańców Wrocławia na Ostrowie Tumskim jako wskaźnik gatunków łowionych w wodach danych okolic lub dobierających tam drogą handlu," *Acta Universitatis Wratislaviensis*, 223 (1974): 3–14; Paul, "Knochenfunde"; Angela von den Driesch, "Fischreste aus der slawisch-deutschen Fürstenburg auf dem Weinberg in Hitzacker (Elbe)," *Neue Ausgrabungen und Forschungen in Niedersachsen*, 15 (1982): 395–423.

[73] Norbert Benecke, "Some Remarks on Sturgeon Fishing in the Southern Baltic Region in Medieval Times," in D. C. Brinkhuizen and A. T. Clason, eds., *Fish and Archaeology* (Oxford, 1986), 9–17. *Acipenser sturio* needs ten years and more to reach spawning size, but it can live a century and attain weights over 100 kilograms. In all fishes, large females have room for many more eggs than do small ones.

[74] Boddeke, *Vissen*, 169–74. Jäger, *Einführung*, 29–30, has recent bibliography on the catastrophic late medieval reflooding of North Sea coastal zones.

[75] *Fleta*, I: 44, H. G. Richardson and G. O. Sayles, eds., Selden Society, vol. 72 (London, 1955), 100; Grégoire Lozinski, ed., *La Bataille de Caresme et de Charnage* (Paris, 1933), 184; Constance B. Hieatt and Sharon Butler, eds., *Curye on Inglysch: English Culinary Manuscripts of the Fourteenth Century (including the Forme of Cury)* (London, 1985), 155–56; *Le Ménagier de Paris*, 239–40; compare Liliane Plouvier, "La gastronomie dans le 'Viandier de Taillevent' et le 'Ménagier de Paris,'" in *Manger et boire au Moyen Age*, Vol. 2 (Paris, 1984), 154.

where plowed fields and watermills multiplied through the twelfth and thirteenth centuries, were distinctly fewer by 1300 than they had been around 1100. Continued "overfishing" thereafter brought near-total destruction of the runs by the mid-1400s.[76] Even in wealthy Parisian households and prosperous Flemish monasteries, consumption of once-favored sturgeon, salmon, trout, and whitefish shrank to nothing by around 1500.[77]

In contrast, the same and comparable evidence reveals other species gaining dietary importance. Especially large increases are noted for eel and for common carp (*Cyprinus carpio*). Eel constitute two-thirds of the remains from twelfth-century Deventer but thereafter fall back to only one third in favor of undifferentiated small cyprinids. After about 1450, eel comprised 20 and carp 40 percent of all fish (and together 90 percent of the local fish) consumed at Sint-Salvators Abbey near Oudenaarde. Of the fish bones identified in twelfth through sixteenth-century deposits at Gaiselberg Castle in Lower Austria, carp provided 60 percent, and most of those postdated 1400. By that time, the species also dominated tables in Paris, Orleans, and La Charité-sur-Loire.[78]

The abundant (and easily recognized) remains of eel and carp lead and stand for general increases in relatively more lentic and heat-tolerant fish varieties. Financial records from the papal court at Avignon (1338–75) trace large shipments down the Rhone and Saône from Burgundy of carp, eel, bream, tench, barbel, and pike.[79] Accounts kept between 1349 and 1413 by managers of waters belonging to the church of St. Etienne at Troyes, Champagne, record large catches of carp, eel,

[76] Halard, "Pêche du saumon," 175–77. On the best-documented river, catches in 1423 were less than a third those of the early 1300s, though the price per fish rose by a factor of twelve.

[77] Desse and Desse-Berset, "Pêches locales, côtières ou lointaines," 125–26; Miriam Sternberg, "L'approvisionnement de Paris en poisson au 16ème siècle: Que disent les sources bibliographiques? Que peut on espérer des données ichtyofauniques des Jardins du Carrousel?" *Anthropozoologica*, 16 (1992): 127–30; Anton Ervynck and Wim Van Neer, "De voodselvoorziening in de Sint-Salvatorsabdij te Ename (stad Oudenaarde, prov. Oost-Vlaanderen) I. Beenderen onder een keukenvloer (1450–1550 A.D.)," *Archeologie in Vlaanderen*, 2 (1992): 425–26. A compilation of fishes identified at fourteen Dutch sites found sturgeon, shad, and/or salmon at six of eight from before 1000 A.D. and at none of the six thereafter. A. T. Clason, W. Prummel, and D. C. Brinkhuizen, "Vogelen en vissen: Een glimp van de Nederlandse vogel- en viswereld uit het verleden," *Westerheem*, 28 (1979): 16–20.

Italian conditions may bear comparison. Fumagalli, *Landscapes*, 137, implies a high and late medieval contraction in the size and numbers of sturgeon taken from the Po, but Marco Vendittelli, "Diritti ed impianti di pesca degli enti ecclesiastici Romani tra X e XIII secolo," *Mélanges de l'école française de Rome: Moyen Age*, 104 (1992): 394–97, 409–10, does not engage possible changes in the important fishery of the Tiber delta, where drainage of marshlands and channels was also under way. Sturgeon did bring the highest price in a 1447 Roman edict, and disputes over claims to several Italian sturgeon fisheries intensified after 1300. Yet Roman physician Paolo Giovio's pioneering zoological investigation, *De romanis piscibus libellus* (Rome, 1524), still celebrated the sturgeon of the Tiber.

[78] G. F. IJzereef and F. Laarman, "The Animal Remains from Deventer (8th–19th Centuries AD)," *ROB: Berichten van de Rijksdienst voor het Oudheidkundig Bodemonderzoek*, 36 (1986): 435–36; Ervynck and Van Neer, "De voodselvoorziening in de Sint-Salvatorsabdij"; F. Spitzenberger, "Die Tierknochenfunde des Hausbergs zu Gaiselberg, einer Wehranlage des 12.–16. Jahrhunderts in Niederösterreich," *Zeitschrift für Archäologie des Mittelalters*, 11 (1983): 139; Desse and Desse-Berset, "Pêches locales, côtières ou lointaines"; Sternberg, "L'approvisionnement"; Marie-Christine Marinval-Vigne, "Consommation d'animaux sauvages en milieu ecclésial à Orléans au XVIe siècle: Données archéozoologiques et livres de cuisine," in Jean Desse and Frédérique Audoin-Rouzeau, eds., *Exploitation des animaux sauvages a travers le temps* (Juan-les-Pins, 1993), 478–82; Audoin, *Ossement animaux*.

[79] Richard, "Transports," 40–44.

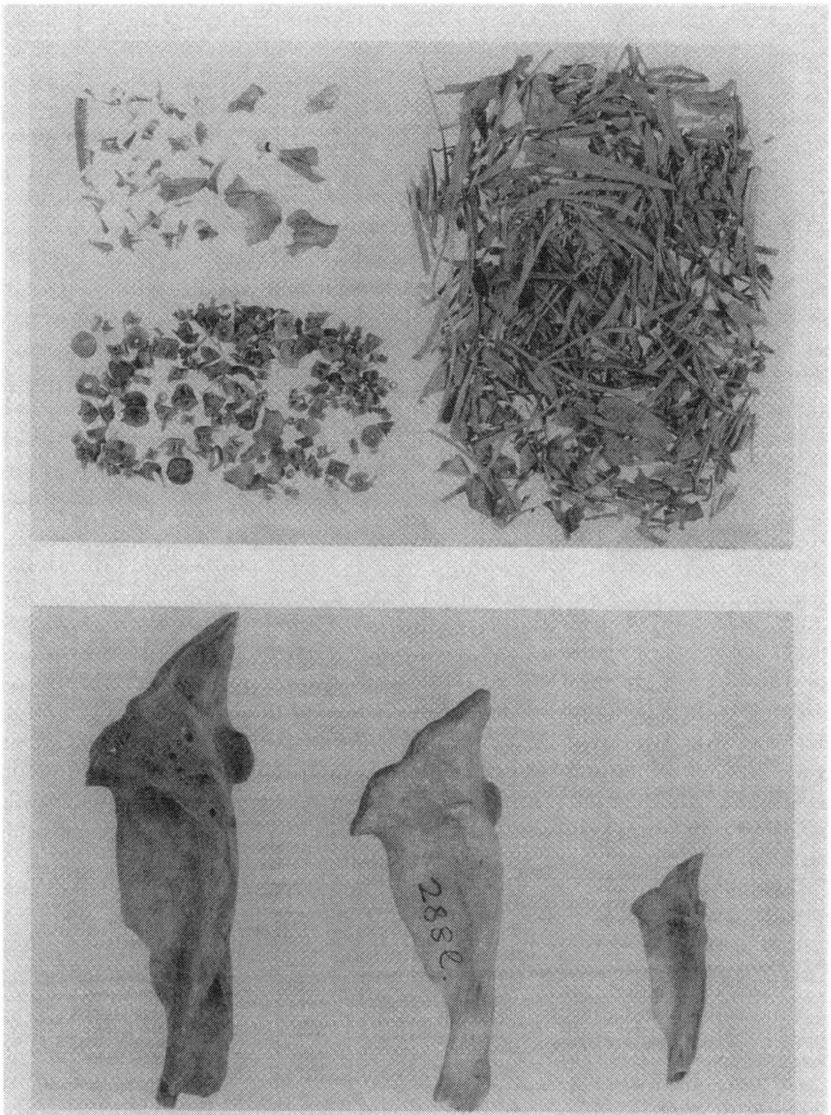

Fish remains recovered in excavation of the late medieval castle site at Plesse near Göttingen in Lower Saxony. Expert analysis of this material can give information about the varieties, origins, and preparation of fishes eaten by medieval people. **Top**: a portion of the finds from water sieving through a fine mesh screen. Vertebrae and some other elements have already been sorted into the two small piles on the left. **Bottom**: a distinctive bone (*hyomandibular*) from the head of the common carp (*Cyprinus carpio*). The center bone is a present-day comparative example from a fish of 38.2 cm. total length. The find on the left is from a much larger, that on the right from a much smaller, type of carp consumed by residents of medieval Plesse. Photographs by Dirk Heinrich. Used with permission.

bream, and pike.[80] As at Deventer, small cyprinids and eel dominated the freshwater component of fishes eaten at a late fourteenth-century palace in Tarquinia.[81]

Characteristic differences between the fishes that rose in importance and those that fell thus argue for human impact on medieval aquatic ecosystems more complex than can be ascribed to overfishing alone. The varieties that increased in dietary importance and apparent natural success may be characterized by greater tolerance, even preference, for warmer, more turbid, and quieter waters. Cyprinids and pike spawn by choice in weedy shallows, and eel leave fresh water when ready to breed. Reproductive success for the fish populations displaying stress (salmonids, sturgeon), on the other hand, requires clean and cool running or estuarine waters, preferably with a gravel substrate. Those were the very aquatic habitats being blocked or diminished by medieval agricultural, urban, and industrial developments. Quite without human forethought, economic development was raising the amounts of silt and nutrients in Europe's watercourses and the proportion of standing water.[82] Some deliberate human responses to a perceived decline and shortage in the fishes long preferred for human consumption would, it will shortly be seen, further accentuate precisely these alterations to aquatic environments and their biota.

MEDIEVAL AWARENESS OF UNDESIRABLE CHANGES to fisheries has already been noted. Actual statements of these perceptions commonly preface purposeful responses to them, but medievalists are well acquainted with many more such actions that people undertook without elaborate written rationale. Demand, pressure, and declining yields of medieval inland fisheries motivated proprietary and regulatory measures directed at controlling human behavior and, furthermore, provoked intentional human intervention in the environment aimed at changing natural relationships. Medieval Europeans both adjusted the social face with which they confronted nature and manipulated nature to fit their own wishes.

Rising demand against a limited, even diminishing, resource often triggers contests for control. Medieval inland fisheries became objects of efforts by landowners, producers, consumers, and territorial authorities to manage exploitation in their own interests.[83] Their measures to privatize, commercialize, and

[80] "Comtes des pêscheries de l'eglise de Troyes, 1349–1413," London, British Library, Additional Manuscript 22496.

[81] G. Clark, *et al.*, "The Food Refuse of an Affluent Urban Household in the Late Fourteenth Century: Faunal and Botanical Remains from the Palazzo Vitelleschi, Tarquinia (Viterbo)," *Papers of the British School at Rome*, 57 (1989): 240–42.

[82] In the termiology of Regier, "Rehabilitation," 93–96, "white fish" were losing habitat and yielding their prior importance in human catches and consumption to "grey fish" and "black fish," whose favored conditions were less damaged and, in certain regions or localities, becoming more common. Although in contrast to postindustrial changes, pre-industrial development had a greater effect on lotic components of aquatic systems, the general ecological outcome was closely similar, as "through their greater flexibility [grey fish] come to dominate within modified ecosystems."

[83] The medieval situation has parallels in the responses to destruction of anadromous Atlantic salmon populations by nineteenth-century New England mill dams as described in Theodore Steinberg, *Industrialization and the Waters of New England* (New York, 1991), chap. 6.

regulate fisheries and fish products helped shape and constrain human impact on the ecosystem. What follows explores each of these three social responses.

A long-term tendency in medieval Europe to transform fishing rights from common or public goods to private property is an axiom of the legal literature. It needs acknowledgement but only short discussion here.[84] By around 1200, royal grants or sheer usurpations had put landowners in possession of fisheries on all but the largest rivers. Later conflicts concerned the authority of princes over fisheries on navigable waters and, of greater social importance, the survival and attempted defense of common access to fisheries under seigneurial control.[85]

Peasants bitterly detested what they saw as lords' usurpation of their just rights to use local waters, and their resistance runs at least from the Norman revolt of 997 through the German Peasants' War of 1525.[86] That long struggle itself confirms that medieval peasants continued to engage in direct subsistence fishing to supplement their grain-based diets. Where detailed—as, for instance, in a court decision at Fontaines in Valois in 1270 or in fifteenth-century customaries from Hainaut and the *Weistümer* precedents from southern Germany—the usufruct rights of ordinary villagers were most often limited to small gear used personally to supply a resident household. Restraints on locations and times (seasons, days) to fish were also the norm.[87] In the long run, then, direct subsistence use of local aquatic resources—

[84] Ernst Cahn, *Das Recht der Binnenfischerei im deutschen Kulturgebiet von den Anfängen bis zum Ausgang des 18. Jahrhunderts*, Ekkehard Kaufmann, ed. (Frankfurt am Main, 1956), 13–90; Jeulin, "L'elaboration par la monarchie," 127–28. Nuanced regional examples include Guido Kisch, *Das Fischereirecht im Deutschordensgebiete: Beiträge zu seiner Geschichte*, 2d edn. rev. [substantively unchanged from the 1932 original] (Sigmaringen, 1978); Władysław Łęga, *Obraz gospodarczy Pomorza Gdańskiego w XII i XIII wieku* (Poznań, 1949), 35–49; Horst Willam, "Die Fischerei des Deutschen Ordens in Preussen bis zu Dietrich von Altenburg," *Jahrbuch der Albertus-Universität zu Königsberg/Pr.*, 11 (1961): 74–137; Freudlsperger, "Fischereigeschichte," 87–122; Roger Grand and Raymond Delatouche, *L'agriculture au moyen âge de la fin de l'empire romain au XVIe siècle* (Paris, 1950), 538–39; Fossier, *La terre et les hommes*, 395–97; J. McDonnell, *Inland Fisheries in Medieval Yorkshire, 1066–1300* (York, 1981), 12–18; Jan Materné, "De verwerving, betwisting en instandhouding van de visserijrechten in de Wase Durmestreek, 13de–18de eeuw," *De Soevereinen*, 22, no. 3 (1991): 1–14.

[85] This is not, of course, the now-proverbial "tragedy of the commons" famously analyzed by Garrett Hardin in *Science*, 162 (1968): 1243–48, which predicts the overexploitation of a resource open to all but controlled by none. Modern managers think regulated entry to the resource is a way to avoid "tragedy." Perhaps ironically, medieval privatization of fishing rights had precisely that effect.

[86] William of Jumièges, *Gesta Normannorum Ducum*, Jean Marx, ed. (Rouen, 1914), 73–74 (Lib.V:2); Hermann Heimpel, "Die Federschnur: Wasserrecht und Fischrecht in der 'Reformation Kaiser Sigismunds,'" *Deutsches Archiv für Erforschung des Mittelalters*, 19 (1963): 474–88; Hermann Heimpel, "Fischerei und Bauernkrieg," in P. Classen, ed., *Festschrift Percy Ernst Schramm zu seinem siebzigsten Geburtstag*, 2 vols. (Wiesbaden, 1964), 1: 353–72; F. Mayer, F. Bischoff, and J. von Zahn, eds., "Kleinere Mitteilungen zur Geschichte der Bauernunruhen in Steiermark, 1478–1515," *Beiträge zur Kunde Steiermärkische Geschichtsquellen*, 14 (1877): 121; Peter Blickle, "Wem gehörte der Wald? Konflikte zwischen Bauern und Obrigkeiten um Nutzungs- und Eigentumsansprüche," *Zeitschrift für württembergischen Landesgeschichte*, 45 (1986): 167–78.

[87] François Blary, *Le domaine de Chaalis, XIIe–XIVe siècles: Approches archéologiques des établissements agricoles et industriels d'une abbaye cistercienne* (Paris, 1989), 95–99; Léo Verriest, *Le régime seigneurial dans le Comté de Hainaut du XIe siècle a la Révolution*, 2d edn. (Louvain, 1956), 320–23; Cahn, *Das Recht der Binnenfischerei*, 51–56, 67–68; Heimpel, "Federschnur," 456–64. Compare the disputes in thirteenth-century English village courts reported in H. S. Bennett, *Life on the English Manor: A Study of Peasant Conditions 1150–1400* (Cambridge, 1937), 270; and the peasant fishing reported by Laszlo Màkkai, "Economic Landscapes: Historical Hungary from the Fourteenth to the Seventeenth Century," in Antoni Mączak, Henryk Samsonowicz, and Peter Burke, eds., *East-Central Europe in Transition: From the Fourteenth to the Seventeenth Century* (New York, 1985), 28–31.

which means the fishes naturally present in Western Europe's ubiquitous streams and small rivers—was surely curtailed.

Fishing rights derive economic value from demand for fish and limited opportunities to obtain them (only certain waters, sites, and seasons are productive), not necessarily from an absolute shortage of fish or decline in their numbers. Even in a largely subsistence economy—which in the Middle Ages included dependent fishers supplying the household needs of their masters—fish flesh on the bank has scarcity value, use value, and value derived from at least the costs of human effort expended in its capture. Great lords and others with a large and steady demand for fish tried to secure stable supplies. Charlemagne instructed his estate managers to see to the employment of fishers. His son possessed thirty-two families of them on the Weser alone until he gave those to Corvey Abbey in 832.[88] Conveyances from lay to ecclesiastical lordship created the surviving record for most such arrangements, such as the six men named at two villages near Kalisz in 1210, whom Duke Władysław gave to Przemęt Abbey together with their individual obligations to fish daily or to provide a dozen fish the length of a forearm three days a week. But for all the gifts to churches and for all the availability of market-supply mechanisms by the thirteenth century, as late as 1265 the duke of Leicester still retained men to send off for two weeks' fishing to cover the needs of his household during Holy Week.[89] Private control over access to fisheries thus became a twig in the bundle of remunerative rights being assembled into lordship over land and men. Actual participants in the indirect subsistence fisheries ranged from more or less skilled part-timers to expert, full-time specialized employees and servants.

Once established in private hands, fishing rights evolved, mainly through rentals and leases, toward a market commodity.[90] Where lords stopped satisfying their own consumption needs through direct exploitation of their resources, exercise of fishing rights came chiefly to sustain production for commercial sale. The transition could often result in what would be temporary arrangements like those about 1300 at Klosterneuburg, where full-time fishers remained abbey dependents. For the right to practice their craft, they owed the prior first refusal rights on large fish, a share

[88] "Capitulare de villis," sect. 45 (A. Boretius, ed. in *MGH, Leges: Capitularia*, Vol. 1 [Hanover, 1883], no. 32); Cahn, *Das Recht der Binnenfischerei*, 91–93. Vendittelli, "Diritti," 427–28, describes other late eighth and ninth-century fishers on the lakes near Rieti in the Apennines who were hereditary serfs of Farfa Abbey. For their counterparts in Bohemia, see Barbara Sasse, *Die Sozialstruktur Böhmens in der Frühzeit: Historische-archäologische Untersuchungen zum 9.-12. Jahrhundert* (Berlin, 1982), 253–54.

[89] *Codex diplomaticus Majoris Poloniae*, Ignacy Zakrzewski and Franciszek Piekosiński, eds., 5 vols. (Poznań, 1877–1908), no. 66; Thomas H. Turner, ed., *Manners and Household Expenses of England in the Thirteenth and Fifteenth Centuries Illustrated by Original Records* (London, 1841), 16, 39, where at least one of the duke's fishers, *Simon Piscator*, was on permanent retainer.

Large consumers who controlled rich local resources, such as the counts of Tirol and the Benedictine monks at Tegernsee Abbey, still employed many full-time fishers in the sixteenth century. See *Das Fischereibuch Kaiser Maximilians I.*, F. Unterkirchner, ed. (Vienna, 1967); Franz Niederwolfsgruber, *Kaiser Maximilians I. Jagd- und Fischbücher: Jagd und Fischerei in den Alpenländern im 16. Jahrhundert* (Innsbruck, 1965), 52–61; Richard C. Hoffmann, "Fishers in Late Medieval Rural Society around Tegernsee, Bavaria," in Edwin B. DeWindt, ed., *The Salt of Common Life: Individuality and Choice in the Medieval Town, Countryside and Church; Essays Presented to J. Ambrose Raftis* . . . (Kalamazoo, Mich. [forthcoming, 1996]).

[90] Cahn, *Das Recht der Binnenfischerei*, 91–103.

A fishmonger's stall. Marginal illumination in a 1290 French antiphonary from the monastery of Beaupré near Gramont, now in Walters Art Gallery, Baltimore, Maryland, MS 759, fol. 108r. Used with permission.

of the catch made with abbey equipment, and fixed money dues.[91] But some generations earlier, fisheries belonging to the count of Namur, to Burgundian lords, and to monasteries from León to Warwickshire to Westfalia were already being rented on fixed terms for annual money dues or, rarely, a share of the catch. Revenues from leases in Picardy exceeded those from equal areas of arable. After the Black Death of 1347–1351, leases everywhere became the norm and continued their steady rise in value.[92] Having paid for the hereditary, lifelong, or terminable privilege of access to the resource, therefore, artisanal fishers lived by serving nearby markets. Their relatively small-scale technologies provided year-round supplies of a fresh local product.

Market price should represent the scarcity value of a commodity relative to effective demand for it. By the later Middle Ages, much quantitative evidence establishes fresh local wild fish as a relatively expensive item. In fifteenth-century Central European towns, for instance, fish cost three to five times more than beef.[93] Fish-producing areas in France and Poland shipped exclusively to the largest cities.

[91] Hartmann Zeibig, ed., *Urkundenbuch des Stiftes Klosterneuburg bis zum Ende des vierzehnten Jahrhunderts*, 2 vols. (Vienna, 1867–68), 2: 169–71.

[92] Generally on leases and their rising value, see Fossier, *La terre et les hommes*, 395–97; and Hitzbleck, *Die Bedeutung des Fisches*, 83–87. Examples include D. D. Brouwers, ed., *Cens et rentes du Comté de Namur au XIIIe siècle*, 2 vols. in 3, *L'administration et les finances du Comté de Namur du XIIIe au XVe siècle*, Sources, vol. 1 and vol. 2: parts 1 and 2, *Documents inèdits relatifs a l'histoire de la Province de Namur publiés par ordre du Conseil Provincial* (Namur, 1910–11, 1926), 1: 105, 114, 156, and 202, and 2: 1, lxix–lii; Jean Richard, "Le commerce du poisson en Bourgogne et les étangs de la région Autunoise," *Mémoires de la Société Eduenne*, 44 (1983): 185–86; Perez-Embid Wamba, *El cister*, 178–79, 524–25; R. A. Hilton, ed., *The Stoneleigh Leger Book* (Oxford, 1960), 39, 163; Van Derveeghe, *Domaine du Val Saint-Lambert*, 110–11 and 118; Wilhelm Vahrenhold, *Kloster Marienfeld: Besitz und Wirtschaftsgeschichte des Zisterzienzerklosters Marienfeld in Westfalen (1185–1456)* (Warendorf, 1966), 128–29.

[93] Hitzbleck, *Die Bedeutung des Fisches*, 104–08.

At festivals and entertainments of important guests, fish such as sturgeon, salmon, and pike graced the tables of papal Avignon. At least on the urban markets of which we are best informed, fresh fish was something of a luxury consumption good, or, as one poet put it, "ein herren speis."[94] Persons of power and wealth claimed preferred access to it.

As operators in what had now become commercial fisheries, fishers and fish dealers had their own interests.[95] These groups were often among the first in a community to organize for recognition by authorities and access to supplies and customers. At Ravenna and Pavia, where possibly precocious concentrations of consumers lived near good-sized rivers, groupings of fishers were recognized in agreements from as early as the tenth century; at Pavia, they were still enforcing their rights over the Ticino River in the late twelfth.[96] A monopoly of fish sales granted by the bishop of Worms to twenty-three named fishers in 1106 ranks among the oldest guild recognitions north of the Alps.[97] Organized fishers at Strasbourg are known by 1139 and had their own statute by 1315. Guilds at Paris appear in market regulations from the 1260s and those at Kraków in the 1360s.[98] Fishers' cartels sought exclusive use of fishing rights for commercial purposes and control over the sale of fresh fish in their town. At a center of market demand without major local aquatic resources, like Bologna with its many students, importing fishmongers played the same role.[99]

94 *Heinrich Wittenwilers Ring*, Edmund Weissner, ed. (Leipzig, 1931), ll. 2905–08; George F. Jones, trans., *Wittenwiler's "Ring" and the Anonymous Scots Poem "Colkelbie Sow": Two Comic-Didactic Works from the Fifteenth Century* (Chapel Hill, N.C., 1956), 38. Many more south German allusions of like tone are listed in Weissner's *Kommentar zu Heinrich Wittenwilers Ring* (Leipzig, 1936), 119. Compare Paul Perceveaux, "Essai sur l'origine des étangs de Dombes," *Bulletin de la Société des Naturalists et Archéologues de l'Ain* (1962): 81–90; Hitzbleck, *Die Bedeutung des Fisches*, 100–09; Ulf Dirlmeier, *Untersuchungen zu Einkommensverhältnissen und Lebenshaltungskosten in oberdeutschen Städten des Spätmittelalters (Mitte 14. bis Anfang 16. Jahrhundert)* (Heidelberg, 1978), 312, 376–78, 397–406; Y. Grava, "Notes martégales sur le revitaillement et la consommation du poisson a la cour pontificale d'Avignon au cours du XIVe siècle," in *Manger et boire au Moyen Age*, 160; Dyer, "Consumption of Fresh-water Fish," 33–35.

95 See in general Cahn, *Das Recht der Binnenfischerei*, 101–19; and Hitzbleck, *Die Bedeutung des Fisches*, 213–15. Compare Daniel E. Moerman, "Common Property and the Common Good: Ecological Factors among Peasant and Tribal Fishermen," in Bela Gunda, ed., *The Fishing Culture of the World: Studies in Ethnology, Cultural Ecology and Folklore*, Vol. 1 (Budapest, 1984), 49–61.

96 Paolo Squatriti, "Marshes and Mentalities in Early Medieval Ravenna," *Viator*, 23 (1992): 12; Carl-Richard Brühl and C. Violante, eds., *Honorantie Civitatis Papiae* (Tübingen, 1983), 20; Elisa Occhipinti, "Fortuna e crisi di un patrimonio monastico: Morimondo e le sue grangie fra XII e XIV secolo," *Studi storici*, 26 (1985): 320–21. A comparable corporate group, the *scola piscatorum stagni*, is well documented from the eleventh century seeking exclusive control over the actual fishing of large estuarine ponds in the Tiber delta and then marketing the catch in Rome. The *scola* paid shares of fish to the churches that owned the fishing rights, and it had to let servants fish for the churches' own use. Vendittelli, "Diritti," 409–22.

97 H. Boos, ed., *Urkundenbuch der Stadt Worms*, Vol. 1 (Berlin, 1886), no. 58, p. 50. Compare Steven A. Epstein, *Wage Labor and Guilds in Medieval Europe* (Chapel Hill, N.C., 1991), 42–44, 53–57.

98 Wilhelm Dettmering, *Beiträge zur älteren Zunftgeschichte der Stadt Strassburg* (Berlin, 1903), 28, 34; Stromeyer, *Zur Geschichte*, 37; Eusèbe de Laurière, *et al.*, eds., *Ordonnances des rois de France de la troisième race recueillés par ordre chronologique*, 21 vols. (Paris, 1723–1849), 2: 583–86; René de Lespinasse and F. Bonnardot, eds., *Les métiers et corporations de la ville de Paris: Le livre des métiers d'Etienne Boileau* (Paris, 1879), 212–22; Stanisław Brzozowski and Mieczysław Tobiasz, "Z dziejów rybactwa małopolskiego," *Studia i Materiały z Dziejów Nauki Polskiej*, seria B: *Historia nauk biologicznych*, vol. 9 (Warsaw, 1964), 78.

99 Antonio I. Pini, "Pesce, pescivendoli e mercanti de pesce in Bologna medievale," *Il carrobio*, 1 (1975): 328–49. Compare the larger role of Parisian *poissonniers* and *marchands* than *pêcheurs de la Seine* in Lespinasse and Bonnardot, *Les métiers*, 212–22, and then René de Lespinasse, ed., *Les métiers*

For consumers, medieval urban authorities took pains to ensure sufficient, safe, and fairly priced foodstuffs, and they commonly maintained relatively strict supervision over the sale of fresh fish. At Ghent and at Paris, for instance, all fish had to be inspected and then offered for immediate retail sale in certain designated areas. Purchase for resale was strictly forbidden.[100] Although high prices should have encouraged fishing pressure on the most-desired fish varieties,[101] barriers to market entry and expansion in turn curtailed it. Price differences also helped minimize direct competition between freshwater fisheries and the sale of preserved marine fishes such as salt herring or dried cod.

Next to privatization and commercialization, public regulation of inland fisheries was the third important social response of medieval Europeans to rising pressures against the resource. Seigneurial measures of this sort, as, for example, the count of St. Pol's 1225 ban on trammel nets, were common by the thirteenth century.[102] Their ambiguous concern for the lord's private supply or profit as well as for preservation and common use makes these a mere half step beyond estate management. But simultaneous royal legislation—in Sicily in 1231,[103] in France in 1268, 1289, and repeatedly thereafter—presaged four subsequent centuries of rising regulation by territorial states.[104]

---

et corporations de la ville de Paris, Tom. 1: *XIV–XVIIIe siècle: Ordinances Générales, Métiers de l'alimentation* (Paris, 1886), 13–20, 407–72.

[100] Lespinasse and Bonnardot, *Les métiers*, 214–18; and Lespinasse, *Les métiers*, 13–20, 448–64; David Nicholas, *The Metamorphosis of a Medieval City: Ghent in the Age of the Arteveldes 1302–1390* (Lincoln, Neb., 1987), 260–61. Compare provisions in the thirteenth-century Scottish town customs (Skene, *Regiam majestatem*, 244–46; Thomson and Innes, *Acts*, 347 red) and in Kraków's municipal ordinances of 1364 and 1408: Franciszek Piekosiński, ed., *Kodeks dyplomatyczne miasta Krakowa (1257–1506)*, 2 vols. (Kraków, 1879, 1882), nos. 262 and 299.

[101] As asserted, perhaps too categorically, by Hitzbleck, *Die Bedeutung des Fisches*, 83–87. I lack at present fully persuasive evidence that fishing for local markets by late medieval artisans itself (apart, that is, from the sheer concentration of aggregate demand in towns) caused greater damage to freshwater fish populations than did the non-market subsistence fishing of local peasants for their own consumption or that of their lords. Both groups of fishers should have known their local resource fairly well and, within the compass of that knowledge, shared comparably ambivalent incentives to maximize their catch *and* to preserve the resource for their future needs. Guild statutes simply do not countenance all-out exploitation and destruction. One could, however, argue that constriction or loss of common rights to fish left members of local peasant communities other than the "lord's fisher" or "master fisher" less solicitous of their aquatic environment and more prepared to countenance loss of habitat as well as illegal and destructive fishing. Consider the endemic (as opposed to openly rebellious) use of poisons and other unlawful methods portrayed in Bennett, *Life on the English Manor*, 94–95; McDonnell, *Inland Fisheries*, 17–18; Richard Jeřábek, "K studiu rybářství v oblasti moravskoslezských Beskyd a Javorníku," *Česky Lid*, 50 (1963): 285–91; Anne-Marie Cocula-Vaillières, *Un fleuve et des hommes: Les gens de la Dordogne au XVIIIe siècle* (Paris, 1981), 132–34; Bela Gunda, "Fish Poisoning in the Carpathian Area and in the Balkan Peninsula," in Gunda, *Fishing Culture*, 1: 181–88.

[102] Fossier, *La terre et les hommes*, 397. In 1260, Salem Abbey obtained judicial confirmation of its legal right to regulate fisheries. X. Staiger, *Salem oder Salmansweiler, ehemaliges Reichskloster Cisterzienser-Ordens* (Constance, 1863), 90. Further examples include Léo Verriest, ed., *Corpus des records de coutumes et des lois de chefs-lieux de l'ancien Comté de Hainaut* (Mons, 1947), 4–5, 11, 42–43, 46, 56, 130, 176–77; Hilario Casado Alonso, *Señores, mercaderes y campesinos: La comarca de Burgos a fines de la edad media* (Valladolid, 1987), 207–10.

[103] *The Liber Augustalis or Constitutions of Melfi Promulgated by the Emperor Frederick II for the Kingdom of Sicily in 1231*, James M. Powell, trans. (Syracuse, N.Y., 1971), 144 (Lib. 3, tit. 72), barred fishing with herbal poisons.

[104] Exemplary or survey treatments of medieval fisheries legislation include S. B. J. Noël de la Morinière, *Histoire général des pêches anciennes et modernes, dans les mers et les fleuves des deux continens* (Paris, 1815), 369–73; Franz J. Mone, "Ueber die Flussfischerei und den Vogelfang vom 14.

The laws openly aimed at preserving fish populations for human use by controlling that use. They typically forbade fishing during spawning season, capture or sale of fish below a minimum size, and gear or methods said to take or kill too many or too small fish. The French ordinance of April 1289, for instance, entirely ruled out nine specified kinds of nets and traps, as well as the use of two more during the months of April and May, when many river species spawn. Legitimate netting gear had to have mesh larger than a *gros tournois*, that is, about 2.5 centimeters (1 inch). Too small for a legal catch were eel worth less than a quarter denier, barbel and carp worth less than a half, and pike valued below two denier.[105] Perugia's statutes of 1342 closed all fishing for tench from May through September.[106] By the late fifteenth century, Bavarian and Austrian rulers were using hand-written, then printed, posters to show the actual smallest legal size for each variety from the Danube and its navigable tributaries.[107] Florentine statutes codified in 1322 prohibited the poisoning of fish and "the capture, sale, or killing of fry."[108] The legislative intent plainly, sometimes explicitly, was to allow desired species to reproduce and grow before human use and to prevent waste.

ON THE SURFACE, PUBLIC LAWS to control fishing dealt with social relations among humans just as much as did private claims to exclusive fishing rights or sales of fish as a market commodity. The necessarily selective protections of law, however, by their differential effects on certain fishes, also entailed semi-conscious human encroachment into natural relationships. Beyond social responses to changes in fish supplies, moreover, medieval Europeans took the further step to active and intentional manipulation of aquatic ecosystems. To serve human purposes, they built new aquatic habitats, modified the mix of fish species, and created new ecosystems, both domestic and wild. The historic vehicle was a particular form of artificial fish farming. Its development and spread both exploited and multiplied

---

bis 16. Jahrhundert," *Zeitschrift für die Geschichte des Oberrheins*, 4 (1853): 67–97; Mira, *La pesca nel medioevo*, 44–55; A. Thomazi, *Histoire de la pêche* (Paris, 1947), 278–80; Grand and Delatouche, *L'agriculture au moyen âge*, 544–46; Sicard, *Les moulins de Toulouse*, 125–28; Cahn, *Das Recht der Binnenfischerei*, 57–60; Kisch, *Das Fischereirecht*, 173–83, 188–92; Willam, "Die Fischerei," 99–137, 145–46; Trexler, "Measures," 460–67; Materné, "Beroeps- en vrijetijdsvisserij," 142–43; and "Exploitatiemetoden, uitrustung en reglementering in de vlaamse binnenvisserij: Een regionale analyze; De Wase durmestreek van de late middeleeuwen tot op het einde van het ancien régime," *Annalen van de Koninklijke Oudheidkundige Kring van het Land van Waas*, 91 (1988): 219–22.

[105] Duples-Angier, "Ordonnances," 49–52; Jeulin, "L'elaboration par la monarchie," 1962–64.

[106] Mira, *La pesca nel medioevo*, 46.

[107] The patent issued for Lower Austria by Emperor Maximilian in 1506 has actual colored drawings of eight species. A published facsimile is in *Archivalien aus acht Jahrhunderten: Ausstellung des Archivs der Stadt Wien*, Historisches Museum der Stadt Wien. 15. Sonderausstellung. Dez. 1964–Febr. 1965, (Vienna, 1965), 34 and plate 8; the 52 x 55 centimeter original is Wiener Stadt- und Landesarchiv, Haupt-Archiv: Urkunden, no. 5825. Older and newer Bavarian examples, including a 42 x 60 centimeter poster printed in 1528, put the names of the fish on oblong bars of appropriate length. Ordinances from as early as 1489 and 1490 survive in Munich, Bayerisches Hauptstaatsarchiv, Ältere Bestände, Staatsverwaltung, Bd. I, Nrs. rot 1608 and 1612b, and Generalregister Fasc. 444 Fischwesen Nr. 1., Nrs. 16–17, 18–19, 389–98.

[108] Trexler, "Measures," 460–61. A Scottish statute of 1318 controlled mesh size and seasons of catch to protect "salmunculi vel smolti seu fria alterius generis piscium maris vel aque dulcis" (Thomson and Innes, *Acts*, 469 red).

what have previously been identified as unintended environmental consequences of medieval economic growth.

Artificial constructions to hold and eventually rear live fish are plainly a response to an inadequacy of natural supply, whether this was understood in nutritional or in cultural terms. Fishponds can equilibrate seasonal irregularities, supplement insufficient wild catches, or even entirely replace wild varieties with preferred domesticates. In some circles, the ponds and a supply of fresh fish for the table were also a way to display wealth and high status. Medieval European fish culture varied in intensity and sophistication along a spectrum jointly determined by growing technical expertise, entrepreneurial priorities, and resources available for investment. Simple storage tanks or cages for seasonally surplus catches were always likely to be found. Heavily capitalized and elaborately managed permanent fish farms were relatively late phenomena. What follows touches mainly on environmental aspects of their evolution.[109]

To build any fishpond is to create a new aquatic habitat. The idealized eighth-century estate of Charlemagne's capitulary *de villis* was to have artificial fishponds (*wiwaria*),[110] but two hundred years later, facilities for raising fish remained very rare, even on monastic estates.[111] Active construction of ponds for this purpose began in the eleventh century and increased rapidly in the twelfth and thirteenth. People built fishponds in regions where human populations and economies were also growing. Disputes over Picard fishponds thus enter the written record around 1100, and major projects in hydraulic engineering there date between the 1170s and 1250s, coincident with such investments in Burgundy and Berry. Across the Channel, from Wiltshire to Yorkshire and the late eleventh century to the late thirteenth, fishponds were made on estates belonging to bishops, major monasteries, and the English crown.[112]

It is important to recognize that, despite the ecclesiastical bias of the high

[109] My discussion here may differ slightly from the overview I sketched more than a decade ago: Richard Hoffmann, "Fish Ponds," in J. R. Strayer, ed., *Dictionary of the Middle Ages*, vol. 5 (New York, 1985), 73–74; it is now further developed in my "Medieval Cistercian Fisheries, Natural and Artificial," in Leon Pressouyre, ed., *L'espace cistercien* (Paris, 1994), 401–14, and "*Carpes pour le duc . . .* : The Operation of Fish Ponds at La Perriére-sur-Saône, Burgundy, 1338–52," *Archaeofauna* [Madrid], 4 (1995): 33–45.

[110] "Capitulare de villis," sect. 21, 62, 65.

[111] The lack of solid evidence for early medieval fishponds and fish culture is confirmed by, for instance, Heinrich Fichtenau, *Living in the Tenth Century: Mentalities and Social Orders*, Patrick J. Geary, trans. (Chicago, 1991), 281. Likewise, the rich records of Cluny at its height of wealth and prestige up to the 1150s refer to catching and temporarily storing fish from the Saône and its tributaries but have no trace of rearing them in fishponds: Ulrich [see note 15 above]; administrative instructions, surveys, and accounts in Auguste Bernard and Alexandre Bruel, eds., *Recueil des chartes de l'abbaye de Cluny*, 6 vols. (Paris, 1876–1903), nos. 3789, 3790, 4132, 4143; Georges Duby, "Le budget de l'abbaye de Cluny entre 1080 et 1155: Economie domaniale et économie monétaire," *Annales: E.S.C.*, 7 (1952): 155–71, and "Un inventaire des profits de la seigneurie clunisienne à la mort de Pierre le Vénérable," *Studia Anselmiana*, 40 (1956): 129–40 [both rpt. in his *Hommes et structures du moyen âge: Recueil d'articles* (Paris, 1973), 61–82, 87–101].

[112] G. de Gislain, "Le role des étangs dans l'alimentation medievale," in *Manger et boire au Moyen Age*, 89; Fossier, *La terre et les hommes*, 366–68; Richard, "Le commerce"; Richard, "Les étangs," 98–99; Devailly, *Le Berry*, 295–96, 556–57; McDonnell, *Inland Fisheries*, 9–12, 19–24; J. M. Steane, "The Royal Fishponds of Medieval England," in Aston, *Medieval Fish*, 1: 39–68; C. J. Bond, "Monastic Fisheries," *ibid.*, 92–95; Edward Roberts, "The Bishop of Winchester's Fishponds in Hampshire, 1150–1400: Their Development, Function and Management," *Proceedings of the Hampshire Field Club and Archaeological Society*, 42 (1986): 125–38.

medieval written record, both lay and clerical landowners built, owned, and operated fishponds in the twelfth and thirteenth-century West. About 1160, while Count Etienne of Sancerre was flooding lands of the cathedral chapter of Bourges to make himself a fishpond, Emperor Frederick Barbarossa was ordering construction of another large one at Kaiserslautern. In 1216, Simon de Joinville, seneschal of Champagne and lord of estates on the upper Meuse, made sure he exempted his fishponds when he allowed the monks of Clairvaux to fish in his river.[113] In particular, recent scholarship is no longer convinced that the Cistercians, whose waterworks became the stuff of later legend, were notably any more innovative than their lay neighbors and kin.[114]

Only later did the active building of fishponds spread vigorously eastward. The Cistercian house founded in 1133 at Waldsassen in the German-Czech frontier zone of the Egerland made its first pond about 1220.[115] A few ponds may be recorded from eleventh or twelfth-century Bohemia, but the first datable construction there was in 1263, and rapid increase came a century after that, when eighty-seven new building projects are recorded between 1347 and 1418. Large and complex hydraulic works were again undertaken by Czech lords between 1450 and 1550, resulting by the latter year in an estimated 26,000 artificial ponds covering thousands of hectares, some of them fed by rivers that had been diverted as much as 35 kilometers.[116] Pond building in southern Poland lagged a generation or so behind that in Bohemia.[117]

Whether made by collecting surface runoff, damming a spring or stream, or diverting part of a river to fill a nearby depression, fishponds are still, not moving, waters. Medieval Europeans managed the fishponds they constructed and other appropriate artificial or enhanced ponds (former river channels, millponds, moats) for production of fish varieties well adapted to lentic habitats with high nutrient levels and warmed water. Probably in the twelfth century and certainly by the thirteenth, careful management included close control over the inflow and outflow of water and a regular (three to five-year) cycle from stocking with breeders or small fish to drainage of the pond for harvest, followed by a dry season and cultivation of

[113] Devailly, *Le Berry*, 361, records the canons' protests; Rahewin's continuation of Otto of Freising, *Gesta Friderici I Imperatoris*, 4: 86, trans. by Charles C. Mierow, *The Deeds of Frederick Barbarossa* (New York, 1953), 333; M. Champollion-Figeac, *Documents historiques inédits tirés des collections manuscrits de la Bibliothèque Royale*, 4 vols. (Paris, 1841–48), 1: 618, as translated in Theodore Evergates, ed. and trans., *Feudal Society in Medieval France: Documents from the County of Champagne* (Philadelphia, 1993), 142. In the summer of 1217, Joinville's lord, the dowager countess and regent of Champagne, was paying to maintain and stock the count's own fishpond at Provins. Felix Bourquelot, ed., "Fragments de Comptes du XIIIe siècle," *Bibliothèque de l'Ecole des Chartes*, 24 (1863): 67. Etienne Fournial, *Les villes et l'économie d'échange en Forez aux XIIIe et XIVe siècles* (Paris, 1967), 687–90, shows like variety among pond owners in that region.

[114] Constance H. Berman, *Medieval Agriculture, the Southern French Countryside, and the Early Cistercians: A Study of Forty-three Monasteries* (Philadelphia, 1986), 89–90; Constance B. Bouchard, *Holy Entrepreneurs: Cistercians, Knights, and Economic Exchange in Twelfth-Century Burgundy* (Ithaca, N.Y., 1991), 111–12, 185–98; Benoit and Wabont, "Mittelalterliche Wasserversorgung," 220–22; Hoffmann, "Medieval Cistercian Fisheries."

[115] Muggenthaler, *Kolonisatorische und wirtschaftliche Tätigkeit*, 129–31.

[116] Jirí Andreska, "Development of Fish-Pond Culture in Bohemia," in Gunda, *Fishing Culture*, 77–83; František Graus, *Dějiny venkovského lidu v cěchàch v době předhusitské*, 2 vols. (Prague, 1953–57), 2: 32–35, 483–86.

[117] Wojciech Szczygielski, *Z dziejów gospodarki rybnej w Polsce w XVI–XVIII wieku* (Warsaw, 1969); Hoffmann, *Land, Liberties, and Lordship*, 365–67.

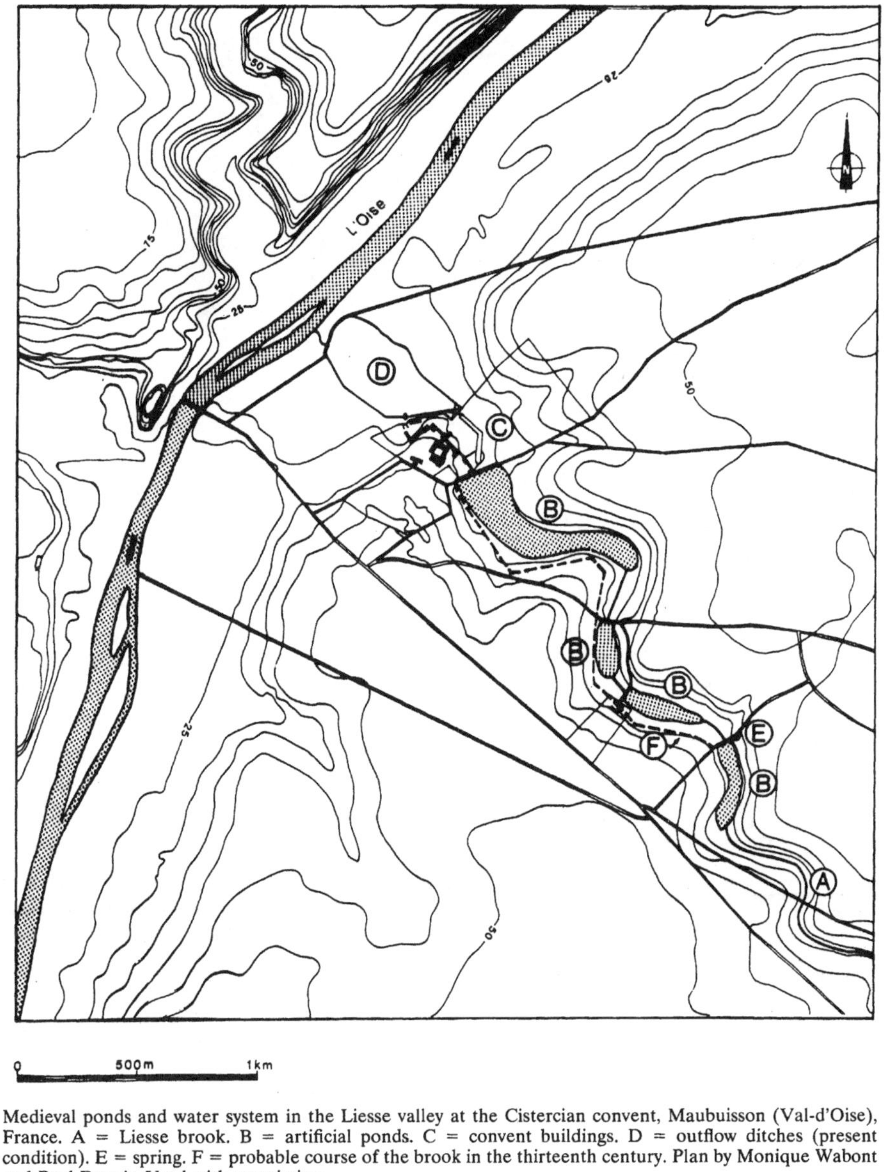

Medieval ponds and water system in the Liesse valley at the Cistercian convent, Maubuisson (Val-d'Oise), France. A = Liesse brook. B = artificial ponds. C = convent buildings. D = outflow ditches (present condition). E = spring. F = probable course of the brook in the thirteenth century. Plan by Monique Wabont and Paul Benoit. Used with permission.

the bottom in order to raise fertility when the pond was refilled.[118] The elaborate hydraulic system built at thirteenth-century Vauclair put the fishpond where it received nutrient-laden outflow from abbey latrines, and the same arrangement fertilized five of Maulbronn's eight nearby ponds.[119]

Anadromous or cold-water fishes had no place in the pond environment. Royal and monastic ponds in thirteenth-century Yorkshire yielded bream, tench, roach, dace, and pike. In the 1384 annual catch from the millpond at Cryfield, Warwickshire, came bream, tench, roach, perch, and pike.[120] Most of the fish species recorded in medieval ponds were these western European natives with preferences for still and weedy waters. They now enjoyed much increased habitat and even deliberate human help as a consequence of medieval economic development. During the 1460s, the duke of Norfolk stocked his half-dozen fishponds with small pike, perch, roach, tench, and bream. He also put in carp. Norfolk's financial account offers the first documented presence of carp in a specific water on the British Isles.[121] The analogous record from France came earlier, so far seemingly as the hundreds of carp Count Thibaut V of Champagne had put into his ponds at Igny-le-Jard on the Marne in 1258.[122]

Carp were not native to Western and Central Europe. Arrival of this exotic species necessarily meant interaction with the ecosystems receiving it.[123] Until the early Middle Ages, all written and archaeological evidence of carp delineates a natural native range in the middle and lower Danubian watershed, where this cold-susceptible organism had been confined by the Pleistocene glaciers and whence its westward movement was curbed by fast and cold headwaters. In the upper Danube, Rhine, and Elbe systems, traces of carp first appear during the eleventh and twelfth centuries, and in the Maas, Seine, and upper Rhone during the late twelfth and thirteenth. Its spread northeast to central Bohemia and southern Poland and west into the Loire and southern England occurred during the later

[118] For clear evidence of these practices on the European continent and in England, see Grand and Delatouche, *L'agriculture au moyen âge*, 541; Devailly, *Le Berry*, 561–62; Roberts, "Bishop of Winchester," 130–35; *Le polyptyque illustré dit "Veil Rentier" de messire Jehan de Pamele-Audenarde (vers 1275)*, Léo Verriest, ed. (Brussels, 1950); Brouwers, *Cens et rentes*, 2: 1, p. lii, and 2: 2, 433–34.

[119] René Courtois, "Quinze ans de fouilles à l'abbaye de Vauclair: Bilan provisoire (1966–1981)," in Chauvin, *Mélanges à la mémoire du Père Anselme Dimier*, Vol. 3 (part 1 [whole number 5]), 339–43. Grewe, "Wasserversorgung," 45–48, and figure 44, treats Maulbronn from the more detailed physical survey of Wolfgang Seidenspinner, "Das Maulbronner Wassersystem—Relikte zisterzienser Agrarwirtschaft und Wasserbautechnik im heutigen Landschaftsbild," *Denkmalpflege in Baden-Württemberg*, 18 (1989): 181–91. Compare the description of Clairvaux remarked in the text above at note 47.

[120] McDonnell, *Inland Fisheries*, 9–12, 19–24; Hilton, *Stoneleigh Leger Book*, 220–21. All of these "grey fish" and "black fish" spawn in still, weedy waters, where trout, for instance, cannot.

[121] Turner, *Manners and Household Expenses*, 560–64; see discussion in Christopher K. Currie, "The Early History of the Carp and Its Economic Significance in England," *Agricultural History Review*, 39 (1991): 101–03 (although the passage includes incorrect assertions).

[122] Bourquelot, "Fragments de Comptes," 71–73, and identified by Grand and Delatouche, *L'agriculture au moyen âge*, 542.

[123] "Regardless of the means by which introductions are effected, successful establishment of an exotic species must necessarily precipitate changes in the physical and biological characteristics of the aquatic ecosystem receiving the introduction . . . That no effects should result from such perturbations strains one's confidence in ecological principles." Jeffrey N. Taylor, Walter R. Courtenay, Jr., and James A. McCann, "Known Impacts of Exotic Fishes in the Continental United States," in Courtenay and Jay R. Stauffer, Jr., eds., *Distribution, Biology, and Management of Exotic Fishes* (Baltimore, Md., 1984), 323, 352.

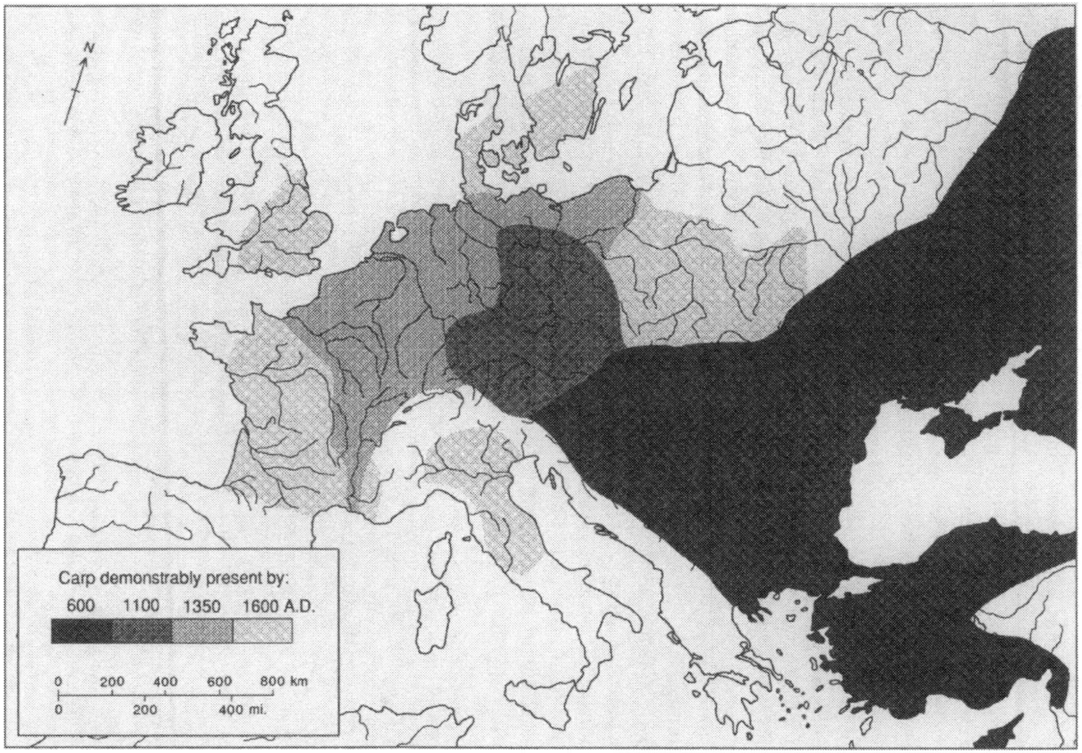

The westward spread of the common carp in medieval Europe. A schematic simplification of information treated in Richard C. Hoffmann, "Remains and Verbal Evidence of Carp (*Cyprinus carpio*) in Medieval Europe," in Wim Van Neer, ed., *Fish Exploitation in the Past: Proceedings of the 7th Meeting of the I.C.A.Z. Fish Remains Working Group* (Tervuren, 1994), 139–50; and Hoffmann, "Environmental Change and the Culture of Common Carp in Medieval Europe," *Guelph Ichthyology Reviews*, 3 (1995): 57–85, and sources there cited. Map prepared in Cartographic Drafting Office, Department of Geography, York University.

Middle Ages.[124] Biologists agree that this movement gained from human help. Captive carp can survive both stagnant store ponds and periods of overland transport. Carp's fecundity and rapid growth to large size attract a pond manager's attention. If, even without much conscious husbandry, medieval fish-keepers thus moved carp into new, more westerly watersheds, the fish were ready to do the rest.

Indeed, carp are remarkably well suited in habitat preferences and reproductive behavior to colonize temperate still-water environments, the very kind that economic development was proliferating in the medieval West.[125] Experiments and observations of the nineteenth-century spread of carp in North America and other territories then new to it verified the unusual ability of this species to colonize explosively in "regions with either simple or relatively fragile fish communities or which are under pressure for other reasons such as excessive fishing or environmental modification."[126] The simple fish communities of medieval Western Europe were under stress from environmental changes and human predation. The foraging behavior of carp, which uproots vegetation and releases nutrients from substrate organisms into the water, accelerated the processes that were altering the environment to the disadvantage of native clear-water species. Competition for food and carp predation on eggs further reduced population densities and species diversity in the native fauna.[127]

By the early fourteenth century, if not before, the best fish culturists on the European continent were emphasizing carp with a "side-crop" of pike. Their standard managerial practices were well documented in many financial accounts kept by estate administrators. The main stock were put in as young fish, whether caught from the wild or spawned by specially selected brood stock, and reared together until ready for harvest as a single age class.[128] Pike of suitable size went

[124] I first inventoried the evidence for westward diffusion in Richard C. Hoffmann, "Remains and Verbal Evidence of Carp (*Cyprinus carpio*) in Medieval Europe," in Van Neer, *Fish Exploitation*, 139–50, and sketched a broader context in "Environmental Change and the Culture of Common Carp in Medieval Europe," *Guelph Ichthyology Reviews*, 3 (1995): 57–85, where I noted some biologists' uncritical use of historical information. For England, compare Currie, "Early History of the Carp." Biological issues in the domestication of this species are most recently summarized in Eugene K. Balon, "The Common Carp, *Cyprinus carpio*: Its Wild Origin, Domestication in Aquaculture, and Selection as Coloured Nishikigoi," *Guelph Ichthyology Reviews*, 3 (1995): 1–55; and, from the perspective of population dynamics, in Jay R. Stauffer, Jr., "Colonization Theory Relative to Introduced Populations," in Courtenay and Stauffer, *Exotic Fishes*, 8–21.

[125] Wheeler, *Fishes of the British Isles*, 178–79. For much more detail, see Otto Heuschmann, *Die Weißfische (Cyprinidae)*, in R. Demoll and H. N. Maier, eds., *Handbuch der Binnenfischerei Mitteleuropas*, Bd. 3, Lfg. 8 (Stuttgart, 1957), 53–63. Regier, "Rehabilitation," 94, lists genus *Cyprinus* as typical "grey fish."

[126] R. L. Welcomme, "International Transfers of Inland Fish Species," in Courtenay and Stauffer, *Exotic Fishes*, 36. See also the discussion and many references in Taylor, Courtenay, and McCann, "Known Impacts," 324–26.

[127] Welcomme, "International Transfers," 33–36. Taylor, Courtenay, and McCann, "Known Impacts," classify the ecological effects of exotic fish introductions (324–26) and then repeatedly specify the known effects of carp (335, 336, 342, 345, 349).

[128] For clearly documented early examples, see Pierre Gresser and J. Hintzy, "Les étangs du domaine comtal en Franche-Comté d'après les comptes de gruerie du XIVe siècle," in *Société d'émulation du Jura: Travaux 1975–1976* (Dole, 1978), 138–46; Isabella Guérin, *La vie rurale en Sologne aux XIVe et XVe siècles* (Paris, 1960), 137–40; Richard, "Les étangs," 99–100; Hoffmann, "*Carpes pour le duc*"; Nuremberg, Staatsarchiv Nürnberg, Rep. 400: IV, Klosterverwalteramt Heilsbronn: Rechnungen, Salbücher und Partikulare, Nr. 1: Jahresrechnungen 1338–1374; A. Heidacher, *Die Entstehungs- und Wirtschaftsgeschichte des Klosters Heilsbronn bis zum Ende des 15. Jahrhunderts: Gründung, Gründer, Wirtschafts und Verfassungsgeschichte* (Bonn, 1955), 119. In 1289, the count of Namur had "queil vivier

into the finishing pond to eat offspring of sexually precocious carp before the fry competed for food with their parents.[129] In well-managed fishponds, therefore, humans had created a complex, domesticated stillwater ecosystem new to Western Europe, while feral offspring of the pond carp joined in the reshaping of wild aquatic ecosystems as well. French writers of the mid-thirteenth century knew carp as both a domestic pond fish and a wild river fish, and so did the first to describe carp in the Polish vernacular, the early sixteenth-century Kraków scholar Stefan Falimirz.[130]

Not only fish were caught up in effects of medieval economic expansion. Unintended changes in habitat and conscious human efforts to eliminate competition and obtain useful food and fur drove down populations of Western Europe's largest aquatic mammals, the herbivorous beaver (*Castor fiber*) and the carnivorous otter (*Lutra lutra*). Drainage of wetland habitats and clearance of the river banks for arable or hay meadows reduced food supply for beaver and availability of denning sites for both species. More turbid water could hamper the otter's ability to detect and capture fish, its principal prey.

Both animals were subject to conscious human predation for consumption and "pest control."[131] As water dwellers, and in view of the shape of the beaver's tail, they were classified as "fish" and thus as acceptable food even during periods of abstinence. Ekkehard IV put *fiber piscis* on his monastic table, and early medieval food waste from both Bavaria and East-Central Europe contains remains of these species. Far more than the beaver's meat or fur, its glands in the groin that secret an oil used in medicines and cosmetics (*castoreum*) made it a valuable quarry.[132]

on a mis d'an en an [carpes] de chief et kewe por rapissonner les autres viviers" (Brouwers, *Cens et rentes*, 2: 2, p. 433), and in 1378 a Bohemian judge mentioned "magnis carponibus, qui ad prolificandum sunt missi in fossatum ibidem" (Augustin Neumann, *Prameny k dějinàm duchovenstva v době předhusitské a Husově* [Olomouc, 1926], 130–33).

The same managerial practices were much later prescribed as the best state of the art in the two definitive sixteenth-century handbooks on fish culture published by a Czech churchman and a Polish pond-master: Jan Dubravius, *De piscinis* (Wrocław, 1547), with a modern edition by Anežka Schmidtovà in *Sbornik filologický ČSAV*, 1, supplement 1 (1953): 11–45, and a facsimile reproduction of the 1599 English translation in *Three Books on Fishing (1599–1659)*, J. Milton French, ed. (Gainesville, Fla., 1962); Olbrycht Strumieński, *O sprawie, sypaniu, wymierzaniu i rybnieniu stawów* (Kraków, 1573) and 2d edn. (Kraków, 1897). An authoritative modern treatment is Stefan Inglot and Aleksander Nyrek, "Jana Dubraviusa i Olbrychta Strumieńskiego działa o gospodarce rybnej: Studium porówznawcze," in Ewa and Karol Maleczyński, eds., *Studia z dziejów polskich i czechosłowackich*, Vol. 1 (Wrocław, 1960), 249–82. Andreska, "Development of Fish-Pond Culture," 83–85, errs on dating.

Carp came late to England, so mid-thirteenth-century ponds of lay and clerical magnates there were stocked with "bremas matrices," pike, and sometimes also perch and roach (McDonnell, *Inland Fisheries*, 11, 26; Steane, "Royal Fishponds," 45–46; Roberts, "Bishop of Winchester," 130–31).

[129] Bourquelot, "Fragments de Comptes," 71, and Fossier, *La terre et les hommes*, 396, may document expectations of this arrangement in northern French ponds as early as 1258 and 1276, respectively.

[130] Bourquelot, "Fragments de Comptes," 71; Lespinasse and Bonnardot, *Les métiers*, 212–18; Józef Rostafiński, *Średniowieczna historia naturalna w Polsce: Symbola ad historia naturalna medii aevi*, 2 vols. (Kraków, 1900), 1: 70.

[131] Most of what follows is in Delort, *Commerce des fourrures*, 108–17; compare Jäger, *Einführung*, 155–58.

[132] Ekkehard, *Benedictiones*; Angela von den Driesch and J. Boessneck, "Haustierhaltung, Jagd und Fischfang bei den Bajuwaren," in Herrmann Dannheimer and Heinz Dopsch, eds., *Die Bajuwaren: Von*

Cistercian monks and Teutonic Knights alike made sure to gain privileges to hunt beaver in thirteenth-century Poland and Prussia. Further west and earlier, the natural dam and house-building habits of this creature so thwarted regionally important efforts of land drainage that it was thought a nuisance. In consequence, the beaver was virtually extirpated from Western Europe by the fourteenth century.[133]

Predators at the top of the food chain make up less biomass and fewer individuals than plant eaters, and the otter, which lived alone, drew less attention than the communal beaver. Otters were thought too few, fierce, and clever for an easy supply of furs, so their usefulness ranked well behind their nuisance role as motive for their pursuit. Otters found proliferating fishponds and their populations of slow, fat stillwater fishes much to their liking. Throughout the later Middle Ages, pond and fisheries owners from the Pyrenees to Prussia hired many a professional otter hunter to protect their property. Despite their efforts, all the good new habitat kept the otters fairly common in the West.[134] Ecological interrelatedness means induced environmental change includes unintended ironies.

Beavers as victims of European markets and ecosystems transformed by European settlers are rather a cliché of North American history. Is anyone still unaware of the environmental price paid in North America for two centuries of capitalist and industrial growth? Human numbers exploded, and so did those of their exotic plants and animals—carp among them—at the cost of indigenous peoples, ecosystems, and organisms. Woodlands and grasslands became simplified agricultural ecosystems. Waters were plundered, befouled, and degraded.

Human use and transformation of natural environments is not confined to these recent events or a "New World." The great economic expansion of medieval Europe, which helped establish the identity of that civilization on that subcontinent, took place with demonstrable environmental impact and among complex interactions between human societies and their neighboring ecosystems. Human numbers and the grain lands and mills needed to feed them brought unintended and long, scarcely seen changes to Europe's watercourses. Culturally formed and socially structured demand stressed stocks of preferred food fishes. When medieval Europeans were alerted by local or regional scarcities, they contested individual

---

Severin bis Tassilo 488–788 (Salzburg, 1988), 203; Daniel Makowiecki, "Materiał kostny zwierząt z grodziska wczesnośredniowiecznego w Lembargu, woj. toruńskie," *Roczniki Akademii Rolniczej w Poznaniu*, 206 [*Archaeozoologia*, 14] (1990): 27–40. In the medieval bestiaries, the beaver bites off its testicles to escape. Willene B. Clark, "The Aviary-Bestiary at the Houghton Library, Harvard," in Willene B. Clark and Meradith T. McMunn, eds., *Beasts and Birds in the Middle Ages: The Bestiary and Its Legacy* (Philadelphia, 1989), 30.

[133] Cornelia Becker, "Die Nutzung von Tieren im Mittelalter zwischen Elbe und Oder," in Herrmann, *Umwelt in der Geschichte*, 13–14; Józef Mitkowski, *Początki klasztoru Cystersów w Sulejowie: Studia nad dokumentami, fundacją i rozwojem uposażenia do końca XIII wieku* (Poznań, 1949), 232–37; Willam, "Fischerei," 74; Bryony Coles, "Further Thoughts on the Impact of Beaver on Temperate Landscapes," in Needham and Macklin, *Alluvial Archaeology*, 92–98.

[134] Delort, *Le commerce des fourrures*, 115–17, 180–81; Joseph Balon, "La pêche et le commerce du poisson dans le comté de Namur au Moyen âge," *Namurcum*, 19 (1942): 29; Erich Joachim, ed., *Das Marienburger Tresslerbuch der Jahre 1399–1409* (Königsberg, 1896), 467.

and collective claims to fisheries and grasped at both market and state mechanisms to allocate or control their demands. Where long familiarity gave good knowledge of the resource, power or common interests could forestall the worst predictions of a self-destructive "tragedy of the commons," though not save every local value or anything resembling equity of access.

By the end of the Middle Ages, indeed, by some time in the thirteenth century, members of European culture had become accustomed to the economic manipulation and transformation of aquatic organisms and ecosystems. They recognized at least some of the unintended consequences of their productive activities, exploiting some and seeking to minimize other environmental changes they had brought about. With conscious and informed purpose, they undertook further to modify physical and biological elements of the aquatic ecosystem. Not everything worked the way they thought it might: recall the over-optimistic fishers of the Pinzgauer Zellersee. Not all eventual outcomes penetrated medieval consciousness: nothing suggests any contemporary awareness of reasons for the collapse of sturgeon catches. But, by and large, later medieval Europeans behaved as if they thought they were somehow in control and able to channel fresh waters to meet human needs. It is now hard to find them verbalizing this capacity but not all that hard to find them exercising it.

In recent years, Denis Cosgrove has argued the importance of Italian Renaissance engineers (and their patrons) in establishing and articulating a new human control over water and the landscapes shaped by it.[135] Cosgrove's assertion is representative of more general scholarly claims that the Renaissance formed a new, unequal relationship between European culture and natural environments, a relationship in which humankind dominated Nature.[136] The evidence here described argues that, where Europeans dealt with water and aquatic life, this relationship was a good deal older than the Renaissance and had evolved in cultural strata quite untouched by Renaissance humanism. One easy, perhaps slightly mythologized, line of development goes back to those twelfth-century Cistercian monks.

Another, arguably more telling, line runs through unlettered but not unthinking generations of peasant pond masters, men with long and cumulative knowledge of fish, water, and ways to bring them to serve human wants. Start, in retrospect, with Stěpánek Netolicky, pond master during 1515–1530 for the Třebon (Wittingau) estate of the Lords Rožmberk in southern Bohemia, who laid out and constructed the 45-kilometer Zlata Stoka ("Golden Drain") to feed nine large and thirty-seven small ponds. Stěpánek consulted on ponds and waterworks for the archbishop of Salzburg and for Count Nicholas of Salm, while a generation earlier, his predeces-

[135] Denis Cosgrove, "An Elemental Division: Water Control and Engineered Landscape," and "Platonism and Practicality: Hydrology, Engineering and Landscape in Sixteenth-Century Venice," in Cosgrove, *Water, Engineering, and Landscape*, 1–11, 35–53; Denis Cosgrove, *The Palladian Landscape: Geographical Change and Its Cultural Representations in Sixteenth-Century Italy* (Leicester, 1993), 135–62.

[136] Keith Thomas, *Man and the Natural World: Changing Attitudes in England, 1500–1800* (London, 1983); John Opie, "Renaissance Origins of the Environmental Crisis," *Environmental Review*, 11 (1987): 2–17; Carolyn Merchant, *The Death of Nature: Women, Ecology, and the Scientific Revolution*, rev. edn. (San Francisco, 1989), 42–191.

Étang de Chaumont, one of a series of medieval ponds surviving at La Trappe Abbey (Orne), Normandy, France. The modern road runs on top of the medieval dam. Photograph by Terryl Kinder. Used with permission.

sor, Żelísko, went to advise the count palatine on the Rhine and the bishop of Passau.[137] Before that and elsewhere, in 1416/17 on the Yorkshire Ouse, one John Copyn had charge of the men who rebuilt a salmon weir at Rosscars for the Benedictines of Selby.[138] Regnault le Tarroillon led work teams on the duke of Burgundy's ponds and fisheries between Dijon and the Saône during 1338–1352; paid by the day or by the job, he and his men stocked and harvested fish by the tens of thousands and constructed sluice gates, overflow channels, and temporary storage tanks.[139] Occasionally, we can even trace such skilled managers back long before the Black Death. Pipe rolls from 1244–1262 record Nicholas "the Fisherman" traveling to supervise local crews working on all the bishop of Winchester's ponds.[140] An older contemporary, William "the King's Fisherman," inspected, advised, and coordinated royal ponds from Westminster to Northampton to York between 1226 and 1272.[141] Might, somewhere on the muddy roads of mid-

[137] Andreska, "Development of Fish-Pond Culture," 80–83; Josef Šusta, *Fünf Jahrhunderte der Teichwirtschaft zu Wittingau: Ein Beitrag zur Geschichte der Fischzucht mit besonderer Berücksichtigung der Gegenwart* (Stettin, 1898), 3–15.

[138] John H. Tillotson, ed. and trans., *Monastery and Society in the Late Middle Ages: Selected Account Rolls from Selby Abbey, Yorkshire, 1398–1537* (Woodbridge, Suffolk, 1988), 170–71.

[139] Regnault is documented in two contemporary castellans' accounts, Dijon: Archives Departmentales de la Côte-d'Or, B 5051 bis and B 5052, and his activities are reconstructed in Hoffmann, "*Carpes pour le duc*."

[140] Roberts, "Bishop of Winchester," 130–35.

[141] McDonnell, *Inland Fisheries*, 19–20; Steane, "Royal Fishponds," 46. We might suspect a French counterpart in Hugh Bernard, who in the autumn of 1258 was handling the stocking of at least three of the count of Champagne's ponds at Igny-le-Jard with carp, chub, and unspecified fishes (Bourquelot, "Fragments de Comptes," 73).

thirteenth-century England, Nicholas and William have met to exchange expertise? How did long unwritten knowledge of pond design pass eastward and of carp pass westward? In medieval Europe, economic exploitation, ecological impact, and environmental mastery were, for good or ill, deeds of human agents.

Richard C. Hoffmann is a professor of history at York University in Toronto and a continuing member of the Centre for Medieval Studies at the University of Toronto. He obtained his BA in history from the University of Wisconsin and his PhD in medieval studies from Yale University in 1970. His *Land, Liberties, and Lordship in a Late Medieval Countryside: Agrarian Structures and Change in the Duchy of Wrocław* (1989), received the Herbert Baxter Adams Prize of the AHA and honorable mention for the Wallace K. Ferguson Prize of the Canadian Historical Association. Since the early 1980s, Hoffmann has been exploring the roles and meaning of fish and fisheries in the environment, economy, society, and culture of medieval and early modern Europe. An analysis of key cultural artifacts, *Tracts on Fishing from the End of the Middle Ages: Fishers' Craft and Lettered Art*, is forthcoming from the University of Toronto Press in 1997. The present article grew from thinking and teaching about early environmental history; it frames issues he is developing into a book-length essay called "The Catch," on the medieval antecedents of today's world fisheries crisis.

6
The Extent of the English Forest in the Thirteenth Century

Margaret Ley Bazeley

I

THE first difficulty which confronts the student of the English forest is to be found in the ambiguity of the terms which are used to describe it. In its proper sense the word " forest " denotes either the whole area in which the king's game is protected by a special law, or a separate administrative district within it. But there are other and looser uses to which the term is put in the records. In the first place, it is frequently applied to mere woods in a forest area. Thus the wood of Islip, near Oxford, known by the distinctive name of " Cauda Aliz " or " La Quealiz," appears at one time as a part of the forest of Brill, at another as a separate forest coupled with it.[1] Brill, in its turn, was merely a part of the forest of Bernwood, which was itself a member of the " Forest between the bridges of Oxford and Stamford ".[2]

Still more misleading is the use of the word " forest " to describe districts where the rights of chace are in the hands of a subject.[3] Over seventy such forests appear in the official records of the thirteenth century. Nor is it always easy to distinguish them at first sight from the forest

[1] *Close Roll*, 1233, p. 345; 1235, p. 111. 33 Hen. III, m 7.

[2] The " wood of Withcote," Leicestershire, so described in an order of 1236 (*ib.*, p. 305) appears three years later as the " forest of Salvey " (*ib.*, 1239, p. 156); Hartley in Great Minterne appears in consecutive orders as a " forest " and as a " park and wood," *ib.*, 1238, pp. 30 and 39.

[3] *E.g.* " the forest of the bishopric of Chester," *Close Roll*, 1244, p. 224.

proper. It is possible that to the ordinary Englishman of the time the distinction did not seem very important. The restrictions of the one were apt to be almost as severe as those of the other. Indeed, if we may judge by the space allotted in the Wiltshire Hundred Rolls [1] to the misdeeds of the foresters of Cranbourne Chase, the private forest was sometimes the more burdensome of the two.

The object of the private owner was always to secure as many as possible of the rights exercised in the royal forests; and the king was occasionally willing to help him. Examples of the privileges conceded in some of the more important private forests are to be found in Mr. Turner's *Introduction to the Select Pleas of the Forest.*[2] We may notice two further cases. A charter of John grants to Geoffrey fitz Peter, Earl of Hereford and Essex, "the forest of Huntingdonshire between the hay of Kimbolton and the park of Melbourn as fully as the king had it, so that a regard be made here when it is made in the forest, and the said Geoffrey shall have the pleas and amercements".[3] A charter of Henry III grants to the Abbey of Whitby the right to have their own verderers in their forest of Whitby to present transgressions before the royal justices for the forest pleas, as the king's verderers: and provides that offenders living outside the liberty who cannot be attached by the verderers shall be attached by the justice of the forest.[4]

As a rule, the grantee of a royal forest would retain some, at least, of the old rights. Thus, a charter of Edmund of Lancaster, confirmed in 1280, grants to the abbess of Tarrant "all his manor of Bere, Co. Dorset, which he had of the gift of his father . . . with the warren and forest of Bere, with all the venison, wood and vert, with power to

[1] *Rot. Hund.*, ii. 245, 248, 249, 253, etc.

[2] Pp. cxi.–cxiii.

[3] *For. Proc. T.R.*, no. 44, m. 1, 45, m. 1. *Cf.* "regard in the liberty of the honour of Kimbolton," 39 Hen. III, *ib.*, no. 40.

[4] *Cart. of Whitby Abbey* (Surtees Soc.), pp. 534–5. *Cf. Chanc. Misc.*, 12/6, 10. Forest law continued to be enforced as of course in the forests granted to Queen Eleanor, *Cal. Pat. Roll.*, 1273, p. 28.

cultivate at will, with attachments, pleas and amercements of vert and venison, and all rents of purprestures".[1] It is probable that many of the royal rights abandoned in disafforested districts fell into private hands in a less legitimate way. Thus the Abbot of Newminster, Northumberland, put "in defense" parts of the district disafforested in 1280, excluding others who had rights in it.[2]

Such proceedings were not confined to those districts which had once been under forest law. It is clear that a great deal of private afforestation went on in the twelfth, and even the thirteenth century. Earl Reginald, brother of Henry II, if the jurors of 1279 may be believed, afforested the greater part of Blackmore, in Dorset.[3] The afforestation of a large part of South Wiltshire was attributed to Richard de Clare at a still later date.[4]

Yet, although the private forest bears many of the marks of the forest proper, it is evident that a distinction was in fact drawn between them. A private forest in royal custody remained a private forest. Only such rights as were already in use were exercised.[5] It may even be doubted whether such forests as passed permanently into the king's hands after the beginning of the thirteenth century were drawn into the full forest system. Thus it is not clear that forest law was ever enforced in its entirety in the forest or chace of

[1] *Cal. Char. Rolls*, 1280, p. 227 : The exact position does not seem to have been clear : in the eyre roll of 54 Hen. III it is stated that "six regarders of the bailiwick of Bere were wont to act with them (*i.e.* the regarders of Poorstock), but Edmund the king's son holds the manor of la Bere and the forest pertaining as disafforested, and will not let them come".

[2] *Plac. de Quo Warr.*, p. 59.

[3] *Chanc. Misc.*, 12 /2 ; *cf. For. Proc. T.R.*, no. 11, m. 16.

[4] *Rot. Hund.*, ii. 249. The verdicts are not consistent, however : elsewhere the afforestation is ascribed to the present earl, *ib.*, p. 265 : much, if not all, Cranbourne Chase was in existence early in Henry III's reign. Randall Meschines is said to have afforested the Wirrall peninsula between 1119 and 1128 (Ormerod, *Hist. of Cheshire*, ii. 353). A letter close of June 30, 1225, shows that private afforestation had been going on in Westmorland and Lancashire.

[5] See the case of Knaresborough Forest, *Select Pleas*, cx,

Keynsham or Kingswood, near Bristol,[1] which had been filched by John from the honour of Gloucester.[2] The pleas were heard, at least in Edward I's reign, by ordinary justices, as in private parks.[3]

While the *forest* so called was not always under forest law, districts otherwise designated were frequently subject to it. Such were the *hays* to be found in great number in the records of the period. In many cases, a fairly small enclosed area is probably to be understood; but it is clear that the term was often used in a much wider sense. The hay of Lythwood, in Shropshire, represented a number of woods and townships.[4] The Hay of Hereford was a forest district some six miles in length, including part of the county town.[5]

The status of the royal parks is more difficult to define. A large number were certainly subject to forest law. Of these the great majority are found to be parks within a forest area or adjacent to it.[6] In some cases—perhaps in many—they formed its original nucleus. It was so, it seems, with Gillingham Park, in Dorset,[7] and North Petherton Park,[8] in Somerset. Sometimes the park wall was broken as a preliminary to the afforestment of the surrounding district. Thus Alan de Neville, according to the verdict of 1279,

[1] Also described as the "chace of Bristol" (*Char. Roll*, 1253, p. 415) and "hay of Kingswood" (*Close Roll*. 1236, p. 242). In M. Petit Dutaillis' essay this Kingswood is confused with that in the forest of Essex. (*Hist. Const. de l'Angleterre*, ii. 760.) The restriction cited by him would apply no less, it seems, in private forests; *cf. Sel. Pleas*, cx.

[2] *Cf. Rot. Litt. Claus*. i. 344, 352, 360, ii. 54, etc.

[3] *Cf. Cal. Pat.*, 1285, p. 153, and 1292, p. 519 : The forests of Cheshire which passed to the Crown in 1237, retained like the county their separate jurisdiction, remaining independent of the Justice of the forest north of Trent. A mandate concerning disafforestment in 1277 is addressed to the Justice of Chester, and the foresters and verderers, *Cal. Pat. Rolls*, p. 193; *cf. Close Roll*, 35 Hen. III m 7 ?

[4] *For. Proc. T.R.*, no. 148.

[5] *Ib.*, nos. 255 and 35.

[6] *E.g.* Woodstock Park, *For. Proc. T.R.*, 136, and *Close Roll*, 1240, p. 234; Guildford Park, *Sel. Pleas of Forest*, p. 54; Ridlington Park, *ib.*, p. 44.

[7] *Cf.* Stowe MSS., 798 f. 6.

[8] *Cf. Chanc. Misc.*, 12/1.

"broke the park of Milchet and caused the beasts to stray, wherefore he has afforested the wood of Milchet, etc".[1] In 1218 the park of North Petherton was reported to have been long unenclosed. It was still so, sixty years later.[2]

One clear example only has been noted of an isolated royal park under the jurisdiction of the justice of the forest—the park of Kenilworth, in the county of Warwick.[3] Elsewhere little has been found to support M. Petit Dutaillis' contention that such parks were subject to forest law in the same way as those surrounded by forest.[4] In one case noted, that of the royal park of Eltham, Co. Kent, the evidence seems to point in the opposite direction. Orders concerning this park are addressed, not to forest officials, but to the keeper of the king's manor of Eltham.[5] Nor has any reference to it been found in the forest proceedings of the period. Kent is noted in 1300 as one of several counties in which the king had no forests, and forest law does not appear to have been in force there at any earlier date.[6] Further evidence is needed before the exact position of the royal park as such can be established.

In a few cases, royal warrens were subject to forest law. Here, too, such warrens, as a rule, were within the metes of a forest, and in one or two cases, at any rate, formed its original nucleus. Such was the warren of Somerton, which included in the thirteenth century a number of the surrounding vills;[7] and the warren of Corfe, which became under John the centre of a forest in Purbeck.[8] Of isolated royal

[1] *Cf. Chanc. Misc.*, 12/2, 4.

[2] *Ib.*, 12/1 and 12/2, 2, and *For. Proc. T.R.*, 154. That the park was not always enclosed in practice is clear from this and other entries. In 1231 the king granted that Woodstock Park should be enclosed on account of the damage done by the beasts to the crops of the men of the neighbourhood (*Close Roll*, p. 500). If the park was closed the enforcement of forest law within it would have made but little difference to the neighbourhood.

[3] *Pat. Roll*, 1222, p. 361 and *Close Roll*, 1244, p. 151.

[4] Stubbs, *Hist. Const. de l'Angl.*, ii. 760.

[5] *Close Roll*, 1246, p. 427.

[6] *Parl. Writs*, I, 91a; *Sel. Pleas*, p. cviii; *cf. Rot. Litt. Claus.*, ii. 212.

[7] *Cf. For. Proc. T.R.*, no. 153, m. 1. *Chanc. Misc.*, 12/2, 2.

[8] The jurors in 1225 stated that "John afforested all Purbeck which

warrens under the jurisdiction of the justice of the forest, we know only of the warrens of Staines[1] and Cambridge.[2] The former was disafforested in 1227: the latter, when it appears in the eyre roll of 13 Edw. I, was certainly not subject to the full forest law.

Within the forest proper we find many varying degrees of afforestment. The forest law was being constantly mitigated by more or less comprehensive exemptions. The commonest of these was exemption from the regard enjoyed by a large proportion of the woods in each forest. Frequently the royal grant specified in addition, " freedom from all forests and all suits of the forest," the forest eyre being implicitly or explicitly excepted.[3]

Beyond this, numerous liberties were enjoyed within the forests, amounting in some cases to practical disafforestment. Thus the Bishop of Winchester secured by charter the rights of chace with complete independence of the forest officials in all his lands, and those of the priory of S. Swithun within and without the metes of the king's forest, the only stipulation being that no nets should be placed for the venison.[4] The Earl Marshall, early in the reign of Henry III, succeeded in withdrawing a large district in the neighbourhood of Chepstow from the jurisdiction of the forest of Dean.[5] The Bishop of Lichfield about the same time appropriated in

ought not to be forest except the warren of hares pertaining to Corfe Castle" (Stowe MSS., 798, f. 6 and Hutchin's *Dorset*, iii. 662). In 1232 Henry III granted exemptions from lawing of dogs to all tenants of his warren of Corfe (*Close Roll*, p. 88 and *Cal. of Chart. Rolls*, 164). The "warren of Corfe" and the "forest of Purbeck" continue to appear in royal orders during the century, *cf. Close Roll*, 1240, p. 217, Inq. a.q.d. 54 Hen. III, iii. 21, *Cal. Pat. Rolls*, 1283, p. 80. The warren does not appear in the eyre rolls of the latter part of Henry III's reign, nor in the perambulations of Edw. I's reign, but an entry on the fine rolls of Aug. 5, 1275, seems to show that it was still under forest law.

[1] *Cal. Chart. Rolls*, 1227, p. 56.

[2] *Sel. Pleas*, cxxxiii.

[3] *Cf.* grant to Evesham Abbey, 26 Hen. III, *Chanc. Misc.*, 12/8, and to Selbourne Priory, *ib.*; and the arrangement with Chertsey Abbey, *Rot. Litt. Claus.*, ii. 56b.

[4] *Cal. Chart. Rolls*, 1284, p. 274.

[5] *Trans. Bristol and Glos. Arch. Soc.*, vol. xxxiii. 160.

right of his manors of Rugely and Cannock, the covert of the forest of Cannock and two of the forest bailiwicks.[1] One of these was recovered by a suit on the part of the Crown. A great deal of friction ensued, and it was not until 1290 that the bishop secured the confirmation of his right to hold the woods in question " as a free chace, disafforested, although within the metes of the forest of Cannock ".[2]

The official view of such chaces is not consistent. The Bishop of Lichfield's liberty is distinguished from the forest in the plea rolls and included within it in a description of the bounds.[3] The Earl Marshall's chace is included in the forest in a regard of 1282 and described as outside it in an eyre roll of the same year.[4] It is clear that the forest system was not so hard and fast as it is often pictured.

II

The Forest had probably reached its widest extent by the end of Henry II's reign. That some afforestation took place under Richard I is clear from the terms of the Great Charter and the Charter of the Forest. That it was not very considerable may be inferred from the silence of the forest records concerning it. On the other hand, losses were certainly sustained during Richard's reign. The disafforestment of that part of Bedfordshire which Henry I afforested, was purchased by the barons of the county for 200 marks in 1191.[5] The knights of Surrey were paying a like sum for the disafforestment of some three-fourths of the county at the same date.[6] In both cases the exemption gained was final.

That John added wide afforestations to his other mis-

[1] *Hist. Coll. for Hist. of Staffs*, vol. v., pt. 1, p. 166.

[2] *Cal. Chart. Rolls*, p. 347.

[3] *Hist. Coll. for Hist. of Staffs*, vol. v., pt. 1, pp. 137–166.

[4] *For. Proc. T.R.*, no. 30, m. 9d, and no. 31. *Trans. Bristol and Glos. Arch. Soc.*, xxxiii. 161.

[5] *Vict. Hist. of Bedfordshire*, ii. 144.

[6] *Sel. Pleas*, p. 118, note 1. For other disafforestments in this reign see *Chanc. Misc.*, 12/5, no. 21; *Sarum Charters and Documents, Rolls Series*, 97, no. lvi.

deeds was the firm belief of a later generation, but contemporary evidence, apart from the reference in the Charters, is of the scantiest. The extant perambulations of the early years of Henry III, representing some nineteen counties, ascribe the wrongful extension of the forests in two cases only to John.[1] In six counties, Cumberland, Yorkshire, Huntingdon, Berkshire, Shropshire and Hereford, the jurors stated, in answer apparently to enquiry under that head, that no afforestations were made by him,[2] though the Cumberland and Hereford jurors go on to say that he put certain woods " in defense " : those in Herefordshire were now out. The jurors of Edward I's reign have much more to say on the subject,[3] but their statements cannot be accepted without some hesitation. Obvious inaccuracies appear more than once. Thus the afforestation of Hewelsfield, in the Forest of Dean, which the jurors of 1300 attribute to John, is recorded in Domesday as the work of the Conqueror.[4] That of Bere, Co. Dorset, laid upon John in 1279, had already taken place according to the perambulation of 1225, under Henry II.[5] The later verdicts are in any case open to suspicion in view of their distance from the events, their dependence on hearsay,[6] and the wild statements to

[1] Certain woods in Oxfordshire and the Isle Purbeck. *Chanc. Misc.*, 11 /1, 19, and Hutchin's *History of Dorset*, iii. 662.

[2] *Chanc. Misc.*, 11 /1, 16, 10. *For. Proc. T.R.*, no. 38, m. 1. Stowe MSS. 798, ff. 8 11, 11d.

[3] Afforestations are attributed to John in Dean (*For. Proc. T.R.*, 255), Hay of Hereford (*ib.*), Feckenham in Warwickshire (*ib.* and *Sel. Pleas*, p. 119), Porchester (*Chanc, Misc.*, 12 /2), Blackmore (*ib.*), Exmoor (*ib.*), North Petherton (*Pat. Roll Supp.* 6a), Selwood (*For. Proc. T.R.*, 154, m. 2), Rutland (*Sel. Pleas*, pp. 116, 117), and Essex (Fisher, p. 398), where " and by the kings Richard and John " is added to the " after the first coronation of King Henry grandfather of the lord the King " of the earlier verdict in respect to about half the district excluded, *Ib.*, pp. 21–24.

[4] F. 167. No mention is made of John in the perambulation of 1298 ; for the similar case of the wood of Ross, *infra* p. 159.

[5] Hutchin's *Hist. of Dorset*, iii. 662. In Rutland the burden of responsibility is shifted in the same way from the shoulders of Henry II to those of John (*Sel. Pleas*, xciv. 116–117).

[6] *E.g.* Warwickshire, *ib.*, 121, Gloucestershire, *Glos.*, *Notes and Queries*, vol. 8, p. 7.

which they occasionally commit themselves.[1] Some afforestation clearly took place under John, but it was probably not enough to balance the very considerable disafforestments to which his necessities drove him.

Large districts in Devon,[2] Cornwall,[3] Staffordshire and Shropshire,[4] Yorkshire[5] and Essex[6] were disafforested in 1204. The disafforestment of Nassaburgh Hundred in Northamptonshire, and part of Trivel Forest, Co. Hereford, was negotiated by the abbots of Peterborough[7] and Abbey Dore[8] respectively, later in the reign. Two hundred marks were paid in each case. The Brewood charter cost the men of Shropshire and Staffordshire 100 marks. 500 marks and five palfreys were paid for the charter to Essex.

The reduction of the forest area was therefore already in progress when the Great Charter of 1215, followed by the Charter of the Forest in 1217, held out hopes of wider concessions. Articles 1 and 3 of the Charter of the Forest promised the disafforestment by verdict of the county of the lands afforested by Henry II, outside the royal demesne, and the summary disafforestment of all such lands afforested by Richard and John.[9]

The perambulations made in accordance with the Charters during the next few years were of a sweeping character.

[1] *Cf.* the statement of the Somerset jurors that John afforested all England, *ib.*, cii. note 1.

[2] *Viz.*, all Devon as far as the metes of Dartmoor and Exmoor, *Sel. Pleas*, p. cvii.

[3] *Viz.*, all Cornwall, except two moors and two groves disafforested later in the reign, *ib.*, and *For. Proc. T.R.*, 249, m. 9 ; how much of the county was previously in forest is not clear.

[4] *Viz.*, Brewood and New Forest, *Rot. Chart.* (*Rec. Com.*), p. 122 and *Hist. Coll. for Hist. of Staffs*, vol. 5, pt. 1, p. 155.

[5] *Viz.*, Ridale, *Rot. Chart.*, p. 121.

[6] *Viz.*, forest north of Stanestreet, *ib.*, 123, and Fisher's *Forest of Essex*, p. 19.

[7] *Rot. Litt. Claus.*, i. p. 381.

[8] *Cal. Chart Rolls*, 1227, p. 2, and *Chanc. Misc.*, 12 /7, 10 ; a marsh in Lincolnshire was also disafforested in 1204, *Rot. Chart.*, p. 128.

[9] *Stubbs' Charters*, pp. 348 ff. No evidence of any summary disafforestment has been found ; as *M. Petit Dutaillis* remarks, it was, in fact, scarcely practicable, *Op. cit.*, p. 802.

The extant verdicts of 1218, 1219 and 1225 claim the exemption of the greater part of the forests under review. There was a natural hesitation on the part of the government in putting them into effect.[1] The earlier perambulations appear to have been actually enforced in some cases,[2] but were annulled by an order of 1224, directing that the forests should be kept as in the time of King John before the war between him and his barons.[3] Of the perambulations of 1225, that of Sussex remained unchallenged, probably because the king had granted away his remaining rights before the moment for revision arrived.[4] The perambulation in Derbyshire was also, it seems, allowed to stand. There is no record of a revision, and the district disafforested does not reappear in the forest records. No evidence is forthcoming with regard to Warwick, Northumberland, and Buckinghamshire, which appear in the list of counties noted in 1227 as " quit ".[5] The Buckinghamshire perambulation, if allowed to pass now, was certainly modified later.[6]

In all the other forest counties a revision was ordered by Henry on attaining his majority in 1227 on the ground that royal demesne and districts in the forest before Henry II's time had been affected.[7] As a result most of the perambulations were greatly modified. In the counties of Lancashire,[8] Huntingdon, Rutland and Leicester, Shropshire,[9] Stafford, Surrey, Worcester and York, the jurors acknowledged their error, and the forests were ordered to be kept as before the war between John and his barons. The

[1] *Cf. Sel. Pleas of the Forest*, pp. xciii ff.

[2] *E.g.*, in Huntingdon, *For. Proc. T.R.*, no. 28, m. 2d.

[3] *Rot. Litt. Claus.*, ii. 1.

[4] *Cal. Chart Rolls*, 1227, p. 8, and Rot. Litt. Claus., ii. 80.

[5] *Ib.*, p. 212.

[6] Compare peramb. in *Chanc. Misc.*, 11 /1, 5, with list of woods given in 40 Hen. III (*For. Proc. T.R.*, no. 2, m. 6,) and 28 Edw. I (*Pat. Roll*, Supp. 6a).

[7] *Rot. Litt. Claus.*, ii. 206. *Sel. Pleas*, p. xcix.

[8] For perambulations in this and the following counties, see Appendix III.

[9] With an insignificant exception.

forests of Somerset and of Gillingham and Bere in Dorset [1] were subsequently recalled to their old state by the royal officials without, apparently, any such acknowledgment. In Essex, Hampshire, Wiltshire, Northamptonshire and Nottinghamshire, the jurors agreed to modify their statements and some concessions were accordingly made.

How far Henry's contention is justified by the facts there is, unfortunately, but little to show. Lands in the king's hands at the time of the Domesday Survey had certainly been affected.[2] There is little evidence that those still belonging to the Crown after 1154 had been touched.[3] It would seem that Henry and his successors held the reservation in the Forest Charter to apply to the former class as well as to the latter. The new afforestations attributed by the jurors to Henry II are so extensive that one hesitates to accept them in the absence of other evidence. In one or two cases the evidence points in the opposite direction. The historical version given by the Leicestershire and Rutland jurors is hard to reconcile with the detailed account presented in the eyre of 1248–9,[4] which, though later, bears the marks of truth. The Buckinghamshire account, on the other hand, carries a certain amount of conviction.[5] In most counties a bare statement is made and no substantiation attempted.

[1] *Chanc. Misc.*, 12/2, 2. *Cf. Rot. Litt. Claus.*, ii. 73, with its reference to an " opportune moment expected " : the two counties had offered, if not actually paid, £100 for a perambulation in 1218 (*Sel. Pleas*, p. xcv.).

[2] *E.g.*, in N.W. Bucks, *Chanc. Misc.*, 11/1, 15.

[3] An example should perhaps be found in Nottinghamshire where certain royal demesnes on the north and west of Sherwood forest appear to have been excluded, *Rot. Litt. Claus.*, ii. 169, 208 ; *Close Roll*, 1234, p. 425 ; *Chanc. Misc.*, 11, 6/10. *Cf. For. Proc. T.R.*, 133. It is not quite clear whether royal demesne noted in the Surrey perambulation was included in the disafforestment or not, *cf. Rot. Litt. Claus.*, ii. 56b. A closer study of local history in each case may bring other instances to light.

[4] *Sel. Pleas*, pp. 45–6.

[5] See, too, the Huntingdon and Cumberland perambulations, *For. Proc. T.R.*, no. 38 and *Chanc. Misc.*, 11/1, 16.

The evidence produced on the king's side is nowhere recorded. Concessions subsequently made in Worcestershire, Yorkshire and Leicestershire show, perhaps, that he was not very sure of his ground. Ombersley and Horewell, in Worcestershire, were disafforested by charter in 1229[1]; the forest between Ouse and Derwent, Co. York, with the exception of the hay of Langwith, in 1234[2]; the forest of Leicestershire, except the manor of Withcote, in 1235.[3]

The results of the revision in the remaining counties are not recorded, but can be traced in part. In Gloucestershire the disafforestment of the greater part of the forest east of the Severn was conceded by a charter of May, 1228,[4] in accordance with a perambulation enrolled on the close roll of 1228.[5] It is not clear how much modification this last had undergone. In Berkshire the district disafforested by charter of 1227[6] corresponds exactly with that described in what appears to be the original verdict.[7] The Cumberland perambulation of 1225 is missing, but probably did not differ greatly from that of 1219. Large districts on the north, east and south, there noted as new afforestments, do not reappear in the later records. It is likely, therefore, that here too much of the 1225 perambulation was allowed to stand. It is possible that Oxfordshire was equally fortunate. The bounds later in use correspond with those of an apparently unrevised verdict of the early years of Henry III.[8] The Lincolnshire men could not have asked for more than the disafforestment of the remaining forest granted to them by a charter of 1230.[9] There is no evidence

[1] *Cal. Chart. Rolls*, p. 102; the Bishop of Worcester had paid 700 marks for a perambulation here eleven years before. *Pat. Roll*, 1218, p. 162.

[2] *Close Roll*, p. 477, and 1237, p. 11.

[3] *Ib.*, 19 Hen. III, p. 82, and *Cal. Chart. Rolls*, 1235, p. 193.

[4] P. 75. [5] M. 10d.

[6] *Cal. Chart. Roll*, 1227, p. 39.

[7] Stowe MSS., 798 f., 8.

[8] *Ib.*, *f.* 7.

[9] *Cal. Chart. Roll*, p. 122.

forthcoming as to the fate of the perambulations in Hereford [1] and Devon.[2]

The disafforestments actually secured were considerable. The counties of Sussex, Lincoln, Leicester and Middlesex obtained total exemption from the forest. In Derbyshire and Oxfordshire, more than half; in Cumberland, Gloucestershire and Worcestershire, more than a third; in Nottinghamshire, perhaps as much as two-thirds, and in Berkshire four-fifths[3] of the forest area was surrendered by the Crown. The men of Essex secured the disafforestment of Tendring Hundred; the men of York, of the forest between the Ouse and the Derwent. In Northamptonshire, Hampshire and Wiltshire districts more or less considerable were exempted.[4]

But if much was granted, more had been refused. In few of the cases just noted were the full claims of the county conceded. In Northamptonshire, Nottinghamshire, Wiltshire, Hampshire and Essex the perambulations had been more or less severely modified. The counties of Huntingdon, Lancashire, Rutland, Shropshire, Stafford and Surrey had been induced to retract the whole of their demand and remained *in statu quo*. The case of Huntingdon was particularly hard. The county had paid 40 marks for a perambulation in 1218.[5] The jurors who made it had been heavily fined and imprisoned,[6] and after three subsequent perambulations the whole county remained in the forest.[7]

[1] The land of Irchenefeld in Herefordshire was disafforested with the exception of three woods in 1251, for a fine of 200 marks. *Cal. Chart. Rolls*, p. 367.

[2] For Devon forests, *see* note at end of Appendix I.

[3] If the identification of the river Lente with the river Cole is correct (*cf. Pat. Roll*, 1221, p. 288 and index).

[4] In many cases, probably in most, the grant of disafforestment was made by charter and a money payment exacted in return.

[5] *Pat. Roll*, p. 162 and *Sel. Pleas*, xcv., note 8.

[6] *For. Proc. T.R.*, no. 38, m. 2d.

[7] *Rot. Litt. Claus.*, ii. 169; *cf.* the case of Somerset and Dorset above. There is no clear evidence, as we have seen, for any disafforestment at this time in Hereford, Devon, Warwick, Northumberland and Buckinghamshire.

Substantial as the concessions had been, a very large proportion of the forests still remained untouched.[1]

Nor were the revised arrangements in all cases strictly maintained. In Nottinghamshire [2] Henry III subsequently reclaimed lands which had once formed part of the royal demesne. In other cases his ministers bore the blame. Robert Passelewe, when justice of the forest, re-afforested certain woods of the Abbess of Ramsey in Wiltshire.[3] In Berkshire, Robert Passelewe and Walter of Eversley, the forester of Pamber, between them, afforested a wood belonging to Stratfield Mortimer, declaring it to be in Hampshire.[4] In the last-named county considerable re-afforestation took place. Many of the woods expressly put out by the revised perambulation of 1228 reappear in the eyre rolls of the period.[5] The woods south of the river Avon there exempted are included in a perambulation of the bailiwick of Chute later in the reign.[6] In the neighbourhood of Alice Holt a number of woods were afforested, according to the verdict of 1300, by Henry III's ministers.[7] The bailiwick of Bagshot, in N.E. Hampshire, which should have ended by the arrangement of 1228 at Crondall, extended in Edward I's reign to Winchester.[8]

[1] A letter close of June 27, 1238, "to all the sheriffs in whose bailiwicks the king's forests are," names Yorkshire, Cumberland, Lancashire, Northumberland, Nottingham and Derby, Warwick, Northampton, Buckingham, Rutland, Huntingdon, Essex, Berkshire, Hampshire, Surrey, Somerset, Dorset, Devon, Wiltshire, Worcester, Stafford, Gloucester, Hereford; Oxfordshire and Shropshire are omitted, probably by a slip. For a list of royal forests in the middle of the thirteenth century, *see* Appendix I.

[2] *Cf. For. Proc. T.R.*, 133, and plea rolls of the period; there is some indication, too, of interference with the revised arrangements in Northamptonshire, *cf. Close Roll*, 1231, Mar. 26 and *For. Proc. T.R.*, 77.

[3] *Wiltshire Inquisitions* (Wilts Arch. Soc.), pp. 66 and 131.

[4] *Chanc. Misc.*, 11 /3, 2 and 12 /10, 2.

[5] *E.g.*, Pappenholt, Itchen, Musholt, 53 Hen. III. *For. Proc. T.R.*, no. 158; compare *Close Roll*, 1228, pp. 102–3.

[6] *Chanc. Misc.*, 12 /9.

[7] *Pat. Roll*, Supp. 6a.

[8] *Ib.* and *For. Proc. T.R.*, 150, where many of the townships between Crondall and Winchester are to be found; compare the statements as to the adjoining bailiwick of Eversley in 26 Edw. 1, D. of Lanc. *For. Proc.* 1 /8.

Such gains, however, did little to compensate for new losses in other directions. Several forests were granted away by Henry in the middle and latter part of his reign. The land between Ribble and Mersey, with the forest of West Derby, was given to Ranulph, Earl of Chester, in 1229.[1] Dartmoor was given in 1239 to Richard, Earl of Cornwall.[2] Edmund, the king's second son, received the forests of Wyresdale, Lonsdale and Pickering in 1267,[3] and two years later the forest of Bere in Dorset.[4] Smaller portions of the forest were granted away elsewhere.[5]

Apart from direct gifts, Henry was lavish in grants of liberties scarcely to be distinguished from complete disafforestment. The Bishop of Winchester's considerable privileges seem to have been conferred, or at least confirmed, and added to by him.[6] Several of the great ecclesiastics and others secured more moderate concessions.[7]

Elsewhere districts were lost to the forest through pure negligence. Such, apparently, were the chaces of the Bishop of Lichfield in Cannock, and of the Earl Marshall in Dean, already referred to.[8] In Huntingdonshire the Bishop of Ely was suffered to appropriate portions of the forest adjoining his chace of Somersham.[9] The eyre roll of 1282 records that when the foresters and verderers went to Benewyk to make inquisition, the bishop's bailiff met them, leading three

[1] *Vict. Hist. Lancs*, iii. p. 3; *cf. Sel. Pleas*, cxii.

[2] *Cal. Chart. Rolls*, i. p. 247.

[3] *Ib.*, ii. p. 78; probably also Amounderness, *cf.* Baines, *Hist. of Lancs*, v. 295.

[4] Hutchin's *Hist. of Dorset*, i. 136; *cf. For. Proc. T.R.*, no. 11, m. 2. Bere had been earlier granted to Simon de Montfort, *Cal. Chart. Rolls*, ii. 8 (1259).

[5] *E.g.*, Dalston in Englewood, *ib.* i. 115; Easingwald in Galtres, *ib.* 122. On the other hand, the king secured the forests of Cheshire on the death of the Earl in 1237, *ante*, p. 143, note 3.

[6] *Cal. Chart. Rolls*, ii. 279 (1284), "temp. Adelmar," *ib.* p. 366 (1286), *Close Roll*, 22 Hen. III, m. 20 and 21; *cf.* terms of John's Charter granting exemption from regard only, *For. Proc. T.R.*, no. 256.

[7] *E.g.* Ramsay (*Ramsay Cart.*, *Rolls Series*, i. 213); Selborne (*Chanc. Misc.*, 12/8); Earl of Chester and Huntingdon, *ib.* 12/3.

[8] *Ante*, p. 145 f.

[9] *Rot. Hund.*, i. 197.

priests with book, cross and candle, to excommunicate the ministers of the lord king, so that no inquisition could be made there that day.[1]

Here and there townships slipped out of the forest. Northover withdrew itself from the pleas of the warren of Somerton in 1268.[2] Huntsham was reported in the early years of Edward I to have been withdrawn from the forest of Dean.[3]

In the forest, as elsewhere, Edward I made some attempt to recover lost ground. Eyre rolls became longer ; fines for default increased in number [4] : liberties were more jealously questioned. The Bishop of Winchester's rights were investigated in 1286.[5] Roger le Bigod's liberty of Chepstow, long a nuisance to the forest of Dean, was ordered to be taken into the king's hands in the eyre of 1282.[6] The Bishop of Coventry had to surrender his chace of Cannock, acknowledge that it was within the bounds of the forest, and pay £1,000 to recover it.[7]

Of actual re-afforestment during the last quarter of the thirteenth century there is little proof in the records. The metes and bounds occasionally described on the eyre rolls seem to correspond roughly with the usage under Henry III. Disafforested lands included in them here and there were perhaps thought too small to be noticed.[8] Liberties, where ignored, were no doubt held to be technically forest.[9] The

[1] *For. Proc. T.R.*, no. 45, m. 6d.

[2] *Rot. Hund.*, i. 139.

[3] *For. Proc. T.R.*, no. 31.

[4] Compare the number of townships fined in the Huntingdon eyre of 14 Edw. I, *For. Proc. T.R.*, 45 and 46, with that in 40 Hen. III, *ib.* 41.

[5] *Cal. Chart. Rolls*, pp. 366–7.

[6] *For. Proc.*, no. 30, mm. 8 and 28d.

[7] *Hist. Coll. for Hist. of Staffs*, v. 166 *et seq.* The Bishop of Salisbury's chace of Le Bisschopebere was appropriated by the warden of Windsor Forest with or without the king's knowledge (*Chanc. Misc.*, 12 /10, 2).

[8] *E.g.* Penyard in Dean Forest, *For. Proc. T.R.*, no. 30, m. 12d, and no. 31.

[9] *E.g.* Tidenham Chace, *ib.* ; Barton and Doddington in Northants, *ib.* on. 74 and *Chanc. Misc.* 12 /3.

only clear attempt to revert to the earlier bounds—that made in Whittlewood forest—was apparently abandoned.[1]

With all his efforts, Edward could but delay the process of dismemberment. Already, in 1277, he had felt obliged to offer new concessions. In that year he issued directions for a "right perambulation, namely that which was made in the time of the lord king Henry our father which has not yet been challenged".[2] It is clear that the king had no intention of undoing the settlement of 1228, and intended the concession to apply only to those forests which had not been included in it, or in which its terms had not been faithfully kept.[3] The jurors, if we may judge from the few verdicts extant,[4] took a different view. In Hampshire and Wiltshire the decisions of 1228 were, in most cases, ignored, and considerable disafforestments demanded.[5] In Dorset, where the revision had apparently not been accepted by the county,[6] the bounds laid down followed in some cases word for word those of 1225. In Somerset,[7] they corresponded for the most part with those of 1219. In Berkshire alone,[8] where the claims of 1225 had been conceded at the time, was the *status quo* maintained.

Edward had no idea of parting with such large portions of his heritage, and the perambulations for the most part

[1] *For. Proc. T.R.*, no. 77; two sets of bounds are given, the first including much put out in 1228.

[2] *Pat. Roll*, p. 237: twenty-four counties are named, including Lancashire and Sussex, in which the king had now no forest. Devon and Cheshire do not appear.

[3] *Cf. Chanc. Misc.*, 12/11, 1 and 2.

[4] Verdicts are extant for Berkshire, Dorset, Hampshire, Somerset, Wiltshire. *See* Appendix III.

[5] *E.g.* the whole bailiwick of Bagshot, with the exception of two or three woods, and a great part of Savernake Forest were disafforested. *Chanc. Misc.*, 12/1, 2. The Wiltshire jurors follow in the main a perambulation of the early years of Henry III. It is possible that the Hampshire jurors had also before them earlier perambulations, now lost.

[6] *Chanc. Misc.*, 12/2, 2.

[7] *Ib.* and 12/1, 1; *For. Proc. T.R.*, no. 154, m. 1: "The jurors say that this perambulation is the same as that made rightly in the time of Henry III."

[8] *Chanc. Misc.*, 12/1, 3.

came to nothing.[1] In one or two cases, however, a concession was made. Blackmore, the largest of the Dorset forests, had been created, according to the verdict, by Earl Reginald, brother of Henry II, and extended by John. It now made good its escape.[2] The disafforestment of Northumberland for a yearly payment of 40 marks,[3] is perhaps connected in the same way with the order of 1277.[4]

Hostility to the forest system grew rapidly in the next twenty years, no doubt as a result of the greater strictness shown. It was an important factor in the political crisis at the end of the thirteenth century. Bishops and barons, attacked in their most treasured immunities, readily became the champions of constitutional freedom. Their victory resulted in an order for fresh perambulations in the autumn of 1297.[5] Those relating to part or the whole of six counties remain.[6] As in 1279, the revised boundaries of 1228 were ignored. Half the forest of Dean was put out, and the whole of the Oxfordshire portion of Bernwood. In Somerset, the jurors followed, in the main, the bounds of 1219; in Exmoor, however, they improved on them.[7] In Buckinghamshire, a part of Bernwood which had been left untouched by the jurors of 1219 and 1225, was now disafforested.[8] In Hampshire, the bounds corresponded roughly with those

[1] The king had ordered that nothing be done, " donee de ipso distincte et aperte et absque calumpnia fact et nobis . . . presentata, preceperimus fieri quod de consilio nostro providerimus faciendum ; " *cf. Sel. Pleas*, cii. *M. Petit Dutaillis'* strictures on Edward in this connection are perhaps unnecessarily harsh (*op. cit.*, p. 820 *et seq.*) ; Edward is here following earlier usage, *cf. Sel. Pleas*, xcv., xcvii. and *Rot. Litt. Claus.*, ii. 157, etc.

[2] *Pat. Roll*, Supp. 6a and *Chanc, Misc.*, 12 /2.

[3] *Cal. Chart. Rolls*, 1280, Dec. 28 : " those beyond the Coket give 23 marks, those south of the Coket 17 marks," *Chanc. Misc.*, 11 /3, 13.

[4] A few small disafforestments were made at other times during the period, *e.g.* Weverham in Cheshire, *Charter Roll*, 1275, p. 197 : land in Over and Sutton, *ib.* 1285, p. 282.

[5] *Sel. Pleas*, p. ciii.

[6] Gloucestershire, Essex, Hampshire, Oxfordshire, Somerset, Bernwood forest, Co. Bucks. *See* App. III.

[7] *Cf. Chanc. Misc.*, 1 /1, 1, and Rawle, *Forests of Exmoor*, pp. 36–40 and map.

[8] If we are right in assigning an early perambulation of Oxfordshire to the year 1219, it may be shown that the same sort of thing happened here.

laid down in 1279. But there was a tendency to ignore the exceptions noted in the earlier verdict.[1] Edward was still unprepared for such sweeping concessions and the perambulations remained a dead letter.

He found it impossible, however, to let the matter rest, and new perambulations were ordered in 1299 and 1300.[2] This time the Crown fared still worse. More than half the remaining forest area was declared to be outside the ancient bounds. In the counties of Huntingdon, Essex, York, Dorset and Somerset, with the exception of Exmoor, the bounds of 1219 and 1225 were followed in the main. In Exmoor, the Buckinghamshire part of Bernwood, and Cumberland these were narrowed still further.[3] In one or two cases the jurors were no longer content with the disafforestments demanded earlier in Edward's reign. In Wiltshire considerable additions were made to the demands of 1279. In Dean, the district wrongfully afforested had altered perceptibly, though not, perhaps, increased since 1298.

In two cases only, where a comparison is possible, do earlier claims appear to have been abated, *viz.* in the counties of Oxford and Surrey. In the last-named county alone was the *status quo* maintained.[4]

Where the encroachments described are of recent date, there is little reason to doubt the care and good faith of the jurors. The same may be said of the comparatively numerous cases where earlier verdicts are followed. Elsewhere it is hard to discover on what authority the dis-

[1] *E.g.* in Bagshot and Eversley bailiwicks, Hampshire *D^y. of Lanc. For. Proc.* 1 /8.

[2] *Sel. Pleas,* pp. civ ff. Verdicts relating to all the forest counties except Cheshire are extant; *see* App. III.

[3] The same is apparently the case in Worcestershire. Compare the 1300 perambulation with that in Stowe MSS., 798.

[4] The perambulation was revised in Edw. III's reign, the county maintaining that unfair pressure had been exercised on the jurors by the Crown (*cf.* Manwood, p. 135 ff.); the Berkshire perambulation excludes only a small district afforested under Hen. III. (*Chanc. Misc.*, 12 /10, 2); in Nottinghamshire, where Henry III's revision was roughly accepted, the subsequent reservation of royal demesne was ignored.

afforestments were made. In some cases, clearly, the jurors had no written evidence before them. In Warwickshire and Gloucestershire they acknowledged as much.[1] Such evidence, where available, was more than once ignored. An example may be found in Herefordshire, where the wood of Ross, noted as "in defensu regis" in Domesday Book,[2] was none the less excluded as an afforestment of John's time. The discrepancies, already noticed, as to the authorship of the original encroachments, show that often but little trouble was taken to verify the facts.

Whether there was any ground for the divergence from earlier demands where these are still further enlarged, it is impossible to say. It is unlikely that evidence unavailable in 1219 and 1225, or even in 1279, was forthcoming in 1300. Much more likely is it that the jurors, ignorant or careless of the earlier verdicts, invented tests of their own. The moment was favourable, and they may well have wished to make the most of it.

Edward's action in the circumstances is perhaps more excusable than M. Petit Dutaillis would allow. The disafforestments confirmed under the strongest pressure at the Parliament of Lincoln, were revoked at the earliest opportunity.[3] The final surrender was averted until the early years of Edward III.[4] With it, the forest system falls into the background of national history.

[1] *Sel. Pleas*, p. 121; *Gloucestershire Notes and Queries*, vol. 8, p. 7.

[2] F. 176b. *See* also the case of Hewelsfield. *ante*, p. 147.

[3] *Sel. Pleas*, p. cv.

[4] *See* Petit Dutaillis, *op. cit.*, pp. 829 ff.

APPENDIX I

LIST OF ROYAL FORESTS IN THE MIDDLE OF THE THIRTEENTH CENTURY

Berkshire, Windsor.
    Savernake (part).
Buckinghamshire, Bernwood (part), including Brill and Panshill.
    Salcey (part).
    Whittlewood (part).
Cheshire, Delamere or Mara and Moudrem, after 1237.
    Macclesfield ,,
    Wirrall ,,
Cumberland, Allerdale, between Alne and Chalk. *For. Proc. T.R.*, mm. 29, 30.
    Inglewood, between Eden and Caldew, *ib.* m. 33. The name is used in 20 Edw. I (Inq. ad Q.D. xviii. 15) of the Allerdale district also.
Derbyshire, Peak.
    Bolsover. *Cf. Close Roll*, 36 Hen. III, m. 14d.
Dorset, Bere, re-afforested *c.* 1250, *cf. Chanc. Misc.*, 12/2, 2, and Cal. Gen. 35 Hen. III, p. 37; alienated 1259.
    Blackmore.
    Gillingham.
    Poorstock.
    Purbeck, *see* p. 144, note 8.
Essex, forest of; many of the woods within it appear as separate forests in the records.
Gloucestershire, Dean.
    Kingswood: It is not certain whether this was under the jurisdiction of the Justice of the forest.
    Minety, a detached part of the county, was in the forest of Braden.

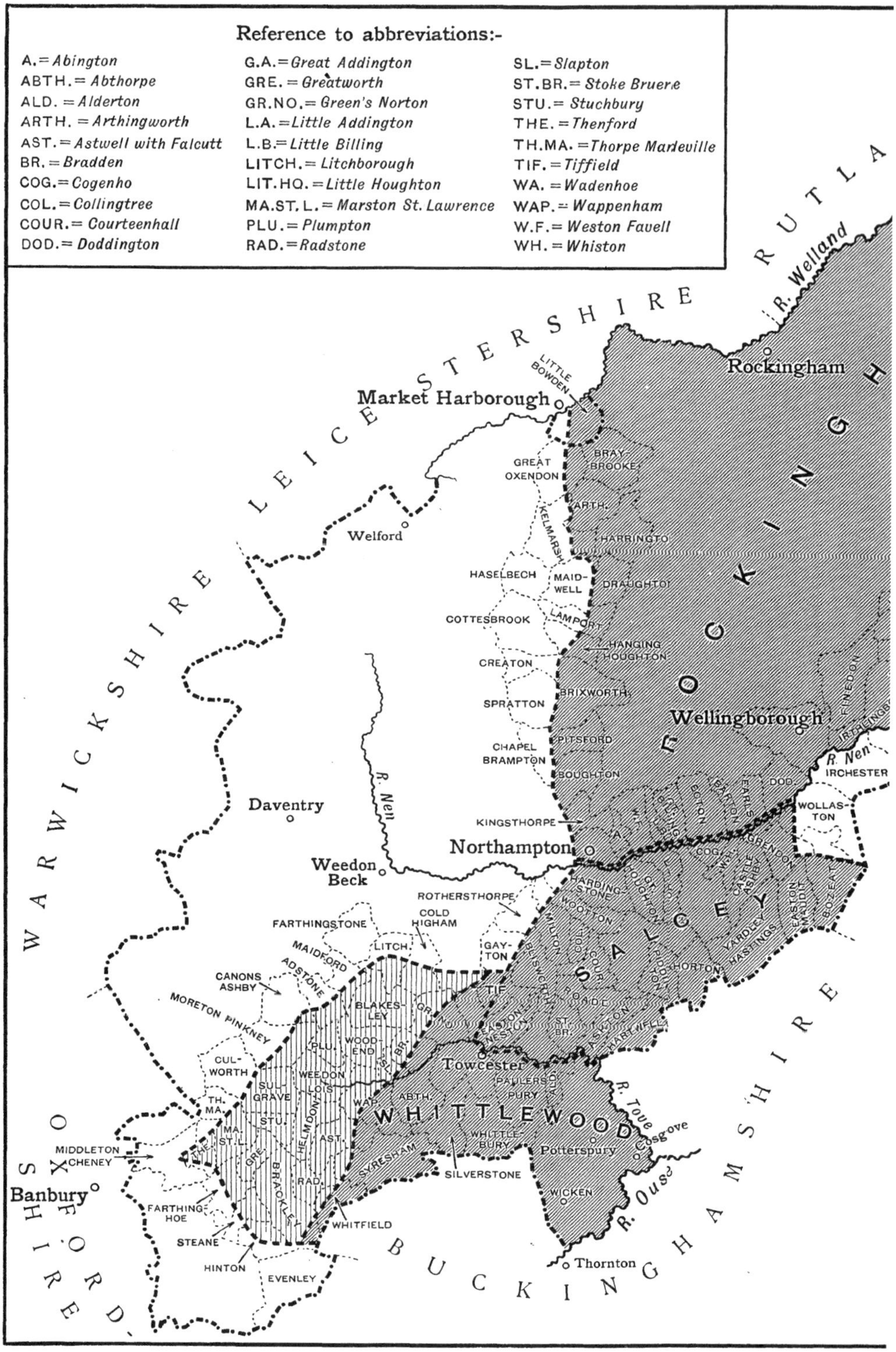
Reference to abbreviations:-
A.=Abington
ABTH.=Abthorpe
ALD.=Alderton
ARTH.=Arthingworth
AST.=Astwell with Falcutt
BR.=Bradden
COG.=Cogenho
COL.=Collingtree
COUR.=Courteenhall
DOD.=Doddington
G.A.=Great Addington
GRE.=Greatworth
GR.NO.=Green's Norton
L.A.=Little Addington
L.B.=Little Billing
LITCH.=Litchborough
LIT.HQ.=Little Houghton
MA.ST.L.=Marston St. Lawrence
PLU.=Plumpton
RAD.=Radstone
SL.=Slapton
ST.BR.=Stoke Bruerne
STU.=Stuchbury
THE.=Thenford
TH.MA.=Thorpe Marleville
TIF.=Tiffield
WA.=Wadenhoe
WAP.=Wappenham
W.F.=Weston Favell
WH.=Whiston
LEICESTERSHIRE
RUTLA
WARWICKSHIRE
OXFORDSHIRE
BUCKINGHAMSHIRE
ROCKINGH
SALCEY
WHITTLEWOOD
R. Welland
R. Nen
R. Toue
R. Ouse
Rockingham
Market Harborough
Welford
Wellingborough
Daventry
Weedon Beck
Northampton
Towcester
Potterspury
Banbury
Thornton
Cosgrove
LITTLE BOWDEN
GREAT OXENDON
BRAYBROOKE
KELMARSH
HARRINGTON
HASELBECH
MAIDWELL
DRAUGHTON
COTTESBROOK
LAMPORT
HANGING HOUGHTON
CREATON
BRIXWORTH
SPRATTON
PITSFORD
CHAPEL BRAMPTON
BOUGHTON
KINGSTHORPE
IRCHESTER
WOLLASTON
FINEDON
EARLS BARTON
ECTON
GRENDON
CASTLE ASHBY
YARDLEY HASTINGS
EASTON MAUDIT
BOZEAT
HARDINGSTONE
WOOTTON
MILTON
HORTON
ROTHERSTHORPE
COLD HIGHAM
FARTHINGSTONE
MAIDFORD
ADSTONE
CANONS ASHBY
MORETON PINKNEY
GAYTON
BLAKESLEY
WOODEND
CULWORTH
SULGRAVE
WEEDON LOIS
HELMDON
MIDDLETON CHENEY
FARTHINGHOE
STEANE
HINTON
EVENLEY
BRACKLEY
SYRESHAM
WHITFIELD
SILVERSTONE
WHITTLEBURY
PAULERSPURY
WICKEN
EASTON NESTON
ASHTON
HARTWELL

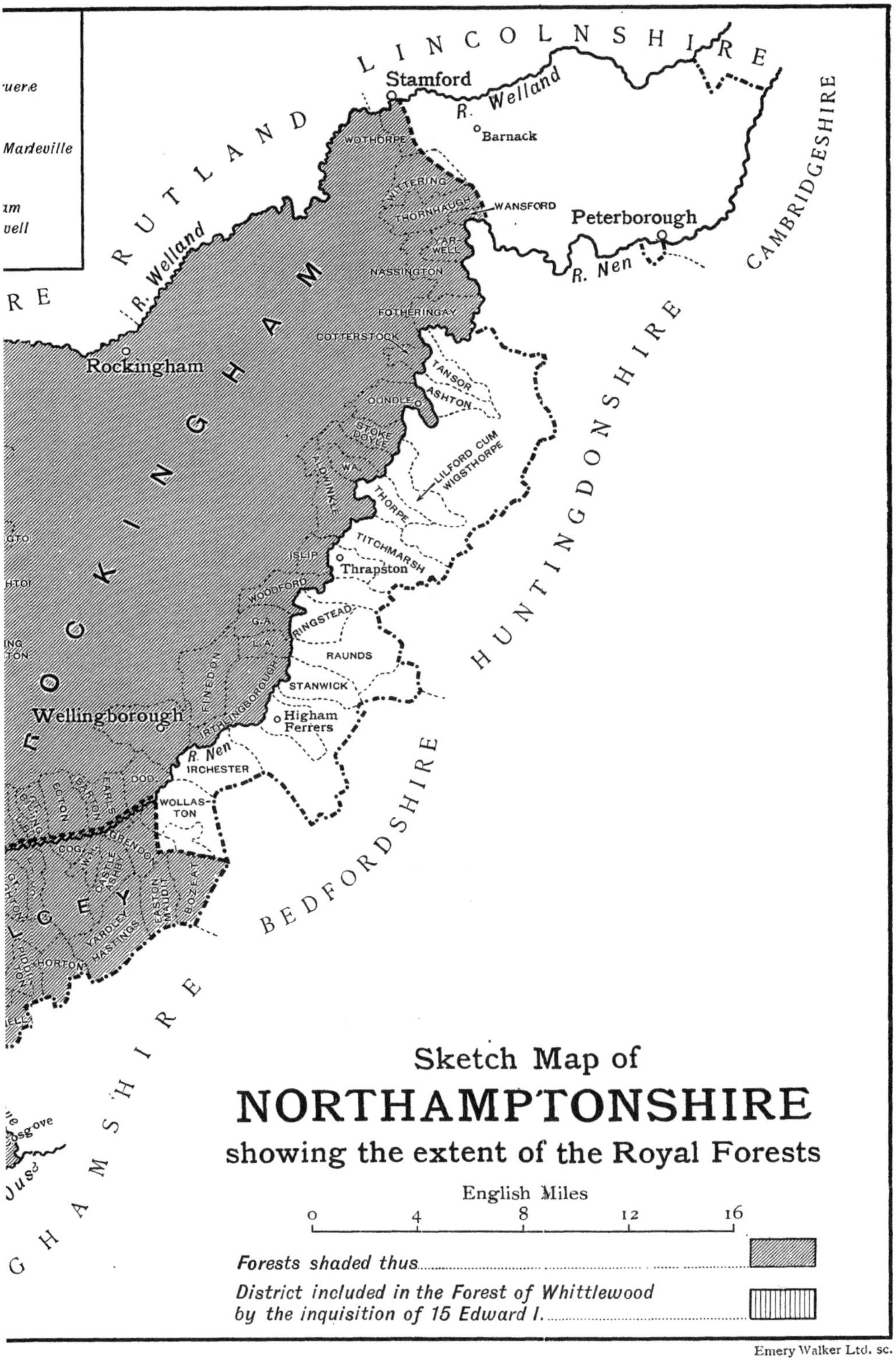
LINCOLNSHIRE
RUTLAND
CAMBRIDGESHIRE
HUNTINGDONSHIRE
BEDFORDSHIRE
ROCKINGHAM
Stamford
R. Welland
Barnack
WOTHORPE
WITTERING
THORNHAUGH
WANSFORD
Peterborough
YARWELL
NASSINGTON
R. Nen
FOTHERINGAY
COTTERSTOCK
Rockingham
TANSOR
ASHTON
OUNDLE
STOKE DOYLE
LILFORD CUM WIGSTHORPE
THORPE
TITCHMARSH
Thrapston
ISLIP
WOODFORD
RINGSTEAD
RAUNDS
STANWICK
Higham Ferrers
FINEDON
IRTHLINGBOROUGH
Wellingborough
IRCHESTER
WOLLASTON
DOD
COTON
BARTON
EARLS
GRENDON
CASTLE ASHBY
YARDLEY HASTINGS
EASTON MAUDIT
BOZEAT
HORTON
Sketch Map of
NORTHAMPTONSHIRE
showing the extent of the Royal Forests
English Miles
0 4 8 12 16
Forests shaded thus
District included in the Forest of Whittlewood by the inquisition of 15 Edward I.
Emery Walker Ltd. sc.

Hampshire, Alice Holt and Wolmer.
Bere Ashley.
Buckholt, connected with Clarendon, Wilts.
Chute (part), including Finkley and Digerley forests.
Freemantle.
New Forest.
Pamber.
Porchester, or Bere Porchester, including Halla Haroldi and Rode.
Windsor (part), comprising bailiwick of Bagshot and Eversley.
Herefordshire, Dean (part).
Hay of Hereford.
Irchenfield, disafforested 1251.
Huntingdonshire, forest of, including forests or hays of Weybridge, Sapley and Herthey.
Lancashire, Amounderness, including Bleasdale, Fulwood, Myerscough, alienated c. 1267.
Lonsdale, including Wyresdale and Quernmore, alienated 1267.
Leicestershire, Sauvey, a small extension of the forest of Rutland, including Withcote.
Northamptonshire, Rockingham, including Brigstock, Cliffe, Geddington, and Northampton Park.
Salcey (part).
Whittlewood (part).
Northumberland, forest of, disafforested 1280.
Nottingham, Sherwood.
Oxfordshire, Bernwood (part).
Shotover, including Stowood.
Whittlewood (part).
Woodstock.
Wychewood.
Rutland, forest of.
Shropshire, Long Forest, in which are occasionally included Long Mynd or Strattondale and Stapelwood, including Buriwood, Lythewood, and Stepelton.
Morf.
Shirlet.
Wrekin or Mount Gilbert, including Wellington and Wombridge.
Haughmond connected with the last named.

Somerset, Exmoor.
Keynsham (part of).
Mendip or Cheddar.
Neroche.
North Petherton.
Selwood.
Somerton warren.
Staffordshire, Cannock.
Kinver.
Surrey, Guildford Park.
Windsor (part).
Warwickshire, Feekenham (part).
Wiltshire, Braden.
Chute (part).
Clarendon, including Panchet, and in wider use, Milchet Park.
Grovely.
Melksham and Chippenham or Pewsham.
Savernake.
Selwood.
Worcestershire, Feckenham.
Kinver (part).
Yorkshire, Farndale.
Galtres.
Langwith Hay.
Pickering, alienated 1267.

NOTE ON THE FORESTS OF BEDFORDSHIRE AND DEVON AND NEW FOREST, HAMPSHIRE

Bedfordshire : No reference to forest in this county in the thirteenth century has been found later than 1219, in which year an inquisition as to assarts was ordered here as elsewhere. But in the patent roll of 6 Edward II (p. 490) woods at Harrold, Carlton, and Wilden are stated to be in the king's forest. Those at Harrold and Carlton may conceivably have formed part of the adjoining forest of Salcey, in Buckinghamshire, though not mentioned in any proceedings relating to it. The reference to Wilden remains inexplicable, unless we imagine it to have been afforested by Edward II. For the forest of Bedfordshire in the twelfth century, *see Vict. Hist. Bedf.*, ii. 144.

Devonshire: This county presents some difficulty. It does not appear in the orders relating to the perambulations of 1277 and 1297, but it does appear in that of 1299 (*Sel. Pleas*, p. civ. and note). A memorandum on the perambulations in the West returned in 1300 states that "nothing has been done in the said county of Devon regarding the forest of Exmoor, because by the said jurors it has been shown to us that the lord king has no forest in the said county whereby any encroachment could have been made" (*For. Proc. T.R.*, no. 154, m. 5, printed MacDermot, *Hist. of Exmoor*). No allusion to forest land in Devonshire after 1239 has been found in the eyre rolls of Henry III's or Edward I's reign (*cf.* MacDermot, *op. cit.*, pp. 6, 19). It is possible, in view of later references to forest in Devon, that debatable land between Devon and Somerset was included in Exmoor Forest (*cf. Sel. Pleas*, p. cvii., note 8). No satisfactory evidence can be derived from claims to common made at a much later date.

New Forest: Mr. Moens (*Archæol. Journ.*, vol. lx., p. 50) marks all Hampshire west of the river Avon, and part of Dorset, as in the New Forest up to 1279, on the ground of claims to commons in the Forest made in the seventeenth century by villages in those districts. No evidence of their inclusion has been found in contemporary records. On the other hand, there is direct evidence that Rockburne, one of the places concerned nearest to the Forest and attached to it at the time of Domesday, had been lost to it by 1236. In that year Rockburne wood was stated to be in Cranbourne Chase (*Close Roll*, p. 280). Subsequently it was discovered that the lord of the manor, John Biset, enjoyed the rights of chace (*ib.* p. 419). Of the Wiltshire places included by the same writer in the New Forest, one or two were in Milchet Forest, (*For. Proc. T.R.*, no. 202). No reference has been found in the forest proceedings to the others. There is no evidence that any disafforestment took place here as a result of the perambulation of 1279. The bounds presented in the eyre of 8 Edward I are clearly not those which the county had laid down as desirable in the previous year.

APPENDIX II

AUTHORITIES FOR THE EXTENT OF THE FOREST IN THE MIDDLE OF THE THIRTEENTH CENTURY, USED IN THE COMPILATION OF THE FOREGOING PAPER AND MAPS

I. *Perambulations and Inquisitions as to metes and bounds.* (For list and references *see* Appendix III.)

(*a*) 1218 *to* 1225; these occasionally give information as to the whole of the existing forest, under one head or another, and provide an authority for the later forest, where the old bounds are maintained. In any case they are useful in supporting other evidence.

(*b*) 1227 *to* 1232; these have been accepted as evidence of extent in the middle of the century, except where subsequent modification is recorded.

(*c*) 1279 *and* 1298 *to* 1300; these in a few cases describe the existing bounds, and are thus valuable as evidence for the earlier forest, where boundaries have remained unchanged, or modifications can be otherwise accounted for. Similar use can be made of those perambulations which give complete lists of "new afforestations" in addition to the "right and ancient bounds." Some caution is, however, necessary, for the lists include here and there woods already exempted from the forests. Such cases are rare and not apparently important. Where, as generally happens, the list of afforestations is incomplete, use may be made of such details as are given, in connection with other evidence.

(*d*) *Notes on the perambulations of Edw. I, temp. Edw. II and Edw. III*; these occasionally supply the names of disafforested districts lacking in the perambulations themselves, and have been used where they are consistent with earlier evidence.

(*e*) *Metes and bounds* enrolled in the eyres; these were probably presentments by the foresters and verderers only. They tend to ignore liberties within the forest bounds and, perhaps, small disafforested districts. Those of Henry's reign have been accepted as evidence; and those of Edward's reign, after general corroboration by other authorities.

II. *Proceedings in the forest courts other than the above.* These are most important as corroborating and supplementing the information given in the perambulations. Places within the forest appear under the following heads:—

(*a*) Townships responsible for making inquisition; the careful restriction of this duty to townships within the bounds is illustrated by the imposition of a fine in this connection on "half" several border townships in a Northamptonshire eyre roll (*For. Proc. T.R.*, 77).

(*b*) Townships making default; these can be taken as in the forest, unless it appears that they have been summoned on some special count. (Art. 2 of Charter of the Forest.)

(*c*) Townships in which expeditation is enforced (*ib.* Art. 6).

(*d*) Lands in which assarts are noted or where trespasses have taken place.

(*e*) Woods mentioned under the heading of "waste" or of "woodwards"; these are taken to be in the neighbourhood of the manors to which they belong, unless there is reason to suppose otherwise.

(*f*) Charters relating to land in the forest, produced in the eyre.

(*g*) Descriptions of forest bailiwicks.

III. *Grants and mandates enrolled among the charters, letters patent and close, fines, etc., and in private cartularies.* They include

(*a*) Grants of disafforestment, exemptions from the regard and other privileges in particular forests.

(*b*) Grants of forest bailiwicks, occasionally with the bounds described.

(*c*) Orders relating to woods and townships stated to be in certain forests; or shown from the context to be under forest jurisdiction, *e.g.* where the order is addressed to the justice of the forest or other forest official.

IV. Inquisitions relating to the forest in Inquisitions post mortem, and ad quod dampnum, Hundred Rolls, private cartularies and elsewhere.

APPENDIX III

LIST OF EXTANT PERAMBULATIONS AND INQUISITIONS AS TO METES AND BOUNDS

1218. *See Pat. Roll, July* 24.

Huntingdonshire : *For. Proc. T.R.*, no. 38, mm. 1 and 2d : dated morrow of St. Swithin, 2 Hen. III.

Leicestershire : *Chanc. Misc.*, bdle. 11, f. 1, no. 5, dated 2 Hen. III.

Nottinghamshire : *Chanc. Misc.*, 11/1, 6, dated Monday after S. Dunstan, 2 Hen. III.

Rutland : *Chanc. Misc.*, 11/1, 7, printed *Select Pleas of the Forest*, xciv. : dated S. James' Day, 2 Hen. III.

1218 or 1219, *see Pat. Roll, April* 22.

Somerset : *Chanc. Misc.*, 12/1, 1, undated, marked "2 Hen. III" in P.R.O. list, but more probably 3 Hen. III when fresh order issued ; *cf.* MacDermot, *Forest of Exmoor*, p. 117.

1219, *see Pat. Roll, July* 20.

Huntingdonshire : *For. Proc. T.R.*, no. 38. *Chanc. Misc.*, 11/1, 9, *D*^{y}. *of Lanc.*, *For. Proc.* 1/11, dated Tuesday before S. Peter in Chains ; *cf.* Rot. Litt. Claus. i. 386.

1219, *Dec.* 13, *see Rot. Litt. Claus.* i. 434*b* ; *Pat. Roll*, 1219, pp. 258–9 ; *Sel. Pleas*, p. xcvi.

Buckinghamshire : *Chanc. Misc.*, 11/1, 14, undated, follows the distinctive lines laid down in the order of Dec. 1219 ; *cf.* inquisition by 24 knights, the reference to Alan de Neville, etc., peculiar to this order.

Cumberland : *Chanc. Misc.*, 11/1, 16, printed *Trans. Cumb. and West. Antiq. and Archæol. Soc.*, vol. 5, N.S., p. 43, undated, by 24 knights before John Marshall and others ; names of the justices are those given in the order of 1219, and the arrangement corresponds with it.

Huntingdonshire : *For. Proc. T.R.*, no. 38, m. 1, undated, by 24 knights, before Hugh, Bishop of Lincoln, Hugh Neville and Walter Malo Clerico ; names of justices those given in order of Dec. 1219, with which the arrangement corresponds.

Oxfordshire : *Chanc. Misc.*, 11/1, no. 19, printed Watney, *Forest of Whichwood*, App. iii., undated, by 24 knights, no justices given : arrangement corresponds with that of the order of 1219 ; probably of this date.

Shropshire : copy in Stowe MSS. 798, f. 1, undated : arrangement as above ; probably 1219.

Yorkshire : *Chanc. Misc.*, 11/1, 10, undated, marked " ? 4 Hen. III. " in P.R.O. list ; by 24 knights, no justices given : arrangement as above.

1225, *see Pat. Roll, Feb.* 16, m. 7d. *Rot. Litt. Claus.* ii. 70, 72.

Berkshire : copy in Stowe MSS. 798, f. 8, undated, by 12 knights : refers to " King Henry, grandfather of the lord king, the son of John " : entered with the perambulations of 1225, and corresponds with the charter of 1227 : gives bounds of Henry II's afforestation only.

Buckinghamshire : *Chanc. Misc.*, 11/1, 15, by 12 knights before Hugh de Neville and 4 others, undated. The names of 4 of the 5 justices are those of the commission of 1225.

Derbyshire : *Chanc. Misc.*, 11/1, 17, before Hugh de Neville, then justice of the forest, and others, undated. The names correspond to the commission of 1225.

Dorset : Stowe MSS. 798, f. 6, Brit. Mus., printed Hutchin's *Hist. of Dorset*, iii. 662, before Hugh de Neville and others, undated : names of justices those of the 1225 commission.

Essex : before Hugh de Neville and Richard son of William, undated, summarised in Fisher, *Forest of Essex*, p. 23, from MS. copy of Bracton, Bod. Lib. Rawl. MSS. c. 158, f. 120 ; probably 1225.

Huntingdonshire : *Close Roll* 11 Hen. III, m. 18d. *Rot. Litt. Claus.*, ii. 206, dated 9 Hen. III, enrolled in connection with an acknowledgment of error (*cf. Close Roll* 11 Hen. III, m. 19, *Rot. Litt. Claus.*, ii. 169, and Stowe MSS. 798, f. 1), before Anselm of Sideham and Ralph de Bray.

Lancashire : Close Roll, 1228, p. 100, undated, resembles the perambulations of 1225 in character and appears to have been enrolled like that of Huntingdon above at the same date as an acknowledgment of error (*Pat. Roll*, Ap. 20, 1228), and in connection with a verdict restoring to the king " all the forest of Lancashire which was before their perambulation ". *Chanc. Misc.*, 11/1, 18.

Leicestershire : *Close Roll*, 11 Hen. III, m. 19d ; *Rot. Litt. Claus.*, ii. 207, before Hugh de Neville and others, undated, apparently of this date and enrolled simultaneously with an acknowledgment of error and restoration of the forest as before, *cf. Close Roll*, 11 Hen. III, m. 19. *Rot. Litt. Claus.*, ii. 169 : in a copy in Stowe MSS. 798, the names of the justices correspond with those of the 1225 commission.

Nottinghamshire : *Rot. Litt. Claus.*, ii. 208, as above, with permission to make further investigation, *ib.* p. 169 : in a copy in Stowe MSS. 798, the names of the justices correspond with those of the 1225 commission.

Oxfordshire : Stowe MSS. 798, f. 7, Brit. Mus., before Hugh de Neville, undated : follows much the same lines as perambulation of Oxfordshire above : probably 1225.

Rutland : *Rot. Litt. Claus.* ii. 208, *cf.* p. 80, undated : enrolled as Leicestershire above.

Surrey : *Rot. Litt. Claus.* ii. 56b, dated Aug. 10, 9 Hen. III.

Sussex : *Rot. Litt. Claus.* ii. 80, dated Aug. 3, 9 Hen. III.

1227–1232. *Records of revision of above and revised perambulations, see Rot. Litt. Claus.* ii. 206, 212 and *Pat. Roll*, 1228, p. 184.

Essex : printed Fisher, *Forest of Essex*, p. 25, *cf.* Close Roll, 1228, p. 102.

Gloucestershire : *Ib.* p. 98, undated, referred to *For. Proc. T.R.*, 284 (temp. Edw. III) as 12 Hen. III : possibly like the Lancashire perambulation above, enrolled at the same time, of the earlier date.

Hampshire : *Close Roll*, 1228, pp. 102–3, acknowledgment of error with corrections.

Huntingdonshire : *Rot. Litt. Claus.* ii. 169, 1227, acknowledgment of error and withdrawal.

Lancashire : *Chanc. Misc.*, 11/1, 18, restoration of all the forest of Lancashire to the king ; dated 12 Hen. III in P.R.O. list.

Leicestershire: *Rot. Litt. Claus.*, ii. 169. Acknowledgment of error and restoration of whole forest.

Northamptonshire: *Close Roll*, 1228, 102. Acknowledgment of error with corrections.

Nottinghamshire: (i) *Rot. Litt. Claus.*, ii. 169. Acknowledgment of error with request for permission to make fresh inquiry.

(ii) *Char. Roll*, 1232, p. 165, and *Close Roll*, p. 86, confirmation of a perambulation undated, " before Hugh de Neville, then justice of the forest, and Brian de Insula ".

Rutland: *Rot. Litt. Claus.*, ii. 169, as Leicestershire above.

Shropshire: *Close Roll*, 1228, p. 102. Acknowledgment of error and restoration of the forest, with one exception.

Staffordshire: *Close Roll*, 1228, p. 101. Acknowledgment of error and restoration of whole forest.

Surrey: *Close Roll*, 1228, p. 102, as Staffordshire.

Wiltshire: *Close Roll*, 1228, p. 103, as Hampshire.

Worcestershire: *Close Roll*, 1228, p. 102, as Staffordshire.

Yorkshire: *Close Roll*, 1229, m. 21d; *cf. Chanc. Misc.*, 11/1, no. 22. Acknowledgement of error and restoration of forests named to the Crown.

Early Henry III?

Essex: Regis. of Waltham Holy Cross, Cott. MSS. Tib. cix., f. 184, part only, undated: extracts in Fisher, *Forest of Essex*, p. 21: refers to the " first coronation of Henry, grandfather of the lord the king ".

Hereford: copy in Stowe MSS. 798, f. 11d, undated: entered with perambulations of Henry III's reign: form resembles in some respects that of 1219: deals with new afforestation only.

Shropshire: (i) *For. Proc. T.R.*, No. 148. A summary of some perambulation, undated: marked " temp. Hen. III " in P.R.O. list. Eyton describes it as the " first perambulation of Edw. I " (*Antiquities of Shropshire*, ix. 147): it corresponds in effect with that of 1300, and may be of the later period.

(ii.) *Ib.* no. 203: undated, headed " these are the forests which were afforested after the coronation of King Henry ' avi regis nunc ' ": corresponds in effect with the above, with two exceptions: the forests, however, are called by different names. The document is included in a bundle of Wiltshire forest claims, dated "temp. Edw. I" in P.R.O. list.

Wiltshire: Stowe MSS. 798, f. 9 ff., by Hugh of Drueys and others, undated, refers to "Henry, grandfather of the lord king". Hugh of Drueys appears several times in connection with Wiltshire in the patent and close rolls of 1219–1232, but not later: *cf.* inquisition in *For. Proc. T.R.*, 225, m. 1, etc.

Worcestershire: Stowe MSS. 798, f. 11, undated, refers to "Henry, grandfather of this Henry": deals with new afforestations only.

Yorkshire: Galtres and Ouse and Derwent Forests, *Chanc. Misc.*, 11/1, nos. 20 and 21; undated, marked (12 Hen. III) in P.R.O. list; may belong to 1225, *cf.* reference to the "king's council" in no. 20: it must apparently have preceded the restoration of the forests in 1229.

Metes and bounds enrolled in the Eyre Rolls of Henry III.

Dorset: Bailiwicks of Blackmore and Gillingham; stated to have been presented in the eyre of 31 Hen. III, enrolled on the eyre roll of 54 Hen. III. *For. Proc. T.R.*, no. 11, m. 1, 1d; Hutchin's *Hist. of Dorset*, iv. 79.

Hampshire: Alice Holt and Wolmer Forest; on eyre roll of 53 Hen. III. *For. Proc. T.R.*, no. 158, m. 3d.

Bere; rough bounds recorded in a grant of the bailiwick before 1226, *Chanc. Misc.*, 12/9, *cf. Rot. Litt. Claus.*, ii. 156.

Bailiwick of Matthew de Columbariis (forests of Finkley, Digerley and Chute). *Chanc. Misc.*, 12/9, included in a roll of transcripts of charters relating to the forest, dated "? 28 Edw. I" in P.R.O. list: contains a reference to the lands of Ralph of Stopham, who was dead in 1241 (*Vict. Hist. of Hants*, iv. 260), and appears therefore to be prior to that date.

Huntingdonshire: Inquisition before W. de Beauchamp and others, by 28 jurors, 28 Hen. III. *For. Proc. T.R.*, no. 38, m. 2: printed *Cart. of Ramsey Abbey* (Rolls Ser. pp. 195, 209).

Rutland: Presented in the eyre of 1269, printed *Select Pleas of Forest*, p. 53.

Surrey: Presented in the eyre of 53 Hen. III, *ib.* p. 61.

Wiltshire: Savernake Forest, inquisition undated, *For. Proc. K.R.*, 2/25. A reference to John Biset, justice of the forest, places it after the year 1238. One to the bailiwick of William de Bonclive, whose inquisition post mortem appears under 36 Hen. III, places it before the year 1252 : it is endorsed in a late hand "43 Hen. III." There is a similar inquisition in *For. Proc. K.R.*, 2/22.

Worcestershire : Feckenham Forest ; the bounds of the different bailiwicks are given roughly in an inquisition ? temp. Hen. III, *ib.* 3/2.

1277–9, *see Cal. Pat. Rolls*, 1277, *p.* 237, *and Sel. Pleas of the Forest*, ci. ff.

Berkshire : *Chanc. Misc.*, 12/2, 3, perambulation by Sir Peter de Codrey and 9 others, dated 7 Edw. I.

Dorset : *Ib.* 12/2, 2, before Walter Scamel, 7 Edw. I.

Hampshire : *Ib.* 12/2, 4, before Walter Scamel and Matthew Columbariis, 7 Edw. I.

Somerset : *Ib.* 2 copies and *For. Proc. T.R.*, no. 154, m. 1, printed Rawle, *op. cit.*, pp. 38–40. Somerton warren, printed *Vict. Hist. of Som.*, ii. 552 : Before the same.

Wiltshire : *Chanc. Misc.*, 12/2, 2, before Walter Scamel, 7 Edw. I : Groveley and Milchet, printed in Hoare, *Hist. of Wilts, Dunworth Hund.*, p. 184, and *Alderbury Hund.*, p. 77, the latter in connection with a perambulation of 1300.

1297–8. *See Cal. Pat. Rolls*, 1298, pp. 323, 329, and *Sel. Pleas of Forest*, p. ciii.

Buckinghamshire : Bernwood Forest : *For. Proc. K.R.*, 1/8, copy of a perambulation dated 26 Edw. I, printed *Vict. Hist. of Bucks*, ii. 132.

Essex : *For. Proc. T.R.*, no. 15, dated 26 Edw. I.

Gloucestershire : Dean Forest, *ib.* no. 255, part given in Rudder, *Hist. of Glos*, App. 2 : dated Feb. 22, 26 Edw. I.

Hampshire : *D^{y}. of Lanc. For. Proc.*, 1/8, before J. Gilberd, Roger of Hegham, etc.

Oxfordshire : *Cart. of Eynsh m Abbey*, ii. 92 ff., by the same.

Somerset : Printed Collinson, *Hist. of Som.*, iii. 56, etc., from a register in Wells Cathedral.

1299–1300, *see Select Pleas of the Forest*, p. civ.

These are to be found for all the counties in which the king had forests, except Cheshire, *see Chanc. Misc.*, 12/10, and *Pat. Roll*, Supp. 6a. A few appear in one or other of these records only : the greater number in both.

Metes and Bounds enrolled in the Eyre Rolls of Edward I.

Derbyshire: Peak Forest, presented in the eyre of 14 Edw. I, printed *Derbyshire Arch. and Nat. Hist. Journal*, xv. 68, and *Vict. Hist. of Derbyshire*, i. 397.

Essex: Bounds given roughly in the eyre of 20 Edw. I. *For. Proc. T.R.*, no. 13, m. 36d: the bounds of the various bailiwicks are also given here, and in the eyre roll of 7 Edw. I, *ib.* m. 36 and no. 12, m. 21.

Gloucestershire: Dean Forest, enrolled in the regard of 10 Edw. I. *For. Proc. T.R.*, no. 31.

Hampshire: New Forest, presented in the eyre of 8 Edw. I, *ib.* no. 161, m. 1d, printed Wise, *New Forest*, p. 40.

Porchester Forest, in the same. *For. Proc. T.R.*, no. 161, m. 8.

Huntingdonshire: Endorsed "*Pleas* of 14 Edw. I, before Roger L'estrange, etc." *For. Proc. T.R.*, no. 43. *Pat. Roll* 14 Edw. III, pt. 1, m. 36. *Cart. of Ramsey Abbey*, i. 211.

Northamptonshire: Rockingham Forest; presented in the eyre of 14 Edw. I. *For. Proc. T.R.*, no. 74, printed Wise, *Hist. of Rockingham Castle*, p. 129.

Salcey Forest, presented in the eyre of 15 Edw. I. *For. Proc. T.R.*, no. 75, m. 2d and 77, m. 1.

Whittlewood Forest: in the same, 2 versions, *ib.* no. 77, m 2.

Staffordshire: Cannock Forest, presented in the eyre of 14 Edw. I, printed in *Hist. Coll. for History of Staffs* (William Salt Society), vol. v. pt. 1, p. 166.

7
The Evolution of Land Transport in the Middle Ages*

R.S. Lopez

I

" ALL ROADS LEAD TO ROME ": LET US THEREFORE BEGIN WITH ROME. For centuries the Roman road system was admired without reserve, but today we have entered a period of severe criticism. It has recently become fashionable to stress the defects of the Roman roads; the reaction is perhaps as excessive as was the praise of the past. At any rate it is easy to account for their good and bad qualities. They were planned and maintained not by merchants, but by soldiers and civil servants, who were chiefly concerned that administrative centres and points of strategic importance should be solidly linked by indestructible and reliable communications. That the network of roads should be convenient and economic was none of their business. That is why the Romans built narrow, precipitous roads along the mountain crests rather than the valley bottoms, sometimes driving straight for their goal over gradients of one in five. But they made the roads indestructible, with a foundation of large stones, one or more layers of gravel or pounded brick, and a surface of large blocks, setts or stones cemented together. Such rigid surfaces, in which sun and rain opened large cracks, needed gangs of slaves, or continuous work by those obliged to furnish road-services to the state, and even so they were unsuitable for heavy or broad vehicles. On the other hand even if nothing was left but the road-bed, infantry, cavalry or pack animals could still pass along it, and if bridges were often lacking it was always possible to ford or ferry rivers — for the Romans, masters of the art of bridge building, preferred to put their bridges in towns rather than along country roads. The transport of provisions in bulk for the army or civil service was exorbitantly expensive, except by water; but the troops lived as far as possible on food produced in their immediate vicinity and the administrative centres were almost all situated either on the sea or on internal navigable waterways. Moreover, when the state could not pay free market rates of prices or wages, it would requisition animals and drivers.

* The substance of this paper was first published in the Bollettino Civico dell' Istituto Colombiano, Genoa, Aug-Sept. 1953. The author has kindly allowed us to reprint it, as few English-speaking readers are likely to have seen it. He has no responsibility for the translation.

Roman roads were not the only benefits which the Empire brought to traders. Peace, low internal customs duties and, at least until the third century, a sound currency, public order and freedom from state interference, all encouraged a notable economic expansion, but did not allow traders to acquire the wealth or prestige which might have enabled them to deflect state policy seriously in their interests. Cicero has vividly summed up the view of the dominant landowning class: " Small-scale trade should be of little account; large-scale trade which imports many goods from all parts of the world to distribute them honestly to many people, is less contemptible. When the merchant, glutted, or rather contented with his profits, retires from the port to become a landed proprietor . . . he seems to me to be worthy of full praise." In other words: only the capitalist merchant deserved consideration. Only the merchant who had abandoned his profession enjoyed respect. In maritime commerce, which Cicero clearly has in mind, it was often possible to pass both these check-points; but for traders on land this was very difficult. In Diocletian's time — to quote only one example — the official price of a cartload of hay was 600 denari and its transport cost 20 denari per mile, which made the cost of transporting it 30 miles prohibitive. It is true that the transport price was determined by the small size of the carts, whose capacity was hardly greater than that of pack animals; and the size in turn was determined by the methods of haulage. Neither horses nor mules were shod at this time, both, like oxen, were harnessed by a sort of yoke, complicated in their case by an elastic collar which constricted the neck with every excessive pull. Nor was it customary to harness a file of animals consecutively to the same cart. These methods might have been improved. In fact we know that in Upper Italy several oxen were yoked in file for farm-labour. But it was useless to increase the number of haulage animals so long as the vehicle remained small, and impossible to enlarge the cart so long as the roads remained narrow. And so long as merchants did not earn enough profits to obtain a voice in the matter with the relevant department of the civil service, roads would not be widened.

This situation was tolerable only so long as peace lasted and so long as the empire had sufficient slaves or at least subjects. From the third century on, with the coming of the barbarians and the decline in population, came the collapse of Roman economy; due at least in part to its transport system. Italy was the first victim. By water, where transport problems were less acute, she could not compete with the wealthier and more advanced eastern provinces. On land, she gradually lost her supremacy over the western provinces, each of which adapted itself to local production, as and when necessary. But the entire empire was finally subverted. Population fell while the demands of the army and civil service rose, and the government was obliged to burden its subjects with ever-growing charges, among others those for the maintenance of the roads and land transport. The increase in the burden of taxes cut into the already small profit-margins of the merchants and transporters. Finally the exhausted subjects were no longer able to maintain the roads and public transport, and the ruin of the state sealed that of commerce.

II

Once the crisis, or at any rate its most acute phase, had passed, the Byzantine empire remained broadly faithful to the fundamental principles of Rome. The roads continued to be constructed and maintained primarily for the needs of army and civil service; the burden of road maintenance and public transport continued to rest at least theoretically on the backs of the subjects. The supply of slaves, however, was rapidly falling, and even the most reckless rulers endeavoured to spare the free peasants. In practice it seems that the state requirements tended to become less imperious, not without consequent great damage to the road system. Though it may be exaggerated, the description of a voyage by land from Constantinople to Lepanto in the tenth century provides some idea of what could happen to the road foundations when maintenance was defective: " On mule-back, on foot, on horse-back, fasting, suffering from thirst, sighing, weeping, lamenting, I arrived after forty-nine days." Fortunately the chief communications of the empire were by sea and not by land.

In the west the collapse was even more rapid though the barbarians did not alter the system. The Germanic codes contain numerous provisions designed to perpetuate the system of roads and public maintenance inherited from Rome. But they were incapable of carrying them out. In Byzantium the government post continued to function along the main roads, in some fashion, in the tenth and eleventh centuries. But all traces of the Visigothic and Merovingian post had vanished by the sixth and seventh centuries, while the Longobardi seem never to have had it at all. The semi-public corporations of carters and muleteers disappeared, the bridges collapsed and were replaced by ferries or boat-bridges (where they were replaced at all), the roads were invaded by vegetation and robbed of their paving. The efforts of the Carolingians hardly sufficed to bind the provinces of their restored " Roman empire " together by a passable, though far from good system of communications. The lack of decent roads was one of the principal reasons for the rapid disintegration of their state. As a matter of fact, the medieval empire consisted primarily of internal provinces, and therefore could not use the Mediterranean as the old Roman empire had done. In the tenth century a chronicler tells the edifying story of a saint who had the utmost difficulty in dissuading the peasants from ploughing up the road which served their village. Such problems arose frequently. The Visigothic laws had already imposed penalties on the powerful man or the serf who closed a public road to traffic. The Burgundian and Bavarian laws contained similar provisions. But the ruin of the lesser Roman roads was not a major calamity in the prevailing economic stagnation. Trade was so shrunken that it would have been a very poor investment to force cultivators to maintain roads for the benefit of a handful of merchants, where they could live in self-sufficiency on their local crops.

But if the surface of the Roman roads in the vast majority of cases failed to survive the Dark Ages, did not their foundations remain as a sort of skeleton which the economic revival of the later Middle Ages might clothe with flesh? For centuries it was believed that the Roman network of roads gave birth to the medieval and modern road-systems. However, this view has lately been contested by many scholars, though others still maintain it. It is true that many late medieval and modern roads follow the same routes as Roman ones, especially in Italy and England. But this is no proof that the apparent continuity was due to the survival of the Roman road-bed rather than to the persistence of the inhabited places which the new roads had to link, to the influence of immutable geographical factors such as fords and mountain passes, valleys and estuaries, or above all to the vitality of the juridical concept of the " public highway". A road so designated was state property, all the more profitable in proportion as the state of the Middle Ages spent less on maintaining it, and drew more revenue from multiplying toll-rights, internal customs, and rights of justice. Whoever claimed such rights over a highway would want people to use it. In spite of this, or perhaps because of this, the documents give innumerable proofs that people did their utmost to avoid the use of the public highways and made use of some path opened by the simple passage of men and animals. It is not pure accident that the signs of continuity are much more numerous in England, where the authority of the sovereign power over the public highway was exercised with greater firmness and discretion than elsewhere, and in Italy, where the cities of Roman origin and the routes fixed by the hydrographic and orographic system of the country were particularly numerous. In France, on the other hand, where the central power underwent a long eclipse and natural obstacles to communication were not great, the roads changed more frequently and more radically.

However, in the high Middle Ages the most redoubtable competition for the " public highways " came not from private paths but from rivers. They were slow and tortuous routes, but required little effort for their maintenance and were well suited to the transport of heavy goods at minimum cost. The Romans had already used the rivers extensively. Roman Arles, on the lower Rhone, had outdistanced Marseille, which had a better port but lacked waterways in its immediate hinterland. Lyons, higher up on the same river, had become the capital of the Gauls; the Rhine and Danube had filled with ships; and even in Italy, Ostia, Pisa and Aquileia, served by rivers and canals, had eclipsed good natural harbours backed by mountains like Pozzuoli, Genoa and Trieste. Between the fifth and tenth centuries internal navigation expanded wherever a rivulet of water offered even the slightest alternative to the beaten path or the ruined public highway. The stony bed of the Scultenna, the stagnant waters of the Sile, the meagre torrents of Gascony, the little mountain lakes of Wallen, the impetuous rivers of the Brescian and Tyrolese Alps became familiar routes to the boatman. Even better where there was a river genuinely adapted to major traffic. The main artery of the Longobard kingdom, and later the Italic one, was not the via Emilia nor the via Postumia, though the ancient cities along these roads continued a modest existence: it was the Po with its numerous tributaries. As in antiquity all roads had led to Rome, so in the high Middle Ages all rivers led to the new capital, Pavia. However, Tuscany created its own system, based on mediocre navigable waterways like the Serchio and the Ozeri which linked Lucca to Pisa and the sea, and therefore eventually broke away from the central administration of the kingdom. Liguria was practically isolated, without trade, with the coastal road in so miserable a state that even in the thirteenth century Dante twice employed it as a simile for the superhuman difficulties encountered in the ascent of the mountain of Purgatory. From Pavia a descent of the Po led to the lagoon ports of Ravenna, Comacchio and eventually to Venice, windows half-opened on the more advanced Arab and Byzantine worlds. Upstream, on the other hand, the river led to the precipitous roads across the Alps. In some cases they were impracticable even for pack animals and had to be negotiated by serfs bent under heavy loads. Only a few traces of this system of transport remain today: barges loaded with salt or sand still move upstream along the lower Po and the women of the Valsesia still carry laden baskets along goat-paths.

The " fluvialization " of land transport (to use a baroque but expressive term) in the high Middle Ages was not confined to the barbarian West. Strange as it may seem, inland navigation played a most important part even in the Arab world, though the Moslems had little water at their disposal and trade among them did not decay as it did in barbarian Europe. This phenomenon has not been sufficiently underlined by historians of the medieval economy. The chief explanation is, I think, that the slow gait of the camel had accustomed the Arabs to patience when faced with the delays of river traffic. Moreover, the orthodox Caliphate and its successors never exercised sufficient autocratic control over their subjects to impose on them the burdensome services which would have been necessary to maintain a road system of the Roman type. What is certain is that the Arabs built few roads and bridges, and allowed some to fall into ruin. The Caliph's posts had 930 stations in the ninth century, but traffic between them was for the most part maintained on paths kept open by the continuous passage of horses and pack animals. Like Venice, Bagdad was built on the water: canals served as streets and the only bridges corresponding to the Rialto were built of boats. The last permanent bridges over the Tigris, inherited from the Sassanid empire whose traditions of road transport were not unlike those of the Romans, collapsed in the tenth century. Only in Spain did the Moslems look after bridges and roads to some extent. At Cordoba, in particular, the old Roman bridge was restored several times and a new one built in the tenth century. But wherever there was a major navigable river — the Guadalquivir, the Nile, the Euphrates or the Tigris, the Hilmend, the Indus, — commerce exexploited it to the full. Indeed Arab geographers list among navigable rivers wadis and torrents such as the " three rivers of Constantine", and that of Bougie in Algeria, and, in Sicily, the " rivers " of Mazzara, Lentini and Ragusa. At this time rivers and canals were the most important internal ways of communication in India and China also. The river-route from the Volga or the Dniepr to the Dvina or the Volkhov formed the principal artery of Russia and the successive capitals of Sweden were built on lakes linked by navigable waterways to the sea. It is thus no exaggeration to say that in the high Middle Ages the chief means of inland transport in the Eastern hemisphere were not carts or pack animals, but boats. This, incidentally, may lend some support to the hypothesis of a connexion between " wet cycles " of climate and economic depressions.

III

The later Middle Ages saw a reversal of this situation, at least in Europe. Water transport was not abandoned — indeed, the building of navigable canals received a new impetus — but it once again took second place to land transport. Little by little a new network of roads was put into effective operation, different totally in structure and methods from the ancient one and used by quite different types of transport and haulage. The changes in transport which accompanied the commercial revolution and the outburst of economic activity in this period can themselves be described as a slow revolution. If we consider them more closely, we find that they reveal the changed political and social face of Europe. For in medieval Europe there was no large and powerful state like the Roman Empire. Slavery disappeared and in many regions, of which Italy was the first, serfdom was abolished. Finally, the dignity of the merchant and of trade won recognition, though with many reservations. Hence private initiative or local associations largely took the place of coercive government action. The routing of roads reflected the needs of commerce rather than the convenience of soldiers and civil servants. Maximum use was made of animal labour in transport, while human labour was so far as possible economized.

When comparing the roads and means of transport of the later Middle Ages with those of the Roman Empire we must bear in mind the society which created both in its own image. The new roads were far more numerous, but also far more modest in appearance: monumental works are more easily constructed by an emperor or a dictator than by an association or confraternity. First came natural paths, scarcely better than those of the early Middle Ages. Later light gravel surfaces were employed, or at most we find flints or stone setts inserted into the earth at short intervals, as may still be seen in many town and village streets of Upper Italy and even on the outskirts of Milan. Occasionally there was a foundation of wood or stone. It is difficult to share the enthusiasm of a French scholar who exalts these unmetalled roads without foundations as greatly superior to the Roman roads with their three or four layers and metalled surfaces. But the medieval roads met their purpose more economically than the Roman ones, since they were more elastic and could be built and repaired with a minimum expenditure of raw materials and labour. Why should one aim at the robustness required of a modern *autobahn*, when only light carts had to be carried? A great lord on his travels might come up against more mud than a Roman senator would have done, and this might well displease him: but a merchant was easily reconciled to it, because his commune did not present him with too exorbitant a bill for road repairs. A metalled road would offer an easier passage to armies, but it was not always clear whether the armies would be friends or enemies. Above all, a merchant wanted to avoid ambushes: an English Statute of 1285 ordered that along highways between market towns "there be no dyke, tree, or bush whereby a man may lurk to do hurt within 200 feet of either side of the way."

However, even medieval men had a certain aesthetic pride as well as practical common sense. In the cities, where traffic, if not heavier, was at any rate more continuous and the drawbacks of casual roads made themselves felt more frequently, paving was soon introduced. By the command of king Philip Augustus, who could not tolerate the mud, Paris streets got stone surfaces before the majority of those in Italian towns; among the latter Genoa was paved before Venice, perhaps because in Venice the canals were always an alternative means of communication. By the end of the thirteenth century the majority of important cities had their streets paved with hard stones or bricks. In the countryside the demand was rather for improvements in the routing and road-widening; all the more since between the tenth and the fourteenth century something like a revolution in the system of haulage took place. Horseshoes, rigid tandem horse-collars and harnessing gradually spread throughout Europe and made possible the use of far larger carts than the Roman. But even in this matter we should beware of exaggerating the importance of the medieval innovations. The new methods spread very slowly, and perhaps their most important result was not the increase in the carrying capacity of the carts but the rapid fall in the cost of mules, which made possible an unprecedented expansion of transport by pack-animals in the later Middle Ages. To multiply the number of mules or carts in a convey it was only necessary for the merchant to pay for them; enlarging the size of carts depended on the prior widening of roads by the public bodies or associations which looked after them. In turn, any expensive road improvement tended to be postponed until the pressure of prospective users had become very great.

The routing of late medieval roads was not always superior to that of antiquity. They followed about the same gradients as the Roman. However, it is likely that the possibility of harnessing additional draught-animals at the steepest points — a thing apparently unknown to the Romans — reduced this disadvantage significantly. Moreover, medieval men had not the same admiration for straight-lined roads as Roman engineers, or modern town architects. On the contrary, in their cities they often manifested a marked preference for winding streets and limited horizons, which allowed cathedrals and palaces to emerge suddenly to the surprised view. As for the country roads, we may quote the case of a road in the Queyras for which five bridges are today sufficient, while in the Middle Ages the route was so tortuous that it required more than thirty, seventeen of which were destroyed by a flood in 1370. But often the Middle Ages simplified the Roman route. Practically all the roads radiating from Florence were gradually removed from the line of the mountain-crests to river lines, and greatly shortened in consequence. Sometimes excessive gradients were smoothed out: at the beginning of the fourteenth century, for instance, the city of Schaffhausen reduced the gradient of the Koblenz road at the cost of expensive rock excavations.

IV

Perhaps the most notable characteristic of the medieval roads, as against the ancient, is the multiplicity of routes which linked the same towns. There are two main roads with innumerable variants between Genoa and Milan, and two main roads to choose from between Genoa and Asti. Four roads lead from Paris to Lyons and four from Clermont to Montpellier. The reasons for this are the same as those which have in modern times led to the construction of different railways linking Milan and Rome or New York and Chicago: the initiative came from autonomous local bodies or independent private companies. Plurality of roads, which is always possible when the dogma of the straight line is abandoned, enabled a greater number of minor centres to be included in the network. Alternative routes allow traffic to be diverted from an overloaded highway or one damaged by the weather or cut by war, blockages or other temporary obstacles, to a free or less busy one. We shall deal with this problem below. First, however, we must see how this system of co-ordinated but autonomous roads of the late Middle Ages could have come into existence on the ruins of the Roman system of the single route.

Most probably it was primarily due to spontaneous generation or regeneration. Adequate public highways were lacking. In the Lombardo-Italic kingdom, for example, the only main artery of traffic which was never completely neglected was the *via Francigena* or *Regia* from the Alps through the Po plain and Cisa to Rome. Travellers were therefore obliged to make themselves paths as and where they could. If they could use such tracts of the Roman roads as were still passable, so much the better; a large part of the *via Francigena* and some of the principal English roads of the fourteenth century incorporated sections of the Roman route; but a road was where people trod. The multiplication of casual paths in the high Middle Ages, like that of semi-rural markets, does not necessarily show that the streams of trade ran far or copiously. On the contrary, it may show that they were too weak to maintain a constant direction and tended to lose themselves in morasses wherever geographical obstacles did not forcibly canalize them. But as commerce grew, so, while lesser markets were eclipsed by greater ones, the pathways became differentiated according to their importance and the degree of their maintenance. The juridical concept of the "public highway" had a certain part to play also; but its effect was not so much to determine which pathways were to remain "public" as to provide protection of public law for such pathways as trade had already picked out from among the rest. In English law of the later Middle Ages not only military roads, but all roads leading to ports or markets were "King's Highways" and enjoyed royal protection. In Italy the emperors asked the advice of merchants before granting sonorous and ineffective decrees of protection to certain roads. In France a thirteenth century jurist distinguished footpaths and secondary roads from "the greater ones, which are called royal roads", but he also recognized that this usage took no account whatever of the purely legal distinctions established in antiquity.

Until the end of the Middle Ages the direct action of kingdoms for the maintenance of regular roads remained rather weak and intermittent. Princes, officers, and officials rode on horseback and had no great need of refinements in road-building. At the very most, ladies might travel in carriages, but for a knight this would have been a great degradation. Even Lancelot, in Chretien de Troyes' romance, hesitated a while to get into one, though this was the only way to save Queen Guinevere. Hence in the eyes of princes and feudatories the fundamental incentive to maintain the roads was the need to ensure the passage of the merchants who paid customs and imported useful commodities. The main burden of road-building and maintenance therefore fell on private associations. Their structure and purpose were not very different from those of the turnpike companies of the early Industrial Revolution, but most of them took on that mixed colour in which utilitarian and religious elements are combined, which is so characteristic of the Middle Ages. Numerous bishops granted indulgences to whoever contributed to road-work. It was a work of piety that incidentally ensured greater incomes for themselves; moreover pilgrims and merchants often used the same roads. Again, the Genoese of all classes who made testamentary provisions for work on bridges and on the harbour, looked after their soul while contributing to the future wealth of their city.

It would take too long to draw up a list of the various kinds of associations, ecclesiastical and lay, semi-public and semi-private, which contributed to the creation and improvement of the road system. Let us rather recall that corporations of merchants and, where they existed, Communes, very soon took the lead in such work and brought to it capital and expertise such as could not be found anywhere else. Yet not even the Communes, with their small territories, could carry out such work over long distances. Moreover, wars between city-states imposed many unnecessary detours. Hence the often rather patchy character of certain main roads, good in the territory of some Communes and extremely bad once they left it. Hence also the abundance of alternative routes which made it possible to avoid one or other of the neighbouring cities if political relations with them should ever be disturbed. However, such rivalry sometimes led to alliances, and these in turn led to agreements for shortening roads. There was — to give only one instance, though not one which deals with roads — the agreement between Cremona and Reggio for the construction of a straight canal of sixty kilometres which would avoid the great loop of the Po between Guastalla and the Panaro and would further cut off Mantua from the main Po traffic.

In the absence of highway authorities capable of regulating long distance traffic, competition between merchants and carriers often led to notable improvements in international communications. The Swiss mountaineers and French carters struggled long to attract to themselves the bulk of the traffic between the Mediterranean and north-western Europe. In the eleventh century the valleys of the Central Alps, and above all the Monte Settimo pass, absorbed a large part of this traffic, even though on the steepest part goods had for the most part to be carried on men's backs or in hand-carts. In the twelfth century the Alpine traffic rapidly lost ground to the sea-route from Genoa, Pisa or Venice to Provence and thence up the Rhone valley (or in barges along the Rhone) and along the Saône to Champagne. The route was at least three times longer, but avoided the mountainous areas and made the most use of the cheaper possibilities of water transport. At the beginning of the thirteenth century the construction of a gallery suspended from the rocks and of daring bridges across the Reuss opened the Gotthard pass to pack-animals and restored part of the lost traffic to the Alps. Then the French carters and the Italian shippers improved their service and lowered their prices. In 1318 a Florentine company of importers of French cloth paid less per transport-mile from Paris to Marseille than for the sea-transport from Marseille to Pisa. This is doubtless an exceptional case, but it indicates the progress achieved. Nevertheless, the Swiss did not accept defeat, and set about building a new road for carts with a capacity of approximately a quarter ton, through the old pass of Monte Settimo. It was the first Alpine road entirely fit for carriage traffic.

V

Let us end at this point. From the middle of the fourteenth century to the middle of the fifteenth new factors announced a new era in the development of transport. The great economic depression which followed upon four centuries of unbroken economic expansion caused the volume of traffic to contract, but for this very reason made a reduction of transport costs essential. The classical spirit of the Renaissance rehabilitated the straight line and the monumental highway. The advent of artillery drew the attention of princes to the advantages of wide and solid roads. The consolidation of absolute monarchies or principalities once again allowed the state to assume a certain amount of control over the main traffic arteries.

This new period need not concern us here. Let us merely point out that the progress of explosives also led to the piercing of the first road-tunnels. Among the oldest and most important was the Foro di Viso, a hundred yards long and eight feet wide, built by the marquess Ludovico II of Saluzzo between 1478 and 1480 with the financial help of the king of France, at a height of 2000 metres below the col de la Traversette. The cutting served for the transport of salt, a cheap commodity which would perhaps in other times have been carried by barge or on the backs of serfs. But a few years after it had been completed, Charles VIII of France had part of his artillery transported across it for use in his invasion of Italy. This too marked the opening of a new era.

Yale. *R. S. Lopez.*

NOTES

Though monographs on individual roads and groups of roads or on special aspects of the history of land transport are numerous, general works are scarce and mostly obsolete. Among the chief ones we may recall: W. Goetz, *Die Verkehrswege im Dienste des Welthandels* (Stuttgart, 1888); G. Schaefer, *Ursprung und Entwickling der Verkehrsmittel* (Dresden, 1908); A. Birk, *Die Strasse: ihre verkehrs- und bautechnische Entwicklung im Rahmen der Menschheitsgeschichte* (Karlsbad-Drahowitz, 1934); A. Uccelli, ed., *Storia della tecnica dal medio evo ai giorni nostri* (Milan, 1945).

Those who wish to study the evolution of land transport not as a chapter of technical history, but as an aspect of the general history of mankind, will find general works of economic and social history of greater importance to them. We may draw attention in particular to the pages dealing with transport in A. Schaube, *Handelsgeschichte der romanischen Voelker bis zum Ende der Kreuzzuege* (Munich, 1906); W. Sombart, *Der moderne Kapitalismus* (2nd edn. Munich, 1916-17); J. Kulischer, *Allgemeine Wirtschaftsgeschichte des Mittelalters und der Neuzeit* (German translation from the Russian, Munich, 1928); G. Luzzatto, *Storia Economica d'Italia* (Rome, 1949); *Cambridge Economic History of Europe*, vol. ii, (Cambridge, 1952); R. S. Lopez and I. W. Raymond, *Medieval Trade in the Mediterranean World* (New York, 1955). All these works contain abundant bibliographical references.

However, the *Cambridge Economic History* is the only general work which takes account of the recent and revolutionary studies on the technique of haulage and road construction. These provided the stimulus for the debatable but suggestive works of Lefebvre des Noëttes — see above all *L'attelage: le cheval de selle à travers les âges* (Paris, 1931) — and the additions made to these works by Marc Bloch, A. G. Haudricourt, J. Sion and others in the special issue of *Annales d'Histoire Economique et Sociale* (Oct. 1935) devoted to the history of technique. For the abundant polemical literature on this question, see the bibliography by L. White, Technology and Invention in the Middle Ages, in *Speculum* XV (1940). The importance of the " inventions " to which Lefebvre des Noëttes has drawn attention, has been much exaggerated by his supporters and even by his critics, but it is nevertheless impermissible to neglect him.

Older, but rekindled by good recent studies, is the controversy on the Roman origins of the medieval roads. F. Imberdis, Les routes médievales: mythes et réalités historiques, a short article with an additional note by Marc Bloch, *Annales d'Histoire Sociale I* (1939) is of great interest for France. M. M. Postan has replied to this in the volume of the *Cambridge Economic History* mentioned above, taking the opposite view; but Postan refers chiefly to England while Imberdis and Bloch had in mind primarily France and Germany. In Italy prevailing opinion still champions Roman origins, even for those roads for which no direct precedents are to be found before the Middle Ages; but recently the thesis of a total renovation of the road system — which the author attributes to agricultural improvements and not to an interruption of the traffic-carrying capacity — has been put forward by J. Plesner, Una rivoluzione stradale nel Dugento, in *Acta Jutlandica* X (Aarhus and Copenhagen, 1938), and welcomed by Luigi Einaudi, Le terre nuove italiane nel Duecento, in *Rivista di storia economica* IV (1939). G. P. Bognetti, *Santa Maria di Castelseprio* (Milan, 1938) seems also to share a similar point of view, though for different reasons.

For the juridical concept of the " public highway " we must consult the works on the history of law, too numerous to be listed here. Let us merely draw attention to the diligent work of C. T. Flower, *Public Works in Medieval Law* in the *Selden Society Publications* (London, 1923).

Since it is impossible to quote even the most important among the national, regional and local monographs, we can only refer the reader to the rich bibliography provided by the general works quoted above, and in A. Sapori, *Le Marchand Italien au Moyen Age* (Paris, 1952), which, though referring chiefly to Italy, also deals with works covering a wider area (pp. 64 and ff.). Finally, since the bibliographies mentioned here confine themselves to Europe, let us recall that L. Bréhier, *Les institutions de l'Empire byzantin* (Paris 1949) contains a learned summary and bibliography of the roads and transport of Byzantium, while scattered information about the quality of roads and the transport of the Moslem world is to be found in A. Mez, *Die Renaissance des Islams* (Heidelberg, 1922) and, for Spain, in E. Lévi-Provençal, *L'Espagne Musulmane au Xe siècle* (Paris 1932).

8

A Day's Journey in Medieval France

Marjorie Nice Boyer

In that delightful book, *Le Livre de la description des pays* Gilles le Bouvier measures the extent of fifteenth-century France by the number of days required to traverse it. It is, he says, twenty-two days' journey in length from the harbor of Sluys in Flanders to Saint Jean Pied de Port at the entry of the realm of Navarre and sixteen days wide from the farthest point in Brittany to Lyons on the Rhône.[1] By road the above distances are approximately 660 and 640 miles respectively and a day's journey between thirty and forty miles. The estimates of Le Bouvier, however, would hardly have been accepted by a certain litigant when he complained in 1375 that, in computing the costs of the case, the court had allowed him insufficient time for travelling. Between Abbeville and Paris, he asserted, there were three long days of journeying.[2] Since the distance is eighty-nine miles by road, thirty miles would be the stretch described as a 'great day's travel.'

The question of the length of a day's journey has been touched upon in passing by several modern authors. Champion considers sixteen miles daily a fast rate of speed and cites as evidence the fact that the news of the fall of Rouen to the French forces on 19 October 1449 reached Charles of Orleans at Blois on 28 October.[3] Other authors mention higher speeds. Grace Stretton states 'Express speed, it has been computed, would mean about thirty-five miles per diem, but a progress would not average more than fourteen or fifteen.'[4] The higher figure is mentioned by an anonymous reviewer in the *Retrospective Review* who points out that the court of John I of England 'very constantly travelled between thirty-five and forty miles a day, and on particular occasions a distance of fifty miles was traversed. . . . Matthew Paris, who wrote about forty years after the reign of John, remarks that he [John] travelled "citius quam fas est".'[5] The above-mentioned litigant would have concurred in Matthew Paris' opinion that thirty-five to forty miles a day was journeying faster than was proper.

Armstrong's study of the speed of news in England at the time of the Wars of the Roses is not strictly comparable with the present study either in the period or the purpose of the work. In investigating how fast it was possible to send messages (rather than how far the individual traveller usually travelled in a day), Armstrong has found that with the help of relays speeds of 100 miles daily were attained.[6]

The only extensive investigation into the problem of how far persons could and did travel in the Middle Ages is that of Ludwig into the speed of travel and marching in the twelfth and thirteenth centuries. His results show that emperors, popes, and noblemen of the period, sometimes accompanied by armies and almost always by large parties of retainers, averaged only eight to nineteen miles daily, sometimes travelled more than twenty miles daily, and occasionally covered distances of thirty-one to forty-eight miles. He concludes that twenty-four miles was a normal day's journey.[7] His book is based chiefly on chronicles and itineraries determined by documents. The accuracy of the former is not above reproach and the latter offer so many lacunae that Ludwig has, in many cases, merely totalled the number of kilometers travelled within a given over-all period, such as a month or a year, and divided by the number of days. Since he has not been careful to exclude periods during which these men sojourned in one spot for days together, the result really has more bearing on the frequency of travel than on the length of a day's journey. The reliability of his results is further impaired by his inexact method of determining distances, for in many cases he merely gives the mileage between two points as the crow flies.

In the present investigation the thorny problem of mileage traversed by travellers has been met by taking distances between points on a modern road map. Admittedly this solution is not ideal, because mediaeval routes were not always identical with their present day counterparts; fourteenth-century itineraries show that in many cases what are now back roads were then the main travelled routes. Nevertheless, distances by road, proving on comparison with those by railroad to be almost uniformly shorter, have been here accepted as the most reliable index in computing mileage.[8]

The present researches are chiefly based on financial documents, the accuracy and contemporaneity of which rank far above those of chronicles. In the use of itineraries the same difficulty, namely lacunae, has been met by eliminating all examples of travel except those in which the actual stop-overs are known for every day or the distance is so great and the number of days so few that the margin of error in computing the average daily speed is small. For instance, Pierre Scatisse, treasurer of France and *général des aides* in Languedoc, journeyed from Nîmes to Toulouse, a distance of approximately 187 miles, from 15 to 19 April 1369 at an average rate of thirty-seven miles daily; the speed is so high that, in the light of other evidence, it is very unlikely that he made any halts of more than overnight.[9] Financial documents offer another advantage over chronicles and itineraries determined by other documents, for the latter are confined to the great, while the former, being mercantile, ecclesiastical, and governmental records, also include messengers, merchants, monks, townsmen, and government officials of all ranks, thus presenting a more rounded picture of travel. This is the more important as the station in life of the travellers seems to have had an effect on their speed.

Cuttino notes that in the case of the English diplomats in France the higher the rank of the travellers the more slowly did they travel.[10] This state of affairs seems to have been due partly to a greater insistence by personages on comfort in travel, partly to prestige, and partly to their custom of travelling in large parties, all three factors being inextricably intertwined. Kings, nobles, and princes of the church almost invariably travelled in large parties, which faced in their peregrinations a series of difficulties much greater than those of small groups. Frequently unable (because of their numerous retinues) or unwilling (because of the inconvenience) to obtain food and shelter at inns, important persons preferred to send retainers on ahead to arrange accommodations at some monastery or at the castle of some lay or ecclesiastical lord. Most of their food was carried with them or servants were dispatched to purchase food and meet the party at some point ahead on its itinerary. The necessity of a pre-arranged route tended to slow down travellers, as did the length of the baggage train, for nobles usually carried around with them most of their furnishings. Further, large parties were inclined to include carts, a form of locomotion slower than horseback.

Most parties, whether large or small, were affected by the widely prevalent custom of travelling in mixed parties of horsemen and pedestrians. The records note groups consisting of 'two schoolmen, two horses, and a valet';[11] or 'a priest, his horse, his valet, another person, his horse, and valet, and packhorses and their conductors';[12] or 'a provost, his clerk, two horses, and a valet on foot';[13] or 'a seneschal and another man, both on horseback, and two valets on foot.'[14] The consuls of Albi habitually travelled on horseback accompanied by a valet on foot.[15]

An example of the journey of a large party is that of Emperor Henry VII, who in October 1310 passed through Chambéry, Montmêliant, Aiguebelle, La Chambre, St Michel, Termignon, and Lanslebourg to Susa on his way to Rome. Eleven miles was his average for the nine days. Perhaps his large retinue, and that of his queen, affected his speed; and probably this was responsible for the fact that more than once the empress spent the night at a village other than that at which the emperor stayed.[16]

Somewhat the same route was traversed by Valentine de Visconti on her way from Italy to France to wed the future Duke of Orleans; but she achieved a slightly higher speed, fifteen miles a day, on those days on which she travelled. Unlike Henry VII, she made frequent stopovers. Leaving Susa with an escort of sixty horses, she was at Chambéry on 13 July 1389, whence she passed via Yenne and Belley to Bourg, where she remained from 17 July to 24 July, journeying to Pont-de Veyle on 25 July and to Pont de Mâcon on 26 July.[17] Henry, Earl of Derby, returning from the Holy Land, passed through much the same territory at only a slight advance in speed. At an average rate of sixteen miles he travelled through Lanslebourg and Chambéry to Mâcon, and thence through Châlon-sur-Saône, Bar-sur-Seine, Troyes, and Provins to Paris, covering the approximately 428 miles between 26 May and 22 June 1393 and, almost without exception, journeying continuously day after day.[18] During this part of his journey his baggage train included carts. However, after he had detached and sent on ahead most of his party, he was able to make the trip from Paris to Calais at an average speed of thirty miles a day. In other words, the smaller group travelled almost twice as fast.

King John II in 1350/51 made the 373-mile trip from Villeneuve-lès-Avignon to Paris in nineteen travelling days, an average of more than nineteen miles a day.[19] Twenty miles daily for twenty-nine days of actual travel was the speed of Charles VI on his return from Languedoc to Paris in 1389/90.[20] On both these journeys the travelling days were interrupted by numerous rest days.

Robert de Fouilloy, bishop of Amiens, travelled with an escort of forty-one horses from Amiens to Paris in three days at the rate of twenty-seven miles in January 1315/16.[21] Slightly faster was the rate of the Count of Forez, journeying from Montbrison to the court of France. Leaving Montbrison 18 February, 1315/6, he spent that night at Riorges, thirty-seven miles away; on 19 February he slept at Varennes, forty-two miles farther; on 20 February at Moulins, nineteen miles farther; on 21 February at Nevers, thirty-five miles farther; on 22 February at La Charité-sur-Loire, sixteen miles farther; on 23 February at Cosne, seventeen miles farther; on 24 February at Montargis, forty-three miles farther; and 26 February at Juvisy, fifty-three miles farther.[22] Despite his high score on individual days, the count's average was only thirty-one miles, the same as that of John II for nine days between L'Abresle and Juvisy.

Probably the most inveterate traveller of the fourteenth and fifteenth centuries was Philip the Bold, Duke of Burgundy, who customarily changed his place of habitation upwards of a hundred times a year. Compared with other persons of his rank, he was also a fast traveller, especially within his own domains. On a trip to Villeneuve-lès-Avignon he averaged twenty-two miles daily on eleven travelling days between Dijon and that city, and the same on the way back in April, May, and July of 1395. In April 1395 he proceeded at the rate of twenty-five miles on a round trip between Dijon and Châtillon. Leaving Paris after dinner on 25 June 1368, he reached Dijon six and a half days later at an average rate of twenty-nine miles daily without any stopovers. At thirty miles daily he travelled between Dijon and Troyes on 2–4 May 1396. His fastest trip, however, was made between Dijon and Paris in April 1364 with an escort of thirty knights and squires. Between Dijon and Provins (where he spent two nights) his speed was thirty-nine miles daily, but between Provins and Paris, which he reached via St Denis, only thirty-two miles.[23] The average for the five and a half days was thirty-seven miles. It should be noted that the route between Paris and Dijon was one which the Duke of Burgundy travelled innumerable times, and much of it lay within his domains. Consequently, he had every opportunity to provide plenty of changes of horses and to equip convenient places for spending the night. Perhaps the far-flung nature of his possessions, stretching as they did from Burgundy to the Low Countries, contributed to his passion for frequent and fast travel. The only example of a still greater speed attained by a person of position is furnished by King Charles VI. When he spent the night of 21 February 1389/90 at Gyé-sur-Seine and was at Paris on 23 February, he travelled 108 miles in two days at an average speed of fifty-four miles daily. Perhaps Froissart's tale of a race between the king and his brother during their return from the trip to southern France, although proved substantially false by Petit's researches, is not entirely without foundation. There exists, in fact, a royal order reimbursing persons whose horses had been impressed by him and his suite 'in coming hastily from Bar-sur-Seine to Paris' on his return from Languedoc.[24]

That no king, noble, or prince of the church approached, on a journey of several days' duration, the speed of the Duke of Burgundy was due to a variety of factors. Valentine de Visconti, John II and Charles VI (in the first case above) were all involved in journeys that partook of the nature of ceremonial or good-will tours. The Earl of Derby's slow speed between Lanslebourg and Paris was due at least in part to the large size of his party and the presence in his baggage train of carts, but it may also have been influenced by the steady pace at which he journeyed, for he travelled uninterruptedly a much greater number of days (twenty-seven days with only one stop-over) than any of the persons considered above. However, it is difficult to escape the conclusion that the determining factor in their slow progress was a lack of interest in fast travel. In contrast, a large proportion of the persons to be considered next were directly interested in efficient speedy travel.

Law officers, treasury officials, town representatives, couriers, messengers, and monks were all employed by, or accountable to, others. Nevertheless, no objection was made by the *Chambre de comptes* to the slow pace of the lieutenant of the *vicomte* of Bayeux and two companions, all three on horseback with three valets on foot, who in September 1345 arrested two prisoners and transported them on hired horses from Neuilly to Caen via Bayeux in something over two days at a rate of about fourteen miles a day.[25] However, a representative of the town of Albi, sent to the seneschal at Toulouse, felt it necessary to explain, in presenting his bill to the town in January 1380/1, that he had been obliged by the terrible weather to spend six days on horseback in making the round trip.[26] This would mean a speed of only fifteen miles per day, whereas the consuls of Albi usually made the journey at a considerably faster rate. Twice they were absent from Albi four days, their speed being twenty-three miles daily; and on three other occasions they were gone three days, their rate being thirty miles daily. One of the latter trips was made to attend a court of law. Between Albi and Carcassonne they twice travelled at a speed of thirty-three miles daily.[27] No wonder the representative of Albi who averaged only fifteen miles a day was embarrassed. At the nearby town of Rodez the consular accounts note a round trip between Rodez and Toulouse, three days of which were spent there and seven en route at the rate of twenty-six miles daily.[28]

At the same speed a courier of the court of Navarre, attended by a mounted valet, travelled from Pampeluna to Bordeaux. They covered twenty miles the first day, twenty-six the second, thirty-three the third, thirty-one the fourth, twenty-four the fifth, and twenty-one the sixth, the day's journeys in mountainous country being shorter than those in more level terrain.[29] Another itinerary through mountainous territory is that for pilgrims to Rome found among the papers of Barthélemy Bonis, merchant of Montauban. The recommended day's journey within France was fourteen miles from Avignon to Carpentras, thirty-six from Carpentras to Séderon, thirty from Séderon to Tallard, twenty-four from Tallard to Embrun, thirty from Embrun to Briançon, and thirty-two from Briançon to Susa, the average being twenty-eight miles a day. This is a fairly high speed, considering the hilly nature of the terrain.[30]

Also for religious reasons, but this time of an administrative nature, a representative of the Hôtel-Dieu of Beauvais travelled between Beauvais and Pontoise in 1378 at the rate of thirty miles daily;[31] and this was the average speed of John Middleton, an English churchman on his way to the curia to procure favors for his home church, on that part of his journey that lay between Paris and Avignon. Landing at Calais, he reached Paris five days later, having travelled between those points at the rate of thirty-six miles daily. There he spent three days before setting out for Avignon, where he arrived after ten more days of travel and six more of rest. He and his servant were both mounted; during the journey he purchased a horse for his attendant, because the latter was ill.[32]

Various officials employed by the royal government were obliged to travel in its service. Pierre Scatisse, a treasurer, of France, was a much travelled man who used a wide variety of speeds in his journeys. Between Carcassonne and Toulouse on 7–9 June 1371 he proceeded at the rate of eighteen miles, between Narbonne and Avignon on 25–29 March 1372/3 at the rate of twenty-three, and between Carcassonne and Toulouse sometimes at eighteen and sometimes at twenty-seven miles.[33] The governor of Dauphiny, Raoul de Louppy, travelled from Romans to Avignon on 18–20 November 1363 at a speed of twenty-nine miles.[34] This was also the rate of a royal proctor between Paris and Gisors, for his receipt (dated January 1412/3) states that three days of his absence were taken up by travel and eight by attendance at Parlement.[35] According to the accounts of the *Argenterie*, persons escorting packhorses loaded with coronation supplies in 1316 required three or four days each way for the journey between Paris and Reims, an average rate of twenty-five or thirty-three miles daily.[36]

Most of the journeys cited thus far have been those in which persons were engaged solely in travel; but a certain number of round trips include also the transaction of the business for which the journeys were undertaken. However, if the trip is long enough and the rate of speed high enough to warrant the conclusion that the performance of the actual errand took up only a small proportion of the absence, the journey still yields valuable data for an inquiry into the length of a day's journey. This is true in the case of the following examples. A consul of Albi went to Gaillac, fifteen miles distant, delivered information with reference to a law suit, and returned in the same day.[37] At a slightly higher figure the journals of the treasury of Philip VI note a two-day round trip (25 September 1346) between Paris and Pont Saint Maixence, thirty-two miles away.[38] Thirty-three miles daily was the average for three days going from Pontaudemer to Paris and three days returning in the case of a tax collector's party containing pedestrians, rather a remarkable circumstance.[39] This was also the speed of an inspector of mints who took four days for the round trip between Tours and Angers;[40] of Raoul de Louppy on 29–30 June 1362, when he travelled from Romans to Chambéry;[41] and of a representative of the Duke of Normandy who went from Rouen to Évreux to appear in court. Probably in the case last mentioned the official act was brief, for with very few exceptions thirty-three miles is the highest figure for trips which included also the transaction of business. From this circumstance and from the relative scarcity of journeys performed at this or a higher speed, it is safe to conclude that thirty-three miles was a long day's journey and that it required a real effort to achieve it, especially several days in a row.[42]

There were, of course, a few trips lasting several days made at this or at a faster rate. During a lawsuit between the town and bishop of Albi, letters from the town to its representatives in Paris were carried by a man who left Albi 23 October 1369 and returned 26 November, after waiting in Paris twelve days for the lawyers' response; the round trip required twenty-five days at a speed of thirty-three miles daily.[43] At the rate of thirty-four miles daily a tax collector's clerk made the journey from Toulouse to Paris in twelve days in September 1336.[44] Thirty-six miles daily was the speed of persons sent from the town of Rodez to Villefranche de Roergue in regard to a subsidy, the journey being a two-day round trip.[45] Pierre Scatisse, if he often travelled rather slowly, could also on occasion achieve great speed. Between Toulouse and Roquemaure on 25–30 November 1373 he proceeded at a rate of thirty-four miles, between Nîmes and Toulouse on 5–19 April 1369 at thirty-seven miles, from Toulouse to Nîmes via Avignon 21–24 December 1370 at forty-two miles, and from Toulouse to Narbonne and back on 1–4 March 1372/3 at forty-five miles.[46] The reason for Scatisse's hurry is unknown, but urgent need of money on the part of the Duke of La Trémoille, scheduled to leave Dijon with the Hungarian expedition 20 April 1396, was evidently the cause for the speedy journey of a man with a packhorse laden with funds who made the journey from Paris to Dijon in only four days at the rate of forty-nine miles daily. Since the date of the man's journey was noted in the duke's accounts as 16 April, the money apparently arrived just in time.[47]

The cause of the high speed used in the four following examples is unknown; the speed is the more remarkable as they were all round trips. However, since their purpose was to perform errands, the actual accomplishment of the mission probably took little time. Thus, the accounts of the royal *Argenterie* include a journey of a mounted man with a valet to escort a packhorse loaded with cloth of gold as the king's offering to St Catherine of Rouen, the round trip between Paris and Rouen taking four days 'going, staying, and coming,' at the rate of thirty-eight miles daily.[48] A tax collector for the region of Lyons, Mâcon, and Châlon, ordered to bring part of his receipts to Nevers, did so, and received payment for nine days 'going, staying, and returning to Lyons.'[49] Since Nevers is about 179 miles from Lyons, he must have averaged forty miles daily. Forty-seven miles daily was the score of a man who in January 1368/9 went from Albi to Rodez to point out the way to a messenger of the Count of Armagnac;[50] and a royal courier attained the average speed of fifty-two miles on the four-day round trip between Paris and Seignelay.[51] The highest speed mentioned in strictly contemporary documents was stated in the records of a lawsuit between the town of Reims and the archbishop as to financial responsibility for the expenses of the royal coronation. An alderman of the town complained that he had been allowed insufficient time to procure additional information. If he had left Paris on Saturday at noon, he insisted, he would have been unable to reach Reims before the following Tuesday at the hour of prime, and even a messenger, he claimed, could not have reached the town before Monday morning.[52] This would involve a rate of thirty-six miles daily for the alderman and fifty-six for the messenger and, in the latter case, obviously implied travelling by night.

From a summary of the evidence, then, a day's journey in France in the fourteenth century was probably about thirty to thirty-three miles. At the rate of thirty-three miles it was possible both to travel and inspect mints, or even to appear in court; but beyond this speed the actual travelling took up so much of the day that any business transacted was in the nature of errands — as the delivery of letters, money, or cloth. Consequently, the litigant who referred to thirty miles a day as a long day's journey was not far wrong, and Gilles le Bouvier's estimate of thirty miles was more nearly correct than his approximation of forty miles. King John of England regularly travelled faster than the French kings were accustomed to do; but Grace Stretton's statement that thirty-five miles was express speed would hardly hold in fourteenth-century France, where royal messengers were accustomed to travel up to fifty-six miles a day. On the other hand, her estimate of the rate of a progress as fourteen or fifteen miles a day adequately describes the speed of Valentine de Visconti. However, the conclusion of the present article that thirty-three miles per day approximated a full day's journey gives a figure considerably higher than Ludwig's. For this there are at least three reasons: the first being his inclusion of days on which a majority of the time was not spent in travelling, and the second his reliance on measuring distances between points in a straight line without taking account of winding roads. Thirdly, his characters were almost uniformly persons of importance — emperors, kings, noblemen, popes, archbishops and abbots, groups which the present researches indicate generally travelled at a slower pace than others.

With the single exception of the Duke of Burgundy (who, despite an escort of thirty knights, went thirty-seven miles daily for five and a half days), no king, nobleman, or important churchman has been found to have averaged more than thirty-three miles for several consecutive days. Persons who did so were mounted messengers, town officials, servants, government employees — in a word, persons under pressure to produce results. This absence of a motive for exertion was one of the reasons why kings, noblemen, and princes of the church were seldom found travelling at great speed, but their movements were hampered also by large retinues.

Large parties very definitely contributed to a slow rate of speed. It was after the Earl of Derby had detached some of his party that he attained his highest speed. Compare this with the escort of sixty horses of Valentine of Milan, who, despite numerous stop-overs, averaged only sixteen miles daily. Baggage tended to increase in geometric progression with the size of the group; where small parties could depend on local inns for food and shelter, large ones could not, and were obliged to carry most of their provisions with them. Groups with extensive baggage trains were also more likely to include carts, a slower form of locomotion than horses. With regard to shelter, also, a numerous party was likely to experience difficulty. Between Chambéry and Susa the consort of Emperor Henry VII sometimes spent the might at villages other than those at which the emperor did, presumably because of the problem of shelter. Important persons attempted to arrange their itineraries so as to spend the night at monasteries, or at the manor houses or castles of friends.

The length of the journey also had its effect on the speed. Most trips made at a speed higher than thirty-three miles were two to six day trips with the three exceptions of a tax collector's clerk who travelled twelve days at thirty-four miles, of Pierre Scatisse who journeyed fourteen days at thirty-seven miles daily, and a tax collector who travelled nine at forty. Long journeys were usually made at a slower rate and frequently included stop-overs. Persons who journeyed on a great number of consecutive days were not only slowed by fatigue but also sometimes by the weather, for they must have taken their chances with rain and mud, snow and ice. Nevertheless, these researches have uncovered hardly any explicit complaints of bad weather. Another consideration, allied to the weather, is that of the time of year, for mediaeval travellers in general avoided night travel. However, there were exceptions. The monk of Fécamp, despite his moderate pace, travelled at night; and the hypothetical messenger who was to arrive at Reims at the hour of prime must have done so; so also must Charles VI on his race of 108 miles between Gyé-sur-Seine and Paris, completed in two days, especially as it occurred in February. It might be supposed, then, that between the autumnal and vernal equinoxes there would have been few journeys over thirty miles a day. On the contrary, out of twenty-one trips, datable with reference to the time of year, which were made at a rate of thirty-one miles or more daily, thirteen were made in the six months between 22 September and 22 March, and only eight in the other half of the year.

The terrain and state of the roads would naturally be expected to influence the speed of travel. A Navarrese messenger on his way from Pampeluna to Normandy proceeded at a slower pace in the mountains than in level country. On the other hand, the Earl of Derby averaged sixteen miles in the French Alps, just as he did between Mâcon and Paris; and in the pilgrim's itinerary between Avignon and Susa the recommended stops do not seem to have been chosen with any regard to whether the country was rugged or level, but probably with reference to convenient accommodations. From the circumstance that both the Earl of Derby and John Middleton travelled faster between Paris and Calais than they did in southeastern France, it is tempting to assume that the roads were better, but this is mere conjecture, for their higher speed may have been due to any one of a variety of factors.

It is, of course, undeniable that pedestrians could not travel as fast as horsemen. For example, mounted messengers took two days to go from Senlis to Paris to fetch papers and return, whereas a foot messenger took three.[53] Nevertheless, since pedestrians accompanying horsemen made a six-day trip at an average speed of thirty-three miles daily, and since the great majority of journeys were made at this or a slower rate, their presence, which was customary, does not seem to have hampered most trips. Journeys at the speed of thirty-four miles or more were made only by mounted men and trips at the rate of fifty miles only by men in a position to requisition horses.

In conclusion, then, it may be said that while most journeys were probably made at a rate between twenty and thirty miles and while it was possible to achieve the speeds of fifty-four and fifty-six miles a day, thirty to thirty-three miles a day approximated a full day's journey; and it required a real effort to achieve this, especially several days in succession.

NEW YORK, N. Y.

[1] Gilles le Bouvier dit Berry, *Le Livre de la description des pays*, edited by E. T. Hamy in *Recueil de voyages et de documents pour servir à l'histoire de la géographie depuis le XIIIe jusqu'à la fin du XVIe siècle* (Paris, 1908), XXII, 30.

[2] H. Lot. 'Des Frais de justice au XIVe siècle,' *Bibliothèque de l'École des Chartes*, XXXIV (1873), 208.

[3] Pierre Champion, *La Vie de Charles d'Orléans (1394–1465)* (Paris, 1911), p. 440. From Rouen to Blois is 142 miles by road.

[4] Grace Stretton, 'The Travelling Household in the Middle Ages,' *Journal of the British Archaeological Association*, New Series, XL (1935), 88, n. 1.

[5] 'Archaeologia,' *Retrospective Review*, Second Series, II, 224.

[6] Charles A. J. Armstrong, 'Some Examples of the Distribution and Speed of News in England at the Time of the Wars of the Roses,' in *Studies Presented to Frederick Maurice Powicke*, ed. R. W. Hunt and others (Oxford, 1948), pp. 429–454.

[7] Friedrich Ludwig, *Untersuchungen über die Reise- und Marschgeschwindigkeit im XII und XIII Jahrhundert* (Berlin, 1897).

[8] The question of what mileage the mediaeval traveller actually traversed is indeed difficult. Take, for instance, the distance between L'Arbresle and Lyons. In a straight line it is eleven miles; according to Ludwig (p. 109) it is ten miles; according to Muirhead (*Northeastern France* 2nd ed., London and Paris, 1930) it is thirteen miles; and according to an undated map put out by La Maison de Dion-Bouton the distance is sixteen miles. (The latter map was probably published very early in this century, because it assumes that the average speed of an automobile is ten kilometers an hour.) The reader should bear in mind the tentative nature of conclusions with regard to mileage.

[9] Léon Ménard, *Histoire civile, ecclésiastique et littéraire de la ville de Nismes*, II (Paris, 1751), 324.

[10] G. P. Cuttino, *English Diplomatic Administration, 1259–1339* (London, 1940), p. 88.

[11] Ménard, II, 324 (7 May, 1373).

[12] Léopold Delisle, *Actes normandes de la chambre des comptes sous Philippe de Valois, 1328–1350* (Rouen, 1871), p. 90 (1334).

[13] Auguste Longnon, *Documents relatifs au comté de Champagne et de Brie, 1172–1361*, III: *Les Comptes administratifs* (Paris, 1914), p. 291 (1340–1341). See also p. 453 (1347–1348): 'A forester, his clerk, two horses, and a valet.'

[14] Dom Claude Devic and Dom J. Vaissette, *Histoire générale de Languedoc avec des notes et des pièces justificatives* (Toulouse, 1872–1893), Vol. x, col. 793 (1336–1337). See also col. 794 (1336–1337) for a royal proctor and clerk travelling with two horses and three servants on foot.

[15] Auguste Vidal, *Comptes consulaires d'Albi (1359–1360)* (Toulouse, 1900), p. 74. References to mixed parties of horsemen and pedestrians are frequent. In the manuscript Collection Clairambault 470, p. 77 (1323–1324) two financial agents set out on a trip with two horses and a servant. A man sent by the town of Provins to obtain letters from the king in 1320 was travelling with a horse and valet. (Maurice Prou and Jules d'Auriac, *Actes et comptes de la commune de Provins de l'an 1271 à l'an 1330* [Provins, 1933], p. 256 [1320].) The consular accounts of Grenoble contain payments to a man travelling with a horse and servant. (A. Devaux, *Comptes consulaires de Grenoble en langue vulgaire* [Montpellier, 1912], p. 61 [1339]. See also p. 145 for three notables travelling with three horses

and three servants in 1339.) In 1346 the *gens des comptes* sent a man with a horse and valet to three different archbishops concerning certain bulls. (Jules Viard, *Les Journaux du trésor de Philippe VI de Valois suivis de l'Ordinarium Thesauri de 1338–1339*, in *Collection de documents inédits sur l'histoire de France publiées par les soins du ministre de l'instruction publique*, Vol. 36 [Paris, 1899], p. 68 [1346]. Two consuls of Rodez, cited to appear before the seneschal at Montpellier in 1350–1351, made the trip with two horses and two valets. (H. Bousquet, *Comptes consulaires de la cité et du bourg de Rodez*, in *Archives historiques de Rouergue*, VI: Premiere partie: *Cité*; I [Rodez, 1925], 130–131; see also p. 252.) Mss 394 of the Collection Baluze in the Bibliothèque Nationale mentions a man as travelling with a horse and valet (p. 700). Examples of mixed parties of horsemen and pedestrians might be multiplied indefinitely.

[16] Francisco Bonainio, *Acta Henrici VII Romanorum Imperatoris et monumenta quaedam alia suorum temporum historiam illustrantia a Francisco Bonaino collecta ac in duas partes divisa* (Florence, 1877), Part I, pp. 286–346. Franz Prowe, *Die Finanzverwahltung am Hofe Heinrichs VII während des Römerzuges, nach den Rechnungsberichten bei Bonaini Acta Heinrici VII*, Part I, pp. 286–346 (Berlin, n.d.). See also Ludwig, *op. cit.* (note 7), p. 74. He was at Chambéry on 14 October; at Montméliant on 16 October; at Aiguebelle, on 17 October; at La Chambre on 18 October; at St Michel on 19 October; at Termignon on 21 October; at Lanslebourg, on 22 October; and at Susa on 23 October.

[17] J. Camus, 'La Venue en France de Valentine Visconti, duchesse d'Orléans et l'inventaire de ses joyaux apportés de Lombardie,' *Miscellanea di storia italiana*, Ser. III, Vol. V (Turin, 1900), p. 28. E. Collas, *Valentine de Milan, duchesse d'Orléans* (3rd ed., Paris, 1911), p. 52.

[18] Lucy Toulmin Smith, ed., *Expeditions to Prussia and the Holy Land made by Henry, Earl of Derby (afterwards King Henry IV) in the years 1390–1391 and 1392–1393, being Accounts kept by his Treasurer during two Years* (London, 1894), p. lxxviii.

[19] Ernest Petit, 'Séjours de Jean II (1350–1356),' *Bulletin historique et philologique du comité des travaux historiques et scientifiques*, Année 1896, p. 587. He was at Villeneuve-lès-Avignon on 30 January and at Paris 19 February.

[20] Petit, 'Séjours de Charles VI, 1380–1400,' *Bulletin du comité des travaux historiques*, 1893, p. 446. He was at Narbonne on 17 January and at Paris on 23 February.

[21] E. Soyez, 'Voyage de l'Evêque d'Amiens, Robert de Fouilloy, envoyé par le roi Louis X en Périgord et en Quercy, durant l'année 1316, pour la réformation du pays,' *Bulletin de la société des antiquaires de Picardie*, XIX (1898), 100.

[22] Delisle, 'Notes sur quelques manuscrits de Baron Dauphin de Verna,' *Bibliothèque de l'école des chartes*, LVI, 687.

[23] Louis Prosper Gachard, *Collection des voyages des souverains des Pays-Bas*, I (Brussels, 1874), 11, 47, 251, and 8–9.

[24] Ernest Petit, 'Séjours de Charles VI (1380–1400),' *Bulletin du comité des travaux historiques* (1893), p. 446. Cf. Froissart, ed. Kervyn de Lettenhove (Brussels, 1863–1877), XIV, 80–82. H. Moranvillé, 'Une course de Bar-sur-Seine à Paris en 1390,' *Bibliothèque de l'École des Chartes*, LIV, 718. According to Froissart, the race was from Montpellier to Paris.

[25] Léopold Delisle, *Actes normandes de la chambre des comptes sous Philippe de Valois*, pp. 331–332.

[26] Vidal, *Douze comptes consulaires d'Albi du xive siècle* (*Archives historiques de l'Albigeois*, Toulouse, Vol. I [1908] and Vol. II [1911]), I, 338.

[27] For twenty-three miles see Vidal, *Comptes consulaires*, p. 71, and *Douze Comptes*, I, 158 (1370). For thirty miles see Vidal, *Douze comptes*, I, 61 (1368–1369), and I, 65 and 161 (1370). For thirty-three miles see Vidal, *Comptes consulaires*, p. 12 (16–17 July 1359), and *Douze comptes*, I, 202.

[28] H. Bousquet, *op. cit.* (note 15 above), p. 252. Rodez is ninety-two miles from Toulouse.

[29] Jean Auguste Brutails, *Documents des archives de la chambre des comptes de Navarre, 1196–1384* (Bibliothèque de l'École des Hautes Études: Sciences philologiques et historiques, fasc. 84, 1890), p. 77, n. 2.

[30] Édouard Forestié, ed., 'Les Livres de comptes des frères Bonis, marchands montalbanais du XIVe siècle,' *Archives historiques de la Gascogne*, Part I, Premier et deuxième trimestres, huitième année (1890), p. xx.

[31] V. Leblond, *Les deux plus anciens comptes de l'hôtel-dieu de Beauvais, 1377–1380* (Extrait du *Bulletin philologique et historique*, Paris, 1914), p. 85.

[32] James E. Thorold Rogers, *A History of Agriculture and Prices in England from the year of the Oxford Parliament (1259) to the Commencement of the Continental War (1793)* (Oxford, 1867) II, 631–634. 1331. Probably more journeys were performed at rates of speed between twenty and thirty miles than at higher or lower speeds. Thus, in the third decade of the fifteenth century a monk of Fécamp on his way to Paris to obtain privileges from the Duke of Bedford for his monastery, travelled from Fécamp to Rouen at the rate of twenty miles daily. (Charles de Robillard de Beaurepaire, *Le Livre de comptes de Thomas de Marest, curé de Saint Nicolas de Coutances, 1397–1433* (Rouen [1905], p. 256. Accounts of Jehan de Saint Riquier, religious of Fécamp.) A horse hired at Montauban for a journey to Toulouse, twenty-six miles distant, was returned the next day in 1346 (Forestié, *Les Livres de comptes*, p. 151), as was done in May 1343 in the case of the mounts of certain schoolmen of Nîmes going to Avignon for the establishment of a school at their town. The travellers themselves, however, made a longer stay. (Ménard, II, p. 324 [7 May, 1373].) The accounts of the royal *Argenterie* note two round trips, one made in 1316 between Paris and Provins, twenty-five miles apart and one in 1380–1381 between Paris and Meaux, separated by twenty-eight miles. (Louis Douët-D'Arcq, ed., *Comptes de l'argenterie des rois de France, publiés pour la société de l'histoire de France d'après des manuscrits originaux*, pp. 10–11. 1316. *Id.*, ed., *Comptes de l'hôtel des rois de France aux XIVe et XVe siècles* [Société de l'histoire de France, Paris, 1865], p. 105 [1380–1381].) In 1387 a clerk of the Chambre aux Deniers went from Senlis, where the court was staying, to Paris, twenty-eight miles away, to fetch money and papers and returned the next day. (Douët-D'Arcq, *Comptes de l'hôtel*, p. 2, and *Nouveau recueil de comptes de l'argenterie des rois de France* [Societé de l'histoire de France, Paris, 1874], pp. 283 and 300.) A royal mounted messenger made the round trip between Melun and Coulommiers to inquire whether there were plague at the latter point at the rate of twenty-nine miles daily. (Douët-D'Arcq, *Comptes de l'hôtel*, p. 43. This was also the rate at which a messenger went from Albi to Castres to deliver a letter and back in July 1393 (Vidal, *Douze comptes*, I, 11 and 30, and II, 144; three different trips are mentioned) and a bailiff proceeded from Rouen to beyond Harcourt to investigate a murder. (Delisle, *Actes Normandes*, p. 85 [1334].)

[33] Ménard, II (*Preuves*), pp. 4, 5, and 6.

[34] Ulysse Chevalier and E. Maignien, 'Compte de Raoul de Louppy, gouverneur du Dauphiné de 1361 à 1369,' *Bulletin d'histoire ecclésiastique et d'archéologie religieuse des diocèses de Valence, Gap, Grenoble et Viviers*, VII (Romans, 1886–1887), p. lv.

[35] David Eugene Smith Library (Columbia University), Manuscript 1412. l.21. (January 1412/3).

[36] Douët-D'Arcq, *Comptes de l'argenterie*, pp. 10–11.

[37] Vidal, *Comptes consulaires d'Albi*, p. 64.

[38] Viard, *Les Journaux du trésor de Philippe VI*, p. 69.

[39] Delisle, *Actes normandes*, p. 90 (1330).

[40] Viard, *Les Journaux du trésor de Philippe VI*, p. 681 (4 February 1349/50).

[41] Chevalier and Maignien, *op. cit.*, p. iii.

[42] Delisle, *Actes normandes*, p. 75 (December 1334).

[43] Vidal, *Douze comptes*, I, 128.

[44] Léon Louis Borrelli de Serres, *Recherches sur divers services publics du XIIIe au XVIIIe siècle* (Paris, 1895–1910), II, 30.

[45] Bousquet, *op. cit.*, I, 247 (11 March 1354/5), and I, 248 (7 March 1354/5).

[46] Ménard, II (*Preuves*), pp. 3–4.

[47] Guy de La Trémoille and Marie de Sully, *Livre de comptes 1395–1406* (Nantes, 1887), p. 40.

[48] Douët-D'Arcq, *Comptes de l'argenterie*, p. 189 (1352).

[49] H. Moranvillé, *Étude sur la vie de Jean Le Mercier 13 . . . –1397* (Mémoires présentés par divers savants à l'Académie des Inscriptions et Belles-Lettres de l'Institut de France deuxième serie: Antiquités de France, VI, 2 [Paris, 1888], p. 305.

[50] Vidal, *Douze comptes*, I, 90.

[51] Douët-D'Arcq, *Comptes de l'hôtel*, pp. 48–49.

[52] Pierre Varin, *Archives administratives de la ville de Reims*, II, 1 (Paris, 1843), p. 205.

[53] Douët-D'Arcq, *Nouveau recueil*, pp. 50, 105, 283, and 300.

9

The Cistercian Order and the Settlement of Northern England

R.A. Donkin

OF THE several reform movements that punctuate the history of Western monasticism, that associated with Cîteaux is in some respects the most remarkable. Cîteaux itself was founded near Dijon in the year 1098. By 1152 (when the general chapter called a halt to the foundation of new colonies), no fewer than 333 houses had been established throughout Europe.[1] The first houses in northern England[2] were Rievaulx and Fountains, both dating from 1132, and all but one of the northern monasteries were in existence by 1152 (Table I). By comparison, only two-thirds of the total of English and Welsh houses had been founded by that time.

The northern plantation was not in itself impressive—thirteen houses out of seventy-five in all England and Wales (Fig. 1)—but it took place early in an area comparatively free from Benedictine influence and it included men of remarkable ability and character. Moreover, the northern houses have a strong collective identity and they may properly be considered together.

The Cistercian Plantation

If there is a connection between the founding of Cistercian houses and the undeveloped condition of the North in the early twelfth century, it is indirect rather than direct and worked through the medium of ordinary landowners who invited the monks in the first place and provided endowments. The plantation was not planned in detail from Cîteaux; it was opportunist in nature, and the monks were usually left with some measure of choice. They favored sites that stood apart from existing settlement; only three of the houses we are considering—Whalley, Meaux, and Byland—are known to have been placed directly alongside a hamlet or village, and in the last two instances the settlements were promptly depopulated and transformed into granges farmed by lay brothers. The remaining houses occupied more or less vacant land and we have brief descriptions of initial, or very

[1] R. A. Donkin: The Growth and Distribution of the Cistercian Order in Medieval Europe, *Studia Monastica*, Vol. 9, 1967, pp. 275–286.

[2] That is, in the six most northerly counties; there were, however, no Cistercian foundations in either Durham or Westmorland.

➤ Dr. Donkin is lecturer in geography in the University of Birmingham, England.

early, clearing operations around Kirkstall,[3] Sallay,[4] and Byland.[5] In the North a site in a small entrenched valley or along the middle reaches of a larger stream was distinctly common. Rievaulx, Fountains, and Newminster provide good examples of the former, and Jervaulx and Kirkstall of the latter. In fact the only two clear exceptions are Meaux in Holderness and Holm Cultram on the Solway, both of which stood in open country and close to extensive marsh and seasonally inundated pasture.

The general chapter of the order laid down a certain procedure for the selection of sites, including close inspection of the ground, but it is doubtful whether this was always followed or, if followed, whether it had much value. Twenty-nine Cistercian houses in England and Wales (that is, more than one-third of the total) changed their sites at least once.[6] Five of these houses were in the North (Table I), and the reason for the move in each case was dissatisfaction with the physical conditions and with the generally poor economic prospects. Not that the monks had grand ideas at this time; it was simply a question of survival. Barnoldswick was exchanged for Kirkstall after five years; the weather, according to the monks, had been consistently bad, and it appears that the years 1151 and 1152 (when the move took place) were particularly wet. The community at Fors in upper Wensleydale was evacuated to Jervaulx "because [it was said] of the intemperance of the air and the unfruitful environment."[7] Sallay nearly decided to seek a new site for the same reason: standing, in the words of the chronicler, "in a foggy and rainy district, its crops, white onto harvest, ordinarily rotted on the stalk."[8] Stanlaw and Tulketh were both abandoned, for Whalley and Furness respectively, owing to recurrent flooding. One of Byland's temporary sites was too confined, and another, near Stocking just below the Hambleton Hills, suffered from lack of water.

How can we account for these errors in siting, which are without parallel in the history of any other order? The answer lies partly in the monks' ignor-

3 J. S. Walbran, edit.: Memorials of the Abbey of St. Mary of Fountains (Vol. 1), *Surtees Soc.*, Vol. 42, 1863, p. 92; J. Caley, M. Ellis, B. Bandinel, edits.: Monasticon Anglicanum, Vol. 5 (London, 1846), p. 531.

4 Monasticon Anglicanum, Vol. 5, p. 515.

5 "Inceperunt assartare viriliter in occidentali parte citra et dejuxta Middleburgam et aedificare subtus moram in dicto territorio de Cukewolde . . ." (*ca.* 1147; *ibid.*, p. 351); and "viriliter extirpare coeperunt de nemore" (*ca.* 1177; p. 353).

6 R. A. Donkin: The Site Changes of Mediaeval Cistercian Monasteries, *Geography*, Vol. 44, 1959, pp. 251–258.

7 Memorials of . . . Fountains [see footnote 3 above], Vol. 1, p. 131.

8 Joseph McNulty, edit.: Sallay Cartulary (Vol. 2), *Yorkshire Archaeological Soc. Record Ser.*, Vol. 90, 1934, p. 128; Monasticon Anglicanum [see footnote 2 above], Vol. 5, p. 512.

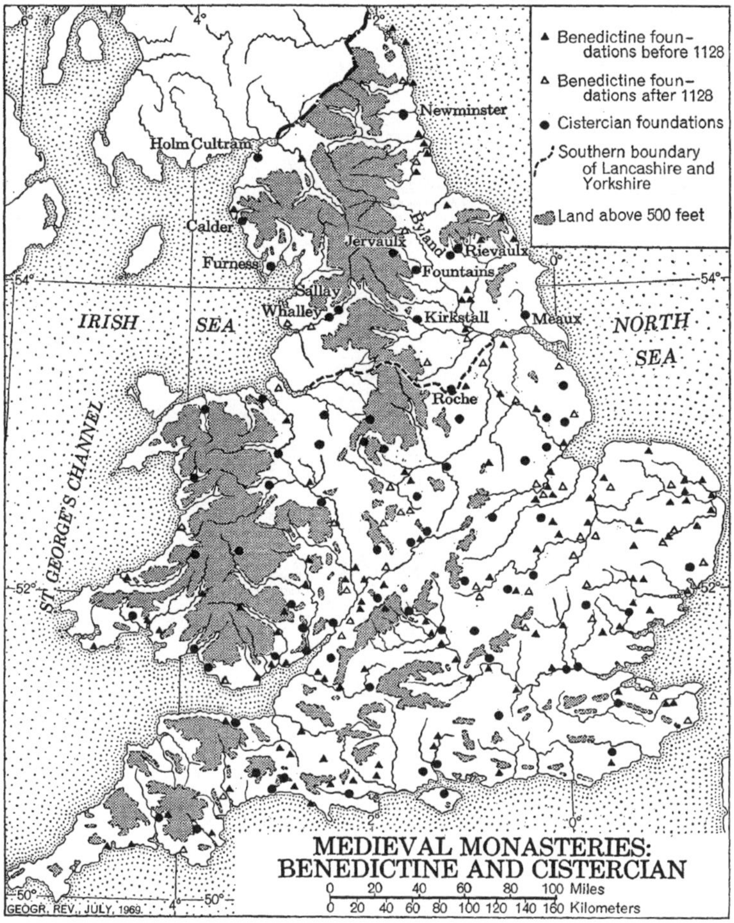

FIG. 1

TABLE I—CISTERCIAN HOUSES IN NORTHERN ENGLAND

PRESENT COUNTY	MONASTERY	DATE OF FOUNDATION	TEMPORARY SITE(S)	
Cumberland	Calder[a]	1135, 1143		
	Holm Cultram	1150		
Lancashire	Furness[a]	1127	Tulketh[a]	(1124)
	Whalley	1296	Stanlaw	(1172)
Northumberland	Newminster	1138	?	
Yorkshire	Byland	1177	Calder[a]	(1135)
			Hood	(1138)
			Byland I	(1143)
			Stocking	(1147)
	Fountains	1132		
	Jervaulx	1156	Fors	(1145)
	Kirkstall	1152	Barnoldswick	(1147)
	Meaux	1151		
	Rievaulx	1132		
	Roche	1147		
	Sallay	1148		

[a] Order of Savigny until 1147.

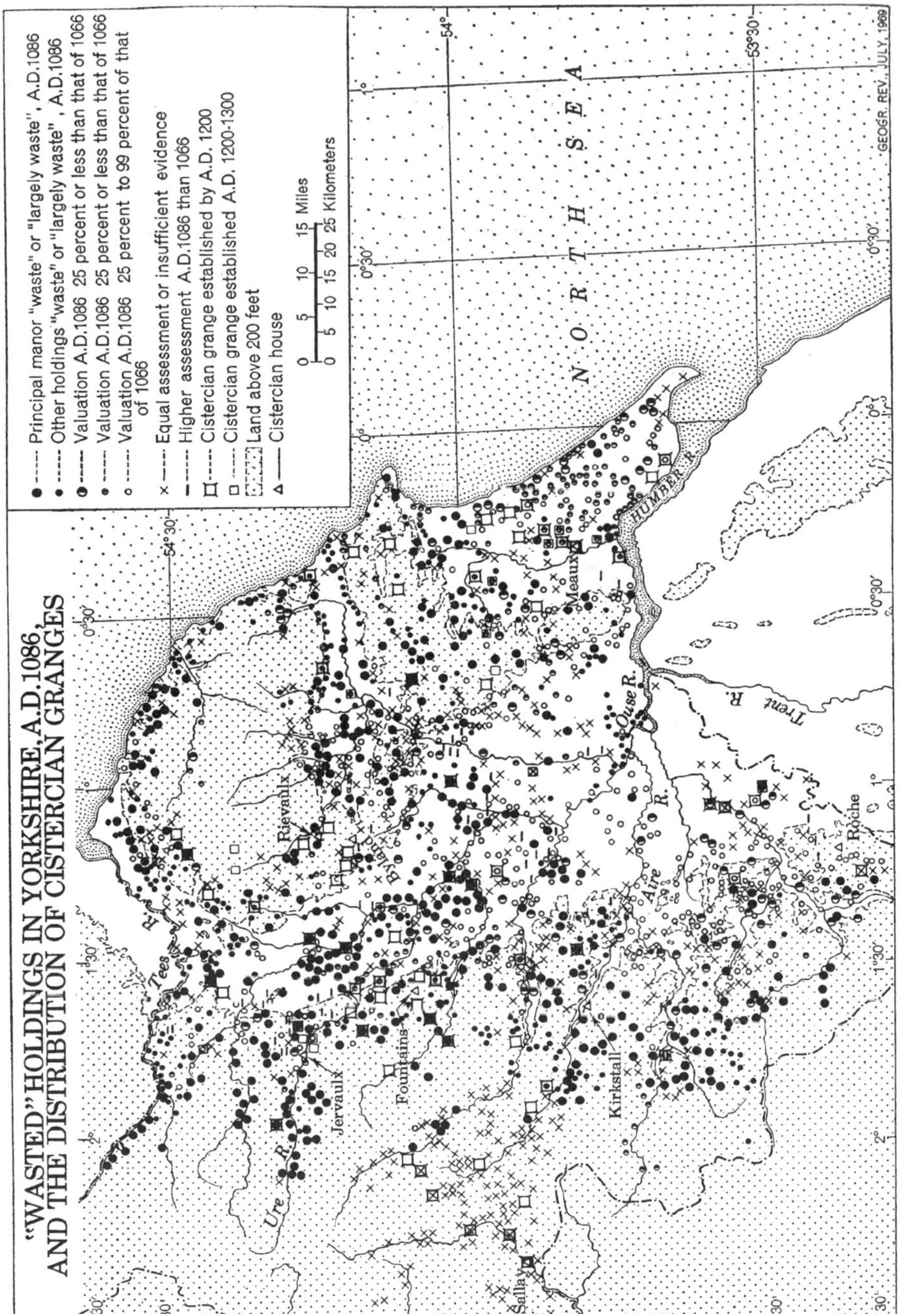
"WASTED" HOLDINGS IN YORKSHIRE, A.D.1086, AND THE DISTRIBUTION OF CISTERCIAN GRANGES
Principal manor "waste" or "largely waste", A.D.1086
Other holdings "waste" or "largely waste", A.D.1086
Valuation A.D.1086 25 percent or less than that of 1066
Valuation A.D.1086 25 percent or less than that of 1066
Valuation A.D.1086 25 percent to 99 percent of that of 1066
Equal assessment or insufficient evidence
Higher assessment A.D.1086 than 1066
Cistercian grange established by A.D. 1200
Cistercian grange established A.D. 1200-1300
Land above 200 feet
Cistercian house
0 5 10 15 Miles
0 5 10 15 20 25 Kilometers
N O R T H S E A
HUMBER R.
Ouse R.
Trent R.
Aire R.
Ure R.
Tees R.
Rievaulx
Byland
Meaux
Jervaulx
Fountains
Kirkstall
Sallay
Roche
GEOGR. REV., JULY, 1969

FIG. 2

ance of local conditions, but more fundamentally in the fact that the question of subsistence, basic to ordinary settlement, received scant attention at first in the prevailing mood of asceticism and religious zeal. Thus for some consider-

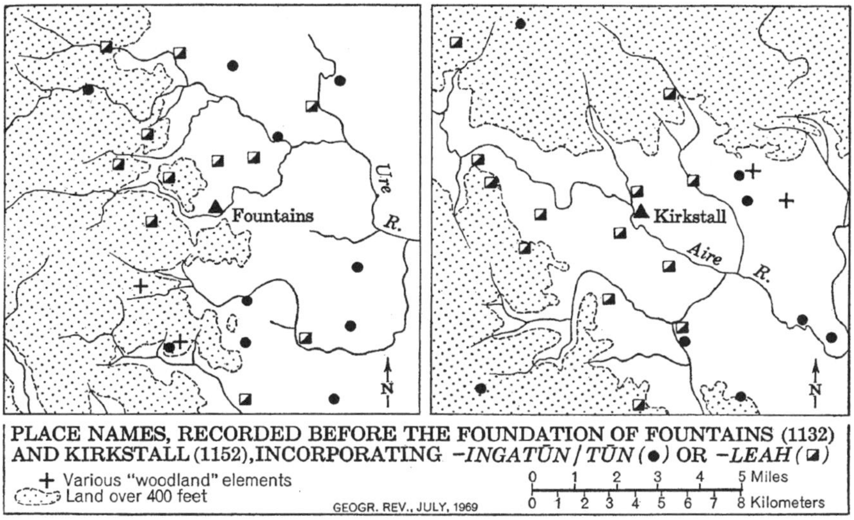

PLACE NAMES, RECORDED BEFORE THE FOUNDATION OF FOUNTAINS (1132) AND KIRKSTALL (1152), INCORPORATING *-INGATŪN / TŪN* (●) OR *-LEAH* (◪)

Fig. 3

able time the Cistercian pattern of settlement changed almost as much through redistribution as through the addition of fresh colonies.

The sites of Cistercian houses in Yorkshire may be studied in relation to the distribution of places mentioned in the Domesday Book (1085–1086). Figure 2 suggests that the monasteries stood within, in some cases just within, the pattern of settlement established by 1066, for which the Domesday Book must be considered a conservative source of information. However, in the winter of 1069–1070 much of Yorkshire had been devastated by the armies of William I, and many manors were reported "waste" or "largely waste" in 1086. We do not know precisely what "waste" meant, nor do we really know what recovery there had been by 1132, or indeed by any other date in the twelfth century. Symeon of Durham and William of Malmesbury suggest that the effects of devastation were widely apparent as late as 1130,[9] and

[9] "Interea, ita terra cultore destituta, lata ubique solitudo patebat per novem annos. Inter Eboracum et Dunelmum nusquam villa inhabitada . . ." (Symeon of Durham [Vol. 2] [edited by T. Arnold; Rolls Ser. 75, 1885], p. 188). "Humus, per sexaginta et eo amplius miliara, omnifariam inculta; nudum omnium solum usque ad hoc etiam tempus . . ." (Willelmi Malmesbiriensis de Gestis Regum [edited by W. Stubbs; Rolls Ser. 90, 1889], pp. 308–309).

Fountains (to quote the account of its foundation two years later) occupied a site "that had long been uninhabited."[10] I think we are justified in believing that the frontiers of settlement had been rolled back significantly and that in the third and fourth decades of the twelfth century some Cistercian houses stood beyond their effective limits—if indeed we can still think in terms of a frontier around the North York Moors and the Pennines during this obscure and difficult period.

That the monks did not make their way into areas entirely undisturbed by settlement, whatever the effects of devastation, is clearly demonstrated by a study of place names in the vicinity of houses founded before 1152. In every case names are recorded, in the Domesday Book or in land charters, before the foundation of the abbey. Fountains and Kirkstall are thickly surrounded by such evidence (Fig. 3), as is Meaux. Peasant colonization, with assarting, had been going on for hundreds of years. William's systematic destruction reversed the process, but it also created opportunities, which the monks, among others, were not slow to grasp.

Cistercian Estates and Rural Settlement

The Cistercian estates, which comprised land of every kind and condition, grew by gifts and, under some disguise, by purchase. For nearly two centuries the monks' aim was to consolidate their holdings by assarting, exchanges, and purchases and to work them directly, avoiding so far as possible the complications of the manorial system and contact with peasant agriculture generally. In this they were only partly successful, but the fact remains that a high proportion of Cistercian arable, probably between 70 and 80 percent in the North, was eventually held in fairly compact blocks. These holdings, known as granges (Fig. 4), formed the basis of Cistercian land planning and may be regarded as the principal contribution of the monks to the landscape and economy of northern England in the twelfth and thirteenth centuries.[11] Cistercian granges were first mentioned during the fourth decade of the twelfth century; there were at least seventy-five of them in Yorkshire before 1200 (twenty-four belonging to Fountains alone) and an additional forty-one by 1350. That granges were more characteristic of the North than of the South of England reflected differences in the ease with which land could be consolidated.

[10] "Locum a cunctis retro seculis inhabitatum" (Memorials of . . . Fountains [see footnote 3 above], Vol. 1, p. 32).

[11] R. A. Donkin: The Cistercian Grange in England in the Twelfth and Thirteenth Centuries, *Studia Monastica,* Vol. 6, 1964, pp. 95–144.

Each of the estates was worked from a cluster of buildings, comprising barns and animal sheds, possibly a grain or fulling mill, accommodation for the *conversi* (lay brothers), and sometimes a chapel. The northern part of the Vale of York and the foothills to the east and west—that is, the area between Fountains, Jervaulx, Byland, and Rievaulx—contained the greatest concentration of granges, of Cistercian arable generally, and, apparently, of wasted holdings at the time of the Domesday survey. Bishop has argued that after 1070 some of the dales were drained of population by landowners anxious to recolonize areas that were potentially more productive, particularly in the Vale of York.[12] Invitations to the Cistercians to settle may also have been made, at least in part, in anticipation of their contribution to the revival of agriculture. In fact, some 44 percent of all known twelfth-century granges in Yorkshire were in territories described as waste or largely waste in 1086, and the proportions were as high as 56 percent and 62 percent in the case of granges belonging to Fountains and Rievaulx respectively. Such run-down properties, even if not completely depopulated, were more tempting than open moor or marsh, and I know of only two or three examples of granges carved largely, or perhaps entirely, out of natural wasteland.

A clue to whether devastated and depopulated land had been reclaimed subsequently is sometimes found in the charter by which it was conveyed. For example, the township of Bramley, waste in 1086, was granted to Fountains early in the twelfth century and transformed en bloc into a grange. The gift of "all Bramley which is of the grantor's purchase" stands alone;[13] no secondary grants or quitclaims by the inhabitants are recorded. The case of Brimham is similar.[14] These places had probably never been resettled; they were certainly the scene of extensive assarting by the monks during the twelfth century. On the other hand, waste did not necessarily imply that no population survived, and the extent of recovery by, say, the second quarter of the twelfth century varied considerably from place to place. Baldersby and Cayton, waste in 1086, were later depopulated by Fountains.

The English Cistercians, even those in the North, never possessed so much arable land that it could not be worked directly, either as manorial demesne or, preferably, as part of a grange staffed by lay brothers. Unlike the Cister-

[12] T. A. M. Bishop: The Norman Settlement of Yorkshire, *in* Studies in Medieval History, Presented to Sir Frederick Maurice Powicke (edited by R. W. Hunt and others; Oxford, 1948), pp. 1–14; reference on p. 6.

[13] W. T. Lancaster, edit.: Chartulary of Fountains (2 vols.; Leeds, 1915), Vol. 1, pp. 140–142; Monasticon Anglicanum [see footnote 3 above], Vol. 5, p. 306.

[14] Chartulary of Fountains [see footnote 13 above], Vol. 1, pp. 145–146.

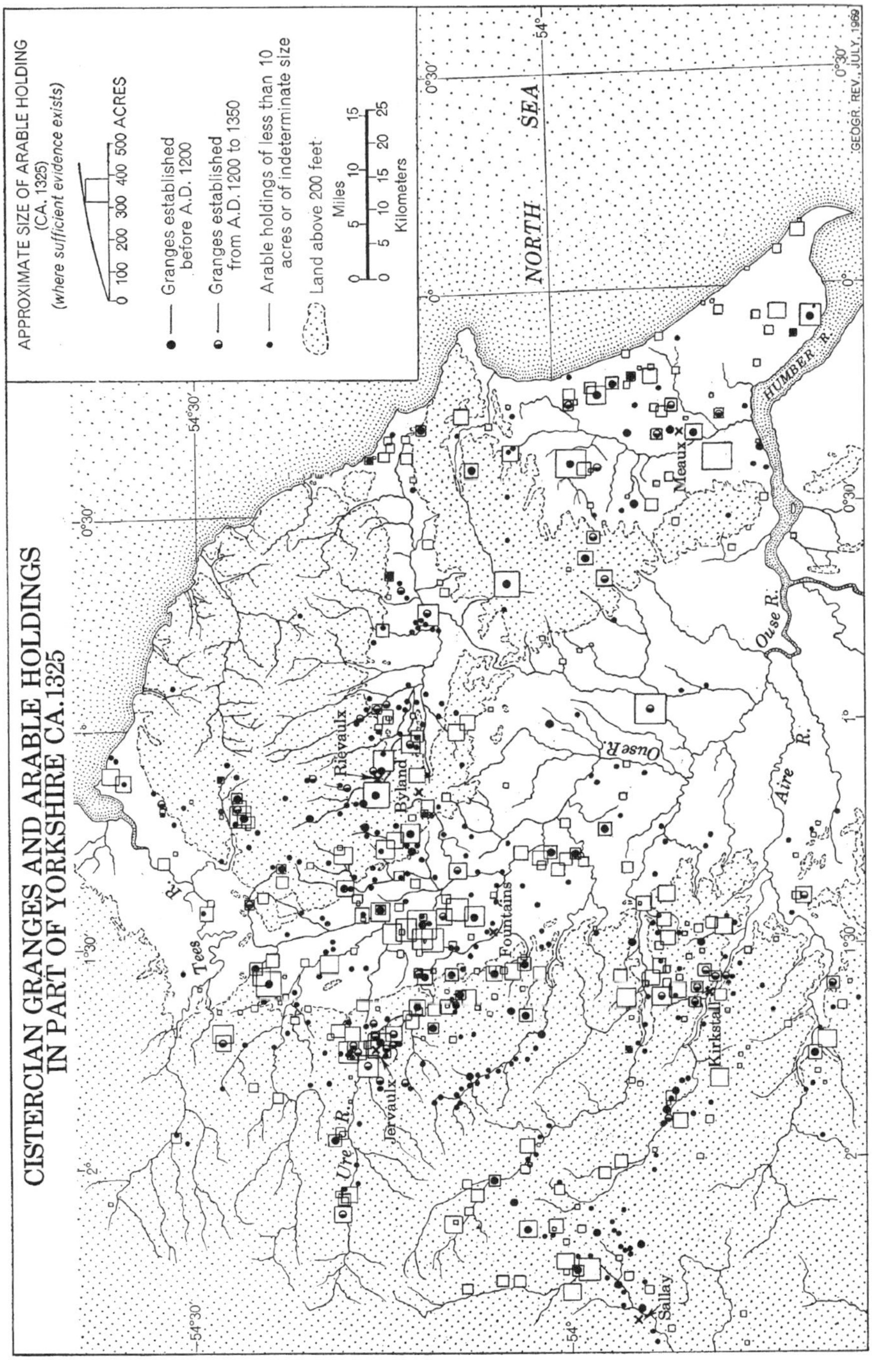
CISTERCIAN GRANGES AND ARABLE HOLDINGS
IN PART OF YORKSHIRE CA.1325
APPROXIMATE SIZE OF ARABLE HOLDING
(CA. 1325)
(where sufficient evidence exists)
0 100 200 300 400 500 ACRES
Granges established before A.D. 1200
Granges established from A.D. 1200 to 1350
Arable holdings of less than 10 acres or of indeterminate size
Land above 200 feet
Miles
0 5 10 15
0 5 10 15 20 25
Kilometers
NORTH SEA
HUMBER R.
Ouse R.
Aire R.
Ure R.
Tees R.
Meaux
Rievaulx
Byland
Fountains
Jervaulx
Kirkstall
Sallay
GEOGR. REV., JULY, 1969

FIG. 4

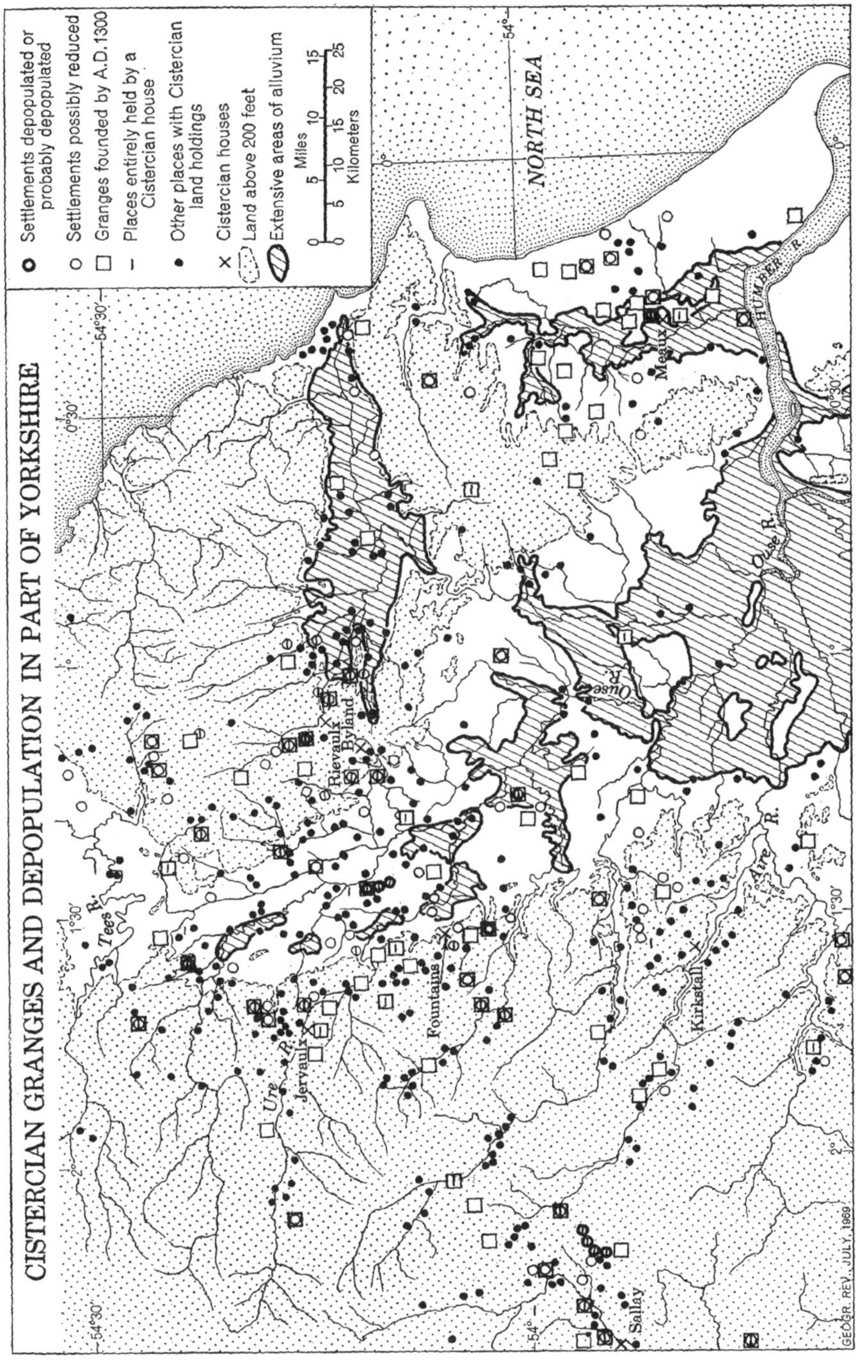
CISTERCIAN GRANGES AND DEPOPULATION IN PART OF YORKSHIRE
Settlements depopulated or probably depopulated
Settlements possibly reduced
Granges founded by A.D. 1300
Places entirely held by a Cistercian house
Other places with Cistercian land holdings
Cistercian houses
Land above 200 feet
Extensive areas of alluvium
Miles
Kilometers
NORTH SEA
HUMBER R.
Ouse R.
Aire R.
Ure R.
Tees R.
Meaux
Rievaulx
Byland
Jervaulx
Fountains
Kirkstall
Sallay
GEOGR. REV., JULY, 1969

FIG. 5

cians of eastern Europe and northern Spain who got involved in vast schemes of reclamation, the English monks had no need, and certainly no wish, to act as agents of peasant colonization. I have found only two unequivocal references to the settlement of peasants by Cistercian houses, and then only in relation to existing centers of population. With the grant of the village of Acton to Stanlaw about 1210 went the right "to settle men there to cultivate the ground."[15] Again, Dieulacres, a Staffordshire house, had land at Rossal in Thornton, Lancashire, from about 1216. There were probably few inhabitants at Rossal in 1086, and some of the charters to Dieulacres (mostly from the first half of the thirteenth century) record grants of villeins (*nativi*) to be removed and settled on its land near Rossal.[16]

We know little about what happened to the peasants dispossessed by the Cistercians: some undoubtedly became lay brothers (but not normally paid laborers), and others were resettled by the previous owner of the land. Only in one case, to my knowledge, did the monastery itself accept responsibility. This was at Byland, where a hamlet (*villula*), now Old Byland, was built to accommodate the evicted. In general, the peasants were probably left to fend for themselves as contemporaries critical of the Cistercians claimed, or, at best, they were dispersed to occupy small parcels of land that the monks found unprofitable or inconvenient to work.

The Cistercian policy of consolidation, where vigorously pursued in areas already occupied, was bound to disrupt existing tenurial and field arrangements. In fact it led to the eviction of peasants (Fig. 5). For Yorkshire alone there are at least three instances of outright depopulation to isolate the abbey itself and to create a home grange.[17] In addition, seven well-documented cases are known of either sudden or gradual depopulation for outlying granges. Finally, for fifty or more other townships, all with granges and with more than half the land owned by the monks, there is evidence of some removal of population and of contracting village communities. Evictions were most common during the twelfth century, but they continued into the second half of the thirteenth century and probably did not cease until the early fourteenth century, when the monks adopted a new economic policy that involved leasing a large part of their estates.

---

[15] "Liceat eis homines laicos si voluerint in villa que dicitur Acton ad terram excolendam ponere" (W. A. Hulton, edit.: The Coucher Book of Whalley Abbey, Vol. 2, *Chetham Soc., Old Ser.,* Vol. 11, 1847, pp. 385–386 and 392). The community at Stanlaw (1172–1296) later moved to Whalley.

[16] G. Wrottesley, edit.: The Chartulary of Dieulacres Abbey, *William Salt Archaeological Soc., Collections for a History of Staffordshire, New Ser.,* Vol. 9, 1906, charter nos. 56–57, 156, and 158–162.

[17] R. A. Donkin: Settlement and Depopulation on Cistercian Estates during the Twelfth and Thirteenth Centuries, *Bull. Inst. of Hist. Research,* Vol. 33, 1960, pp. 141–165.

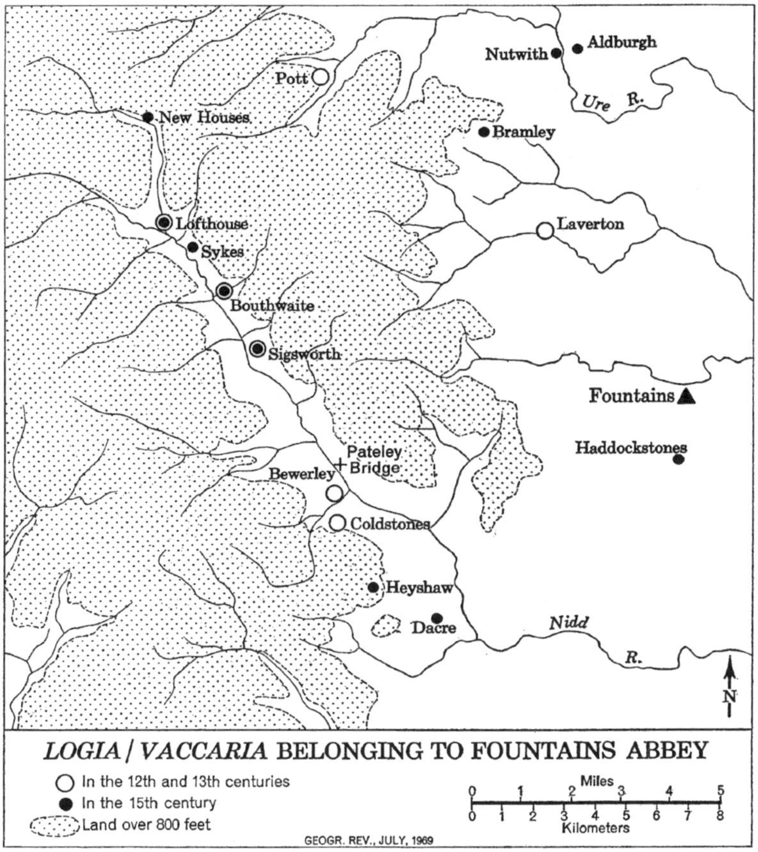

LOGIA / VACCARIA BELONGING TO FOUNTAINS ABBEY

FIG. 6

The typical grange comprised several hundred acres of arable and pasture for a considerable number of sheep. However, sheep were not everywhere and at all times first among the monks' farm animals and probably stood well to the fore only from about 1175 to 1325. Dairy cattle were mostly kept on holdings known as vaccaries (*vaccariae*).[18] Many of these lay within private forests and chases on both sides of the Pennines, around the North York Moors, and in the Cheviots. In fact, cattle rather than sheep were associated with the frontiers of monastic settlement. The buildings, for both men and animals, were called *logias*. Some may have been mere shielings, occupied only in summer, but what evidence there is suggests permanent occupation.

[18] R. A. Donkin: Cattle on the Estates of Medieval Cistercian Monasteries in England and Wales, *Econ. History Rev.*, Vol. 15, 1962–1963, pp. 31–53.

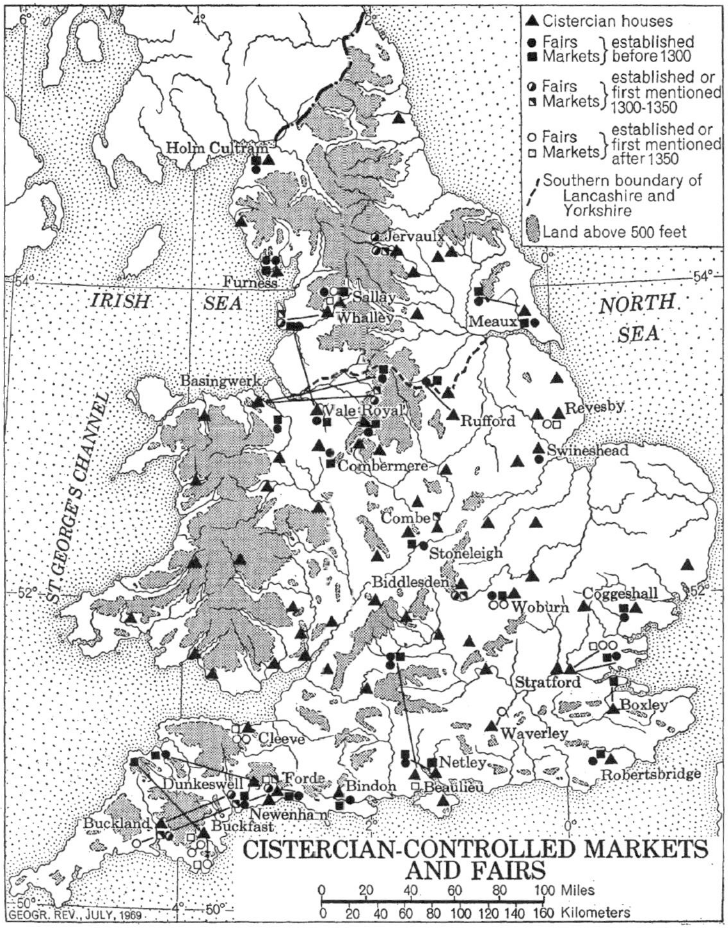
Cistercian houses
Fairs, Markets established before 1300
Fairs, Markets established or first mentioned 1300-1350
Fairs, Markets established or first mentioned after 1350
Southern boundary of Lancashire and Yorkshire
Land above 500 feet
Holm Cultram
Jervaulx
Furness
Sallay
Whalley
Meaux
IRISH SEA
NORTH SEA
Basingwerk
Vale Royal
Rufford
Revesby
Swineshead
Combermere
Combe
Stoneleigh
Biddlesden
Woburn
Coggeshall
Stratford
Boxley
Waverley
Cleeve
Forde
Dunkeswell
Newenham
Buckland
Buckfast
Bindon
Netley
Beaulieu
Robertsbridge
ST. GEORGE'S CHANNEL
CISTERCIAN-CONTROLLED MARKETS AND FAIRS
0 20 40 60 80 100 Miles
0 20 40 60 80 100 120 140 160 Kilometers
GEOGR. REV., JULY, 1969

FIG. 7

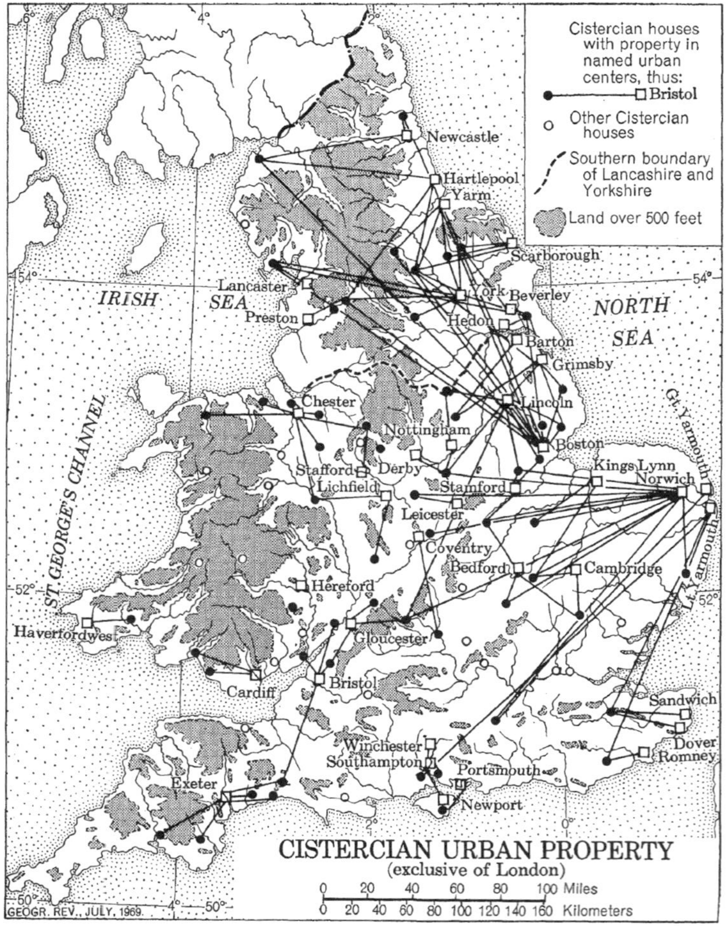
Cistercian houses with property in named urban centers, thus:
Bristol
Other Cistercian houses
Southern boundary of Lancashire and Yorkshire
Land over 500 feet
Newcastle
Hartlepool
Yarm
Scarborough
Lancaster
Preston
York
Beverley
Hedon
Barton
Grimsby
Lincoln
Boston
IRISH SEA
NORTH SEA
Chester
Nottingham
Stafford
Derby
Lichfield
Stamford
Leicester
Coventry
Kings Lynn
Norwich
Gt. Yarmouth
Lt. Yarmouth
Bedford
Cambridge
Hereford
Haverfordwest
Gloucester
Cardiff
Bristol
Sandwich
Dover
Romney
Winchester
Southampton
Portsmouth
Newport
Exeter
ST. GEORGE'S CHANNEL
CISTERCIAN URBAN PROPERTY
(exclusive of London)
0 20 40 60 80 100 Miles
0 20 40 60 80 100 120 140 160 Kilometers
GEOGR. REV., JULY, 1969

FIG. 8

Vaccaries were established toward the close of the twelfth century in several of the northern dales. In Nidderdale (Fig. 6), there is no evidence of settlement above Pateley Bridge before certain logias belonging to Fountains were named in a charter issued by Richard I, and in 1308 permission to reside in a large part of the dale was confined to the abbey's own servants who "look after the cattle in winter."[19] If the present settlements with the same names occupy the sites of former monastic buildings—and this seems probable—the most characteristic position for the logias was at the meeting of the floodplain and the steep valley walls, close to richer pasture and invaluable water meadow. In the second half of the fourteenth century, Fountains' estates in Nidderdale, and its vaccaries elsewhere, were managed by keepers who had to deliver fixed amounts of butter or cheese (or their monetary equivalent) to the abbey.

During the fourteenth century and later, some Cistercian granges were leased intact, but most were dismembered. We are sometimes told explicitly that the grange was transformed into a village, for which of course there was a nucleus of buildings. Between 1336 and 1363 Fountains demised at least eleven granges that had been ruined in the wars between England and Scotland, and Jervaulx in 1342 "made towns (*villas*) of the four great granges of Newstead, Rookwith, Aikbar and Didderston."[20] By this time the wheel of fortune had turned full circle with a vengeance.

Urban Properties

The Cistercians neither settled in towns nor encouraged towns to develop outside their walls. Half a dozen houses, including Furness and Holm Cultram in the North, established boroughs at some distance from the abbey, and all but Calder among the houses of the Northwest acquired market and fair franchises before the middle of the fourteenth century[21] (Fig. 7). It is hard to say if this was to compensate for generally inadequate trading facilities, but the contrast with the houses east of the Pennines is rather striking. None of the eastern houses attempted to establish boroughs, and only two, Meaux and Jervaulx, exercised the right to hold a market and fair. In any event, arrangements for marketing Cistercian wool regularly bypassed the local market and centered on the main towns. At the end of the twelfth century the commercially important eastern houses began to acquire property in such towns, and

[19] Memorials of . . . Fountains [see footnote 3 above], Vol. 1, pp. 210–226.

[20] Calendar of Inquisitions (Miscellaneous), Vol. 2 (1307–1349) (London, 1916), p. 445, no.1797.

[21] R. A. Donkin: The Markets and Fairs of Medieval Cistercian Monasteries in England and Wales, *Cistercienserchronik*, Vol. 69, 1962, pp. 1–14.

particularly in the ports[22] (Fig. 8). The properties included cellars, warehouses, wharfs, shops, and ordinary burgages, some in central locations, others in developing suburbs. There are also occasional references to the monks building houses for their own use.

After about 1350 urban holdings, like other Cistercian property, were mostly leased and served merely to swell the rent roll. But at the height of the monks' interest in the wool trade, during the twelfth and thirteenth centuries, when some houses were exporting on their own account and had agents as far afield as France and Italy, it was probably convenient, not to say essential, to have premises in such places as Newcastle, York, and Boston. Interestingly enough, none of the northern houses appears to have held property in London. The pull of the capital extended no farther north than Vale Royal in Cheshire.

In summary, then, the association between the Cistercian order and the settlement of the North of England is merely one aspect of a more self-contained theme: the monastic economy. Members of the order nowhere actively promoted peasant colonization, but rather the reverse: granges and logias were strictly monastic properties, and although some occupied abandoned village sites, most of the rest expanded at the expense of peasantry. In short, the monks' connection with settlement developed almost wholly in the detailed implementation of a policy of land management that had direct exploitation as its central principle.

---

[22] R. A. Donkin: The Urban Property of the Cistercians in Medieval England, *Analecta Sacri Ordinis Cisterciensis,* Vol. 15, 1959, pp. 104–131.

10
The Chronology of Labour Services[1]

M. Postan

I

THE chronology of labour services in the Middle Ages has been agitating agrarian historians for nearly a hundred years. In view of this it is surprising to find how many of the dates are still a matter of assumption. On the whole, economic historians know much more about the final demise of labour dues than about their previous history. They may disagree as to the exact dates of the fourteenth-century commutation, or as to the extent to which England had been manorialised and was therefore likely to be affected by the dissolution of the manor. But, on the whole, they are agreed that commutation did take place in those parts of the country which were manorialised ; and it would be generally accepted that commutation was rare in the first quarter of the fourteenth century, that labour services were exceptional in the last quarter of the fifteenth century, and that consequently the final substitution of money for labour dues took place some time between the first quarter of the fourteenth century and the first quarter of the fifteenth.

This may not be much to show for half a century of research, but little as it is, it is a great deal more than is known about labour services in the preceding periods. Were they rising, stationary, or falling, and if they fell or rose how are the ups and downs to be dated ? None

[1] The author intends to deal with some of the topics discussed in this paper at greater length in his forthcoming book on Manorial Profits.

of these questions has been answered, and for England as a whole they have not even been asked. And in the absence of definite knowledge, economic and constitutional historians have been thrown back on a series of purely conventional assumptions.

Economic historians have been inclined to assume a gradual dissolution of the manorial structure, which extended over two or three centuries and was due to a gradually expanding money economy. This assumption usually enters their language and thoughts in the form of an adverbial figure. When students find money rents on thirteenth-century manors they regard labour services as "already commuted"; when they find them still enforced in the fifteenth century, they say that commutation has not "yet" begun. The adverbs are employed to register surprise, or to record what is thought to be a "local peculiarity."

On the other hand, the general assumption of the constitutional historians, is that labour services in the twelfth and thirteenth centuries were growing, in consequence of the clarification of the feudal and manorial structure under the Normans and Angevins. Services, it is held, became generalised and intensified as the manorial organisation crystallised and spread in the two or three centuries following the Conquest.

These two assumptions may appear to clash, though a useful chronological device for reconciling them can be, and has been found. It is indeed possible to hold both, by assigning the extension and the increase of labour services to a period which terminates with the Hundred Rolls; and their disappearance to the end of the thirteenth and the fourteenth centuries, when economic forces began to play on the framework of the manor, gradually dissolving it.[1] But even if these two assumptions can be recon-

[1] This appears to be Vinogradoff's view, though on occasions he appears to assume a constant tendency to commutation "checked during the feudal period by the scarcity of money." *Growth of the Manor*, p. 329. Cf. *Villeinage in England*, pp. 297–8, 307 and 181.

ciled with each other, they are difficult to reconcile with the results of recent studies in other fields. The assumption of the increasing uniformity and rigidity of manorial forms in the twelfth and thirteenth centuries does not tally with what historians have recently told us about the active market in land in that period, the rapid process of sub-infeudation, the morcellation of manors and vills, the traffic in land (especially in free land), amongst villeins and other tenants, and the traffic in manors, tenements and fees among the landlords. It is even more difficult to reconcile recent studies with the assumption of the gradual disappearance of labour services under the pressure of an expanding money economy. If services were disappearing with the growth of money economy, how is it that in the more backward parts of the country, farthest from great markets, above all in the north-west, labour services were shed first, while the more progressive south-east retained them longest?

Indeed, the explanations underlying the assumed chronology of labour services are even more difficult to accept than the chronology itself, and the chief fault is not so much with the dates, as with the logic on which they are founded. That logic is simpler than is sometimes imagined; indeed, so simple as to be almost a truism. If labour services varied in quantity from manor to manor or from time to time, the cause of that variation was much more local and direct than the cosmic forces which historians have been in the habit of invoking. Given the social conditions of medieval England, a legal and political organisation dominated by feudal landlords and a working population largely composed of occupying landholders, labour services were a natural and easy way of meeting the landlord's demand for labour. Where these social conditions were present, and as long as they were maintained, the fluctuation of labour services requires no other explanation than that which is provided by the ordinary interplay of supply and demand—demand for villein service and supply of villein labour. And in so far as the cultivation of the demesne accounted for the demand, and the extent of villein settlement determined the supply, the differences between labour services exacted in different places were inevitably influenced by the relative areas of villeinage and demesne.

For England as a whole this connection may be impossible to establish. Differences in social structure and economy, in soil and methods of cultivation, could produce local variations in services, which overshadowed and concealed their relation to the size of the demesne. But within areas marked by similar geographical and social conditions labour services stood in an unmistakable relation to the needs of the demesne. The relation is evident in Professor Kosminsky's analysis of the large and small estates in the *Hundred Rolls*, but it would have stood out more clearly still, had he illustrated his arguments by the measurements of demesne lands in manors belonging to the same vills or the same lordships.[1] Take for instance the entry in the *Hundred Rolls* for Cottenham in Cambridgeshire. The village contained six manors, belonging respectively to the Abbot of Crowland, Gilbert of Cottenham, Robert de Insula, Simon le Waleys, Walter de Pelham and the village rector. On four of these roughly the same amount of money, rent and labour services is imposed on each unit of villein land. The rent may vary from 4*s*. 6*d*. on one manor to 5*s*. 9*d*. on another, the value of the services from 1*s*. to 10½*d*., but roughly they are the same, especially if compared with those prevailing on the remaining two manors. These two manors stand in sharp contrast both to each other and to the rest of the village, for on one of them 1*s*. 9*d*. is paid in rent and 4*s*. 9*d*. is the value of labour services, while on the other only money rent is paid and no services are demanded or evaluated. The cause of the variation is not difficult to find: the proportion of villein to demesne land on the four similar manors is

[1] Kosminsky, *The English Village in the Thirteenth Century*, Moscow, 1935 (Russian); "Rents and Labour Services, etc.," *Economic Hist. R.*, vol. v, No. 2.

roughly the same, while the demesne is altogether absent from the manor which does not exact labour services and is proportionately larger than anywhere else on the one manor on which services are valued at the exceptionally high figure of 4*s*. 9*d*.

The same is true of most vills on estates for which a similar comparison is possible, e.g. the Hertfordshire estates of St. Paul, the Fitz Hamme manors in Buckinghamshire, the Beauchamp estates in the South Midlands or the western group of the Peterborough estates. All these are groups of manors, each of which is situated within the same geographical and social area and belongs to the same lord; yet we find that within each group the labour services vary from manor to manor and that the variations reflect the differences in the relative sizes of the demesne.[1]

But if this is the true logic of the labour services it should account not only for differences between them, but also for their evolution. The changes from time to time, as well as the variations from place to place, are affected by the exigencies of demesne agriculture. When and where these exigencies change more quickly or more slowly than the supply of villein labour, the labour services should change accordingly. And such evidence as we have shows that they do.

II

The dimensions of both demesne and villein land fluctuated throughout the Middle Ages, but on the whole the fluctuations of the area under demesne cultivation were far more marked than those of the area in villeinage. Much as the village population may have changed, the core of villein land, at least before the fourteenth century, remained relatively stable. Therefore of the two elements in the

[1] P.R.O. Inq. Post Mort., *Hen. III* 7/3. Maxwell-Lyte, *Two Registers, etc.* Somerset Rec. Soc., vol. xxv, 1920. These and other examples will, I hope, be available in greater detail elsewhere.

equation—demesne and villeinage—the demesne was bound to exercise the stronger influence upon the evolution of labour dues. When the demand of the demesnes declined, the lords could dispense with some of the services previously required and the manorial documents would either contain the rubric of "services sold" or else record the progress of commutation. *Mutatis mutandis*, when and where the demand grew, the lord would not only exact the services in full, but would also try to impose additional obligations. This connection is generally admitted for the fourteenth and fifteenth centuries; it is understood that the letting out of the demesne at the close of the Middle Ages, with a consequent curtailment of demesne cultivation, was accompanied by the commutation of labour services. What is not so well understood is that the connection was also responsible for certain general movements in the earlier centuries.

Isolated and exceptional changes in labour services could occur at any time; a spendthrift heir, too long a vacancy, a slack and careless landlord, might lead to a decline of the demesne, and consequently to a relaxation of labour services. On the other hand a new broom, a reforming landlord or a competent abbot, might in time lead to the intensification and improvement of demesne cultivation, and to an increase in the customary services performed by the villeins. But in addition to these exceptional and sporadic movements in both directions, there were, in the four centuries for which reliable evidence exists, movements which were so general and so widespread as to suggest the possibility of distinct phases in the history of labour services.

Of these phases the least known and most unexpected is that which is revealed by the earliest manorial surveys. Manorial documents of the twelfth century show, on the bulk of the manors which they cover, labour services declining and the cultivation of the demesne receding. Some ten or eleven surveys compiled in the twelfth century, and two or three later surveys reflecting twelfth century conditions, have been investigated for the purposes of this enquiry, and nearly all of them exhibit the same trend.[1]

If historians of the last generation have failed to notice or to emphasise the direction of the twelfth-century changes, this has perhaps been due to the accident that the surveys best known to them happened to be those on which the trend is least noticeable. One of these is the twelfth-century survey of the estates of the Abbey of Peterborough, the so-called *Liber Niger Petroburgensis*, which was apparently compiled at some time in the third decade of the century. This document depicts manorial economy at its most robust.[2] With the sole exception of the sokemen on the Lincolnshire and on some of the Northamptonshire manors, and perhaps of the burgage tenants of Oundle and Kettering, the bulk of the Abbey's tenants are villeins dis-

[1] *Liber Niger Petroburgensis*, MS. 60 of the Soc. of Antiquaries. A photostat has been placed at my disposal by Mr. W. Mellows, whose generous assistance throughout my work on the Peterborough documents has been invaluable. The Camden Society's printed version has not been used here. *An Inquisition of the Manors of Glastonbury Abbey of the year* 1189, Roxburgh Club, 1882. W. H. Hart and P. A. Lyons (ed.), *Cartularium Monasterii de Ramseia*, 3 vols., Rolls Series, 1884–93. W. Greenwell (ed.), *Boldon Buke*, Surtees Society, vol. xxv, 1852, and *Bishop Hatfield's Survey*, *ibid.*, vol. xxvii, 1857. W. Hale (ed.), *The Domesday of St. Paul's*, Camden Soc., 1857. B. Lees (ed.), *Records of the Templars in England in the Twelfth Century*, 1935. L. B. Larking (ed.), *The Knights Hospitallers in England*, Camden Soc., 1857. *The Red Book of Worcester*, MS. Eccl. Com., 2/121/43698, partly printed in M. Hollings (ed.), *The Red Book of Worcester*, part I, Worc. Hist. Soc., 1934. *The Shaftesbury Cartulary*, B.M. MS. Harl. 61; I am much indebted to the generosity of Prof. Stenton, who lent me his own transcripts of the MS. *The Cartulary of the Abbey of the Trinity of Caen*, Bib. Nationale MS. Lat. 5650; a photostat of this has been procured, through the kind assistance of the Prof. M. Bloch and Prof. Eileen Power.

[2] On some of the Peterborough manors, however (e.g. Irthlingborough), we find labour services partly or wholly commuted in 1308. The commutation apparently took place earlier, but how much earlier we shall not be able to tell until we know something about the Peterborough estates in the second half of the twelfth century: *Peterborough Account Rolls* for 1292 and 1308. Photostats of the Accounts have been made available through the kind generosity of Mr. Mellows and Miss Wake of the Northamptonshire Record Society.

charging full labour services. But the fact that historians have been inclined to overlook the tendency towards commutation in the other well-known and most widely read twelfth-century survey, that of Glastonbury, is probably due more to the uncommunicative nature of the document, than to the actual conditions on the manors. Unlike the Black Book of Peterborough, the survey of Glastonbury reveals the existence of very large bodies of rent-paying tenants holding wholly or chiefly for money rent, especially on the outlying manors of the Abbey in Wiltshire, Dorset and Berkshire. Unfortunately the document, like most surveys, depicts a static condition, but unlike most of them contains very little evidence of recent changes. In the absence of these indications, to assume that the numerous money-paying tenants were a product of recent commutation would perhaps be to beg the question. Yet an observer with his eyes wide open, and his theories suspended, will find some indications even here ; for the documents contain more than a score of references to land-grants and changes in tenurial conditions carried out during the rule of Abbot Henry of Blois (1126–71) and his successor, and with one or two exceptions all of these are grants of land to be held for money and commutation of villein tenures. Even more pointed are the references to the changes on the demesne. With the exception of two small additions to the demesne, most of the references concern leases to tenants. In the Wiltshire estate of Grittleton the whole manor is let out to the villagers, and there is hardly a manor on which portions of the demesne have not been leased, mostly by Abbot Henry.

It is somewhat more difficult to understand the insufficient attention which has been paid to the evidence of the long-available twelfth-century surveys of the estates of the Ramsey Abbey (which are the very estates which Vinogradoff chose to cite as an example of the " immutable " manorial custom) and to those of the Bishop of Durham. On the Ramsey estates the manors not only contain large bodies of tenants described as *censuarii* and discharging the bulk of their obligations in money, but, what is still more important, they have undoubtedly been affected by a recent process of commutation. Not everywhere is the evidence as clear as on the manor of Holywell, about which we are told that in the time of King Henry I there were twenty-three virgates *omnes ad opus,* and *nunc autem quindecim tantum ex hiis operantur et cetere sunt ad censum.* But even where the changes have been less wholesale, as in Cranfield, or Shitlington and Pegsdon, they have all been in one direction—from labour services to rent.

More significant still is the evidence of the famous "Boldon Book" of the Bishopric of Durham. The fifty-five manors, for which this survey (c. 1183) gives sufficient information to justify a verdict, fall into three distinct groups. One of these is made up of some twenty manors organised on the pattern of the manor of Boldon, on which manorial institutions function with undiminished vigour. Villeinage with heavy labour services characterises their social structure and conditions of tenure, the demesne is either farmed out as a single unit or, as in at least eight manors, managed directly by the Bishop. Then there is an intermediate group of some eighteen manors, such as West Auckland or Stockton-on-Tees, on which the manorial organisation is not so complete, and the labour services are not so heavy, as on the manors of the Boldon type. But the real contrast is provided by a third group, consisting of nineteen odd manors, Newton-juxta-Boldon, South Bidick, Warden-Law, Morton, Trillesden, Mainsforth, Carlton, Darlington, Blackwell, Cockerton, Redworth, Lanchester, Ryton, Crawcrook, Winlaton, Westow, Bedlington, Whickham, and Haughton Parva. In none of these do we find villeins burdened with week-work, on some of them the very name of villein has disappeared and the bulk of the population consists of money-paying *molmen,* or more commonly *firmarii.*

On nearly all of the manors in the last group the money-paying tenants have arisen from what once upon a time was ordinary villeinage. The twelve molmen of Newton-juxta-Boldon are described in a fourteenth-century survey as erstwhile villeins, the eighteen bovates held by *firmarii* of Wardon are described as *terre bondorum* in the fourteenth century survey and so also are the lands of men who figure as *firmarii* in the 1183 survey of the manors of Morton and Carlton (Carleton). But the most significant indication of the change is to be found in what we can glean of the fate of the demesne. With the exception of Haughton Parva, the manors in this group do not contain any functioning demesnes, though they must have possessed them at some time. In Darlington, which is the only place where the holdings of the *firmarii* are differentiated from those of the other rent-paying tenants, the twelve bovates held by them in 1183 correspond exactly to the twelve bovates of the erstwhile demesne, as described in the later survey. More transparent still is the position on the Ryton group of manors. We are told in the 1183 document that the men of Ryton, Crawcrook, Winlaton and Westow hold their manors, demesnes and works at farm, while in the later survey each of the men is holding his customary tenement *cum parcellis dominicis* pertaining to it. The process is described best—for it has apparently taken place most recently—in the 1183 survey of the village of Whickham. The entry in the Boldon Book tells us that the "*dominium . . . erat tunc in manu episcopi, nunc autem predictum manerium est ad firmam cum dominico,*" and then, as in Ryton, we find the later survey showing the demesne held in parcels attached to the customary holdings.

One other familiar survey, the so-called Domesday of St. Paul's, though later in date, throws backward glances, which are numerous enough to give us an insight into twelfth-century conditions. What we learn does not differ much from what we have observed in the surveys already mentioned. Not only were rent paying tenants of every sort and description predominant at the time of the principal survey of 1222, but many of them had obtained their holdings and established a purely monetary connection with the landlord in the course of the preceding century. Some of them appeared as a result of assarting, which on the St. Paul's estates was continuous throughout the greater part of the Middle Ages. But in addition to holders of assarts, there are also numerous money-paying tenants, whose tenures bear witness to the transformation of either the land in villeinage, or the demesne, or both. In Kensworth the territory of the village is very largely made up of holdings of this kind. In Caddington nearly twenty virgates of demesne land are let out—12 to rent-paying tenants and another 7½ to tenants owing labour services. Large portions of the demesne arable are also let out in Ardleigh, Sandon and Luffenhall, Beauchamp, and Heybridge.

Somewhat rarer are references to commutation of villein holdings and it would, indeed, be wrong to suppose that all the tenements *ad censum* need necessarily have arisen as a result of commutation. Yet occasional references show that some must have appeared in that way, and while there are also a few instances of money rents which have been turned into labour services only very recently (which, as we shall see further, was to be expected), there are in the manors of Kensworth, Ardleigh, Luffenhall, and Runwell clear traces of somewhat less recent changes in the direction of commutation.

That these changes must have taken place in the twelfth century is shown by a number of chronological indices. The evidence is clear in the case of the manor of Beauchamp in Essex, for which we possess a survey of 1181, revealing roughly the same proportion of land held for rent in the demesne, land let out and land asserted as we find in the survey of 1222. Elsewhere indirect evidence is provided by the names of men responsible for the innovation. In "Adulfsnasa," the men chiefly responsible for the letting of the demesne and of the "assessed" hide were Richard Rufus and Hugh de Runwell, who were active in the second half of the twelfth century, and Allard who probably administered the manor at the turn of the century. In Runwell the additions to the rent-paying holdings on the lands of the *antiquum tenementum*, the wholesale letting out of lands described as "East Strete" and the letting out of parcels of demesne elsewhere, are associated with the names of the same Richard Rufus and of Gilbert de Arches, another twelfth-century administrator. In Heybridge it is the predecessors of the 1222 farmer who are responsible for the letting of demesne land. In Ardleigh some of the demesne was let by Ralph de Diceto, who was active in the eighties of the twelfth century and Richard of Stapleford who, though alive in 1222, was no longer farming the estate at the time. In the list of tenants *ad censum* we are referred to the activties of Master Alberic and Nicholas the Archdeacon, both twelfth-century men. It would take too long to enumerate all the references of the same kind on the other estates of St. Paul's, but the evidence of Navestock (Knavestock) is perhaps worth singling out. On that manor the "new demesne" was largely let out by Richard Rufus and his successors, but the list of tenants also contains a large number of men holding portions of the "old demesne," which must have been let out even earlier.

The significance of these familiar documents would perhaps have been realised more fully, had the earlier writers been able to study them in conjunction with other surviving surveys of twelfth-century estates, some of which have only come to light or become easily available quite recently. Of these the most important are the surveys of the estates of the Templars, the Bishopric of Worcester, the nuns of Shaftesbury and the nuns of the Trinity at Caen. These in conjunction with several smaller and more fragmentary surveys [1] provide a great deal of new and important

[1] E.g. the Survey of Binham in Douglas, *The Social Structure of Medieval East Anglia*, 1922, app. ii, no. 3; or the Survey of the Lands of the *Camerarius* of the Abbey of Abingdon; T. Stevenson (ed.), *Chronicon Monasterii de Abingdon*, Rolls Series, 1858, vol. ii, pp. 297 *seq.*

evidence supporting the impression made by the more familiar sources.

Some of this information merely adds supplementary instances of the same kind as those which have already been observed elsewhere. Thus the description of the estates of the Bishop of Worcester in the "Red Book" of Worcester shows the manors of the Bishopric in Worcestershire and adjoining counties in 1182 containing both typical tenures *ad opus*, and large bodies of peasant, i.e. non-military, tenures for money. Anything in the nature of an exact enumeration of these is made difficult by the ambiguous term of *geld* which the compilers employ to denote money payments. Yet those instances in which the word unmistakably describes money payments to landlords alone account for some 225 virgates, as compared with 255 which may or may not have been held for labour services.

As elsewhere, the bulk of money tenures on the Bishop's estate may well have been older than the survey, possibly older than the bishopric itself; but, as elsewhere, many of the rents were undoubtedly a result of recent commutation. In Hartlebury, a manor on which money-paying tenants are relatively more predominant than on almost any of the other possessions of the bishop, we are told that they *deberent esse operarii*, that is, should be, but are not. We are told the same about Wodmancote, a hamlet of Bishop's Cleeve. In Tredington most of the money virgates are described as men *que solent operare*. About Newton, the hamlet of Ripple, we are told that 8½ virgates, listed in the survey, *novissime tenentur pro gabulo*. In most of the manors we are also given some indication as to the dates at which the lettings for money occurred. They are those of the mid-century bishops, John, Alverd and Simon.

Different in character, though similar in implication, is the evidence of the Templars' Inquest of 1190. The immense landed properties of the Order were distributed all over the country, covered every possible variation of geographical and social background, and included, side by side with well-rounded and perfectly articulated manors, a miscellaneous collection of fragmentary estates forming part of no clearly recognisable manorial units. Moreover, unlike most of the monastic estates surveyed in the twelfth century, those of the Order were administered primarily with a view to the money revenue which they yielded, rather than to the direct sustenance which could be derived from them. Hence it would be natural to expect the Inquest to reveal a development of rent far more extensive than elsewhere. Indeed, so marked is this feature of the document, that Vinogradoff, who saw it in manuscript, was impressed by its similarity with the rentals of a much later age.[1] And with the exception of a few estates, chiefly those in Gloucestershire and Oxfordshire for which the evidence of the document is not clear, the Survey has very little beyond rents and very light services to record.

Needless to say, many of the rent-paying tenures on the Templars' manors, especially on their non-manorialised properties in Lincolnshire and Yorkshire, are part of the inherited social order and require no explanation. Yet something in the nature of commutation will be required to account for the almost entire absence of tenures for full labour services in the manorialised areas of Warwickshire and Essex, and a process of commutation is in fact indicated by a few traces of recent changes which the document contains.

Thus in the Warwickshire manor of Balsall we find, in addition to the main group of tenants who hold for rent and light occasional services, a group of tenants who pay a higher rent than the rest and therefore *quieti sunt de omnibus consuetudinibus ville*. On a large number of manors rent-paying tenements have been carved out of the demesne lands. In Newton we are told that *una duarum hidarum qui erant in dominico est assisa* at 5*s*. a virgate. In the Sherbourne group the demesnes of Newbold and Tysoe are

[1] *Villeinage in England*, p. 207.

let out, and so are portions of the demesne in Balsall and in most of the Essex manors.

Yet it is not the evidence of the Worcester survey or of the Templars' Inquest that historians of Seebohm's or Maitland's age would have found most revealing. Of the documents which have recently become available by far the most important are two or three surveys describing their respective manors at several successive points in the twelfth century, and thus giving an image less static and consequently more significant than that which historians have been able to derive from the better known documents. A typical document of this kind is the Cartulary of the Abbey of the Trinity at Caen.[1] The English estates of the nunnery are described in three successive twelfth-century surveys. The first, which apparently belongs to the early years of Henry I, shows in the Gloucestershire manor of Minchinhampton, 26 virgates *ad opus* and 9 *ad censum*. The second, belonging to the early years of Henry II, enumerates in the same manor, 9 virgates *ad opus*, 11 wholly commuted, and 11 with the option of performing the work or paying rent. The third survey, made some twenty years later, shows all the virgates of this manor commuted for a money rent. The same thing apparently happened at the Abbey's manors of Avening, near Minchinhampton, Felstead in Essex, Tilshead in Wilts, and probably also at Horstead in Norfolk.

A view at two successive points of the century is also available for a number of Dorset and Wiltshire estates belonging to the nuns of Shaftesbury. The manuscript in the British Museum contains copies of two surveys, of which one has apparently been drawn up in the late twenties or early thirties, and the other in the seventies.[2] The

[1] The dating of the manuscript will be discussed elsewhere. The dates adopted here are roughly those suggested by Miss T. Birdsall in her essay on the English manors of the Abbey in *Anniversary Essays in Medieval History by Students of C. H. Haskins* (Boston and New York, 1929), pp. 25–44.

[2] For the dating of the two texts I am indebted to Prof. Stenton.

comparison between the two is made somewhat difficult by changes in the areas of some of the manors and by numerous mistakes in the medieval copy. Yet there is little doubt that the forty or fifty years which elapsed between the two versions, witnessed a considerable extension of money rents. Thus in the manor of Iwerne Minster, at the time of the first survey, there were 55 odd tenements, of which some 35 virgates and 60 acres were held for full labour services and about two virgates were held for money combined with somewhat substantial autumn services. By the time of the second survey there were only nine virgates on full labour services, while the rest were held either for money only or for money and autumn services. The same process occurred in the interval between the surveys on the manors of Tisbury, Chiselborough, Fontmell and Handley (Sixpenny) and of all the Shaftesbury manors for which comparable evidence is available, the manor of Holt in Bradford-on-Avon, alone fails to provide clear evidence of the process.

The most eloquent sequence of surveys is probably that of the Burton Cartulary, though its evidence is perhaps too eloquent to be dismissed with a passing mention and must be reserved for special consideration at the end of this essay. But even without that evidence the conclusions should be clear. The twelfth-century surveys available at present deal with more than three hundred manors differing in almost everything in which it is possible for manors to differ—geographical environment, social background, density of settlement, methods of cultivation, type of land-ownership and system of management. Where the differences are so striking the similarity of local changes suggests a general transformation at work. The exact magnitude of the transformation cannot, and probably never will, be properly measured, for it would be wrong to assume that the bulk of the money-paying tenures enumerated in the surveys. are of recent origin. But even if the magnitude of the change can be disputed, its direction cannot. To unprejudiced eyes every sign points to a movement towards the commutation of services and the dissolution of the demesne.[1]

III

If what the twelfth-century surveys demonstrate is true, and the period did in fact witness a general movement of commutation, does this not mean that the founders of economic history were right after all? Can we say that what now emerges is not fundamentally different from the old assumption of a slow and gradual commutation, which began almost as soon as the manor came into existence and continued as long as the manor functioned? Unfortunately this is exactly what we cannot say as a result of the foregoing discussion. A continuous and uninterrupted process is the one thing the available evidence does not exhibit, and the failure of the twelfth-century commutation to remain equally general and strong in the thirteenth, is one of its most conspicuous features.

On some estates it may indeed have continued into the beginning of the thirteenth century, as it did on a few of the St. Paul's manors. The Survey of the estates of St. Mary's Priory, Worcester, compiled in the first half of the thirteenth century, describes a number of manors on which services had been commuted and the demesne leased. At least some of them (e.g. Tibritton) must have undergone the change much earlier, but it is quite possible that the lettings under the "new assize" were very recent.[2] In the more backward parts of the country the movement may have gone on unchecked. Thus it is likely, though by

[1] Vinogradoff could not help noticing that a process of commutation was at work on the estates of Glastonbury, St. Paul's and Burton: *Villeinage in England*, p. 307, 327, 330. He was however prevented from drawing the conclusion, which the texts suggest, by his general theories of the development of feudalism and the absence of money economy. More emphatic are the references to twelfth century commutations in Prof. Douglas's book: *op. cit.*, pp. 83, 123–9.

[2] W. Hale Hale (ed.), *Registrum Prioratus Beate Marie Wigorniensis*, Camden Soc., vol. xci, 1865.

no means certain, that the wholly commuted estates depicted in the fourteenth-century survey of the Bishopric of Durham stand in direct succession to the half-commuted estates of the twelfth century. But on almost all the other manors for which we possess thirteenth-century documents, and above all on manors situated in the more progressive parts of England, in the heart of the arable and populous south, south-east and south-west, what the evidence reveals is not only the absence of a general commutation, but the action of a diametrically opposite process. The period following the commutation of the twelfth century and preceding the return of commutation in the fourteenth, is one of stabilisation and even of increase in labour services.

In the agrarian history of England the thirteenth century is a period of *Hochkonjunktur*—an age of rising production, expanding settlement, technical improvements, the investment of capital, the application of a greater amount of labour to the same amount of land. It was accompanied by the growth of the demesne on the bulk of the estates for which we have evidence. Out of about eight hundred manors investigated, over six hundred and fifty show clear signs of an extension or intensification of demesne cultivation.[1] This growth of the demesne was unaccompanied by any considerable increase in the amount of land subject to villein labour. It was therefore bound to lead to a full exaction, or even an increase of the labour services borne by each unit of villein land.

The relevant facts have been known to historians for a long time; but, as most of them have been collected in the course of local studies, they have been commonly treated as local phenomena. Maitland noticed a tendency to increasing labour services on his Cambridgeshire manor, Miss Neilson pointed it out on the Ramsey estates, Mr. Feiling discovered it on an Essex manor of Battle Abbey, Professor Douglas on some of the estates of Ely. A depression

[1] A list and an analysis of these will be included in the book on which the present paper is based.

of a different kind has been described in Mr. Bishop's study of the Cistercian granges in Yorkshire, while Professor Kosminsky and Professor Petrushevsky have drawn our attention to the general feudal reaction of the thirteenth century, and Vinogradoff found instances of it in the *Hundred Rolls.*[1] There is thus nothing in the so-called "manorial reaction" to surprise scholars who have studied rural conditions in detail, though it is only when the local evidence is brought together that the prevalence and the ubiquity of the reaction becomes evident.

The ubiquity of the process may sometimes escape attention, owing to the variety of ways in which the increased demand for labour services could be met, and additional burdens imposed. One of the ways was to subdivide units of villein tenure without decreasing the services attaching to them. This was one of the methods by which Glastonbury Abbey raised the amount of labour available on a number of its manors. The commonest way, however, was by the addition of new services, as on the estates of the Bishopric of Winchester, where we find new *precaria* introduced and enforced, or on the estates of Ramsey, for which Miss Neilson has tabulated the additions made to the customary services of the tenants during the century.[2]

A method equally common, though even more likely to escape the attention of students, was the "definition" of services, formerly left undefined. It is a common

[1] Maitland, "The History of a Cambridgeshire Manor," *Coll. Papers*, II, pp. 366 *seq.*; Neilson, *Economic Condition of the Manors of Ramsey Abbey*, 1898, pp. 26, 45–52; Feiling, "An Essex Manor in the Fourteenth Century," *Eng. Hist. Rev.*, 1911; Douglas, *op. cit.*, p. 112; Bishop, "Monastic Granges in Yorkshire," *Eng. Hist. Rev.*, 1935; Vinogradoff, *Villeinage in England*, p. 204; Kosminsky, *op. cit*, p. 206, *seq.*

[2] E.g. the fardellers of East Pennard and East Brent, half-virgaters of High Ham: Elton and others (ed.), *Rentualia et Custumaria . . . abbatum . . . Glastonie*, Somerset Rec. Soc., vol. v, 1891; B.M. MS. Vesp. F. xi. Hall, *Pipe Roll of the Bishop of Winchester*, 1209, and MS. Eccl. Com. 2/159447: (e.g. Brightwell and Taunton). Neilson, *op. cit.*, pp. 26, 45–52. Also Douglas, *op. cit*, app. ii, no. 3 and MS. B.M. Claud. D. xiii. fo. 7 *seq.*

assumption that this earlier indefiniteness was against the peasant's interest. But, as a matter of fact, that was not always so. Frequently, the translation of the undefined week work into a definite task to be done in a day was and was meant to be a far heavier burden on the villein than an undefined day's work. By way of definition a number of new burdens were imposed on some of the estates of Ely between 1222 and 1277, on some of the estates of Peterborough before 1308 and on the estates of the Bishop of Worcester.[1]

The method, however, which most merits the term "reaction" was the abolition of earlier commutation and the imposition of full labour dues on tenants who used to hold for money rent. Instances of this which are easiest to trace are those of destroyed "options." The earlier surveys of estates frequently provide the tenants with an option of either paying their rent in money or performing services. The choice was in most cases the lord's, but whenever the lord chose to take money the full labour services were *eo ipso* foregone. In the thirteenth century however we find survey after survey destroying the option and both imposing a rent, as if the tenure were *ad censum*, and exacting labour services far heavier than those which had accompanied rent tenures in the past—commonly the full labour services. This indeed was the method adopted in the thirteenth century by Glastonbury, and a number of smaller estates.[2]

Most significant of all, however, are instances of reaction in the narrowest sense of the word—the simple revocation of the earlier concessions and a return to the heavier terms of the dim and distant past. By a lucky accident, one of our documents has preserved obvious signs of some such reaction in preparation. The twelfth-century survey of Glastonbury bears on its margins notes in what appears to

[1] Hollings, *op. cit.*; MS. Eccl. Com. 2/121/43698.

[2] Documents cited *above*, p. 27, footnote 1: (e.g. Mere, Winterbourne. Bradbury). Maxwell-Lyte, *op. cit.*: (e.g. Stoke-under-Hamden).

be a somewhat later hand, suggesting alterations in the conditions of tenure recorded in the text. In almost every case the note is against entries of parcels of demesne let out or of services commuted, and in almost every case the comment on the former is that they had better be drawn back into demesne (*utilius esset in dominicum*) and on the latter that they had better be let again for work (*utilius esset ad opus*).[1] And even a cursory reading of Abbot Michael of Amesbury's survey in the thirties of the following century will show how closely the spirit of the instructions was followed, though it was left to the compilers of the survey of Abbot Roger Ford, a generation later, to record a yet further increase in the needs of the demesne and a yet further augmentation of services.[2]

IV

Thus the typical sequence is from labour services to partial or complete commutation, and then back again to partial or complete return of labour services. To say that this sequence was typical is also to insist on the fact that it was not universal. We have noted complete estates, such as those of Peterborough, or individual manors in other estates, which were not affected by the twelfth-century commutation ; there were also estates, such as those of Durham, which may not have been affected by the reaction of the thirteenth century. Moreover, a number of manors which were not subject to the action of the early commutation, were nevertheless visited by the later urge to expansion and saw their labour services intensified. Above all special circumstances could produce local deviations. Professor Stenton has noted the creation of demesnes on some of the Lincolnshire sokes in the twelfth century. At Wargrave, one of the manors of the Bishopric of Winchester, services were commuted in the year 1252, when the bulk

[1] Jackson (ed.), *op. cit.* [2] *Supra*, p. 187, footnote 2.

of the other Winchester estates were imposing them. At St. Ives, a Ramsey manor, the proportion of holdings for labour service was falling in the thirteenth century, at the very time when the Abbey was imposing new labour dues on the bulk of its estate.[1] For the two latter manors the explanation is obvious; St. Ives was a market town, Wargrave was engaged in a piece of large-scale colonisation. But for the Lincolnshire case an explanation will be difficult to find, and a diligent search would doubtless reveal others equally difficult to explain. In short, exceptions there were, and it would be strange if there had been none, but numerous as they may be they do not obscure the general trend, which no statistical test, however simple, will fail to exhibit. Nor do they overshadow the typical instances of manors, or whole estates, going through the entire sequence of alternating stability and dissolution.

It is because the estates of Burton Priory in Staffordshire and Derbyshire provide one such typical instance that a consideration of them has been deferred until now. The earliest condition of the estates is portrayed in the first of the twelfth-century surveys of the manors of Bromley, Stretton and Burton, belonging, probably, to the first quarter of the century. In this survey we find the core of the village consisting of tenants subject to full labour dues and described as villeins. The second description of these estates, the date of which is a generation or two later, shows the demesne let out, mostly to the former villeins, and the latter turned *censuarii*. But a third, a thirteenth-century reference, is concerned with litigation between the Prior and his tenants, the tenants complaining to the royal courts that the landlord is treating them as villeins and not as *censuarii*, and is demanding from them villein service. The cycle is thus complete, though it is destined to be broken again in the

[1] Stenton, *Danelaw Charters*, p. cviii; *idem*, *Types of Manorial Structure, etc.*, p. 26. For Wargrave, see Eccl. Com. 2/159447. For St. Ives, see the Ramsey Surveys referred to above.

late fourteenth and fifteenth centuries, when a new, and this time a final, wave of commutation lays for ever the ghost of manorial order on the lands of the Prior of Burton.[1]

In this Burton example the social relations implied in the reaction, are as characteristic as the reaction itself. In many instances the re-imposition of the old labour services or the addition of new ones, was brought about by something resembling a bargain and was accompanied by compensating concessions to the tenants. It has been tacitly assumed in this essay that rents and labour services stood in a complementary relation to each other, and that an increase in one would, in normal circumstances, be accompanied by a decrease in the other. This was certainly so whenever labour services were remitted, and it was occasionally so in cases when labour services were re-imposed. A very illuminating illustration of this is provided by the manorial accounts of the Crowland manors.[2] When, in the second half of the thirteenth century, the landlords required additional labour from their customary tenants, the accounts contain allowances of rent in compensation for the extra labour performed. The arrangement continues for years, until at last, at the beginning of the fourteenth century, the additional services are merged into the customary ones and the rent is permanently lowered. A similar procedure was adopted on the manor of Brightwell in Hampshire, belonging to the Bishop of Winchester. There are traces of similar transactions on some of Hospitallers' manors in Oxfordshire, which had formerly belonged

[1] Wrottesley (ed.), *The Burton Cartulary*, Wm. Salt Soc., pp. 20 and 26 (Bromley), 22 and 28, 19 and 25 (Stratton, Mickle Over and Little Over); *idem*, *Staffordshire Plea Rolls*, Wm. Salt. Soc., vol. vi, part 1, pp. 60, 98, 109 and 116; for the dating of the Survey, see Round, *Burton Abbey Surveys*, vol. ix, N.S., pp. 272–6. Round was unnecessarily puzzled by the differences in the amounts of farm in the two surveys.

[2] Page, *op. cit.* Cf. the rents on p. 284 with the table of services on p. 84, and the accounts of Cottenham and Oakington and Drayton, pp. 21 *seq.*, 233 *seq.*, 176–9. Also *idem.*, *Wellingborough Manorial Accounts*, Northampton Rec. Soc., vol. viii, p. xxvi and text.

to the Templars, and on some of the Battle Abbey manors.[1]

Very often, however, the procedure was simpler, shorter and more like that of Burton. The lords imposed additional services without a *quid pro quo* of any kind, cancelled earlier commutations, reduced their tenants to simple villeinage, refused to recognise customary contracts. Thirteenth-century instances of complaints brought by tenants before the royal courts are frequent enough, but they are much less frequent than the cases of oppression which must actually have taken place, since the only ground on which royal interference could be claimed was the plea that the manor was on ancient demesne, and the estates on which the peasants had any reason at all to believe themselves to be on what was once King's land must have been very few. As in the very similar movement of the German *Bauernlegen* three hundred years later, the will of the lord prevailed.

The parallel with the East German *Bauernlegen* applies also to what is the most important feature of the process, as well as the most important omission in this paper. Nothing has so far been said here of the causes of the movements, of forces responsible for the expansion of the demesne, and for the rise and fall of services. The object of this essay has been to indicate the main chronological landmarks and only incidentally to question the assumption of a continuous evolution towards free tenure. If, as a mere by-product, a doubt has emerged as to the effects of the so called rise of money economy, we shall do nothing here to remove it. For it is a salutary doubt. The rise of money economy has not always been the great emancipating force which nineteenth-century historians believed it to have been. In the absence of a large reservoir of free landless labour

[1] Cf. the terms of virgate tenures in Merton in the twelfth century Templars' Inquest with those recorded in the Hundred Rolls. Also Scargill-Bird, *The Estates of Battle Abbey*, pp. 58–82 (Bromeham and Bright Walton).

and without the legal and political safeguards of the liberal state, the expansion of markets and the growth of production is as likely to lead to the increase of labour services as to their decline. Hence the paradox of their increase in Eastern Germany, at the time when the production of grain for foreign markets was expanding most rapidly, and hence also the paradox of their increase in England, too, at the time and in the places of the highest development of agricultural production for the market during the Middle Ages.

11
An Italian Estate, 900–1200

P.J. Jones

I

It is generally known that by 1200 the 'classical' manorial or *villa* organization of Carolingian times, if not already broken up, was fast disintegrating in most parts of Europe where it had once prevailed. Thereafter, it is said, for many centuries the agrarian system of Western Europe was essentially stable. The great landowners rarely exploited their lands directly: instead of the labour services and miscellaneous dues of the past they drew rents, increasingly money rents, from a dependent peasantry whose rights in the land varied from hereditary tenure to a mere temporary leasehold, and whose status had long ceased to conform to the older categories of free, 'half-free', and servile. Peasant status in fact was commonly determined by the incidence of certain seigneurial rights, like *heriot* or *merchet*, which with rights of justice, of tallage, and so on, were often now as profitable to the lord as any rents he derived from the land.

In this development, as in so much else, Upper and Central Italy were precocious. To begin with, historians have long been agreed that the large self-contained estate was at no time so common and rarely so well developed here as north of the Alps. From Roman times the tendency had been for indirect to prevail over direct exploitation, and during the post-Carolingian period that tendency triumphed. As in the north many great properties were broken up, those of laymen by partition and enfeoffment, those of the church by lay usurpation or grants to the nobility of long-term leases. As in the north too the disintegration of the great estate was accompanied by the disintegration of the traditional unit of 'manorial' tenancy, the *mansus*.[1] As a result the Italian lord was soon a mere receiver of rents, usually fixed rents, to which, however, might be added the more valuable revenues of seigneurial authority or the tithes and other dues pertaining to a church.

As in the north once again it was such seigneurial authority, with its powers of justice and claims to 'fealty', which had helped to create from the various groups of dependent cultivators of earlier times a great common class of peasant *massarii* or *manentes*. The great majority of these, whatever their name or origin, stood in much the same relation to their lord and their land. They consisted of families settled on their holdings from time immemorial and paying rents and services controlled by local custom (*consuetudo fundi*); but many among them were tenants, or descended

[1] In places the *mansus* persisted until the fourteenth century (C. Cipolla, 'Per la storia della crisi del sistema curtense in Italia', *Bull. Ist. Stor. Ital. per il Medio Evo*, 1950), though not in Tuscany (*infra*). Beyond the Alps the *mansus* and its derivatives vanished from northern France in the twelfth century, but survived until the thirteenth in Burgundy and Lorraine, until the fourteenth in Germany (C. E. Perrin, *Recherches sur la seigneurie rurale en Lorraine* (Strasbourg, 1935), p. 648; A. Déléage, *La Vie Économique et Sociale de la Bourgogne dans le Haut Moyen Âge* (Macon, 1941), p. 524; P. Dollinger, *L'Évolution des Classes Rurales en Bavière* (Paris, 1949), p. 111).

from tenants, holding by hereditary grants (*libelli*) often premonitory in form of the leases (*freie Leihe* and so on) which later became common in the north with the collapse of demesne farming. The agrarian economy of Northern Italy therefore was a peasant economy and small-scale farming, even on large estates, the rule.

In descriptions of Italian rural society evidence from Lucca is usually prominent. This evidence is uncommonly abundant from an early period, but has so far been used in detail only to illustrate conditions on the bishop's estates at the opening of the Middle Ages. It shows that by the late tenth century these estates, composed in large part of scattered gifts from small freemen, included only a small demesne, which was increasingly reduced by perpetual grants to members of the local nobility. By the same period the assimilation of the various peasant classes was far advanced and the typical tenants were *massarii* or *residentes* holding by leases (*libelli*) in practice hereditary. Rents were fixed and so were services where they survived. Rents to begin with were in kind, extending even to the products of domestic industry (cheeses, linen cloth, etc.), but commutation for money became more and more the rule. No *heriots* were claimed, nor *merchet*, but hospitality (*albergaria*) was commonly owed and attendance at the lord's court. Briefly the bishop's economic position was not strong: his properties were dissipated in the hands of the lay aristocracy and his rental was modest and fixed.[1]

If such were conditions about 1000 on church lands at Lucca, it may be useful to trace what changes if any took place in the two following centuries, centuries of political and social revolution, which witnessed the rise of the commune and great commercial and industrial growth. This may be attempted first by examining the records of the cathedral chapter.

At Lucca no precise date is known for the division of income between bishop and *mensa canonicorum*, but at the turn of the ninth century donations to the chapter begin,[2] and once begun continue uninterruptedly down to the thirteenth century. The earliest gifts to S. Martino were fairly substantial, though small enough beside grants to churches north of the Alps or even elsewhere in Italy. They began when Berta, wife of Adalbert II margrave of Tuscany (898–925), assigned to the chapter twenty-two *mansi* at Massa Maciniaia, to which the kings Hugh and Lothair in 932 added forty-one *manentes* in the curtis of Massarosa and its neighbourhood. Thereafter grants of *mansi* or parts of *mansi* were fairly common to the end of the eleventh century and recurred intermittently in the twelfth.

Large though some of these properties were, they were not normally consolidated. Sometimes they lay scattered through a wide district, and often only a 'portion' or part of a 'portion' was granted. The usual type

[1] R. Endres, 'Das Kirchengut im Bistum Lucca vom 8. bis 10. Jahrhundert', *Vierteljahrschrift f. Sozial- und Wirtschaftsgeschichte*, XIV (1916–18).

[2] *Regesto del Capitolo di Lucca* (*Regesta Chartarum Italiae*), ed. P. Guidi and O. Parenti, 1910–39 (hereafter cited as *RL*). E. Kittel, 'Der Kampf um die Reform des Domkapitels in Lucca im 11. Jahrhundert', *Brackmann Festschrift* (Weimar, 1931). Cf. L. Santifaller, 'Papsturkunden f. Domkapitel bis auf Alexander III', *ibid.* M. Giusti, 'Le Canoniche della Città e Diocesi di Lucca al Tempo della Riforma Gregoriana', *Studi Gregoriani*, III (Rome, 1948).

of gift, however, even from early times consisted not of *mansi* but of simple 'pieces of land'. 'Pieces' could be of any size, from a few *staia* to a 1000 *modia* and more; one 'piece' might include several 'pieces' or contain *casae et res massariciae*, and a *mansus* might be described as merely two pieces. There is usually no hint whether a piece was tenanted or where precisely it lay. Even the character of pieces is sometimes vague, but mostly they were cultivated lands, arable fields, vineyards, *oliveta*, and gardens. There were few gifts of woodland or waste and the signs of active land reclamation to be found elsewhere in Tuscany and Northern Italy during this period are almost wholly wanting here.[1]

Beside rights in land the chapter inevitably attracted into its grasp a number of churches, with their appurtenant holdings, tithes and other revenues, and in certain places developed or acquired rights of jurisdiction as well. Before 1200 S. Martino had come to own nearly thirty churches in and out of Lucca. By that time, it has been shown, tithes had become the principal source of wealth to many a religious house in Europe, partly because they remained proportionate to the yield of the soil.[2] At Lucca there is no doubt that ecclesiastical property supplied a valuable part of the chapter revenues, but unfortunately there is no means of exactly assessing its importance.

The same must be confessed of the chapter's seigneurial dues. What profit the chapter drew from these is nowhere indicated, but it was probably slight. Compared with the rights of other lords in the region, the capitular franchises were not extensive. Unlike the bishop the chapter received no grant of the imperial tax, *fodrum*, and while the bishop exercised blood-justice the judicial powers of the chapter were doubtless confined to *basse justice*.[3] Beside jurisdiction the chapter could also claim *albergaria*, *masciamentum*,[4] and *guadia* (watch), but apart from *albergaria*, which was so common an incident in Tuscany as to seem inseparable from the holdings of

[1] References to reclamation do occur (*RL*, nos. 907, 1054, 1094), and certain place-names indicate reclamation, though perhaps at an earlier time; leases, however, cease in most cases to be addressed in this period to improvement or assarting.

[2] F. L. Ganshof in *Cambridge Economic History of Europe* (1941), I, 313.

[3] Cf. G. Salvioli, 'L'immunità e le giustizie delle chiese in Italia', *Atti Memorie R. Dep. Stor. Pat. prov. Moden. e Parm.* (Modena, 1890), pp. 148 *seq.*; A. Lattes, *Diritto consuetudinario delle città lombarde* (Milan, 1899), p. 371. At Massarosa *fodrum* was reserved to the emperor: F. Schneider, *Entstehung v. Burg u. Landgemeinde in Italien* (Berlin, 1924), p. 227 n. 1. The inhabitants of Massarosa, Gualdo, and Montigiano likewise paid *data* and *prestantie* to the commune: *RL*, no. 1454 (a. 1181?). Although *datie* were commonly due from *manentes*, etc., in Tuscany, there is no evidence they were imposed by S. Martino.

[4] *Ammasciamentum* (normally coupled with *dismasciamentum*) was taken by Salvioli to mean military service, but there is abundant evidence from Tuscany and outside to suggest it denoted the right to invest with a *mansus* in return it would seem for a sum of money: *RL*, nos. 1400, 1497; *Memorie e Documenti per servire all'istoria del principato Lucchese* (Lucca, 1813 *seq.*, hereafter cited as *MD*), III, 122 *seq.*; P. Idelfonso, *Delizie degli eruditi toscani* (Florence, 1770), X, 201, 208; J. Lami, *Sanctae ecclesiae florentinae monumenta* (Florence, 1758), I, 56, 60, 164; *Regesto di Camaldoli* (*Reg. Chart. It.*), ed. L. Schiapparelli, etc. (1907–22), nos. 1201, 1253, 1273; O. Hartwig, *Quellen u. Forschungen z. ältesten Geschichte d. Stadt Florenz* (Halle, 1880), II, 67 n.; R. Davidsohn, *Geschichte v. Florenz*, IV/1, 181; P. Sella, *Glossario latino emiliano* (Città del Vaticano, 1937), *Glossario latino italiano* (1944) s.v. *amasare, amaxare, dismasare*; Salvioli, *loc. cit.* p. 113. Taken together *ammasciamentum* and *dismasciamentum* recall the *ius instituendi et destituendi* (*stiften, entstiften*) of German records (Perrin, 'La société rurale allemande du Xe au XIIIe siècle', *Rev. Hist. de Droit*, 1945; Dollinger, *loc. cit.* (pp. 392, 397)), and suggest also the *gersuma* of English manors.

manentes,[1] these rights are clearly attested only on certain estates, and even there were not always secure.[2] There was, it is true, a strong tendency to assume that a lord would have some power of constraint over all his *manentes*, a power descended from the *iustitia familiaris* of an earlier time, and safeguarded still by oaths of fealty, which S. Martino like other lords regularly took from its dependents, but this power may have been restricted to litigation among tenants and was clearly threatened by the consular tribunals of Lucca.[3]

Churches or *castella* with rights of justice were not at any time typical gifts to S. Martino, but this was not because the chapter's benefactors were mostly men of humble condition. Frequently they were members of the feudal middle class or of families who rose to social eminence through notarial and judicial office, members of the first citizen aristocracy of Lucca, the *milites*. It is naturally impossible to establish the identity of all donors to S. Martino, but it is clear that in the tenth century the aristocracy preponderated, that during the eleventh and twelfth more than half were members of great families, lawyers, notaries, or clerks, while some who cannot be traced further were well enough endowed to grant *mansi*, *castella*, or churches. The status of the rest can only be conjectured. Few are described as artisans, and they may rather be taken to indicate the persistence here as elsewhere in Italy of a class of small proprietors or *alloderii*.

The great families brought no unqualified benefit to the chapter. On the lands of S. Martino, as everywhere else, they took as much as they gave, and sometimes more. During the twelfth century it was quite common for donors to reserve an interest in property they granted.[4] In effect if not in form this was not new, for the same process can be traced from the earliest period. The very families which gave so generously 'pro remedio anime' frequently came to hold of the chapter the same or other

[1] Thus *albergarie* were owed to S. Martino and other landowners from their *manentes* in places where seigneurial powers are not otherwise attested (*RL*, nos. 32 n., 1150–1, 1205, 1329, 1387, 1729) and are obviously similar to the *pascioraticum* which many peasants paid their lords (*infra*). Cf. Endres *ubi supra*, pp. 275–6.

[2] *RL*, nos. 796, 1186, 1188, 1303, 1352, 1443, 1497–8, 1521, 1575; *MD*, III, 94, 96–7. In the tenth century S. Martino had been granted an immunity (or rather *mundiburdium*, but this is generally assumed to be the same thing), and immunities are said to have applied to all lands, including those subsequently acquired (G. Seeliger, 'Soziale u. politische Bedeutung d. Grundherrschaft im früheren Mittelalter', *Abh. phil.-hist. Klasse sächs. Gesell. Wiss.* XXII, (1904), 124); yet the jurisdiction of S. Martino is only proved, and in the twelfth century was only confirmed, at Massarosa (with Fibbialla, Gualdo, Ricetro and Montigiano) and Massa Macinaia. The chapter did receive gifts of other *castella* or parts of *castella*, but at only one of these, Gragno, are there signs that seigneurial authority may have followed (*RL*, nos. 487, 1027, 1179, 1278, 1281, 1293, 1524). A brief entry for the year 1189 states that the 'homines S. Martini et casalini eis assignati' in the *castellum* of Maggiano 'sint suprascripte ecclesie S. Martini in proprietate, allodio, et *dominatione*' (*ibid.* no. 1603).

[3] *RL*, n. 1826, shows a *manens* winning a case in a consular court of Lucca (for his status, cf. nos. 1521, 1582), and well before the end of the twelfth century grants of land by S. Martino, even to *coloni*, are made 'ad penam... consulum et treuganorum Luc.', the magistrates of the commune (e.g. *RL*, nos. 1687, 1700, 1725).

[4] The practice is still more evident in gifts to Pozzeveri (*infra*). It has been noted that elsewhere in Tuscany such 'donazioni improprie' tended to increase: M. Modigliani, 'Studi e doc. ad illustrazione degli stat. del comune di Anghiari', *Arch. Stor. It.* ser. IV, 6, 230–1. Cf. the 'pseudo-conversi' on the lands of S. Maria di Montepiano: *Carte del mon. di S.M. di Montepiano* (*Reg. Chart. It.*), ed. R. Piattoli, 1942. Once a donor stipulated that the land was not to be leased to his relatives, but this led to conflict later: *RL*, nos. 695, 1013, 1480.

lands *libellario nomine*. Often they received grants in several places and most of them held episcopal and other church land as well. All kinds of property had, by 1100, been made over in this way to the greater and lesser nobility, although there is a tendency for these 'great *libelli*' as they are called to occur in distant places or in villages where S. Martino had only parcels of land.[1]

Great *libelli* exacted only fixed rents, often nominal, in kind or money. They were almost always granted to a man and his heirs, and were in practice perpetual.[2] Their effect, like that of the emphyteusis elsewhere in Italy, was virtually to alienate the land granted and create between the peasant cultivators and the chapter a powerful class of mesne tenants, who were tempted to treat as allodial property what belonged to S. Martino. In time usage allowed the *libellarius* to sell his holdings if the chapter's rights were safeguarded;[3] but on occasion certainly he disposed of them 'per alodium'. Of some lands there is no later record after the original *libellus*.

It was to be expected that the canons would sooner or later attempt to resume what they could of such properties. In the twelfth century many churches sought to avoid new grants of fiefs to the powerful and revoke those already made. The bishops of Lucca had tried to do this from a very early period. The chapter followed their example, though perhaps with less energy, and was able to obtain the surrender, sometimes by gift, more often by sale, of a number of possessions held by great families, the Avvocati, Dombellinghi, and others, as well as by less important tenants whose identity is elusive. Laconic notes also record *libelli* 'finiti et non renovati' and others which have elapsed ('vacat', 'non valet').[4] At the same time the evidence implies an increasing reluctance to grant or renew *libelli*. In the eleventh century 150 grants were made to men of all classes (of whom more than one-third were clerks, lawyers, and men of substance), but during the twelfth only fifty or so are recorded, of which scarcely

[1] At Massa Macinaia on the other hand there were few, at Massarosa only one, while at Sorbano del Giudice, where the canons were evidently anxious to consolidate an estate, no grant of the sort is recorded.

[2] On the bishop's land *libelli* were commonly renewed on the death of the tenant or the lord. This practice may be traced in the capitular documents, but not so often as to suggest it was the rule. Acts described as *renovationes* frequently prove to be grants to wholly different families: *RL*, no. 1586; *MD*, v/1, 201; Endres, *ubi supra*, p. 269; F. Schupfer, *Diritto privato dei popoli germanici* III/2 (Città di Castello, 1907), 476–7; Pertile, *Storia del diritto italiano* (Turin, 2nd ed.), IV, 305; *RL*, no. 1473 (a. 1182), the record of a lawsuit, makes it plain that custom prescribed renewal and that perpetual inheritance could not be assumed. Few great *libellarii* were ever compelled to surrender their holdings for non-payment of rent, but some examples there are (*RL*, nos. 1145, 1275, 1355, 1473), though the grants merely threatened a money penalty (cf. Schupfer, *loc. cit.* III/2, 477).

[3] So at least certain records in the register and other Lucchese collections would suggest (*RL*, nos. 289 n. 4, 629–30, 737–8, 893, 967, etc.), though traditionally alienation was not allowed (P. S. Leicht, *Studi sulla proprietà fondiaria nel. M.E.* I (Verona, 1903), 102; Pivano, *Contratti agrari in Italia* (Turin, 1904), p. 215. In the twelfth century a few *libelli* forbade alienation, but these were not granted to notabilities (*RL*, nos. 693, 772–3, 783), while others, probably granted to humble people, permitted it, reserving a right of pre-emption to the lord (ibid. nos. 556, 805, 830, etc.). This tendency towards freedom to alienate led to the doctrine that *libelli* conferred a *dominium utile* (Leicht, *loc. cit.*; Schupfer, 'Precarie e livelli', *Riv. It. Scienze Giurid.* XI, 167; P. Torelli, *Un comune cittadino in territorio ad economia agricola* (Mantua, 1930), p. 242).

[4] *RL*, nos. 758–9, 952, 958, 966, 1091, 1169, 1290–1, 1433, 1439; *MD*, v/1; Endres, *ubi supra*, p. 256. The *RL* provides some parallel instances (usually by sale) from other Lucchese churches and monasteries, as do the *Regesti del R. Archivio di Stato in Lucca*, ed. degli Azzi (Lucca, 1911).

twenty fall between 1151 and 1200. Of these twenty, at least nine were renewals of old grants, four of them after litigation. In many places few or no *libelli* occur after 1100.

Taken together these facts certainly suggest a tendency to reduce the number of mesne tenants, but they are not enough to show that more than a minority of the great *libellarii* was affected. It is plain that the policy of resumption was not evenly sustained. Some surrenders were incomplete, some new grants were made, while many leases to the aristocracy are known to have persisted into the thirteenth century, either as *libelli* or as *feuda*. The assimilation of great *libelli* and fiefs is a development well attested from the late twelfth century on, and can be illustrated on these estates.[1] The terms of a feudal grant were not onerous—an oath of fealty and a money-rent—and only once involved military service. Clearly the *libellarii* were not to be easily displaced; and we know that in many parts of Italy laws were passed to prevent their dispossession and make their tenure secure, belonging as they did in great numbers to the very class which ruled the commune and made its statutes.

II

Originally the *libellus* was a peasant lease, intended largely for land improvement and reclamation. It imposed a duty to reside and develop the land (*ad meliorandum*), to come and 'do justice' and to pay certain rents and often services as well. In this primitive form it occurs fairly frequently in the bishop's records until the tenth century, when it gradually disappears. Small grants to humble people continue, but now only involve rents. In the chapter records *libelli* of this modified type, granted to peasants, are attested down to 1100. They relate to a number of places, but principally to one, Massa Macinaia, and all are grants of *mansi*. Like the great *libelli* they were hereditary—a solitary late example in 1195 is called *perpetua locatio*[2]—and demanded only a fixed rent, with perhaps recognition dues at Christmas or Easter.[3] In one case only does the clause appear requiring

[1] *RL*, nos. 260 n., 1469, 1471, 1477, 1805 n., 1834. For this process on the episcopal lands see *RL*, no. 28; *MD*, III, 101, 167, 183, 212, 226, 231–2, 237–9; V/1, 201; P. Guidi, E. Pellegrinetti, *Inventari del vescovato della cattedrale e di altre chiese di Lucca* (Rome, 1921), 3 *seq.*, 36 *seq.* Cf. Pertile, *loc. cit.* IV, 319; F. Schneider, *Reichsverwaltung in Toscana* (Rome, 1914), p. 203. *Entstehung* etc. p. 282. Leicht, *Diritto privato preirneriano* (Bologna, 1933), p. 252. Torelli, *loc. cit.* pp. 224 *seq.*

[2] *RL*, no. 1725. Such 'perpetual' *libelli* appear about this time in other parts of Tuscany, and the thirteenth-century law-books seem to contemplate no other kind: Gaudenzi, *Bibliotheca Iuridica Medii Aevi*, II, III. In the past the *libellus* had threatened eviction for failure to pay rent; this clause no longer appears, but a lawsuit of 1178 suggests the Roman rule could be applied compelling surrender if rent went unpaid for three years: *RL*, no. 1392 (originally a *libellus*). On this rule and its gradual application in Lombardy and Tuscany see Lattes, *Studi stor. sopra il contratto d'enfiteusi* (1868), pp. 148–9; *Diritto consuetudinario*, p. 317; Pertile, *loc. cit.* IV, 327. It occurs also north of the Alps: Dollinger, *loc. cit.* p. 9.

[3] At one time *libelli* had forbidden the raising of rents. The grants of S. Martino only once mention this, but the clause may be found in other Tuscan collections still in the thirteenth century. Sometimes if lands were laid waste by war or bad weather the rent would be reduced: *RL*, no. 404, cf. nos. 40, 649–50, 693; *Regesti cit.* 1/2 n. 141; C. Sardi, *Le contrattazioni agrarie del M.E. studiate nei doc. lucchesi* (Lucca, 1914), pp. 78 *seq.* Cf. L. Zdekauer, 'Degli statuti della Rocca di Tintinanno', *Bullettino Senese* (1896); Schupfer, *Diritto privato*, III/2, 471; Leicht, *Storia del diritto privato* (Milan, 1948), III, 80.

residence, only once the old stipulation that the peasant shall not be removed, and none at all of these *libelli* is granted 'ad meliorandum'.[1] It is obvious that many features of the early peasant *libellus* had been abandoned in Lucca. But some of them recur in a new kind of lease, new at least in name, which becomes increasingly prominent in the twelfth century, the *tenimentum*. Except for the single grant of 1195 there are no certain instances of peasant *libelli* after 1100. The *tenimentum* had taken their place.

The word 'tenimentum' appears in Tuscan cartularies during the eleventh century to describe both a holding and a form of tenure. Its meaning is often vague; but the tendency is clear as time goes on to associate it with peasant holdings; an Aretine law-book of about 1250 represents the *tenimentum* as a perpetual grant to peasant dependents who render works and may not leave the land.[2] That such was the character of most *tenimenta* on the estates of S. Martino there can be little doubt. In general they were rustic leases, imparting a new name to the peasant *libellus*, with some of its older characteristics revived, just as the fief lent a new name and nature to the great *libellus*.

The grants were made 'per tenimentum' or 'per tenimentum et perpetuam locationem' and were hereditary. In a good number (about one-third) conditions reappeared reminiscent of the original *libellus*: obligatory residence, fixity of tenure, a duty to improve, and often too a promise not to raise the rent. Failure to pay rent might entail a fine or forfeiture or both,[3] but in the main *tenimenta* were held to confer as secure and lasting a tenure as *libelli*,[4] and if alienation was sometimes forbidden, it was also sometimes allowed, with the first refusal saved to S. Martino.

By 1200 nearly all the leases granted by the chapter had become *tenimenta*. From the last twenty years of the twelfth century there survive more than forty, and from the last decade over twenty. The contrast with conditions one hundred years before is emphatic. To the place of *libelli* bestowed in generous numbers upon local magnates have succeeded grants made more and more to men who work the land themselves. An important if imperfect change has occurred in the capitular economy.

Among the complex class of people holding land on lease from S. Martino the records show that some, perhaps no mean proportion, were dependent

[1] *RL*, nos. 31, 531. The clause imposing 'residence' persists longer in other regions of Tuscany, e.g. the Casentino: *Reg. Camald. cit.* Only the *libellus* of 1195 was granted 'ad meliorandum' (*RL*, no. 1727), but the phrase survives until much later in other Tuscan *libelli*.

[2] Gaudenzi, *loc. cit.* III, 308–9. This conclusion contradicts the findings of Leicht (*Dir. priv. preirn.* pp. 121, 171). The evidence is too ample to be quoted, but for good examples see *Reg. Camald.* nos. 447, 532, 666, 706, 970, 994, 1198, 1353, 1416, 1602, 1754, 1965, 2072, etc.; *Regesto di Coltibuono* (*Reg. Chart. It.*), ed D. L. Pagliai, 1909, no. 531; *Regestum Pisanum* (*Reg. Chart. It.*), ed. N. Caturegli, 1938, no. 221; *Cartulario della Berardenga, Bull. Sen.* 1915 *seq.*, nos. 90, 115, 130, 137–40, 159, 201, 307 etc.; C. Calisse, 'Doc. del mon. di S. Salvatore sul Monte Amiata', *Arch. della Soc. Rom.* vol. XVII, no. 59; Lisini, *Inventario delle pergamene conservate nel diplomatico di Siena* (1908), 98, 121; Rumohr, *Ursprung d. Besitzlosigkeit d. Colonen im neueren Toscana* (Hamburg, 1830), pp. 29 *seq.*, 31 *seq.*, 49, 71–3, 81, 89; F. Soldani, *Historia mon. S. Michaelis de Passiniano* (Lucca, 1741), pp. 117–18; Zdekauer, *ubi supra*, pp. 374 *seq.* Cf. Piattoli, in *Carte Montepiano*, *op. cit.* p. l.

[3] Forfeiture after two or three years' withholding of rent: *RL*, nos. 1638, 1676, 1695, 1703.

[4] A lawsuit of 1200 shows certain landlords trying to evict a tenant on the grounds that though he has held of them for many years, it was not 'per tenimentum vel libellum': *RL*, no. 1826, cf. no. 1747.

cultivators. What they do not show is how the mass of such dependents held their lands and whether all were leaseholders. The register gives a pattern of landownership, not of landholding or landworking. It is generally agreed that many tenants of the twelfth century were descended from *libellarii* who had become assimilated to the vague class of *manentes*. For this reason it was still sometimes stipulated in grants by S. Martino that tenants were not to be treated as *manentes* or *coloni*, even after thirty years residence;[1] and a lawsuit of 1195 distinguished sharply between tenure 'per manentiam' and 'per tenimentum'. The grant was not enough in law to create dependent status, though it might have that effect.[2] Some land therefore must have been cultivated by peasants who were not bound to the chapter by specific contracts and whose rents and services were controlled only by custom.[3] Even so the documents sometimes class together *manentes*, *libellarii*, and *tenitores*, as though there was little practical difference among them. Economically they were one.

Libelli and *tenimenta* combine with other records to confirm what is known of the Tuscan peasantry at this time. They show that by far the most important obligation owed by *massarii* was the fixed rent from the land which they or their ancestors had been given to work (*ad regendum et laborandum*). Other servitudes might be *albergaria*, *commestio*, or *pascioraticum*, and certain seasonal gifts,[4] but of labour services there is no trace at all on the chapter's estates, and very few appear on the lay properties which the documents casually illustrate. Without exception they were slight and infrequent.[5]

The main condition of the *manens*' status was his bond with the soil: he was bound to reside on a definite holding.[6] He also swore an oath of submission (*comandamentum*, *fidelitas*) to his lord, who gained thereby a theoretic right to dispose of his person and goods and a power of discipline over him: 'ius manentie' and 'ratio de placito' were closely associated.[7] The typical holding of the *massarius* or *manens* during most of this period remained the *mansus* (*masium*, *mascia*), and in general one family, one

[1] *RL*, nos. 1535, 1708, 1770; cf. no. 1409. All are *tenimenta*, but a *libellus* granted in 1190 by the hospital of Ponte S. Pietro contains the same condition: *ibid.* no. 1610. For other Lucchese examples see Sardi, *loc. cit.* pp. 112–13; P. Vaccari, *L'affrancazione dei servi della gleba* (Bologna, 1926), p. 39. A lawsuit of 1195 (*RL*, no. 1729) shows that the place of birth and thirty years residence were important in determining the status of *manens*. The thirty-years rule was very old, and is repeated still in the statutes of Bologna (a. 1250).

[2] *RL*, no. 1729. Cf. Sardi, *loc. cit.* p. 115. 'Ammasiare' could be the word for putting a *manens* to work land: *RL*, no. 1400; cf. p. 20 n. 4 *supra*.

[3] The chapter possessed extensive lands at Massarosa and Fibbialla, yet very few surviving leases, either *libelli* or *tenimenta*, relate to them, though all but one of those that do are to *coloni*, etc.

[4] Notably the *spatula de porco*, common all over Tuscany and described by Schupfer as a recognition due (*Diritto privato*, III/2, 468). Cf. the *porcus donativus* on certain northern estates: C. E. Perrin, 'Une étape de la seigneurie. L'exploitation de la réserve à Prüm au IXe siècle', *Annales Hist. Ec. Soc.* (1934), p. 459.

[5] *RL*, no. 1387 (a. 1178: 'una die ad raunandum fenum', 'viii operas et duas ascinatas de fieno recare de campo et ii operas cum duobus asinis de tertio in tertio anno' etc.), cf. nos. 900, 1121, 1130.

[6] Occasionally members of the family might leave, but whoever did so forfeited all profit from the land: *RL*, no. 1687.

[7] *RL*, nos. 1239, 1400, 1540, 1542, 1729; *MD*, V/3, no. 1813; Kovalevsky, *Die ökonomische Entwicklung Europas* (Berlin, 1901–14), II, 349; Vaccari, *loc. cit.* and 'Ancora della servitù della gleba', *Studi Università Pavia* (1937).

massarius and his 'consortes', continued to cultivate one *mansus*. But from an early time there is evidence of subdivision, and the partition of *mansi* was probably common.[1] In any case the holdings were not of uniform size, nor were they compact; the same property might be described in one context as a *masium*, and in another as 'pieces' of land. *Massarii* appear holding simple 'petie terre', and there are more leases of pieces than of *mansi*. Not all lands therefore were accounted *mansi* nor all holdings, and the *mansus* itself may have been a loose and fragile unit, of which the components could change.[2] Perhaps for this reason we find in the second half of the twelfth century a new word coming into use to describe the peasant holding: '*podere*'. The *podere* was often the old *mansus* with a new name; but the new name (the modern Italian for 'farm') was more comprehensive than the old and during the thirteenth century began to displace it everywhere in Tuscany.

The *manens* did not necessarily cultivate only one holding or work the land of only one lord.[3] More important, he could himself own property,[4] and the rights in his holding also came to be considerable. Not merely was his tenure in effect hereditary; he was described as possessing a 'peculium', as having 'iura et actiones' in his land—the customary phrase to denote rights of property. *Massarii* could therefore deal in land, saving the rents due to the lord, and accumulate money to buy their liberty. From 1174 comes a deed of manumission in which a lay lord (and *libellarius* of S. Martino) sells for £6 to a *manens* his freedom 'de aliqua colonaria ascripticia atque originaria conditione'. This was a fairly common procedure; but in most of the acts of manumission preserved in the chapter registers the tenant either buys his holding or surrenders it in return for freedom.[5] The number of such acts is not great before 1200 and beside them must be set examples of men consenting still to receive land 'ut coloni et manentes'. There is no sign of any general policy of manumission, although some unrest among the peasantry there may have been. In the neighbouring *contado* of Pisa all the villages had acquired their communes and consuls by the middle of the twelfth century, and the development was clearly similar round Lucca.[6]

[1] *RL*, no. 34 shows that two *masia* first mentioned in no. 6 (a. 898–925) have now (a. 987) four *casaline* with four *massarii*; no. 32 records the gift of two *masia* and a thirteenth-century note adds: 'modo vero multiplicata sunt ipso duo masia et sunt plura masia'. There are further instances and all can be matched with evidence from other Tuscan cartularies.

[2] In a grant of land ('vinea et sterpetus atque silva') *per tenimentum* in 1167 it is stipulated 'quod suprascripta terra aliquo iure non debet pervenire ad aliquod masium': *RL*, no. 1258. On the instability of the *mansus* see Déléage, *loc. cit.* pp. 248, 329, 456; Perrin, 'Le manse', *Annales Hist. Soc.* (1945), pt. II, p. 45. [3] *RL*, no. 807 (a. 1123) would suggest *massarii* could also sublet.

[4] *RL*, nos. 1435, 1725. Cf. P. Santini, 'Condizione personale degli abitanti del contado nel sec. XIII', *Arch. Stor. It.* (1886), p. 184. Other Lucchese and Tuscan sources show that *villani*, etc., could have an allod, distinct from their *tenimentum*, although the lord seems to assume a right over both indiscriminately: *Reg. Camald.* no. 2079; Rumohr, *loc. cit.* pp. 71–3, 86–9; Vaccari, *loc. cit.* p. 200.

[5] *RL*, nos. 1472, 1672–3; cf. nos. 1318, 1329, 1774; Sardi, *loc. cit.* pp. 113–14; Vaccari, *loc. cit.* pp. 65 *seq.*

[6] At Massarosa the community obtained a temporary grant of liberties from Henry VI, but he withdrew them in 1191 and confirmed the chapter's rights there and 'dominium': *RL*, nos. 1629, 1642; Volpe, *Studi sulle istituzioni comunali a Pisa* (Pisa, 1902), p. 56.

III

Of demesne farming by the chapter there is no evidence.[1] The word 'donnicatum' continues to be used, but its meaning is vague and, where not simply traditional, refers only to buildings or land not granted away by fief or *libellus*. Demesne had always included more waste than cultivated land and at Massarosa the chapter drew revenue from the woods, marsh, and 'terre de culmatis' leased to the community.[2] Most properties were leased as soon as they passed to the chapter; even those recovered from tenants in the twelfth century were often straightway leased again, and what mills the chapter owned were also leased. Some manorial officers (*castaldi*) there certainly were, drawn mainly if not entirely from the class of *manentes*; they had land attached to their office and sometimes a regular payment (*pascioraticum*) from certain tenants. Their main work presumably was to supervise the payment of rent and tithe;[3] yet the rents from *libelli* and *tenimenta* were almost invariably owed, not to any local official, but directly to the chapter. There is nothing to suggest the organization in regional groups for economic and judicial purposes perfected on other great properties where demesne farming had been abandoned.[4] Most of the capitular lands were in or near Lucca and rents could easily be carried to the city.

Rent was paid in both money and kind, but there is no doubt that by the twelfth century rents in kind were much the more usual. It is commonly believed that in Italy as well as Northern Europe the tendency at this time and later was to replace food-rents by payments in money; on these estates the development is clearly the reverse. Down to about 1000 all rents paid by *libellarii*, of whatever class, were money-rents. During the next two centuries, however, food-rents and money-rents were almost exactly equal in number, while rents paid for *tenimenta* and by the peasantry in general were predominantly rents in kind. In the twelfth century rents were sometimes commuted, but again more frequently from money to kind than kind to money. Food-rents consisted mainly of grain, wine, and beans. Oil is scarcely mentioned, though the chapter had its *oliveta* and in 1281, when establishing separate prebends for the canons, assigned to

[1] Only one document suggests the canons might 'work' lands 'ad eorum manus': *RL*, no. 917 (a. 1137).

[2] *RL*, nos. 1497, 1642; cf. nos. 1278, 1281 (Gragno).

[3] Hence the *castaldus* had to control the tenant's agriculture: *RL*, no. 1719 (a. 1194), a *tenimentum* granted two brothers for a rent of forty *staia* of wine, 'et non debeant calcare sine parabola castaldi'. In Lombardy and some parts of Northern Europe the *gastaldus* (or *villicus*) exercised also *basse justice* (M. Handloike, *Die lombard. Städte unter d. Herrschaft d. Bischöfe* (Berlin, 1883), pp. 40 *seq.*; Déléage, *loc. cit.* p. 525; Dollinger, *loc. cit.* pp. 393–4). This may have been so at Lucca where we see *castaldi* occasionally doing the advocate's work of defending the legal rights of the chapter, but the social status of the *castaldi* makes it unlikely.

[4] As in Bavaria: Dollinger, *loc. cit.* pp. 136 *seq.*, and in *Le Moyen Âge* (1950). In Tuscany the records of Camaldoli reveal a similar organization, but the chapter's leases, even in places like Massarosa, where a manorial centre might be expected, still obliged the tenant to bring his rent to Lucca.

each one rents in oil as well as grain, wine and money.[1] Products of domestic industry are never mentioned. The range of commodities is small, simpler than that on the bishop's estates earlier, and much less various than that attested north of the Alps. With a flourishing urban market at their door the canons needed to draw only the basic produce from their lands of which they could easily sell the surplus.

Rents in kind were preferred because they were obviously economic. All rents were fixed, by contract or by custom, and there is evidence enough of the same rents persisting for more than one hundred years. In time such fixity of income could bring distress upon the chapter. The value of money in Lucca began to decline sharply toward the end of the twelfth century and caused the canons to try and increase their revenues, notably from Massarosa where they were forced to promise in 1191 not to impose new exactions 'pro deterioratione monete Lucensis'.[2]

The same fall in money values will account for the occasional raising of rents when leases were renewed or granted to different tenants, and will give fresh point to the chapter's endeavour to reduce the number of mesne holders. By removing the *libellarius* the canons could draw the heavier rent paid by the peasant on the land—once again usually a rent in kind. In addition the chapter had even before 1200 begun to let some of its lands for a mere term of years, share-cropping (*mezzadria*) had made a hesitant appearance, and occasionally an entry-fine (*servitium*) was being charged.[3] These practices were new. It was new also when in the later years of the twelfth century the canons, like other Tuscan landowners of the time, started to compile exact statements of their rents and prerogatives in various parts of their domains.[4]

The chapter was plainly anxious to make the most of its rights, but there is nothing to suggest it was forced to do so by economic debility. On occasion the canons certainly borrowed money. They also had to sell land sometimes to meet a sudden and unexpected cost—'pro dato Lucensis civitatis', 'pro facto placiti'.[5] At the same time they acted themselves as

[1] Guidi, Pellegrinetti, *loc. cit.* pp. 129 *seq.* The cultivation of olives was relatively rare in the Middle Ages and became a Lucchese speciality only later: Sardi, *loc. cit.* pp. 139 *seq.* G. Luzzatto (*I servi nelle grandi prop. eccles. ital. dei sec. IX e X* (Senigallia, 1910), p. 153), using Lucchese documents of the ninth and tenth centuries, detects a major difference between the *manentes* of Tuscany and Lombardy, in that the former rarely owed corn and other cereals among their food-rents. Wine was the most usual product rendered (cf. Endres, *ubi supra*, p. 273), and the chapter documents show this still to be so in the eleventh and twelfth centuries. Cf. M. Luzzatto, 'Contributo alla storia della mezzadria nel M.E.', *N. Riv. Storica* (1948), p. 73. Wine was easier and better to sell, easier to conserve: Déléage, *loc. cit.* pp. 607–8.

[2] *RL*, no. 1642. It was said the coinage of Lucca had lost half its value in thirty years: *ibid.* no. 1728 (a. 1195). Cf. V. Pfaff, 'Die Einnahmen d. römischen Kurie am Ende des 12. Jahrhunderts', *VSWG* 1953. On the other hand S. Martino could sometimes benefit by a rise in the measure of the bushel (*staio*) which took place in the twelfth century (compare *RL*, nos. 1088 and 1103), although some leases provided that changes of measure should not affect the rent: *ibid.* no. 1712.

[3] For grants of 18, 20, 24 years, etc.: *RL*, nos. 1529, 1535, 1545–6, 1646, 1699, 1751; for entry fines: nos. 812, 1134, 1687, 1717, cf. 975; for *mezzadria*: no. 1680, cf. 748? A few earlier examples of share-cropping (not in grants by S. Martino) do not include the grain crop: nos. 401, 531.

[4] *RL*, nos. 1497–8, 1547, 1568. Cf. Rumohr, *loc. cit.* p. 42. This development was common to the whole of Europe: Perrin, *loc. cit.* pp. 657 *seq.*; *Camb. Econ. Hist.* I, 304–5.

[5] *RL*, nos. 1165, 1232, 1337 (this land was later bought back), 1379, 1634.

creditors, taking land as security for their loans, while the debts they contracted were small when measured beside the sums they spent on property to consolidate their holdings. Most of their purchases were made after 1100, particularly from 1160 to 1180, and in the last decade of the century and later, when the price of land had risen acutely in Lucca.[1] Although some money to buy land was given to the chapter, or supplied by individual canons, the larger part of these transactions must have been paid for out of current revenue. If so, the twelfth century may be described as a time of real though moderate prosperity for S. Martino.

IV

It remains to inquire whether these conditions were typical of ecclesiastical lands at Lucca or in Tuscany at large. At Lucca certain contrasts with S. Martino are offered by the monastery of S. Pietro di Pozzeveri, established in 1056–8. As an eleventh-century foundation Pozzeveri seems to have escaped the cupidity of the great leaseholder, and was not therefore compelled to resume lands lost to its control.[2] The monastery lay not in Lucca but some ten miles to the east. For this reason probably it was not enriched by donations from many different lords and magnates, but like other religious houses, came under the influence of one great local family, the Porcari, and most of its benefactors were men of slight substance, small freemen it may be supposed, whose modest gifts of land were scattered across a wide area. The grants include much more woodland than those to S. Martino, but are otherwise similar in being mainly grants of pieces; *mansi* are rare.

The economic practice of Pozzeveri was precisely that of the chapter. Lands were let on hereditary tenancies (there are no short-term leases) and most rents were fixed rents in kind—mainly oil or grain, but never wine. There were *castaldi* who leased out some of the lands and collected some of the rents; but most rent according to the leases was brought 'ad monasterium'. There is no sign of demesne farming or of labour services; even so by this regime Pozzeveri, no less than S. Martino, seems to have prospered enough to buy land and build up its holdings.

As far as may be judged conditions were similar on most church lands near Lucca. The records are of hereditary grants for fixed rents in money or kind.[3] Labour services, still attested on the bishop's estates

[1] Only the roughest reckoning can be made of land prices during this period, but there is no doubt that the rise already noticed by Endres in earlier centuries (*ubi supra*, p. 251) continued at an increasing rate between 1000 and 1200. Whereas 2*s*. to 4*s*. per *staio* was a common price before 1050, 5*s*. to 15*s*. was the usual range a century later, and between 1175 and 1200, 15*s*. or 20*s*. to 35*s*., 50*s*. and more being sometimes charged in the 1190's. Other Tuscan sources bear this out. Cf. Torelli, *loc. cit.* p. 256, who observes a similar rise at Mantua.

[2] Only one *libellus* granted by Pozzeveri survives, and that to men of whom one may have been a *massarius: RL*, no. 662 (a. 1106), cf. no. 959; all other grants are *tenimenta*. Pozzeveri did of course, like S. Martino, resume lands by purchase from humble tenants.

[3] However, on the lands of some Lucchese churches examples occur in the later twelfth century of contracts in the modern style: the proprietor takes an active interest in the working of the land, and shares the expenses and crops with the tenant. The grants are not perpetual and compensation is made for improvements: Sardi, *loc. cit.* pp. 167 *seq.*

in the late tenth century, are rarely mentioned in the twelfth, and demesne farming is in abeyance. Once again this system seems to have yielded profits. The bishop of Lucca particularly was able during the twelfth and early thirteenth centuries to spend large sums on purchase and recovery of property.[1] Some churches certainly became embarrassed by debt, perhaps through maladministration and waste: such were the monastery of Sesto in 1135 and the convent of S. Frediano di Tolli in 1181. In 1191 the priest of S. Quirico had to sell land to Pozzeveri to pay usurious debts incurred by the previous incumbent.[2] Sales of this kind by churches are not uncommon, but normally they are made to other churches, and often land is sold merely to raise money for a purchase somewhere else. The market in land was brisk and there is much to suggest that more property was being bought by the church than sold.

Outside Lucca in other parts of Tuscany general tendencies are much the same. However, variations occur in local detail, too important to overlook. To begin with labour services are more widely attested in certain regions both before and after 1200 than at Lucca—on estates of the bishop and chapter of Florence for example, at Camaldoli, Vallombrosa, and Monte Amiata.[3] Such vestiges of the old manorial system were destined, many of them, to disappear in the thirteenth century with the commutation of services, but as yet the change is barely announced. Nor was it until the thirteenth century that the manumission of unfree peasants became frequent; at the end of this period and even beyond it the gift, sale, or pledge of *coloni* was still fairly common, and individual families continued to enter the class of *manentes*.[4]

Where defined labour services are not heavy: thirty-seven works annually is a high number. They consisted of various kinds of seasonal 'opere manuales'; 'opere boum' do occur, but are slight in amount and need indicate only carrying services. Nonetheless the persistence of works implies the persistence of some sparse demesne farming. Where labour services continued it fell to the local *castaldi* to control and supervise them, but the cartularies ignore this side of the *castaldus*' work and his

[1] *MD*, III, 205; IV/2, nos. 118–19, 122, 127, 140, app. nos. 94, 98, 100, 106 ,115; V/1, nos. 417, 421, 424 *seq.*, 431 *seq.*, 485, 497, 501–4; V/3, nos. 1808, 1813, 1820, 1829. Cf. Guidi, Pellegrinetti, *loc. cit.* pp. 23–5.

[2] *MD*, IV/2, app. no. 113; *Regesti*, ed. degli Azzi, I/2 nos. 436, 444; *RL*, no. 1626; cf. *ibid.* no. 1532 for a list of debts to tradesmen and others owed by the church of Ponte S. Pietro in 1185.

[3] Lami, *loc. cit.* I, 165–7, 176, 291–7; Rumohr, *loc. cit.* pp. 49 *seq.*; Santini, 'Nuovi documenti', etc., *Arch. Stor. It.* (1897), p. 287; Bonaini, 'Statuto della Val d'Ambra del MCCVIII del Conte Guido Guerra III e Ordinamenti dei fedeli di Vallombrosa degli anni MCCLIII e MCCLXIII', *Annali Università Toscane*, II, 115–16, 135–7; Zdekauer, *ubi supra*, pp. 374 *seq.*; *Reg. Camald.* nos. 708, 724, 997, 1609, 1754, 2009, 2079, 2150–1, 2237, 2326, 2556; *Carte della canonica della cattedrale di Firenze* (*Reg. Chart. It.*), ed. R. Piattoli, 1938, no. 159.

[4] *Reg. Colt.* nos. 486, 526, 530–2; *Reg. Camald.* nos. 1113, 1402, 1463, 1613, 1704, 1754, etc.; *Regestum Volaterranum* (*Reg. Chart. It.*), ed. F. Schneider, 1907, no. 241; 'Cart. Berardenga', *loc. cit.* nos. 90, 113, 128, 130–3, 139–40, 159, 196, 201; Lisini, *loc. cit.* pp. 98, 102, 125, 189, etc.; Lami, *loc. cit.* I, 162, 165, 171, cf. 168. Davidsohn, *Forsch. z. älteren Gesch. v. Florenz* (1896), I, 159; Rumohr, *loc. cit.* p. 70 n.

main office as illustrated there was as usual to receive rent and buy or let land.[1]

Even when the peasant remained subject to services, they were rarely his main obligation. He owed rents as well, in money and kind, and on all these Tuscan estates fixed rents from customary or leasehold tenures had plainly become the principal source of income. Some contrast with the practice of S. Martino is suggested by the *libelli* of other Tuscan churches, for which it remained the custom to demand only money rents, but this may be deceptive. For one thing the number of leases in some registers is very small. For another the terms of such *libelli* are no safe guide to the rent paid by the mass of peasant dependents. Rents, as all the sources show, were rendered in money and kind and by the thirteenth century more in kind than money. In 1263 the cathedral chapter of Arezzo laid it down explicitly that grants of land should be made for food-rents, not money rents, wherever possible.[2] And so the contrast with S. Martino is only apparent, and the correspondence between Lucca and the rest of Tuscany is reinforced by the gradual appearance elsewhere of *mezzadria*, entry-fines, and leases for a few years only.

More difficult to find are parallels to the policy of resumption at Lucca. It was the older churches which had been plagued most by magnate *libellarii*. At Pistoia both bishop and chapter had to resume lands, and according to Schneider the bishops of Volterra also, though the documents merely show them buying property from the local aristocracy. On this they spent generously and by a policy in other ways ambitious fell gravely into debt.[3] This, it has been said, was the unavoidable fate of feudal institutions overtaken by a money economy, and it cannot be denied that during the twelfth century a number of Tuscan churches accumulated heavy debts. Davidsohn long ago drew up a list of them, which could easily be extended; but it would be wrong to deduce destitution from debt, and wrong as well to overlook local circumstance. At Pistoia the bishop was impoverished while the chapter flourished. At Arezzo the bishop incurred his debts by political adventure, and so at Volterra.[4] Religious houses were in the habit of borrowing small sums of money, which were normally repaid, and even the larger debts need offer no true indication of economic conditions. Monasteries did not cease buying land because they

[1] *Reg. Camald., passim*; Bonaini, *ubi supra*, pp. 135–7; Davidsohn, *Forsch.* I, 149 (a. 1170); Lami, *loc. cit.* I, 272; R. Caggese, 'Note e doc. per la storia del vescovado di Pistoia nel sec. XII', *Bull. Stor. Pistoiese*, IX (1907), 158. The *castaldi* of Camaldoli were usually lay *conversi* (Modigliani, *ubi supra*, IV, 6, 229–30) and so apparently were the *vilici* of Coltibuono. On the chapter lands of Siena Cathedral they were *villani*: Rumohr, *loc. cit.* pp. 31 *seq.*

[2] 'Et quod poderia et terre cum locabuntur, non locentur ad censum vel pensionem sed affictentur ad frumentum vel bladum': *Doc. per la storia della città di Arezzo*, II (ed. U. Pasqui, Florence, 1916), p. 369. From the late twelfth and early thirteenth centuries come examples of money rents being converted into food-rents: Rumohr, *loc. cit.* pp. 23, 31 *seq.*, 66–70. It has to be added that grants for rents in kind are common after the late eleventh century in the records of Pistoia Cathedral chapter: *Libro Croce* (*Reg. Chart. It.*), ed. Q. Santoli, 1939.

[3] Caggese, *ubi supra*; *Libro Croce*; *Reg. Volat.* nos. 164–5, etc.; F. Schneider, 'Bistum u. Geldwirtschaft', *Quellen u. Forsch. aus Ital. Archiven u. Biblioteken* (1905), pp. 92 *seq.*

[4] Davidsohn, *Geschichte*, I, 408, 512 n. 3. Caggese, *ubi supra*; *Libro Croce*, p. xvi. Schneider, *ubi supra*.

owed money. In fact there is abundant witness to purchase of land by the church—often from feudal families. Purchases indeed gained in number upon gifts as the twelfth century advanced.

Conditions at Lucca then were not exceptional, nor was the modest prosperity of S. Martino and Pozzeveri. In the following period, many churches did have to endure financial strain, but even this, it has been shown, must not be exaggerated. Contemporary language was often hyperbolical, and it would be dangerous to take as typical of the Tuscan church at this time a complaint by the abbot of S. Andrea di Candeli who in 1217, to pay a debt, sold freedom to a peasant cultivator—'ne usurarum insatiata voracitas grandes ipsius monasterii possessiones celeriter attenuet et consumat'.[1]

The University of Leeds

[1] Soldani, *loc. cit.* pp. 214 *seq.*; cf. Davidsohn, *Forsch.* III, reg. 7, IV, 283.

12
Lords and Peasants: A Reappraisal of Medieval Economic Relationships

M. Toch

I

In the present paper we shall challenge some views and assumptions commonly held about the economic development of agriculture in the central and later Middle Ages. These views and assumptions, whether explicit or implicit, will be shown to touch upon some broader issues of social relationships in the countryside. A brief review of the research literature will reveal the main issues to which we shall address ourselves.

"In the fifteenth century, agriculture was in most cases, no longer conducted by the masters, but rather by the peasantry".[1] This was Georges Duby's conclusion to his analysis of the decay of manorial economy in the later Middle Ages. After his discussion of lords and manors, Duby devoted to the subject of the peasants the closing chapters of his great synthesis of a hundred years of research into the agrarian economy and rural life of the medieval West.[2] Similar views and structuring of the subject may be found in any recent major work on the topic.[3] The general consensus is that the XVth century, or at latest the

The following abbreviations are used:

CEH	Cambridge Economic History of Europe, 2nd ed., Cambridge 1966
HStAMünchen	Bayerisches Hauptstaatsarchiv München
MGSL	Mitteilungen der Gesellschaft für Salzburger Landeskunde
MIÖG	Mitteilungen des Instituts für österreichische Geschichtsschreibung
VSWG	Vierteljahrschrift für Sozial— und Wirtschaftsgeschichte
ZAA	Zeitschrift für Agrargeschichte und Agrarsoziologie
ZBLG	Zeitschrift für bayerische Landesgeschichte

[1] G. Duby, *L'économie rurale et la vie des campagnes dans l'Occident médieval,* Paris 1962, engl. transl. by C. Postan, *Rural Economy and Country Life in the Medieval West,* London 1968, p. 331.

[2] Duby, *Rural Economy,* pp. 332-357.

[3] Cf. F. Ganshof, A. Verhulst, M. Postan and L. Genicot in *CEH* I, pp. 305-339, 581-632, 705-739; G. Fourquin, *Le paysan d'Occident au Moyen Âge,* Paris 1972, pp. 112-141, 171-179; and most recently J.A.van Houtte, E. Miller, A. Verhulst, J. Favier, W. Abel in H. Kellenbenz (ed.), *Handbuch der europäischen*

XVIth, saw the final stages of an extended and complex process — the restructuring of the organization of northwestern and central European agriculture. From the XIIth century onwards control over production was gradually transferred from the lords (here used in the most general sense, including both lay and ecclesiastical landlords) to the peasants. As major elements in this transformation, which, coupled with the infusion of urban capital, was to "launch the rural economy and the whole country life of western Europe into a new leap forward",[4] can be seen the following:
(1) the contraction of the demesne and of direct cultivation by the lords; (2) the partition and leasing of demesne lands to the peasants under increasingly favourable conditions of tenure; (3) the commutation of labour services and the concomitant freeing of peasant resources; (4) a slow strenghtening of the peasants' community vis-à-vis the landlord.

Most of these trends were already dealt with by late XIXth — and early XXth — century scholars. The local and regional research conducted intensively and with increasingly sophisticated tools over the last forty years has made us aware of both the diversity and the uneven distribution of these phenomena and of their relation to general economic and demographic trends. In various periods, this general process was sometimes accelerated, as for example, during the XIIth century with its crisis in and the restructuring of lordly incomes. At times, direct cultivation of demesnes once more gained ground, as in the XIIIth century, when land was scarce and prices high. England remained a "bastion of manorialism" much longer than the continent. The Cistercians made a virtue out of direct cultivation and local research has lately revealed that all over Europe lords were busily managing what was supposed to have been disintegrating for years. Still, the process went on, accelerated finally by the late medieval "agrarian depression" when war, pestilence, rising wages, and tumbling grain prices made direct cultivation by lords economically unviable.

There can be little doubt that between the XIIIth and the XVth centuries in most parts of western and central Europe a major change had occurred in the management and organization of agriculture. The landlord economy of the early and high Middle Ages, which had been subject to a large extent to the will and whim of the lord, had developed into a kind of structure which could be termed a "peasant economy" as defined by T. Shanin. Namely, the family farm was the basic unit of production, seconded by the economic frameworks of the peasant community. Land husbandry was the principal means of livelihood directly providing the major part of consumption needs. There was a frequent need for credit, met outside the scope of homestead and community. The peasantry was

Wirtschafts— und Sozialgeschichte, II, Stuttgart 1980, pp. 113f., 238, 264, 274f., 316, 542-544. For a dissenting view but a similar structuring see J. Heers, *L'Occident aux XIVe et XVe siècles,* 2nd ed. Paris 1973, pp. 128-161.

[4] Duby, *Rural Economy,* p. 357.

politically and economically dominated by outside forces.[5] In this structure of production, the landlords appear as outsiders, mere rentiers, whose economic functions were increasingly eroded. Yet these "rentier-landlords" did not relax their grip on the peasantry. From the XIIIth century on there was a tightening of rent-collection, as witnessed by the abundance of property and rent registers all over Europe. Lords likewise increased their incomes from taxation, jurisdiction, banal monopolies and, in some places, the revival of peasant bondage — all prerogatives derived from extraeconomic sources. Thus, the line of reasoning goes, the withdrawal of the lords from the soil created a dynamic movement which further emphasized the political-legal, rather than the economic, aspect of late medieval lordship. To complete the symmetry of the picture, the peasantry is seen as having emerged from the tribulations of the late medieval crisis economically and demographically revitalized, ready to assume the tasks of modernization awaiting it in the Europe of early modern times.

The flaw in this picture would seem to lie neither in the evidence nor the conclusions concerning economic processes, but rather in the inferences regarding the relative position of lords and peasants. For these inferences seem scarcely reconcilable with indications of the vitality and strongly felt presence of lords in rural life which we see in the late Middle Ages and early modern period in many parts of Europe.[6] It is difficult to see how such a high profile could be sustained by a rent-collecting lordship through extraeconomic means of control, many of which were available only to the higher and highest ranks of lay and church aristocracy. We would like to suggest, therefore, that there were complementary means of influence upon and control of the peasant economy. The application of these means by the lords counteracted the tendency toward withdrawal inherent in the discontinuance of demesne production and made for the continued, or in some places renewed, involvement of the lords in agrarian economy and rural life.

The evidence for this thesis has been drawn mainly from German sources, a fact which might seem to militate against drawing any conclusions regarding the rest of Europe. Morever, most scholars consider the German experience to have been special, if not unique, as in Marc Bloch's dictum about "that singular

[5] TH. SHANIN, *Peasant and Peasant Societies*, Harmondsworth 1971, p. 14f., and in full in his: The Nature and Logic of the Peasant Economy, *Journal of Peasant Studies* 1(1973), pp. 63-80.

[6] For England and Germany the evidence is unambiguous. See K.B. MCFARLANE, *The Nobility of Later Medieval England*, Oxford 1973, esp. pp. 41-60; the case studies in H. PATZE (ed.), *Die Grundherrschaft im späten Mittelalter*, 2 vols., Sigmaringen 1983; H. RÖSSLER (ed.), *Deutscher Adel 1430-1555*, Darmstadt 1965; Österreichische Akademie der Wissenschaften (ed.), *Adeliges Sachleben des Spätmittelalters*, Vienna 1982. For France see the indications in G. BOIS, Noblesse et crise des revenues seigneuriaux en France aux XIVe et XVe siècles: essai d'interpretation, in: PH. CONTAMINE (ed.), *La noblesse au Moyen Âge*, Paris 1976, pp. 219-233.

quality of archaism, which through almost the entire feudal era seems the distinctive mark of German society".[7] Yet if we leave on one side the idiosyncrasies of learned terminology, most of the structural features as well as the main lines of development of German agrarian history fit very well into the larger European framework.[8] This is especially true of the former Frankish and Frankish-dominated areas of northern, western and southern Germany which form the geographical framework of the present study. In this old-settled Germany developed manorial structures, although to a somewhat lower density and with obvious regional differences, which were structurally akin to the ones found further to the west. The process of decay which began in the XIIth century, as well as the concomitant growth of the peasant economy developed here along the same lines encountered in northwestern Europe.[9] The opening of woods, wastelands, and mountains in the XIth-XIVth centuries was undertaken in the same manner as elsewhere, by peasants settled on homesteads and under the direction of the lords. Even in more technical aspects, such as the evolution of common fields and the economic frameworks of the peasant community, Germany tends to conform to the European type.[10] To be sure, there were differences, but they are mainly found in the political aspects of lordship, which were part and parcel of the specific development of the German territories,[11] and in the legal differentiations within the body of the peasantry.[12]

What, then, were the means of lordly influence and control in the peasant economy of northern, western and southern Germany? As we shall show, they were part of the interlocking institutional arrangements of landlordship and peasant tenure prevalent in these regions. We shall proceed in order of increasing generalization, starting with fully documented institutions found only in southern Germany, passing on to arrangements prevalent in most parts of Germany

[7] M. BLOCH, *Feudal Society*, transl. by L.A. MANYON, London 1961, p. 270.

[8] CEH I, passim.; DUBY, *Rural Economy*, passim; F. LÜTGE, *Geschichte der deutschen Agrarverfassung*, 2nd ed. Stuttgart 1967, pp. 45-56; Ch. Perrin, La société allemande du Xe au XIIIe siècle d'après un ouvrage récent, *Revue hist. de droit fraincais et étranger* Ser. 4, 24 (1945), pp. 84-102.

[9] See the studies in Patze (note 6) and the penetrating analysis by PH. DOLLINGER, *L'évolution des classes rurales en Bavière depuis la fin de l'époque carolingienne jusg'au milieu du XIIIe siècle*, Paris 1949, thenceforth cited in the updated German translation ed. by F. IRSIGLER, *Der bayerische Bauernstand vom 9. bis zum 13. Jahrhundert*, Munich 1982.

[10] R.C. HOFFMANN, Medieval Origins of the Common Fields, in: W.N. PARKER-E.L. JONES (eds.), *European Peasants and their Markets*, Princeton 1975, pp. 23-72.

[11] O. BRUNNER, *Land und Herrschaft*, 5th ed., Vienna-Wiesbaden 1965; H. PATZE (ed.), *Der deutsche Territorialstaat im 14. Jahrhundert*, 2 vols., Sigmaringen 1970-71.

[12] K.F. BADER, *Studien zur Rechtsgeschichte des mittelalterlichen Dorfes*, 3 vols., Vienna 1957-67; TH. MAYER (ed.), *Die Anfänge der Landgemeinde und ihr Wesen*, 2 vols., Konstanz-Stuttgart 1964; Dollinger (note 9).

and western Europe, and concluding with a general discussion of investment in agriculture. Our final remarks will deal with the revisions which our findings require in the widely accepted thesis outlined at the beginning of this paper.

II

The *Gericht,* the first institution which we shall discuss, is mentioned in southern German and Alpine Austrian sources from the late XIIth to the XVIIth century. Its last remains disappeared only in the early XIXth century. But the bulk of references dates from the period between the XIIIth to the XVth centuries. They are found by the thousands in the property and rent-registers known as *Urbare,* the German equivalent of the rentals and censiers-coutumiers of Western Europe.[13] Most of the surviving *Urbare* are of course of ecclesiastical origin, as are almost all other pertinent types of sources.[14] Still, the very few preserved records of lay landlords have similar entries using the same terms as those employed in ecclesiastical sources. This fact and the geographical distribution of the institution justify us in viewing it as a general phenomenon prevalent all over "Upper Germany", comprising Swabia and Bavaria, as well as in present-day Austria, in the regions of the Tyrol, Salzburg, Styria and Carinthia. It is mentioned also in Upper and Lower Austria, Franconia, German Switzerland and Alsace.

The *Urbare* refer to this institution by various names,[15] all used interchangeably. We shall term it *Gericht,* by the noun derived from the verb *richten,* to fix, to arrange. A typical entry of *Gericht* in an *Urbar* follows upon the rents and dues accruing from a certain property. It opens with the phrase "habet, debet zu gericht", followed by a list of five elements: (1) a sizable sum of money sometimes designated "viehgericht" or "pro jugalibus", in place of the draught animals which some earlier sources mention; (2) smaller amounts of grains, under the rubric "pro semine", or sometimes only "semen sufficiens", all of which clearly denote seedgrain; (3) some pigs and poultry; (4) essential agricultural equipment, such as a plough, cart, harrow and yoke, sometimes also

[13] See in general R. FOSSIER, *Polyptiques et censiers* (Typologie des sources du moyen âge occidental 28), Tournhout 1978. On the German Urbare see K.Th.v. Inama-Sternegg, Über Urbarien und Urbarialaufzeichnungen, *Archivalische Zeitschrift* 2(1877), pp. 26-52; H. OTT, Probleme und Stand der Urbarinterpretation, *ZAA* 18(1970), pp. 159-184; G. RICHTER, *Lagerbücher— oder Urbarlehre,* Stuttgart 1979.

[14] Mainly "Leihereverse", letters of tenure issued by the lord, counter-signed by the peasant and preserved in the lord's copyregister, and a few surviving account books. CF. J. WILD, *Beiträge zur Registerführung der bayerischen Klöster und Hochstifte im Mittelalter,* Kallmünz 1973.

[15] In Latin institucio, expedicio, iudicium, ius, procuratio, regimen curie, pro jugalibus; in German Recht, Gericht, Berichtung, Richtung, Hofgericht, Hofrecht, Hubrecht, Hubgericht, Samrecht, Stift, Weglos.

numerous smaller tools; (5) hay in sufficient quantities, sometimes with the number of beasts to be fed for a given time span. Some of the entries are long, detailed inventories, while others are concise lists of essentials. Some specify amounts of cash, others only one lump sum. Pastoral holdings state numbers of cattle or sheep, a fisherman's tenure will list a boat and nets, a miller's millstones. There is even one rare reference to a bridge-warden's *Gericht*.[16]

Earlier scholars already identified these entries as formalized inventories of the material assets needed to keep in working order the holdings owned by the lord and cultivated by the peasant.[17] The most recent and detailed treatment of this subject is by J. Hopfenzitz,[18] whose interpretation is close to our own in that he stressed the legal point: that the homestead is entitled to or has an inherent right to the objects listed in the *Gericht* entries. We feel, however, that he erred in attempting to link the massive presence and fullness of these entries in XIVth-century sources to the "late medieval crisis", which he sees as having forced landlords to resort to decisive measures in order to make their depopulated possessions more attractive to new cultivators.[19] Such an explanation not only disregards the rapid development and diffusion of *Urbare* in this period. More important, it ignores some well-published and very detailed XIIIth-century references, in which the *Gericht* is already a fully developed institution.[20]

The origins of the *Gericht* go back to the XIIth/XIIIth centuries, the period of transition from direct cultivation by lords to peasant tenure. To be sure, nowhere is this transition explicitly described, but the earliest and, up to the XVth century, fullest *Gericht* entries refer to the big, well-equipped "curiae" and "Maierhöfe", the former centres of manorial administration where old structures were often preserved for centuries.[21] In this transitional period, with

[16] H.J. Busley (ed.), *Die Traditionen, Urkunden und Urbare des Klosters Neustift bei Freising*, Munich 1961, p. 226.

[17] F. Hundt, *Kloster Scheyern, seine ältesten Aufzeichnungen, seine Besitzungen*, Munich 1862, p. 76f.; S. Herzberg-Fränkel, Wirtschaftsgeschichte des Stiftes Niederaltaich, *MIÖG* Ergänzungsband 10, 1916, p. 225f.; A. Dopsch (ed.), *Die landesfürstlichen Urbare Nieder— und Oberösterreichs aus dem XIII. und XIV. Jahrhundert*, Vienna 1904, p. CXI; A. Gstirner, Das Gericht oder die Stift in Steiermark, *VSWG* 28(1935), pp. 313-347; Dollinger (note 9), pp. 127, 168, 359, 392; I. Bog, Neue Quellen zur Agrarverfassung geistlicher Herrschaften in Bayern, *ZAA* 9(1961), p. 60f.

[18] J. Hopfenzitz, Hubgericht-Hofgericht-Hubrecht. Eine Untersuchung zum mittelalterlichen Besitzrecht in Oberdeutschland, *ZAA* 24 (1976), pp. 8-53.

[19] Hopfenzitz, p. 39.

[20] Exactly the sources used by the earlier authors and overlooked by Hopfenzitz, which are cited in note 17. To them should be added O. Stolz, *Die Schwaighöfe in Tirol*, Innsbruck 1930, passim., and A. Hochholzer, Grundherrschaftliche Fronhöfe und Ämterverfassung im niederbayerischen Raum, *ZBLG* 31(1968), p. 55.

[21] Cf. the earliest reference, from the Swiss monastery Muri (mid-12th century): H. Wopfner (ed.), *Urkunden zur deutschen Agrar-Geschichte*, Stuttgart 1928, p. 139.

landlords oscillating between direct cultivation, short-term farm, and peasant tenure, the equipment, livestock and grains belonging to the curiae were transferred too. These holdings were let "berichtet", i.e. equipped with the inventory. Their equipment, the *Gericht*, was then entered in the *Urbare* as part of the lord's property, at the appropriate place near to the rent and dues. For holdings acquired later, a new *Gericht* would have to be provided, as illustrated by some direct evidence from the XIIIth century.[22] Smaller holdings, the "hubae, beneficiae, feuda", especially those situated at some distance from the manorial centres, usually show much shorter and schematic entries, indicating that their *Gericht* must be dated later. Thus we can assume a slow spreading of this usage, integrating at different times various components of the lordly property into local custom, which then developed into part of the customary law of the manor.

It is in this completed form, the "Hofgericht" as part of the "Hofrecht", that the *Gericht* presents itself in the XIVth and XVth centuries. Formally, as with other aspects of the law of the manor, there is a due process of law-finding, in which lord and peasantry cooperate.[23] In content, there was a reciprocal responsibility: the obligation of the peasant about to leave the homestead to safeguard the *Gericht*, and the commitment of the lord to continue to provide it. To be sure, in most of the sources, which originated, it should be remembered, from the side of the lords, only the former is mentioned.[24]

There was in fact good reason for this obligation. Up to the XVIth century the greater part of the area under discussion was subject to "Freistift", a type of non-hereditable short-term tenancy of a few years, terminable at the lord's will. This made for a high turnover of peasant cultivators, while providing little incentive to safeguard soil and equipment.[25] For this reason, and similar to so

[22] For instance in Niederaltaich (Lower Bavaria): J. CHMEL (ed.), Die Besitzungen des Benediktinerklosters Niederaltaich in der Passauer Diöcese, *Notizenblatt d. kaiserl. Akad. d. Wissensch.* 4 (Vienna 1854), p. 575.

[23] HStAMünchen, Geisenfelden Lit. 23 f. 13 (end of XIIIth century). Similar in Scheyern (Monumenta Boica X, Munich 1763, nr. 225, XIVth century) and Neustift (Busley, note 16, p. 251, 1st half of the XVth century). On the late medieval development and structure of manorial law see P. BLICKLE (ed.), *Deutsche Ländliche Rechtsquellen*, Stuttgart 1975.

[24] See the references from Urbare in Hopfenzitz (note 18), pp. 18-20, the sections in the laws of the manor in Wopfner (note 21), p. 321, and in G. FRANZ (ed.), *Quellen zur Geschichte des deutschen Bauernstandes im Mittelalter*, Berlin 1967, pp. 450-452, 505, 599; letters of tenure: Monumenta Boica X, 1763, nrs. 74, 158, 211, 225; Staatsbibliothek München Clm 1052 ff. 13, 16, 21', 22; A. WEISSTHANNER (ed.), *Die Urkunder und Urbare des Klosters Schäftlarn*, Munich 1957, p. 155; M. THIEL-E. ENGELS (eds.), *Die Traditionen, Urkunden und Urbare des Klosters Münchsmünster*, Munich 1961, p. 208; H.C. FAUSSNER-A.V. GROTE (eds.), *Urbarbuch des landesfürstlichen Kastenamtes Burghausen*, Munich 1983, p. XLVIII. On the ongoing debate about the lordly vs. peasant origin of the Weistümer, the rural documents of law-finding, see Blickle (note 23).

[25] On systems of tenure in the area see Bader (note 12); H. LIEBERICH, Die Rechtsformen des bäuerlichen Besitzes in Altbayern, *Mitteilungen f.d. Archivpflege in*

many battles of lordly power against peasant ruse,[26] the attempt to hold the peasant responsible was doomed to failure. To little avail were the variety of clauses inserted in the *Urbare*, laws of the manor, and letters of tenure cited above, as well as the periodical checks and inquiries instituted by the more conscientious lords.[27] Wherever we obtain a direct glimpse into the actual workings of manorial administration, we see that the lords had to invest in the upkeep of the *Gericht* on the peasant tenures.[28] As stated sometimes explicitly, the lords were prepared to do so in order to see their property produce, so that rents and taxes could be raised.[29] With no other incentive to the cultivator, it is precisely in those areas which clung longest to "Freistift" that the *Gericht* survives into the XVIth and XVIIth centuries, whereas it withered away wherever hereditary tenancy finally prevailed in the course of the XVth century, as in the Southwest, and on the ducal properties in Bavaria.[30] But for three centuries at least, this institution was economically viable indeed.

The institution of the *Gericht* then, as developed in the XIIth and XIIIth centuries and institutionalized in the laws of the manor in the succeeding period, must have played a considerable role in the transition from landlord to peasant production. This drawing upon the lords' stocks of equipment, livestock, grains and capital, effected a redistribution of the means of production which enabled peasant tenures to "go into business". Later, the *Gericht* served as a prop to the

Oberbayern 6(1941), pp. 159-176; O. STOLZ, *Rechtsgeschichte des Bauernstandes und der Landwirtschaft in Tirol und Vorarlberg*, Bozen 1949, pp. 82-126; H. KLEIN, Die bäuerlichen Lehen im Erzstift Salzburg, *MGSL* 69(1929), pp. 145-168.

[26] Cf.M.-Th. Lorcin, Un musée de la ruse paysanne, *Études rurales* 51 (1973), pp. 112-124.

[27] For instance in Scheyern, cf. the marginal annotations in HStAMünchen, Scheyern Lit. 54 (ca. 1300), 55 (ca. 1315), 56(1400), passim, or in Neustift: Busley (note 16), p. 251.

[28] Cf. in Niederaltaich: Chmel (note 22) 4(1854), p. 575; 5(1855), pp. 168, 263; Scheyern: HStAMünchen, Scheyern Lit. 54 ff. 15, 36, 70; Lit. 77 ff. 5, 316; Kaisheim: H. HOFFMANN (ed.), *Die ältesten Urbare des Reichsstiftes Kaisheim 1319-1352*, Augsburg 1959, pp. 106, 112; convent of Augsburg: R. DERTSCH (ed.), *Das Füßener hochstiftische Urbar von 1398*, Kempten 1940, p. 10; Ellwangen: Hopfenzitz (note 18), p. 20; Langheim: F. GELDNER (ed.), *Das älteste Urbar des Cistercienserklosters Langheim*, Würzburg 1952, p. 59. For numerous, slightly ambiguous, references see note 27 above, where frequent mention is made of new cultivators installed on holdings and acknowledging for the abbey's officials the Gericht in place.

[29] Chmel (note 22), 4(1854), pp. 473, 507; 5(1855), pp. 192, 259, 309-311, all from the mid-XIIIth century. Similar in Geisenfeld at the end of the XIIIth century: HStAMünchen, Geisenfeld Lit. 23 f. 14, and in Neustift in 1403: Busley (note 16), pp. 204, 205, 207, 208, 212.

[30] For the former see Bader (note 12) and the regional case studies in Patze (note 6). For the latter G. Kirchner, Probleme der spätmittelalterlichen Klostergrundherrschaft in Bayern, *ZBLG* 19(1956), pp. 1-94.

peasant economy by putting the lords' resources at its disposal, while at the same time guaranteeing the lords a decisive voice in the administration of agricultural production. It is this last aspect which is most striking as one moves from the grain-producing Swabian-Bavarian lowlands to the Alpine regions, where the same principles were applied in different environmental and economic circumstances.

The Bavarian and Austrian Alps, in whose river valleys Bavarian peasants, led by their lords, had superseded a sparse Rhaeto-Romanic and Slavonic population in the course of the early and central Middle Ages, underwent a second phase of agricultural settlement during the XIIth-XIVth centuries.[31] At fairly high altitudes, often above the line where grain can be grown, there arose within a relatively short time many hundreds of *Schwaighöfe*. These represented a new type of dispersed peasant settlement devoted to animal husbandry and dairy production. Unlike the "Alm" with its temporary huts and exposed pasture used only during summer, the Schwaigen were true homesteads provided with sturdy buildings, extensive grazing lands, cultivated meadows for winter fodder and, wherever possible, small plots on which some grain could be grown for home consumption. Due to the difficulty of communication in this rugged terrain, which prevented the development of true transhumance, and on account of the relatively late date of their construction, we found no mention of *Schwaigen* worked directly under lordly management. In other words, of small and medium size, inhabitated and cultivated by peasant families, and held in inheritance, the *Schwaigen* were from the outset genuine elements of the peasant economy. Yet at the same time they reflect more clearly than any other agricultural institution the strenght of lordly influence on this peasant economy.

Schwaighöfe were established in two ways. One was the conversion of an existing grain-producing homestead into a stock-raising one, by the provision of cattle and the allocation of meadows and pasture from the lord's demesne or out of the commons (as a result of pressure upon the peasant community). The second, most common way was the erection of *Schwaigen* similarily equipped by lords, on newly asserted slopes belonging to the lords by virtue of their "ban" over virgin soil. As in other large-scale clearing projects, the peasants doing the actual work were provided with food and tools and then settled on the newly created tenures. They then enjoyed several years of reduced rent and

[31] The literature and source references for the following in: O. Stolz, *Schwaighöfe* (note 20); H. Wopfner, Beiträge zur Geschichte der alpinen Schwaighöfe, *VSWG* 24(1931), pp. 36-70; H. Klein, Über Schwaigen im Salzburgischen, *MGSL* 71(1931), pp. 109-128; O. Stolz, Beiträge zur Geschichte der alpinen Schwaighöfe, *VSWG* 25(1932), pp. 141-157; A. Gstirner, Die Schwaighöfe im ehemaligen Herzogtume Steiermark, *Zeitschrift des historischen Vereines für Steiermark* 31(1937), pp. 1-86; E. Krausen, Die Schwaigenwirtschaft des Klosters Raitenhaslach, *Mitteilungen der Geograph. Gesellschaft München* 53(1968), pp. 339-351; W. Fresacher, Wirtschaftsgeschichtliche Erkenntnisse aus den Gurker Urbaren, *Carinthia* I 161(1971), pp. 138-149.

later, improved conditions of tenure, in this case inheritability as mentioned above. But lords played a leading role not only in the creation of *Schwaigen*, but also in the assurance of their continued existence and ability to pay rent. Using the very terms employed in the lowlands for *Gericht*, there are constant references to lords regularly supplying cattle, salt, seed-grains, and to homesteads situated at altitudes too high to enable cultivation, even of food-grains. This principle of lordly responsibility embodied in the institution of *Gericht*, then, was also rigorously applied to the Alpine regions. Up to the XVIth century local customary law held that only *Schwaigen* properly equipped with cattle by the lord carried the obligation to pay rent.

Naturally, such a far-reaching commitment on the part of the lords was attended by vastly augmented possibilities, amounting at times to a virtual *dirigisme*, of interference in the peasant economy. In the XIIIth century, the chapter of Gurk (Carinthia) converted most of its possessions in one particular valley into cheese-producing *Schwaigen*. Since the soil, climate and elevation of this valley seem to have been the same as those in neighbouring possessions of the chapter, administrative convenience must have motivated this step. This is borne out by the fact that another group of holdings near Gurk cultivated mainly grains, while a third and distant one paid mainly cash rents.[32] A different principle seems to have guided the arrangements of the Styrian abbey of Admont, whose immediate vicinity was especially suited to meadowland. By providing a *Gericht* suited solely to animal husbandry, over several hundred years Admont built up an export trade in cheese, cows and oxen which was still thriving in the XVIIth century.[33] Finally, we have the case of the archbishopric of Salzburg, which had gradually converted the *Gericht* on its *Schwaigen* from sheep to cows, until, by the end of the XVth century, a group of only some twenty distant holdings continued to raise sheep. In 1498 the decision was taken to replace all sheep with cows. Within two years these holdings were producing melted butter instead of cheese, paying rent to the annual rate of some 5000-6000 huge chunks weighing up to ten pounds each.[34]

For both the grain-producing holdings in the lowlands and the stock-raising Alpine *Schwaigen*, provision by the lords of the means of production was the key to the very functioning of the peasant economy. There were of course obvious differences, the most important one being the marked prominence of *Gericht* in the latter as compared to its more obscure character in the former. In lowland grain-production *Gericht* seems to have played its main role in the XIIth - XIIIth centuries, during the poorly documented transitional phase from manorial to peasant production. In the later Middle Ages it continued to be

[32] Fresacher (note 31), pp. 141-143.

[33] Gstirner, *Gericht* (note 17), p. 323.

[34] H. Dopsch, Wandlungen und Konstanz der spätmittelalterlichen Grundherrschaft im Erzstift Salzburg, in: Patze (note 6), II, pp. 258-261.

employed mainly on larger holdings, many of which were still exercising former manorial functions, such as rent-collecting and the lodging of the visiting lord and his officials. By contrast, the *Schwaigen*, established in a later period when written accounting was commoner, are much better documented. But more than anything else, the isolated nature of the settlements and the adverse climatic and topographic conditions of the Alpine regions must have created the strong dependence of peasant upon landlord, and consequently, the marked vitality of *Gericht* in this area, which continued into the early modern period. Beyond differences of timing and degree, the arrangements involved in *Gericht* in both areas served basic needs of agrarian society, so well that they were institutionalized and legitimized in customary law.

III

In the foregoing discussion we indicated a convergence of needs which gave rise to the institutionalization of landlord interference in the direction of the peasant economy. It remains to be shown that this state of affairs was not confined to only one, albeit sizable, part of Germany, but was, rather, a basic configuration in agrarian society as a whole. To this end we shall examine the institution of share-cropping known in Germany as *Teilbau* or *Teilpacht* and in other parts of Europe as *facherie, métayage, mezzadria* or *tâche*. As is well known, its main feature was the contractual, short-term cooperation between landlord and peasant, matching in agreed proportions land, equipment, and stocks to the latter's labour, the fruits of which were to be divided accordingly. Historians have shown special interest in this type of commercial lease which is found in abundance in the notaries' registers of southern Europe. They see it as a channel for the influx of urban capital into the rural economy.[35] As suggested in the title of a much-cited study,[36] share-cropping is viewed as the primary instrument for tendencies towards intensification and modernization in late medieval agriculture. But, as recently pointed out, this concentration upon the urban features of *mezzadria* is prejudicial to an understanding of its northern counterparts.[37] True, nothing comparable to the large-scale investigations in Italy and southern France [38] has yet been undertaken for northwestern continental Europe, where the chronology and diffusion of *métayage* and *tache* are

[35] Duby, *Rural Society*, p. 326f.; Heers, *L'occident* (note 3), pp. 255-262.

[36] P.J. Jones, From Manor to Mezzadria: A Tuscan Case Study in the Medieval Origins of Modern Agrarian Society, in: H.A. Rubinstein (ed.), *Florentine Studies*, London 1968, pp. 193-241.

[37] G. Duby-A. Wallon, *Histoire de la France rurale*, vol. I, Paris 1975, p. 588 f., following Duby, Rural Society, p. 326 f.

[38] I. Imberciadori, *Mezzadria classica toscana*, Firenze 1951; G. Sicard, *Le métayage dans le Midi toulousain à la fin du Moyen Âge*, Toulouse 1957.

far from established.[39] Yet for a smaller area in central France, the role of *métayage* in the process of a more rational regrouping of holdings initiated by local lords after 1450 has been convincingly demonstrated.[40] We now know that wherever instituted, such arrangements became part and parcel of the traditional social framework of landlords and peasantry.[41]

The state of the research into the German *Teilbau* is even more disappointing, despite copious references in faultlessly printed sources and an abundance of local and regional studies mentioning it. Only very recently has there been an awakening of interest in the subject, focusing on *Teilbau* leases employed since the mid-XIIIth century in the Lower Rhine area by urban ecclesiastical institutions and possibly by landowning burghers.[42] Cases of town-dwelling merchants preferring to lease their landed property in this way have also been noted in Lübeck and Regensburg.[43] Similar references can probably be found in many more places.[44] In these contracts, in exchange for half the annual produce, the landlord provides, in addition to the land, all or part of the seed-grain, draught animals, and cattle, and often tools, and nearly always half the wages paid to the harvesters. Other clauses stipulate details of cultivation, bind the lessee to keep the soil in good heart, and mention inter alia the sowing of the fallow, and the growing of industrial plants.

But do these facts, however remindful of southern *métayage*, really necessitate an urban commercial modernizing source, originating in heavily urbanized neighbouring Flanders, for the diffusion of leases involving landlord-owned capital and stocks?[45] A look at the evidence would seem to require a different approach. Indeed, tenures held in return for part of the produce are found all

[39] Ganshof-Verhulst in CEH 1, 2nd ed., p. 324 f.; M.-Th. Lorcin, *Les campagnes de la région Lyonnaise aux XIVe et XVe siècles*, Lyon 1974, pp. 94-96. See also note 41 below.

[40] L. Merle, *La métairie et l'evolution agraire de la Gâtine poitevine de la fin du moyen âge à la Revolution*, Paris 1958.

[41] D. Nicholas, *Town and Countryside: Social, Economic and Political Tensions in 14th Century Flanders*, Brugge 1971, p. 338; G. Despy, Un domaine seigneurial au bas Moyen Âge, *Le Moyen Âge* 69(1963), p. 873 (Brabant); L. Genicot, *La crise agricole du bas Moyen Âge dans le Namurois*, Louvain-Gent 1970, p. 72; G. Bois, *Crise du féodalisme*, Paris 1976, p. 219 (Normandy); G. Fourquin, *Les campagnes de la région Parisienne a la fin du Moyen Âge*, Paris 1964, pp. 80, 480; G. Fournier, La création de la Grange de Gregovie, *Le Moyen Âge* 56(1950), p. 332f. (Burgundy).

[42] F. Irsigler, Die Auflösung der Villikationsverfassung und der Übergang zum Zeitpachtsystem im Nahbereich niederrheinischer Städte während des 13./14. Jahrhunderts, in: Patze (note 6), I, pp. 295-310.

[43] J.M. Wülfing, Grundherrschaft und städtische Wirtschaft am Beispiel Lübecks, in: Patze (note 6), I, pp. 498-502; W. Eikenberg, *Das Handelshaus der Runtinger zu Regensburg*, Göttingen 1976, pp. 261-270.

[44] Cf. Kirchner (note 29), p. 13.

[45] Irsigler (note 42).

over Germany, with the earliest texts dating from the late XIth and early XIIth centuries,[46] the most numerous references from the XIIIth-XVth centuries, and the latest from the XVIIth-XVIIIth centuries.[47] True, most of them state nothing but the bare fact that some piece of property owes a specified part of the annual produce, usually one third to one half. But, as already pointed out, the sole function of *Urbare* is to record the lord's rights, not his duties. These are found elsewhere. Wherever individual contracts or account books with detailed expenditures specify the terms of leases, there is an obligation of the lord corresponding to that of the peasant.[48]

Despite inevitable variations in so widespread a phenomenon, certain common features stand out. In arable husbandry *Teilpacht* was never universal. It seems to have been most prevalent in the XIIth-XIVth centuries and to have been employed largely on the great curiae let out for short periods, rather than on smaller holdings usually held in inheritance.[49] Again, it was on the former manorial centres still provided with some visible attributes of lordship, that considerable rights of direction and interference were preserved by way of *Teilbau* leases. Only in the XVth-XVIth centuries were they replaced in many areas by fixed rents, increasingly longer terms, and finally inheritability of tenures. On the properties of Cistercian abbeys where the transition from direct cultivation to peasant tenure was made only in the XIVth-XVth centuries, *Teilpacht* continued much longer.[50] Thus share-cropping in arable husbandry seems to have been connected mainly with the cessation of direct cultivation, a long process heavily dependent on the ongoing commitment of landlords to

[46] Wopfner (note 21), pp. 112, 117, 128; Kirchner (note 29), p. 13; Dollinger (note 9), p. 131.

[47] W. Abel, *Geschichte der deutschen Landwirtschaft vom frühen Mittelalter bis zum 19. Jahrhundert*, 3rd ed., Stuttgart 1978, pp. 201, 250-255.

[48] Contracts: HStAMünchen, Passau-St. Nikola Lit. 7 f. 15; Chmel, Niederaltaich (note 22) 5, pp. 115, 216; 6, p. 427; Eikenberg, *Regensburg* (note 43); R. Braun, *Das Benediktinerkloster Michelsberg 1015-1525*, Kulmbach 1978, pp. 100, 102-104; M. Schaab, Die Grundherrschaft der südwestdeutschen Zisterzienserklöster, in: Patze (note 6), II, p. 77f.; W. Rösener, Grundherrschaften des Adels in Südwestdeutschland, ibid. II, p. 127f.; Th. Zotz, Grafen von Leiningen, ibid. II, pp. 196f., 201-205; Irsigler (note 42), p. 303f.; W. Janssen, Kölner Erzbischöfe, ibid. I, p. 335f.; Wopfner (note 21), pp. 194-197 (lower Rhine); Franz, *Quellen* (note 24), p. 366 (lower Rhine); Wülfing, Lübeck (note 43), p. 498f. For account-books see Eikenberg, *Regensburg* (note 43); E. Wisplinghoff, Untersuchungen zur Wirtschafts— und Besitzgeschichte der Benediktinerabtei Brauweiler bei Köln, *Jahrbuch des Kölner Geschichtsvereins* 43(1971), pp. 146-152, 164f., and my forthcoming study on the economy of Bavarian monasteries.

[49] Cf. the case studies of Ph. Dollinger, Les transformations du regime domanial en Bavière au XIIIe siècle d'après deux censiers de l'abbaye de Baumburg, *Le Moyen Âge* 56(1950), pp. 294-298, and Zotz (note 48), pp. 201-205.

[50] Schaab (note 48), p. 66.

provide peasant tenures with the means of production. In this sense, throughout most of Germany, the function of *Teilpacht* was similar to that of *Gericht* in the south of the country. Indeed, we have found no instance of a homestead featuring both institutions at one and the same time, although lords might employ both on different parts of their property.

In other branches of agriculture *Teilpacht* assumed an even more critical importance. It made its earliest appearance in viticulture,[51] that branch of agriculture most dependent on constant and heavy inputs of labour and capital.[52] There it remained long the most prevalent type of lease, to be replaced by less onerous forms of tenure only in the XVIIth-XVIIIth centuries. The lord's contribution included not only grape-vines, props, manure, and outlays for the gathering of the vintage, but also grain liveries and cash advances for the sustenance of the vine-growers.[53] These extensive needs of the viticulturer are explained not only by the high cost of viticulture, but also by its vulnerability to bad seasons and its close dependence on the market. Apparently the peasant economy of the later Middle Ages and early modern period was incapable of conducting this branch of agriculture on its own.

A similar situation is found in the area of animal husbandry. Except for the Alpine regions, old-settled Germany by and large lacked the necessary space for pastoral husbandry. The peasant homestead with its meagre meadows [54] was unable to graze any sizable number of beasts. Nor could it rear the breeding animals necessary for proper stock-raising, as we see from the clauses in manorial law obliging the lord to provide breeding stock of all sorts for the use of the villagers.[55] With the marked expansion of animal husbandry in the XIVth-XVth centuries, another and more widespread solution was found in arrangements based on the principle of *Teilpacht*.[56] These short-term leases of livestock,

[51] See the references in Wopfner and Kirchner (note 46) and Wisplinghoff (note 48), p. 135.

[52] Cf. the expenses and works listed in L. Strebl, Mittelalterlicher Weinbau in den Rechnungsbüchern des Stiftes Klosterneuburg, *Unsere Heimat* 30 (Klosterneuburg 1959), pp. 11-21. In general see R. DION, *Histoire de la vigne et du vin en France*, Paris 1959, and FR. BASSERMANN-JORDAN, *Geschichte des Weinbaues*, 1923.

[53] E. NEUSCHELER, Die Klostergrundherrschaft Bebenhausen, *Württembergische Jahrbücher f. Statistik* 1928, p. 161f.; R. ZIRNGIBL (ed.), S. Emmeramische Kloster-Rechnung (1326, 1328), *Westenrieders Neue Beiträge* 1(1812), p. 257; 2(1818), p. 183; Germanisches Nationalmuseum Nürhberg, ST. Emmeramer Rechnungsbuch 1338, ff. 6, 13; F. BASTIAN, Das älteste Aldersbacher Rechnungsbuch, *Festgabe für K.A.v. Müller*, 1933, p. 33; K. LAMPRECHT, *Deutsches Wirtschaftsleben im Mittelalter*, III, 1886, p. 527f.

[54] See for instance the Urbar of Scheyern of 1400, which lists the abbey's arable and meadows by size: HStAMünchen, Scheyern Lit. 56, passim.

[55] Lamprecht (note 53), I, 1885, p. 541; Wopfner (note 21), pp. 224, 245, 325, 339; H. DUBLED, Les grandes tendances de l'exploitation au sein de la seigneurie rurale en Alsace du XIIIe au XVe siècle, *VSWG* 49(1962), pp. 73-75, 111-114; idem., L'administration de la seigneurie rurale en Alsace du XIIIe au XVe siècle, *VSWG* 52(1965), p. 446f.

[56] Abel (note 47), pp. 252-254.

cultivated meadows and grazing lands employed by rural and urban landlords up to the 18th century, are closely akin to the Italian "soccida" and French "gaisalle", which scholars have viewed as another avenue of urban investment in agriculture.[57] In Germany they developed out of the needs of rural society, as did the share-cropping arrangements prevalent in arable husbandry and viticulture. Of course, this is not to say that they could not have served as a vehicle for intensification and modernization, by channeling urban resources into agricultural production.[58]

Teilbau in Germany should thus be viewed primarily as a rural phenomenon. Like *Gericht*, it gave the lords a powerful tool for the organization of production in accordance with their particular needs and interests.[59] But above all, it is a further and more general indication of the basically underequipped and impoverished state of the medieval peasant economy and society. *Teilbau* like *Gericht* developed and spread as an answer to the problem of the uneven distribution of the means of production. As this imbalance was gradually corrected in the early centuries of the modern era, *Teilbau* disappeared from arable husbandry. However, like *Gericht* in the adverse circumstances of the Alps, *Teilpacht* continued, in the more demanding economic environment of viticulture and stockraising, to provide a solution to the problem of the provision of capital and capital goods, which the peasant economy was unable to generate on its own.

IV

Despite its overriding importance for such basic issues as levels of production and economic growth, the nature of investment, capital formation and capital goods in medieval agriculture has received surprisingly little attention. The significant exception is English rural historiography, which, building upon an unrivaled richness of sources, has provided a viable conceptual framework as well as hard facts.[60] Both Prof. Postan and Prof. Hilton, the former on the basis of his general analysis, the latter with the backing of precise figures from a sizable number of English estates, arrived at a pessimistic view of the level of

[57] DUBY, *Rural Economy*, p. 150f.

[58] For instance the case of sheep-rearing modernized in the vicinity of Augsburg, or the special cultures developed around Metz: R. KIESSLING, Bürgerlicher Besitz auf dem Land, in: P. FRIED (ed.), *Bayerisch-schwäbische Landesgeschichte an der Universität Augsburg*, Sigmaringen 1979, p. 135; J. SCHNEIDER, *La ville de Metz aux XIIIe et XIVe siècle*, Nancy 1950, p. 406f.

[59] Cf. Schaab (note 48), p. 70f.

[60] R. HILTON, Rent and Capital Formation in Feudal Society, *2nd International Conference of Economic History 1962*, vol. II, Paris 1965, pp. 33-68; M.M. POSTAN, Investment in Medieval Agriculture, *Journal of Economic History* 27(1967), pp. 576-587.

investment by landlords. On the estates checked, an investment "of not more than 5% of total income in buildings, stock and equipment seem to have been common in the thirteenth century...".[61] Outside England, similar or even lower figures have been noticed in the French Alps du Sud, Flanders and western Germany of the XIVth-XVth centuries.[62] As to capital formation by the peasant economy, the picture seems to have been even bleaker. What can be inferred from the English material points to such a level of impoverishment as to leave the vast majority of the peasantry with virtually no opportunities for saving.[63] Only in the XVth century, when more substantial peasants were finally able to augment their holdings and increase livestock did the peasant economy begin to contribute to capital formation.[64] Here again it is the late medieval agrarian depression which is seen as breaking the vicious circle of demographic pressure and technological stagnation, laying the groundwork for the early modern breakthrough achieved by additional investment and technical progress.

There is no reason to doubt the validity of this analysis as presented by Postan and Hilton. It corroborates, from a different angle, our conclusions as to the underequipped and impoverished state of the peasantry. Its one flaw lies in the clear-cut division made between investments in the landlord economy, i.e. in the working of demesnes, and investments in the peasant economy, i.e. in the peasants' holdings. This becomes evident when the conceptual framework underlying the analysis is applied to the German situation. As defined by Hilton, the constituents of capital include "(1) the tools and equipment of landlord and peasant economies; (2) buildings; (3) other permanent improvements such as enclosures, drainage etc.; (4) industrial premises and equipment; (5) mines and forges; (6) herds of livestock".[65] *Gericht* and *Teilbau*, when considered in these terms, thus clearly provided for constituents (1) and (6). Although Hilton excludes current expenditures on farming operations, for example on seed, from his definition of capital, we maintain that there are grounds for including them. As Postan and Hilton themselves point out, "it is as a rule very difficult to draw a line between the lord's outlays in the nature of investment and those in the nature of current disbursements on the running of the manor".[66] The problem is even thornier in the case of current expenditure on the peasants' homesteads, where investment in seed and harvesters' wages was

[61] Hilton, p. 53.

[62] G. Duby, La seigneurie et l'economie paysanne. Alpes du Sud, 1338, *Études rurales* 1(1961), p. 306; Nicholas (note 41), p. 36; H.P. Lachmann, Die Höfe der Katzenelnbogener in der Obergrafschaft, *Archiv f. hessische Geschichte und Altertumskunde* 32(1974), p. 178f.

[63] Postan, p. 585f.; Hilton, pp. 53-56.

[64] Postan, p. 586f.; Hilton, pp. 58-60.

[65] Hilton, p. 34.

[66] Postan, p. 578; Hilton, p. 44.

not one among several options, but rather a precondition for production. Through *Teilpacht* and *Gericht* lords met a good part of the peasants' needs for livestock and draught animals, tools and equipment, industrial premises such as mills not maintained directly on the manor, as well as part of seed and seasonal expenditure. The lords covered in most places even building expenses, as a matter of routine unconnected with the more elaborate arrangements of *Gericht* and *Teilpacht*.[67]

Teilpacht and Gericht are thus to be considered, together with more irregular forms of assistance, as institutionalized channels of lordly investment in the peasant economy. The needs leading to this engagement in the creation of capital goods have already been dealt with. What remains to be shown is its significance for the agricultural economy as a whole. In order to arrive at a realistic estimate of the overall capital formation carried by landlords, we must add, in the light of our findings, to demesne investments the outlays of londs on the peasants' holdings. In the few instances where figures are available, overall rates of investment much higher than the 5% mentioned — somewhere in the vicinity of 10-15% of total income from agriculture — become evident.[68] Given the manifold impediments to capital formation in medieval society,[69] this is quite an impressive rate. It is hard to see how lords, with so many more other claims to be satisfied out of their income, could have invested more.

Bearing these facts in mind, the question of low productivity, which is attested for the German as for other medieval agricultural economies,[70] assumes quite a different dimension. As even this low level of output depended on continuous investments by landlords, any reduction in landlord inputs must have caused farreaching repercussions. For instance, is it too farfetched a notion to suggest some connection between the crisis of income felt by many German landlords on the turn from the XIIIth to the XIVth century,[71] and the disastrous

[67] Instead of a mass of references cf. O. SIGG, "SPÄTMITTELALTERLICHE AGRARKRISE". ASPEKTE DER ZÜRCHER GESCHICHTE..., *Schweizerische Zeitschrift für Geschichte* 31(1981), pp. 123-133.

[68] Schaab, Südwestdeutsche Zisterzienserklöster (note 48), p. 77; Wisplinghoff, Brauweiler (note 48), p. 179f., and my own forthcoming study on Bavarian monasteries.

[69] Hilton, Postan, op.cit.

[70] The work on Germany is still behind research done on northwestern Europe: H. van der Wee-E. van Cauwenberghe, *Productivity of Land and Agricultural Innovation in the Low Countries (1250-1800)*, Louvain 1978. But see Abel (note 47), pp. 106-109; W. ACHILLES, Die Getreidewirtschaft der Kirche zu Hedeper und Bornum, *ZAA* 8(1960), pp. 138-158; idem., Überlegungen zum Einkommen der Bauern im späten Mittelalter, *ZAA* 31(1983), pp. 5-26.

[71] R. SABLONIER, *Adel in Wandel. Eine Untersuchung zur sozialen Situation des ostschweizerischen Adels um 1300*, Göttingen 1979, pp. 224-232. See also the case studies by E. WISPLINGHOFF, Brauweiler (note 48); idem., Beiträge zur Wirtschaftsgeschichte der Abtei Siegburg, *Rheinische Vierteljahrsblätter* 33(1969), pp. 78-138; H.P. SATTLER, Die Ritterschaft der Ortenau in der spätmittelalterlichen Wirtschaftskrise, *Die Ortenau* 42, 44-46 (1962, 1964-1966).

returns of agriculture in the first decades of the XIVth century, for which bad harvests have been commonly held as solely responsible? Considering the investments necessary to keep both landlord and peasant production going, the margin between incomes and outlays was just too small to leave room for a significant accumulation of capital. In other words, agricultural society as a whole does not seem to have been able, up to the end of the Middle Ages, to muster the resources needed to advance beyond the level of subsistence economy.

V

All this applies to conditions in Germany. Is there any evidence that a similar situation prevailed in the rest of Europe? It may be argued that the basic framework existed in every agricultural system passing from a landlord to a peasant economy. Indications of an impoverished and underequipped peasantry abound in the literature. Indeed, the spread of southern European *métayage* and *mezzadria* may be linked directly to the miserable state of the peasantry in these regions where it was practised.[72] The diffusion of share-cropping arrangements in the lands farther north has already been mentioned.

Other forms of letting land together with all or part of the inventory are well attested.[73] The understocking of peasant tenures is a well-known fact of English peasant life,[74] and livestock leases were much in use in rural Flanders, France and Italy. Even a minor detail like the widespread covering of building expenses is also found in England, where it was viewed by Hilton as an indication of a rise in the rate of investment by lords.[75] This rise is attributed to the landlords' distress during the crisis of the late XIVth and the XVth centuries. In England this crisis brought on the transition from demesne to peasant production, a transition which, on the continent, had long before prompted the pronounced forms of landlord assistance discussed in this paper. In Hilton's own words, "the creation of estate capital was as much the result of peasant demand as of landowners' inclinations".[76] Finally, let us consider the low rate of investment by landlords. As recently pointed out, on small English manors where the demesne was the major component and the lords had little authority over

[72] DUBY, *Rural Economy*, p. 327.

[73] Nicholas (note 41), p. 336; M. MATE, The farming out of manors: a new look at the evidence from Canterbury Cathedral Priory, *Journal of Medieval History* 9(1983), p. 339.

[74] M. POSTAN, Village Livestock in the Thirteenth Century, *Economic History Review* 2nd ser. XV (1962), reprinted in idem., *Essays on Medieval Agriculture and General Problems of the Medieval Economy*, 1973, pp. 214-248.

[75] Hilton (note 60), pp. 48-52.

[76] Hilton (note 60), p. 52.

adjoining villages, rates of investment have been found to be considerably higher than on great manors with numerous peasant tenancies.[77] In other words, in England, whenever landlords were not burdened with the usual obligations towards their tenants, they could and would direct a higher percentage of their income toward capital formation. Indeed, it is the smaller cohesive estate and holding, which was for a time to be in the forefront of agricultural progress.

One might also speculate whether the early lead of modern English agriculture is not, in some way, related to the fact that, having passed from demesne to peasant production so much later than the continent, the landlords' capital resources were less exhausted by the demands of the peasant economy.

Most of the factors constituting the background and problems of German agricultural economy discussed in this paper, were present to some degree in the other rural societies of Europe. However, the question as to the means adopted in these societies to deal with such problems, can hardly be determined within the scope of this paper. The following questions, which come to mind when attempting to judge the implications of our findings, are thus first and foremost adressed to German conditions, although some parallels outside Germany have already been indicated.

Bearing in mind the constraints of capital formation in general, and of the contribution of the landlord in particular, we should perhaps take a more tolerant view of the backwardness and inflexibility of which medieval agriculture has been rightly accused.

Perhaps, too, we ought to re-examine the concept of the "late medieval agricultural crisis". During this period considerable parts of the peasantry, mainly the ones engaged in arably husbandry, left the tutelage of lordly assistance and control.[78] This would imply that by then they were able to conduct their affairs on their own, freeing landlords from the need for constant investments in the peasant economy. It seems that the results of this process are clearly visible in the period of economic growth which followed the late medieval centuries.

Turning to social relations, one wonders whether the concept of "Alpine freedom" evoked for the Swiss peasants as well as the Tyrolians of the German Peasants' War is really applicable to the Alpine peasantry subject for such a long time to such stringent economic control, as has been demonstrated above.

[77] R.H. Britnell, Minor Landlords in England and Medieval Agrarian Capitalism, *Past & Present* 89(1980), pp. 14-18. Cf. Also the very similar situation described by F. Irsigler, Adelige Wirtschaftsführung im Spätmittelalter. Erträge und Investitionen im Drachenfelser Ländchen 1458-63, *Festschrift H. Kellenbenz,* I, Stuttgart 1978, pp. 455-468.

[78] For the legal and institutional aspects of this process see P. Blickle, Grundherrschaft und Agrarverfassungsvertrag, in: Patze (note 6), I, pp. 241-261.

Finally, we would do well to avoid rash judgements of the landlord of the central and late Middle Ages. Far from becoming a "rentier-landlord", his involvement in peasant affairs gave new meaning to the old protective and, at the same time, possessive attributes of lordship — "huld und munt", "tuitio et warrantio". Deeply influencing the countryside in many more ways than the purely economic one, the German "Herr" was to remain a most decisive factor in the agrarian society of the ancien régime.

13

An Industrial Revolution of the Thirteenth Century[1]

E.M. Carus-Wilson

IT has been commonly supposed that the thirteenth century witnessed a decline in the nascent cloth industry of England, a decline which was only to be checked and converted into renewed advance and yet more spectacular progress under the vigorous patronage of Edward III. We read, for instance, of the "impoverished state" of the industry "on the eve of the great experiment"; of how "something was wrong with the industry, and if it was to be given fresh life something must be done."[2] Such a conception of arrested growth and even of decay is not, however, borne out by a close investigation of the sources. On the contrary, they reveal rather the expansion and rapid development of the industry up to the eve of the accession of Edward III. The reason for this discrepancy is not that the sources themselves have been misinterpreted, but that only one group of them, the urban records, has been hitherto explored in this connection. It has been too readily assumed that the history of industry in England at this time was to be found in the history of her towns and their gilds, and that symptoms of decline evident here signified a decline in the industry as a whole. In reality, however, rural records also throw a flood of light on the industrial history of the time, and when they are considered in conjunction with those of the towns it becomes apparent that the century was one of striking progress industrially, though of equally striking change and upheaval. It witnessed, in fact, an industrial revolution due to scientific discoveries and changes in technique; a revolution which brought poverty, unemployment and discontent to certain old centres of the industry, but wealth, opportunity and prosperity to the country as a whole, and which was destined to alter the face of medieval England.

In the early Middle Ages the various processes of cloth-making were all strictly "handcrafts." The chief processes, apart from dyeing and finishing, were four. First the wool was carded or combed by hand; then it was spun on the rock or distaff. Next the yarn thus prepared was woven on a loom worked by hand and foot, and finally the loose "web" thus made was fulled by hand

[1] Owing to war conditions it has proved impossible to check and to complete all the references in this article, particularly those to MS. sources in the custody of the Public Record Office.

[2] E. Lipson, *The History of the English Woollen and Worsted Industries* (1921), p. 11; L. F. Salzman, *English Industries of the Middle Ages* (1923), p. 203.

or foot. The process of fulling, that is to say, of beating or compressing the cloth in water, served first of all to shrink the cloth, reducing it in width by anything from a fifth to a half, and in length to a corresponding extent.[1] This so increased the density and weight per unit of length as to give it much greater resistance to weather and wear. Secondly, it served to " felt " the cloth, so inextricably entangling the fibres that the pattern of the weaving often ceased to be visible. This not only gave the cloth greater fabric strength, but also a smoother and softer surface, and it was an essential preliminary to the finishing processes of raising and shearing applied to the finer cloths. In addition to shrinking and felting the cloth, making it close and firm, the fulling process also scoured it and cleansed it, with the aid of various detergents[2] such as fuller's earth, removing especially the oil with which the wool had been impregnated before spinning. Now the mechanising of the first three cloth-making processes during the eighteenth and nineteenth centuries is a commonplace of history, but the mechanising of the fourth during the thirteenth century, though it gave rise to an industrial revolution not less remarkable, has attracted scarcely any attention. It is with this that the present article proposes to deal.

Three primitive methods of fulling " by might and strength of man," without any mechanism, have been most commonly used in western Europe : beating with the feet, with the hands, or with clubs wielded by hand. Most suited to long heavy broadcloths is some method of fulling by foot such as is vividly portrayed in the paintings on the piers of the *fullonica* at Pompeii, and in those of the house of the Vettii there. In these we can see the fuller at work, standing almost naked in a trough, trampling the cloth under foot, while his hands rest on low side walls by which he can support and raise himself. Traces of what may have been fulleries such as these in Roman Britain have been revealed in three places : at Titsey and Darenth in Kent, and at Chedworth in Gloucestershire. Here have been found very similar troughs, circular in form, with low side walls and drainage facilities.[3] Their close proximity, in

[1] For the purpose and nature of fulling, see J. and J. C. Schofield, *The Finishing of Wool Goods* (1935), and J. Schofield, *The Science and Practice of Scouring and Milling*. The medieval assize of cloth sometimes quoted a different standard for cloth " watered" and cloth " unwatered," *e.g.* Statute 11 Henry VI, c. 9.

[2] Cf. G. Espinas, " Essai sur la Technique de l'Industrie Textile à Douai aux xiiie et xive siècles." *Mémoires de la Société nationale des Antiquaires de France*, t. LXVIII (1909), p. 42.

[3] *Archæologia*, vol. LIX (1904), G. E. Fox, " Notes on some probable traces of Roman Fulling in Britain," pp. 208-9 ; *Guide to Chedworth Roman Villa* (1926), pp. 12-13.

each case, to beds of fuller's earth and to what later became flourishing centres of the industry, would seem to lend some support to the theory that they were fulleries, though the matter cannot be considered as finally determined. From Roman Gaul we have an actual representation of a fuller at work in a trough, carved on the " fuller's tomb " at Sens.[1] So for a thousand years and more fullers trod the cloth underfoot, as indeed they have long continued to do in outlying parts, such as the Hebrides, untouched by the mechanical inventions of the thirteenth or of the eighteenth centuries. The early fourteenth century ordinances of the fullers' gilds both at Lincoln and at Bristol mention this working " in the trough,"[2] and later on in *Piers Plowman* we read of cloth that is " fulled under fote."[3]

Sometimes hands were used instead of, or in addition to, feet. A visitor to Skye in 1774 thus described the Luaghad, or fulling of cloth, there : " Twelve or fourteen women, divided into equal numbers, sit down on each side of a long board ribbed lengthways, placing the cloth on it : first they begin to work it backwards and forwards with their hands, singing at the same time as at the quern : when they have tired their hands, every female uses her feet for the same purpose, and six or seven pairs of naked feet are in the most violent agitation, working one against the other : as by this time they grow very earnest in their labours, the fury of the song rises ; at length it arrives to such a pitch that without breach of charity you would imagine a troop of female demoniacs to have been assembled."[4]

Hand fulling alone, or fulling with clubs wielded by hand, has probably always been used for smaller articles. Indeed methods of fulling even in the same locality seem commonly to have varied according to the size and character of the articles to be fulled. A traveller to Iceland in 1814-15 thus describes two different methods in vogue there : " Both ends being knocked out of a barrel, it is filled with articles to be fulled, when it is laid on the side, and two men lie down on their backs, one at either end, with their feet in the barrel, and literally *walk* the cloth, by kicking it against each other. Smaller articles they full by placing them between their knees and breast, and then moving backwards and forwards with

[1] C. Roach-Smith, *Collectanea Antiqua*, vol. V (1861), plate XX, fig. 1.

[2] Toulmin Smith, *English Gilds* (1870), p. 180, " *in alveo* " ; *Little Red Book of Bristol*, ed. F. B. Bickley (1900), vol. II, p. 12, " *ouveraunt en le stok.*"

[3] *Piers Plowman* (B), XV, 445. Angus Pirie, a skilled weaver of Dornoch, used to full his cloth by foot in a trough but has given up this method as too strenuous and too chilling now that he is old.

[4] Quoted in E. Lipson, *History of the English Woollen and Worsted Industries* (1921), p. 139.

the body, turning them always with their hands till ready. This accounts for the very awkward motion which the Icelanders almost always fall into when sitting, and from which many of them cannot refrain even in church."[1] In France in the eighteenth century fulling by hand was frequently used for hosiery, and fulling with clubs wielded by hand for hats and caps.[2] We may infer a similar use of clubs in Roman times from the account of the martyrdom of Saint James the Less, written in the second century: "*Quidam autem ex eis, accepto fuste ex officina fullonis, quo comprimebat vestes, valide infligit ejus capiti.*"[3] For this reason the fuller's club became the emblem of St. James and is to be seen in many medieval representations of him, as for instance in the east window of Gloucester Cathedral, on the rood screen at Ranworth, on one of the stall panels at Blythburgh, and on the font at Stalham.[4]

In medieval records it is not easy to distinguish this method of using clubs from that of fulling by hand alone, since both could be described as " fulling by hand " in distinction to " fulling by foot." At any rate it seems that in England one or other of these methods of hand fulling was commonly used for hats and caps. Thus in London long after mechanical fulling had commonly been adopted for broadcloths, the Hurers successfully petitioned against this method being allowed for hats and caps, and ordinances were passed to this effect in 1376;[5] several citizens were fined for breach of the ordinance and, during the hearing of a case against one John Godefray, a jury of cappers and hatters declared that caps could not and ought not to be fulled under the feet or in any other way than by the hands of men.[6] It is clear that the hatters and cappers were as much opposed to fulling by foot as to mechanical fulling; thus again in 1404 they petitioned that their work should not be fulled in mills *or by feet*, but only by the hands of men, and again offending citizens were punished.[7] Most probably hand fulling was reserved for small articles such as hats and caps, made usually of felt, while the long, heavy broadcloths which came to form the staple of the English export industry were fulled by foot.

[1] E. Henderson, *Iceland* (Edinburgh, 1818), vol. I, p. 365.

[2] Savary des Bruslons, *Dictionnaire Universel de Commerce*, vol. II, p. 526; Postlethwayt, *Universal Dictionary of Trade and Commerce* (4th edition, 1774): " Fulling."

[3] *Acta Sanctorum*, vol. XIV, p. 35.

[4] For other examples, see C. Cahier, *Caractéristiques des Saints dans l'art populaire* (1867), p. 547; F. C. Husenbeth, *Emblems of Saints*, 3rd edition, ed. A. Jessopp (1882), p. 110.

[5] H. T. Riley, *Memorials of London*, p. 400.

[6] A. H. Thomas, *Calendar of Plea and Memoranda Rolls, 1364-1381*, pp. 230, 233; Riley, *ut supra*, p. 529. [7] Riley, *ut supra*, p. 667.

Such were the primitive methods of fulling in use when the English woollen industry was first established. Most important of them is fulling by foot, since this method was applied to the long, heavy broadcloth which came to form the staple of the English export industry.

The mechanical method of fulling invented during the Middle Ages, and in use for many centuries, was evolved from the primitive method of fulling by foot. The invention was a twofold one. In the first place the action of the two feet was replaced by that of two wooden hammers, alternately raised and dropped on the cloth as it lay in the trough, and controlled probably by a revolving drum on the tilt- or lift-hammer system.[1] In the second place this revolving drum was attached to the spindle of a water-wheel, and this supplied the motive power. Thus, by a simple contrivance, water power was made to replace human labour, and a series of hammers could be set to work with but one man standing by to watch the cloth and see that it was kept properly moving in the trough. The whole was then spoken of as a *molendinum fullericum*, or " fulling mill,"[2] since, though it was not strictly a mill (*molendinum*) in that it did not grind (*molere*), it bore a resemblance in one part of its mechanism to the water corn mill. Indeed the building itself, down by the water, with its leet and its revolving wheel, would be difficult to distinguish externally from a corn mill. Henceforth, just as there had hitherto been a distinction in rentals, surveys, etc., between the windmill, the watermill and the horse-mill (*molendinum ventricum*, *molendinum aquaticum* and *molendinum ad equos*), so now there appears a further distinction between the water *corn* mill and the water *fulling* mill (*molendinum aquaticum blaericum* and *molendinum aquaticum fullericum*).

The question now arises as to the date of the invention of the water fulling mill. This would seem impossible to fix with any certainty. M. Bloch asserts that there was a fulling mill at Grenoble " about 1050,"[3] but the actual evidence does not seem to support

[1] This revolving drum could be turned by hand, and such a device may still be seen in use in parts of Scotland to-day, though it is very heavy to work.

[2] While " fulling mill " is the most widely used term, certain parts of England had their own local terms, derived from words of different origins describing the same fulling process. Thus in place of " full," " fuller," " fulling mill," we find " tuck," " tucker," " tucking mill " in the west country, especially in Cornwall, Devon and Somerset; and " walk," " walker," " walking mill " (or " walkmill ") in the north, especially in the Lake District, while in Wales a fulling mill becomes a " pandy." Many of the sites of these ancient mills can be identified by the fact that they have one or other of these expressions attached to them.

[3] *Annales d'histoire Économique et Sociale*, No. 36, Nov. 1935, M. Bloch, " Avènement et conquêtes du moulin à eau," p. 543.

his conclusion. The charter to which he refers speaks of certain rights "*in unum quodque molendinum, quando edificatur, et in bateorium, similiter quando edificatur.*"[1] Now a *bateorium, battorium, batatorium* or *baptitorium* is certainly a place where beating or hammering is carried on, but we are not justified in assuming that this beating was done by water power, or that it was necessarily the beating of cloth. Ducange defines *Bateria* as, "*Ars tundendi pannos, terendi cortices et alia similia facienda*, and in a charter quoted by him there are enumerated "*furnos, torcularia, molendina, baptitoria, et fullonos.*" Clearly, then, a *baptitorium* or *bateorium* is not even synonymous with a fullery, much less with a mechanical fulling *mill*, and there is as yet no evidence that the fulling mill was known on the continent in the eleventh century. In England, at any rate, it seems as though water fulling mills were introduced in the latter part of the twelfth century. The earliest reference to one so far discovered is that in the survey of the Templars' lands made in 1185. This mentions a "*molendinum fulerez*" at Newsham in Yorkshire and another, built by the Templars themselves, at Barton, close to Temple Guiting, in the Cotswolds.[2] Four years later a charter to the Abbey of Stanley in Wilts speaks of the "*molendinum monachorum fullericum.*"[3] The absence so far of any earlier references to fulling mills does not, of course, prove their non-existence, and how far the lack of other evidence for the twelfth and earlier centuries is due to lack of documents comparable to those of later centuries it is impossible to say. But a significant change in nomenclature points also to the change having been introduced in the late twelfth century. For from the opening of the thirteenth century not only do references to such mills increase, but so also does the use of the phrase *corn* mill in distinction to *fulling* mill, while the word *fullonia* disappears, giving place to *molendinum fullericum*. Certainly the fulling mill cannot have been at all widely used until the thirteenth century, and it is in the late thirteenth century that we come across the first evidence of opposition to its use on the part of the handworkers.

The origin of the invention is even more obscure than its date. We know neither in what country, nor by whom, water power

[1] *Cartulaires de l'Église Cathédrale de Grenoble*, ed. M. J. Marion (Paris, 1869), p. 119.

[2] Dugdale, *Monasticon* (1661), vol. II, p. 540; B. A. Lees, *Records of the Templars in England in the Twelfth Century* (1935), pp. ccxiii, 50, 127, cxxv. There was also a derelict fulling mill at Witham, Essex, in 1308, and this may, it is suggested, represent the " mill " in the survey of 1185, *ibid.* p. lxxix.

[3] W. de G. Birch, *Collections towards the history of the Cistercian Abbey of Stanley, Wilts*, p. 43, quoting Harleian MS. 84, f. 273b; see also pp. 15, 17, 33, for later references.

was first applied to fulling, nor whether the idea spread from a common source or was evolved independently in different regions. It is conceivable that the Templars may have introduced the fulling mill into England. At any rate the religious orders were among the first to take advantage of it and to develop its possibilities. In monastic cartularies many early references, not all of which can be precisely dated, are to be found to fulling mills. About the year 1200 the Abbey of Winchcomb possessed a fulling mill at "Clively," and when the Abbot made a grant of another mill it was on condition that it should not be converted into a fulling mill to compete with his own.[1] The monks of Evesham held a fullers[2] mill (*molendinum fullonum*) at Bourton-on-the-Water in Gloucestershire in 1206;[2] the Augustinian friary of St. John the Baptist at Ludlow had one before 1221, probably on the Teme;[3] Newminster had one on the Wansbeck very early in its history;[4] St. Albans had established one by 1274,[5] and in an extent of the Abbey of Kirkstall of 16 Edward I a fulling mill is mentioned as well as a tanning mill.[6]

Nor were the great episcopal estates behind the monastic ones. The earliest Pipe Roll of the Bishop of Winchester (1208-9) shows that he then possessed four fulling mills (described as "*fulleraticum*" and "*foleraticum*"): at Waltham, Sutton, Brightwell and New Alresford; mills to which Dr. Hubert Hall called attention as "perhaps the earliest fulling mills in England of which we have mention."[7] Later rolls show the Bishop possessed of a fulling mill at Downton in Wiltshire by 1215, of two in Oxfordshire, at Witney, by 1223, and of one in Somerset, at Taunton, by 1224.[8] The Bishop of Bath owned a fulling mill at Kidderminster in 1293,[9] while early in the following century the Bishop of Exeter agreed to join with the Mayor and Commonalty of Barnstaple in erecting mills, including fulling mills, on the river which divided their property.[10]

[1] *Monasterium Beatae Mariae Virginis et Sancti Cenhelmi: Landboc*, ed. D. Royce, I, p. 195. [2] *Chronicle of Evesham* (Rolls Series), p. 213.

[3] British Museum, Harleian MS. 6690, f. 89 ff., quoted in T. Wright, *History of Ludlow* (1852), p. 98. [4] *Newminster Cartulary* (Surtees Society, vol. 66, 1878), p. 3.

[5] *Walsingham, Gesta Abbatum Monasterii Sancti Albani* (Rolls Series), ed. H. T. Riley, vol. I, p. 410 ff. [6] P.R.O. Ancient Extents 86 (1).

[7] *Pipe Roll of the Bishop of Winchester*, ed. Hubert Hall (1903), pp. xxvii, 1, 13, 41, 61.

[8] P.R.O. Ecclesiastical Commission, Various, II, 159273, 159278 ff. References given by Miss M. Wretts-Smith.

[9] *Inquisitions Post Mortem for the County of Worcestershire*, edited for the Worcester Historical Society by J. W. Willis Bund (1894), pt. I, p. 43; *Cal. Inquisitions Post Mortem*, vol. III, p. 45 (21 Edward I).

[10] *Reprint of the Barnstaple Records*, ed. J. A. Chanter and T. Wainwright (1900), I, p. 110, no. xx.

It must not, however, be assumed that, since many of the earliest surviving references are to mills on monastic and ecclesiastical estates, laymen lagged behind. Indeed in the monastic cartularies themselves we get glimpses of lay owners of fulling mills, for such mills often happened to be part of endowments bestowed by laymen upon a monastery. About the year 1200, for instance, Robert of Seckworth owned two "myllis fuleree" in Seckworth and granted the tithes of them to the nunnery of Godstow.[1] Godstow also claimed tithes in 1235 of the mill called "pannmylle" (probably a "cloth mill") at Wycombe.[2] Again, when Peter Undergod founded the hospital of St. John the Baptist near the bridge over the Teme at Ludlow, he endowed it, *inter alia*, with the fulling mill which he had bought from Gilbert de Lacy.[3]

The fulling mills on lay estates for which most early records survive are, not unnaturally, those of the king himself. One of the first royal mills was that near Marlborough, at Elcot. This was in existence in the reign of John and was rebuilt by the king's orders in 1237. The task was entrusted to William de Pretsch and Vincent Carpentar', who had workmen under them, and cost altogether £4 17s. 4d. Most of this money was spent on felling and carting timber from Savernake forest; the rest on remaking the mill-pond, the weir, the mill-wheel and its enclosure, the mill-race and also the "*flagella et baterella*"—probably the hammers for beating the cloth.[4] In 1251 Henry III ordered a fulling mill to be built in his park at Guildford;[5] the royal manor of Steèple Langford in Wilts had one in 1294,[6] and by the beginning of the following century there was a royal fulling mill in the West Riding at Knaresborough.[7]

When we turn to trace fulling mills on estates other than monastic, episcopal or royal, there is, unfortunately, no comparable evidence available. The sources are on the whole later in date and different in character. The mandates and instructions on Royal Close Rolls and Liberate Rolls have, for instance, no parallel, and in place of the twelfth and early thirteenth century monastic cartularies we have only scattered deeds, scarcely ever so early in date. Nor are there any early consecutive series of manorial

[1] *Register of Godstow Nunnery* (Early English Text Society), vol. I, p. 43.

[2] *Ibid.*, p. 89. [3] *History of Ludlow, ut supra*, p. 98.

[4] *Calendar of Liberate Rolls*, I, p. 278; *Great Roll of the Pipe, 1241-2*, p. 175; *Rott. Litt. Claus.* (Record Commission), II, p. 23.

[5] *Calendar of Liberate Rolls*, III, p. 376; T. H. Turner, *Domestic Architecture in England*, I (1851), p. 233, II (1853), p. 149.

[6] P.R.O. Rentals and Surveys, General Series, portf. 16, no. 66.

[7] *Calendar of Close Rolls*, 1302-7, p. 35.

accounts such as those enrolled on the great pipe rolls of the Bishop of Winchester or on the royal pipe rolls, but only separate accounts, surviving in fragments. The principal sources are threefold: first the Inquisitions Post Mortem taken on the death of a supposed tenant-in-chief for the information of the king; secondly, Rentals and Custumals of individual manors drawn up for the information of the lord of the manor and his officials; and, thirdly, year to year Accounts kept of the administration of such manors and records of their Courts. These three sources are extensive from the latter part of the thirteenth century, though not until then. The first is the most accessible in print, through the *Calendars of Inquisitions Post Mortem*, but these are deceptive for the present investigation since they do not always reproduce the detailed extents in which the fulling mills are usually to be found. In these printed calendars, for instance, no fulling mills appear for Wiltshire before the reign of Edward III, but the more detailed *Abstracts of Wiltshire Inquisitions Post-Mortem* (1242-1326) give five.[1] Hence, for counties where we have no such thorough survey, the originals must constantly be consulted. It must further be remembered that these inquisitions may not always record the state of affairs at the moment that the return was actually made; they may reproduce earlier surveys. Thus when a fulling mill appears we can only be certain that it existed either at that or at an earlier date. Nor do Rentals and Custumals always give precise dates; often their date can only be inferred from their handwriting, and even then it is possible that they are sometimes copies of earlier surveys. None of these sources are sufficiently comprehensive to form any basis for statistical analysis, but from them and other records we can at least gain an impression of the rapid extension of the fulling mill during the thirteenth century and its widespread distribution at the beginning of the fourteenth century. And it must be borne in mind that the mills of which record has survived can be only a small proportion of the total, and that the present investigation cannot claim in any way to be exhaustive.[2]

The accompanying table attempts to set out geographically the evidence which has so far come to light as to the distribution of fulling mills in England before the reign of Edward III. All the mills noted here date from the thirteenth or early fourteenth centuries (before 1327), except for the three already mentioned as

[1] *Abstracts of Wiltshire Inquisitions Post Mortem*, ed. E. A. Fry, vol. I (1242-1326) (1908), pp. 119, 227, 246, 257, 350.

[2] Further evidence is constantly coming to light, and collections of local deeds still have much to yield. The writer would welcome information as to other early mills than those listed below.

dating from the late twelfth century; most of them belong to the reigns of Edward I or Edward II.[1]

The Pennines		**The Lake District**	
Yorkshire: West Riding		Kendal	P.R.O. Assize Roll, 979, m. 2 (40 Hen. III)
Almondbury	M.A., 29/2 (32-3 Ed. I); 1145/21 (Ed. [II])	Millom	I.P.M., Ed. II, 50
Alverthorpe	Yorks Archæological Soc., Record Series, XXIX, *Wakefield Court Rolls*, I, 250 (1296)	Penrith	M.A., 824/28 ff. (1 Ed. I ff.)
Bradford	M.A., 29/2, 1145/21	Sowerby	*Ibid.*
Castleford	M.A., 1145/21	Staveley	Lancs & Cheshire Record Soc., vol. 54, *Lancs Inquests, Extents and Feudal Aids*, II, 148
Kirkstall	Anc. Ext., 86 (1)	**The Midlands**	
Knaresboro'	*Supra*, p. 46	*Derbyshire*	
Leeds	M.A., 1145/21	Hartington	*Cal. I.P.M.*, III, 300 (26 Ed. I); M.A., 29/3 (7-8 Ed. II)
Newsham	*Supra*, p. 44	Wirksworth	*Cal. I.P.M.*, III, 291 (25 Ed. I); M.A., 29/3
Rothwell	M.A., 29/2, 1145/21	*Nottinghamshire*	
Thorpe Arch	*Cal. I.P.M.*, IV, 25 (29 Ed. I)	Warsop	*Notts I.P.M.*, 128 (1268)
Wakefield	*Wakefield, ut supra*, I, 176, 252 (1277, 1296); II, 185 (1316)	*Northamptonshire*	
North Riding		Wellingboro'	
Burton Constable	I.P.M., Ed. II, 63	*Staffordshire*	
Masham	*Cal. C.R.*, 1302-7, 164	Barton	M.A., 29/3 (7-8 Ed. II)
Lancashire		Himley	*Cal. I.P.M.*, VI, 470 (20 Ed. II)
Burnley	Chetham Soc., CXII, *Two Compoti of the Lancs and Cheshire Manors of Henry de Lacy, 24 and 33 Ed. I*, 4, 8, 15, 16	Rolleston	M.A., 29/3
Colne	*Ibid.*	*Worcestershire*	
Manchester	*Ibid.*, p. xxii	Hartlebury	M.A., 1143/18 (30-1 Ed. I)
Wyresdale	I.P.M., Ed. II, 69	Kidderminster	*Worc. I.P.M.*, I, 43 (1293); *Cal. I.P.M.*, III, 45
The Lake District		Mitton	J. R. Burton, *Kidderminster*, 21
Applethwaite (Windermere)	I.P.M., Ed. II, 81	Overbury (*see* Cotswolds)	
Brampton	*Cal. I.P.M.*, III, 184 (23 Ed. I)	Shelsley (*see* Welsh Marches)	
Carleton	M.A., 824/28 ff. (1 Ed. I ff.)	**The Welsh Marches**	
Carlisle	C. Gross, *Gild Merchant*, II, 39	Alvington	*Tax. Eccl.*, p. 172
Clifton	*Cal. I.P.M.*, III, 432 (28 Ed. I)	Caerleon	M.A. 1202/6 ff. (7 Ed. II, ff.)
Cockermouth	Surtees Soc., CXXVI, *Register of St. Bees*, 48, 449 (27 Ed. I); R. & S., 730; M.A., 460/24	Ludlow	T. Wright, *Ludlow*, 98; Brit. Mus. Harl. MS., 6690 f., 89 ff.
Crosthwaite	I.P.M., Ed. I, 32 Ed. II, 81[1]	Monmouth	*Tax. Eccl.*, 172
Dacre	I.P.M., Ed. II, 82	Painscastle	I.P.M., Ed. II, 50
Egremont	*Cal. C.R., 1288-96*, 402	Shelsley	*Worc. I.P.M.*, II, 7
Embleton	I.P.M., Ed. II, 75	Talgarth	*Cal. C.R.*, 1307-13, 200.
Glassonby	I.P.M., Ed. II, 76	Usk	M.A., 1202/6 ff. (7 Ed. II ff.)
Grasmere	I.P.M., Ed. I, 5, 32; Ed. II, 81[2]	Wilton	I.P.M., Ed. II, 82
Greenriggs	I.P.M., Ed. II, 17	**The West of England**	
Grizedale	I.P.M., Ed. II, 82	*Cornwall*	
		Heskyn	*E.C.H.*, 207 (1307)
		Lawhitton	*Mon. Ex.*, 429 (1308)

[1] For abbreviations used in the references, see list at end of article.

The West of England	
Legha in Buryan	*E.C.H.*, 208, n. 8 (1316-17)
Penryn	*Mon. Ex.*, 430 (1308)
Sheepstall nr. Ruan	*E.C.H.*, 207 (1260)
Talgarrek in Camborne	*E.C.H.*, 206 (1260)
Treclego	*E.C.H.*, 207 (1291)
Tremodret	*E.C.H.*, 207 (1291)
Trewithian in St. Wenn	*E.C.H.*, 207 (1313)
Tybesta	I.P.M., Ed. I, 95
Devon	
Bovey Tracey	I.P.M., Ed. II, 100 (19, Ed. II)[3]
Chudleigh	*Mon. Ex.*, p. 428
Crediton	*Mon. Ex.*, p. 427
Harpford	I.P.M., Ed. I, 42 (27 Ed. I)
Hartland	I.P.M., Ed. I, 32 (27 Ed. I)[3]
Molton, North	I.P.M., Ed. II, 36, 59 (7 & 10, Ed. II)[3]
Molton, South	I.P.M., Ed. II, 100 (19 Ed. II)
Moreton Hampstead	*Cal. I.P.M.*, III, 282 (25 Ed. I)
Sampford Courtenay	I.P.M., Ed. I, 21 (23 Ed. I)[3]
Slapton	I.P.M., Ed. I, 32 (35 Ed. I)[3]
Somerset	
Cheddar	M.A., 1131/3 (1301)
Dulverton	Brit. Mus. Add. MSS., 16332
Dunster	Maxwell-Lyte, *Dunster*, I, 297
Taunton	Eccl. Com.
Wells	M.A., 1131/4 (1308-9)
Wiveliscombe	*Ibid.*
Wookey	*Ibid.*
The Cotswold District	
Barton-on-Windrush	*Supra*, p. 44
Bourton-on-the-Water	*Supra*, p. 45
Hawkesbury	C.R., Gen. Series, 175/41 (19 Ed. [II])
Hinton	*Cartulary of the Monastery of St. Peter of Gloucester* (Rolls Series), III, 60
Minchin-hampton	R. & S., 238
Overbury	*V.C.H., Worc.*, II, 301
Stanway	*Tax. Eccl.*, 234 (1291)
Wheatenhurst	R. & S., 245 (15Ed. I)
Winchcomb	*Supra*, p. 45

The Middle Thames Region	
The Kennet Valley	
Benham Valence	*V.C.H., Berks*, I, ~~198~~ 388
Burghfield	*Ibid.*, III, 403; Brit. Mus. Harl. MS., 1708, f. 209
Chilton Foliat	*Wilts I.P.M.*, 350 (1307)
Elcot	*Supra*, p. 46
Hampstead Marshall	*V.C.H., Berks*, IV, 182; I.P.M. 54 Hen. III, 25
Newbury	*V.C.H., Berks*, I, 388, IV, 136
Reading	*Ibid.*, III, 344
Speen	*Ibid.*, IV, 107; M.A., 750/23 (5-6 Ed. I)
The Thames Valley	
Medmenham	I.P.M., Hen. III, 30 (1263)
Purley	*V.C.H., Berks*, III, 421
Seckworth	*Register of Godstow*, I, 43
Witney	*Supra*, p. 45
The Chilterns	
Wendover	Anc. Ext., 79 (2) (24 Ed. I)
Wycombe	*Register of Godstow*, I, 89 (1235)
Wiltshire	
North	
Castlecombe	
Chilton Foliat (*see* Kennet Valley)	
Chippenham	*Wilts I.P.M.*, 246, 300 (1300)
Stanley-on-the-Marden	*Supra*, p. 44
South	
Downton	Eccl. Com.
Harnham	*Wilts I.P.M.*, 227 (1299)
Mere	*Ibid.* 257; M.A., 1055/21 (1300)
Sarum, Old	*Cal. I.M.*, I, 328 (1277-8)
Steeple Langford	R. & S. Gen. Ser., 16/66 (1294)
Hampshire	
Alresford, New	*Supra*, p. 45 (1208-9)
Sutton	*Ibid.*
Waltham	*Ibid.*
Winchester	*Infra*, p. 51
South-Eastern England	
Guildford	*Cal. L.R.*, III, 376 (1251)
Tonbridge	*Hundred Rolls* (Record Comm.), II, 219
The London District	
Enfield	*Cal. I.P.M.*, V, 192 (5 Ed. II)
Stratford	*Cal. Letter Books of London*, ed. R. R. Sharpe, C. 51 (1299)

East Anglia		**East Anglia**	
Lawford, Essex	*Cal. I.P.M.*, II, 380 (15 Ed. I)	Hadleigh, Suffolk	H. Pigot, *Hadleigh*, 229 (1305)
Witham, Essex	*Supra*, p. 44[2]	Aby (*or* Strubby), Lincs	*Cal. I.P.M.*, VI, 158 (1321-2)
		Tothill	*Cal. I.M.*, I, 238 (1264-5)

[1] See also J. Somervell, *Water Power Mills of South Westmorland*, where the probable sites of several of these mills are identified.

[2] Cf. M. L. Armitt, " Fullers and Freeholders of Grasmere," *Westmorland and Cumberland Archæological Society*, New Series, vol. 8, p. 139.

[3] See also *Devon Association for the Advancement of Science, Literature and Art*, vol. XLIV (1912), R. Pearse Chope, " The Aulnager in Devon."

From this survey, inadequate though it must be, it is evident that the use of the fulling mill had become widespread over England and the borders of Wales between the end of the twelfth and the beginning of the fourteenth century. The fulling mill was, indeed, destined to supersede almost entirely the primitive fulling " under the feet of men," though its final triumph was not yet assured, and a veritable revolution in one of the chief branches of cloth manufacture was in progress. Foot fulling was giving way to mechanical fulling ; human labour was being displaced by water power ; the industry was being carried on at the mill rather than in the home ; it was dependent as never before upon considerable capital equipment, and was already passing out of the gild system of control. Moreover, changes in technique and organisation, striking enough in themselves to warrant the use of the word revolution, were giving rise to changes in location no less striking —changes which were to affect the distribution of the whole English woollen industry. For the survey, it will be seen, reveals remarkable concentrations of mills in the West Riding of Yorkshire, in the Lake District, in Cornwall, Devon, Somerset and the Cotswolds, in Wilts and in the Kennet Valley, with a corresponding dearth of mills in the eastern parts of England. Further, it shows that the mills were almost entirely in the country districts rather than in the towns. Now in both these respects a startling change has taken place since the twelfth and thirteenth centuries. Then the chief centres of cloth manufacture were not in the hilly northern and western regions of England but in the eastern lowlands ; not in the rural districts but in the cities. York, Beverley, Lincoln, Louth, Stamford and Northampton[1] were then famous for their fine quality cloth, and next to them in importance came London,

[1] See, *e.g.*, Newcastle Records Series, II, *Pleas from Curia Regis and Assize Rolls*, p. 307 ; *Cal. Patent Rolls*, 1247-58, p. 309 ; F. D. Swift, *James I of Aragon*, p. 229 ; *Cal. Close Rolls*, 1234-7, pp. 73, 301 ; 1247-51, pp. 154, 157, 301, 375.

Oxford, Winchester, Leicester and Colchester. In all these cities there was a large-scale industry supplying London and, in many instances which we can trace, the export market, and many have left record of their organised groups of fullers[1] as well as weavers. Now, however, with the invention of the fulling mill, water power was becoming a decisive factor in the location of the industry, and it began to concentrate on the swift, clear streams of the north and west, in remote valleys far beyond the bounds of the ancient chartered cities of the plains.

Hence it comes about that this chapter in the development of England's woollen industry is written largely in the records of the manor rather than of the borough. Indeed, in many instances which we can trace, the initiative in the new developments was taken by the lord of the manor, and the capital equipment provided by him. Thus, as we have seen, King Henry III reconstructed his fulling mill at Elcot, using timber from his forest of Savernake,[2] at a cost of £4 17s. 4d., while the Bishop of Winchester built a new fulling mill at Brightwell costing £9 4s. 4d.[3] Similarly the fulling mill at Burnley was built anew (" *de novo constructo* ") for £2 12s. 6d. at the expense of the lord of the manor, and money was also spent on the repair of that at Colne.[4] Such instances could be multiplied.

The incentive to such enterprise on the part of the lord of the manor was that the fulling mill was an investment from which considerable profit could be derived. For, like the corn mill, the oven, the wine press, the dye pan, or any other such equipment erected by the lord, it could be made a manorial monopoly, to which the tenants owed suit.[5] Its value varied not only according to its own efficiency, but also according to the size, population and industry of the area it served. Thus, for example, a half share in the fulling mill at Kendal was at one time worth 10 marks a year,

[1] *E.g.*, Lincoln, 1200 (*Curia Regis Rolls*, I, p. 259). Stamford, 1182 (F. Peck, *Stamford*, p. 17). Northampton, 1275 (*Hundred Rolls*, II, p. 3). London, 1298 (*Liber Custumarum*, I, p. 128). Leicester, 1260 (*Records of the Borough of Leicester*, I, p. 89). Winchester, 1130 (*Pipe Roll, 31 Henry III*, p. 37).

[2] *Supra*, p. 46.

[3] *Pipe Roll of the Bishop of Winchester, ut supra*, p. 13 : " *in unum molendino foleratico facto de novo* " (1208-9).

[4] *Two Compoti of the Lancashire and Cheshire Manors of Henry de Lacy, 24 and 33 Edward I*, Chetham Society, Vol. CXII, pp. 15, 16.

[5] On this subject see *Beitrage zur Geschichte der Technik* (1913), C. Koehne, " Die Mühle im Rechte der Völker " ; *Annales d'histoire Économique et Sociale*, no. 36, *ut supra*, and cf. G. Espinas, *La Draperie dans la Flandre Françoise au Moyen Age* (1923), II, p. 213, n. 6 : the Duke of Burgundy writes to his receiver concerning his corn mills at Bruay, suggesting that for his greater profit one of them should be made into a " molin foleur de draps."

but in 1274 its value was considered to have fallen to 8 marks.[1] The reason alleged was that the tenants at Kentmere no longer did suit to it, and probably what had happened was that the mill at Staveley had now been built[2]; and since Staveley is half-way between Kentmere and Kendal, this would mean for the tenants a journey of only about four instead of eight miles down the Kent valley with their cloths. It is perhaps not a mere coincidence that the development of the fulling mill took place during the century which saw the crystallisation and culmination of the manorial system with seignurial rights and privileges at their height.

How eagerly such monopolies were coveted may be seen from Jocelin de Brakelond's story of Herbert the Dean, who thought that "the profit which may come from the wind ought to be denied to no man." When Herbert excused himself thus for erecting his own windmill the Abbot was speechless with rage, and when Herbert pleaded that it was only to grind his own corn and not other men's, he retorted, "I thank you as much as if you had cut off both my feet; by the face of God, I will never eat bread until that building be overturned."[3] If even the wind could be thus monopolised, it was still more easy to enforce control over the water, to insist that the lord alone had the right to use it for profit-making, and that no one else could do so without a licence purchased from him. Even before the introduction of the fulling mill, the lord claimed the right to dispose of the watercourse as he pleased for fulling and dyeing, reserving it wholly to himself, or leasing it out, often as a monopoly, to others. Thus for instance at Hadleigh one John Garleberd was granted for an annual rent ten feet of land along the bank of the mill pond, with permission to wash his dyed wool there and draw out water, on condition that no one else should have access there.[4] Later on two dyers were fined at Hadleigh for washing dyed wool in the lord's pond without licence.[5] Similarly the cellarer of Bury St. Edmunds claimed the right to prohibit the town fullers from using the water. So profitable were such monopolies that frequently when some measure of freedom was granted to tenants the lord expressly reserved the right to maintain them in his hands. So, for instance, in the charter of 1228 granted by the Archbishop of York to Sherburn in Elmet, the

[1] P.R.O. Inq. P.M., Edward I, 5. [2] See Table p. 48.

[3] *Chronicle of Jocelin of Brakelond*, ed. L. C. Jane, p. 94; cf. the dispute at Hesdin-le-Vieux over the fulling mills of the Prior of S. Georges (G. Espinas and H. Pirenne, *Recueil de documents relatifs à l'histoire de l'industrie drapière en Flandre*, II, p. 690).

[4] P.R.O. Ecclesiastical Commission, Various, I, 16/2.

[5] *Ibid.*, 16/9.

" burgesses in our borough of Shireburn " were forbidden on pain of forfeiture to have an " oven, dye-pan or fulling stocks." Those who made use of the Archbishop's dye-pan might have, in any week they pleased, " a cartload of dead wood from our wood at Shireburn."[1] Or again, a charter of King John to Ulverston reserved in the king's hands the oven, dye-pan and fullery ("*furnum*, *tinctoriam et fulloniam* ").[2]

Nor did the lords of the manor claim merely the exclusive right of erecting and possessing such fulleries or fulling mills. They insisted also that all cloth made on the manor must be brought to the manorial mill and there fulled by the new mechanical method, and no longer at home " by hand or foot " ; just as they insisted that all corn must be ground in their wind mills or water mills, and not at home by hand mills. Such a claim would seem as difficult to justify as it certainly was to enforce. Never, perhaps, was it wholly conceded, and both manorial court rolls and monastic chronicles bear witness to the constant opposition it aroused, and to the hatred which it inspired. At Hawkesbury, for instance, in 1325-6, one Matilda, daughter of Adam the Carter, was fined for fulling a piece of cloth " *alibi quam ad molendinum domini*."[3] Other such cases occur on manorial court rolls, but most striking is the evidence from monastic sources, and most vivid of all is the account of the struggle over the fulling mills at St. Albans in 1274. At this time the abbey of St. Albans was evidently as proud of its mills as of its conventual buildings. Abbot John (1235-60) spent, it is said, no less than £100 on their reconstruction, taking them back into his own hands after they had been leased out at farm and allowed to fall into disrepair. His successors were evidently determined to make a goodly profit out of them and claimed that no grinding of corn or fulling of cloth, even of small pieces,[4] could be carried out anywhere except at the abbey mills. The people of St. Albans, however, resisted what they considered to be an unwarranted usurpation; they gave the abbey mills a wide berth and preferred to grind and full at home, free of charge, by the primitive old-

[1] *Old Yorkshire*, 2nd series, 1885, W. Wheater, " The Ancient Cloth Trade."

[2] T. West, *Antiquities of Furness* (1813), pp. 85, 418; *fulloniam* cannot strictly be interpreted as fulling *mill* as it is here, and often elsewhere, translated: it would seem to denote almost always the primitive non-mechanised fullery, and by the fourteenth century the word has virtually disappeared. Cf. charter, quoted by Ducange, reserving "*furnos, torcularia, molendina, et fullonos.*"

[3] P.R.O. Court Rolls, General Series, 175/41.

[4] " *Pannos viles* " in contrast to "*pannos grossos*," *i.e.* probably small pieces woven for use at home rather than whole broadcloths woven for sale; this restriction would be peculiarly irksome.

fashioned methods.[1] In 1274 matters came to a head in what the chronicler describes as a great insurrection, provoked by the zeal of Abbot Roger in enforcing his monopolies by entering the houses of offenders and levying distraint. The people of St. Albans determined to contest the case in the king's court, opened a fighting fund to which rich and poor contributed, and, when Queen Eleanor was passing through St. Albans, staged a great demonstration to enlist her support. The Abbot tried to outwit them by diverting the royal route and taking the Queen by a back way to the abbey, but his stratagem failed, and the Queen was intercepted by an angry crowd consisting mainly of women, whose attack, said the monkish chronicler, was formidable "since it is difficult happily to compose the anger of women." Weeping and lamenting and stretching forth their hands, the women complained bitterly of the Abbot's tyranny, crying "Domina, miserere nobis." It was not easy, however, for an English mob to make their grievances intelligible to a foreign queen and her entourage, and the sympathy aroused by their tears seems quickly to have been dispelled by the assurances of the astute Abbot that the light words of such women were really unworthy of credence. At any rate when the people of St. Albans brought their case into the king's court, judgment was given against them, and, despite an appeal, the abbot won the day and the judgment was proudly entered in the chronicle for future reference.[2]

The story of the gradual emancipation of the industry from seignurial control does not concern us here, for it belongs to the later middle ages and is part of the larger story of the disintegration of the manor and the transition from medieval to modern. Indeed the development of the cloth industry mirrors the rise and decline of the manor as it does that of the gild. Let us turn rather to consider the effects of the invention of the fulling mill and its extension in rural districts upon the old-established urban centres of the cloth industry.

[1] One of the fullers, Henry de Porta, living in Fullers Street, was accused of erecting in his house a "*truncum ad fullandum pannos*"; this may perhaps imply some partly mechanised device such as wooden hammers attached to a revolving drum worked by hand. Such a device is still used to-day, *e.g.* in the "Clansman Mills" at Killin. Cf. *supra.* p. 43.

[2] *Gesta Abbatam Monasterii Sancti Albani*, ed. H. T. Riley, Rolls Series (1867), I, pp. 323, 410 ff. The struggle continued, here as elsewhere, for more than a century, and was one of the causes contributing towards the Peasants' Revolt. Cf. the struggle at Evesham during the fourteenth and fifteenth centuries over ovens and cornmills; in 1307 a private oven erected in his house by William de Tettebury was thrown down by the Abbey steward with the aid of the town bailiffs, and in 1388 the hand mills of other tenants were destroyed, as was a horse mill in 1430. (G. May, *History of Evesham* (1845), p. 83.)

The development of the fulling mill affected decisively the location of the industry, in that it determined that it should be dispersed over the countryside rather than concentrated in the towns.[1] For though at first these mills, often in remote rural valleys, dealt no doubt with the cloth woven for the needs of the rural population, ultimately they came to cater for the needs of the industrialists. Since cloth could be fulled in the mills mechanically, and therefore more cheaply, inevitably much of the work that had been done in the cities came to be sent out to them, and more and more they took over the fulling branch of the cloth industry, threatening the handcraft fullers in the towns with unemployment and starvation. In London, for instance, so serious was the competition of the country fulling mills that complaint was made to the king in 1298. It was said that certain men of the city had sent cloths " outside the city to the mill of Stratford and elsewhere, and caused them to be fulled there, to the grave damage of those to whom the cloth belonged and also of the men using this office in the city."[2] Round these mills grew up groups of industrial workers entirely outside the jurisdiction of the urban gilds. In many little rural hamlets in valleys where water power had been turned to account we find colonies of fullers in the late thirteenth century, working evidently to supply no merely local demand. Thus there were fullers scattered throughout the West Riding valleys ; at Calverley, for instance, there seem to have been at least five in about 1257.[3] Or again in Gloucestershire, in the Stroud valley region, there is evidence of several fullers in the manor of Minchinhampton, and in about 1300 seven men paid rent there for leave to dig fullers' earth.[4] The tendency for one of the chief branches of the woollen industry to shift from the town to the

[1] In this respect the English industry offers a striking contrast to that of Flanders.

[2] *Liber Custumarum*, I, p. 127 ; Letter Book C, f. xxxvii (*Calendar*, p. 51).

[3] H. Heaton, *The Yorkshire Woollen and Worsted Industries* (Oxford Historical and Literary Studies, vol. 10, 1920), p. 5, quoting *Calverley Charters*, Thoresby Society Publications, vol. VI, p. 8-55.

[4] P.R.O. Rentals and Surveys, 238. Though it is dangerous to assume that anglicised surnames such as " Fuller " indicate at this time the trade of their owner, and not merely of his forbears, it is most probable that " Rogerus Fullo, Ricardus Fullo, Reginaldus Fullo and Symon Fullo," who pay rent for digging *argilla*, are actually fullers, as very likely are others with non-occupational surnames, *e.g.*, William Dygge, who pays rent for a watercourse and for digging *argilla* ; Thomas de Rodebere, who rents a fulling mill, and John de Dodebrug', Robert de Brystoll and William Hocvale, who rent diggings. For the dating of this custumal, see *Bristol and Gloucestershire Archæological Society Transactions*, vol. LIV (1932), C. E. Watson, " The Minchinhampton Custumal and its place in the Story of the Manor."

country gave a great stimulus to the development of the industry as a whole there, and doomed to failure the attempt of the cities to concentrate it within their walls to their own profit. To the advantages of water power were added the advantages of freedom from the high taxation in the towns and from the restrictions of the gilds. Colonies of weavers also began to settle round the fulling mills, and, as the industrial population of the rural regions increased, so that of the cities decreased, and the once mighty weavers' gilds sank into insignificance and poverty. The industry, in fact, was deserting the towns for the countryside. There is clear evidence of this decay in the case of at least seven of the leading cloth-producing cities, and others may yet be found to have been in similar case.

Winchester, for instance, in the twelfth century had a considerable number of both weavers and fullers, each organised in their own gild, and each paying £6 yearly to the crown in the time of Henry I.[1] But by the time of Edward I it was becoming increasingly difficult to collect the money, and the reason given for this was that large numbers of the clothworkers had left the town.[2] At Oxford also there was a weavers' gild paying £6 to the crown in the twelfth century.[3] But in the reign of Edward I they successfully petitioned that the sum should be reduced to 42s. on the ground that, while there used to be sixty or more weavers in the town, there were now only fifteen. Later they asked for a further reduction to 6s. 8d., since there were only seven weavers left, and those were poor; finally, in 1323, they pleaded that all these were dead and had no successors.[4] The Lincoln weavers also were finding difficulties about paying their annual £6 to the crown in the early fourteenth century and alleged the same reasons, stating that there were no weavers left in Lincoln between 1321 and 1331 and from then until 1345 only a very few, though when Henry II granted their gild there were more than two hundred.[5] In London the number of looms was said to have fallen from 380 to 80 early in the fourteenth

[1] *Pipe Roll 31 Henry I*, p. 37.

[2] *Victoria County History, Hampshire*, vol. V, p. 477. Complaints of financial stringency are, of course, a commonplace of the public records, but the reason here given for the difficulty, read in conjunction with the Bishop of Winchester's records, seems to bear the stamp of truth.

[3] *Pipe Roll 31 Henry I*, p. 2; see also *V.C.H. Oxfordshire*, vol. II, for an account of the fluctuations of the weavers' gild (p. 242 ff).

[4] *Oxford Historical Society*, vol. XXXII, pp. 99, 123-4; P.R.O. Ancient Petitions, 132/6569.

[5] *Cal. Close Rolls*, 1348-50, p. 120 (Petition of 1348); *Telariorum*, given as "spinners" in the calendar, is a synonym for *Textorum* "*Weavers*."

century.[1] York was in very similar difficulties. In the twelfth century its weavers' gild had paid a larger sum than any other—£10 annually, but during the thirteenth century it fell into more and more serious arrears, pleading in excuse that " divers men in divers places in the country, elsewhere than in the city or in the other towns and demesne boroughs—make dyed and rayed cloths." [2]

The decline of the industry in all these five boroughs is easily apparent, since each had an old-established weavers gild, paying annually to the crown as lord of the borough. It is less easy to trace developments in the six other leading cloth-making cities, for four at least of these were not royal boroughs, none of them had privileged early gilds, so far as can be discovered, and comparable evidence is not therefore available. Yet here too we can find signs of decay. Northampton, for instance, complained in 1334 that formerly 300 clothmakers had worked there, but that now the houses where they used to live had all fallen down.[3] Leicester in 1322 declared that there was only one fuller left in the town " and he a poor man,"[4] and it is significant that from the end of the thirteenth century the very extensive Leicester records contain less and less about the cloth industry and more and more about the marketing of raw wool.

Competition from the country districts was not, of course, entirely new. Some clothmaking had always been carried on in the villages. But hitherto the " great industry " for export had been to a marked extent concentrated in the cities and controlled by them; there lived the capitalist entrepreneurs, carrying on the dyeing and finishing processes, often in their own houses, and employing the colonies of skilled weavers and fullers settled within the walls, though they would also buy the rough unfinished webs brought in for sale by the country people. Now, with the invention of the fulling mill, the balance was tilted in favour of the country districts, and the cities were faced with constantly intensified competition. How then did they strive to maintain or recapture their supremacy?

Where circumstances were favourable some set up their own mills, as did Winchester in 1269, when the town granted permission to nine fullers to construct a fullers' mill.[5] But the slow-moving courses of the rivers on which most of these towns lay were less

[1] Lipson, *op. cit.*, p. 11; no reference given.
[2] Heaton, *op. cit.*, p. 29 (Petition of 1304).
[3] *Rot. Parl.*, II, p. 85.
[4] *Cal. Inq. Misc.*, II, p. 138.
[5] *The Black Book of Winchester*, p. 190.

adapted to mills than were their swift upper courses, nor can the requisite space for the diversion of the watercourse have been always readily available. Moreover, there would tend to be strong opposition to an innovation which would throw so many out of work, and all the forces of conservatism would be arrayed against it.

Other towns therefore resisted the adoption of the new methods, urging the inferiority of machine work as well as the unemployment it caused. Thus a complaint from certain Londoners to the king in 1298 declared that, according to the accepted custom, cloths should be " fulled under the feet of men of this office, or their servants, in their houses in the city and not elsewhere," but that certain fullers had sent such cloths " outside the city to the mill of Stratford and elsewhere and caused them to be fulled there, to the grave damage of those to whom the cloth belonged and also of the men using this office in the city."[1] The petitioners did not, however, secure the prohibition of fulling at mills, but only an ordinance that no cloth should be sent outside the city to be fulled at mills (" *pur foller as molins* ") except by those who actually owned the cloth, and that six men should watch at the city gates, arrest the cloths, and keep them until the owners came and avowed them as theirs.[2] Twelve years later one Godfrey de Loveyne was heavily fined for sending three cloths outside the city to be fulled at mills.[3]

Most towns, however, concerned themselves primarily with confining the industry within the city walls. Their own civic ordinances could at least compel clothmakers in the city to employ city labour only and thus to maintain the wealth and prosperity of the city. Thus when the craft ordinances of Bristol were first written down in the city records in 1346, that of the fullers decreed " *qe nul hom face amesner hors de ceste ville nule manere drap a foler qe home appele raucloth sur peyne de perdre xld. pur chescun drap.*"[4] In the same ordinance there is mention of cloth being sent " to the mill " (" *al molyn* "), so that clearly the opposition was not to milling as such but to the work going out of the city. The prohibition was repeated later in the century,[5] and similar prohibitions continued to be made in other towns. At Winchester, for instance, in 1402, clothmakers of the town were forbidden to employ either fullers

[1] *Liber Custumarum*, I, p. 127.

[2] *Ibid.*, I, pp. 127, 128; *Letter Book*, C, f. xxxvii.

[3] *Letter Book*, D, p. 239 (" *pannos crudos* " is probably raw, *i.e.* unfulled, cloth, not " undyed ").

[4] *Little Red Book of Bristol*, ed. F. B. Bickley, II, p. 7.

[5] *Ibid.*

or weavers outside the town.[1] A somewhat similar ordinance seems to have been made at Leicester in 1260, and citizens were punished for breach of it.[2]

Such ordinances might do something to prevent city manufacturers from having dealings with workers outside, but they could not prevent an independent industry from flourishing in the country districts. Some cities therefore turned to an authority higher than that of the city and prayed the king to aid them in securing the monopoly they coveted. The York weavers, with those of other royal boroughs in Yorkshire, had already, by their charter of 1164, been granted a monopoly of making dyed and rayed cloth in all Yorkshire. At the end of the thirteenth century their monopoly was, as we have seen, being seriously infringed, so in 1304 they petitioned the king and he ordered the Exchequer to have enquiries made and to compel all found plying the craft in illegal places to refrain.[3] We do not know what effect, if any, was given to this order, but we do know that it did not, any more than did the cities' own ordinances, succeed in the impossible task of confining the cloth industry within urban walls.

The decline of the industry in the thirteenth century in what had been its most flourishing urban centres is as striking as is its expansion in rural regions during the same period, but it is the urban side of the matter which has hitherto attracted the attention of historians, and from it they have falsely deduced a decline in the industry as a whole. The real significance of this decline now becomes clear. The industry was developing, and developing rapidly, but outside the jurisdiction of those cities that had once taken the lead in it. The decay of the once famous cloth-making cities of the eastern plain and the rise of the country fulling mills shows not only that the rural industry was gaining over the urban, but also, when we consider the preponderance of fulling mills in the north and west of England, that the broadcloth industry as a whole was tending to shift from east to west, to new centres in the West Riding, the Lake District and the West of England. For here were to be found ample supplies not only of fine wool but also of water power. In the twelfth and early thirteenth centuries the fine quality English cloths specially in demand abroad were cloths "of Stamford," "of Lincoln," "of Louth," "of Beverley," "of York"; but in the fourteenth and fifteenth centuries there was no demand at all for these cloths, but much for "Kendals," "Ludlows," "Cotswolds," "Mendips," "Castlecombes,"

[1] *Black Book of Winchester*, p. 8.

[2] *Records of the Borough of Leicester*, ed. M. Bateson, I, pp. 91, 347.

[3] Heaton, *op. cit.*, pp. 28-9.

" Stroudwaters," or " Westerns," and the primary, though not the only, factor in this change was the invention of the fulling mill.

Abbreviations in Table of Mills

M.A.	=	Public Record Office, Ministers Accounts.
C.R.	=	,, ,, ,, Court Rolls.
R. & S.	=	,, ,, ,, Rentals and Surveys.
Anc. Ext.	=	,, ,, ,, Ancient Extents.
Eccl. Com.	=	,, ,, ,, Ecclesiastical Commission, Various, II, 159273 ff.
I.P.M.	=	Public Record Office, Inquisitions Post Mortem.
Cal. I.P.M.	=	*Calendar of Inquisitions Post Mortem.*
Cal. I.M.	=	,, ,, *Inquisitions Miscellaneous.*
Cal. C.R.	=	,, ,, *Close Rolls.*
Cal. L.R.	=	,, ,, *Liberate Rolls.*
V.C.H.	=	*Victoria County History*
Tax. Eccl.	=	*Taxatio Ecclesiastica, circa 1291* (Record Commission 1802).
Mon. Ex.	=	Oliver, *Monasticon Exoniensis.*
Wilts I.P.M.	=	*Abstracts of Wiltshire Inquisitions Post Mortem*, ed. E. A. Fry (1908), 1242-1326.
Worc. I.P.M.	–	*Inquisitions Post Mortem for the County of Worcestershire*, ed. for the Worcester Historical Society by J. W. Willis Bund (1894).
Notts I.P.M.	=	Thoroton Society, Record Series, Vol. IV, *Inquisitions Post Mortem for Nottinghamshire*, Vol. II (1279-1321), ed. J. Standish (1914).
E.C.H.	=	Charles Henderson, *Essays in Cornish History* (1935), p. 206, " Cornish Tucking Mills and Windmills."[1]

[1] This gives no references, but is based mainly on the author's own extensive collection of Cornish deeds, now in the Truro Museum.

14
Urban Evolution during the Middle Ages*

Maurice Lombard

[7] It is traditional to focus the urban problem of the early Middle Ages almost exclusively on north-western Europe, France, the Netherlands, England, the Rhinelands and, thus focused, to contain it between two irrefutable determinants: neatly defined points of departure and of arrival. At the beginning, there was urban decay, starting with the economic crisis of the Roman Empire in the third century and marking the gradual disappearance of the ancient city, of urban institutions and of the urban way of life in the West, which was barbarised and ruralised to an increasing extent. At the other extreme there was urban renewal which took shape in the West from the tenth and eleventh centuries onward. Cities and urban patterns reappeared, sporadically at first and then on a more substantial basis. The movement proceeded at a gradual rate and the city took shape, and this may correctly be dubbed the medieval city. However, even when it seemed to be rekindling the ashes of the ancient city, and was installed on the very site of the Gallo-Roman city or in close proximity to it, the characteristics of this town were entirely different.

The Roman city took the form of a monumental nucleus, relatively confined, the site of the forum, the temple and the *praetorium*. All the rest of the urban space, which may be called the ancient city, presented a diverse appearance: villas, shanties, gardens and cultivated land formed a poorly defined urban zone. There was no perimeter wall to establish physical separation between town and countryside, and the suburb did not exist. The notion of the suburb is a medieval one, a space which is situated beyond the urban enclosure. In the Roman city, on the other hand, the impression is of an indefinite expanse of new residential quarters. The ancient city was thus thoroughly permeated by rustic life. This Roman city, in the West, was inhabited by functionaries living on their salaries, and by landowners drawing rent from their estates, in other words from the surrounding countryside. These landowners, controllers of the countryside, formed the ruling class, the wealthy element of the ancient city. We may also note the presence of various artisans and merchants, attracted by the markets for

*This brief survey is the text of a conference paper, delivered in March 1951 at the University of Toulouse, for the Marc Bloch Association. It forms the starting-point and the first draft of several chapters of a work entitled *Les Villes du haut moyen age et le Rythme urbain*, currently in preparation.

consumer goods opening up the time, and the improved opportunities they offered. Thus, **[8]** the city was an administrative and military installation, initially at least, a city created alongside the Roman strategic routes and especially at their intersections, but also alongside the ancient Gallic routes which pre-existed the Roman network. Small-scale commerce and small-scale urban industry were not slow to develop, catering for the needs of this population of administrators and soldiers. Then the landowners of the periphery tended to settle within the new towns, attracted by a superior standard of living, by the commodities available through the presence of suppliers, also by the appeal of spectacles, theatre and amphitheatre, finally by the opportunity to take up positions in the municipal administration, positions which though onerous were very prestigious.

If we are to summarise the whole process of evolution, the medieval city was built on a pattern which was both very different and quite familiar: individualised by its surrounding wall, enclosing houses pressed close together; suburbs developed outside the wall, manufacturing suburbs and commercial suburbs which, little by little, were absorbed into the urban perimeter. Urban design then typically showed a series of successive rebuildings of the outer walls. It was thus a case of urban patterns which continually overlapped the rural patterns of the environs, and absorbed a substantial proportion of the countryside. Even the zones which, topographically, were not touched by the construction boom unleashed by urban prosperity, were subject to the influence of the city and were penetrated by urban influences. This new city was inhabited by the bourgeois, who made their living primarily from commerce and industrial production and formed an urban patriciate, a wealthy ruling class. It was inhabited, also, by an urban proletariat which enabled the city to play the role of a manufacturing centre. In a word, this medieval city was above all a city with an economic function.

How and why, in our western world with its ancient rural, even sylvan traditions, did the transition take place from this first urban form, that of the old city, to the second, that of the medieval city? In particular, at which moments, in the barbarian West, are this urban decadence and then this revival to be located? And finally, precisely what trajectory and chronology are to be attributed to the curve of the graph of urban evolution between the third and the eleventh century? This curve, as we know, descends to a certain point, yet to be determined, and then rises again. What is the lowest point of the curve, in terms of the places considered, and what is the spatial progression of this urban renewal, which extends like an oil-stain?

It is this comprehensive and very broad problem of urban evolution during the early Middle Ages, and not the other problems of urban history, immense and numerous as they are, that I propose to examine, confining myself to the highpoints of the question.

When attempting to retrace with the greatest possible precision the curve of urban evolution, its chronology and its geography, it is necessary to move beyond the narrow confines **[9]** of the western horizon. During the early Middle Ages the rhythm of urban development was not a factor exclusive to the lands of the Occident. Leaving the Occident in the third century to return there in the eleventh, a relatively long journey needs to be undertaken, through Mediterranean and oriental lands, and we will gain a better understanding of what has been called the urban renaissance, its chronology and its itineraries.

A relatively long journey, made particularly difficult by the multiplicity of languages employed by our sources: Latin and Greek, but also Arabic, Hebrew, Syriac, Persian, etc. While the medievalist tends to have a very sound knowledge of Latin and Greek as well, most of the time, with a few happy exceptions, he does not have the same knowledge of oriental languages. It is precisely this linguistic ignorance of a part of their documentation which accounts for the error of those who have introduced the 'Oriental', 'Islamic' or 'Mohammedan' factor, without extricating themselves from the tight framework imposed on them by the western sources; and more specifically, the error of Pirenne. The great Belgian historian translated as a break in the story of relations between Orient and Occident, what was only a break in his sources and in the data which he was capable of drawing from them. Another mistake appears in Pirenne's work (and I am thinking in particular of his two books of synthesis, *Mahomet et Charlemagne* and *Les Villes du Moyen Age*, where he sets out his general theories): a lack of historical perspective which induces him to adopt a chronology which is too short and too compact for the influences which he believes he can detect and which cannot have been propagated as quickly as he claims, in the general economic conditions of the early Middle Ages. For him the 'Arab' conquests would not even have been accomplished unless, *ipso facto*, the economy of the West had come to a standstill: the city, which had survived there since Antiquity, went into a state of decadence. We may note in passing that he had very little time at his disposal to situate this descent of the curve, provoked according to him by the expansion of Islam, before perceiving, thanks to the sources at his disposal which he knew well, the beginning of the revival, the urban renewal of the West. This rapidity, which he attributes to the repercussions of the Islamic conquests on the economy of the barbarian West, is to be explained, in my view, by the ill-considered projection of theories of contemporary economics into a very distant past. The economists of today live in a part of our modern world. The economies of Central Asia, of Black Africa or of the Polynesian Islands, barely feature in treatises of political economy. The subject matter of economists is above all the most developed and most frenetic part of our planet, where an event taking place in New York can have an immediate reaction the same day in London or in Paris. It is in this context of actions and almost instantaneous reactions that our economists have elaborated their theories and their laws. Historians owe them a great deal; there is no question here of minimising the importance of their contribution to the new points of view now accepted by historical science. It is simply that a distinction has to be drawn between the method of work and the results of the work. **[10]** These results, valid for our times in the majority of cases, cannot be transported into the past, especially into a past as distant as the early Middle Ages, with a totally different economic climate, of which the principal characteristic is precisely the extreme slowness of the processes, of economic cycles, of actions and reactions; a slowness naturally due to the difficulty of communications, the immensity of spaces characterised still by an economy showing very little differentiation. If, today, the zones of primitive economy seem to us like islands in the middle of the flood-tide of modern circulation, in the period which concerns us – the early Middle Ages – these zones of primitive life extended over the whole of the globe. On the other hand, the points where a certain technique of general relations and a relative economic differentiation had already been attained, were of an infinitesimally small number. They were only very small islets linked together by the most tenuous relations in the middle of immense spaces which were wild and almost empty.

It is essential to take account, when economic problems are projected into the past, of material conditions so different from ours and also to take account of mental frameworks which may be even more different. It is at this moment that the historian should turn towards the sociologist, who will enlighten him on these mentalities so foreign to ours. Thus a continual collaboration is instituted between the 'pure' economist, the 'pure' sociologist and the historian who could in contrast be dubbed 'impure', because blended in him are all the approaches and all the inquiries, with the object of 'bending theories according to the graph of reality' as Bergson said. Aware of the latest works of the economists, the historian projects into the past the problems which the latter pose for our times, the problems and not the results, the methods and not the fully developed theories, taking the fullest account of the moment and the social place whither these problems are transported or, better, transposed.

Now, one of the conclusions reached in the course of our researches is the close correlation which exists between the influx of precious metals and the growth of the volume of currencies in circulation, on the one hand, and on the other, urban development, the proliferation and expansion of cities. In other words, monetary and urban rhythms are blended during the early Middle Ages. Any restriction in monetary circulation (decline in the exploitation of mines, cutting of the routes used for the importation of new gold, flight abroad caused by a deficient commercial balance, hoarding) is reflected by urban decadence, a slump in the economic activity of the cities and a loss of their social power. On the other hand, any new influx of monetary metals (discovery of new seams, seizure of commercial currents bringing in the products of new mines, influx of currency caused by a commercial balance in surplus, return into circulation of hoarded gold) is reflected by significant urban prosperity, a revival of economic activity and of the social power of the city, to the detriment of the countryside and of the rural estates. A veritable problem of connected vessels: when monetary circulation **[11]** becomes more intense, rural forms and the social power of the countryside are progressively eclipsed. On the other hand, these rural forms dominate when the phenomenon is inverted – as when a monetary economy necessarily overlaps an urban economy.

This affirmation of an intimate connection between monetary circulation and urban development is hardly revolutionary. It will simply enable us to fix more precisely the chronological stages, the geographical extension and the modalities of urban evolution during the early Middle Ages, or at least to tackle the overall problem more effectively.

First Phase (Third-Fourth Centuries)

Urban Decadence in the Roman West and Urban Prosperity in the Eastern Sector of the Empire

M. Andre Piganiol, summarising his ideas in a volume of the Glotz collection,[1] tells us of the ruin of towns in the third and fourth centuries: these towns were ruined by barbarian invasions and by governmental exploitation. In the West, these invasions were facilitated by the conflict between the rival armies of the Rhine and the Danube; their troops abandoned outposts on the *limes* and returned to Italy, to continue the battle on behalf of the competing candidates for the imperial throne. The barbarians were then enabled to launch large-scale incursions across the Roman world of the Occident: thus the Franks in Gaul and Spain, from 253 to 268; the Alamans in Gaul and in Italy, in 268; the Souabes in northern Italy, in 270–271. Then, there was the terrible invasion of Gaul by the Germans, in 275. The emperor Probus was obliged to recapture seventy towns before driving the barbarians back across the Rhine. Combined offensives of the Alamans, the Vandals and the Burgonds, in 285, 288, 291 became common. The towns suffered pillage, and substantial damage; some were sacked and razed, etc. As was said by an author of the period, 'the barbarian hordes transported into Germany the riches of Gaul'. A series of movements followed, with episodes of brigandage and uprisings in the countryside, throughout the fourth century. 'Amid the debris of the great cities, only sparse groups of miserable people, witnesses to past calamities, still attest for us to the names of former times'.[2]

The East was under attack as well, from Iranian peoples, the Sarmatians, or Caucasians, the Alains, and most of all from the eastern Germans, the Goths. The Goths, in 256, advanced as far as Thessalonica. From the Black Sea, the Gothic and Sarmatian ships launched attacks across the Hellespont: almost all of the towns of the coast of Asia Minor were destroyed. In 269, a veritable coalition of all the barbarians of the steppes crossed the Danube. They were defeated only with great difficulty by Claudius II at Naissos, in upper Serbia.

[12] To resist the barbarians and the brigands who took over the role of the barbarians, in the third and fourth centuries cities surrounded themselves with walls. In Gaul, they were confined within very tight enclosures and these enclosures, interestingly enough, often restored the outline of the old Gallic *oppidum*. The city, insofar as it could still be called a city, then

1 *Histoire romaine*, IV, 2, *L'Empire chrétien*

2 OROSE, *Adversus paganos*, VII, 22

took on the appearance of a fortress, in the form so characteristic of the cities of the Middle Ages, the *castrum*, the *burgus*.

The ruination of the cities was thus, initially, the result of pillage on the part of barbarian invaders. But in addition, we are told by M. André Piganiol, exactions extorted by governments, and the policies of the emperors towards the cities, had the effect of depriving them of their wealth and their human resources. They deprived them of their wealth by suppressing the revenues that they drew from the land surrounding them, and by appropriating this land and making it a part of the imperial domain. On the other hand, the municipal offices were now nothing more than *munera*. The wealthy were required to provide services free of charge, and the poor were expected to contribute manual labour. Both groups, to escape these increasingly onerous impositions, fled the cities. The rich man relocated to his rural estate, and the poor man also took refuge in the countryside. They both abandoned the city where they had been subjected to the scrutiny of the state. The urban population was impoverished, and the city progressively deprived of its human material, its social resources. If the Barbarian invasions demolished the cities materially, it was the policy of the emperors which demolished them socially. Hence: urban decadence, continuous expansion of the imperial estates, ruralisation.

This analysis is substantially correct, with only one omission: it fails to take account of the very real urban rejuvenation to be observed in the eastern sector of the Empire. The creation of Constantinople,[3] which was to be one of the greatest cities of the Middle Ages – for a certain period of time, the greatest – and would only be superseded by Baghdad from the ninth century onward, took place between 324 and 33. This is a fact of immense importance for urban history in general, which does not accord with the idea of generalised urban decay from the third century onward.

The underlying cause of the urban decay of the Roman West and, on the other hand, of the urban buoyancy perceptible in the Roman East, is to be sought elsewhere, in the unequal distribution of stocks of gold between East and West. The economic activity which declined in the West but was sustained in the East testified to the discrepancy in economic and urban conditions between the two extremities of the Mediterranean world in the third and fourth centuries. The article by G.I. Bratianu on the distribution of gold in the final phases of the Roman Empire[4] casts light on this difference in the volume of stocks of the yellow metal in the two halves of the Roman world. The West was to an ever increasing degree stripped of the gold which the Roman conquests had accumulated there, at the time of the systematic pillage of the treasures amassed in the Hellenistic East. This gold, from the end of the second century, and especially during the third and the fourth, flowed towards the East to finance the purchase of oriental luxury goods, which had become essential to Mediterranean civilisation. Control

3 C. EMEREAU, 'Note sur les origines et la formation de Constantinople' (*Revue Archéologique*, 1925): R. MAYER, 'Byzantion, Konstantinopolis, Istambul, eine genetische Stadt-Geographie' (*Denkschr. Akad. Wiss. Wien, Phil.-Hist. Klasse*, LXXI, 1943).

4 In: *Etudes Byzantines d'histoire économique et sociale*, 1938.

of this lucrative oriental trade was entirely in the hands of Levantines, Greeks, Egyptians and especially Syrians. The cities of Egypt and Syria were the centres of transit between the lands producing the luxury goods (that is, the Indian Ocean and Asia in general) and the major consumer markets which were still, before the fourth century, constituted by Rome and the cities of the West. It was at this time, from the third century, that Levantines embarked on their role as masters of commerce in the West. Before the third century, their activity had been mainly directed towards the East. They traversed and dominated the routes of the Red Sea, of Mesopotamia and of Iran. The Parthian empire was exploited by them, and the Indian Ocean ploughed by ships from Alexandria. Now, in the third century, in the East, the empire of the Persian Sassanids was inaugurated, replacing the empire of the Arsacid Parthians. A domination which could be called phil-Hellenic, which allowed foreigners from the *Pars Orientis* of the empire to encroach on its territory and trade there profitably, was succeeded by a xenophobic state, with a strictly nationalistic base, and in the course of the third century Levantine businessmen were gradually excluded from the eastern routes. They then turned to the west, and this was the time that western commerce began to be dominated by these Levantines, the *Syri* of the early Middle Ages. This was also the time when, as a result of their efforts, the haemorrhaging of western gold began, leading to the virtually total exhaustion of the reserves, at the end of the sixth century and the beginning of the seventh. The gold which was the motivating force behind an active economic life and the maintenance of a prosperous urban life fled from the Roman West.[5]

On the other hand, the circulation of gold in the eastern sector of the empire, in the third, fourth and fifth centuries, remained active. It was this which was to enable the old Hellenistic metropolises, Alexandria and Antioch to continue their economic activity, and would also pave the way for the foundation, and then the burgeoning prosperity, of the new great city, Constantinople. This Constantinian creation should be linked to another factor, which was also the work of Constantine: the striking of a solid currency, the *solidus aureus*, which in the eastern provinces was called *denarion chrusoun* or gold denier, the designation behind the Arabic word dinar, the major monetary unit of the caliphate.

The urban movement was fuelled in the East by this monetary circulation which remained intense, while in the West it halted and decreased causing urban anaemia, which is nothing other than the corollary of monetary anaemia.

[14] Second Phase (Fifth – Seventh Centuries)

Accentuated Urban Decadence in the Barbarian West.

---

5 Marc BLOCH, 'Le probleme de l'or au moyen age' (*Annales d'histoire économique et sociale*, V, 1933); Maurice LOMBARD, 'L'or musulman du VIIe au XIe siècle' (*Annales E.S.C.*, II, 1947).

Stagnation, then Recession of the Urban Movement in the Byzantine Empire; Urban Prosperity in the Sassanid Orient.

A new wave of invaders launched attacks on the West, completing the destruction of those cities of the *Pars Orientalis* which had already been sorely tested in the third and the fourth centuries and which, for the most part, had been unable to restore their ruined sectors. The difficulties of reconstruction in a period of economic depression are self-evident, such reconstruction proving impossible when the money is lacking. The cities – or what was left of them – were once again sacked and pillaged in the course of the great invasions of the fifth century, especially the cities of Gaul in 406–7. One author tells us that the whole of Gaul burned like a torch: *Una fumavit Gallia tota rogo*. The cities of Spain and North Africa were sacked by the Vandals, the cities of Italy by the Huns, the Visigoths and the Vandals. In 451 Aquilae was completely destroyed and, in the following century, even the site of this once powerful city, for many years the leading commercial centre of northern Italy and the great supplier of the Danubian *limes*, was unrecognisable. The inhabitants of Aquilae fled in all directions, many of them taking refuge among the lakes of the delta of the Po and of its tributaries. There they established themselves on a rather more elevated site, dominating the lowlands, *rivum altum*, Rialto, the future Venice. But Venice did not immediately begin to flourish; its magnificent urban development is attributed to another time, the time when money flowed into this region from the lower Adriatic, enabling Venice to play the role of arbitrator between the western world, on the silver standard and the eastern, Byzantine or Muslim world, on the gold standard. For the moment, only a few fishermen's huts marked the territory where one of the first cities to be reached by the renewal movement was to emerge. The two sacks of Rome, in 410 by Alaric's Visigoths, in 455 by Genseric's Vandals, complete the list of new ruins added to old.

But what made these ruins irreparable was the acceleration in the outflow of gold from the West to the East. If money had been available in this part of the world, sacked by the barbarians, the task of reconstruction would have been facilitated, and the ravaged cities, after the first brutal moment of conquest, might well have risen again from their ruins. But the volume of gold in circulation dwindled more and more in the Germanic kingdoms. It was diminished first as a result of large-scale hoarding, taking place during the period of the invasions; many hoards have been found buried in the neighbourhood of the enclosures, adjoining the urban perimeter of the *castra* and the *burgi*. This gold was totally lost, as far as the monetary circulation of the period was concerned, while the non-hoarded gold was used to buy **[15]** certain luxury goods from eastern countries, goods which the West was no longer capable of producing itself, owing to the decadence of its technological processes. In addition, the barbarians acquired a taste for fine clothing and expensive jewellery. This commercial importation, seen from the perspective of the West, was to a growing extent the monopoly of the *Syrians*. This was a one-way trade, without the exchange of merchandise, the West having nothing to export to the East which the latter could not procure for itself on the spot, in Egypt, in Syria, in the lands of the Black Sea or the Balkans.

Concentrating on this aspect of western commerce, we note that the major commercial effort of western countries, at the height of the Roman era, was essentially the export of commodities and raw materials, destined in the majority of cases for the great consumers' market of Rome (with its population of almost a million, the capital constituted an irresistible mercantile magnet), trading in what we would call heavy materials. This commerce was to disappear with the decline of the urban market of Rome, with the abandonment of Rome for Constantinople. Evidence of this is provided by, among other things, Monte Testaccio on the bank of the Tiber, a hill entirely constructed from the debris of amphorae originally containing Spanish olive oil imported for consumption in the capital: these amphorae are dated, and the last date appearing on a shard is 257.[6]

On the other hand, the trade in oriental luxuries was to survive. This was the commerce in objects that were very light and at the same time very precious, guaranteeing a large profit for a small volume of merchandise, and this commerce was to be maintained as long as there remained in the West the ability (and not just the desire) to buy the ornaments and the lavish costumes offered by oriental manufacturers, inasmuch as a class of wealthy individuals, sovereigns, the landowners or the churches, having access to gold, was to survive in the West. It was they who demanded the luxury products of the Orient, supplied by the *Syrians*. This commerce lasted, although at a steadily diminishing level, until around the end of the sixth century. At this time, we witness the total obliteration of commercial activity in the Barbarian West. The *Syrians* no longer came to the West, because the West could no longer supply them with the gold currency which they had been accustomed to seeking there. We can then point to a state of veritable monetary inertia, reflected in the wretched standards of the coinage,[7] in a circulation reduced to the minimum, in the severing of commercial ties. It is at this moment that we can place the bottom of the economic curve, marking the lowest point attained by urban decay, the late sixth century–early seventh centuries. The rural, domanial aspect emerges victorious in all regions of the West, England, Gaul, Spain and Italy. The rural basis, which is that of the Occident, the sylvan basis even, which is that of the northern part of the Occident, reappear more and more often. In Africa, it is not the rural domain which holds sway, but the encampment, nomadism; the savannah turning to desert which reappears and proves invasive. The mounted nomad **[16]**, the 'Numid', on his Berber horse, had been driven away or sedentarised by urban development, first introduced by Carthage, subsequently and predominantly by Rome. But he was to regain and extend his sphere of operations from the

6 R. THOUVENOT, Essai sur la province romaine de Bétique, Paris 1940.

7 P. LE GENTILHOMME, Mélanges de numismatique mérovingienne, Paris 1940.

third century onward, the moment when he had a new and powerful instrument at his disposal, the camel, which had just been introduced into Barbary via Cyrenaica.[8] The husbandry of the dromedary was developed and, with it, the camel-riding tribe. Zones of more and more importance were taken over for the pastoral life, for caravan routes, crops cultivated for the nourishment of urban populations were uprooted; the great struggle commenced between the nomad and the sedentary, between the camel-rider and the cultivator; a conflict still in progress but currently being resolved to the detriment of the camel-riding nomad. The city, in North Africa, was not devoured by the countryside. It died because it no longer had countryside around it, because the cultivated land had reverted to pasturage, to savannah, to the favoured haunts of nomads. African cities contracted and were depopulated in confrontation with the nomads, exactly the fate that befell the cities of western Europe in confrontation with the great rural domains.

Ruralisation on one side, nomadisation on the other, urban deflation and barbarisation on both sides. The city no longer had the appropriate means to defend itself, i.e. money. Later, with no changes to the natural conditions, with the return of money, when the land would again be irrigated by this privileged medium of exchanges, urban life would be reborn, in ruralised Europe as in nomadised Africa.

Passing on now to the eastern seaboard of the Mediterranean, we note first of all the halting of the great urban movement marked by the creation and the early progress of Constantinople, then stagnation and before long, a decline in urban activity in the Byzantine Empire. Urban growth slowed in the second half of the sixth century, then stopped at the beginning of the seventh. Then followed a diminution and contraction of urban activity and, in parallel, an evolution towards the large estate, towards domanial anchylosis. In the social context, the feudal system was in process of construction, and the great manorial house was making its appearance. In an economic context, the closed domanial cell was being formed. In the seventh century, in the eastern Mediterranean, the almost perfect form which feudalism was taking on at this time in the Barbarian West had not yet been achieved, but progress was being made. We can follow the stages of it in the Egyptian papyri, a mass of documents emanating for the most part **[17]** from the offices of the major landowners.[9] Another source of testimony also enables us to understand this evolution for Byzantine territories as a whole, the imperial reports, outlining the incessant struggle waged by the emperors against encroachments on the part of the great feudal aristocracies, and in their parallel efforts to restore new life to the cities. In the Byzantine East, which retained its governmental structures, its economy directed by central offices, the *basileis* were at pains to restrain, with varying degrees of success,

8 St. GSELL, in *Mémoires de l'Académie des Inscriptions et Belles-Lettres*, XLIII, 1926.

9 E.R. HARDY, *The large estates of Byzantine Egypt*, New York 1931; H.I. BELL, 'An epoch in the agrarian history of Egypt' (*Recueil d'études égyptologiques dédiées a la mémoire de Champollion*).

the natural evolution towards the domanial formula. They could not prevent the decline of the urban movement. The towns of the Egyptian delta, formerly so rich and so densely populated, were impoverished financially and demographically. The bourgeois of the towns of the interior, those first affected, streamed towards Alexandria, which remained a still-active economic centre and which, more and more, seemed to be a world apart when juxtaposed against Egyptian territory which, for its part, was reverting little by little to its primitive rural forms. In the hinterland, all that remained was the mass of indigenous peasants (Copts, fellahs), the priests and monks who had appropriated all the land surrounding their fortified monasteries,[10] and also the landed gentry who lived on their estates with their officers, their guards and their servants, in other words, the serf and his master, whether this master be lay or ecclesiastical.

Syriac ecclesiastical chronicles tell a similar story. In Syria, as in Egypt, activity was still maintained in the commercial cities of the coast, but inland there were no longer towns of any real importance. Nothing was to be found there other than rural populations enslaved by the great feudal proprietors, among whom nomadic Arabs were beginning to infiltrate.[11]

The same evolution was evident in Asia Minor, where the towns of the Anatolian plain declined, while some ports remained relatively active on the Aegean Sea. In the interior, great manorial houses were being built for the feudal lords whose independence and instability were subsequently to trouble the Byzantine Empire so deeply. Forms of nomadisation were also developed there: extension of zones of pasturage and the proliferation of larger flocks of sheep, a whole pastoral way of life, spreading at the same time that the urban aspect so characteristic of Asia Minor was beginning to fade, in the period which saw the beginnings of Christianity and the first councils.

The same developments were observed in the Balkan Peninsula, where all economic and urban activity was concentrated at Constantinople and at Thessalonica, the rest of the country being subjected to a very clear ruralisation, further accentuated by the settlement of the Slavs, from the sixth century onward, in Macedonia, central Greece and the Peloponnese. The latter brought with them particular forms of settling **[18]** the land: a dispersed village with small houses separated by cultivated ground, the Slavic *Zadrouga* has neither the appearance nor the function of a town in the sense that we understand, that is a built-up nucleus with economic worth.

In the Byzantine East of the late sixth and early seventh centuries, the towns thus appear to be no more than islets in the middle of vast spaces which are dominated more and more by a rural and pastoral economy: full-blown recession, despite the desperate struggle of the emperors to maintain the urban movement, combat the great seigneurial houses and keep the

10 U. MONNERET DE VILLARD, 'Descrizione generale del monasterio di San Simeone presso Aswan' (*Annales du Service des Antiquités Egyptiennes*, XXVI, 1926.

11 R. DUSSAUD, *Les Arabes en Syrie avant l'Islam*, Paris 1907.

nomadic hordes in check. These are the major apparent features of the Byzantine urban history of the sixth and the seventh century. The underlying reason has to be sought – here too – in the restriction of monetary circulation. It was at this time that the routes transporting the gold of the Urals and of Nubia to the Byzantine workshops were cut off by nomadic incursions. It was the time that the flow of coined gold, arriving from the West through the intermediary of the *Syrians*, was dwindling, and the time that the outflow of gold became accentuated: to the interior of the Empire as a result of hoarding; outside the frontiers, towards the East, towards the Sassanid Empire which was then the obligatory transit-point dominating all the commercial routes between the Indian Ocean and the Mediterranean. These two processes overlap each other: urban decadence and at the same time, contraction of the volume of gold in circulation.

Continuing further to the East, we move on now to the Sassanid Empire. Iran, like Mesopotamia, is a dry region: these are desert zones dotted with oases which extend continuously from Central Asia to the Mediterranean and to the Persian Gulf. In these oases a particular way of life was evolved, dependent entirely on irrigation which facilitated the cultivation of palms, fruit-trees and also of plants of a tropical nature, rice, sugar-cane, cotton. These irrigated crops were farmed intensively, introducing immense possibilities for the provision of goods to large urbanized regions, in terms of food and clothing. It could be said that the oasis inspired and maintained the city. While the western forest has always been hostile to the town (in that the large clearings set aside for cultivation have done nothing to aerate or enrich it), the oriental oasis favoured the development of great metropolises. In the vast central oasis constituted by Mesopotamia, the great capitals of the Orient have existed in succession: Babylon, then Seleucia, then Ctesiphon. Every urban impetus is accompanied by an extension of the cultivated land.

The Sassanid period was characterised by development of irrigation and plantations and, at the same time, by a full-scale urban movement. This is a significant fact which in the past has not been sufficiently stressed. Numerous cities were created by the Sassanid sovereigns, who were great builders, and in Iranian place-names **[19]** their names are still to be found followed by the termination *abad*, 'the city': Firouzabad, Bahramabad... or incorporated in the name of the new city: Rev-Ardachir, Nev-Chahpouhr, Ram-Kavadh... Between the fourth and sixth centuries, around the double ancient nexus of Seleucia-Ctesiphon new satellite urban communities developed: Veh-Ardachir, Mahoze...[12]

These Sassanid cities were inhabited by a population of artisans, of merchants, a bourgeoisie enriched by trade, a population which, while not of the highest social class was nevertheless free, which paid personal taxes to the State but was not subject to the corvée, nor to military

12 Cf. the accounts of German archaeological expeditions to Ctesiphon: O. REUTHER, *Die deutsche Ktesiphon-Expedition 1928-1929* (Berlin 1930); E. KUHNEL and O. WACHSMUTH, *Die Ktesiphon-Expedition 1931-1932* (Berlin 1933); J.-H. SCHMIDT, 'L'Expédition de Ctésiphon en 1931-1932' (*Syria*, XV, 1934).

service. It was at this time that the traditional classes of the Avesta, priests, warriors and farmers, came to be supplemented by a fourth class, that of the *Hutukhsh* ('the industrious' in Pahlavi)[13] which included both artisans and tradesmen. This active class of the population did not assert itself then, but the endorsement which it gained in religious circles clearly illustrates the growth of its economic and social power. In the sixth century, the widespread and deeply rooted movement of Mazdakism – a movement tinged, as always in the Orient, with religious Messianism – took full account of the growing importance enjoyed by the urban masses in the Sassanid Empire.

In parallel, we witness a progressive decline of the landed gentry, the *dihqans* ('the landowning aristocracy'). They lost more and more of their social influence and their economic wealth, and in Sassanid Iran and Mesopotamia a veritable crisis of the nobility took place, a crisis of the assets of the nobility, of the feudal system, in confrontation with the new rising force, that of the citizens, the 'bourgeois', merchants with personal fortunes.[14]

In the Sassanid Empire the sense of evolution was thus quite different from that which we have observed in the Byzantine Empire and in the Barbarian West. Here, the dominant note was provided by the prosperity of the cities and the decline of the great feudal estates. This was a domain of large-scale monetary circulation. It was not gold coinage which was legal tender, but silver coinage. Gold was hoarded in the form of ingots, jewellery and other precious possessions; the coin in the widest circulation was the Sassanid drachma, the *direm*. These silver coins were issued in enormous quantities by numerous mints, virtually throughout the Empire. In his excavations of Susa, J. de Morgan collected a great many drachmas of Chosroes II (590–628), showing a variety of designs, representing most of the major cities of **[20]** the Sassanid Empire,[15] proof of very active monetary circulation and a significant development of commerce in the Sassanid East, in the early seventh century, on the eve of the Muslim conquests. This was the time when the Persian silver *direm* circulated not only within the great Sassanid Empire, but also far away towards the South-East and the North-West, to the the Indian Ocean and the Ponto-Caspian steppes where it took over the positions formerly occupied by the Byzantine *nomisma*.

From the fifth to the seventh century, we may thus observe a kind of monetary withdrawal from the West towards the East, and this monetary withdrawal goes together with the urban movement: an urban rhythm accorded a monetary rhythm.

---

13 E. BENVENISTE, 'Les Classes socials dans la tradition avestique' (*Journal Asiatique*, 1932.)

14 A.CHRISTENSEN, L'Iran sous les Sassanides, Copenhagen-Paris 1936.

15 J. DE MORGAN, *Manuel de Numismatique orientale*, Paris 1936.

Third Phase (Seventh – Eleventh Centuries)

Urban Prosperity In The Muslim World
Beginnings Of Urban Renewal In The Barbarian West
Urban Development Of Byzantium

If we position ourselves in the very interior of the Muslim world once constituted, we witness prodigious urban growth everywhere and, where it was in progress, the halting of the domanial process which the Egyptian papyri have enabled us to trace in some detail. The testimony of these papyri is also useful to us for the first centuries of the Muslim period; it is a valuable tool for the purpose of sketching the trajectory of the curve on the graph which, at this time, changes its appearance and its meaning.

On the eve of the Muslim conquest, in Egypt, the domain, the seigniory, was in the process of being organised economically and socially: the seigneur and his serfs. We find in the papyri of Aphrodite, before the conquest, formulas of this type: 'The wretched serf Anoup (Anubis) prostrates himself before the great patrician; he grovels over the immaculate footsteps of the mighty duke Athanasios'. In the wake of the conquest, this evolution was aborted. The domanial cell, which was on the way to its complete realisation, was shattered and henceforward, the serf and the seigneur, the magnificent duke Athanasios and his wretched slave Anoup were placed, in terms of the new Muslim state, in a virtually identical position. Both paid capitation and the property tax levied on non-Muslims. The proceeds of the taxes collected in this manner were distributed among the members of the Muslim community. The latter lived in the cities, did not till the soil and had the status of stockholders where the land was concerned, living on the revenues paid by the people of the countryside. Thus the domanial regime, consolidated during the preceding period, was dismantled and transformed.

[21] This defeat of the domanial system was further accentuated by the growing importance of the role played by money, by consumer goods. As is the case with many of our burgeoning contemporary cities, the rapid growth of Muslim metropolises was provoked to a large extent by inflation – metallic in this case – and the consequent increase in prices. The abrupt enrichment of the merchant class of the cities enabled it to invest its gains in purchase of property in the countryside. The proprietor received the revenues for his land, but he stayed in the city; he too was a stockholder. Thus, to an increasing extent, economically and socially, the city dominated the surrounding countryside: the city-dweller imposed his control on the rustic. An active scheme of exchanges led to a renewed tightening of links between the countryside and the prosperous urban market sector: demand for agricultural produce to feed the city; demand for rural manpower for urban building projects. The capital epoch for a city is in fact the moment of its creation, and the construction sector, from an economic and social point of view, exerts a powerful appeal and makes its influence felt over long distances. The old adage 'When the building comes, everything comes', is entirely applicable to this urban construction, which brought together thousands and thousands of workers, hastily recruited from everywhere for the rapid erection of the new city. Regarding this movement of population from the countryside towards the city in the process of construction – rural workforce, snapped up by the city – we see a great many examples in the lists, furnished by the Egyptian papyri, of countrymen recruited in the villages of the Nile Valley for urban construction. They were sent to Fustat to erect public buildings, the governor's palace, the mosques; then even further, to Damascus, to participate in the construction of the Great Mosque of the Umayyads; to Tunis, to construct the buildings and the ships of the new maritime arsenal. To provide the workforce of the Syrian arsenals, whole populations were transported from the coasts of the Persian Gulf and of the Red Sea towards the Mediterranean ports.[16]

Thus there was a blending of populations, of technical processes, of mental perceptions essentially contrary to the domanial process, then pending completion. The ever more tight exchanges between the city and the countryside changed the meaning of evolution; the domanial cell disintegrated under the impact of intense demand for labour emanating from the expanding urban centres.

This urban expansion, this prodigious development of cities, of the economy and the civilisation which they represent, appears to us the essential characteristic of the Muslim world between the seventh and the eleventh centuries. This 'Muslim period' is one of the great moments in the general history of the urban movement – a capital fact which is seldom put under the spotlight. Other moments in the development of the cities have been broadly **[22]** studied. Not the Muslim moment. Attempts at synthesis[17] listed 'the great urban periods': the Hellenistic period, the Roman Empire, the thirteenth century West, the nineteenth century. What is forgotten, between the Roman Empire and the thirteenth century West, is the remarkable urban development experienced by the Muslim world of the seventh to the eleventh century.

What is the meaning of the propagation of the urban movement across the immense economic domain which had just been created by the Muslim conquests? We see it travelling from the East towards the West. It was amplified in the ancient Sassanid Empire (Iran, Mesopotamia) already enjoying a period of prosperity before the Muslim conquest; it started again in the former Byzantine provinces (Syria, Egypt) where it slowed; it was reborn in the countries of the Muslim West (Africa, Spain, Sicily), where it had long since disappeared.

This intense urban impetus in the Muslim world takes two forms: either the development of ancient centres which took on a new lease of life and expanded topographically and

16 In this context it is possible to associate with this migration of maritime populations (transfer of *nakhoda*, 'pilots', from the Persian Gulf and the Red Sea to the Syrian ports in the eighth century) with the introduction of the type of sail known as 'Lateen', moving from the sphere of the Indian Ocean to that of the Mediterranean.

17 For example: G. CHABOT, *Les villes*, Armand Colin.

demographically, economically and socially (Damascus, Cordova, Palermo); or the creation *ex nihilo* of new cities (Kairouan, Baghdad, Fez).

In the former Sassanid domain, built successively were: Kufa, on the Euphrates, Basra, the great port at the base of the Persian Gulf (637–638); and in particular the great Abbasid foundation, Baghdad, on the Tigris, in 762. From the ninth century onward, less than a hundred years after its creation, Baghdad was the greatest city in the world. In 836 a new city for the caliph was established on the Tigris, up-river from Baghdad, Samarra, which also became, very quickly, an important economic centre. Muslim commerce, with its warehouses on the eastern coast of Africa, introduced urban forms into this part of the Black Continent: Mogadishu, Barawa, Melinda, Mombasa were created, cities to which the contingents of Negro porters brought their loads of gold and ivory and from which the currents of Islamisation set out towards the heart of Africa.[18]

In the former Byzantine domain, everywhere an urban revival was noted: cities developed, which had been almost obliterated in the preceding period (Damascus, Aleppo), and numerous small towns burgeoned in Syria and in Egypt. Urban history in the Valley of the Nile is dominated by the massive development of the formerly small nucleus of Egyptian Babylon, at the point of the Delta, which proliferated by projecting around it a whole series of populous new cities: Fustat (seventh century), Al-Askar (eighth century), the Tulinid al-Qata'i (ninth century), Al-Qahira, the Fatimid Cairo (tenth century).

In the western Mediterranean, the cities created were: Kairouan (670), Tunis (698), Madia, Tahert (761), Tlemcen, Fez (867), Algiers (946), the Qala'a of the Beni Hammad (1007), of Marrakesh (1077). To the South of the Maghrib, the great caravan cities arose at the desert approaches, **[23]** points of arrival for the gold of Sudan: Sidjilmasa (787), Ouargla, the towns of Mzab, Ghadames, etc. From there, at the other extremity of the Saharan routes, Muslim commerce introduced urban forms into the Sudanese world: cities of gold and of slaves were born in the Nigerian Sahel, Awdaghost, Tadmekka, Tombouctoo.[19] And, as a repercussion, the opening of this immense new commercial horizon did not fail to play a role in the urban renewal experienced by Muslim North Africa between the eighth and the eleventh centuries: an urban renewal more important and more extensive than the urbanisation of the land had been in the Roman period.

In Spain, Cordova, Toledo, Saragossa, Seville, Malaga, ancient centres reduced to nothing during the Barbarian period, regained life and vigour, and expanded as never before. The great port of Almeria – the Aumarie of the medieval epics – was created in the Muslim period. Around Cordova, as around Kairouan, residential towns grew up: Madinat al-Zahra, Madinat al-Zahira. In Sicily, Palermo reached its apogee, monumental and economic.

---

18 L.M. DEVIC, *Le Pays des Zendjs ou la Côte orientale d'Afrique au moyen age*, Paris 1883.

19 E.F. GAUTIER, 'L'or du Soudan dans l'histoire' (*Annales d'histoire économique et sociale*, VII, 1937).

And only the metropolises, the most important cities,[20] have been cited here. Around them, an infinite number of urban conglomerates, more or less populous, and subsequently to enjoy varying degrees of success, all contributed, for the moment, to augmenting the density of the urban network.

What were the general aspects of this Muslim city in the full flush of growth, and first of all its demographic aspect? Within the urban perimeter, a very high concentration of population was the rule. Many of these metropolises became, within a few decades, the greatest cities in the world. In the absence of precise censuses, it is possible to arrive at an approximation of size, taking account of something which we have often encountered; we are dealing not with low-level housing, laterally extended, but on the contrary, with what the Latin-speakers called *insulae*: large housing blocks **[24]** of seven or eight storeys, each accommodating as many as 250 or even 300 persons.[21] At the end of the ninth century and in the tenth century, its period of apogee, Baghdad certainly attained and even exceeded one million inhabitants. Its surface area would fit within the city limits of Paris, minus the boulevards. Damascus and Cordova formed agglomerations of three to four hundred thousand inhabitants. Cairo's population was slightly smaller, at around half a million. If these figures – which are approximations – are compared with those that may be attributed to the medieval cities of the West at the time of their full economic development, i.e. in the thirteenth century – the huge gulf that separates them is striking. The most populous cities of northern Italy or of Flanders barely exceeded the total of thirty or forty thousand inhabitants at that time, and it was not until the fourteenth century that Paris, a unique case in terms of the Christian West, attained a figure of three hundred thousand. We make an exception here of Byzantium, with a population definitely approximating to a million, which is an oriental city and the great rival of Baghdad; Baghdad and Byzantium, 'the two eyes of the world' as they were called by the Byzantine historians, thus recognising the pre-eminence of the capital of the caliphs.

---

20 Several monographs on the great Muslim urban centres – of variable interest for the history of cities – have already been published. We may mention: G. LE STRANGE, *Baghdad during the Abbasid Caliphate*, Oxford 1900; E. HERZFELD, 'Geschichte der Stadt Samarra' (*Die Ausgrabungen von Samarra*. VI, Hamburg 1948); J. SAUVAGET and J. WEULERSSE, *Damas*, Paris 1936; J. SAUVAGET, *Alep, essai sur le développement d'une grande ville syrienne des origins au milieu du XIXe siecle*, Paris 1941; M. CLERGET, *Le Caire, étude d'histoire et de géographie urbaines*, Paris 1934; R. LE TOURNEAU, *Fès avant le Protectorat, étude économique et sociale d'une ville de l'Occident musulman* (Publ. de l'Institut des Hautes Etudes marocaines, Casablanca 1950; G. MARCAIS, *Tunis et Kairouan*, Paris 1937; R. CASTEJON, 'Cordoba califal' (*Boletin de la Real Academia de Córdoba*, 1924); E. LEVI-PROVENÇAL, *L'Espagne musulmane au Xe siècle*, Paris 1932: chap. vi, *Cordoue, capitale du califat umayyade d'Occident*; R. VELASQUEZ BOSCO, *Excavaciones en Medina Azzahra (Junta Superior de excavaciones y antiguedades*, 1923–1924 and foll.).

21 Our sources indicate this explicitly for Fustat-Cairo; cf. for example: NASIR-I-KHUSRAW, tr. Scheffer, p. 146–147.

As for the economic and social aspects: these great Muslim cities were before all else centres of commerce, locations with an essentially economic role. This is shown in the very design of the city. In the middle, often traversing it from one gate to another: the *souq*, the market, the commercial and industrial street where objects were manufactured and offered for sale before the very eyes of the customer. Even today, the *souq*s of the major cities of the East and the Maghrib gave an authentic impression of their originals. In the middle of the *souq* stands the great mosque, the moral centre of the market, its protective shadow rendering transactions more honest. Alongside, extend the *fondouq*s, hostelries for merchants, and the Kaisaria, a large and enclosed hall, its heavy doors reinforced with iron, serving as a depot for precious commodities emanating from the exterior. Opposite the Kaisaria stand the *souq al-sagha*, the market for currency exchanges and, if the city is important enough, the Mint, the *dar al-siqqa*. All around this central nucleus of commercial organisms, the various bodies of professionals are based, each group occupying its own quarter, its own street. The *souq*, as the pole of urban activity, supports an industrious and commercially active population, leading hectic and turbulent lives, from the porter, the artisan, the broker, to the wealthy merchant, to the controller of the market. This was the setting for the emergence of the stereotypical tycoon, enriched by long-range commerce, living lavishly in his opulent urban establishment, with an entourage of slaves and retainers: the 'financial backbone' of the urban society of the Muslim world. At the same time there was a worsening of the wretched state of the lower classes of the urban population, slaves or freemen, an urban proletariat whose revolts were sometimes ferocious: in the early ninth century the 'naked' took control of the streets of Baghdad and sacked several **[25]** quarters of the capital; social ferment, brutal confrontations, which testify to the intensity of urban life in this period.

A final aspect of this urban expansion in the Muslim world of the seventh to the eleventh century, the least known and, perhaps, the most important, on account of the explanatory elements which it entails for our benefit: the monetary aspect. Money was, in fact, the medium whereby this powerful urban activity was created, maintained and also best characterised: material construction of the city and the buoyancy of this sector; purchases of goods in the countryside for current consumption and of precious merchandise from distant centres of production for luxury consumption; manufacture and sale *in situ* or at a distance of the products of local industry; purchased by the wealthy classes of property in the countryside... In the general economy, the urban market is a preferential centre for the acquisition and redistribution of monetary assets. And, in its turn, the urban prosperity of the Muslim world was facilitated and supported by the influx of gold and the increasing intensity of its circulation: stockpiled gold put back into circulation and especially the influx of new gold, mined gold and in particular Sudanese gold, in quantities which were to be boosted over the course of time, from the eighth-ninth centuries onward.

The capital fact, for the history of the urban movement during the early Middle Ages, is the reintroduction of cities, i.e. of major centres of consumer demand, in the western

Mediterranean, on the very doorstep of the Barbarian West . And this movement of profound urbanisation, of city life, of urban civilisation and expansion, experienced in the ninth-tenth centuries by the Maghrib, Spain and Sicily, was virtually created by the importation of gold from the Sudan. The lands of western Islam – united by Arab authors under the name of Maghrib 'lands of the West' – were, for the easterners, a veritable Eldorado which attracted adventurers, mercenaries, scholars, in a quest for gold, prebends and pensions. It was the gold of Sudan which brought to Andalusia, from the Orient and particularly from Baghdad which was the great centre of diffusion, the poets of the Court, the musicians, the artists, those who have been called the pioneers of oriental culture,[22] and thanks to whom the techniques and forms of refined thought – in short, urban civilisation – passed from the East to the Muslim West, to the gates of the Barbarian West.

The demand for consumer goods initiated by the great cities of the Muslim world was to permit commerce and the urban movement to propagate and to develop in the Barbarian West.

The Muslim urban centres needed certain kinds of merchandise **[26]** (slaves, wood for shipbuilding, iron and weapons, tin, furs) which only the Barbarian West was capable of supplying; and in return for these they sent the latter gold: infiltration of gold, development of commerce and urban renewal, from the ninth-tenth centuries.

When medievalists began to write the history of the urban renewal of the West, they initially said that the urban renewal was the consequence of the Crusades and it became apparent in the twelfth century. Then, pursuing their studies in greater depth, they dated this renewal back to the eleventh century. Then, they found some very clear indications as early as the tenth century. The most recent researches speak of the end of the ninth century and, at certain very localised points, which are precisely the points of arrival of the commercial and monetary routes emanating from the Muslim world, the first manifestations of the renewal of cities, of urban growth, appear from the end of the eighth century and the beginning of the ninth, the time at which Muslim gold, in the form of *mancus*, began to irrigate the Barbarian West.

Thus it is that this period saw the beginning of the development of the cities of Italy: Amalfi, Naples, Gaeta on the Tyrrhenian Sea, and especially Venice on the Adriatic, Venice which owed its precocious economic prosperity to its location at the meeting point of three commercial domains, of Byzantium, of the Muslim world and of the Barbarian West. It contributed to the revictualling of Constantinople, deprived by the Muslim conquests of the provisions which it had hitherto drawn from its provinces of Egypt and of Syria. It pursued a profitable traffic in contraband with the Muslim ports. It imported the precious products of

22 Cf. R. BLACHÈRE, 'Un pionnier de la culture orientale en Espagne au Xe siecle, Sa'id de Bagdad' (*Hesperis*, X, 1930).

Byzantine industry which it passed on to the trade fairs of Pavia[23] where its merchants held the monopoly of the commerce in the oriental objects which the West was now capable of acquiring, thanks to the input of Muslim gold. It could be said that the initial and rapid progress of Venice in the eighth-ninth centuries was the consequence – direct and indirect – of the Arab conquests and of the commercial demands emanating from the great urban centres of the Muslim world.

It was the turn, subsequently, of the cities of northern Spain, of Languedoc and of the corridor of the Rhone, continuing via the Saone and the Meuse to the Rhineland and Flanders.

At the same time, from the other end of the Islamic world, also making itself felt was the commercial appeal launched by the great oriental centres, created or revived in the Muslim era, especially by Baghdad, its influence radiating and extending: an appeal directed towards the Barbarian West, via the northern routes, the routes of the Volga, of the Baltic and of central Europe. Muslim funds entered the system by the same route. Massive depots have been found stretching along the Russian rivers, on the shores of the Baltic and as far afield as Iceland! The creation of commercial centres, of embryonic cities, was the next step, and thus the 'Land of cities' was born, *gardariki*, as the Scandinavians called the region of the Russian rivers **[27]**: cities of wood constructed alongside navigable waterways, at the points chosen by higher commerce, at the places which were the destination of the financial currents emanating from the Muslim world: Itil (subsequently Astrakhan) on the delta of the Volga, Boulghar (near the site of the future Kazan) at the confluence of the Volga and the Kama, the 'City of the Bourtas' (later Nijni-Novgorod) at the confluence of the Volga and the Oka, Novgorod-the-Great on the Volkhov to the North of Lake Ilmen, and especially Kiev[24] on the Dnieper, with a commercial horizon simultaneously embracing the Muslim world to the East, Byzantium to the South, the Germanic lands of the upper Danube to the West and the shores of the Baltic to the North. Via the continental routes of central Europe and the maritime routes of the Nordic seas, the commercial and urban influx spread towards the Rhinelands, Flanders and England, where it combined with the currents emanating from the Mediterranean.

Thus, urban prosperity in the Barbarian West was localised at a very early stage at the zones of entry of the monetary currents emanating from the Muslim world.[25] This was the time that saw the appearance of terms such as portus, 'market-place', *Vic, Vicus*, 'commercial

---

23 On the fairs of Pavia and the Venetian commerce taking place there, see the *Honorantie civitatis Papie*, published by A. SOLMI in: 'L'Amministrazione finanziaria nel regno italico nell'alto medio evo' (*Bolettino della Società Pavese di Storia Patria*, XXXI, 1931).

24 Cf. E. SIMOES DE PAULA , *O comercio varegue e o Grão-Principado de Kiev*, São Paulo 1942. Cf. my account in *Annales E.S.C.*, IV. 1949.

25 Maurice LOMBARD, 'La route de la Meuse et les relations lointaines des pays mosans entre le VIIIe et le XIe siecle' (in: *L'Art mosan*, Paris, A. Colin, 1953). See the map.

zone';[26] the time when the city moved beyond its tight confines, and commercial and industrial zones were constituted. The traces of this expansion, if they are sought in the zones where the commercial links between the Muslim East and the Barbarian world were sealed, may be detected from the end of the eighth century.

Byzantium, in the same period, experienced a similar renewal, prefiguring the prosperity of the tenth-eleventh centuries, the second golden age of Byzantine art, the urban apogee of Constantinople, as is illustrated by the details supplied in the *Livre des Cérémonies*, by the description of Constantine of Rhodes who celebrates its beauties in the tenth century, by the effusive expressions of the rabbi Benjamin of Tudela who visited Byzantium at the beginning of the twelfth century, by the sense of wonder that the Crusaders of 1204 displayed when they entered the city 'of marble, of silk and of gold'.[27]

The beginnings of this new prosperity of the old Constantinian creation are to be placed at the end of the eighth-ninth centuries, when Muslim gold, after a detour through the Barbarian West, arrived to revitalise the luxury industry, offering new outlets for Byzantine products and for merchandise transferred via Byzantium from the Muslim East towards the Christian West. Here, **[28]** as in Venice, the profitable position of intermediary between the eastern world and the western world – and the monetary influx resulting from it – was the origin of the urban impetus.

In its turn, Byzantium exported a portion of its gold towards the Muslim world to buy there the primary materials necessary for luxuries and for industry: spices, perfumes, raw silk, ivory, pearls, precious stones etc. And this gold was to sustain and amplify still further the activity of the great Muslim cities.

From the Muslim East to the Muslim West, from the Muslim West to the Barbarian West, from the Barbarian West to Byzantium, from Byzantium to the Muslim East: the circuit was closed, monetary circuit and urban circuit. Geographically and chronologically, the urban evolution of the early Middle Ages overlaps monetary evolution very precisely.

The Muslim world of the seventh century to the eleventh, with its abundance of gold, thus appears to be the centre – and the origin – of a vast movement of urban renaissance which spreads along the great commercial routes, revived or newly created by the consumer demand emanating from the metropolises of the Islamic East: expansion of urban prosperity in the former Sassanid domain; renewal of cities in the former Byzantine domain, in ruralised Spain and nomadised North Africa; the progress of Constantinople; creation of urban forms in the

---

26 H. PLANITZ, 'Frühgeschichte der deutschen Stadt' (*Zeitschrift der Savigny-Stiftung für Rechtsgeschichte, Germ. Abt.*, LXIII, 1943).

27 Ch. DIEHL, *Constantinople*, Paris 1924. Map of the city, in A.M. SCHNEIDER, 'Byzanz, Vorarbeiten zu Topographie und Archäologie der Stadt' (*Istambuler Forschungen*, VIII, Berlin 1936).

Black world (coasts of East Africa and the Sudan), in the region of the Russian rivers and of the Baltic; finally the revival of urban activity in the Christian West.

Through its breadth, its intensity and also through the new era which it inaugurates for western Europe, this movement marks an epoch of supreme importance in urban history.

15

Settlement Patterns, Urban Functions and Capital Formation in Medieval Flanders

D. Nicholas

The mercantile settlement hypothesis of medieval urban origins made famous by Henri Pirenne and his disciples was based on the example of Flanders and particularly Ghent, its largest city. Pirenne saw the cities developing in the post-Viking age as merchant agglomerations centered around a fortification and expanding by a European-wide trade in fine woollen textiles. The cities' prosperity had ledto the precocious development of Flemish agriculture by providing markets for the peasants, with inflationary prices that enabled them to commute their servile obligations. The prosperity of Flanders in the eleventh and twelfth centuries was also furthered by a series of counts, statesmen who perspicaciously founded "new towns" or agrarian villages on their estates and cooperated with other lords who were doing the same. One of these foundations, Ypres, developed into the third great industrial city of Flanders.

Yet Pirenne's explanation is less than persuasive in treating the origins of urban functions: trade, crafts, finance, and public administration. The wandering merchant whom Pirenne made the prototype of a class certainly existed, but a resident population was necessary to provide for his needs when he was at home; for while the presence of fortresses at strategic points undoubtedly furthered the prosperity of the places in which they were situated, they could hardly have provided either the population base or the main markets of the enormous Flemish cities. Pirenne furthermore never adequately explained the source of the luxury articles that made the cities' fortunes. The intensive colonization of western Flanders postdates by two to three centuries the development of the basic urban configuration of the county, and of the new foundations only Ypres had a glorious future. We must thus dismiss facile assumptions of a necessary direct connection between regional agricultural surplus and urban development, for the leading cities were clustered in areas that by the thirteenth century if not earlier were so overpopulated that food generally had to be imported over a considerable distance. Still, the city in its initial stages needed to attract a substantial population before it would transcend its immediate hinderland to obtain food.

The Chronology and Forms of Settlement

I am concerned here less with the physical origin of the Flemish cities

2

than with the question of how the settlement patterns and environmental circumstances within an economic region caused certain agglomerations to develop into major cities, while others remained satellite towns or agrarian villages. We must therefore begin by considering Germanic primary settlement to about 900 A. D. In Flanders. The Flemish cities were produced by subsequent elaborations on a settlement pattern that was clearly discernible by that time. Our best source is toponymic material. Archaeological data are necessarily incomplete, while toponymic evidence at least has the virtue of consistency, and it appears probable that written reference to a community would not appear until it was of at least some local importance. The data are plotted on Map 1 and are based on first mentions of settlement in the communities, even in cases where the eventual permanent name of the place appears later. I have limited the map to the modern Belgian provinces of West and East Flanders and Dutch Zeeland. Except for some small territories in the southwest, most of which were French-speaking by the eleventh century, this represents the frontier of Germanic linguistic domination in the early Middle Ages. Germanic Flanders was the only major region of Europe west of the Rhine that developed large cities in the absence of a substantial prior Roman presence (although the Romans did have several small *castella* there). It thus affords distinct advantages for the study of urban origins from purely Germanic roots.[1]

Germanic primary settlement centered on two poles: coastal Flanders, and the Dender, Scheldt, and Lys valleys. While we know rough population densities only for the parishes in the southwest around Poperinge, extrapolation from these suggests that the primary areas could have supported a maximum population of some 60,000-75,000, a fact implying reasonably continuous settlement.[2] There was also some habitation in the southwest along the Mandel river, a tributary of the Lys that was eventually a center of linen manufacturing, and in a belt extending from the Lys over Tielt and reaching the coast through the polder areas northeast of modern Ostend. This was sandy and covered

---

[1]Discussion based on my compilations from M. Gysseling, *Toponymisch Woordenboek van België, Nederland, Luxembourg, Noord-Frankrijk en West Duitsland (vóór 1226)* (Brussels, 1960). Information on commune areas is taken from Eugène de Seyn, *Geschied- en Aardrijkskundige Woordenboek der Belgische Gemeenten*, 2 vols., 2nd ed. (Turnhour, n.d.). Since the coastline has changed constantly, I have plotted the chronology of settlement on a modern map.

[2]My calculations from M. Gysseling and A. C. F. Koch, *Diplomata belgica ante millsimum centisimum scripta*, I (Brussels, 1950), 60-61, based on a *bunuarium* size of about 1.25 hectares. The suffix *-inge* or *-inga* suggests Germanic settlement at the place before Saint-Bertin colonized extensively.

3

largely by heath in the early Middle Ages, and it seems probable that the inhabitants had an essentially pastoral economy. The presence of substantial sheep raising later in this part of Flanders, together with the importance of 'Frisian' cloth production in the early period lends credence to this supposition. Flanders only began importing wool at the end of the eleventh century, a fact suggesting that much of the great expansion of arable noticeable at that time was at the expense of pasture needed for the textile industries.[3] A similar soil type is found north of Ghent, and evidence from the later Middle Ages suggests that this region was pastoral even then.[4]

In northwestern Flanders there was primary settlement around the count's fortress at Bruges, which was made a port only by coastal flooding in the early eleventh century. Indeed, the appearance in the sources of communities northeast of Bruges during the next two centuries is a chronology of the receding of the water. There was little primary settlement in the northeast. Most was along the Durme, a tributary of the Scheldt that ran east and came about five kilometers north of Ghent.

The core of primary habitation was in southeastern Flanders, the Lys and Scheldt valleys, which produced considerable grain and gave access to the farms of France and southwestern Flanders. The region between the two rivers east of Courtrai was almost completely settled by 900, as was a belt between the two streams farther north near the divergence of the Mandel from the Lys. North of Ghent, away from the great streams, there was primary settlement in a belt ranging northwest. In the Alost region there was habitation in a western area near no large center and in three nuclei around Ninove, Grammont, and Alost itself. Despite the obvious importance of the place, there was little settlement in the district of Dendermonde, at the junction of Dender and Scheldt, a fact almost certainly due to the fact that the sandy coastal plain bends abruptly south at Ghent to include much of the territory between Lys and Scheldt near Ghent but follows the course of the Scheldt farther east. The cores of primary settlement were thus along rivers that were important for grain production and transport. Large towns tended to develop downstream from the grain supply and on the edge of a belt of less productive territory, in this case the sandy coastal plain, which presumably would need the food which the terminal point received coming downstream, and which in its turn, with its more

---

[3]A. Verhulst, "La laine indigène dans les anciens Pays-Bas entre le XIIe et le XVIIe siècle," *Revue Historique*, DIV (1972), 283, 289.

[4]See below, and A. Verhulst, *Het Landschap in Vlaanderen in Historisch Perspectief* (Antwerp, 1966), pp. 56, 58, 11-51; and Verhulst, *Histoire du paysage rural en Flandre de l'époque romaine au XVIIIe siècle* (Brussels, 1960), pp. 60-61, 68-69.

4

pastoral economy, could provide animals for leather and textile industries.

Elaboration of these settlement patterns between the tenth and thirteenth centuries also has important implications for the early history of urban functions and suggests that parts of Flanders were already experiencing a version of an overheated economy by the eleventh century. Primary settlements tended to be nuclei around which later communities developed, and settlement existed before 900 in 180 communes, whose modern borders, which are usually quite close to those of the Middle Ages, encompass nearly one-third of the land area of Flanders and just over one-third of the eventual totalnumber of parishes. The tenth century was a period of consolidation, as the larger centers grew into the functions that the primary patterns had suggested for them. During this time only twenty-two new communities are mentioned (4.1% of the eventual total), but they were large, involving 7.68% of the land area. By the last quarter of the tenth century some parishes in eastern Flanders were assuming peculiar shapes, suggesting that they were on the edge of or between previous settlements. The only substantial growth at this time was near Ghent, particularly south and east along the Scheldt, despite the infertility of the region. A comital castle had been erected there during the Viking attacks, and Ghent had a thriving merchant settlement and was the chief place of eastern Flanders, an agglomeration that could help determine as well as be determined by alterations in rural settlement patterns.

In summary, therefore, on the eve of the great clearance endeavors of the High Middle Ages, there was extremely heavy settlement throughout most of eastern Flanders. The large towns except Ypres had existed by 900 as villages; but between 900 and 1050, or just before the great era of reclamation was to begin, several major secondary centers of Flanders--Dixmude, Audenarde, Termonde--appear in the sources. The increase in agricultural productivity of the late Carolingian period had furthered the development of centers that were peculiarly favored by geography, and the same thing was about to happen in the central Middle Ages. By now, however, there was not room in eastern Flanders for more large cities, with the result that the growth of such places as Termonde, which was similar to Ghent in many respects, was stunted.[5]

The diffusion of settlement quickened in the eleventh century. Roughly one-fifth of the total parishes and land surface are attested. Patterns are now quite discernible. One-third of the new land was in the district of Ghent, mainly

[5]As with Ghent, Termonde was settled on the smaller of the two streams serving it, in this case the Dender, expanding as did Ghent toward the source of its food supply. The Scheldt only touched the northern edge of the town.

5

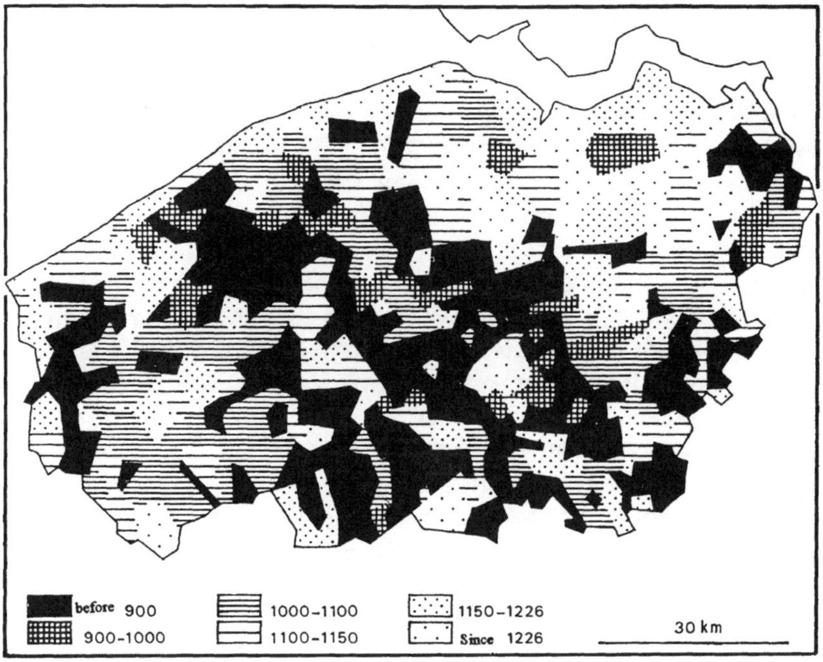

Fig. 1. Chronology of settlement in medieval Flanders: the evidence of toponyms

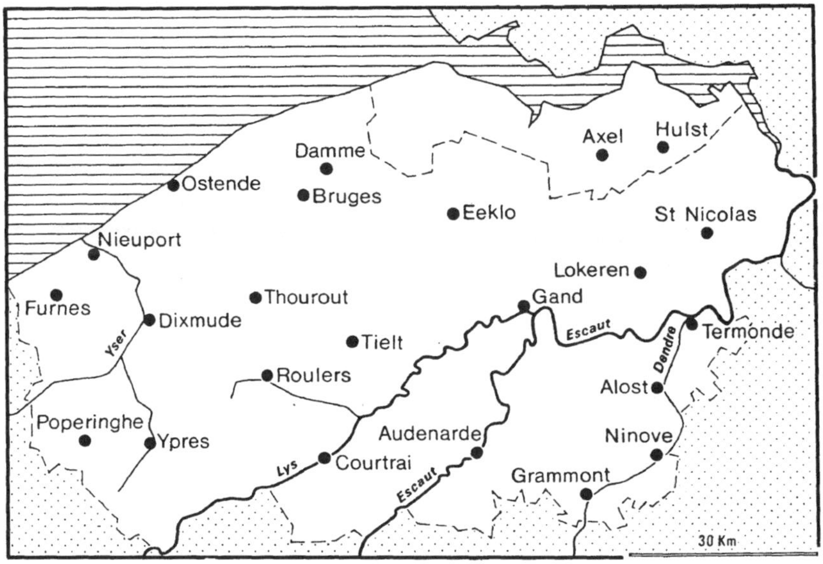

Fig. 2. Chief towns of Flanders

6

north of the town, while one-fifth was in that of Bruges. But the focus was shifting. Between 1001 and 1050 the district of Termonde saw the appearance of six new parishes of a total of thirty, with a land area over one-third of the total surface of the circumscription. The economic region of Ghent was thus continuing to fill out on the east, a prelude to the great expansion of settlement in northeastern Flanders during the twelfth and thirteenth centuries. Of considerable importance too is the expansion around Ypres. Before 900 this district had known settlement in only five parishes, all of them in the Saint-Bertin estates around Poperinge. In the second half of the eleventh century alone, Ypres itself was established, with eight communities that involve one-third of the area of the district. In the century between 1051 and 1150 nearly half of the total surface of this area is first mentioned in written sources, while between 1051 and 1100 alone ten of twenty-one communities in the neighboring district of Dixmude appear. The great expansion of settlement in the interior of southwestern Flanders thus preceded the more famous efforts at polder reclamation along the coast in the twelfth century and produced one great city. Settlement also continued to grow during the eleventh century in eastern Flanders, at a fairly constant rate and in nearly all cases involving small communes on the edge of previously recorded settlements.

The first half of the twelfth century was a great age of colonization throughout Flanders, even in the more thickly settled east. In this single half century 102 new settlements are recorded, involving just under one-fifth of the total parishes and land area. Of particular interest is the growth of two areas that had been economic backwaters, the southwest and northeast, far from the developing urban networks and not particularly well situated for transport to them. The polder reclamation has for years excited the admiration of historians as an example of princely initiative and private enterprise conquering the environment and bringing democracy and liberty to the unenlightened. In the coastal district of Furnes, only six of thirty-seven parishes are first mentioned in the first half of the twelfth century, but they involve 41.64% of the land surface. In the northeastern district of Saint-Nicolas, the figures are seven of twenty-nine parishes with 33.64% of the land. Yet the already heavily populated vicinity of Alost witnessed greater areal expansion in the twelfth century than did that of Bruges.

Rural overpopulation thus was already becoming a serious problem, and the signs of this are clear by the late twelfth century. Between 1151 and 1226 colonization slowed somewhat *except in the older settled districts* of Alost, Ghent, and Ypres, which accounted for over half the total expansion. It is particularly striking in the case of Ghent, and again involved mainly the northern part of the area, the sandy coastal plain. The arable surface of Flanders

7

was being used up except in the unproductive areas. Fifty-four communities (10.2%) still had not been mentioned in the sources by 1226, but save two that were created by modern divisions of earlier settlements and several that originated in later reclamation in Zeeland, all were noted in the later medieval sources. Of the land whose parishes were not mentioned in the sources before 1226, or roughly one-tenth of the area of Flanders, two-fifths are in the northeast, while another one-fifth is in the areas of Ypres and Furnes.

Correlating the urban map with these schedules of settlement leads to important conclusions on the nature of urban origins. Three-quarters of the places ever mentioned in neighboring Picardy had been settled by 1000.[6] Flanders only reached this stage in the third quarter of the twelfth century. It was obviously still a frontier area much later than the regions of northern France from which it was eventually to draw much of its grain supply. Since there is no evidence that wool was imported before the late eleventh century or grain before the mid-twelfth, the presence of a prosperous agrarian hinterland almost certainly contributed to the rise of the Flemish cities. But the combination of industry and available raw materials eventually caused the Flemish cities to become a depressant on Flemish agriculture. The fact that the rich land of the southwest developed so late and produced only one large city, and that one much smaller than Ghent and Bruges at their apogee, suggests the importance of commerce and of producing even for the small pre-urban markets in eastern Flanders. There was undoubtedly a tremendous population growth in the twelfth century. Until then, the southeast had been able to feed Ghent, but now the metropolis began to import grain from France along the Lys and the Scheldt. The agricultural expansion of the southwest in the twelfth century was thus directed toward producing for towns that were already large, and in that sense the Pirenne school was correct in arguing the primary importance of the cities for the Flemish economy. But they failed to see that the cities had been created and fed by dense settlement in the fertile lands of eastern and central Flanders. When the great cities became so large that they had to obtain their food from a wider area, the rural southwest developed no large towns because a market for its farm produce was already assured. The rural and urban sectors of the Flemish economy were thus in a rough equilibrium in the twelfth century.

But this situation was of short duration, for the cities of the late Middle Ages found it easier to import French and German grain than to rely on the

---

[6]R. Fossier, *La Terre et les hommes en Picardie jusqu'à la fin du XIIIe siècle*, 2 vols. (Paris and Louvain, 1968), I, 163

8

Flemish farmers. They thus forced native grain prices down and contributed to a depression of Flemish agriculture. On the surface this may seem unlikely, but it is made possible by local hydrography. As Ghent became too large to be fed by southeastern Flanders, the Lys and Scheldt, which had brought grain from rural Flanders in the early period, were now used to import it from France. Since a convoy network and toll arrangement would have had to be established anyway to import what could not be obtained locally, importing most of the grain was actually easier than patronizing local Flemish markets that were farther from navigable streams. The Zwin fulfilled the same functions for Bruges, which imported German grain in the late Middle Ages, while the Lieve canal, which was built from Ghent to Damme in the thirteenth century, also provisioned Bruges with French grain. Such a developing situation would obviously have important effects on social geography within the cities themselves and can only be explained in the light of population density that was so high in the cities that the countryside could not support it, and of a countryside that had reached its productive limits.

The Density of Rural Population

Unfortunately, the only reasonably comprehensive enumeration of population for medieval Flanders is a hearth tax record of 1469, and by that time the basic urban landscape had long since been established.[7] Map 3 represents the density of population given in this survey, using a multiplier of 4.5 for the rural hearth. The surviving returns are not complete, but they do suggest heavy population in areas of primary settlement save in the immediate vicinity of the large cities. Yet even the poor and much later settled northeast had extremely dense population, as did some areas in the western polders.

This suggests a considerable pressure on resources; yet several considerations cause me to doubt seriously the validity of these figures as indices of total population. First, the extreme variations between adjacent localities make the entire picture suspect. Secondly, it seems virtually certain that the inhabitants of ecclesiastical seigniories were not included in the 1469 enumeration. Fourteenth-century land books of St. Bavo's abbey of Ghent show that this monastery alone had more dependents in several of its villages

---

[7]Totals of the hearths by parish, but not a formal edition of the documents, are found in J. De Smet, "Le dénombrement des foyers en 1469," *Bulletin de la Commission Royale d'Histoire*, XCIX (1935), 105-150.

9

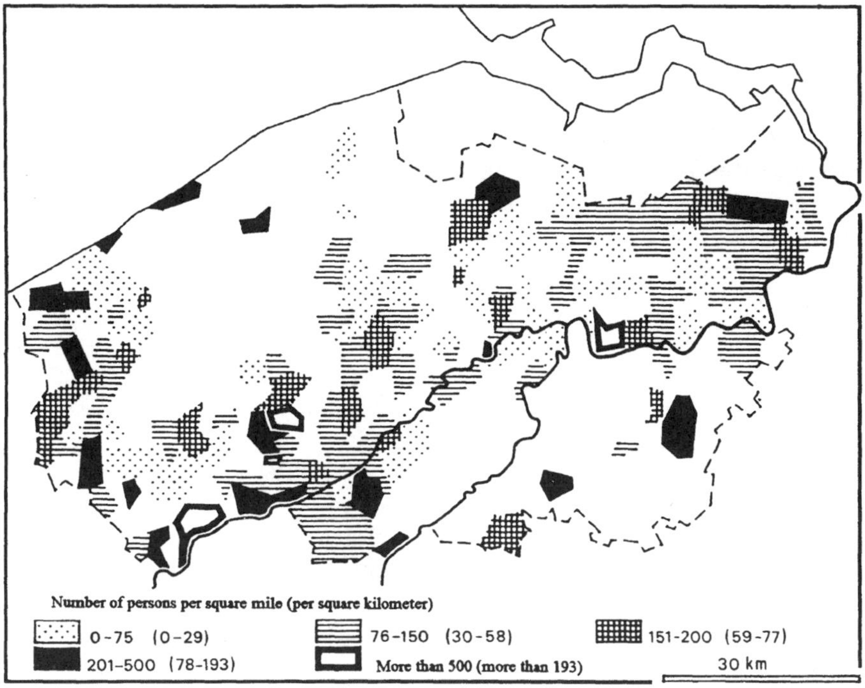

Fig. 3. Density of population in Flanders according to the survey of 1469

than the count had in 1469.[8] If the descendants of these persons were included in the later survey, it suggests a frightful population drop within a century. That Flanders did experience population decline brought on by general economic depression, plagues, and the civil war of 1379-85 is undeniable, but I doubt that it was this drastic. Accordingly, all recent calculations of the medieval

[8]See landbook of abbey of St. Bavo of Ghent, State Archive of Ghent, R43, fo. 18-19r, 20r-25r, 16r-17r. The decline would have been as much as 68% in a single century in the village of Kluizen; R 43, fo .72v-74r.

10

population of Flanders based on the figures of 1469 are probably too low. While even on their face they suggest serious pressures on available resources, they indicate a much less critical situation than was actually the case.

A final element of the population question is the number of "poor" hearths within the overall totals of 1469. The problem was worst in the northeast, in some instances involving over 50% of the total hearths reported. This was the least naturally fertile and the most recently settled part of Flanders, and an area of heavy population but probably less severe than in other regions.[9] The conclusion is obvious: Flanders could not even support the cities that it had. To feed themselves, the large cities had to gain control of sources of supply of foreign grain, and this in turn prevented the smaller places from turning the frequent grain shortages to their own advantage. The condition that in the early Middle Ages had led to the growth of towns and had caused the cities to expand toward their sources of food, inevitably the interior, had ceased to be. Flanders instead was plagued by chronic shortages and fragmentation of farmers' holdings.

The Cities in Their Primary Phase

It is thus important to establish how the cities grew in reaction to the situation of the early Middle Ages and to see how the later condition, which made Flanders unviable as an economc region and forced the cities to turn to other sources of supply, altered settlement patterns and social structures within the cities themselves.

The prosperity of Bruges was always derived from foreign trade, which was originally facilitated by the floods. The Franc (castellany) of Bruges had room for an agricultural expansion that could feed the metropolis during most of the central Middle Ages. Settlement at Bruges developed, however, not from the comital castle that was its nucleus toward its seaport, but along a land route leading toward the interior.[10] It thus followed a pattern that was standard for virtually all towns evolving out of primary settlements in northern Europe: the city expanded toward its source of food supply, which was also the source of its earliest trade, and which fed it and provided it with goods to reconsign,

---

[9]W. P. Blockmans and W. Prevenier, "Armoede in de Nederlanden van de 14e tot het midden van de 16e eeuw: bronnen en problemen," *Tijdschrift voor Geschiedenis*, LXXXVIII (1975), map p. 514. Compare D. Nicholas, "Weert: a Scheldt Polder Village in the Fourteenth Century," *Journal of Medieval History*, II (1976), 256.

[10]J. B. Ross, "Introduction," *The Murder of Charles the Good, Count of Flanders*, by Galbert of Bruges (New York, 1967), pp. xvi, 51-63, and literature cited.

11

often to peasants of areas less favored by soil conditions: for we have seen that the major cities developed on the edge of fertile areas. Ultimately, however, Bruges would prefer to import grain and other basic raw materials from sources outside its immediate hinterland. Bruges' future was as an artificial seaport, and accordingly the city was provisioned mainly by sea in the late Middle Ages, although it was important for the rural grain economy of Flanders at least through the twelfth century. The pull of Bruges was such, however, that only secondary centers developed beside it in northwestern Flanders during the age of city gestation.

The topographical development of Ypres, the only "new town" that became a major metropolis, was similar. It could be reached by water from Bruges as well as overland and was only a few kilometers from the Lys. Ypres was thus the connecting link between two hydrographic systems, for the Yperlee was not navigable south of Ypres. It thus followed the pattern of development on the edge of a local region. The halls and market were just south of the church of St. Martin, at the outlet of the road leading to Dixmude, with the road to Thourout leading directly to the market but slightly east. The town then backed down the Yperlee; it does seem probable here that the small stream was more important than the land routes in determining settlement patterns.[11]

Ghent , the largest city of Flanders and probably the earliest to develop important urban functions, is an obvious paradigm. It was the product of "natural" forces of the primary settlement period, while Ypres came later and in some measure as the result of deliberate planning. Bruges was a unique case, owing its position to conditions extraneous to Flanders.

Several nuclei formed the basis for the eventual city of Ghent, illustrated on Map 4. There had been a Roman fortification on the right bank of the Scheldt on the site where St. Bavo's abbey was later built. An agrarian settlement developed by the eighth century several hundred meters downstream from this near the church of St. John (now St. Bavo's cathedral), on the site called *portus* in tenth-century documents. But the second and more important pole of settlement was on an island in the bend of the Lys. It consisted primarily of leather workers, a fact that confirms my suggestion of a strongly pastoral economy north of the city. This was later called the *vetus burgus (Oudburg)*, a term which at that time did not necessarily mean a fortification but could

---

[11]J. Dhondt, "Développement urbain et initiative comtale en Flandre au Xie siècle," *Revue du Nord*, XXX (1948), 152; G. Des Marez, *Étude sur la propriété foncière dans les villes du Moyen-Age et spécialement en Flandre* (Ghent and Paris, 1898), p. 216 ff.; and A. Verhulst, "De Vroegste Geschiedenis van het Sint-Maartenskapittel en het ontstaan van de stad Ieper," *Handelingen der Maatschappij voor Geschiedenis en Oudheidkunde te Gent*, n.s. XI (1957), 31-48.

12

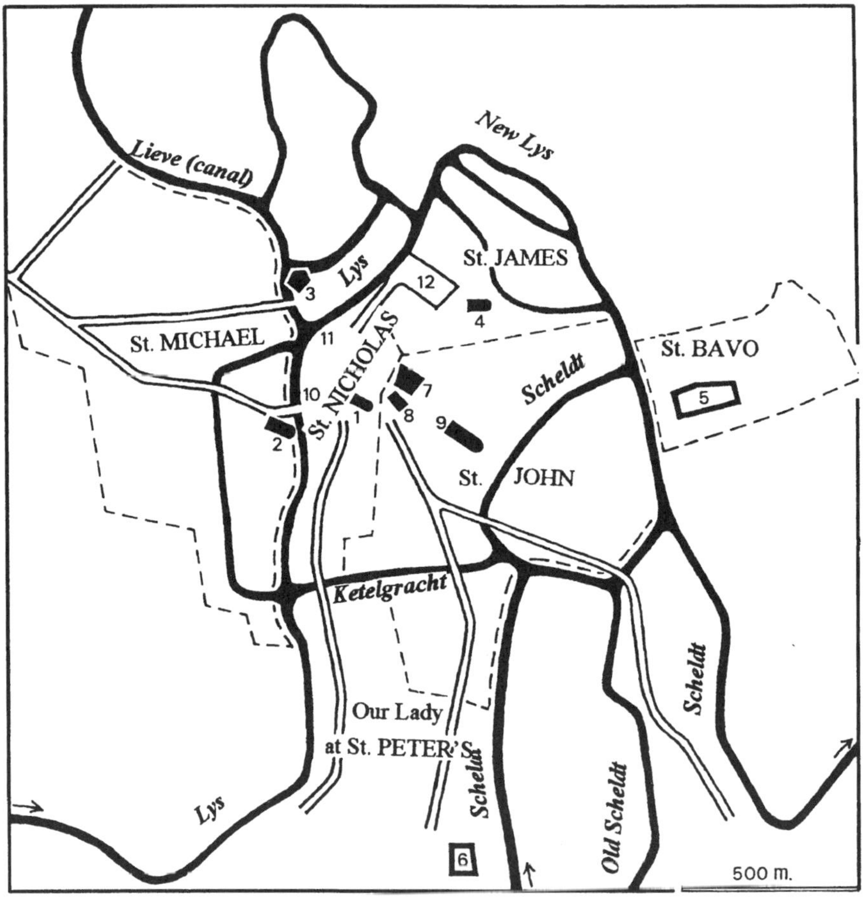

1. Church of St. Nicholas
2. Church of St. Michael
3. Castle of the counts of Flanders
4. Church of St. James
5. Abbey of St. Bavo
6. Abbey of St. Peter
7. City hall
8. Cloth hall
9. Church of St. John
10. Grain Market
11. Fish Market
12. Friday Market

Fig. 4. Ghent in the fourteenth century

denote a settlement outside a fortress, of more recent date than the fortress itself. This agglomeration was considered by contemporaries to be older than those parts of the settlement located due south of it, in the vicinity of the then course of the Scheldt.[12]

The *portus* around St. John's was annihilated during the Viking attacks, and the center of settlement seems then to have moved toward the fortification on the Lys. It was predominantly merchant even by the early tenth century, but there is no evidence that the previous *portus* settlement expanded to link Scheldt and Lys; rather, this was a new settlement, on the right bank of the Lys south of the count's castle. The left bank of the Lys, the later parish of St. Michael, was settled by the mid-tenth century. During this century two water links between Lys and Scheldt were dug, the Ketelgracht and the New Lys, and a land axis was provided. The central city at Ghent thus became an artificial island, later called the "barrel" (*cuip, cuve*).

With food markets, which were the main markets of the city, just outside the walls of the fortification, Ghent conforms to the general pattern of the cities of northern Europe. This, however, suggests that the main business of the inhabitants of the suburb was not provisioning the lords of the castle with luxuries, but furnishing the suburbs themselves with grain and other necessities and in reexporting grain down the Scheldt; for Ghent was on the northern edge of a belt of sandy loam land, near the edge of the coastal plain and the natural terminus for the prosperous agriculture of the open field areas of eastern Flanders. There simply was not enough market in the small forts of the pre-urban nuclei, or indeed among the nobles in general to suggest that a town the size of Ghent could have based its prosperity on producing fine textiles for the aristocracy. The essential business of most townspeople was provisioning other townspeople, a characteristic of the city that, as we shall see, would eventually lead to self-perpetuation of the city and its growth beyond bounds that could be sustained by the local economy.

Settlement at Ghent did not initially expand toward the Scheldt. For although the Scheldt was the better artery for long-distance trade, grain shipped along it was provisioning large centers south of Ghent, notably Tournai and Cambrai. The "barrel" was walled during the eleventh century, and settlements extending south down the left bank of the Lys were incorporated into the city before 1199. But the Scheldt area was essentially suburban and was not densely settled before the twelfth century. With the money derived from their original

[12]Discussion based on A. Verhulst, "Die Frühgeschichte der Stadt Gent," in *Die Stadt in der europäischen Geschichte. Festschrift Edith Ennen* (Bonn, 1972), pp. 108-137, which supersedes previous literature.

14

profits in victualling, the urban wealthy were able in a second stage to invest in industry. Only in 1254 was the Overscelde quarter, between the medieval and modern beds of the Scheldt, brought within the city walls, and this was the quarter where textile artisans were most numerous. While it is true that the presence of the seigniorial jurisdictions meant that these areas were not annexed to the city until they were quite populated, it does seem clear that substantial settlement along the Scheldt at Ghent postdated the settlement of the central city along the Lys by at least a century and a half.[13]

The tax and militia records of Ghent are the best means of determining settlement patterns, but there are problems with them. Few sources expressly mention individuals' professions. It is known that the frames for stretching textiles were located Overscelde and that it was thus primarily a working class section of town. But for tax purposes Ghent was divided into parishes, and the St. John parish, which included Overscelde, also contained the aristocratic streets on the *portus* side of the Scheldt. The quarter of St. Bavo was outside the city wall until the 1380s and included little settlement. St. Nicholas is the smallest geographically, but it included the food markets. St. Michael was that part of the *portus* west of the Lys, but it included pasture areas west of the city, while St. James was in the northeastern part of the *portus*.[14]

The weavers were the largest single element of the city population and certainly were the most important of the textile trades. At various times during the fourteenth century they were placed under civil disabilities and fined. In 1325 and following years, and again after 1349, these levies were collected in the parishes according to the pattern elucidated by Table 1. I have also included the parish distribution of drapers who pledged in 1362 never again to rebel against the count of Flanders.

---

[13]Des Marez, *Propriété foncière*, pp. 183-203; M. Gysseling, *Gent's Vroegste Geschiedenis in de Spiegel van zijn plaatsnamen* (Ghent and Antwerp, 1954), pp. 30-32.

[14]W. Blockmans, "Peilingen naar de sociale strukturen te Gent tijdens de late 15e eeuw," in *Studien betreffende de sociale strukturen te Brugge, Kortrijk en Gent in de 14e en 15e eeuw* (Heule, 1971), map 4.

TABLE 1[15]

	1325-26	1349-50	1362
Overcosterie St.John	15.55%	12.79%	9.12%
Nedercosterie St. John	16.37	13.24	12.77
Overcosterie St. Michael	25.38	27.40	29.29
Nedercosterie St. Michael	8.09	5.48	14.26
Sts. Nicholas, James, Bavo	15.00	10.05	12.41*
St. Peter	19.60	31.05	21.53

Sts. Nicholas and James only.

These figures do not correspond exactly, but they do suggest that while the weavers may have tended after the 1320s to migrate to the suburbs, there was considerable continuity in the relative strength of the weavers in the parishes of Ghent during the fourteenth century. It is obvious that there were very few weavers in the areas of Sts. Michael and Nicholas that bordered the food markets, while most were concentrated in the southern suburbs. A fair number lived in St. John.

The chief rivals of the weavers within the textile industry were the fullers. Our best source for the social geography of the fullers is an enumeration by ward of 775 fullers who did military service in 1356-57, presumably on the basis of a city-wide assessment. The percentages are as follows:

[15]For the earlier period the percentage is taken from the fiscal year 1325-26, but there is little variation before the tax was ended in 1333-34. Sources of table: G. Espinas and H. Pirenne (eds.), *Recueil de documents relatifs à l'histoire de l'industrie drapière en Flandre*, 4 vols. (Brussels, 1906-24), II, 436-53, 504-10; J. Vuylsteke (ed.), *Gentsche Stads- en Baljuwsrekeningen, 1280-1336* (Ghent, 1900), pp. 407-08, with my calculations.

16

TABLE 2 [16]

St. John	377	48.6%
St. Michael	126	16.3%
St. James	214	27.6%
St. Peter	58	7.5%

Of interest here is the fact that the most strongly weaver quarter of Ghent, the suburban village of the abbey of St. Peter, had by this assessment only one-eighth the number of fullers as weavers at mid-century. The fullers were stronger in St. James, while the two groups were roughly equal in the parish of St. John, with the fullers congregating near the Scheldt and the weavers somewhat farther away. The fullers, however, seem to have found life in St. Peter's village dangerous, for their wards were in two streets that were near the St. John parish. These figures suggest that most fullers lived in or near the old city or in the parish of St. Michael, which was adjacent to it on the west, while the weavers were concentrated in a belt from St. Michael's through St. Peter's village and into St. John and Overscelde. There were few weavers in St. James, a site of fuller strength in north Ghent; for most of the fullers living in the parish of St. John were in wards along the Scheldt near St. James.

Just as the food markets and earliest settlements at Ghent were located on the Lys upstream from the count's castle, toward the source of food, so the Reep, cloth halls, and Overscelde and St. Peter's village workers' quarters were all along the Scheldt, which was the normal transit route for English wool in the central Middle Ages, before the great development of Bruges. The presence of many textile artisans in the parish of St. Michael does not really alter this, for much will happen in two and a half centuries, and the halls, expensive equipment, and most settlement remained on the Scheldt in the fourteenth century as they had been in the beginning. Yet while the textile industry was undoubtedly the major export trade of the city and was the major employer of its people, it represents a second stage both of settlement and of capital formation.

---

[16]A. Van Werveke (ed.), *Gentse Stads- en Baljuwsrekeningen (1351-1364)* (Brussels, 1970), pp. 290-91. I have grouped the wards into parishes and made the appropriate calculations.

17

Settlement Patterns and Capital Formation

The textile industry of Ghent was thus quite weak in the central city, an extraordinary circumstance if clothmaking was as important in the overall economy of the city as the traditional view would have us believe. The question can be elucidated in part by considering the sources of taxable wealth and profit margins.

Several forced loans were assessed during the troubled period between 1336 and 1349, but the amounts vary considerably between years. A better index of the geographical distribution of wealth in Ghent is a list of 1327 detailing persons in each parish from whom the city could expect to collect a loan in case of emergency, and the amount payable by each. The data are summarized in Table 3.

TABLE 3[17]

Parish	Wealth in lb.and %	Parish % of weversgeld, 1325-26	Number of taxpayers, with average amount owed
John	2170: 34.31%	31.92%	47: 46.17 lb.
Nicholas	1220: 22.39	4.41	30: 40.67
Michael	810: 14.86	33.47	22: 36.82
James	970: 17.80	9.46	24: 40.42
Peter	280: 5.14	19.60	8: 35.00

These figures suggest that the wealthy were concentrated in the largest parishes, Sts. John, Michael, and Nicholas, but so was the rest of the population, save that there were few artisans in the parish of St. Nicholas, which contained the great markets. The average assessment for the forced loan was highest in St. John, which housed most of the city's textile merchants as well as a substantial artisan population, followed closely by St. Nicholas, which thus seems to have had the most aristocratic social composition of any of the parishes. St. Michael's tended to be working class, while St. James was dominated by the aristocrats and the fullers, who were generally allied

[17]Source of table: F. De Potter (ed.), *Petit Cartulaire de Gand* (Ghent, 1885), pp. 321-23.

18

politically with the counts of Flanders against the weavers. Still, all parishes save St. Peter had a substantial number of wealthy persons.

These suggestions from the loan assessment of 1327 are corroborated by an examination of the occupations of the wealthy. The city leased excises and rents to brokers, who collected them and generally made substantial profits. This was the major source of income for the city each year. Of 131 persons included in the loan list, sixty-three at some time leased an excise or had relatives who did so. In Table 4 I have grouped these men by parish and the type of excise leased. Several taxes were owed on cloth and wool at various stages of the clothmaking process. The excise of the gates involved in principle a tax on virtually allcommodities imported, while grain, beer, meat, and fish were taxed inside the city. Many of the brokers who controlled the sources of supply of the city by leasing these taxes, and who accordingly had opportunities for enormous monopolies and profits, leased several excises, suggesting diversified operations, and where this was the case I have so indicated.

TABLE 4

Parish	Gates, food	Textiles	Textiles and Gates, food	Other	Total
Nicholas	14	1	3	1	18
Michael	7	--	2	1	10
John	12	6	--	2	20
James	7	4	1	1	13
Peter	1	1	--	--	2
Total	41	12	6	4	63

Table 4 confirms our earlier findings: that most textile wealth and settlement was in the parishes of Sts. John and James; that there substantial settlement of textile artisans in St. Michael's parish but little wealth, suggesting that workers who found housing there because none was available on the east side; and that the brokers who leased the gates and the food excises lived principally in the parishes of Sts. Nicholas and John but with a substantial number also in Sts. Michael and James. The parish of St. Nicholas had a comparatively small population, for the markets, guild halls, and docks took up much of the area. This, along with the Scheldt grain trade by the fourteenth century, explains the presence of many victuallers in the parish of St. John, which bordered St. Nicholas on the east and where many undoubtedly resided whose business establishments were in St. Nicholas. It seems clear that the city continued in the fourteenth century as earlier to import much of its strategic material along the Lys; grain brought along the Scheldt had to be transported along the Ketelgracht to the grain market on the Lys.

Thus two-thirds of the wealthy persons of 1327 whose precise economic orientation can be identified made their money by provisioning the city. Only 19% were exclusively in textiles, while another 9.5% were active in both textiles and provisioning. The extent to which provisioning, particularly with food, was an important source of capital formation is even more pronounced among the wealthiest, those liable for loans of between 50 and 100 lb., than among the more modestly well-to-do. The biggest operators concentrated on the grain and gate excises, while persons who leased only textile taxes were generally not from the more established families of Ghent.

The gaps in these figures are obvious, but the corroboration of the several sources is sufficiently strong to suggest that while wool and textile merchandising was unquestionably a major source of income for Ghent, it seems to have been as much a source of population, and hence of markets for the grain merchants, as of capital. Smaller numbers of persons making higher per capita profits concentrated on brokerage in raw materials, particularly along the Lys but also on the Scheldt. Most of the prominent shipping magnates of Ghent, the Yoens, Maihuus, and Eeckaerds for example, had their houses near the Lys, although scattered near the Lys bridges throughout the city.[18] There is a corresponding and not surprising tendency for persons with backgrounds and interests in northeastern Flanders to have houses in Ghent near the Scheldt, as did various textile magnates.[19] The moneychangers were in the Korte Munt and Lange Munt, which are near the Lys adjacent to the food markets and linked them to the Friday Market, which was the general merchandise mart of Ghent and obviously attracted customers from throughout eastern Flanders. Had there not been substantial foreign capital involved in the grain trade, it is unlikely that the moneychangers would have been situated there.

The physical environment and the need to provision the city with food, wool, spices, beer, wine, and other commodities that were not available locally thus determined both economic geography and patterns of capital formation. It seems clear that the Pirenne school has drastically underestimated the extent to which the greatest industrial city of northwestern Europe in the Middle Ages

[18] Municipal Archive of Ghent, Ser. 301, III, I, fo. 18r.

[19] Municipal Archive of Ghent, Ser. 301, III, I, fos. 4r, 22v, 23r.

20

remained bound to the basic conditions of its environment. Towns in theory should be fed by their immediate hinterlands, and in such a period as the early Middle Ages, with primitive transport and small towns, this was almost certainly the case. But there are two problems. One would need a reasonably large population before the grain trade would bring much profit, unless a major part of the grain merchants' business was in reconsignment. In the case of Ghent this can be demonstrated for the late Middle Ages and was almost certainly true earlier.

Secondly, the city, barring total demographic catastrophe, is self-perpetuating. Urban agglomerations are composed of persons who fulfill "basic" and "non-basic" productive functions. Basic elements are positions produced by outside income, such as textile merchants and artisans and ecclesiastical and governmental institutions. Non-basic are those who are supported by serving the needs of the basic producers. One basic factor generally needs one non-basic to support him, with the result that depending on the household multiplier that one uses, themigration of a textile artisan to a city should theoretically increase the population by between seven and nine persons.[20]The demand for the services of non-basic persons would tend to force prices upward. The population of Ghent in the fourteenth century corresponded rather closely to this theoretical model.[21]

This essential nature of the medieval cities of Flanders and elsewhere has several interesting corollaries. First, because of the large number of persons congregating to serve the needs of those elements of the population whose economic function was producing for export or was in some other way external to the city, the city absorbed population from the surrounding countryside, a demographic drain that would initially relieve rural overpopulation, but which could and did lead to the creation of oversized cities that would put unnatural stress on the rural economy. The larger centers would continue to exist, for their function was essentially bound to the locality itself. The demand for goods from the nobility, as we have seen, could hardly explain the great growth of merchandising in the cities, and much of what the farmers used was produced locally. Until the cities developed substantial distant markets, in most cases not before the twelfth or thirteenth centuries, most townspeople produced or consigned mainly for othertownspeople, even with food. The takeoff of the "commercial revolution" of the Middle Ages was thus due to forces internal to

---

[20]J. C. Russell, *Medieval Regions and Their Cities* (Bloomington, Ind., 1972), pp. 34-35.

[21]D. Nicholas, "The Population of Fourteenth-Century Ghent," *Handelingen Gent*, n.s. XXIV (1970), 109; W. Prevenier, "Bevolkingscijfers en professionele strukturen der bevolking van Gent en Brugge in de 14de eeuw," in *Album Charles Verlinden* (Ghent, 1975), pp. 276-77.

the city. This feature also explains why the early settlements were generally the largest and most prosperous.

The cities, however, had to establish a mechanism to obtain food from outside their walls. Since the immediate area often could not support a large city by the second stage of development (the appearance of industrial artisans producing for an export market), and as the non-basic elements drove the city populations upward, the towns had to make certain that a source of food was available from outside the immediate area. As security against a bad local harvest, this was always necessary, but it only became an urgent problem when the Flemish countryside became extremely overpopulated after the twelfth century. Not only did the Ghent grain staple on the Lys and Scheldt ensure food for the city, but it also made very simple the question of reconsignment, which could only be overland or along the Scheldt. By transcending Flanders as their natural economic region, the cities were seriously weakening the economic potential of their hinterlands. The entire county was made to suffer in the late Middle Ages by the grain staple of Ghent.

Thus the weight of our evidence suggests that the monopoly of raw materials, chiefly grain and wool, was sufficiently lucrative to provide the basic wealth of the urban upper classes. Textiles created enough income to provide work for the masses, who in their turn were dependent on the monopolists for their food and drink. We shall see that the cloth industry also managed to create a generally positive balance of trade for Ghent, but it was no more important in the calculations of the *haute bourgeoisie* than were the supply monopolies.

We have seen that a regular excise was collected on all important raw materials. The only rate schedule that has survived for Ghent is from November, 1335.[22] It specified a tax of 2d. *payment* per halster (53.65 liters) on all grains and vegetables. The grain excise was leased in the following year for 6604 lb. *payment*.[23]This figure remained relatively stable in succeeding years. The 1336 figure would assume that at least 792,489 halsters of grain and vegetables were consumed in Ghent during this year, even without allowing for the profit that the leaseholder expected to make. Since 6.32 halsters of grain per person was a minimum necessary to sustain life,[24] enough tax was collected to

[22]Espinas and Pirenne, *Recueil*, II, 417-18.

[23]N. De Pauw and J. Vuylsteke (eds.), *De Rekeningen der stad Gent. Tijdvak van Jacob van Artevelde*, 3 vols. (Ghent, 1874-85), I, 2. The conversion to modern measure is according to M. J. Tits-Dieuaide, "La conversion des mesures anciennes en mesures metriques. Note sur les mesures à grain d'Anvers, Bruges, Bruxelles, Gand, Louvain, Malines et Ypres du Xve au XIXe siècle," *Contributions à l'histoire économique et sociale*, II (1963), 74.

[24]Blockmans and Prevenier, "Armoede," p. 505.

22

provide food for 132,080 persons, which would be roughly double the size of Ghent at that time.[25] Unless the leaseholders operated at a loss, there was a substantial reexport of grain.

But the leaseholders who controlled the supply of grain on the city market were also able to charge high prices there. We have only one continuous series of grain prices for Ghent in the fourteenth century, a wildly fluctuating group from 1320-26,[26] but figures from the 1380s suggest that rural prices in Flanders were only about one-third the sale prices in Bruges and Antwerp.[27] The ratio was probably less extreme in the 1330s, for the cities then needed Flemish grain, but the monopolists who controlled supply could still have charged whatever the market would bear. Some relative figures from the 1350s and 1360s are instructive. Most grains on the ecclesiastical estates around Ghent at that time cost about 10d. *gr. tor.* per halster,[28] while in 1362 at Bruges the mean on rye was about 27d. *gr. tor.* per hoed and 47d. in 1363, an average of 21.46 d. *gr. tor.* per Ghent halster.[29] At this rate the cost of grain for a family of five would be some 2 lb. 16s. *gr. tor.* annually. The wage of a continuously employed master carpenter in Ghent in the 1360s was about 7 lb. *gr. tor.*[30] It is difficult to measure the income of a textile artisan, for the work was even more subject to seasonal variation and the uncertainty of the wool supply. At Courtrai, which used some of the same industrial ordinances as Ghent, the fullers in 1348 were demanding a customary wage of 15s. 2 d. *par.* (15.16d. *gr. tor*) per cloth, a figure that had risen nearly 2.5 times, to 36d. *gr. tor.*, by 1390.[31] An average textile took 3.5 days to full, according to statutes of Ypres from the early fourteenth century,[32] and at this rate a fuller employed full-time (about 240 days annually) would have earned just over 5 lb. *gr. tor.* under the 1348 schedule at Courtrai. Ghent may have been higher, and the weavers

---

[25] D. Nicholas, "Economic Reorientation and Social Change in Fourteenth-Century Flanders," *Past and Present*, no. 70 (1976), p. 25.

[26] Blockmans and Prevenier, "Armoede," p. 505.

[27] D. Nicholas, "The Scheldt Trade and the 'Ghent War' of 1379-1385," *Bulletin de la Commission Royale d'Histoire*, CXLIV (1978), 256-57.

[28] K. De Blonde-Cotternier and others, "Prijzen en lonen in de domeinen der Gentse abdijen (St. Pieters en St. Baafs) (13e-14e eeuw)," in C. Verlinden and others, *Dokumenten voor de geschiedenis van prijzen en lonen in Vlaanderen en Brabant*, 4 vols. (Bruges, 1959-73), IV, 253, 266-67.

[29] Blockmans and Prevenier, "Armoede," pp. 505-06.

[30] Nicholas, "Economic Reorientation," p. 14.

[31] Espinas and Pirenne, *Recueil*, I, 655, 668-69.

[32] Hans Van Werveke, *De Omvang van de Ieperse lakenproduktie in de veertiende eeuw* (Antwerp, 1947), p. 11.

generally received higher wages than the fullers. But many and probably most earned much less than this maximum, and it seems clear that the poor were paying nearly half their wages for grain alone in the mid-fourteenth century. The poorer an area, the higher the percentage of their income that its inhabitants will spend on food. No figures survive from the period of urban origins, but some statistics have suggested that many poor burgesses in the fifteenth and sixteenth centuries were spending between sixty and eighty per cent of their income on food, and the indirect evidence of Ghent corroborates this.[33]

Thus the brokers who controlled the grain supply of Ghent in the fourteenth century could have made enormous profits, involving even in a normal year (and this figure would be higher during scarcities) at least 10d. *gr. tor*. Per halster, or 16,000 lb. *gr. tor*. per annum, a sum roughly quintuple the expenditure of the city government in 1360-61.[34]This figure is based on rural prices around Ghent, and the merchants seem to have been using mainly French grain, but it is doubtful that they would have done so if the total cost, including shipping, had been more than the price on local grain markets. Ghent alone would have needed some 20,344,080 liters of grain in the mid-fourteenth century to sustain a population of roughly 60,000. Yet so well had Ghent come to monopolize a grain trade that benefitted mainly French farmers, to the considerable depression of Flemish agriculture, that documents of the 1380s suggest that not only were the magnates importing enough to provision Ghent, but they were also reexporting a like amount of French grain toward Brabant, Antwerp, and possibly northeastern Flanders. A combination of the amount reexported with the amount needed in the city brings the total rather close to the hypothetical amount suggested by the excise figures, and the profits of the grain merchants, a rather small group, would accordingly have been at least 32-35,000 lb. *gr. tor*. annually, and probably more.

Our figures show the stranglehold that the non-basic producers, those who provided services to exporters and their employees, had on the economy of Ghent by the fourteenth century, and this fact alone indicates the extreme pressure that the overpopulated cities placed on the Flemish economy as a whole. Militia figures of 1356-57 suggest that as segments of the entire town population including textile workers, victuallers comprised 9.1%, shippers and dockworkers 12.25%,and brokers 1.1%, a total of 21.45% of the households

---

[33]Carlo M. Cipolla, *Before the Industrial Revolution. European Economy and Society, 1000-1700* (New York, 1976), pp. 28-31. See also Fernand Braudel, *Capitalism and Material Life 1400-1800* (New York, 1973), pp. 87-97.

[34]Van Werveke, *Rekeningen*, p. 492.

24

of the city.[35] We have seen that these trades controlled immense wealth; and since the shipping trades had a high percentage of unskilled laborers, it seems clear that the small number of grain merchants and others who controlled sources of supply dominated the textile artisans, who formed the mass of the city population and accordingly were dependent upon a narrow circle of monopolists for raw materials for food and industry. The shipping magnates of the cities obtained cheap foreign grain, dumped it on the city markets where the masses had no choice, and thus contributed both to the depression of the urban masses and of the Flemish farmers, who could not undersell their foreign competitors and had to turn to other lines of work, such as linen manufacture.

My conclusion is thus that the wealthiest Flemish townsmen in the late Middle Ages were using previously developed settlement patterns and their unfortunate consequences to make much or most of their money by monopolizing domestic markets. This is completely contrary to most historiography of the medieval Flemish economy. But I do not in any sense mean to suggest that the textile industry was unimportant. The accounts of the 1380s mention the merchants of Ghent exchanging French coin into Flemish at the toll of Termonde. This certainly indicates that they were reconsigning French grain, but also that there was a favorable balance of trade toward France, probably in textiles, so that the merchants of Ghent were not only making great profits by avoiding the Flemish grain markets, but were also profiting from the labor of the urban masses.[36] The textile industry must thus be placed into perspective.

First, it has been assumed that the great Flemish cities reached the second stage of their prosperity by using wool from England, after beginning with a native Flemish product. This cloth had been marketed in northern Europe, but a great source of profit was the Italian trade at the Champagne fairs. The share of the three great Flemish cities in the Italian textile trade diminished in the late thirteenth century and continued to do so for the rest of the medieval period. The Pirenne school has assumed that this was due to a combination of the expansion of the Italian industries themselves and the increasing competition from the smaller Flemish towns, whose textiles are found in greater profusion on the Italian markets than are those of the great cities, and this caused serious crises and led the cities to lash out at rural and small town textiles in a defensive reaction.

Such assumptions, which I have shared in earlier works, are weakened

---

[35]Calculated from Van Werveke, *Rekeningen*, pp. 296-97.

[36]Nicholas, "The Scheldt Trade," based on General Archives of the Realm, Brussels, Chambre des Comptes 22798, fos. 6v-7r, 9r, 15v.

by two considerations. Only in the mid-thirteenth century did the great cities of Flanders begin to make "wet" textiles, which were heavier, smoother, and finer than their previous types.[37]The smaller towns continued to market the cheaper cloth, as indeed did the artisans of the great cities. It is precisely at this point that few textiles of Ghent, Bruges, and Ypres are found in Italy. The Italians continued to patronize the textiles of the smaller Flemish towns throughout the Middle Ages, for they were light, cheap, and of comparatively high quality. The cities made no attempt to hinder the small centers from making and marketing this cloth, but they did try to prevent them from imitating their own specialties.

Furthermore, the great cities did not concentrate exclusively on luxury textiles. There was a considerable domestic market for ordinary cloth. There had to be: citizens of Ghent and Ypres were forbidden by their city governments to purchase cloth not made in the home town,and I cannot believe that every dockworker in Ghent went to work in a fine woolen suit. The great towns were trying to insure a captive market for the merchants of the cloth halls among the poor of the native city, just as they did with the grain monopolies. They were not attempting to hinder the smaller towns from developing their own less extensive spheres of influence.

Hence cloth of every conceivable weight and price was manufactured, and this makes it very difficult to form an accurate estimate of the total production of each type or the extent of profit margin. Just as the Flemish grain merchants preferred French grain at this third stage of city development and thereby depressed local agriculture, so they preferred English wool, which was of higher quality than the native product. The cost of a sack of fine English wool at Calais in 1371 was about 12 lb. *gr. tor.* But this is a wholesale price, and on some grades it was this high in the late 1330s.[38]A schedule for the costs of transporting 229 sacks of English wool from Bruges to Ghent in 1339 has survived; including freight, the excises at Ghent, and butter for greasing the cloth when finished, the cost was raised an average of 10s. 11d. *gr. tor.* per sack.[39] The municipal accounts give prices of cloth purchased by the magistrates for uniforms for the city officials, but they do not include the luxury

---

[37]G. De Poerck, *La Draperie médiévale en Flandre et en Artois. Technique et terminologie*, 3 vols. (Bruges, 1951), I, 259.

[38]Espinas and Pirenne, *Recueil*, III, 775; E. B. Fryde, *The Wool Accounts of William de la Pole. A Study of Some Aspects of the English Wool Trade at the Start of the Hundred Years War* (York, 1964), Appendix; Eileen Power, *The Wool Trade in English Medieval History* (Oxford, 1941), pp. 22-23. The 12 lb. *gr. tor.*figure is derived from Municipal Archive of Bruges, Charter 616, fo. 31r.

[39]De Pauw and Vuylsteke, *Rekeningen*, I, 339; Espinas and Pirenne, *Recueil*, II, 613.

26

specialty of Ghent, the *strijpte halflakene*. Rather, they show several varieties of less fine cloth whose prices varied between 1 lb. and 2 lb. *gr. tor*., and there was even some variation in the price of the same grade of cloth. The more lightweight textiles sold for 8-10s. *gr. tor.*[40] In view of the price of the English commodity, which was quite scarce at that time, domestic wool was probably being used for most textiles. During the 1360s, when the supply of foreign wool was just as expensive but more secure, the luxury cloths of Ghent were priced between 7 lb. and 9.5 lb. *gr. tor*.,[41] and about five fine textiles could bemade from a 364 pound sack of English wool.

The excises may give some indication of total production, for most textiles paid a tax of 4-5s. *payment*. The textile frames were leased for 3672 lb. in 1338-39, somewhat higher than in previous years, and this suggests a production of 18,360 pieces of domestic cloth.[42] Yet an average of 30-35,000 textiles received aseal on the frames at Ypres, a city roughly half the size of Ghent, in the late 1330s and 1340s.[43] In addition to the excise cost, the merchant would have to pay about 13 lb. *gr. tor*., including transport and finishing materials, for a sack of English wool that might optimally make five export textiles that could retail for an average of 8 lb. *gr. tor.* We have only indirect indices of the wages of the various textile artisans, but it seems highly unlikely that the total cost in machinery, wages, taxes, inspection, and transport in the city could have been much less than 3 lb. *gr. tor*., and it was probably more. Even if we assume the most favorable circumstances for the cloth merchants, a textile that sold for 8-10 lb. Could not have cost less than 5.5 lb. from sheep to market. If Ghent produced 70,000 textiles each year, which the population difference with Ypres would suggest, we are left with an export capital of 175,000 lb. *gr. tor.* Yet this is obviously far too high, for domestic textiles would realize much less profit and would not be involved in the positive balance of payments. It seems clear that the textile magnates brought more capital into Ghent, even using imported wool, than the grain merchants disbursed, but the textile industry involved a vastly larger work force and smaller per capita profits, for masters and artisans alike, than could come in the grain trade.

Citizens of Ghent had two other major sources of capital investment. They made considerable profit exploiting the peat bogs of northeastern Flanders in the fourteenth century. But although this certainly contributed, perhaps

---

[40] De Pauw and Vuylsteke, *Rekeningen*, I, 275-76.

[41] Van Werveke, *Rekeningen*, pp. 387-88; Municipal Archive of Ghent, Ser. 400, IX, fo. 237v (municipal account of 1365-66).

[42] De Pauw and Vuylsteke, *Rekeningen*, cited Espinas and Pirenne, *Recueil*, II, p. 624.

[43] Van Werveke, *Lakenproduktie*, p. 12.

almost as much as textiles, to the favorable balance of trade,[44] it does not seem to have had much effect on either rural or urban settlement patterns. The wealthy townspeople only began using significant amounts of peat after the Flemish wood supply had been depleted, and this meant after the basic settlement patterns and urban landscape had been determined. The townspeople exploited the moors directly to sell the peat on the city market, but they also speculated in the property, buying it cheaply from the ever impecunious counts of Flanders, particularly in the 1290s and 1350s, and selling it more expensively to rural speculators and other townsmen.

Another source of income for the townspeople was rent. But while this undoubtedly contributed to the development of settlement patterns, we know little about it. Even at Ghent, which has by far the best surviving records among the Flemish cities, there are insuperable problems, and the information that we do have suggests that urban rents in the *portus* of Ghent were surprisingly low in the fourteenth century.[45] Rents had a great deal to do with settlement in the early days of the town, undoubtedly keeping population lighter and more aristocratic in the central city than in the suburbs. They were an important element of capital formation in the pre-urban period, when a rent of as much as 2s. *par.* per *bunder* was a good rate on rural land, and the cities were much higher.[46] But the unchanging rates were totally unrealistic by the fourteenth century, and ownership of land in the city was more a source of social prestige, and perhaps a means of keeping the lower classes out of some wealthy quarters, than an important source of income. Rural land, acquired more recently by townspeople and generally leased for a term of years rather than in perpetuity by the fourteenth century, brought greater profits, but even here the lords were not making immense returns on their investments.[47] The great elements of capital formation in Ghent in the fourteenth century, just as in the period when

[44] In 1362-63 the peat excise realized 2880 lb. *payment* for the city, while the combined taxes on textiles, mainly on local sales, involved just under 3880 lb. Van Werveke, *Rekeningen*, pp. 546-48.

[45] Rents on land around the Hudevettershoek, primarily small apartments (*gariten*), in 1330 averaged 11s.6d. *par.*, or just under 1s. *gr.tor.* A probably more representative figure comes from the ward around the Schaapbrug, in the parish of St. James, where the fullers were strong and rents averaged 1 lb. 1s. 8d. *par.*, or 2s. 1d. *gr. tor.*, in any event only a small part of the yearly income of a continuously employed master artisan as noted above. Figures from Vuylsteke, *Rekeningen*, pp. 740-45.

[46] A. Verhulst, *De Sint-Baafsabdij te Gent en haar grondbezit* (Brussels, 1958), pp. 215-16.

[47] Rural land investment by the Flemish townspeople is treated in detail in D. Nicholas, *Town and Countryside: Social, Economic, and Political Tensions in Fourteenth-Century Flanders* (Bruges, 1971), pp. 267-329.

28

the city began to transcend its immediate hinterland, continued to be grain merchandising and textile manufacturing. The profits were realized mainly by a narrow group, probably of no more than five hundred persons, from the need of the masses for food, for wool that would create jobs, and for a sale market of the only commodity produced in large enough quantities to support the population of a major metropolis.

Summary, Perspective, and Conclusion

We thus find that the Flemish cities developed in regions with prosperous agriculture, areas of dense Germanic primary settlement, but they needed a stimulus to trade and industry. Places that were surrounded by prosperous farmland, however, remained of secondary imaportance, for there was little need for their services in reconsigning food to regions lacking adequate supply. The inhabitants of the original fortification or the ecclesiastical complex could not have accounted for enough non-basic producers to explain the great growth of the cities, for the total population of most agglomerations consisting simply of castle and suburb would scarcely exceed 1000-1500. Flanders proper contains no good example of the stunted fortification that failed to become a major city, but nearby Thérouanne, the French bishopric to which much of western Flanders owed allegiance in the Middle Ages, is a classic case. Flanders had perhaps a dozen places by 1300 with a population larger than this. Provisioning the fortification with luxuries and food, however, provided capital to the inhabitants of the suburb, as settlement expanded toward the source of food supply, which was as important for the survival of the merchants as of the occupants of the fortress.

The capital thus formed, together with the presence of good transport facilities, a convenient market, and pastoral areas in northern Flanders that could provide leather and wool, led the towns into their second stage of development. In this phase the population that had been largely concerned with basic provisioning now began to find some employment in industry, but the essential means of production were owned by those who had the greatest capital concentration and possibilities for still more accumulation: the landowners in the original *portus*, who formed a municipal aristocracy. The central city by now was given over largely to provisioning the growing settlement with food and industrial raw materials. The towns in this stage attracted settlers from the surrounding countryside and gave both an outlet for surplus population in the more densely settled regions of eastern Flanders and a market on which the farmers of the immediately contiguous economic region might sell their produce. With the prior settlement of the central city by the victuallers and the marketplaces, the industrial workers generally settled on the outskirts of the town, which were then brought within the walls in the late twelfth and thirteenth centuries. But settlement began to diffuse at this stage, so that no one area of the town had a total concentration of a single occupation or occupational type. Demand for export textiles and other goods to feed and clothe the local aristocracy was substantial, but it was essentially secondary asan element of capital formation to the business of providing goods and services to other townsfolk. Since those who producied for an exterior market needed the services of other residents of the town, the cities grew beyond what their immediate environs could support.

Cities tended to develop in Flanders as elsewhere in a rough rank-size pattern, with market towns that drew on a radius of ten to fifteen kilometers in turn serving a regional capital that provided more specialized services over 80 to 150 square kilometers.[48] In an arc southeast and east of Ghent there were five towns with populations of 3000-5000, one-fifteenth to one-tenth the size of Ghent in the mid-fourteenth century,and in each case 30-40 kilometers from the metropolis. A similar statistic is true of the satellites of Bruges, which had three-fifths the population of Ghent and was the center of several towns of 1500-3000 souls at a distance of only 10-25 kilometers. The pattern is less true of Ypres, the smallest of the major cities and the last to develop, for southwestern Flanders had several other moderately large towns. Professor Josiah Russell has developed a formula for devising the populations of cities within the economic region by using a rigid rank-size hypothesis. While there is considerable truth to these ideas, I prefer not to think in terms of immutable laws or patterns, and certainly not of a region that must conform to a theoretical model.[49]

---

[48]C. T. Smith, *An Historical Geography of Western Europe Before 1800* (New York, 1967), p. 298.

[49]It is appropriate here to consider the theories of Professor Russell, for whose work I have the utmost respect and admiration even as I am forced to take issue with specific points. He tends to juggle the populations of cities in economic regions in terms of his rank-size formula; and when he cannot find enough cities of the proper appropriate size to fit, he merely enlarges the region. In his *Medieval Regions and Their Cities*, pp. 112-121, he discusses an economic region of which Ghent is the leading city. He includes Picardy and Artois, quite appropriately for the late Middle Ages (though not for the period before the twelfth century), but also territory as far south as Reims, east to Cologne and Aachen, and north through the Netherlands. It is true that the Flemish cities had commerce with these areas, but they also traded with the Italians and Castilians. To obtain his regional scaling of size populations, he takes statistics of 1356 for Ghent, 1340 for Bruges, but 1412 for Ypres, by which time that city had been in decline for nearly a century, but no corrective is suggested. Professor Russell also estimates total population of these areas in the fifteenth century as 1.5 million, which in my opinion is far too low.

30

In a third stage of development export continued to be a source of foreign capital that contributed to the growth of the cities and caused them to transcend their immediate hinterlands. The cities were forced to look beyond Flanders for grain and wool by this time, the twelfth and particularly the thirteenth and fourteenth centuries, for the pressures of urban growth in the second stage had led to the colonizing of most of the fertile land left in Flanders, but the creation of only one new metropolitan area, although several secondary centers had also appeared. The citizens in the third stage began to invest in land and raw materials outside the city, but often for reasons as much social as economic. The cities also placed artificial constraints on rival towns that might more adequately have served the needs of local farmers. They hindered the development by the smaller towns of export industries that might have drained still more excess population from the Flemish countryside, although the extent to which the countryside and the smaller Flemish towns did export lightweight woolens and fine linen in the late Middle Ages is quite remarkable. Such centers could even have provided a service for the citizens of the great cities themselves, for as the cities became so large that their food supplies had to be secured in large measure from distant growers, the masses became as dependent on monopolists who controlled the grain trade as on magnates who imported the fine English wool upon which the major export industry of Flanders, and accordingly their jobs, depended. A stifling situation had thus developed that even the demographic catastrophe of the late Middle Ages could not alleviate. Not even the extension of the economic region, facilitated by the creation of the Burgundian empire in the late fourteenth and fifteenth centuries, could provide an outlet.

Index